Urban Politics

This popular text mixes classic urban theory and research with a review of the most recent developments and trends in the urban and metropolitan arena. The book's balanced and realistic approach helps students understand the nature of contemporary urban problems and the difficulty in finding effective "solutions" to those problems in a suburban and global age.

The ninth edition, thoroughly rewritten, maintains its focus on questions of economic development and race and gives enhanced attention to the changing patterns of the American city, including the impacts of globalization and gentrification. Boxed case studies of both current political controversies and urban-related films provide material for class discussion. The concluding sections demonstrate the trade-off between "ideal" and "pragmatic" urban politics.

Key changes to this edition include:

- thoroughly updated and rewritten chapters, reflecting the most current census data and evidence in areas such as the "new immigration," changing patterns of suburbanization, gentrification, and community development;
- a new opening chapter providing a sharper focus on the differences between industrial and post-industrial communities;
- coverage of cities in crisis, including the politics surrounding municipal bankruptcy in Detroit and Stockton and the big-city pension problems of Chicago and other cities;
- increased attention on policies for sustainable urban development;
- new photos and boxed material throughout the book illustrating important themes.

Myron A. Levine is Professor in the Department of Urban Affairs and Geography at Wright State University, USA. In addition to authoring *Urban Politics*, Dr. Levine is the editor of two volumes, *Annual Editions: Urban Society* and *Taking Sides: Urban Affairs*. His writings have appeared in various journals, including the *Urban Affairs Review* and the *Journal of Urban Affairs*. His research focuses on national urban policy, urban revitalization, and efforts at regionalism and local government collaboration. He has received NEH and NSF awards to study and teach in France, Germany, the Czech Republic, Slovakia, and Latvia.

Urban Politics

Cities and Suburbs in a Global Age

Ninth Edition

Myron A. Levine

Routledge
Taylor & Francis Group

NEW YORK AND LONDON

Ninth edition first published 2015
by Routledge
711 Third Avenue, New York, NY 10017

and by Routledge
2 Park Square, Milton Park, Abingdon, Oxon, OX14 4RN

Routledge is an imprint of the Taylor & Francis Group, an informa business

Eighth edition published by M.E. Sharpe, Inc., 2012

Library of Congress Cataloging-in-Publication Data
Levine, Myron A.
   Urban politics : cities and suburbs in a global age / by Myron A. Levine.—Ninth edition.
      pages cm
   Includes bibliographical references and index.
   1. Municipal government—United States.   2. Metropolitan government—United States.   I. Title.
   JS323.R67 2015
   320.8′50973—dc23
   2014026934

ISBN: 978-1-138-85357-7 (hbk)
ISBN: 978-0-7656-4625-5 (pbk)
ISBN: 978-1-315-71970-2 (ebk)

Typeset in Times
By Apex CoVantage, LLC

To Nancy

For her love, support, caring, and wisdom.
For showing me the beauty of life.
For being fabulous.

Contents

Preface

Much popular commentary has focused on the "comeback" of America's cities. Once-ailing downtowns have bloomed as centers of global corporate offices, entertainment, night life, and tourism. Previously declining inner-city neighborhoods have experienced extensive upgrading, with new housing and trendy stores that serve capable young professionals attracted to the dynamism of city life. These knowledge workers, in turn, provide the creative talent that serves to draw prestigious national and global firms back to the city.

But these images of urban prosperity disguise an elementary truth: all is not well with the American city. Despite the evidence of an urban rebound, many communities—suburban as well as central city—are not thriving. Local growth trends are very uneven; while some communities exhibit significant gains, others suffer unabated decline. Cities—and increasingly suburbs as well—continue to face the "wicked" problems of urban poverty, family dissolution, homelessness, worsening inequality, housing abandonment, crime, and the resegregation of public school systems. A new immigration, primarily from Latin America and Asia, too, has added to the service burdens of cities. Even economically booming cities—New York, San Francisco, and Chicago, to name only a few—suffer serious problems of housing affordability, displacement, ghettoization, school segregation, traffic congestion, and environmental harm. The nation's suburbs have become new centers of immigration, poverty, closed storefronts, vacant properties, and resegregated school systems. The 2014 protests and riots in Ferguson, Missouri, that occurred in the aftermath of a police officer's shooting of an unarmed young black male, serve as testimony to the inequality and racial tensions that continue to exist in the contemporary metropolis. The urban crisis never really left the city; yet, somehow, it has moved to the suburbs.

The 2013 bankruptcy of Detroit underscored the depth of the problems that major urban areas face. Detroit was not the only city in the nation to face the prospect of bankruptcy, only the nation's biggest. In Detroit, Harrisburg (Pennsylvania), Stockton (California), and a fairly large number of other communities, fiscal crisis appears to have become a permanent part of the local condition.

In an age when population and political power have shifted to the suburbs, urban leaders have had to become more creative in their coalition-building and problem-solving efforts. In a global age, effective urban leadership is made even more difficult as cities and suburbs are affected by events and decisions from beyond their local borders. Local communities now compete for new jobs not only with one another but also with communities located overseas. The intensified economic competition has led local officials to anticipate the needs of business leaders, even at the price of diverting spending away from residential neighborhoods, reducing municipal responsiveness to other needs.

The 9th edition of *Urban Politics* argues that it is important to look at the interaction of public and private power in the local arena. The formal rules of local government remain important, as they define what cities can and cannot do. The formal structure of local governing and electoral systems also help to determine "who gets what" from politics, just who is—and is not—represented in city hall. Yet a description of the formal rules and institutions of city government—city charters, the mayor, city manager, city council members, and other top municipal officials—by itself yields only a very incomplete and misleading understanding of how politics is played in the local arena. City officials are often constrained by the decisions made by private actors and by concerns for local competitiveness.

It is not easy for public officials to get important things done. Yet, while public leadership is difficult, it is not impossible. Private power counts, but so does local politics! Creative and inspired public leadership—at the neighborhood level as well as in the top offices of city hall—can get results.

Urban Politics remains quite pragmatic in its overall orientation. It identifies the root sources of urban problems, but it does not call for idealistic policy changes that are impossible to achieve. Instead, it seeks to identify targets of opportunity where urban advocates can hope to fashion a winning coalition behind practical—albeit at times rather small—measures that will improve the urban condition. The book also concludes by examining the possibilities of a "green politics," where a commitment to environmental protection and sustainability can offer keys to building a better city.

Urban Politics draws on current work in a number of fields: political science, geography, urban sociology, urban economics, urban planning, and public administration. It draws the reader's attention to "current affairs" that reveal the relevance of more scholarly academic works to the contemporary urban debate.

Over the years, this book has been the beneficiary of the insights and support offered by numerous colleagues. I will name only a few. Bill Peterman and Janet Smith showed me the extensive changes taking place in Chicago. Innisfree McKinnon generously shared her knowledge of regional planning in the Pacific Northwest. Jack Dustin tutored me as to the possibilities inherent in regional partnerships and collaborative action. Jack further underscored the critical importance of public-private partnerships and performance measurement and management systems as cities and suburbs attempt to do more with less. Jack has proven to be a quite supportive and exemplary chair of Wright State University's Department of Urban Affairs and Geography. At Wright State, Dean Kristin Sobolik, too, deserves thanks for her celebration of faculty scholarship.

I would never have been so deeply involved with writing *Urban Politics* were it not for the late Bernard M. Ross, who asked me to co-author the book's earlier editions.

Bernie was a lover of cities, a believer in the virtues of professionalized urban management, and an advocate of citizen participation. He was also a true gentleman.

The Urban Affairs Association also deserves a word of appreciation for its work in giving greater prominence to a field of study that, for many years, suffered a degree of neglect as it lacked an agreed-upon disciplinary core. The UAA is a rarity among the academic professions; its journal articles are relevant and readable, and its annual conferences are lively and interesting—and worth attending!

Very special thanks go to Harry Briggs at M.E. Sharpe, the publisher of previous editions of *Urban Politics*, for his continued support and enthusiasm for this project. Harry's belief in *Urban Politics* helped to keep the book alive at a time when it seemed to be on the verge of disappearing amid the rubble of the continuing consolidation, restructuring, and shakeout of the book publishing industry. Thanks a lot, Harry! Elizabeth Parker also provided detailed editorial assistance and help with photo permissions while the manuscript was at M.E. Sharpe.

I am extremely pleased that *Urban Politics* has a new home at Routledge, a publisher renowned for its list of titles in the fields of Political Science and Urban Affairs. A number of people at Routledge have extended their enthusiastic support and a kind welcome. Michael Kerns, the Acquisitions Editor at Routledge, was solicitous of my concerns from the very beginning. Emma Elder at Taylor & Francis Books in England took charge of the entire production process and assembled a most capable team behind the volume. Lillian Rand took charge of various details. My thanks also go to Alice Sparks for her close eye in proofing the volume and to Alan Rutter for providing the volume's index. Leigh-Ann Bard has been extremely helpful in marketing the volume. Harbour Fraser Hodder has my special thanks for meeting deadlines, for keeping me on deadline, and for the extremely positive way by which she extends editorial advice. Nicola Platt was also wonderful, joining Taylor & Francis and taking charge of production as the volume neared completion.

Of course, my deepest thanks go to Nancy, my partner over the decades in this and every other important project in my life. And now our son Alex, his wife Marisa, and our daughter Evie show us the continuing wonders of cities like Chicago and Minneapolis, even in the dead of midwinter.

1 The Urban Situation

Global City, Tourist City, Bankrupt City

A time traveler from the 1950s who woke up in 2015 would be struck by the unfamiliar appearance of urban America. Important changes took place during the time in which the time traveler slept. Our time voyager left an era where cities were industrial centers; manufacturing and related industries (including port-related activities, warehousing, and distribution) dominated the urban economy of midcentury. The American city of the twenty-first century, by comparison, is much different, having lost much of its industrial base and character.

New York City in the 1950s was defined by its numerous small factories, warehouses, and shipping, with "finger piers" jutting into the Hudson River from Manhattan. By the twenty-first century, the gritty industrial nature of large sections of New York had disappeared, giving way to a "new city" of internationally connected corporate offices and soaring office towers. Entertainment centers sprouted up on former manufacturing sites. New York was no longer the manufacturing center of old; instead, the city had become a hub of global corporate headquarters, banking, financial services, information technology, digital and other "new media" firms, and entertainment activities.

New York was not the only city to undergo such a transformation. The change was even apparent in prototypical industrial cities like Pittsburgh. By the beginning to the twenty-first century, civic leaders in Pittsburgh had torn down the idle, rusting hulks of the city's famed steel mills and removed the industry's slag heaps in order to build a new postindustrial infrastructure: riverfront bike paths and parks, office and shopping complexes, and modern professional sports stadiums.

Big-city downtown enjoyed a new revival, as did many of the "core" residential neighborhoods located nearby. The urban comeback was all the more notable as during the latter half of the twentieth century, the same downtown business districts and core-city neighborhoods suffered extensive decline as middle-class families left the city in search of the "good life" of the suburbs. Businesses, both retail and manufacturing, soon followed. Our urban time traveler would be surprised to find that in many cities the central business district and surrounding residential neighborhoods no longer appeared to be dying; instead, these areas have blossomed as the site of new investment, with

1

THE POSTINDUSTRIAL TRANSFORMATION OF PITTSBURGH

The Industrial City: Steel Mills and the South Slopes Neighborhood of Pittsburgh, 1940.

Photo taken by Jack Delano, January 1940. From Library of Congress Prints & Photographs Division, Washington, DC, http://commons.wikimedia.org/wiki/File:Mill_District_-_Pittsburgh.jpg.

Pittsburgh's Postindustrial Transformation. The city has redeveloped its riverfront, previously the site of idle steel mills and slag heaps, into a place for recreation and commerce, with parkland, bike paths, riverside restaurants, new offices, and two stadiums for the city's professional baseball and football teams.

From Wikimedia Commons, User PerryPlanet, June 28, 2009, http://en.wikipedia.org/wiki/North_Shore_Riverfront_Park

upgraded residences, sidewalk cafés, fashionable bistros, upscale boutiques, and even new shopping complexes that offered the convenience that previously could only be found in suburban malls. In a transformation process that came to be called **gentrification**, technologically competent workers, young professionals, and newly married couples took up residence in core neighborhoods, in some cases converting vacant warehouses to residential use, having rediscovered the virtues of living in close proximity to the job opportunities and the nightlife of an active city.

Suburbia, too, underwent considerable change during the more than half a century that our time traveler slept. In the 1950s, at a time when many Americans still did not own an automobile, suburban development was in its relative infancy. Suburbia was largely viewed as an expanse of leafy, affluent, single-home communities, although closer observation also revealed the existence of numerous industrial and working-class communities that did not fit the upscale-bedroom-suburb stereotype. Over the decades that followed, however, suburbia exploded (Figure 1.1), gaining extensive population and new economic activities. The United States of the twenty-first century has become a suburban nation: census data reveals that since the 1970s the total population of U.S. suburbs outnumbers that of central cities.

Contemporary suburbia is also considerably more varied in its economic and demographic makeup than it was in the 1950s. Economic activities once confined to the Industrial City are now commonly sited in the office and industrial parks and shopping malls and big-box retail stores of the suburbs. Factories, warehouses, and commercial centers have sprouted at beltway exits and along the roadways near airports. Highways

Figure 1.1   **The 1990s: A Decade of Continuing Suburban Expansion.** The Rate of Population Growth of the Nation's Suburbs Was Twice That of Central Cities (Percent Change in Metropolitan Population and Families, 1990–1997)

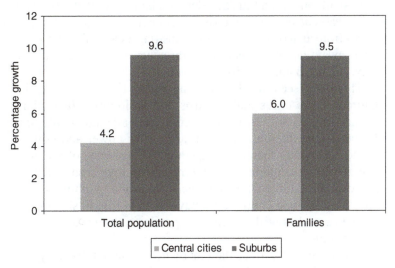

Source: U.S. Department of Housing and Urban Development (HUD), *The State of the Cities*, 1998, p. 7; available at www.huduser.org/Publications/PDF/soc_98.pdf.

Note: The HUD figure is based on the U.S. Bureau of the Census Current Population Study.

and airports serve as important transportation nodes in an increasingly national and globalized economy; businesses no longer have to locate, as they once did, along rail lines and near the river and ocean ports of the Industrial City.

Continuing advances in computerization and telecommunications have further served to liberate national and global corporations from central-city locations. Corporations can now site much of their office and support activities in **edge cities**, the relatively dense concentrations of office parks, technology-related firms, restaurants, shopping, and entertainment centers that can be found in contemporary suburbia. But new suburban development is not limited to the "new suburban downtowns" of edge cities. Substantial new economic growth is also located in the **edgeless development**[1] located along suburban roads on the outskirts of the metropolis. Suburban "strip malls" have become the sites of new offices, restaurants, and entertainment facilities, further weakening not just a region's central city but also many inner-ring suburbs located in closer proximity to the central city.

As the economy of suburbia changed so did its demography. In the 1950s, suburbia was primarily a bastion of white prosperity; in contrast, suburbia of the 2000s is considerably more diverse. Contemporary suburbia has become the home to numerous ethnic groups and even newly arrived immigrants from oversea. The numbers of low-income families residing in the suburbs have also increased; the stalled national economy and the collapse of the housing finance bubble of the early 2000s further added to suburban poverty rates. By the early twenty-first century, the total number of poor families living in suburbs surpassed the number living in central cities—even though poverty rates (the chances that a person will be poor) remain higher in central cities.[2]

The family structure found in the suburbs also changed noticeably. The two-parent family norm of suburbia in the 1950s gave way to an increase in the numbers of female-headed families and also to gay and lesbian households.

In short, our urban time traveler would discover that cities and suburbs in the United States had changed with the rise of globalization and with the transition of the United States from an industrial to a postindustrial society. The Industrial City to a great extent faded away[3] and was replaced by three new urban forms: the Global City, the Tourist City, and the Bankrupt City.

This book seeks to describe the forces that have shaped the transformation of United States cities and suburbs and to identify just what strategies can—and cannot—reasonably be undertaken to help alleviate contemporary urban problems. It makes a simple but important argument: power and politics count! The changes in the American urban landscape and the problems of urban communities were not, and are not, inevitable. They are not the simple result of inescapable demographic and economic forces. Instead, decisions made by public officials and private actors have played—and continue to play—a great role in shaping the geography of urban problems and how the nation responds to the urban situation. In short, political power counts.

This chapter describes the emergence of the Global City, the Tourist City, and the Bankrupt City. It will then begin to explore the role that public decisions and private power have played in forging the contemporary urban situation.

GLOBAL CITY

The decline of the Industrial City left former manufacturing centers in desperate search for new economic possibilities. The most successful communities adapted and found a new role to play in an increasingly **globalized economy**, a world where the organization of production transcends a nation's borders. Cities sought to attract the headquarters and production facilities of multinational corporations. Cities also made investments that they hoped would lead to the development of jobs in health care, education, and advanced technology, growth fields in a new service economy.

New York City, badly hurt by the decline of its manufacturing base and by the exodus of both population and commercial activity to the suburbs, skirted on the edge of fiscal default in the mid-1970s, unable to find the revenues necessary to pay off its creditors as municipal loans came due. The intervention of the state and federal governments helped New York gain access to funds (especially new borrowing through the municipal bond market) that the city needed to maintain operations while implementing various fiscal reforms. New York, despite its fiscal problems, also still enjoyed important advantages as a critical national and global center. As a result, the city was able to dig itself out of the hole, escape the specter of default, and reemerge as a top-tier **Global City**, a world center of corporate headquarters, banking, and financial services firms in a world where economic activities transcend national borders.

New York City's decline and rebound point to the importance of *globalization* and the position of a city in the *global city* hierarchy. **Globalization** denotes the eroding significance of national and local borders. Contemporary cities exist in a global system of interconnected relationships. Economic global competition helps to explain the financial problems that cities like New York suffered beginning in the mid-century, as multinational corporations shifted manufacturing and back-office support jobs to lower wage sites located overseas.

But globalization of the economy does not only pose problems for cities, it also presents cities with opportunities. Of course, certain cities are in a better position than others to find an important role to play in the new global economy. Contemporary New York—along with London and Tokyo—is generally regarded as one of the world's three top-tier cities, cities that have a large concentration of business firms that are critical to business decisions around the globe. The credit and investment decisions made by corporate officials in a global city like New York can affect the opening or the shutting down of a manufacturing plant half a world away. Global cities are vital centers of commerce, corporate control, knowledge, creativity, communications, and entrepreneurship.[4]

What opportunity did a globalizing economy offer New York? Major multinational and national firms find great value in **agglomeration**, which is locating a firm in close proximity to other corporations doing similar work. Cities also offer the advantages that industries receive from **cluster patterns of development**: by locating in relatively close proximity to similar firms, a corporation can tap a large pool of qualified workers as well as draw on the specialized support services provided by financial accounting, legal, and managerial assistance firms that work in their field.[5] Simply put, a firm enjoys benefits

The Freedom Tower, New York City. The soaring 1776-foot Freedom Tower, the centerpiece of the 9/11 rebuilding site, is actually taller than the Twin Towers that fell during the 9/11 attacks. The Freedom Tower was built despite great cost and concerns for safety. Critics also objected to a building that commercialized a memorial site. The office space provided by the Freedom Tower and other new World Trade Center buildings helped to reinforce the position of Lower Manhattan as a financial center of the global economy.

From Wikimedia Commons, User Hakilon, December 30, 2013, http://commons.wikimedia.org/wiki/File:One_World_Trade_Center_im_Dezember_2013.jpg.

from locating in the same general geographic area as other firms in its industry. New York rebounded, as the city provides one of the world's premier clusters of banking, finance, and corporate activities.

Los Angeles ranks a rung or so below New York on the global city ladder, especially in terms of its reach on the world economic stage. Los Angeles, of course, is an important center of communications (especially the film industry) and Pacific Rim banking. It is also a multicultural, multilinguistic city. Still, the city still lacks the concentration of world-class firms found in New York.

Chicago, Houston, Denver, Miami, and San Francisco are other U.S. cities with global connections. These cities are important national and regional commercial centers. But, compared to New York and even to Los Angeles, the cities are less critical command-and-control centers of the global economy.

A city's position in the global hierarchy helps to determine the opportunities it has available and even its ability to rebound from disaster. In the global hierarchy of cities, New Orleans ranks lower than the national and regional centers named above. During the age of the Industrial City, New Orleans was an important port city, a result of its advantageous location near the mouth of the Mississippi River. But even before Hurricane Katrina hit the city, New Orleans' economic importance had already begun to slip. In the new postindustrial global economy, Miami, not New Orleans, became the primary locus of United States finance and trade with the Caribbean.[6] As New Orleans does not occupy a critical position in the global economy, in the wake of the flooding and devastation wrought by Hurricane Katrina, there was no equivalent sense of national urgency to rebuild New Orleans as there had been to rebuild Lower Manhattan after the terrorist attacks of 9/11 and the collapse of the World Trade Center. New Orleans remains an important center of tourism but is not as essential to the health of the national economy as is New York; New Orleans does not occupy a critical position in the global economy.

Globalization denotes the permeability of national borders not just to capital investment but also to population flows. The urban time traveler from the 1950s would undoubtedly be astonished by the variety of languages spoken on the streets of the twenty-first century American city. A **new immigration**, primarily from Latin America and Asia, has brought greater population diversity to cities. Immigrants help provide the investment funds, the creative talent, and the physical labor that can fuel the dynamism of cities and suburbs. Post-Katrina New Orleans experienced a record increase in its Mexican population, as thousands of Hispanic workers came to New Orleans seeking work in the rebuilding of the flood-ravaged city.[7]

A brief look at a list of the persons who died in the 9/11 attacks on New York's World Trade Center (WTC) underscores the importance of immigration to the Global City. The homelands of the victims ranged from the Dominican Republic to Canada to Poland.[8] The dead on 9/11 included both legal and undocumented immigrants, a large number who came from Mexico and who worked as window washers, custodial staff, and food-service personnel in the WTC's below-ground eateries and its top-floor world-renowned Windows on the World restaurant. Mexicans are New York's fastest growing minority and an important source of labor in the city's service industries.

TOURIST CITY

In numerous urban areas, the Industrial City has given way to the **Tourist City**. In a postindustrial age, municipal officials no longer focus their efforts exclusively on "smokestack chasing," offering tax reductions and other incentives in the hope of winning the location of a major new factory. Cities also attempt to generate new economic activity through the construction of sports stadiums, convention centers, casinos, and distinctive tourist and shopping districts. (See Box 1.1, "Baltimore's Harborplace: Reclaiming the Old Dock Area.")

Local leaders recognize that the offering of such subsidies does not constitute the only tool that a city can use to spur economic growth; the provision of urban amenities—that is, making the city a better place in which to live—can help drive local economies. Economist Richard Florida, most notably in *The Rise of the Creative Class*,[9] argues that a city's investment in lifestyle amenities will do more than merely increase tourism: cities need to provide interesting living spaces and a quality of life that can attract computer programmers, Web designers, media specialists, and other knowledge-based workers and members of the **creative class**, a pool of talent that, in turn, will help a city attract major corporations seeking a highly skilled workforce.

An amenities-driven development strategy represents a distinct break with the urban development policies of the Industrial City. For many years, cities wooed manufacturing plants by promising tax cuts and by offering the infrastructure improvements—increased sewage processing capacity, expanded airports, and strengthened city streets that can handle heavy trucks—demanded by businesses. The amenities-driven approach, by contrast, focuses on building more livable neighborhoods. Neighborhoods with sidewalk cafés, Starbucks coffee houses, restaurants offering diverse cuisines, bookstores, rock and jazz concerts, edgy local theater, and access to cycling, river

Box 1.1
Baltimore's Harborplace: Reclaiming the Old Dock Area

Like many other industrial centers, Baltimore over the decades lost industry and population. Baltimore's Inner Harbor, virtually next door to the city's central business district, itself suffering decline, was marred by empty warehouses and closed factories. The city's shallow shipping channel could not handle big ships; as a result, port-related activities migrated outside the city.

Baltimore's civic leaders sought to transform the city's image and bring new activity to the Inner Harbor area. The State of Maryland and the city invested heavily in tourist attractions: Baltimore opened the Maryland Science Center and planetarium in 1976, a new convention center in 1979 (which, years later, was rebuilt and expanded), the "National Aquarium" in 1981, a "retro" Camden Yards ballpark for the Orioles in 1992, and a 71,000-seat football stadium for the NFL Ravens (1998). The city

The Tourist/Entertainment City: Baltimore's Harborplace, with the USS Constellation.

From Wikimiedia Commons, User Cszmurlo, March 6, 2007, http://commons.wikimedia.org/wiki/File:USS-Constellation-Szmurlo.jpg.

Sources: Costas Spirou, *Urban Tourism and Urban Change: Cities in a Global Economy* (New York: Routledge, 2011); Marc V. Levine, "Downtown Redevelopment as an Urban Growth Strategy: A Critical Appraisal of the Baltimore Renaissance," Journal of Urban Affairs 9, no. 2 (June 1987): 103–123.

built—and later rebuilt—a downtown convention center. A new light rail line served the football stadium, ballpark, convention center, and parts of the old downtown. New hotels sprouted on land that was previously disused or underutilized. Expensive townhomes and condominiums took the place of abandoned warehouses.

Without a doubt, the pivotal project in the Inner Harbor's transformation and revival was the 1987 opening of Harborplace, a postindustrial, pier-side entertainment/shopping/dining complex. Visitors can walk along the harbor, watch jugglers and mimes, visit historic ships, and eat and drink in the project's crab houses and Irish-themed bars. Desirable townhouses were soon built on the site of rotting warehouses. Harborplace signaled that Baltimore had "come back."

Critics point to the public cost of all of these projects and ask "who benefits?" and "who loses?" from such heavy public investment in tourist-bubble projects. All of the new development brought little improvement in the lives of people living in Baltimore's more poverty-stricken neighborhoods. Critics also observed that the various Inner Harbor projects led to an increase in land prices and rents in immediately adjacent residential neighborhoods. The gentrification of neighboring areas has been accompanied by the displacement of the working class and the poor.

rafting, and other recreational activities all help to make a city attractive to members of the creative class. Municipal officials hope that if a city attracts talented workers, businesses will soon follow.

The transformation of Chicago provides a case in point. For a long time, Chicago was the prototypical Industrial City, the "City of the Big Shoulders," to use the words of poet Carl Sandburg. Over the years, however, Chicago's position as a manufacturing center began to slip. By the 1960s, Chicago had entered a period of sharp decline, losing both jobs and population.

Mayor Richard M. Daley (who served six terms in office, from 1989 to 2011) responded with programs to reestablish the city's downtown, to strengthen neighborhoods to make them ripe for gentrification, and to make the city more attractive to tourists as well as to creative-class professionals, and to national and global corporations. Daley removed a large antiquated railroad yard located on the lakefront in the heart of the city's downtown in order to build Millennium Park, with its concert venues, exciting public art, skating rink, active water feature, ample space for major public festivals, and acres of underground parking. The city made improvements in up-and-coming residential neighborhoods, planting trees, introducing wrought-iron fences, upgrading softball fields and lakefront beaches, and providing trails for jogging, cycling, and rollerblading. The city introduced clearly marked bicycle lanes on streets that connected the city's "hip" neighborhoods with its downtown; where necessary, the city removed a lane of automobile traffic in order to make way for bicycles. The Chicago River, for many years the site of vacant warehouses and underutilized industrial land, became the location of pricey new waterfront condominiums and even a site for such leisure activities as kayaking; Mayor Daley "wanted the Chicago River to become as lively as the Seine in Paris." By the time Daley left office in 2011, entertainment had become the city's Number One industrial sector.[10] Mayor Rahm Emanuel, Daley's successor, continued the focus on

Box 1.2
The Wire: HBO's Portrait of Baltimore

The Wire, the 2002 Home Box Office (HBO) drama that ran for five years, took television viewers into the poor neighborhoods of Baltimore, a much different world from the tourist bubble of the Inner Harbor and the stadium-related development projects of downtown. *The Wire* presented a fictionalized view of life in the city's most devastated neighborhoods, sections of the city where residents confronted the ills of gang-related activity, illicit drugs, teenage pregnancy, a failing school system, dilapidated housing, lead poisoning, homelessness, and AIDS. In these impoverished neighborhoods, children see no promise of a good future and, instead, turn to drug sales and gang membership as means of advancement. *The Wire* revealed the dreams and aspirations of inner-city residents and how young people adapted to an unforgiving urban environment.

The Wire also provided an indictment of the inability of public institutions to tackle the serious problems and inequalities of the contemporary city. Yet, despite the good intentions of the show's creators, the visuals and storylines of *The Wire* helped reinforce stereotypes that white middle-class Americans have of the central-city poor. The series focused on some of the more salacious elements of Baltimore's inner-city life, while neglecting to reveal more positive elements, such as the extensive activities of BUILD (Baltimoreans United in Leadership Development) and other bottom-up, grassroots community organizations (as this book describes in Chapter 7).

Little in the series focused on Baltimore's downtown—except for shots of police headquarters, city hall, the docks, and newspaper offices as public servants and reporters attempted to do their jobs. The series gave even less attention to Harborplace, an insular bubble of tourist privilege that is separate from, and almost alien to, life in the "real" Baltimore.

Source: Peter L. Beilenson and Patrick A. McGuire, *Tapping into* The Wire: *The Real Urban Crisis* (Baltimore: Johns Hopkins University Press, 2012); Peter Dreier and John Atlas, "*The Wire:* Bush-Era Fable about America's Urban Poor," *City & Community* 8, no. 3 (September 2009): 329–240.

amenities, dedicating additional bicycle lanes and breaking ground for the three-mile elevated Bloomingdale Trail along a disused rail line.

Critics argue that strategies aimed at enhancing amenities and building the Tourist City and the Global City do not necessarily help a city's poorer residents and more distressed neighborhoods. Critics charge that city officials have too often responded to the demands of business interests in constructing a **tourist bubble**, an island of privilege for visitors, young professionals, and major corporations that flourishes in the midst of a larger urban landscape still characterized by extensive ghettoization, urban poverty, and distress.[11] (See Box 1.2, "*The Wire:* HBO's Portrait of Baltimore.")

BANKRUPT CITY

Not all is well with America's cities. The so-called urban renaissance does not extend to all cities and neighborhoods. In the early 2000s, a sluggish national economy and the collapse of the mortgage finance market led to a flood of home foreclosures and boarded-up properties. Decline was not confined only to distressed neighborhoods in the inner city. Fashionable "main-line" suburbs that were once the most desirable communities in a metropolis suffered vacant storefronts and had "For Rent" signs pop up in front of once-attractive single-family homes. Sprawling communities on the edge of the metropolis saw condominium projects left partially built.

In 2013 Detroit became the largest city in United States history to file for bankruptcy. Once the nation's most important automobile manufacturing center, Detroit was unable to manage the transformation to a postindustrial, globalized, and suburban age. In just a single decade, Detroit lost a half million residents, its population of 1.2 million in 1980 shrinking to just 700,000 in 2010. Extensive areas of vacant properties, razed homes, and closed storefronts testified to Detroit's dramatic descent.

One of Thousands of Abandoned Houses in Detroit. Detroit has hemorrhaged population and has no hope of regaining its former size. Note the vacant lots on the sides of the house and dominating the block. As the city no longer needed the extensive housing stock that it had at its peak population, over the years it razed houses that were abandoned and suffering from extensive disrepair. Detroit has physical infrastructure much larger than it presently needs, a "footprint" inherited from the days of the city's Industrial Era vitality.

From Wikimedia Commons, User Notorious4life, May 20, 2010, http://commons.wikimedia.org/wiki/File:AbandonedHouseDelray.jpg.

Declarations of municipal bankruptcy in the United States have historically been rare events. In recent years, however, a number of municipalities have sought Title IX bankruptcy protection. Detroit's move followed bankruptcy filings by two California cities: Stockton (with a population of 296,300) and San Bernardino (population 212,600). Vallejo and Orange County are other large California municipalities that filed for bankruptcy after imposing cutbacks in service provision and attempting to negotiate repayment agreements with the municipality's creditors.[12] Harrisburg, Pennsylvania, similarly began the steps necessary to file for bankruptcy, only to face the intrusion of the state government, which enacted a new law to prohibit the filing. With no other alternative readily available, Harrisburg received state assistance and worked out a deal with the city's creditors, making payments to bondholders while substantially reducing the services provided to local residents.[13]

In each of the cases mentioned above, the municipality's economic well-being had been severely weakened by long-term trends, including deindustrialization and the exodus of the local jobs and tax base to the suburbs. In Detroit, Stockton, and Harrisburg, past labor agreements had further undermined municipal financial stability, saddling the city with generous pensions and expensive health care benefits that were not fiscally sustainable. Stockton permitted police officers to retire and draw benefits at age fifty.[14] Even seemingly prosperous cities like Chicago, Philadelphia, New Orleans, Omaha, and Portland discovered that they were facing a looming pension crisis, and that they were likely to have great difficulty in finding the monies to cover the unfunded pension liabilities owed municipal workers.[15]

Detroit's downfall was largely the result of the city's lack of economic diversification. The city was reliant on an automobile industry that had reduced the number of assembly-line jobs and that was undergoing a restructuring as globalization enabled American manufacturers to assemble automobiles from parts produced overseas. Detroit also faced a greater exodus of wealth and population to the suburbs beyond that experienced by other major cities in the Northeast and the Midwest.[16]

Simple descriptions of the shake out of the automobile industry and the shift of population and economic activity to suburbia, however, do not tell the full story of Detroit's fall. Race also played a role in Detroit's problems, setting the stage for political polarizations, extremes of rhetoric, and a politics of blamesmanship, scapegoating, and distrust that made it impossible for civic leaders to forge coalitions that could provide meaningful responses to the city's mounting problems.[17] The Detroit metropolitan area is arguably the nation's most divided metropolis by race, with white flight to the suburbs leaving a central-city population that is 92 percent nonwhite.[18]

Short-sighted and corrupt leadership, too, exacerbated Detroit's problems. Mayor Kwame Kilpatrick was found guilty in U.S. District Court of bid-rigging in the issuance of city contracts to enrich himself, family members, and friends. Misguided pension managers handed municipal retirees a "13th check" or bonus check in a year, resulting in a loss of nearly $2 billion that could have helped shore up the shortfalls in pension accounts.[19] Such salient episodes of blatant corruption and mismanagement allow critics to place the blame for the city's downfall on the errant behavior, incompetence, and shenanigans of its political leaders.

But corruption and mismanagement, however deplorable, are *not* the root cause of Detroit's decline. The city had hemorrhaged jobs and population during the decades before Kilpatrick assumed office, even during years when the city balanced its budget. The 50-year "downward economic trajectory" of Detroit (and of other large cities) suggests that "no single policy regime"[20]—no single political administration or set of policies—bears the full responsibility for the downfall of Detroit and for the long-term decline of other cities with an antiquated industrial infrastructure. As Chapter 2 documents in greater detail, a vast range of government policies and the self-interested actions of private actors both contributed greatly to the downhill slide of Detroit and other cities.

POWER AND THE STUDY OF URBAN POLITICS

Urban patterns are not inevitable. Patterns of growth and decline are not simply the product of human desires (for a better life, a larger home, and a safer neighborhood) and the workings of an unfettered free market. Rather, government policies and the exercise of private power, too, play a great role in determining just which communities grow and which decline.

As Chapter 2 describes, a great many governmental regulatory and spending programs contributed to the shift of population and economic activity from central cities to the suburbs, and from communities in the **Frostbelt** (the Northeast and Central regions of the United States) to the **Sunbelt** (the South and Southwest). Government policies also helped facilitate the movement of capital to locations overseas. Government tax policies, too, served to incentivize, oftentimes unintentionally, important economic and population shifts.

Even the more recent renaissance of central business districts and core neighborhoods in many cities, is not simply the result of unfettered individual choice operating in a free market. Instead, private interests took actions and demanded public policies that contributed to the revival of a city's downtown and the gentrification of nearby residential areas. A **growth coalition** of interests that benefit from new development—major corporations, property developers, real estate firms, construction unions, and their political friends in office—worked to secure programs committed to downtown revitalization and neighborhood transformation. As Chapters 3 and 4 describe, cities invest heavily in new sports stadiums, convention centers, casino gambling, and historic-themed districts in response to the demands of private actors who gain financially from the emergence of the Tourist City. Municipal governments also invest heavily in the Global City, for instance, in "wiring" the city and in providing the advanced telecommunications infrastructure demanded by multinational and technology-oriented firms. New York City gave extensive tax breaks and other subsidies to create "Silicon Alley," a new and lively area of Internet-related and "new media" firms in the old Flatiron district of Lower Manhattan. Such investment, however, often does little to improve conditions faced by the residents of a city's lower- and working-class neighborhoods.

Private institutions also play an important role in the onset of municipal fiscal crises. Certainly, as discussed above, public officials deserve blame for mismanagement, corruption, short-sightedness, and a reluctance to make politically difficult decisions, when necessary, to cut back services and to restrain the demands of public workers for costly pension and health care benefits. But the blame is not the city's alone. Private lending houses often encouraged debt-ridden cities to issue more bonds—that is, to

Box 1.3
Orange County's Bankruptcy: A Story of Public Imprudence and Private Manipulation

There certainly is nothing natural or inevitable about the 1994 filing of bankruptcy by a municipality as affluent as southern California's Orange County. The county should have had no great problem paying its bills. But when county voters continued to reject new taxes, local officials decided to look for creative ways to maintain public service levels without having to raise taxes. The county treasurer turned to a high-risk borrowing-and-investment strategy; the county borrowed funds to invest in the stock market, with the expectation that the return on the investment would be sufficient to repay the sums borrowed while also yielding sizable additional sums to be used for public service provision.

But the investment scheme did not work out as planned. When the stock market unexpectedly turned sour, the county did not earn the profits that it had anticipated. Worse yet, the county discovered that it could not repay the money it had borrowed.

County officials deserve blame for engaging in such a speculative strategy. But that risky course of borrowing was encouraged by private investment houses and bond rating firms that ignored warning signals that the county was overextended and might have difficulty in paying off its obligations. As the county ran up its debt, brokerage houses continued to encourage private investors to buy the county's bonds, that is, to lend more and more money to the county. By ignoring the warning signs and encouraging more and more loans, these financial houses reaped high loan placement fees and considerable profits.

When the county's debt situation reached the point that it could no longer be ignored, Wall Street financial institutions began to seize collateral and sell off the Orange County portion of their investment portfolios. Moody's and other bond rating houses downgraded the county's credit rating. Private investors saw these actions as a clear signal not to buy new county bonds, a shutoff of funds that precipitated the county's 1994 filing for federal bankruptcy protection.

Source: Marc Baldassare, *When Government Fails: The Orange County Bankruptcy* (Berkeley, CA: University of California Press, 1998); Milan J. Dluhy and Howard A. Frank, *The Miami Fiscal Crisis: Can a Poor City Regain Prosperity?* (Westport, CT: Praeger, 2002), 82–83.

borrow more and more money despite fiscal warning signs—as the bond houses and private financial firms earned considerable fees from the continuing issuance and sale of municipal bonds. (See Box 1.3, "Orange County's Bankruptcy: A Story of Public Imprudence and Private Manipulation.")

When a municipal fiscal emergency occurs, private institutions act to ensure that their interests are served, even at the price of drastic cuts in the level of municipal services provided city residents. In Vallejo and Stockton, more conservative interests used the looming threat of municipal bankruptcy to force local officials to adopt a more business-like model of operation, downsizing government, reducing public services, dismissing public workers from their jobs, and making past labor contracts "rewritable,"[21] in essence forcing municipal unions to accept reductions in the level of health care and pension benefits to which the municipal employers had previously agreed. Vallejo shrunk the size of city staff, closed fire stations, cut services to senior centers, and lowered the funding of libraries.[22]

POWER: THE ABILITY TO GET THINGS DONE

The particular focus of this book is on power and how it is exercised in the urban arena. The study of cities and suburbs requires that we look not only at the decisions made by public officials but that we also look behind the scenes to the influence of private actors.

Power is too often viewed simplistically only in terms of **social control**; a political actor possesses power when he or she can force others to comply with his or her wishes. Under this elementary definition of power, an actor has "power over" others who fear sanctions or punishments should they fail to behave as expected.

In the study of cities, however, power does not refer only to situations of social control, to situations where a person has "power over" someone else. Rather, **power** also denotes **social production** or the "power to" get important things done. The exercise of power does not always entail conflict and the use of overt or even hidden threats. An actor also has power when he or she can organize things and get important projects accomplished. Power is exercised by someone who is successful in arranging coordination and joint action in the pursuit of goals.[23]

In the urban arena, we need to find out whose cooperation is necessary for social production, that is, whose active participation or consent is necessary to get things done and who possesses the ability to stop or thwart important courses of action. The study of urban politics must go beyond descriptions of the formal structures of city government and the *powers* (that is, the formal bits of authority) that a mayor, city manager, city council members, and other officials possess. A critical examination of the urban arena requires that we also look at how these actors get things done, despite their oftentimes quite limited formal authority or powers of office. The study of local politics also requires a focus on nongovernmental actors and institutions to discover the degree to which public officials are constrained in their decision making. Just whose cooperation—both inside and outside of government—do municipal officials require in order to get important things done?

In Detroit, municipal officials simply lacked the ability to organize social production; they lacked meaningful power, that is, the "power to" get major things done. Detroit officials could not put in place policies to constrain suburbanization; they had no ability to enact regional land-use plans to limit the outmigration of jobs and population. They lacked the formal authority to impose the taxes that would yield the funds necessary to tackle the city's many deep-seated problems. They could not force independent suburban governments to enter into meaningful collaborative arrangements with the city to increase racial integration or otherwise improve conditions in the city's public schools. Nor was the city able to offer the financial inducements necessary to attract and retain major corporations in the city and thereby improve the city's fiscal position. A major corporation could simply turn to other jurisdictions that offered subsidy packages that were the equivalent of—or even superior to—those offered by Detroit.

PRIVATISM: THE LIMITED POWER OF GOVERNMENT

In sharp contrast to Europe, cities in the United States lack strong public authority and planning powers. In Europe, government officials enact strong regulations on land use; local and regional governments in Europe also rely on public investment—even having the municipality buy up available land—to guide urban development and to ensure the achievement of public purposes. Compared to the United States, European governments have much stronger tools that they can use to curb urban sprawl, to preserve historic areas and the city streetscape, to construct effective mass transit systems, and to build extensive affordable housing. European governments not only invest heavily in mass transit systems; European planners establish pedestrian-free zones in the center of cities, limit parking in the downtown, and even set the timing of stoplights to slow the movement of traffic—all measures intended to limit automobile use and to promote the livability of cities.[24] Planners in Europe often require that the developers of new commercial projects provide subsidized housing units for the poor.[25]

Such policies, widely adopted throughout Europe, are, with few exceptions, alien to the American city. In Europe, governments play a strong role in shaping metropolitan areas; private developers and free-market forces do not dictate the geography of urban development.

In the United States, in contrast, a prevailing culture of **privatism** serves to keep public planning and governmental authority to a minimum while maximizing private-sector freedom. The privatist culture of the United States views cities narrowly as places where private actors engage in profit-making activities. In the American "private city,"[26] homeowners and the heads of business possess great leeway to develop and dispose of their property as they see fit. Many of the most important decisions that affect a city's health are in the hands of private actors, including business leaders, real estate developers, mortgage lenders, and homebuyers, not public officials. Americans resist strong urban planning requirements and the imposition of land-use restrictions that they view as violations of an individual's freedom and property rights.

In a privatist system, city officials lack the ability to dictate "good" urban development and actions to correct urban problems. Instead, public officials in the United States must gain the involvement of private actors, persuading them to undertake actions that are important to the city. In the United States, more so than in Europe, urban problem solving requires effective partnerships that entail action by both government and private-sector actors.

Privatism also denotes a system that gives great deference to private contracts and the concerns of private investors. In cases of municipal bankruptcy, a city's first obligation is not to its citizens but to its creditors. A city is legally required to take steps to repay its creditors, even if such repayment forces a city to make steep cutbacks in police protection and other important neighborhood services. The necessity of repaying creditors (or at least certain types of creditor) may even require that a city make sharp reductions in the pensions and health benefits provided to retired municipal workers.

A municipality in fiscal distress must obey the legal requirements of a privatist system that protects investors. Municipal bondholders are "superior claimants"[27] who stand first in line to get paid. When the small city of Central Falls, Rhode Island, declared bankruptcy, municipal workers found that they had little alternative but to accept reductions of up to 55 percent in their pensions, at the same time that the city was initiating steps to repay bondholders in full. The State of Rhode Island even gave bondholders the right to place liens on municipal tax revenues, a step that further protected creditors and forced steeper cuts in other service areas. In Stockton, California, a U.S. federal bankruptcy judge ruled that the city, seeking to emerge from bankruptcy, could reduce its contributions to worker pension plans despite having agreed to the benefits in past labor agreements.[28] In the privatist city, profit-seeking investors often enjoy a privileged position that is denied to municipal workers and ordinary citizens.

Yet, a city's creditors do not always come out ahead. Detroit's financial stewards pursued a more balanced approach to bankruptcy, not one that repaid investors while making deep cuts in the pensions of retirees. New pacts with labor unions led to some cuts in retirement benefits, including the elimination of cost-of-living increases and a reduction in health benefits. But the city also went to court arguing that some of its obligations to creditors should be voided. The city justified its move claiming that the Bank of America, UBS, and other financial institutions had prompted the city to make complicated interest-rate swaps, transactions that the city said were illegal, decisions that further eroded the long-term ability of the city to meet its pension obligations. Detroit's fiscal manager offered the holders of certain types of bonds only 20 cents on the dollar. Stockton had offered a major creditor only a penny on a dollar to settle outstanding debts.[29] The formal rules of bankruptcy privilege some bondholders, but not all bondholders. Private financial interests cannot simply dictate to the city. In the contemporary city, skilled public leadership also counts.

THE SUBTHEMES OF THIS BOOK

As already noted, the major focus of this book is on the interrelationship of public authority and private power in the American metropolis. Six important subthemes further guide this book's study of politics in United States cities and suburbs:

1. GLOBALIZATION EXERTS A POWERFUL INFLUENCE ON CITY AFFAIRS

Globalization—the cross-border flow of investment, the outsourcing of production to sites located in other countries, the rise of internationally based as opposed to locally rooted businesses, and heightened immigration—has had a great influence on the contemporary urban situation. The competition for business no longer takes place only among the cities and suburbs of a single region; instead, economic competition has become national and global in its scope. The actions of private managers have always had an impact on a locality's affairs; but in a global age, managers handed a local assignment by multinational corporations will often lack the sense of civic loyalty that an earlier generation of locally rooted downtown business leaders had displayed.

Globalization entails the trans-border flow of population. Modern transportation enables large numbers of people to travel to the United States from abroad. The long-term relaxation of the nation's immigration laws, too, has altered the demography and politics of U.S. cities. Twenty-four large- and medium-size cities have a population that is more than one-fifth foreign born (see Table 1.1). Over 60 percent of the population of Miami was born outside the United States, as was nearly half the population of Santa Ana and 40 percent of the populations of Los Angeles and Anaheim. Over one-third of New York City's population was born outside the United States. In a global age, immigrants, both

Table 1.1

Top 25 Cities Ranked by Percent of City's Population That Is Foreign Born, 2002 (and 2009 Census estimate for the nations' largest cities)

Rank	City	Percent Foreign Born, 2002	Percent Foreign Born, 2009[†]
1.	Miami, FL	60.6	*
2.	Santa Ana, CA	48.4	*
3.	Los Angeles, CA	41.3	39.7
4.	Anaheim, CA	40.3	*
5.	San Francisco, CA	36.7	34.1
6.	San Jose, CA	36.5	38.1
7.	New York, NY	36.0	35.7
8.	Long Beach, CA	30.9	*
9.	Houston, TX	28.1	28.5
10.	San Diego, CA	27.9	24.9
11.	Oakland, CA	27.1	*
12.	Boston, MA	27.0	25.1
13.	Dallas, TX	26.5	24.8
14.	Sacramento, CA	26.4	*
15.	Honolulu CDP, HI	25.5	*
16.	El Paso, TX	24.9	24.1
17.	Stockton, TX	24.2	*
18.	Riverside, CA	23.9	*
19.	Fresno, CA	22.7	*
20.	Chicago, IL	22.6	20.6
21.	Newark, NJ	22.4	*
22.	Phoenix, AZ	21.1	21.7
23.	Las Vegas, NV	21.1	*
24.	Denver, CO	20.2	24.8
25.	Austin, TX	19.6	20.2
26.	Aurora, CO	17.7	*
27.	Minneapolis, MN	17.6	*
28.	Seattle, WA	17.2	17.1
29.	Arlington, TX	16.6	*
30.	St. Paul, MN	16.3	*

Source: Extracted from U.S. Census Bureau, American Community Service Office, "Percent of Population That Is Foreign Born," September 2, 2003, www.census.gov/acs/www/Products/Ranking/2002/R15T160.htm; and U.S. Census Bureau, Statistical Abstract of the United States: 2012, Table 39, www.census.gov/compendia/statab/2012/tables/12s0039.pdf.

[†]Estimate reported only for the nation's 25 largest cities.

*The 2009 *American Community Survey* estimate presented data only for the 25 largest cities in the United States. An asterisk indicates that the city was not one of the nation's 25 largest in terms of population in 2009 and hence no data was reported.

legal and undocumented, represent an infusion of capital and labor into the local economy. Particularly in states along the border with Mexico, however, the arrival of unauthorized immigrants can strain budgets for schools, law enforcement, and health care.[30]

The new immigration is not only reshaping the politics of big cities; it is also altering politics in suburbs and smaller cities. Immigrants to the United States now reside in a more widely dispersed set of communities than did waves of immigrants who came to America during earlier eras in the nation's history. Foreign-born families are no longer found solely in port-of-entry cities; today, recent arrivals also turn to heartland cities like Denver, Indianapolis, Minneapolis, and St. Paul, and to smaller cities and the suburbs in a search for jobs. By 2010, over half of the nation's immigrant population was living in suburbs.[31]

2. *FORMAL RULES AND STRUCTURE CONTINUE TO HAVE AN IMPORTANT IMPACT ON LOCAL POLITICS*

This book stresses the critical role played by private power in the local arena, that nongovernmental institutions and players are key participants in urban decision making. Yet the formal rules and structures of local government remain important. The formal structure and processes of local government help determine just whose interests are represented in city hall and just what does and does not get done. This book shall examine the extent to which alternative electoral rules (including voter registration requirements and at-large versus district-based council systems) and alternative local governmental structures (i.e., city-manager-led systems versus strong-mayor cities) favor different interests. This book will also examine alternative arrangements for interlocal cooperation in metropolitan areas.

The formal position of local government in the American federal system is set by the United States Constitution. To be more precise, the U.S. Constitution makes no explicit mention of the existence of cities and lists no constitutionally protected powers for cities. Instead, each of the fifty states decides just what units of local government it will create and just what exact authority each unit may—and may not—possess. In general, the state-imposed rules serve to fragment local authority, creating numerous and relatively autonomous general-purpose governments (cities, counties, townships, etc.) and more specialized local political bodies, including school districts and the bistate Port Authority of New York and New Jersey.

Constitutionally speaking, municipalities are mere administrative subdivisions of a state's government. Each state determines the exact powers of its various local governments. State laws tend to strictly limit the taxing and borrowing capacities of local governments. Even the question of municipal bankruptcy—whether or not a city or county may file for federal bankruptcy protection—is a matter that is left up to each state; nearly half (twenty-three) of the states prohibit municipal filings for bankruptcy protection.[32]

3. *THE INTERGOVERNMENTAL CITY: STATE AND FEDERAL GOVERNMENTS PLAY AN IMPORTANT RULE IN URBAN AFFAIRS*

Cities and suburbs exist in an intergovernmental setting where the decisions of the national and state bodies help determine the formal powers and the resources available to local governments. The ability of cities and suburbs to solve problems is highly dependent on decisions made by the state and national governments.

The concept of the **intergovernmental city** points to the significant impact that state and national government decision making has in local affairs. State and national financial assistance accounts for nearly 40 percent of local government revenues.[33] Financially distressed communities are even more greatly dependent on intergovernmental assistance for the continued provision of basic municipal and social services.

State and federal **mandates** can also burden a city with the cost of providing specific required services. New York State law, for instance, mandates that New York City pay for half the state share of federal Medicaid program benefits provided for poor people. This is the largest Medicaid burden that any state in the nation imposed on its local governments. In 2008 alone, this single mandate saddled New York City with $4.6 billion in spending obligations.[34]

The actions taken by state and local governments can be critically important to cities facing fiscal failure, as a comparison of the 1975 New York City fiscal crisis and the 2013 Detroit bankruptcy will make clear. In the mid-1970s, New York City teetered on the edge of fiscal insolvency, unable to pay creditors as its loan obligations became due. But the city did not technically file for bankruptcy. Instead, the federal and New York State governments intervened in quite helpful ways, especially with "guarantees" that they would assure the repayment of bonds issued by New York City. In effect, the national government and the State of New York acted to assure creditors that these higher governments would take on much of the responsibility for loan repayment should the city itself prove unable to meet its repayment schedule for newly issued bonds. These guarantees led creditors to extend new flows of cash to New York, giving the city time to undertake the necessary reforms to put its fiscal house in order.[35] The State of New York created the Municipal Assistance Corporation to sell state-backed bonds to help the troubled city borrow the money it needed to maintain the provision of public services. New York's governor also met with the leaders of local labor unions—especially the teacher's union—to convince labor officials to use union funds to buy city-issued bonds and, by doing so, to keep the city financially afloat. The United States Congress voted to extend the city over $2 billion in loans.[36]

However, times had changed considerably by 2013, when Detroit filed for bankruptcy. The state and federal governments did not extend to Detroit similar levels of assistance that had decades earlier been extended to New York City. Republican Governor Rick Snyder even faced great difficulty in trying to convince Michigan's Republican-controlled legislature to approve a commitment of $350 million over twenty years as the state's piece of a "grand bargain" to resolve the city's pension crisis. Under the grand bargain that had been struck, if the state would commit $350 million and retirees would agree to a reduction in benefits, donations from philanthropic foundations would cover nearly a half billion dollars of additional pension obligations.[37]

Why were federal and state governments more reluctant to help Detroit than New York? To a great extent, the answer lies in the fact that the two cities occupy different positions in the global hierarchy of cities. A functioning and vital New York City is critical to the good health of the nation's economy. Detroit, by contrast, is no longer even a lively industrial center; its days as a critical national economic hub had clearly passed. State and federal officials aided New York out of fear that a New York City bankruptcy would have severe repercussions that would cripple the entire United States economy.

Few national actors shared similar sentiment regarding the repercussions of a Detroit bankruptcy.

Partisan perceptions, too, make a different. Michigan's Republican legislators were reluctant to set a precedent where other communities would demand that the state intercede to help them with their debt. State legislators were also reluctant to saddle people living in other parts of the state with the costs of aiding Detroit. Some high state officials had even argued that municipal bankruptcy was fairly desirable, a means of forcing the city to curb its excess spending and to introduce new policies that would help attract businesses.

But even the Democratic administration of President Obama was reticent to step in and offer Democratic Detroit broad-scale assistance. In a suburban age, especially at a time of divided government in Washington (the Republican Party controlled the House of Representatives), there was simply no great willingness by the federal government to step in with a major assistance package to help Detroit get back on its feet.

Detroit "is no longer self-governing."[38] Its elected officials lost power as the State of Michigan placed much of the governing authority for the city in the hands of a state-appointed fiscal manager, an unelected official who does not answer to Detroit's elected officials or to the city's voters.

4. *SUNBELT V. FROSTBELT: REGIONAL DIFFERENCES IN URBAN PATTERNS*

During the second half of the twentieth century, Sunbelt communities in the South, the Southwest and the West generally grew and prospered while the aging Frostbelt communities in the Northeast and Midwest suffered long-term decline. The problems typical of growing communities in the Sunbelt—increased traffic, gaining access to water supplies in the arid Southwest, and controlling land use to protect the natural environment—differ markedly from the problems faced by declining communities.

The 2010 census confirmed the continuing shift of population to the Sunbelt (Figure 1.2 and Table 1.2). California, Arizona, Texas, and Florida enjoyed the fastest rates of growth in the nation. Of the nation's ten largest metropolitan areas, the Dallas-Fort Worth-Arlington metroplex and greater Houston were the fastest growing.[39] The nation's most quickly growing communities—Gilbert, Chandler, and Peoria (Arizona); North Las Vegas and Henderson (Nevada); and Irvine, Rancho Cucamonga, and Chula Vista (California)—are in the Sunbelt.[40] Other rapidly growing communities were found in Arizona, Nevada, Utah, and Washington, as families in metropolitan areas on the West Coast and in the Southwest began to look inland for affordable housing and a lower cost of living.[41]

The regional shift in population has also led to a regional shift in political power: The voting power of Frostbelt states has declined while that of the Sunbelt continues to grow. The 2010 census count indicates that Texas is in line to pick up an additional 4 seats in the United States House of Representatives. The Sunbelt as a region was expected to gain an additional 12 congressional seats, an increase that would solidify the region's congressional dominance; 263 of the 435 House of Representative seats are in the South and the West.[42]

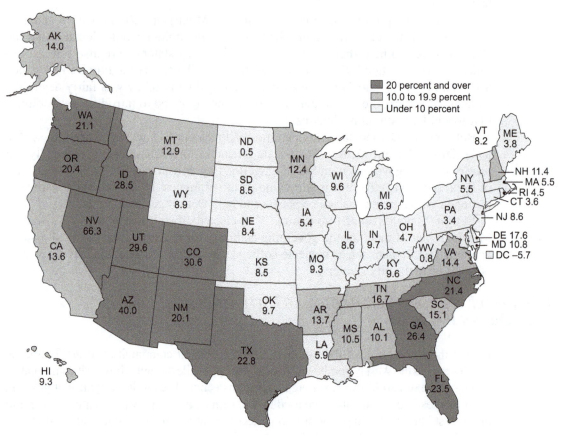

Figure 1.2 **The Regional Shift: Percent Change in Population by State, 1990–2000**

Source: U.S. Census Bureau.

Table 1.2
Population Change in the United States by Region, 2000 to 2010

Region	Population		Percent Change, 2000–2010
	2000	2010	
Northeast	53,594,378	55,317,240	+3.2
Midwest	64,392,776	66,927,001	+3.9
South	100,236,820	114,555,744	+14.3
West	63,197,932	71,945,553	+13.8

Source: Extracted from U.S. Census Bureau, "Population Distribution and Change, 2000 to 2010," *2010 Census Briefs* (March 2011), www.census.gov/prod/cen2010/briefs/c2010br-01.pdf.

Ann Markusen uses the term **gunbelt** to underscore the importance of defense-related expenditures to the growth of Sunbelt communities, especially in California, Texas, and Florida. But the "gunbelt" is not strictly confined to the Sunbelt. The list of communities that have benefited from defense-related and aerospace spending also includes Seattle, Colorado Springs, Washington, D.C., and the high-tech suburbs of Boston.[43]

In pointing to the important differences between regions, special care must be taken to avoid stereotyping the communities located in each region. A region is not a homogeneous entity; Sunbelt communities are not all alike, just as Frostbelt cities are not all alike. Sunbelt communities are not uniformly prosperous. Even before Hurricane Katrina, New Orleans experienced the sort of urban problems—deindustrialization and the loss of jobs, large concentrations of inner-city poverty, and the racial segregation of schools and neighborhoods—that are typically associated with big cities in the Northeast and Midwest. Even relatively prosperous communities in the South and Southwest contained large concentrations or "pockets" of poverty: Miami (26.5 percent poverty); Memphis (26 percent); New Orleans (24 percent); Dallas, El Paso, Tucson, and Fresno (23 percent); Atlanta (22.5 percent); Stockton (22 percent); and Houston and Phoenix (21 percent).[44] In the states of the former Confederacy (the "Old South" as distinct from the growing Southwest), much of new local dynamism was confined to resort and retirement communities. Despite its general reputation as an economic "boom" region, the Sunbelt is not a region of uniform urban growth and prosperity.

Frostbelt cities similarly exhibit considerable variation. The economic resurgence enjoyed by New York and a number of other Frostbelt success stories is barely evident in cities like Detroit, Buffalo, St. Louis, and Youngstown. Over one-third of the population of Detroit (36 percent) and Cleveland (35 percent) fall below the poverty line. Other Frostbelt cities have poverty rates that are nearly as debilitating: Buffalo (29 percent); Milwaukee and St. Louis (27 percent); Cincinnati (26 percent); Philadelphia (25 percent); Newark and Toledo (24 percent); Pittsburgh, Columbus, Minneapolis, and St. Paul (23 percent); Chicago (22 percent); and Baltimore and Boston (21 percent). In so-called "disaster cities," poverty rates are so high as to be almost unbelievable: Benton Harbor, Michigan (56.7 percent, over half of the city's population!); Camden, New Jersey (38.2 percent); and East Cleveland (37.7 percent).[45]

Despite important Frostbelt-Sunbelt differences, the urban crisis in the United States is a national phenomenon. Home foreclosures and property abandonment are not confined to distressed Rustbelt cities like Detroit, Indianapolis, and Cleveland. In 2009, the highest foreclosure rates in the nation were actually reported by four Sunbelt states—California, Florida, Nevada, and Arizona.[46] The economic recession and housing finance meltdown of the early 2000s brought an end—or at least a temporary halt—to what had appeared to be an unstoppable Sunbelt boom.[47]

5. *THE DOMINANCE OF LOCAL ECONOMIC DEVELOPMENT CONCERNS*

Concerns for job creation and economic development have come to dominate local politics. City after city and suburb after suburb have pursued a variety of strategies in their efforts to win the competition for the location of industry. Postindustrial dislocation, advances in telecommunications, and the globalization of corporate structures have all increased capital mobility, adding to the sense of economic insecurity felt by local communities. By the beginning of the twenty-first century, economic development was clearly the Number One issue on the agenda of most cities.

This was not always the case. In the 1960s, battles over school busing, community control, big-city riots, civilian-police review boards, and anti-poverty programs defined urban politics. A half century later, these competing issue concerns have largely fallen to the wayside as local officials give priority to efforts aimed at attracting new industries.

Of course, "crime" remains a salient issue in many communities. Younger and more upscale voters also exhibit a new concern for **ecological sustainability**, for having the city take actions to preserve energy resources and to protect the natural environment. Cities in the arid West are also concerned with water, as the limited availability of this critical resource can impose severe constraints on industrial and residential growth. In the early 2010s, the debate over immigration and the status of undocumented workers also gained new prominence in the local as well as the national arena.

Still, despite the attention demanded by other policy issues, a general sense of local economic fragility has given American urban politics in the twenty-first century its defining character. Local voters and municipal officials have both given renewed emphasis to projects aimed at local economic growth and job creation.

6. *THE CONTINUING IMPORTANCE OF RACE AND ETHNICITY IN THE URBAN ARENA*

In the United States, city politics is intertwined with the politics of race. A "new immigration" from Latin America and Asia has further added to the complexity of ethnic and racial relations—and politics—in the American city.

There is much good news when it comes to race in the metropolis. Statistical evidence points to increases in residential integration. The all-white suburb has virtually disappeared from the metropolitan landscape. Yet, despite these gains, the data also point to continuing racial discrimination, imbalances in housing, and the persistence of ghettoization. While federal fair housing laws have succeeded in helping to eradicate the most blatant forms of housing discrimination, more subtle discriminations still mar the housing market. African-American home seekers, for instance, are shown fewer available homes than are shown comparable white homebuyers.[48]

Statistical evidence also documents the worsening racial balances found in public school classrooms. In recent years, racial integration in the public schools has not been increasing but has been decreasing, especially as judicial decisions have given localities across the United States new permission to terminate desegregation efforts.[49] The Supreme Court has even limited the ability of local school boards to use race as a substantial criterion in setting the enrollments for "magnet schools," schools that have such attractive specialized programs that they can serve as a tool for voluntary integration. Instead of continuing progress toward integration, the statistical evidence points to an increasing **resegregation of public schools**, with African-American and Latino students learning in environments that are racially isolated. Much of the new school resegregation is found in the suburbs, places of refuge for families who have chosen to move away from school districts that are receiving an influx of lower-income and nonwhite children.[50]

Americans overwhelmingly condemn *de jure* **segregation**, that is, the noxious practice of requiring segregation by law. The famous 1954 U.S. Supreme Court decision ***Brown v. Board of Education*** began the prolonged process of bringing an end to *de jure* segregation, that is, the end of state-ordered school segregation. But *Brown* did not end the extensive segregation of public school classrooms that existed "in fact" but was not ordered by state or local law. Despite the *Brown* ruling, inner-city schools of many big cities have either no white enrollment or only a handful of white students. Similarly, while many suburbs have integrated schools, a great many others have schools with only a quite minimal African-American enrollment.

While Americans overwhelmingly approve the dismantling of *de jure* segregation, there is no equivalent public willingness to combat *de facto* **segregation**, patterns of residential and school segregation that exist "in fact" even though racial separation is not mandated by law. The racial imbalances that exist in public schools are largely a reflection of residential patterns, the differences in the racial and ethnic composition of different city neighborhoods, and the different racial composition of cities and suburbs.

Race Still Shapes the Metropolis: "Thank You" Sign to the Local Sheriff in Gretna, Louisiana. After Hurricane Katrina, residents of the white working-class suburb of Gretna placed such signs in their front yards to express their support for the local sheriff. Sheriff Arthur Lawson had gained national notoriety when he used armed local officers to block entry by poor African Americans who were seeking to cross the bridge into Gretna, to flee the devastation and death wrought by the flooding of New Orleans.

From Wikimedia Commons, photo taken by Infrogmation, November 25, 2005, http://commons.wikimedia.org/wiki/File:Gretna23NovThankChiefLarson1.jpg.

Race still shapes the American metropolis, a truth revealed by the response of different communities to Hurricane Karina. In the midst of the storm, vigilantes, and in some cases even the local police, barred entry into the neighboring suburbs by black New Orleansians attempting to flee the destruction and death of their flooded city.

In 2014 riots broke out in Ferguson, Missouri, a suburb outside of St. Louis, as protestors vented their anger over the shooting of an unarmed black youth by a white officer. Two-thirds of Ferguson's population is African American, evidence of the new population diversity of suburbia. Yet the city had a white-dominated government. Protestors complained about the city's militaristic approach to policing and the irresponsiveness of government to African-American concerns in a city where the mayor, the police chief, and five of the six city council members are white. In Ferguson and other American communities, questions of racial justice and severe racial cleavages and tensions lie just beneath a surface veneer of public normalcy.

CONCLUSION: THE URBAN SITUATION

Despite downtown revivals and neighborhood gentrification, the urban crisis continues. Not all American cities, suburbs, and communities have "come back." The nation's most distressed communities may even lack the ability to come back on their own. Once-industrial centers continue their steep decline. Big and small cities alike are vigorously looking for a niche that the city can occupy in a postindustrial global economy. Housing affordability and homelessness remain salient urban problems, even in an era of widespread home foreclosures and vacant properties. Homeland security has burdened communities with costly protective services. An underperforming national economy and cutbacks in federal and state aid have compounded the difficulties that cities and suburbs face in maintaining adequate levels of public services. Ghettoization persists and, in important ways, the problems of school segregation and isolation are getting worse.

One of every six central-city families lives in poverty. The poverty rate in primary cities (18.2 percent) in 2007 was nearly twice that found in suburbs (9.5 percent).[51] Despite the much-celebrated renaissance of major cities, job growth in central cities continues to lag behind that of the suburbs. The revival of downtown business districts has blinded more casual urban observers to the continuing fragility of big-city economies; core cities continue to lose private-sector employment market share to the suburbs.[52] Cleveland, Youngstown, and other hard-hit Frostbelt cities have so little hope of attracting industry and population that civic leaders have turned to a **shrinking cities strategy**, turning large areas of the city over for use as community gardens, urban agriculture, and green space. Detroit has similarly turned to a shrinking cities strategy, seeking to save money by taking certain neighborhoods "off line," that is by reducing the service levels provided to depopulated neighborhoods.

Urban problems have also spread to the suburbs. From 2000 to 2008, suburbs saw a 25 percent increase in the number of people living in poverty.[53] Many inner-ring **first suburbs**, a city's oldest and nearest suburbs, exhibit new weaknesses: the shutdown of aging manufacturing plants; vacant storefronts in once-exclusive suburban shopping strips; and the appearance of vacant homes and "For Rent" signs in communities that were once among the most exclusive in the metropolis. Today's young homebuyers are bypassing first suburbs for homes located in newer communities, homes with large kitchens, multiple bathrooms, and vast backyards.

The next chapter tells the story of how the great cities of the United States began to weaken during the years following World War II. The demographic shifts and economic dislocations that buffeted cities were not all "natural" or foreordained. Public and private power helped to shape just which communities grew and which declined. The focus of this book is on power: Who has the power to get things done in the local arena? Whose cooperation is essential for effective governance? Who is—and is not—effectively represented in the metropolis? Just whose interests do municipal governments serve?

KEY TERMS

agglomeration (an economics concept) (*p. 5*)
Brown v. Board of Education (*p. 25*)
cluster patterns of development (*p. 5*)
creative class (*p. 7*)
de facto segregation (*p. 25*)
de jure segregation (*p. 25*)
ecological sustainability (*p. 24*)
edge cities (*p. 4*)
edgeless development (*p. 4*)
first suburbs (*p. 26*)
Frostbelt (*p. 13*)
gentrification (*p. 3*)
Global City (*p. 5*)
globalization (*p. 5*)

globalized economy (*p. 5*)
growth coalition, a city's (*p. 13*)
gunbelt (*p. 23*)
intergovernmental city (*p. 20*)
mandates, state and federal (*p. 20*)
new immigration (*p. 7*)
power as social control (*p. 15*)
power as social production (*p. 15*)
privatism (*p. 16*)
resegregation of public schools (*p. 24*)
shrinking cities strategy (*p. 26*)
Sunbelt (*p. 13*)
tourist bubble, a city's (*p. 10*)
Tourist City (*p. 7*)

2 | **The Evolution of Cities and Suburbs**

The choices made by developers, business investors, and homebuyers all help determine patterns of urban growth and decline. Yet the "free market" does not tell the full urban story. This chapter details how government programs—including "hidden" urban policies—have shaped metropolitan America. The chapter also describes how manipulations by self-interested private actors impede the workings of a free market to produce urban problems that cannot be viewed solely as the "natural" results of free choice.

THE NATURAL FACTORS THAT SHAPE THE GROWTH AND DECLINE OF CITIES AND SUBURBS

In a classic essay on urban development, political scientist Edward C. Banfield pointed to three sets of natural forces or "imperatives" that determine urban growth and decline.[1] The first is **demographic**: increases in population, for instance, push a city to expand outward. The second is **technological**: the available transportation and communications technology determines just how far outward residents and businesses can move. The third is **economic**: more affluent people have the means to seek the "good life" in communities located far away from the congestion, cramped housing, and crime of the central city, while poorer people will tend to occupy the less desirable sections of the metropolis.

Clearly, such natural forces have shaped the American metropolis. The oldest part of most cites can be found by a major locus of transportation—a harbor, river, canal, or important railroad or trail junction—that provided the commercial access necessary for a community's economic growth. Cities in the West such as Fort Worth (Texas) and Fort Collins (Colorado) are exceptions: they sprouted near the protection of army outposts in a hostile environment.

The American city of the 1700s and early 1800s was relatively small in size. Walking was a major form of urban transportation. Hence, urban historian Kenneth Jackson refers to these preindustrial communities as **walking cities**.[2]

Steam Trains and Electric Trams, The Bowery, New York City, 1896. In the pre-automobile age, cities were the center of economic activity, with trains and electric streetcars providing the essential transportation lifelines.

Originally published in 1896 in *The New York Times*. http://commons.wikimedia.org/wiki/File:The_Bowery,_New_York_Times,_1896.JPG

The primitive nature of transportation technology limited the territorial expanse of the walking city. Workshops and residential spaces were often located in the same neighborhood. Wealthy merchants, shippers, manual workers, and the poor all lived inside the city, close to work. During this early era, cities had not yet lost population and wealth to suburbs. The hamlets and farm villages outside the city were rural, not suburban; residents of the countryside had little interaction with the city.

Cities grew in a process called **urbanization**: migrants left the poverty and economic vagaries of life in the countryside for the promise of jobs, education, and opportunity offered by the city. During the industrial age, factories in the city attracted job seekers from the countryside and immigrants from overseas. The population pressures forced the city to expand.

Suburbs did not even appear as part of the American landscape until the latter half of the nineteenth century.[3] The movement of population away from the center city had to await progress in transportation technology. In the early and mid-1800s, workers could move only as far out as a horse-pulled streetcar could take them. Successive transportation innovations—the electric trolley, the steam railroad, electric commuter trains, and the automobile—each enabled more and more residents to move farther and farther away from the city center.

But even during the age of the electric streetcar, urban areas were relatively compact, quite unlike the sprawling megalopolises of today. Advances in building technology, including the introduction of the elevator, reinforced the urban core, with the first skyscrapers constructed in the late 1880s. The American city expanded upward before new transportation technology allowed it to spread outward.

For a long while, permissive state laws enabled the city to extend its political boundaries to reflect the outward movement of population. Cities used the power of **annexation** to adjoin neighboring areas to the city, with the city swallowing up an abutting community and making it part of the city. The residents of underdeveloped outlying communities, where streets were barely paved and service provision was quite poor, often looked to the larger city for road paving, street lighting, and the provision of municipal water and gas. There was not yet massive resistance to annexation.

A turning point came in 1893 in a **political revolt by Brookline, Massachusetts**, a growing suburb that was surrounded by Boston on three sides. Brookline spurned annexation by Boston. Brookline residents saw their community as a "refuge" from the dirt and corruption of the industrial city. They feared that joining the city would lead to higher taxes. Ethnocentrism, the distrust of foreigners, also played a role in the suburb's rejection of the city. Brookline residents opposed to annexation "frankly stated that independent suburban towns could maintain native American life free from Boston's waves of incoming poor immigrants."[4] After the Brookline revolt, suburbs across the United States began to fight to maintain their independence from the city.

Changes in state laws began to favor the suburbs, making it increasingly difficult for cities to expand via major annexations. Urban populations continued to grow and move outward, but central cities in many states could no longer easily extend their political boundary lines. **Streetcar suburbs** sprouted along the electric trolley tracks, beyond the borders of the central city. As historian Sam Bass Warner Jr. summarized, "the metropolitan middle-class abandoned their central city."[5]

While the middle class began its move to the suburbs, poorer residents from rural areas continued to pour into cities in search of economic opportunity. In the **Great Migration** (roughly from 1910 through the 1940s), millions of poor African Americans—and whites—left the rural South to go to Chicago, Detroit, Pittsburgh, and other big cities in the North. The mechanization of agriculture and the end of the sharecropper system in the South pushed the rural poor off the land. To meet the production needs of both World Wars I and II, city factories sent recruiters to the South in search of workers. Appalachian and rural whites as well as African Americans moved northward, searching for both economic security and social freedoms.[6]

The automobile revolutionized urban form; suburbanites no longer needed to live in close proximity to streetcar and railway lines. The automobile enabled home seekers to fill in the spaces between the "fingers" of development that already existed along streetcar and rail lines. The automobile also enabled commuters to reside at a considerable distance from the city center.

Industrial and commercial enterprises soon accelerated their own move to the suburbs. Manufacturers, seeking the space necessary for assembly-line production, were attracted by the relatively low price of undeveloped land located on the rim of urban areas. The rise of the trucking industry enabled the exodus of warehousing and distribution activities out of the central city. Older manufacturing and warehousing sections of the core city, areas such as New York's SoHo and Lower East Side, suffered a steep decline. Beginning in the 1970s, advances in cargo containerization further accelerated the suburbanization of warehousing and distribution activities, as narrow and congested cities streets and the small loading docks of old central-city warehouses could not handle the new shipping technologies.

Retail and entertainment establishments followed the middle class and its buying power to the suburbs. Suburban residents did not want to be bothered with long drives for shopping, traffic jams, and the difficulties in finding parking downtown. Commercial developers responded by constructing open-air plaza-type shopping centers and, later, enclosed shopping malls in the suburbs. By the 1950s and 1960s, retail sales in the central city plummeted. In 1983, Hudson's department store, long associated with Detroit, closed the doors of its downtown flagship store, having opened new stores in various suburban shopping malls. Detroit gained the dubious distinction of being the largest city in the country not to have a major department store within the city's borders. Baltimore, Toledo, Dayton, Davenport, Charlotte, Fort Worth, and a great many other cities soon saw long-established department stores close, signaling the decline of the downtown core.

Advances in telecommunications would soon free white-collar offices from the need to be located in a region's central business district. They, too, began to move to the suburbs. Orange County, California, witnessed an office boom south of Los Angeles. Outside Chicago, the office towers of Schaumburg comprise a virtual second downtown in greater Chicagoland. Similar concentrations of offices, shopping centers, and hotels sprouted in **edge cities** that sprang up on the rim of virtually every major metropolitan area: Route 128 outside of Boston; White Plains (New York) and the New Jersey suburbs of New York City; King of Prussia (outside of Philadelphia); Rosslyn, Crystal City, and Tyson's Corner (in northern Virginia in the Washington, D.C. metropolitan area); Troy and Southfield (just north of Detroit); the Houston Galleria; the Perimeter Center north of Atlanta's beltway; and various communities on the Silicon Valley peninsula lying between San Francisco and San Jose, to name only a few. **Technoburbs**, high-technology-oriented suburbs, mushroomed as the sites of globally oriented and foreign-owned firms.[7] The **multicentered metropolis** emerged as the new urban reality; the central city and its downtown no longer dominated the urban region.

In the 1950s and 1960s, when the movement to the urban rim was still in its relative infancy, suburbia was stereotyped as a land of relatively tranquil **bedroom communities** where husbands commuted to the central city for work. Industrial and factory suburbs also existed but did little to mar the overall perception of a serene, predominantly white and middle-class suburbia.

Over the decades that followed, suburbia would continue to mature. Today, suburbia is clearly much more diverse and dynamic than the 1950s stereotype. Suburbs have become the site of high-tech industry, office campuses, entertainment venues, cultural centers, universities, and fine dining. For most suburban residents, life on the city's rim no longer seems "sub" to that of central cities.

Today, the all-white suburb, which had no African-American residents, has largely disappeared. The racial integration of suburbia has increased. Lower-income residents, too, are increasingly found in the suburbs. Yet, despite these important gains in diversity, suburbia is not fully open to minority citizens and the poor, populations that continue to disproportionately reside in the central city and in declining inner-ring suburbs. Conditions in the most troubled inner-ring suburbs, including East Cleveland, Trenton (New Jersey, just across the river from Philadelphia), East St. Louis (Illinois), and East Palo Alto (California), are in many ways indistinguishable from those of the urban core.

The latter half of the twentieth century also saw a major shift of population and economic activity from the older **Frostbelt** cities of the Northeast and the Midwest to the growing **Sunbelt** communities of the South and West. The nation's most dynamically growing cities were in the Sunbelt, while cities in the Northeast and North Central regions continued to lose population (see Table 2.1). At the beginning of the twenty-first century, the nation's fastest-growing metropolitan areas—Las Vegas, Phoenix, Austin, Boise, and Santa Ana (California), to name just a few—continued to be found in the Southwest and the West.

As Edward Banfield theorized, advances in technology help to explain Sunbelt growth. The introduction of jet travel and other innovations in transportation and telecommunications allowed citizens and corporations to move to Sunbelt communities with their warm weather, sunny skies, good beaches, and promise of escape from the congestion and social ills of northern communities. Businesses were also attracted to the region's relatively cheap land. The introduction of air-conditioning was essential for the growth of cities in the torridly hot South. With the marvel of machine-cooled air, northerners could even move to Miami, a city built on a mangrove swamp.

Fax machines, satellite communication, e-communication, and the new digital technology enabled businesses to leave the city and move to small towns across the country

Table 2.1

Growing and Declining Cities by Region: Cities over 100,000 Population, 1980

U.S. region	Number of cities with 100,000+ population	Number of cities gaining population	Number of cities losing population
Northeast	23	—	23
North Central	39	8	31
South	60	46	14
West	47	39	8
Total	169	93	76

Source: Bureau of the Census, U.S. Department of Commerce News (Washington, DC, June 23, 1981), x.

and even out of the country. Business CEOs (chief executive officers) relocated data entry and other clerical and support operations to less costly sites in far-off small towns and overseas sites. Rosenbluth Travel, one of the nation's largest travel agencies, relocated its 200-employee reservations center from downtown Philadelphia to low-wage Linton, North Dakota. American Airlines moved its ticket-processing center from Tulsa to Barbados. New York Life shifted insurance processing operations to Ireland, where workers are well educated but are paid less than workers in the United States.[8]

A number of former manufacturing centers were able to reemerge as postindustrial **global cities**, the office and financial centers of the knowledge-based world economy (an emergence that Chapter 3 describes in greater detail). New York, Los Angeles, Chicago, and San Francisco, no longer the factory cities of old, now serve as centers of corporate headquarters, banking, conventions, trade shows, and tourism.

Other former manufacturing centers, however, were unable to break their downward trajectory. In many cases, distressed cities lack the highly educated, professional workforce that global firms value. These cities continued to suffer such extensive population losses that their inner-city neighborhoods are marred by extensive abandoned housing and vacant lots. Cleveland lost over half of its population, dropping from 915,000 in 1950 to 391,000 in 2012. **Shrinking cities** like Cleveland, Detroit, Flint, Dayton, Youngstown, Buffalo, Rochester, Syracuse, and New Orleans no longer expect that they will ever recover their former population and status. Instead, these cities have begun to cope creatively with their decline, turning to extensive **greening strategies**—demolishing dilapidated buildings and turning vacant properties into side lots, expanded parks, natural swales to aid storm-water retention, and community gardens and urban farms—in order to create a new urban living environment with a greater appeal to residents and corporate investors.[9]

HIDDEN URBAN POLICY: HOW THE GOVERNMENT SHAPES METROPOLITAN DEVELOPMENT

As just described, natural factors—population pressures, technology, and affluence—have a great impact on determining where people live and where businesses locate. But contrary to Edward Banfield's claim that these forces are "imperatives" that dictate the exact patterns of urban growth and decline, government policies and the actions of powerful private actors—including banks, lending institutions, real estate firms, and land developers—intrude on and distort the operations of the market. Numerous government programs have accelerated the disinvestment in older cities and the shift of activity to the suburbs and the Sunbelt.[10]

The federal programs with the greatest impact do not always have an explicit urban orientation. Many of these programs have quite laudable objectives: building the interstate highway system; helping Americans to buy homes of their own; rewarding veterans for their service; promoting the construction of much-needed hospitals and sewage plants; and incentivizing business expansion. Yet these programs constitute a **hidden urban policy** as they also have a tremendous, albeit often unintended, influence on the growth and decline of American communities.

THE FHA AND VA: FEDERAL HOMEOWNERSHIP PROGRAMS SHAPE URBAN GROWTH AND DECLINE

Federal assistance helped millions of working-class and middle-class families to buy homes of their own. The **Federal Housing Administration (FHA)** sought to make America a nation of homeowners by incentivizing banks and other mortgage lending institutions to extend home loans to borrowers for whom the financial institutions would normally deny credit.

FHA loan insurance provides protection for up to 80 percent of the value of an approved property. The FHA essentially guarantees that a credit institution will be repaid 80 percent of a loan if an FHA-certified homeowner defaults on scheduled payments. By removing most of the risk that a lender faces in issuing a home loan, FHA insurance spurred financial institutions to give mortgages to millions of Americans who would not, in the program's absence, have received credit. Facing less risk with FHA-backed loans, lenders could also reduce down-payment requirements and interest rates, putting home ownership within the reach of the working and middle classes.

The **GI Bill of Rights of 1944** extended similar assistance through the **Veterans Administration (VA)** to millions of soldiers returning home from World War II. As "the VA very largely followed FHA procedures and attitudes … the two programs can be considered as a single effort."[11] Together, the FHA and VA programs offered prospective homebuyers a very attractive package of low or no down payment, easy credit, and a twenty-five- to thirty-year period of very manageable monthly payments.[12]

These federal programs accelerated suburban development and central-city decline. The programs backed the purchase of new homes; the programs did not offer similar insurance for the purchase of apartments or for the renovation of older housing in the central city. The FHA was guilty of **redlining** large portions of central cities, refusing to approve loans in inner-city areas even from qualified homebuyers.

The anti-city bias of the FHA was codified in the agency's 1939 *Underwriting Manual.* The *Manual* instructed FHA underwriters to minimize homeowner defaults by looking for "economic stability" when making neighborhood evaluations. As the *Manual* explicitly declared, "crowded neighborhoods lessen desirability."[13] The FHA wrote off the "graying" areas of the inner city and instead chose to finance suburban development.

The suburban bias of the government programs is well evident. From 1934 to 1960, home seekers in the suburban portions of St. Louis County received five times as many FHA-backed loans as applicants in the city of St. Louis. The FHA redlined entire cities it saw as risky; in New Jersey, no loans were approved in Camden and Paterson.[14] By shutting off mortgage money, the FHA virtually guaranteed the precipitous decline of already-fragile communities.

A second FHA bias was even more pernicious; the agency pursued policies that mandated racial segregation. Until its policies were finally changed in the 1950s and 1960s, the FHA—a government agency—explicitly endorsed a policy of racial segregation as a means of protecting the value of government-insured homes.

The agency's *Underwriting Manual* stated, "If a neighborhood is to retain stability, it is necessary that properties shall continue to be occupied by the same social and racial classes."[15] The *Manual* instructed federal underwriters to give a low rating to mortgage applications that would lead to the "infiltration of inharmonious racial or nationality groups" into a neighborhood.[16] In other words, the government required residential racial segregation before it would approve a loan! The FHA even endorsed the use of **restrictive covenants**, legally binding agreements that prohibited a buyer from reselling the home in the future to someone of a different race.[17] This was government-enforced racial segregation.

The FHA also practiced **racial steering**, using its process of loan approvals to ensure that black and white homebuyers would reside in different neighborhoods. The FHA did not approve loans to minority applicants who sought to buy homes in all-white suburbs. In fact, very few African Americans even won FHA backing. A paltry 2 percent of the homes built with FHA mortgage insurance in the post–World War II era were sold to minorities, and half of those involved homes that African Americans bought in all-minority subdivisions.[18] In the 1940s, the FHA even required the developer of an all-white subdivision to build a six-foot-high, half-mile-long concrete fence—a wall—along the border with Detroit in order to seal off the new housing development from a nearby black neighborhood.[19]

Why did the FHA, an important federal agency, practice segregation? FHA administrators feared that racial integration would jeopardize local property values, with white families fleeing neighborhoods undergoing racial change and defaulting on their loans. The FHA also reflected a point of view that, largely unthinkable today, was popular at the time. The National Association of Real Estate Boards in its code of ethics encouraged practices to preserve the racial homogeneity of a neighborhood.

"The Wall," Detroit, 1941. A half-mile long concrete wall constructed along Detroit's outer boundary was designed to keep African Americans from the city out of a new housing development that was built in the suburban community on the other side.

From the Library of Congress Prints & Photographs Division, Washington, DC 20540, http://www.loc.gov/pictures/item/fsa2000044373/pp/.

Outcries from civil rights groups eventually led the FHA to end its blatantly discriminatory practices. By 1949, the agency deleted from its manual the references to "racial groups" and "infiltration." But the harm that the FHA had done could not be undone. The FHA had helped to underwrite the growth of a racially homogeneous suburbia and the decline of minority-dominated central-city neighborhoods.

The agency's pro-suburban lending biases also incentivized new sprawled development. In Los Angeles and other metropolitan areas, the FHA examiners approved home loans for "leap-frog" housing projects built on the edges of the metropolis in previously undeveloped natural areas.[20]

To its credit, the FHA in the 1960s reversed course and began to aggressively approve home loans in the inner-city areas it had previously ignored. Unfortunately, even this U-turn in FHA policy unintentionally hastened the decline of numerous inner-city neighborhoods as the FHA approved loans to applicants who lacked strong work and credit histories. FHA properties in the inner city deteriorated as these owners lacked the financial means and readiness to assume the responsibilities of home ownership.[21]

The agency also failed to provide the necessary oversight to prevent unscrupulous lenders and real estate firms from recruiting buyers who would prove unable to make orderly payments. As a review of one FHA program in the late 1960s reported, "the well-intentioned program turned into a scam for unethical real-estate speculators who bought decaying inner-city dwellings, slapped on coats of paint, and haphazardly made other superficial improvements before selling the houses at grossly inflated prices to unsuspecting buyers."[22] Many homeowners, dissatisfied with the structural problems of their "unfit" homes, walked away from the properties. As a result, FHA-backed properties wound up in default, boarded up and abandoned, accelerating the decline of core urban neighborhoods.

Critics also blame the FHA for many of the home loan defaults that plagued the banking and housing markets in the early 2000s. The critics argued that the FHA was exceedingly lax in its standards for mortgage approval, a process that put families into homes they could not afford, leading to foreclosure and abandonment.[23] In 2007, at the height of the home finance crisis, nearly 411,000 FHA mortgage holders were in default, and an estimated 24 percent of FHA-backed loans faced "serious problems."[24]

Yet this indictment of the FHA is overly harsh. The agency was not responsible for the great bulk of home foreclosures in the inner city. In the early 2000s, large numbers of low-income families circumvented the FHA approval process, obtaining "subprime" loans from private lenders that offered the promise of unrealistically low monthly payments. The FHA was more stringent in its underwriting standards than were the new private lenders who earned fees as a result of each loan that was issued. In the midst of the mortgage market meltdown of the early 2000s, FHA-approved loans actually had a better record of repayment than did the loans issued by the new private mortgage firms.[25]

Republican-era deregulation of the credit industry enabled new and more unscrupulous private lenders to offer homebuyers non-FHA-backed mortgages at quite advantageous terms. The foreclosure crisis was the result of "high-cost, abusive, and often fraudulent transactions designed to trap homeowners and homebuyers into usurious obligations."[26] This time, the "bad guys who stuck up the cities were not using federal mortgage insurance to 'FHA' entire neighborhoods with vacant foreclosed homes."[27] The predatory lending practices of unregulated lenders, more so than the negligence of the FHA, led to the rash of mortgage foreclosures and the collapse of housing markets.[28]

FEDERAL TAX SUBSIDIES FOR HOMEOWNERS: A HUGE HIDDEN URBAN POLICY

The federal tax code encourages homeownership, allowing homeowners to deduct mortgage interest and property taxes from their taxable gross income. In 2012 alone, homeowners received more than $117 billion in assistance through the tax code. The $117 billion in **tax expenditures** provided to homeowners (the amount that the federal treasury lost as a result of the deductions and credits claimed by homeowners) surpassed by far the $62 billion that the federal government spent on its various programs to assist low-income renters.[29]

The tax write-offs have helped millions of Americans to buy a home of their own. Critics argue, however, that the programs do not really increase homeownership as much as they enable people to buy more expensive homes.[30] The great bulk of the deductions do not promote homeownership; rather, sizable tax benefits are claimed by families who have the wealth to buy a home even without the assistance of special federal tax provisions.[31]

The deductions have an urban impact. They have clearly helped to fuel suburban development, making it easy for the middle class to flee the central city. As the tax advantages can only be claimed by homeowners, the programs do not really provide any great transfusion of money to central-city neighborhoods with large stocks of rental housing. The programs offer very little assistance to the inner-city poor. Even poor families who own a home will have incomes so low that they do not itemize deductions and hence cannot claim the mortgage deduction. The mortgage interest deduction is of no value to them.

What does all of this mean? The tax expenditures give the greatest subsidies to more affluent homeowners while failing to target aid to families most in need of housing assistance. The program is often criticized as being **Robin Hood in reverse**; unlike the legendary Robin Hood who stole from the rich to give to the poor, the homeowner provisions of the tax code "give to the rich." The tax provisions are a **mansion subsidy** that critics deride as **welfare for the rich**. Nearly two-thirds of the program's subsidies go to people who make more than $200,000 a year.[32] Wealthier families buy the most expensive houses, pay the biggest mortgages, and hence receive the biggest subsidies. By comparison, the middle-class homeowners and the poor get relatively little from the program. The tax credits are worth on average $7,200 a year to a person who earns $200,000 a year. A lower-middle-class taxpayer who earns between $50,000 and $75,000 receives only a mere fraction of that amount, $1,150 in homeownership incentives.[33] Renters get no tax subsidy at all.

The tax deductions for homeownership have also helped stimulate **condominium and cooperative apartment conversions** in the city. As a tenant receives a subsidy only for buying—and not for renting—a dwelling unit, the program serves to create an incentive that leads landlords to convert apartment buildings into condominiums and cooperatives, displacing tenants who cannot afford to buy their apartments in a building that is "going condo."

THE ANTI-URBAN BIAS OF HIGHWAY CONSTRUCTION AND FEDERAL AND STATE PLANNING

During the days of the Cold War with the Soviet Union, the United States government committed itself to completing a national highway network for the quick and efficient transport of military personnel and materiel. The National Defense Highway Act of 1956 increased the federal share of funding for highway construction projects from 50 percent to 90 percent.

The new highways did more than facilitate military and interstate travel. They also opened outlying areas in a metropolis to development. Federally-funded highways were the "main streets" of a growing suburbia. The intersections of major highways with the "beltway" road that encircled the city became the obvious choice for shopping centers, enclosed malls, power stores, and office parks, facilities that enabled people to move still further away from the central city.

Federal highway construction destroyed the vitality of numerous inner-city neighborhoods.[34] The new highways divided communities, displacing tenants and erecting physical barriers that made it difficult for residents who lived on one side of a highway to reach neighborhood stores located on the other side. The stores closed, the neighborhoods decline, and, where they could afford it, residents moved to the suburbs.

In city after city, local decision makers turned to highway construction as a tool to remove a city's black population from areas located near the city center. In Florida in the mid-1960s, highway planners built a leg of the I-95 expressway that "tore through the center of Overtown," Miami's large African-American community. The construction displaced more than ten thousand residents and razed Overtown's business district, destroying an inner-city community that was once renowned as the "Harlem of the South." In Nashville, Tennessee, highway planners put a "kink" in the route of I-40, destroying hundreds of homes and putting a divider through black North Nashville.[35]

African Americans were not the only victims of highway construction. In order to build new highway capacity to help suburban commuters, highway planners also destroyed working- and middle-class communities. The 1950s construction of the Cross Bronx Expressway in New York City tore apart a solid working-class, Jewish neighborhood. Forced from their homes, many residents left the city, never to return. The construction led to the social descent of the South Bronx.

Even more modern regional planning efforts, despite their stated commitment to neighborhood and environmental protection, oftentimes wind up using federal funds to support suburban development. In metropolitan Atlanta, ARC (the Atlanta Regional Commission) planned new roads and set a framework for new high-quality development (i.e. single-family homes built on cul-de-sacs with adequate setbacks and stream buffers) that provided the infrastructure for new development on the suburban rim.[36]

THE URBAN AND REGIONAL IMPACTS OF MILITARY AND AEROSPACE SPENDING

Defense-related spending also helped promote the growth of both suburbs and the Sunbelt. During World War II, decision makers sought spread-out production sites that could not easily be bombed by the enemy. Rather than expand production in Detroit, the war planners built new plants outside the city. Even after the war's end, the U.S. Defense Department continued its preference for dispersed production sites, providing the employment base for continued suburban development.[37]

World War II production contributed to the economic dynamism of Sunbelt cities, including Los Angeles, San Diego, Phoenix, Fort Worth, San Antonio, Oklahoma City, New Orleans, and Atlanta.[38] Warm-weather locations provided ideal locations for port activities, troop training, and airplane testing. The corporate executives who served on the War Production Board also preferred cheap-labor Sunbelt locations that lacked the strong labor unions found in the manufacturing centers of the North.

During the Cold War military and aerospace spending continued to fuel Sunbelt economies. From 1951 to 1981, Defense Department spending for prime contracts (that is, the amount of money that the government spends on the construction of military facilities and the purchase of goods from the private sector) increased by 810 percent in the South and 402 percent in the West, but fell by 1.5 percent in the Midwest.[39] The Defense Department closed the New York and Philadelphia naval yards, deciding to retrofit its Atlantic and Pacific fleets in lower-cost nonunion Norfolk (Virginia) and San Diego. Massive governmental expenditures for space exploration led to an economic boom in Florida (the Cape Canaveral launch site) and Texas (especially in the area near the NASA Johnson Space Center located in Houston). Government contracts for missile-guidance systems and other high-tech computerized and electronic components propelled the growth of communities in California's Silicon Valley and the Pacific Northwest, especially the Seattle region, which at the time was the headquarters for Boeing aircraft. Defense contracts even helped pay engineers to relocate in northern California's Silicon Valley.[40]

THE URBAN IMPACTS OF OTHER FEDERAL PROGRAMS

Generous **federal grant programs for hospitals and sewage processing facilities** helped to underwrite the infrastructure costs of new development in the suburbs and the Sunbelt. Federal **tax incentives to businesses** to promote private investment in more modern machinery and physical plants similarly spurred commercial construction in the suburbs and the Sunbelt; the government did not give a similar array of tax benefits to firms to rehabilitate and remain in the aging manufacturing plants of central cities in the Northeast and Midwest. Critics derisively referred to the government's investment tax credit to businesses as an **urban disinvestment tax credit**, as the incentives led businesses to abandon older central-city plants.

Federal tax incentives for the oil and gas industries helped catalyze economic development in the South and West. Houston's dynamic growth can be attributed at least in part to the quite favorable tax treatment accorded the petrochemical industry. Federal grants for port development and highway construction also helped provide the infrastructure for Houston's growth.[41]

The federal **urban renewal** program in the 1950s and 1960s was intended to help troubled cities. But in clearing large parcels of land for expanded business districts and new university campuses, urban renewal displaced low-income and minority residents and destroyed existing neighborhoods. Urban renewal tore down more housing than it built.

Urban renewal has often been referred to as **Negro removal**: local governments used federal renewal assistance to tear down the homes of African Americans who resided too close to a city's central business district or to privileged white neighborhoods. In Pittsburgh, city planners relocated African-American families from urban renewal areas to housing projects built in other black sections of the city, a relocation program that sought to reduce the objections of white neighborhoods to the city's urban renewal agenda. City planners also reinforced racial boundaries in the city, creating a "buffer zone" of open space between Pittsburgh's central business district and nearby neighborhoods that had a sizable African-American population.[42]

Hispanic areas, too, have been the targets of urban renewal programs. In San Antonio, renewal efforts cleared neighborhoods in the Central West project, nearly 70 acres of land adjacent to the downtown and HemisFair '68, San Antonio's World's-Fair-style exhibition intended to raise the city's profile and to attract new investment to the city. The redevelopment projects accommodated institutional interests; the city built a new convention center and a new court house. Public officials showed little concern for relocating the displacees. Very little of the new housing that was built could be considered affordable.[43]

The Chicago suburb of Addison in 1997 agreed to pay $1.8 million to Hispanic families whom the local redevelopment agency had pushed out of their homes in the city's designated renewal area. The city had razed a number of structures that could not be considered blighted. "It was Mexican removal in the guise of urban renewal," said the lead attorney representing the Leadership Council for Metropolitan Open Communities.[44]

LOCAL GOVERNMENTS CHOOSE SEGREGATION: BUILDING THE "SECOND GHETTO"

As the Pittsburgh, San Antonio, and Addison stories suggest, local governments have often used their powers to reinforce residential segregation. In Chicago, during the decades that followed World War II, the city council and various public agencies pursued a course of action to reinforce the city's racial boundaries. The Chicago Housing Authority (CHA) discriminated in tenant assignments on the basis of race. The CHA did not automatically award a vacant public housing unit to the next family on a waiting list. Instead, the CHA looked to the applicant's race in an effort to ensure that a new tenant would be compatible with the population of the surrounding neighborhood. Whites were admitted to housing projects in white areas; blacks were sent to housing projects in black areas. The city council also gave each individual alderman (Chicago's name for a member of its city council) the power to reinforce segregation. Each member of the city council possessed the authority to veto the placement of a new public housing project in his or her ward. White council members barred the construction of public housing projects that would introduce racial minorities into their neighborhoods.

Chicago, Miami, and a sizeable number of other cities can be seen to have chosen the construction of a **second ghetto**. Of course, each major city has an area of dilapidated housing that became a ghetto when better-off families moved away. But the second ghetto was different; it was not a natural phenomenon but a government creation.

"We Want White Tenants in Our White Community: Sign Opposite the Sojourner Truth Housing Project, Detroit, 1942. Racism and segregated housing were found in northern cities, not just in the South. In Detroit, a riot by white neighbors prevented African Americans from moving into a federal housing project.

From the Library of Congress Prints and Photographs Division, Washington, DC 20540, http://www.loc.gov/pictures/item/owi2001018484/pp/.

Local governments essentially chose to pursue a course of action that created a new or expanded ghetto area with boundaries that did not match those of a city's older or more natural ghetto. In Chicago, civic leaders sought to prevent blacks, displaced by urban renewal projects, from moving into neighboring white areas. The city relocated African Americans in immense high-rise public housing that it built in isolated industrial areas or on the edges of the city's existing black neighborhoods.[45] A half century later, living conditions in the segregated high-rises proved so awful that Chicago, with financial assistance from the federal government, finally decided to tear down much of the high-rise ghetto that the city had previously constructed.

Other cities, too, have a hidden history of segregative actions. New York City, for instance, violated the federal Fair Housing Act, setting racial quotas for certain public-housing projects and steering black and Hispanic applicants away from projects with largely white populations. The city also established a policy of giving preferential treatment to applicants who lived in the area surrounding a housing project. Whatever its merits, the policy effectively prevented black families from gaining entrance to public housing in white neighborhoods.[46]

SUBURBAN ZONING POWERS AND THE ABILITY TO "KEEP OUT" UNWANTED POPULATIONS

A vast number of suburbs refuse to take the steps necessary to allow the construction of subsidized housing units within their borders. Of even greater significance, as Chapter 9 will describe in greater detail, suburbs use their **land-use and zoning powers** to exclude

Box 2.1
**The Uses and Abuses of Zoning: The New York
Metropolitan Area**

In 1916, New York became the first city in the United States to adopt a zoning ordinance, a move so revolutionary that it was hailed as opening "a new era of civilization."[1] The New York ordinance regulated the use, height, and bulk of all new buildings, an effort to protect residential neighborhoods against the intrusion of new skyscrapers.

Zoning helps to assure orderly land development by preventing incompatible land uses. No homeowner wants to see a factory or an automobile repair station built next to his or her home. Zoning prevents such incongruous development by designating different sections or zones of a community for different uses. Certain land parcels are designated for industrial and commercial uses; other parcels are reserved for residential development. Light industry can be kept separate from heavy industry. Apartment buildings may be allowed in certain areas, while other sections of the city are zoned only for single-family homes.

Suburbs utilize their zoning and land-use powers to keep out both "nuisance" and heavy industrial activities; they also use these powers to keep out lower-income people. Communities in Westchester County, just north of New York City, have relied on zoning and other land-use restrictions to prevent the "Bronxification" of their area; they did not want their communities to become like the neighboring borough of New York City. Suburban ordinances typically restrict (or even ban) the construction of apartment buildings. Suburban ordinances typically require that new homes be built on large lots with large-size rooms and other expensive construction features. In many communities, such local ordinances wind up putting the price of a home beyond the reach of middle- and working-class families as well as the poor.

What would happen if a locality could not use zoning and land-use powers to constrain new development? One hint is provided by the 1964 opening of the Verrazano Narrows Bridge, which connected Staten Island to the rest of New York City. Staten Island is a part of New York City; it is not a suburb with the legal authority to enact zoning and other land-use controls. As a result, new construction on Staten Island differed from that found in nearby suburbs in New Jersey: "Compared with the region's typical suburb, Staten Island has been a paradise for the home building industry"; a typical home on Staten Island is "smaller, less expensive, more crowded, and less attractive than that built during the same period in the suburbs of the New York region."[2] The pace of new construction threatened green space and "the suburban neighborhood character" of Staten Island.[3]

As the comparison of development on Staten Island and New Jersey reveals, local zoning has obvious virtues. New Jersey communities were able to use the tools of zoning to prevent the levels of overdevelopment and overcrowding that can diminish the quality of local life.

> Yet critics observe that local zoning controls also have a downside. Stringent zoning regulations diminish the production of good-quality affordable housing. Suburbs often use zoning as a potent weapon of exclusion, a means to "keep out" less-advantaged people.
>
> 1. Robert M. Fogelson, *Downtown: Its Rise and Fall, 1880–1950* (New Haven, CT: Yale University Press, 2001), 160. See Fogelson's larger discussion, 160–166.
> 2. Michael N. Danielson and Jameson Doig, *New York: The Politics of Urban Regional Development* (Berkeley: University of California Press, 1982), 79, 106–107.
> 3. "New York City Council Stated Meeting Report, December 3, 2003," *Gotham Gazette,* December 3, 2003, www.gothamgazette.com/searchlight/council.2003.12.03.shtml.

subsidized housing for the poor. Middle- and upper-income communities use their zoning powers to restrict housing opportunities for lower-income and working-class families. More affluent communities maintain their exclusivity by limiting the construction of apartment buildings and townhomes, housing units that would be within the financial reach of working- and lower-middle-class families. A suburb can drive up the price of entry into a community by requiring that new homes are built on excessively large lots of land and meet expensive construction requirements that exceed concerns for health and safety. (See Box 2.1, "The Uses and Abuses of Zoning: The New York Metropolitan Area.") Such zoning practices are a root cause of the racial and income imbalances of communities in the contemporary metropolis; they serve to concentrate poorer and minority citizens in the central city and in a region's more distressed "first suburbs."[47]

SUNBELT GROWTH: FREE-MARKET GROWTH OR BUSINESS SOCIALISM?

In the Sunbelt, urban growth has not simply been the result of the region's good climate and innovations in transportation. Rather, local governments undertook expensive public programs to attract growth. Local governments did not simply step aside and allow the free market to work. Instead, Los Angeles, Houston, San Antonio, and San Jose incurred huge debts in order to provide the sewer, street, highway, and other infrastructure improvements demanded by businesses.

Local governments, acting at the behest of business influentials, played an important role, devoting public monies to building the infrastructure that business desired. In the years that followed World War II, Houston boosted its debt eightfold in order to finance the city's municipal construction boom: in Houston, the "public sector actively fueled and sustained the urban development process with public dollars."[48] In Los Angeles, the "local state" similarly invested heavily in the region's port, airport, and rail facilities, enabling the region to emerge as a center of global trade.[49] Despite the claims of advocates of American capitalism, it was not the workings of an unfettered free market that by itself lured businesses to the Sunbelt. Corporations in the Sunbelt enjoyed the substantial business-friendly investments provided by government, a sort of business-oriented municipal socialism!

SUMMING UP: THE GOVERNMENT'S ROLE ASSESSED

In his review of American urban development, historian Kenneth Jackson asks, "Has the American government been as benevolent—or at least as neutral—as its defenders claim?"[50] The answer must be a resounding "No!" Urban problems are not purely the result of natural ecological evolution; they are also the consequence, often unintended, of various government policies and actions.

Government policy—especially its "hidden" urban policy—has played a great role in shaping the metropolis. An advocate of cities may reasonably argue that the government has an obligation to remedy the urban problems it helped to create.

THE IMPORTANCE OF CORPORATE AND PRIVATE POWER

Private decision makers, oftentimes working hand in hand with public officials, also played a critical role in dictating patterns of urban growth and decline. Urban trends that at first glance seem "natural" may, under closer examination, reveal the manipulation and influence of private sector actors.

Even the Great Migration was not entirely the result of the aspirations of African Americans who left the South in search of a better life in the cities of the North. Rather, industrial owners in the North helped promote the migration for their own purposes. In need of labor, the owners of mills and foundries in the early 1900s sent their agents to the South to hire poor black tenant farmers: "Poor rural blacks with little understanding of industrial conditions and no experience with unions were recruited in the South and transported directly to northern factories, often on special trains arranged by factory owners."[51] The recruiters promised the migrants an ideal life, which, in reality, was nowhere to be found, especially as the new arrivals were often shunted into segregated worker dormitories. The mill owners found a particular advantage in utilizing African Americans as **strike breakers**, a means of containing labor union organizing and militancy.

WHY PRIVATE INDUSTRIALISTS INITIALLY CHOSE SUBURBAN LOCATIONS

The initial move of industry to the suburbs was prompted, at least in part, by the efforts of factory owners to contain labor militancy. The industry did not simply follow its workforce to the suburbs. Instead, in the early twentieth century, a number of industrial giants built **company towns** to house their workers in areas outside the city that otherwise had no significant residential population:

> Between 1899 and around 1915, corporations began to establish factory districts just beyond the city limits. New suburban manufacturing towns were being built in open space like movie sets. Gary, Indiana, constructed from 1905 to 1908, is the best-known example. Other new industrial satellite suburbs included Chicago Heights, Hammond, East Chicago, and Argo outside Chicago; Lackawanna outside Buffalo; East St. Louis and Wellston across the river from St. Louis; Norwood and Oakley beyond the Cincinnati limits; and Chester and Norristown near Philadelphia.[52]

Why would owners choose to locate manufacturing plants in relatively remote sites in an era when transportation was primitive and the suburbs were not easily accessible? Quite simply, central cities in the 1880s and 1890s were sites of union organizing and labor unrest. Choosing a factory site away from the city allowed an owner to control workers and **contain labor militancy**.

In the manufacturing suburb of Pullman, just south of Chicago, industrial magnate George Pullman, inventor of the railway sleeping car, exerted strict control over his workers. He offered good-quality company-owned cottages as a reward to cooperative employees. But as the owner of all housing in his company town, Pullman was also able to evict union organizers and other "troublemakers," ousting outspoken workers from their homes as well as from their jobs.

PRIVATE POWER AND THE MARKETING OF THE SUBURBAN IDEAL

The "natural forces" theory of urban development highlights how new technology changed the shape of the American metropolis. The introduction of the automobile determined the sprawling character of development in the Los Angeles region. Los Angeles and other cities in the West that grew rapidly during the age of the automobile followed a pattern of spread development. Their development is in sharp contrast to metropolitan areas in the Northeast and Midwest that have a more compact urban form, as they largely developed before the age of the automobile.

But a closer look at the evolution of Los Angeles reveals that a technology-based or automobile-focused explanation of the region's development is incomplete. Los Angeles took on much of its "spread city" shape before the automobile gained popularity, *before* the region's famed freeways were built.

Fringe development outside Los Angeles actually began in the early years of the twentieth century. Local real estate developers, including Henry Huntington who also owned a private streetcar company, the Pacific Electric Railway, sought to make their fortunes in real estate. Huntington built his system of electric interurban streetcars as a means to bring potential buyers to his suburban home sites. The finest mass transit system of its day, Huntington's Red Cars (featured in the cartoon movie *Who Framed Roger Rabbit?*) traveled at speeds of forty-five to fifty-five miles per hour. Huntington's streetcars operated at a loss, but the monetary losses did not matter. The streetcars were there to help him sell homes; the streetcar losses were the subsidy that Huntington was willing to pay in order to generate a demand for the homes that he was building on the outer edges of Los Angles. The demand was not purely natural; it was not there until Huntington and his advertising helped to create it.[53]

Private real estate interests across the nation vigorously promoted the ideal of suburban living. The Irvine Company touted the rural tranquility of its new community, Irvine, California, located forty miles south of Los Angeles: "Come to Irvine and hear the asparagus grow." The company, interested in profits, marketed a highly exaggerated picture of the tranquil, idealized life of suburbia. The reality was far different from what the company advertised to the public. As one company executive recalled, "When you live between two highways, it's hard to hear the asparagus grow."[54]

PRIVATE INSTITUTIONS AND RACIAL STRATIFICATION OF U.S. CITIES AND SUBURBS

Differences in group buying power explain only part of the reason why there exists a racial imbalance of urban neighborhoods, why people of different races and ethnicities tend to live in different geographic locations. Residential patterns are not simply a reflection of group buying power and the preference of people "to live with their own kind." Private institutions also undertook a series of actions that interfered with the workings of a free market; the actions of private institutions prevented minority families from moving to neighborhoods they had the means to afford.

As previously mentioned in this chapter, during the first half of the twentieth century, restrictive covenants or binding deed restrictions prohibited a property owner from selling or renting a housing unit to the members of specified ethnic and racial groups. Depending on the part of the country, restrictive covenants banned home sales to African Americans, Hispanics, Asians, and Jews. Local real estate boards insisted that racial restrictions be included in sales contracts. The Chicago Real Estate Board even formulated a model restrictive covenant to be included in property contracts.[55]

Racial ghettos and Chinatowns expanded as restrictive covenants barred minorities from residing in other parts of the city. This was not a natural segregation but a segregation imposed by private-sector practices that prevented housing markets from operating as they should. Restrictive covenants produced a segregated city, with patterns of segregation that continued well after 1948 when the Supreme Court in its **Shelley v. Kraemer** decision ruled that the judiciary could no longer enforce restrictive racial covenants.[56]

Shelley v. Kraemer did not put an end to the various discriminatory practices that maintained residential segregation. Many real estate agents practiced racial steering, refusing to show homes in a white neighborhood to a minority buyer. Mortgage lenders and home finance institutions similarly would not approve loans or home insurance to a minority buyer seeking to move into a white neighborhood. Instead, the agents working for these institutions directed minority home seekers to different neighborhoods. As previously observed, private institutions were not the only ones to engage in this discriminatory practice. The Federal Housing Administration, too, endorsed racial steering, instructing home-loan examiners only to approve loans that preserved a neighborhood's racial homogeneity.

In Pittsburgh, white brokerage boards blocked membership by black brokers, denying them access to property listings that would have enabled African-American agents to show desirable properties to prospective African-American buyers and renters. The city's white-owned newspapers facilitated steering, with listings in classified ads that indicated if a home or rental unit was "for Colored," that is, open to African Americans. The absence of a "for Colored" designation in ads for homes in an outlying area of the region indicated that a community was "closed," that a black person could not buy or rent a home there. In Mt. Lebanon, a suburb of Pittsburgh, real estate agents refused to show properties to blacks and Jews.[57]

In Austin, Texas, deed restrictions similarly specified "white" or "Caucasian only." Such wording served to keep out both Latinos and African Americans; Latinos in Texas, at the time, were considered "mostly" nonwhite. The system of property restrictions helped keep parts of the city exclusive while concentrating racial minorities in East Austin.[58]

As the work of urban historian Thomas Sugrue reminds us, residential segregation in the United States was limited neither to the South nor to central cities: "the history of northern suburbia" has been defined by "patterns of entrenched segregation." Outside New York and Philadelphia, developer William Levitt in the 1950s built large tracks of mass-produced houses that put a three-bedroom home within the financial reach of the working class. The **Levittowns** were often viewed as a suburban working-class paradise, but "by William Levitt's orders, not a single resident was black." The racial homogeneity of Levittown did not represent the workings of a free market: "The absence of blacks was not the result of a shortage of potential black buyers." African Americans who worked the region's factories could easily afford a home in Levittown. But Levitt refused to sell to blacks, fearing that whites would be unwilling to buy homes in a mixed-race suburb. Levitt's sales agents even refused to sell to African-American war veterans, who were informed that Levittown was an "all-white community." Even after the Supreme Court's *Shelley v. Kraemer* decision seemingly barred enforcement of Levittown's racially restrictive actions, Levitt's agents still acted to evict a black family for being an "undesirable" tenant. In the Pennsylvania Levittown, white residents turned to violence—a grassroots community riot—in their attempts to oust the first African-American family to move to the suburb, having bought a home from a willing white seller.[59]

The Working-Class Suburban Paradise: Levittown, Pennsylvania, 1950s. FHA- and VA-insured loans enabled the lower-middle class and the working class to flee the cities for the suburbs. The mass-produced tract housing of Levittown further helped to put the suburban dream within the reach of the working class. Levittown, however, was racially restricted in order to maintain the community's attractiveness to white buyers. In the community's early years, African Americans were denied the right to buy homes in Levittown.

From http://commons.wikimedia.org/wiki/File:LevittownPA.jpg

The **1968 Fair Housing Act** made racial steering and other forms of housing discrimination illegal. The law has succeeded in eliminating the most blatant forms of housing discrimination. Yet, while discrimination against minority home seekers has decreased over the years, it has not disappeared. Contemporary housing discrimination takes a more subtle form. In an estimated 20 percent of cases, for instance, African Americans and Hispanics are denied information regarding the availability of home loans, information that is provided to comparable white home seekers. Such actions serve to constrain choice and to steer minorities away from more desirable neighborhoods.[60]

Chapter 9 will describe in further detail the more subtle and not-easy-to-detect forms of racial steering that continue to exist. Home seekers who feel that they are the victims of discrimination have a very difficult time proving in court that racial steering actually occurred. A minority home seeker does not know for sure exactly which houses an agent has shown, and exactly what information the agent has given, to white buyers. Nor is it easy for a buyer to prove that any differences in treatment were the result of race and not simply a response to the size of a home seeker's family or to the home seeker's buying power.

BANKS AND THE REAL ESTATE INDUSTRY: BLOCKBUSTING, REDLINING, AND CORE-CITY DISINVESTMENT

While large segments of the real estate industry practiced racial steering, there were other real estate agencies that sought to profit by increasing tensions in a residential area facing the prospect of racial transition. In a process that is often referred to as **blockbusting** or **panic selling**, real estate agents would publicize that a black family had moved into an all-white neighborhood. Real estate agents would then go door to door, preying on the fears of white owners and the elderly, pushing owners to sell their homes before the neighborhood underwent further change and the value of homes plummeted. The frightened owners, worried about the loss of the investment value of their homes, would list their homes with the real estate dealers, who would then go to their neighbors urging them, now even more fervently, to sell before it was too late. The real estate dealers profited from the sales fees they earned in the neighborhood's turnover. Their manipulations, however, led to extensive white flight and undermined the residential stability of inner-city neighborhoods.

Blockbusting did not lead to racial integration; rather, the creation of a panic led to white flight and ultimately to a neighborhood's **resegregation**. All-white areas quickly became all-minority areas as the whites sold their homes and fled.

Other real estate speculators sought to capitalize further, buying houses cheaply and **subdividing single-family homes** into small, shabby apartments that could be rented at inflated prices to black families who had few other neighborhoods open to them. The overcrowded and poorly maintained structures quickly deteriorated.

Redlining by private financial institutions, too, was a major contributor to core-city disinvestment and decline: banks and other credit institutions simply refused to make loans in large areas of the city that credit officers viewed as posing greater-than-desired financial risks. Even good applicants with excellent job histories and credit records found that they could not get loans for properties in redlined neighborhoods. At one time, banks, insurance companies, and other financial institutions literally took a map and drew a red line around the areas of a city where the company would not make loans or insure properties. The result was neighborhood **disinvestment** and decline, as redlining cut off the economic blood for new construction, major structural repairs, and a community's rejuvenation.

Since the 1970s, federal law has prohibited redlining. Banks and other financial institutions can no longer crudely draw a line on a map or otherwise refuse credit to an entire section of a city. The **Community Reinvestment Act (CRA) of 1977** put further pressure on lending institutions to advance credit to homebuyers and small business owners in underserved areas of the city. Under the CRA, banks must make loans in communities, including poorer communities, from which they receive deposits.

The CRA has been extremely important in extending credit for homes and business expansion in inner-city communities. Yet despite the mandates of federal law, redlining persists, albeit in modified form. A financial institution may offer financing for condominium and cooperative conversions while denying loan applications to groups seeking to renovate older buildings for affordable housing. Race continues to be an unacknowledged factor in lending decisions.[61]

A Richmond, Virginia, jury in 1998 ordered Nationwide Insurance to pay more than $100 million in damages as a result of the company's reluctance to insure homes in black neighborhoods. Nationwide's practices were not as blatant as the crude redlining of the 1950s and 1960s. The company did not reject all applications from inner-city black neighborhoods. Instead, the company instructed its agents to avoid "black urbanite households with many children."[62]

Credit and insurance institutions have the ability, despite the CRA, to deny loans to applicants with low credit scores. The CRA also does not require private insurers to reveal how they came to a judgment on an applicant's credit score. As a result of these provisions, the CRA is not easily enforceable. State departments of insurance seldom give priority to fighting insurance redlining.[63]

The CRA, however, does require mortgage-finance institutions to disclose the geographical area of each loan. Community groups have used this information to document the areas of a city that are underserved, putting pressure on banks to extend credit to applicants in disadvantaged communities. The CRA gave community organizations the right to challenge bank mergers if they could prove that a bank had failed to meet its lending obligations under the Act. ACORN (the Association of Community Organizations for Reform Now) and various other community groups used the threat of opposing bank mergers as leverage to convince financial institutions to commit millions of dollars to affordable home mortgages and loans to inner-city businesses. Republican Senator Phil Gramm of Texas criticized the CRA for allowing "professional protest groups" to extort benefits from financial institutions.[64]

Critics of the CRA often overstate the threat that the Act poses to banks. Banks have had little difficulty in meeting the law's requirements. In 1998, only 15 of the 772 banks examined—just 2 percent—received less than a satisfactory grade from regulators.[65] To meet CRA requirements, a bank simply has to take positive steps in advertising its lending services in disadvantaged neighborhoods. Banks work with community groups that help identify potential homebuyers and counsel prospects in how to budget funds for home repairs and the other demands of homeownership.

Box 2.2
Did the CRA Produce the Housing Foreclosure Crisis?

When the nation's housing markets collapsed in the early 2000s, political conservatives blamed one of their favorite bogeymen, the Community Reinvestment Act (CRA). The conservatives charged that the CRA's lending requirements virtually coerced mortgage lenders to make loans to unworthy applicants in inner-city neighborhoods. The accumulation of bad loans, they argued, led the bankers to panic, which affected the housing market nationwide. The conservatives argue for further **deregulation**, that the government should repeal or modify the harmful provisions of the CRA that intrude on the ability of home lenders to make sound business-like decisions.

The evidence, however, does not support the conservatives' charges. The CRA had been in effect for a quarter of a century before the housing finance crisis hit. It is a bit absurd to put the blame on a policy twenty-five years after its enactment and not give the policy credit for the revival of inner-city neighborhoods and the boom in housing markets and the national economy that took place during the intervening quarter of a century.

Core urban neighborhoods in cities such as Cleveland and Detroit did suffer extensive foreclosures. Yet the housing crisis was not confined to areas of CRA activity. In fact, most defaults did not involve properties in the inner city. Overextended borrowers walked away from the loans they had taken to finance new Florida condominiums, $300,000 Arizona villas, and luxury suburban dream houses. The home foreclosures and distress sales in these areas cannot be blamed on the provisions of the CRA.

Loans subject to CRA supervision suffered fewer defaults than did comparable non-CRA loans. "Bad" loans were disproportionately issued by the smaller credit institutions and speculators who were not subject to CRA regulations. New and more unscrupulous businesses had entered the housing field when the previous era of Republican deregulation removed large chunks of the home mortgage industry from CRA supervision.

It was deregulation, not the CRA, that led to the rash of ill-advised mortgages and subprime loans that resulted in the housing finance crash. The most abusive **predatory lending practices**—loans that incurred outrageously high placement fees; loans with super-low monthly payments but with an excessively high final **balloon payment** that buyers could not meet; high prepayment penalties that prevented homeowners from refinancing with a loan at a lower rate of interest—were all the work of lending institutions not subject to the CRA's provisions.

Sources: Gregory D. Squires, "Predatory Lending: Redlining in Reverse," *Shelterforce Online* 139 (January/February 2005), www.nhi.org/online/issues/139/redlining.html; Traiger & Hinckley LLP, "The Community Reinvestment Act: A Welcome Anomaly in the Foreclosure Crisis—Indications that the CRA Deterred Irresponsible Lending in the 15 Most Populous U.S. Metropolitan Areas," January 7, 2008, www.traigerlaw.com/publications/traiger_hinckley_llp_cra_foreclosure_study_1-7-08.pdf; and Traiger & Hinckley LLP, "The Community Reinvestment Act of 1977: Not Guilty—Mortgage Data Refute Charge that the CRA Is at the Root of the Financial Crisis," January 26, 2009, http://traigerlaw.com/publications/The_community_reinvestment_act_of_1977-not_guilty_1-26-09.pdf.

Overall, the CRA has been an amazing urban success story, producing tens (if not hundreds) of billions of dollars in loans to homeowners and businesses in low-income and minority neighborhoods. In Cleveland, Chicago, Pittsburgh, and other cities, the CRA led banks to "'rediscover' the inner city as a viable and profitable market."[66]

Despite this record of success, credit officers and free-market conservatives continue to complain about the intrusiveness of the law. As a result, political conservatives have pushed for deregulation, attempts to loosen the requirements of the Act and to exempt numerous institutions from CRA requirements and oversight. The 1999 Gramm-Leach-Bliley Act limited the scope of the CRA, exempting many credit institutions—especially smaller banks and savings institutions—from compliance. The amendments severely weakened the CRA, allowing an increasing number of home loans to be issued by businesses that do not have to meet CRA requirements.[67]

Nonetheless, talk-radio hosts and prominent political conservatives showed little hesitation in blasting the CRA for causing the foreclosure crisis of the early years of the twenty-first century.[68] But their attempt to pin the blame for the crisis on the CRA lacks merit, especially as more than 90 percent of subprime loans were not subject to the CRA![69] The Act had also been in operation for a quarter of a century before the housing finance crisis flared. Also, the CRA does not deserve blame for the flood of mortgage defaults that involved condominiums and single-family homes and properties in well-to-do Sunbelt communities, loans that were outside the CRA's area of responsibility. (See Box 2.2, "Did the CRA Produce the Housing Foreclosure Crisis?")

Unscrupulous private **predatory lenders**, not the CRA, undermined the mortgage market. In a process called **push marketing**, lenders target high-cost loans with disadvantageous terms to minorities who may not be aware of the availability of less-costly alternative credit. Studies have found that, even when the income and credit risk of an applicant are controlled, minorities are disproportionately pushed into high-interest and riskier **subprime mortgages** as opposed to the lower-cost conventional loans offered to other home seekers.

Mortgage agents out to make a quick profit may seek to convince buyers of the affordability of a low monthly payment in an adjustable rate mortgage where payments rise and fall depending on the rate of inflation. But when such a loan contains an unrealistically low **teaser rate**, the homeowner may face the prospect of foreclosure when, much to his or her shock, the required monthly mortgage payment soon doubles.[70] Unable to meet such payments, low- and moderate-income owners faced the prospect of losing their homes and much of their life savings and good credit rating.[71]

PRIVATE INTERESTS AND THE ECONOMIC GROWTH OF THE SUNBELT

The move of industry to the Sunbelt was more than a search for a sunny climate and warm-weather ports. Factory owners were also motivated by their worries about labor costs and unionism. In the middle of the twentieth century, manufacturers moved to the South in order to escape the high-wage, high-tax, pro-union environment of northern cities. **Right-to-work laws** in the South undermined labor organizing. As workers in right-to-work states cannot be forced to join a union, employers can undermine union organizing efforts by hiring only nonunion workers.

States and municipalities in the South offered a pro-business climate. Taxes on business were kept low as welfare benefits and social services were kept to a minimum. Business owners in the South also did not have to comply with the extensive and costly regulations for worker benefits and environmental protection that were more typical of northern states.

HOW PUBLIC POLICIES AND PRIVATE-SECTOR ACTIONS CONTRIBUTE TO HOMELESSNESS

There are numerous reasons why people are homeless. Some individuals are drug and alcohol abusers who cannot hold steady employment. Others have developmental disabilities or suffer mental illness. Young people may be seeking escape from abusive homes. Still others wind up homeless because they can no longer pay the monthly rent due to a disruption of income caused by the loss of a job or a marital breakup.

Yet personal failings are not the sole cause of homelessness. Homelessness is also a result of government programs that deinstitutionalize psychiatric patients while reducing social welfare and public housing budgets. There is an insufficient supply of halfway houses, community centers, and support programs that provide an alternative to the streets for people who have difficulties in functioning.

Increases in homelessness are also the result of the disappearance of low-cost housing. Both private interests and local governments share responsibility for the virtual disappearance of the **single room occupancy (SRO) hotel,** the cheap by-the-night or by-the-week housing that offered a city's most marginal residents a last-chance refuge from the streets. An SRO, with its tiny rooms and toilets down the hall, is not what any tourist would deem an acceptable hotel. SROs tend to be rather run-down residency hotels located in undesirable parts of town. Still, an SRO offers a poor person with a few dollars a place to sleep for the night or the week.

Today, the supply of SRO housing has dropped dramatically as private developers and public redevelopment officials built new office and retail complexes, convention centers, and luxury apartment buildings in areas where SROs once stood. Private developers and public officials have succeeded in their goal of bringing new life to large parts of the inner city. In the process, some of the most vulnerable residents of the city lost their residences, their only alternative to the streets and municipal-provided shelters.

CONCLUSION: HIDDEN URBAN POLICIES, PRIVATE POWER, AND THE CONTEMPORARY URBAN SITUATION

Natural forces—population pressures, technological advances, and affluence—have had a great influence on the shape of U.S. cities and suburbs. Yet these natural forces do not dictate the exact urban patterns and problems found today. Government policies—often unrecognized or "hidden" policies—and the exercise of private-sector power, too, have a great influence on urban development. Public policies and private sector actions contributed to numerous contemporary problems, including urban sprawl, the decline of older manufacturing centers, the disappearance of SRO housing, and the racial and class stratification of communities and public school classrooms.

The forces that shape urban and suburban development have produced a number of contemporary problems, three of which deserve special emphasis:

1. THE SEPARATION OF RESOURCES FROM NEED

In a process called **dual migration**, the poor move into cities while the well-to-do middle class moves out to the suburbs. Government policies, including the tax breaks given to homeowners, continue to encourage the outflow of middle-class and better-off families to the suburbs.

In recent years, however, the suburbs have begun to become home to an increasing number of poor people. The suburbs have a larger population than do central cities; they now also have more poor people than do central cities.

Still, the growth of suburban poverty should not draw attention away from the larger patterns: On the whole, the residents of suburbia are generally wealthier than the residents of central cities; central cities continue to provide services to a population that has greater needs than the population residing in the suburbs.

Poverty remains a more prominent fact of central-city than of suburban life. In 2013, the nation's largest central cities suffered a 21.7 percent poverty rate, as compared to the 12.1 percent poverty rate of their suburbs.[72] New York City in 2010 had a poverty rate of 20 percent compared to 9 percent for its suburbs. Los Angeles had a rate of 22 percent poverty compared to 14 percent for its suburbs. Atlanta's poverty rate was 26 percent; its suburbs only 14 percent.[73] People in need of public services are disproportionately concentrated in the nation's cities, while the metropolitan area's taxable wealth is disproportionately found in the suburbs.

2. RACIAL IMBALANCE IN THE METROPOLIS

Dual migration, exclusionary land-use practices, racial steering, and discriminatory lending practices set in motion the creation of a contemporary American metropolis that is marred by racial imbalances. Despite the success of the Fair Housing Act, racial imbalances in metropolitan America remain. Some communities have large concentrations of ethnic and racial minorities, while others do not. These differences are not simply a reflection of the differences among groups in terms of their buying power, education, and housing preferences. Statistical evidence shows that increased income and education do not enable African Americans to move to better neighborhoods to the same extent that such gains in income and schooling enhance the residential choices available to whites and even to Latinos.[74]

More subtle discriminations in the housing market are difficult to detect. A lack of political will also undermines enforcement. In a suburban nation, state and national officials do not give great priority to programs aimed at the racial integration of the suburbs.[75]

3. URBAN SPRAWL AND QUESTIONS OF SUSTAINABILITY

The American metropolis is marked by extensive **sprawl** or low-density, spread-out patterns of development that eat up green space and agricultural land and increase residents' reliance on the automobile. In Germany and countries in Europe, governments have enacted strong policies to limit the extent of suburban development outside of major cities.[76] European nations promote the population densities that are necessary for public transit.

The United States, by contrast, has made no equivalent commitment to constraining sprawl and reducing its associated environmental problems.[77] In the United States, public programs, especially highway programs, tax incentives, and local zoning and land-use policies, continue to support the construction of single-family homes and automobile-reliant development.

KEY TERMS

annexation (*p. 30*)
balloon payment (*p. 50*)
bedroom communities (*p. 31*)
blockbusting (*p. 48*)
company towns (*p. 44*)
Community Reinvestment Act (CRA)
    of 1977 (*p. 49*)
condominium and cooperative
    apartment conversions (*p. 37*)
contain labor militancy (*p. 45*)
demographic factors in urban
    development (*p. 28*)
deregulation (*p. 50*)
disinvestment (*p. 49*)
dual migration (*p. 53*)
economic factors in urban
    development (*p. 28*)
edge cities (*p. 31*)
Fair Housing Act of 1968 (*p. 48*)
federal grant programs for hospitals
    and sewage processing facilities
    (*p. 39*)
Federal Housing Administration
    (FHA) (*p. 34*)
federal tax incentives for the oil and
    gas industries (*p. 39*)
FHA loan insurance (*p. 34*)
Frostbelt (*p. 32*)
GI Bill of Rights of 1944(*p. 34*)

global cities (*p. 33*)
greening strategies (*p. 33*)
Great Migration (*p. 30*)
hidden urban policy (*p. 33*)
land-use and zoning powers (*p. 41*)
Levittowns (*p. 47*)
mansion subsidy (*p. 37*)
multicentered metropolis (*p. 31*)
Negro removal, urban renewal
    as (*p. 40*)
panic selling (*p. 48*)
political revolt by Brookline,
    Massachusetts (*p. 30*)
predatory lenders (*p. 51*)
predatory lending practices (*p. 50*)
push marketing (*p. 51*)
racial steering (*p. 35*)
redlining (*p. 34*)
Republican-era deregulation (*p. 36*)
resegregation (*p. 48*)
restrictive covenants (*p. 35*)
right-to-work laws (*p. 51*)
Robin Hood in reverse (*p. 37*)
second ghetto (*p. 40*)
Shelley v. Kraemer (*p. 46*)
shrinking cities (*p. 33*)
single room occupancy (SRO) hotel
    (*p. 52*)
streetcar suburbs (*p. 30*)

3 | Recent Trends

Gentrification and Globalization

This chapter discusses two important recent trends in the evolution of urban areas: **gentrification** (the rediscovery of inner-city neighborhoods, often referred to as the back-to-the-city movement) and **globalization** (the vulnerability of cities to forces from beyond their borders and from beyond the nation's borders). The two concepts, while distinct, are interrelated. Globalization intensifies the pressures underlying neighborhood gentrification; the well-paid professionals employed by major international firms seek homes in relatively close proximity to a city's downtown; their actions contribute to a price inflation that helps drive out the poorer residents of these neighborhoods. Gentrification, in turn, helps to make a city attractive to global corporations that seek a talented workforce. Charlotte, North Carolina, and a great many other cities have pursued a conscious strategy of gentrification, with the hope that the new vibrancy of core neighborhoods will attract both upscale workers and major corporations.[1]

GENTRIFICATION

In the late 1970s and early 1980s, journalists began to take note of an emerging "back to the city" movement as so-called **urban pioneers** bought and renovated housing in distressed inner-city neighborhoods. Gentrification refers to the upgrading of a core neighborhood that occurs when young professionals—especially singles and childless couples—place new value on city living. The term itself denotes the arrival of a relatively well-heeled urban "gentry" who have discovered the value in living close to the job and entertainment opportunities of an active downtown. In the initial phases of gentrification, urban pioneers view homes in low-priced inner-city neighborhoods as a "good buy."

Writers have many synonyms for gentrification: neighborhood renewal, inner-city revitalization, urban rebirth, the back-to-the-city movement, neighborhood reinvestment, and urban invasion.[2] When used very precisely, the term *gentrification* refers to a

Gentrification: New Development in Minneapolis' Warehouse District. Once an area of disused warehouses left over from the era when Minneapolis was a vigorous mill and industrial city, this area on the edge of the city's central business district has in more recent years become the site of new restaurants, shopping, and loft and condominium development.

From Wikimedia Commons, User Mulad, July 15, 2005, http://commons.wikimedia.org/wiki/File:Minneapolis_Warehouse_District.jpg.

transformation process that "operates in the residential housing market,"[3] a process of class (and often racial) succession where upscale home seekers displace the poor. Today, the term gentrification is also used more widely to refer to nonresidential investment projects, such as the opening of a luxury shopping galleria or a new multiplex cinema, that are part of an area's upgrading and transformation.

Critics often charge that gentrification constitutes a white "invasion" of poor black and Hispanic neighborhoods. Yet a number of cities have also begun to experience black gentrification. African-American professionals have moved into New York's Harlem and Brooklyn's Clinton Hill as well as Chicago's historic Bronzeville neighborhood and areas of the city bordering the lakeshore on Chicago's South Side, areas that, not too long ago, were overwhelmingly black and poor.[4] In New York and Chicago, the opening of a Starbucks signaled a change in the class composition of inner-city African-American areas.

Today, a great many inner-city areas are gentrifying. Alan Ehrenhalt argues that gentrification is part of a "great inversion" that is taking place in metropolitan areas. According to Ehrenhalt, central cities are becoming home to professional and technologically competent workers while the poor and the working class are increasingly being consigned to the city's outskirts.[5]

Yet, while gentrification is widespread, it would be misleading to conclude that gentrification has fundamentally altered the balance between central cities and suburbs. Cities continue to suffer poverty rates two to three times that found in the suburbs. Philadelphia, for instance, has a poverty rate of 23.8 percent compared to 7.4 percent for its suburbs; New York City has a 21 percent poverty rate as contrasted to 9 percent for its suburbs.[6]

Gentrifying neighborhoods are also more prevalent in corporate headquarters cities with downtowns that offer high-paying jobs and an abundance of cultural and nightlife opportunities.[7] Detroit, Cleveland, Newark, and Buffalo, by contrast, have experienced only the most minimal gentrification. Gentrification also does not take place in all neighborhoods; neighborhood revival is least likely to occur in those areas of the city that have the greatest concentrations of poverty and that suffer the highest rates of social disorganization.[8]

WHO TRANSFORMED THE INNER CITY: URBAN PIONEERS OR CORPORATE DEVELOPERS?

Gentrification is often portrayed as an individualized and market-driven process: urban pioneers ventured into troubled neighborhoods, rehabilitating solid homes that they bought at bargain prices. Artists soon followed, seeking lofts, vacant warehouses, and other large workspaces in neighborhoods that offered low rents. The presence of the pioneers and artists soon served to signal others that a once troubled inner-city neighborhood was now relatively safe and "open" to other newcomers interested in taking up residence in the "hip" and newly "discovered" areas of the city.

The early gentrifiers often had a romanticized sense of community. This largely white and highly educated group of professionals valued the population diversity and "authentic" feel of inner-city neighborhoods, especially when contrasted to the "sameness" and soulless nature of the modernistic housing that dominated most suburbs.[9] Of course, not all urban re-settlers valued the lifestyles of their inner-city neighbors. The first wave of gentrifiers also included newcomers who believed that their presence would serve to introduce much-needed change into poor neighborhoods.[10]

Initially, banks and other financial institution were reluctant to extend loans and other financial support to the first-wave gentrifiers. Banks redlined inner-city areas that were deemed as too risky for investment. Early gentrifiers often had to look elsewhere for creative means of home financing.

Over the decades that followed, however, the members of the city's growth coalition—developers, real estate agents, and insurance companies—changed their tune as they began to see the enormous profits that could be gained from neighborhood transformation. In city after city, financial and real estate interests began to play a more active role promoting neighborhood transformation, even "branding" communities as distinctive and quite fashionable areas with names that gave cachet to the take-off areas. New York City developers and landlords advertised the attractions of life in SoHo (south of Houston Street), NoHo (north of Houston), NoLIta (north of Little Italy), and DUMBO (down under the Manhattan-Brooklyn Bridge overpass), aggressively marketing inner-city areas to upscale buyers.[11] In Cincinnati, developers built and sold condominiums in the extremely poor Over-the-Rhine (OTR) district, located just north of the city's downtown. They advertised the areas as the city's "Gateway District," as if it were not part of the OTR ghetto, the site of the city's last major riot.

Box 3.1
Chicago: A Neighborhood Changes, and So Do Its Coffeehouses

In the Wicker Park section of Chicago, the opening and closing of coffeehouses stands as visual testimony to how different waves of gentrification have transformed the neighborhood. When Wicker Park was a Polish working-class neighborhood, residents gathered at Sophie's Busy Bee, the local "greasy spoon" that had a photograph of the Pope prominently displayed on the wall. The first wave of gentrification saw the appearance of a new coffeehouse, the neo-bohemian Urbus Orbis, which served as a hangout for the area's artists and young "hipsters." The presence of these newcomers, however, soon served to signify that the neighborhood was "in;" it was soon also "discovered" by newcomers who were less fond of the area's gritty urban texture. Developers built new housing for young professionals who sought to live near Chicago's downtown offices and its various nightlife areas. The new supergentrifiers valued neither art nor urban authenticity. They frequented the newly-opened Starbucks. The Busy Bee and Urbus Orbis both closed.

Source: Richard Lloyd, *Neo-Bohemia: Art and Commerce in the Postindustrial City* (New York: Routledge, 2006), 107.

In SoHo in Lower Manhattan, many of the artists who had converted empty manufacturing lofts into working and living spaces were later displaced as landlords and developers rehabbed properties for more profitable clienteles. Local officials and real estate developers promoted the growth of a "Destination Culture" that re-made SoHo as a place of consumption for younger and more upscale customers. Today's SoHo is the site of upscale residences, high-end boutiques such as Chanel, retail chain stores including Banana Republic, and even an Apple computer store with a "genius bar" in back. These corporate-led developments have driven out many of the art galleries, individually owned boutiques, and dance companies that dominated SoHo during earlier stages of its revival.[12]

Loretta Lees uses the terms **financifiers** and **supergentrifiers** to denote the quite different character of the second invasion wave that took place in New York's SoHo and other inner-city areas.[13] Supergentrifiers move to a neighborhood because of its fashionableness and convenient location. The supergentrifiers welcome the convenience of Starbucks and other chain stores. Unlike the urban pioneers who preceded them, the supergentrifiers do not prize urban grit and authenticity. (See Box 3.1, "Chicago: A Neighborhood Changes, and So Do Its Coffeehouses.") In Chicago, new residents demanded that strip shopping malls offer the convenience of parking lots, even though such suburban-style development was out of character with the historic cityscape. Supergentrifiers bought units in high-rise condominiums and built fortified modern homes that were incongruous with an area's existing housing stock and character. Their efforts to upscale a neighborhood were met by the resistance of other gentrifiers, "social preservationists" intent on preserving the authenticity of inner-city communities.[14]

The phrase **new-build gentrification** points to how corporate investment in major projects—high-rise residential towers, inner-city shopping centers, and big-box retails stores—is transforming core urban communities. Where the new facilities are built on **brownfield sites** (the vacant or underutilized properties of industrial-era warehouses and manufacturing plants), construction does not directly lead to residential displacement. Still, such projects increase the attractiveness of inner-city living, generating an escalation of rents in nearby properties than can push out the working class and the poor.[15]

WHY CITIES PROMOTE GENTRIFICATION DESPITE ITS COSTS

Gentrification brings a new sense of vitality and a number of more specific benefits to cities.[16] New investment helps to stabilize declining neighborhoods, upgrade residential structures, and increase an area's attractiveness to future investment. Gentrified areas also help a city to attract workers with advanced technological and specialized skills, the sort of talented workforce that a city needs in order to compete for high-tech, legal, and financial service firms. Neighborhood upgrading expands the municipal tax base, yielding higher property-tax revenues and local income-tax receipts (that is, in states that allow municipalities to levy a local earnings tax).

New shops and restaurants add to the quality of daily urban life. Even low-income African-American residents of transition areas generally report that they are happy with how their neighborhood is improving. The poorer residents who continue to reside in gentrifying neighborhoods tend be optimistic when it comes to their neighborhood's future.[17] Long-time residents appreciate the gains that accompany a neighborhood's takeoff.[18]

The low-income and minority residents of areas undergoing gentrification find that they are living in areas with greater public safety, more varied shopping opportunities, improved municipal services, and new cultural and job opportunities. Gentrification brings once-neglected neighborhoods more into the mainstream of American life.[19]

Gentrification also appears to bring increased physical safety to inner-city areas. Gentrified areas generally experience a reduction in homicide rates, but not necessarily a decline in property crimes as the rise in wealth creates new opportunities for burglaries. The gains in physical safety are more apparent in areas experiencing white gentrification as opposed to black gentrification.[20]

Critics, however, weigh the costs and benefits of gentrification much differently. The critics argue that growth advocates do not give adequate consideration to gentrification's more harmful impacts, especially the **displacement** of poor and working-class families and racial minorities who are "pushed out" to house newcomers with greater buying power. Soaring property values and rents make gentrified neighborhoods unaffordable to the working class and the poor.[21] (See Box 3.2, "Gentrification and the Movies of Spike Lee.") Unscrupulous developers fail to maintain properties or, in extreme cases, resort to arson and other illegal actions in efforts to oust existing tenants in order to convert properties to more profitable uses.[22] It should come as little surprise that African Americans tend to be less positive than whites in their assessment of the changes being brought to gentrifying communities.[23]

Box 3.2
Gentrification and the Movies of Spike Lee

Celebrated American movie director Spike Lee has for a long time been troubled by gentrification. His 1989 classic *Do the Right Thing* traces how simmering racial tensions coupled with police brutality explode into a spasmodic race riot on a hot summer day. An early scene in the film, set in the predominantly black Bedford-Stuyvesant section of Brooklyn, gives voice to the resentments over gentrification which, at the time, was still in its initial pioneering phase. A minor altercation ensues when Clifton, maybe the first young white person to move into the neighborhood, returns home and accidently scuffs the "Jordans" (the basketball sneakers) worn by Buggin' Out, a young man with a strong sense of Black Pride:

Buggin' Out: Who told you to step on my sneakers? Who told you to walk on my side of the block?
Clifton: I own this brownstone.
Buggin' Out: Who told you to buy a brownstone on my block, in my neighborhood on my side of the street? Yo, what you wanna live in a black neighborhood for, anyway? Man, motherfuck gentrification!

Over the years, the pace of gentrification speeded up, transforming Brooklyn neighborhoods like Bedford-Stuyvesant, Cobble Hill, and Fort Greene (Lee's childhood home). The influx of whites diminished the presence of the African-American poor, introducing wine bars and organic markets, and otherwise making poorer residents feel like aliens in their own neighborhood.

In a series of interviews produced for YouTube and other platforms, Lee in 2013 announced his concerns over the changes being brought to Brooklyn's neighborhoods. Lee professes to having "mixed" feelings about gentrification. Lee recognizes that gentrification can lead to a greater police presence, improved public schools, and better garbage pickup. But he is troubled by what he labels the "Christopher Columbus syndrome," where the new arrivals show little respect for the people who already live there. The gentrifiers impose their behavioral expectations on their neighbors.

Lee reports the disappearance of African drummers who had for decades played on Sunday mornings in a Harlem park in Upper Manhattan. He also describes the disrespect shown his father, a noted jazz musician who for decades had played music in his Fort Greene brownstone, when newcomers called the cops to complain that the noise was too loud: "That's not making good neighbors. That's not coming in a neighborhood and being humble."

Sources: Spike Lee, *Do the Right Thing: A Spike Lee Joint* [includes the movie script] (New York: Fireside, 1969), 167; the dialogue presented above is how it was spoken on screen, in a dialect that differs slightly from the words of the original script. "Spike Lee Keeps It Funky About Gentrification & the 'Christopher Columbus Syndrome'" (video), July 21, 2013, http://hiphopwired.com/2013/07/31/ spike-lee-keeps-it-funky-about-gentrification-the-christopher-columbus-syndrome-video/.

Urban geographer Neil Smith characterized gentrification as a process of **neighborhood invasion**, where the city's better classes expropriate low-income and minority areas of the city.[24] Other urban observers have similarly observed that gentrification is a process that is fundamentally rooted in "class" and "class transformation."[25] Gentrification can entail cultural clashes between newcomers and long-term residents, especially in cases when gentrifiers demand policies to "manage neighborhood behaviors" such as public drinking, the blaring of loud music, and playing basketball at night.[26]

Gentrification also severs lower-income individuals from **neighborhood networks**—the church- and community-based organizations, youth groups, and self-help ethnic associations—that provide assistance to poor people, especially poor women, who depend on them for assistance. In Chicago, gentrification-induced displacement wound up adding to the barriers that Mexican and Puerto Rican families faced in gaining support from social service programs sited in Hispanic areas of the city.[27] Elderly displacees suffer a lost sense of place.

Gentrification does not bring the racial and class intermixing that the proponents of gentrification promise. Gentrifiers often profess to value being part of a diverse community. Yet the daily routines of most gentrifiers typically show little interaction across lines of class and race. Poorer residents and gentrifiers reside in the same geographical neighborhood but nonetheless inhabit vastly different worlds,[28] as one observer reported when describing the changes taking place in inner Washington, D.C.:

> Over time the neighborhood's revitalization engineers a rigid caste system eerily reminiscent of pre-1965 America. You see it in bars, churches, restaurants and bookstores. You see it in the buildings people live in and where people do their shopping. In fact, other than public space, little is shared in the neighborhood. Not resources. Not opportunities. Not the kind of social capital that is vital for social mobility. Not even words.[29]

In Chicago, the demolition of high-rise public housing and the construction of new HOPE VI mixed-income housing projects (a program that is discussed in greater detail below) did not lead to interactions across class lines and the creation of "social capital" that would give new life chances to lower-income residents. The former residents of public-housing were allocated relatively few units in the new mixed-income developments that were built on the city's near north side. Chicago's efforts "generated displacement and racial containment, not mixed-income living, for most public housing residents."[30] Another review of HOPE VI efforts similarly underscores that the construction of mixed-income housing resulted in very little community-building and race-mixing. Instead, the new housing developments were characterized by a "social compartmentalization" by class, and sometimes by race, where the buyers of market-rate units and the former tenants of public housing tended to associate only with their peers.[31]

After the destruction wrought by Hurricane Katrina, officials in New Orleans and the U.S. Department of Housing and Urban Development promoted gentrification as a means of attracting residents and new investment to the storm-ravaged city. But their projects did not produce the results that had been anticipated. Once again, the evidence revealed that gentrification resulted in little positive intermixing and community building. The native "insiders" and "outsiders" (the professionals who moved to New Orleans to help rebuild the city after the storm) seldom crossed lines of class and race.[32]

HOW PUBLIC AND PRIVATE INSTITUTIONS PROMOTE NEIGHBORHOOD TRANSFORMATION

Gentrification is often portrayed as the product of free-market forces, where venturesome homebuyers take advantage of bargain-priced properties in the inner city.[33] But as the HOPE VI and post-Katrina New Orleans experiences demonstrate, this is not always the case. Government policy, often in response to the demands of influential private actors, has promoted gentrification.

The perspective that neighborhood transformation is the result of the free-market choice made by individual homebuyers may actually be a fairly accurate description of the early stages of gentrification, where urban "pioneers" bought homes in the inner city and rehabilitated them through their own hard work or **sweat equity**. But the far-reaching transformation of inner-city neighborhoods apparent in more recent years cannot be attributed solely to the venturesome actions and "incumbent upgrading" by individual homeowners. Instead, major private institutions, working with the cooperation of local governments, made extensive capital investments that reshaped inner-city neighborhoods.[34] (See Box 3.3, "3CDC: A Civic Elite Remakes Cincinnati's Riot Corridor.")

Sections of New York City, such as fashionable SoHo, have "been submerged by a tidal wave of new luxury apartments and chain stores." As sociological Sharon Zukin details, "Global investment firms have bought thousands of low-cost apartment houses and prepare to raise the rent or sell them as condos, driving out older and poorer residents."[35] As Zukin continues, "tenement dwellers, mom and pop store owners, whole populations of artists and workers, and people of color" were driven out, displaced by "gentrifiers, cocktail bars, Starbucks, and H&M." New York "lost its soul."[36]

Government officials often promote and subsidize the process of neighborhood transformation. In New York, municipal officials joined with real estate interests to give birth to "Silicon Alley," an emergent "technobohemian" district in Lower Manhattan. Public officials and real estate interests sought to lure "new media" firms to the city by rebranding a Lower Manhattan district of small offices and aging warehouses as an emergent high-tech "paradise."[37] Cities across the country "up-zoned" areas to allow the construction of high-rise residential towers and chain store outlets favored by developers and well-off consumers.[38]

Local governments also took advantage of federal **HOPE VI** funds to demolish hulking public housing projects in order to accelerate the gentrification of nearby areas.[39] Chicago tore down the infamous high-rise towers of the Cabrini-Green housing project, an action that opened surrounding areas to investors seeking to build new townhouses and condominiums located quite close to the city's Gold Coast and Magnificent Mile.

Municipal governments promote neighborhood transformation through a variety of actions, big and small. The City of Chicago supported new residential and retail development in the University Village project located adjacent to the University of Chicago-Illinois; the project led to a rise in housing pressures not only in the area adjoining the project but also in nearby Pilsen, the city's historic center of Latino population.[40] A bit further north, Chicago granted historic landmark status to Wicker Park neighborhood,

Box 3.3
3CDC: A Civic Elite Remakes Cincinnati's Riot Corridor

In 2001, Cincinnati's Over-the-Rhine (OTR) neighborhood was the site of a major urban riot, an event that scared off investors and sent the already distressed community into even further decline. The riot brought to a halt the limited pioneer gentrification and incumbent upgrading that was occurring in the area. But in the decades that followed the disturbances, the southern portion of Over-the-Rhine came back; its vacant properties and boarded-up storefronts gave way to expensive new condominiums, fashionable bars and eateries, and a flourishing night life.

The leaders of Cincinnati's top corporations orchestrated the rebirth of the area. Pulling together investment funds (which received the advantage of federal tax credits) and working with the assistance of local governmental officials, the city's top business leaders created a nonprofit corporation that pursued a strategic plan for the block-by-block transformation of the troubled area. Cincinnati's civic elite believed that conditions in OTR, which adjoined the city's downtown on its northern edge, were scaring off investment in the city's central business district. They saw the building of a "safe" and "clean" OTR as "essential" to changing Cincinnati's image and to bringing conventions, new investment, and development to the city's central business district.

Population figures underscore OTR's steep descent; OTR had shrunk from a population of 44,500 in 1900 to a mere 7,600 in the year 2000, 80 percent of whom were African American. The area was scarred by approximately 500 vacant residential buildings and 700 vacant land parcels.

The Cincinnati Center City Development Corporation (or 3CDC, as it is commonly called) was created in 2003 to spur real estate development and new investment in Cincinnati's downtown and in the adjacent OTR neighborhood. 3CDC is a corporate-led organization with a board of directors that in 2007 included the top executives of the Western & Southern Financial Group, the Kroger Company, Proctor and Gamble, PNC Bank, Fifth Third Bank, and Cincinnati Bell.

3CDC and local developers rebranded the southern portion of OTR as Cincinnati's "Gateway Corridor." 3CDC spent $30 million to become the owner or "preferred developer" of over 200 vacant properties acquired as part of a "land banking" strategy to give the organization greater control over new construction in the neighborhood. The corporation also bought up and closed liquor stores and other "hot spot" properties that had been an impediment to new development. 3CDC also managed streetscape improvements, financed with city assistance, to build an attractive new restaurant strip. As the popularity of the area increased and crime in 3CDC's target area declined, developers even began to once again use the Over-the-Rhine name as a brand that reflected the urban feel of the city's newly hip area.

Municipal agencies aided efforts to reposition the southern section of OTR, an area that had a number of small theater companies and galleries, as an emerging arts district. The city built a gleaming, modern School for the Creative and

Performing Arts to connect the district with the Music Hall, the city's German-style opera house located on OTR's western edge. Across from the Music Hall, the Parks Department reconstructed Washington Park to serve as a new "civic lawn" for music, outdoor film showings, and festivals. 3CDC, which had pushed for construction of the new park and its underground garage, was given charge of programming events to make Washington Park an entertainment destination. The City Parks Department and 3CDC partnered in a $40 million effort that turned a neglected park, a haven for drug abusers and the homeless, into an active public space that served the larger city and not just the area's residents.

3CDC also managed the distribution of Cincinnati Equity Funds and New Market Funds, $400 million in gap financing and below market-rate loans that served as an impetus for its projects. The corporation worked to relocate the Drop Inn Center, the city's largest shelter for the homeless, to a less central location. Drop Inn residents often spilled from the shelter into the park, with a boisterous behavior that decreased the area's attractiveness to visitors and homebuyers.

The transformation of Over-the-Rhine was a well-financed and carefully coordinated enterprise where planners even paid close attention to the construction of parking lots and garages to support the area's new commercial enterprises and residential condominiums. As 3CDC reclaimed one block, the organization shifted its attention to the next block. Local activists criticized that the city should be investing in the neighborhood's poor people, not in garages.

Source: Original case study, based on 3CDC annual reports and various other 3CDC documents and presentations, www.3cdc.com Web postings, personal interviews, and attendance at community meetings.

a designation that developers and real estate firms had sought as part of their efforts to rebrand the area and sell new homes. Historic landmark designation also meant that homebuyers could obtain tax credits for housing rehabilitation.[41] Developers in Wicker Park also went to the city council to thwart the plans of a nonprofit group to rehabilitate nearby housing units for the poor; developers worried that new low-income housing would anchor the poor in the neighborhood, diminishing the area's attractiveness to market-rate homebuyers.[42]

In Philadelphia, governmental planners and the city's downtown real estate sector collaborated on plans that produced the upgrading of Society Hill. A joint public-private civic elite virtually willed a revitalized, upscale Society Hill area into being. The city expelled all but a few of the residents living in the area to make way for the creation of a new neighborhood that was marketed to higher-income tenants.[43]

Urban universities, too, have often been active in plans to upgrade the neighborhoods that surround their campuses. In Philadelphia, city officials worked cooperatively with the University of Pennsylvania to reduce crime and improve the physical appearance of the ghetto area that surrounded Penn's campus. The university pursued the place-based revitalization of the near-campus area; the university-led project did not seek, as its main goals, poverty reduction and improvements in the lives of low-income residents.[44]

COPING WITH GENTRIFICATION

In a privatist society that defers so greatly to market forces, there is no realistic prospect of bringing a halt to gentrification. Nonetheless, there are strategies that can temper some of the ill effects that accompany neighborhood transformation.

In a number of cities, **grassroots organizing efforts** have fought unfettered, market-led gentrification. In Washington Heights in New York's Upper Manhattan, a multiethnic coalition of community groups battled to ensure that housing opportunities for the poor were included in institutional plans to bring new development to the area. By contrast, in the Park Slope section of Brooklyn, grassroots groups were weakly organized. As a result, property developers in Park Slope enjoyed greater freedom as they bought up properties and converted apartments into cooperatives and condominiums, actions that led to substantial displacement and greatly altered the neighborhood.[45]

In Bernal Heights in southern San Francisco, progressive community organizations pressed the city government to acquire land for new public housing so that the neighborhood would be able to retain its income diversity even in the face of gentrifying pressures.[46] In San Diego, a coalition of community groups mobilized to oppose the construction of Ballpark Village, a mixed-use bayfront development located just outside the fences of the new Padres baseball stadium. The grassroots groups dropped their opposition only after the city and the developer agreed to increase the number of affordable housing units being built on-site and elsewhere in San Diego's downtown.[47]

Also in San Francisco, grassroots organizations fought for **measures to limit the conversion of single room occupancy (SRO) hotels.** Advocates for the homeless sought to minimize the loss of dwelling units that house the large number of transients who reside in the city's Tenderloin district.[48] Activists feared that, in the absence of strong municipal regulation, this vulnerable population would be driven out as the city's growth coalition extended development from the adjoining financial district into the Tenderloin.

On the South Side of Chicago, African-American activists pursued a strategy of "defensive development" to limit the harm brought by gentrification. Rather than have development projects controlled by outsiders, these activists promoted black-owned restaurants and African-American heritage tourism in a revived historic Bronzeville, projects that promised to deliver a greater number of new jobs to neighborhood residents. But critics contend that even African-American controlled growth projects lead to displacement. New townhome construction in the city's poor Douglas/Grand Boulevard neighborhood, for instance, resulted in rising rents for nearby properties. The sponsorship of new projects by African-American leaders also serves to insulate new development from local criticism.[49]

Cities can aid the efforts of **community development corporations (CDCs)** to provide affordable housing and thereby mute displacement in poor neighborhoods facing new growth pressures. As Chapter 7 will describe in further detail, CDCs are neighborhood-based groups that work with bankers, public officials, and other partners in order to increase the number of quality housing units within the financial reach of low-income and working-class tenants. In Chicago, the Bickerdike Redevelopment Corporation joined various partners to amass the funds necessary to acquire and rehabilitate older apartment buildings in neighborhoods undergoing transformation, apartments that were then rented to low-income families. In Atlanta, the Reynoldstown Redevelopment Corporation (RRC) pursued a similar course of action. RCC not only built new rental units, it also constructed owner-occupied homes on vacant lots, part of a strategy intended to keep new home prices as low as possible.[50] Municipalities can assist affordable housing efforts by giving government-held properties to CDCs at greatly reduced cost.

Affordable housing advocates also argue for **mandatory set asides**, legislative requirements that new residential developments include a certain percentage of affordable units. Mayor Bill de Blasio proposed a "mandatory inclusionary housing program" to require housing developments in New York City to increase the number of dwelling units within the financial reach of low- and middle-income families. Critics of the mayor's program worried that the regulation would cut the number of market-rate units upon which developers depended for revenues. De Blasio also promised to increase public support for the construction of affordable housing and to allow new housing to be built at higher densities, steps intended to alleviate some of the pressures underlying rent inflation. The mayor also sought to offer landlords new incentives to continue rent stabilization.[51]

Boston and San Francisco utilize an alternative strategy, imposing **linkage fees** on the construction of new office buildings, collecting funds that are then used to support affordable housing projects elsewhere in the city. Boston's program has provided assistance for more than 5,000 units of affordable housing.[52] Seattle has a special **housing levy** that provides funds for the preservation of rental apartments, the construction of affordable rental units, and the development of mixed-income residential projects.[53]

Public policy can also aid neighborhood stability by **promoting residential ownership** in transition neighborhoods.[54] Boston, Philadelphia, Pittsburgh, and Washington, D.C. are among the cities to **freeze property taxes** for existing working- and lower-middle-class residents who reside in areas where gentrification has led to soaring property values and tax bills.[55]

All of the efforts described above are quite noteworthy and often reflect the activism and bottom-up efforts of neighborhood groups. Still, while more progressive cities have encouraged the expansion of affordable housing, cities in general are reluctant to commit to the expense required by such housing efforts. Municipal officials also fear that restrictions on development will deter private investment and impair a city's economic growth.

WORLD CITIES AND THE GLOBAL HIERARCHY: THE POSITION OF CITIES IN A GLOBAL ECONOMY

A **world city** (or **global city**) is an important **command-and-control center** of an interconnected global economy. A global city has a dense concentration of corporate headquarters, banks, and other financial institutions. The decisions made by major corporations and financial institutions located in a global city have an impact on the well-being of cities around the world. Global cities are also centers of telecommunications technology.

Not too long ago, many urban theorists predicted that advances in transportation and telecommunications would continue to weaken big cities by giving corporations the ability to relocate facilities to small towns and suburban areas. So why do many world-class firms continue to locate their headquarters and front offices in major cities even though advancing technology would seem to have liberated businesses from the city?

Box 3.4
Is Los Angeles a Global City?

New York, London, and Tokyo clearly meet anyone's definition of a global city. But is Los Angeles, the second largest city in the United States, also a global city?

To a great many observers, the answer is an obvious "Yes!" Los Angeles' downtown is a center of banking where decisions are made that influence development on both sides of the Pacific Ocean. The economic health of Los Angeles is to a great degree dependent on foreign capital, as seen in the deep investment by Japanese corporations in real estate in the city. Los Angeles mayors have led trade missions overseas to tout L.A. as the "gateway for the Pacific Rim." The Los Angeles region expanded its port and airport facilities to accommodate increased international commerce. City leaders encouraged immigrants to maintain business contacts in their countries of origin, connections that could help promote new trade opportunities for, and investment in, Los Angeles.[1] L.A. is also a multicultural mecca, where the local culture has been enriched by new arrivals from Mexico, El Salvador, Guatemala, India, Pakistan, China, Korea, Japan, and other Latin American and Pacific Rim nations.

Yet urban sociologist Michael Peter Smith argues that despite these obvious international connections, Los Angeles should *not* be regarded as a global city. Smith observes that Los Angeles is more "a receiver rather than a sender of global commands and controls."[2] L.A. lacks the density of headquarters and banking firms found in a global command-and-control city like New York. Unlike New York, decisions made by firms in Los Angeles do not have an equivalent reach into the economies of cities overseas. Instead, L.A. is more typically the victim of, rather than a master of, global forces.

Yet Smith's conceptualization of a global city may be overly strict. Urban geographer Edward Soja argues that many commentators who rank global cities give too much consideration to the presence of command-and-control corporate headquarters. Soja argues that other aspects of globalization deserve an equivalent weight. Los Angeles, with more than 40 percent of its population foreign born, is a global city where many citizens maintain bicultural identities and where issues of multiculturalism often dominate the local arena.[3]

Los Angeles is not one of the world's top-tier command-and-control centers. But in other ways, L.A. is clearly a global city.

1. Steven P. Erie, *Globalizing L.A.: Trade, Infrastructure, and Regional Development* (Stanford, CA: Stanford University Press, 2004), 224–227.

2. Michael Peter Smith, "Looking for Globality in Los Angeles," in *Articulating the Global and the Local*, ed. Ann Cvetkovich and Douglas Kellner (Boulder, CO: Westview, 1997), 55–71; the quotation appears on p. 55.

3. Edward W. Soja, *Postmetropolis: Critical Studies of Cities and Regions* (Maiden, MA: Blackwell, 2000), 222–232.

Cities provide corporations with the advantage of density; corporations seek the advantages of **agglomeration** or dense sectoral development. Firms in an industry find it advantageous to locate close to businesses that provide the specialized financial, legal, and other support services that the various members of an industry require. Firms that work in the same field also draw from the same pool of professional talent in specialized labor markets. A new computer firm, for instance, will find it highly desirable to locate in an area that has other computer firms, giving the new entrant access to an existing pool of experienced and talented information-technology specialists and designers.

New York, London, and Tokyo are generally seen to be at the very top of the **world cities hierarchy**; each has an extensive concentration of corporate headquarters, financial offices, and telecommunications that makes the city an important hub in the global economy.[56] Decisions made in these cities affect businesses and communities around the world. In the United States, Los Angeles, Chicago, and Washington, D.C. lack an equivalent density of corporate development and hence rank below New York in terms of their overall significance on the world economic stage.[57] Still, these cities have global connections. Los Angeles is an important center of Pacific Rim banking and multicultural media development. The growth of textile manufacturing in L.A. has been fueled by the immigration of low-wage workers from Mexico and Asia. (See Box 3.4, "Is Los Angeles a Global City?") Chicago similarly enjoys great "global connectivity" as the headquarters site of a number of major national and international firms.[58] Chicago's emergence as a global corporate center led to the expansion of corporate offices and upscale residential development into the South Loop, West Loop, University Village, North Park Village, and River North, areas located just outside the borders of the city's traditional central business district.[59]

Miami's Downtown: The city has grown as a global corporate finance center for Central and South America. Copyright © by Tom Schaefer. http://commons.wikimedia.org/wiki/File:Miami_downtown_by_Tom_Schaefer_-_Miamitom.jpg.

Millennium Park, Chicago: Chicago leaders built Millennium Park on the downtown lakefront site of the old commuter railyards. The construction of Millennium Park was part of the effort by civic leaders to transform the image of the city and to promote Chicago as an attractive "world class" city. Millennium Park, Pritzker Pavilion band shell.

From Wikimedia Commons via user Adrian104. http://commons.wikimedia. org/wiki/File:Jay_Pritzker_Pavilion_Chicago.jpg.

Other U.S. cities occupy more specialized or limited positions in the global economic hierarchy. Third-tier global cities include Houston (with its connections to Mexico and Latin America), Miami (with its Cuban enclave and its emergence as a center of Caribbean banking and finance), and San Francisco (which stands as a competitor to, and by some estimates even surpasses, Los Angeles as a Pacific Rim financial center). Boston, Dallas, and Philadelphia can be considered fourth-tier cities, clearly important in their regions but with limited international ties. A fifth tier would likely include Atlanta, Rochester, Columbus, and Charlotte (an important regional banking center), cities where aggressive entrepreneurs have just begun to carve out global connections.

GLOBALIZATION: THE PERMEABILITY OF CITY BORDERS

Even communities not commonly regarded as global cities are influenced by globalization, that is, by forces from beyond their borders and from overseas. *Globalization* denotes the permeability of local borders.

International flare-ups, changes in currency exchange rates, and the attractiveness of investment opportunities in other countries all affect the well-being of U.S. cities. In a global age, a city's growth and continued economic well-being are dependent not only on the city's "fit" in the global economy but also on investment decisions made by institutions overseas.[60]

Five important characteristics underscore the increased vulnerability of cities in a global age.

1. ADVANCES IN TRANSPORTATION AND TELECOMMUNICATIONS INTENSIFY THE REGIONAL AND GLOBAL COMPETITION

Telecommunications, satellite uplinks and downlinks, fiber optics, and advances in computerization and information technology have joined with jet travel to give a corporation the ability to locate its headquarters and financial services divisions at some distance from its production facilities and back-office support operations. A multinational firm can locate its headquarters at a prestige address in New York, London, Tokyo, Paris, Frankfurt, or Hong Kong while siting manufacturing plants and support operations in low-cost smaller cities and suburbs. Such activities can even be shifted overseas. Automobile companies, for instance, have established supply chains allowing parts manufactured in Mexico, Brazil, or even South Africa and Central Europe to be shipped to the United States for final assembly. In India, Mumbai, Bangalore, and Hyderabad have become important centers of software engineering and information technology development.

Increasingly, multinational firms are engaged in **offshoring**, shifting production and support tasks to lower-cost subsidiaries located overseas, and **outsourcing**, signing contracts to have important work performed by firms located overseas. Major retailers, for instance, have established customer service **call centers** in India; English-speaking phone operators in Mumbai, Bangalore, and Hyderabad respond to questions from a firm's customers in the United States and other countries around the globe. Mexico, China, the Philippines, and the former communist countries of Eastern Europe, too, offer low-wage, low-tax sites as an alternative to U.S. cities. Cities are confronted by the demands of technology-oriented corporations that threaten to contract out work to firms overseas, should a city prove irresponsive to its demands.[61]

Of course, not all firms can easily relocate production overseas: many firms find it important to be located close to suppliers, customers, and skilled labor markets in the United States. The mobility of capital can be overstated. Yet it remains undeniable that major firms have a greater variety of geographical options today than at any time in the past.

MindSpace Campus, HiTec City, Hyderabad, India: U.S. cities are losing jobs as American firms digitalize and outsource work to well-educated workers in lower-wage nations.

From Wikimedia Commons via Flickr and user peculiar235. http://commons.wikimedia.org/wiki/File:Hydabada.jpg.

U.S. localities find they compete economically not just with one another but also with communities overseas. Cities invest in airport expansion and modernization in order to maintain their gateway to the global economy. A city with an airport that provides a central hub for air travel will be a convenient locational site for business meetings, conventions, tourism, and corporate headquarters.[62]

2. THE GROWING IMPORTANCE OF ADVANCED TECHNOLOGY AND THE "KNOWLEDGE INDUSTRY"

In a postindustrial age where knowledge work has superseded factory work, cities can no longer stake their futures solely on "smokestack chasing." Instead, cities invest in the telecommunications infrastructure and in human resource development (education and job training), and the provision of service amenities that can attract postindustrial businesses and their workforces.[63]

California's **Silicon Valley**, the region centered on Stanford University, emerged as a center of information technology as a result of the area's concentration of highly educated professionals who possessed advanced competencies in mathematics, computer programming, and digital technologies. San Francisco, just to the north, responded with its own efforts to assist the start-up of entrepreneurial "dot-com" firms. Austin, Texas, similarly adopted an economic growth strategy that built on the advantages afforded the city as the home of the University of Texas and Dell Computers. New York City, too, sought to emulate the success of Silicon Valley, upgrading teleport facilities and other telecommunications infrastructure in order to promote the development of **Silicon Alley**; the city helped transform the former warehouses of the old Garment District into a takeoff site for software, Web advertising, and other digital and "new media" firms.[64]

As already noted, the new telecommunications technology has freed multinational corporations from having to locate in the central city. A multinational corporation (MNC) can choose to site its headquarters or various branch offices and back-office support operations in the office parks of "self-contained high-end suburbs," suburban **nerdistans** with their "concentrations of skilled workers."[65]

The new technology even enables firms to shift activities to smaller communities and to communities located at great distances from major urban centers. American Express moved its back offices from New York to Salt Lake City; Metropolitan Life relocated back-office operations to Greenville (South Carolina), Scranton (Pennsylvania), and Wichita (Kansas).[66]

In Utah, Salt Lake City joined with a dozen or so other communities to build the UTOPIA (Utah Telecommunication Open Infrastructure Agency) fiber-optic network. The region's boosters promote UTOPIA as one of the largest capacity ultra-high-speed digital networks in the world. Utah's civic leaders argue that the $470 million investment will make the region attractive to technology-oriented businesses: "The best network in the U.S. will be in Utah—not in New York, not in Chicago, not in Los Angeles."[67]

Chattanooga, Tennessee, reports that its ultra-fast connection has helped to attract business start-ups and creative talent. The city claims to offer the fastest fiber-optic

Internet service in the nation, transferring data at one gigabit per second—fifty times faster than the average speed for home networks.[68]

3. THE VALUE THAT PROFESSIONALS PLACE ON LEISURE, ARTISTIC, AND CULTURAL ACTIVITIES

Municipal leaders have come to realize that an offer of tax inducements—the promise to cut a business' taxes—in a great many cases will not be sufficient to win the location of a firm that has such a wide choice of sites. Instead, a so-called "smart city" will offer a prospective firm more than the promise of tax advantages; a smart city also offers a good quality of life, an attractive living environment that will appeal to a corporation's top executives and to technology-oriented workers.

The continued growth of North Carolina's "Research Triangle"—the Raleigh, Durham, and Chapel Hill area—is in no small part due to planning efforts that have helped to maintain the region's high quality of life. The region's planners guided new development into mixed-use activity centers along highways, enabling the population densities that sustain urban business and entertainment while also preserving green and recreational spaces even amid the region's mounting growth pressures.[69]

4. A NEW IMMIGRATION: CHANGING DEMOGRAPHY AND POLITICS IN CITIES AND SUBURBS

Capital in a global age is mobile; so too is labor. Media images of American prosperity coupled with advances in transportation have produced a new immigration, with incomers from Latin America, South Asia, East Asia, the Near East, and Africa seeking opportunity in the United States. U.S. foreign policy commitments also wound up bringing new arrivals from Korea, Vietnam, Laos, the Philippines, Russia, Cuba, and El Salvador. Businesses in New York, Los Angeles, and other port-of-entry cities hire immigrants to perform low-wage and part-time jobs, often "off the books," a characteristic of the **informalization** or **casualization of work** in a postindustrial economy.[70]

Economist Edward Glaeser argues that immigration has been "essential" to the renaissance enjoyed by New York, Chicago, and other major cities: "Cities are good for immigrants and immigrants are good for cities."[71] Immigrant entrepreneurs connect their new city with their home country, providing access to foreign markets as well as alternative sources of capital for ethnic-owned business start-ups. More skilled immigrants help drive technology-oriented industries. In Los Angeles, a large labor force of Asian American and Latina immigrants contributed to the city's resurgence as a low-wage, textile manufacturing center. (See Box 3.5, "Film Images of the City—Immigrant Los Angeles: *Real Women Have Curves* and *Bread and Roses*.") Los Angeles is just one of many cities where the availability of immigrant labor has helped to breathe life into local manufacturing.[72] In communities across the country, new arrivals do much of the kitchen work and table service in restaurants; it is almost impossible to imagine a smooth-working restaurant industry in the contemporary United States without immigrant labor.

Box 3.5
Film Images of the City—Immigrant Los Angeles: *Real Women Have Curves* **and** *Bread and Roses*

Director Patricia Cardoso's *Real Women Have Curves* (2002) focuses on the struggles of Ana, an eighteen-year-old Latina (played by America Ferrera) who attempts to cope with the conflicting demands of her Mexican and U.S. worlds. Should she defy the expectations of her family, leave Los Angeles, and take a scholarship to attend Columbia University in far-off New York City? Or should she remain in L.A. and play the traditional supportive role expected of Latina women? Initially, Ana bows to her family's wishes and helps out in the small dressmaking business run by her sister.

The film points to the casualization of work in a global city, especially the low-paid jobs often performed by women. The small factory is literally a sweatshop where the ladies strip down to their underwear in order to cope with the suffocating heat. Ana rails against the exploitation of the immigrant women; corporations sell the women's hand-crafted gowns for hundreds of dollars but pay the women only a pittance for their work.

Ken Loach's *Bread and Roses* (2000) is a more strident, unvarnished indictment of the social and work conditions suffered by immigrants who occupy the bottom-rung positions in global Los Angeles. Loach starts by showing the dangers that the migrants face in crossing the border, including the possibilities of rape. The undocumented migrants pay a "coyote" high fees to smuggle them across the U.S. border. The coyotes, however, abandon their human cargo when things go wrong; the human-cargo smugglers often "rip off" their paying customers.

Maya (played by Pilar Padilla) escapes the coyotes and, with the help of her sister, finds a job cleaning offices in one of Los Angeles' gleaming downtown office towers. The film reveals the low-wage, no-benefits, insecure jobs that make up the underside of the city's glitzy global economy. The women put up with all sorts of abuse on the job for fear of losing their livelihood. The city's downtown corporations contract with smaller firms to clean their offices. The contracted firm stands as a buffer between the women and the city's giant corporations which, by outsourcing the janitorial tasks, deny responsibility for the low pay and poor work conditions of the largely Latina workforce. Even though the cleaning firm is run by Mexican Americans, it, too, exploits the women, with the men in charge demanding a portion of the women's wages and even sexual favors in return for giving them work. The film underscores the **dualism** of the global city, contrasting the harsh lives of the workers with scenes of the flamboyant excesses of a lavish Hollywood party.

By the late twentieth century, changes in U.S. national law effectively opened the country's doors to a **new immigration** from the Caribbean, Latin America, the Pacific Rim, and Africa, a sharp contrast to the earlier waves of immigration that came to United States cities primarily from Europe. The reforms abolished the old system of country-by-country quotas that favored European nations and sharply limited immigration from other regions of the world. New rules for family reunification allowed family members from overseas to join a breadwinner working in the United States. Amnesty provisions, which sought the humane goal of regularizing the status of undocumented families already living in the United States, also served to spur an influx of new arrivals, especially from Mexico.[73] U.S. foreign policy and political commitments resulted in the arrival of Soviet Jews and Vietnamese, Cambodian, Laotian, and Cuban refugees.

The new immigration is changing the demography of the American metropolis. Phoenix, located in a border state, provides a dramatic example. In just two decades, from 1980 to 2000, Phoenix experienced a startling two-thirds increase in its population, largely a result of new arrivals from Mexico. By 2010, 41 percent of Phoenix's population were of Hispanic or Latino ancestry. The economic downturn of the early 2000s, however, reduced immigration pressures on Phoenix, at least a bit. Between 2007 and 2009, Phoenix actually saw a drop in the number of residents who had been born outside the United States. In the midst of a continuing economic recession, Phoenix simply had fewer job opportunities to attract newcomers.[74]

Even communities located far from the border with Mexico are being reshaped by a new immigration, not just from Latin America but from Asia and Africa. In 1970, 17 percent of the population of New York City was foreign born. By 2011, the figure more than doubled, with 37 percent of New York's population having been born in other countries.[75] The city's Chinese population spilled over the borders of its Lower East Side Chinatown into neighboring Little Italy. New Chinatowns emerged in the city's outer boroughs, in Jackson Heights and Flushing (Queens) and in Sunset Park (Brooklyn).[76] Likewise in Chicago, the city's burgeoning Chinese population spread well beyond the city's South Side Chinatown into the adjoining Bridgeport neighborhood. A second Chinatown expanded on Chicago's North Side, along Argyle Street and Broadway, a port-of-entry neighborhood for new arrivals from China, Vietnam, and Southeast Asia.[77]

The new immigration has also reshaped smaller cities and suburbs, communities that have not traditionally served as a port of entry for new arrivals. Denver, Nashville, Oklahoma City, Wichita, and St. Paul and other heartland cities have all had a substantial increase in their foreign-born populations.[78] One-fifth of Denver's population is foreign born, with immigrants from Mexico accounting for virtually all of the city's population growth during the 1990s. Over the same decade, Kansas City saw its immigrant population double.[79] Smaller cities in Minnesota (Rochester) and Wisconsin (Wausau, Green Bay, Sheboygan, Appleton, LaCrosse, and Eau Claire) saw the growth of a local Hmong population, an ethnic group from Laos that resettled in the United States as a result of the Vietnam war.[80]

In contrast to the earlier arrival of immigrants from Europe, many of the new immigrants skip the central city and move directly to the suburbs, especially when they are welcomed by members of their extended family. Immigrants look for jobs and housing

The New Immigration and Chicago's New Chinatown: The Argyle Street area in the center of the Uptown neighborhood on Chicago's North Side is a port-of-entry area for new arrivals from China, Vietnam, Thailand, and other Asian countries. Locals refer to the area as the "New" Chinatown as it is located at quite a distance from the city's more established and historic Chinatown on Chicago's South Side.

From Wikimedia Commons, User JeremyA, July 29, 2010, http://commons.wikimedia.org/wiki/File:Argyle_CTA_20100729.jpg. Copyright © 2010 by Jeremy Atherton.

that in the contemporary United States are increasingly to be found in the suburbs. Los Angeles is ringed by various Mexican, Korean, Chinese, and Vietnamese communities. Westminster, south of Los Angeles in Orange County, is popularly known as "Little Saigon." Similarly, on suburban Long Island outside New York City, Hempstead and Hicksville have become centers of the region's Indian population, with Hicksville popularly referred to as "Little India."[81] In the greater Chicago area, Naperville, Schaumburg, Skokie, Hoffman Estates, Glendale Heights, Hanover Park, and Palatine are among the region's suburbs with a large concentration of South Asians.[82]

As has just been discussed, there are growing numbers of immigrants who can be found in suburbia. However, the nation's new arrivals are still disproportionately concentrated in central cities. Immigration imposes a special burden on **port-of-entry** or **gateway cities**. Over 60 percent of Miami's population is foreign born, as is half the population of Santa Ana, California. Los Angeles (41 percent), New York (37 percent), and San Francisco (35 percent) have immigrant populations that are nearly as large. Boston (29 percent); Houston (28 percent); Dallas, El Paso, and Phoenix (26 percent each); San Diego (25 percent); and Chicago (22 percent), also have large immigrant concentrations.[83]

In port-of-entry cities, the low-paid clerical, janitorial, and assembly jobs are to a great extent performed by immigrant women. These low-wage and part-time jobs have taken the place of the former well-paying jobs that in an earlier era were found on the docks and in factories of the Industrial City. The informalization of work in the new urban economy is also marked by the rise of small migrant-owned shops and the reemergence of **piecework** (where workers are paid by the piece of work they finish, not by the hour), sweatshops, and even manufacturing at home.[84]

Critics point to the costs that cities and local school systems bear in communities that have large numbers of new immigrants. The costs are particularly severe in cities in the Southwest.[85]

Yet the new arrivals also contribute to neighborhood well-being and to the growth of local economies. Immigrants add to the demand for housing in otherwise weak housing markets, helping to preserve home values, stem abandonment, and otherwise stabilize weak inner-city neighborhoods.[86] (See Box 3.6, "Are Cities Better Off as a Result of Immigration? Chicago's Killer Heat Wave and 'Little Village.'") The new arrivals help fill inner-city public school classrooms. The new immigration has even led to the growth of a number of Rustbelt cities in the Northeast and the Midwest that were in the throes of long-term postindustrial decline. In New Jersey, Latino arrivals led to a noticeable rejuvenation in Paterson and other former industrial centers that had fallen on hard times. In contrast to the "barrio urbanism" pattern found in the Southwest, the Hispanic communities in New Jersey are not as dominated by Mexicans but are more multicultural, including Puerto Ricans (the dominant Spanish-speaking group in New Jersey), Dominicans, Columbians, Cubans, and Peruvians.[87]

Baltimore, Chicago, Philadelphia, Pittsburgh, Detroit, Cleveland, and Dayton have all advertised themselves as a **Welcome City** that seeks immigrants as a means of reversing population decline and filling vacant properties. Baltimore Mayor Stephanie Rawlings-Blake announced her hopes to recruit 10,000 immigrant families to Baltimore. The mayors of Baltimore and Philadelphia issued orders that barred the local police from inquiring about a person's immigration status.[88] Chicago Mayor Rahm Emmanuel said a city ordinance that prohibited police from detaining undocumented immigrants unless they were involved in a serious crime helped to make Chicago the most immigrant-friendly city in the United States.[89] The Pittsburgh Promise, a nonprofit organization, pursued an alternative strategy, targeting $40,000 college scholarships to lure immigrant families residing elsewhere in the region to move to the city and have their children fill the city's schools.[90]

Advances in transportation and communications have enabled immigrants to maintain bicultural and binational identities. Unlike the arrivals from Europe a century or so ago, the new immigrants do not sever relations with their old homelands and become totally "American." Satellite television brings the new immigrants programs in their native language. E-mail, Skype, cheap telephone calling cards, and relatively affordable transportation allow immigrants to keep in constant contact with family and friends back home, feeding a sense of bicultural loyalty and identity. Even the seemingly far-off reaches of the world are not all that far off. By nonstop jet, Chicago is only eleven hours to Turkey and eighteen hours to India.[91]

Box 3.6
**Are Cities Better Off as a Result of Immigration? Chicago's
Killer Heat Wave and "Little Village"**

Does immigration help or hurt a city? Immigration can actually add to a city's well-being, as demonstrated by a review of the death toll of Chicago's 1995 killer heat wave. That summer, over 485 people died in Chicago from heat-related causes. The elderly were especially vulnerable.

But the deaths were not distributed equally throughout the city. As a quick look at a city map readily reveals, the deaths were concentrated in certain neighborhoods and not in others.

Not all lower-income communities suffered high death rates. The mortality rate was actually fairly low in the predominantly poor Mexican-American community of South Lawndale, an area of the city commonly called "Little Village." Public-health authorities began to ask why the death rate in Little Village was so low, especially when the death rate in neighboring North Lawndale, a poor African-American area, was so high.

Continuing immigration from Mexico had made Little Village a lively neighborhood, with an active shopping district and a well-supported network of churches. The elderly in Little Village were able to escape the heat of their old apartments by frequenting the area's air-conditioned stores. The elderly were not scared to venture into the busy 26th Street shopping district, with its stores, bakeries, restaurants, and pushcart vendors selling juices and churros. The community's well-financed and socially active churches also provided outreach services, with church members visiting homes and tending to the needs of the elderly.

North Lawndale, by contrast, was a distressed community pockmarked by boarded-up buildings, abandoned lots, and drug dealing on the streets. North Lawndale had few air-conditioned stores that the elderly could frequent to escape the blast-furnace conditions of their apartments. The elderly in North Lawndale lived in fear; even in the heat, they were reluctant to open first-floor windows, venture out into the streets, or even unchain the door when municipal officials inquired as to their health. The elderly were afraid to open the door to strangers. The elderly died in their apartments, behind locked doors and windows bolted shut. Even the churches of North Lawndale exhibited advanced distress; they lacked the membership to provide the home visits and networks of support evident in Little Village.

Both Little Village and North Lawndale are poor neighborhoods, and both suffer serious problems of gang activity. Yet there is a vast difference between the two communities. Continuing immigration gave Little Village a vital street life and an active network of churches. North Lawndale experienced no such immigration and, as a result, suffered an exodus of population that emptied streets, closed churches and stores, and diminished residents' sense of personal safety. Without new arrivals, North Lawndale suffered abandonment and steep decline.

Source: Eric Klinenberg, *Heat Wave: A Social Autopsy of Disaster in Chicago* (Chicago: University of Chicago Press, 2002), chap. 2.

Technology and transportation have shrunk the globe and created **transnational communities**. The nature of immigration itself has changed over the years. In a "back-and-forth migration" new arrivals seek economic opportunity in the United States but do not relinquish their home ties.[92] In Chicago's Pilsen and Little Village neighborhoods and in Detroit's Mexicantown, immigrant workers send a part of their paychecks to family members in Mexico; the workers return home for frequent visits.

The diversity of the new immigration has also affected voting patterns. New arrivals can undercut racial and ethnic "block voting" as they do not share the same experiences and political attitudes of their ethnic brethren who have resided in American cities for a much longer period of time. In New York, African Americans and African Caribbeans have not been able to form a sturdy political alliance. Instead, the two groups have clashed over such matters as just which group is most deserving of the next open city council seat.[93]

5. THE VULNERABILITY OF CITIES TO TERRORISM, INTERNATIONAL POLITICAL TURMOIL, AND DISEASE

Globalization also denotes a heightened vulnerability of cities,[94] a reality underscored by the attacks of 9/11. Even cities that have not been the direct targets of terrorist assaults have had to divert spending for activities related to homeland defense. Cities must also take action to prevent attacks by computer hackers and other malcontents whose intrusions can paralyze a city's digital enterprises.[95]

International crises—famine, civil war, and political turmoil—produce waves of immigration that, too, add to municipal service burdens. Cities are also susceptible to pandemics. With modern jet travel, diseases such as AIDS and Ebola can quickly cross from one continent to another.[96]

CONCLUSION: GLOBALIZATION, POWER, AND DEMOCRACY

The competitive pressures of globalization have led cities to give great attention to local economic development, slighting social welfare and housing priorities. As Thomas Friedman provocatively phrases it, in the face of global pressures and uncontrollable global forces, "Your politics shrinks." Countries and communities put on a "Golden Straightjacket," pursuing economic growth and neglecting social policy and other priorities.[97]

A number of U.S. cities, however, have attempted to break out of the Golden Straightjacket and pursue a more balanced approach to future development.[98] In Seattle, neighborhood groups play a vigilant role in the local arena. Their presence helps to ensure that corporations will not dictate the exact shape of Seattle's postindustrial transformation.[99] In Seattle, global competitive pressures are not deterministic. Local politics still counts; a city ultimately decides how it will respond to the new competitive global setting.

In Seattle, Boston, and other cities that have large numbers of well-educated and affluent professionals, the local political culture stresses environmental protection and preservation of the quality of urban life. In these cities, public officials do not simply cede to the demands of multinational corporations. Activism by gays and lesbian and by other countercultural groups also appears to contribute to a willingness of municipal officials to deviate from a growth agenda set by global corporate interests.[100]

How do cities compete in a global age? A city can no longer hope to win businesses by relying only on a strategy of tax cuts and other business subsidies. Hundreds of competitor communities can offer a prospective firm the same, or even a better, package of benefits.

"Smart" communities do not rely only on tax cuts and incentives; these cities also invest heavily in their telecommunications infrastructure, upgrading fiber-optic networks and wireless access to the Internet in an effort to improve their competitive position. Rather than reduce business taxes across the board, these municipalities target assistance to small businesses and to business start-ups, enterprises where the city's favors are likely to have a substantial impact on job creation.

Local leaders have begun to recognize the importance of joint actions that can enhance the competitiveness of the larger city-region. No city and no region can expect to "win" the competition for businesses in all industrial sectors. Instead, cities and regions will find their greatest chances of success when they seek to expand an existing *industry cluster*.

An **industry cluster** refers to a group of "linked" or interconnected firms that tend to locate in relative close proximity to one another as they share specialized supply networks and support services and recruit from the same pool of skilled labor.[101] Clustering enables **knowledge transfer** where the members of an industry can exchange technical know-how and otherwise share ideas that lead to greater productivity and growth. Industry clusters are "the new engines of metropolitan economies."[102] Communities in a region enjoy their greatest chances of economic success when they seek to expand an existing regional cluster.[103]

Local universities are often **institutional anchors** that provide the research, the specialized training, and sometimes even some of the investment dollars necessary to grow an industry cluster. In Ohio, the University of Akron's nationally ranked polymer science and engineering program helped Akron, the home to B.F. Goodrich and once "the rubber capital of the world," to reverse its long-term decline and reemerge as a globally important center of polymer chemistry and related technology.[104] The economic growth of California's wine country in the Napa and Sonoma valleys was aided by the viticulture and enology programs of the University of California at Davis.[105] Universities anchored in inner-city communities often lead revitalization projects in surrounding neighborhoods.[106]

In a globally competitive age, cities are increasingly coming to recognize the critical importance of investing in human resources. Cities with an educated, technologically competent, and adaptable workforce have the best chances of attracting knowledge-based industry.

Finally, an outstanding local quality of life helps to make a community attractive to both professional workers and technology-oriented firms. In San Francisco, the creation of a "hip" and "trendy" neighborhood in place of the aging warehouses of SOMA (South of Market Street) helped the city to attract "new media" and other creative businesses.[107] Other cities concentrate on parks facilities, bicycle trails, river rafting, and the availability of concerts and cultural and entertainment activities to attract creative workers.

Globalization constrains local choices. Yet no city is a mere prisoner of global economic forces.[108] As the next few chapters of this book will further describe, neighborhood groups, ethnic minorities, taxpayer associations, and environmentalists can provide a substantial challenge to business-led urban growth agendas.

KEY TERMS

agglomeration (*p. 69*)

brownfield sites (*p. 60*)

call centers (*p. 71*)

casualization of work (*p. 73*)

command-and-control center in a global economy (*p. 67*)

community development corporations (CDCs) (*p. 66*)

displacement (*p. 60*)

dualism (*p. 74*)

financifiers (*p. 59*)

freeze on property taxes as a means to counter displacement pressures (*p. 67*)

gateway cities (*p. 76*)

gentrification (*p. 56*)

global city (*p. 67*)

globalization (*p. 56*)

grassroots organizing efforts (*p. 66*)

HOPE VI (*p. 63*)

industry cluster (*p. 80*)

informalization of the economy (*p. 73*)

knowledge transfer (*p. 80*)

linkage fees (*p. 67*)

mandatory set asides as an affordable housing strategy (*p. 67*)

measures to limit the conversion of single room occupancy (SRO) hotels (*p. 66*)

neighborhood invasion (*p. 62*)

neighborhood networks (*p. 62*)

nerdistans (*p. 72*)

new-build gentrification (*p. 60*)

new immigration (*p. 75*)

offshoring (*p. 71*)

outsourcing (*p. 71*)

piecework (*p. 77*)

port-of-entry city (*p. 76*)

promoting residential ownership as a strategy for neighborhood stability (*p. 67*)

Seattle's special housing levy (*p. 67*)

Silicon Alley (*p. 72*)

Silicon Valley (*p. 72*)

supergentrifiers (*p. 59*)

sweat equity (*p. 63*)

transnational communities (*p. 79*)

universities as institutional anchors of economic development (*p. 80*)

urban pioneers (*p. 56*)

Welcome City (*p. 77*)

world cities hierarchy (*p. 69*)

world city (*p. 67*)

4 Who Has the Power?

Decision Making, Economic Development, and Urban Regimes

Who has the power to "get things done" in the urban arena? Whom do local governments serve? Why do cities subsidize sports stadiums despite numerous academic studies that point to the waste and economic inefficiency of such investments?

A review of the formal structure of local government—the formal authority of mayors, managers, and council members—cannot provide a full answer to these questions. A thorough examination of urban power also requires a look "behind the scenes" to determine the extent to which off-stage actors constrain the actions of municipal officials.

MOVING BEYOND THE OLD "POWER ELITE" VERSUS "PLURALISM" DEBATE

For too many years, two polarized schools of thought dominated the debate over urban power. **Power elite theory** argues that "big business" and other behind-the-scenes notables effectively control the local arena. According to power elite theory, city council debates and public decision making are little more than public theater; for the most part, public officials implement courses of action that business leaders and other local notables had determined in private.

Power elite theory views urban politics as extremely undemocratic; cities are dominated by "the few;" important policy areas are effectively closed to the voice of the people.[1] The popular culture, including movies like *Roger and Me*, reinforce the perception of elite rule, that corporate chief executive officers (CEOs) have a stranglehold on local affairs. (See Box 4.1, "Urban Films—A Corporate Power Elite: *Roger and Me*.")

Of course, private actors and corporations possess considerable influence in the American urban arena. No one seriously contends that the average citizen possesses the same effective voice as the chief executive of a major corporation. Business dominance also characterized politics in Sunbelt communities for much of the twentieth century, as public officials largely pursued an agenda formulated by business-led civic associations such as the Dallas Citizen's Charter Association, San Antonio's Good Government League, and the Phoenix 40.

Box 4.1
Urban Films—A Corporate Power Elite: *Roger and Me*

Michael Moore's 1989 "guerilla" documentary *Roger and Me* provides a clear statement of the view that corporate elites possess immense and unaccountable power in the local arena. Moore, a native of Flint, Michigan, traces the decline of his beloved community, a city once known as an auto factory worker's paradise. Flint slid over the years into postindustrial decline, becoming a city marred by extensive joblessness, poverty, evictions, housing foreclosures, and property abandonment. Moore points to the villains he sees as responsible for Flint's decline: General Motors (GM) and its then-CEO Roger Smith, who closed automobile plants in the city while shifting production to low-wage plants in Mexico and overseas. Thousands of workers in Flint lost their jobs as a result of the global corporate strategy of plant closings.

Roger Smith and other CEOs answer to a corporation's stockholders; their primary concern is the corporate bottom line, not the health of the communities in which they are located. The managers of national and global corporations lack the sense of local roots and civic patriotism exhibited by an earlier generation of home-grown business owners and managers. Working in security-guarded headquarters building and playing in private clubs, the new executives have no real knowledge of the residents of Flint and their daily lives and sufferings. Moore contrasts pictures of Smith and other GM officials celebrating the Christmas season at a corporate party while a poor Flint family faces eviction, unable to pay their monthly rent.

Moore's viewpoint is clear: The "people" have no meaningful control over what happens in Flint. The decisions made in corporate boardrooms doomed Flint and its hard-working people.

In Houston, the borderline between business and government was not easy to discern. Oscar Holcombe, a real estate dealer and developer, served twenty-two years as mayor, serving eleven nonconsecutive times over a mayoral career that spanned from 1921 through the 1950s. During this era, property developers and appointees with ties to the real estate industry populated Houston's planning commission.[2] Houston's government pursued priorities set by the business community: public officials built the sewers and infrastructure necessary for growth while keeping taxes and social services to a minimum.

In more recent years, the city's changing demographics have led municipal officials to give greater consideration to the demands of Latinos, the gay and lesbian community, and other new arrivals. Still, the concerns of the business community continue to shape Houston, with municipal efforts focused on downtown development: the construction of a new convention center, subsidies for sports-related development, and government-supported gentrification. Public policies that promoted the upscaling of Houston's core area led to the virtual disappearance of older ethnic neighborhoods: Chinatown, Little Saigon, and historic African-American "Freedmen's Town."[3]

Clearly, businesses exert considerable influence in the municipal arena. Power is not evenly distributed in the city; cities are not perfectly democratic. Yet elite theory overstates the power of the business community and, as a result, fails to provide an accurate description of power relations in the American city. In most cities, there is no unified business elite capable of extensive, coordinated action across a broad range of municipal affairs. "Business" does not even comprise a unified bloc capable of coordinated political action. Business leaders do not all share the same interest; downtown revitalization projects, for instance, are likely to face opposition from small business owners and from business interests located outside the city center. In city after city, business executives can cite numerous instances where local officials did not cede to their demands. Whatever its insights, power elite theory presents an overly simplified view of urban power.

A competing school of thought, **pluralism** (also called **pluralist theory**), offers a quite different perspective: that power in the urban arena is not held only by a select few "big mule" interests; instead, power is spread more widely, albeit unevenly, throughout the community. Pluralists do not contend that cities are fair and democratic; they recognize that wealthy developers like Donald Trump enjoy greater access to decision makers than do ordinary citizens. Still, pluralists argue that cities are not the puppets of corporate officials and other powerful behind-the-scene interests.

Pluralists contend that, while local democracy is imperfect, municipal decision making is not a "closed" process but is actually relatively "open" to a diversity of (that is to "plural") voices. Environmentalists, middle-class homeowners, taxpayer associations, racial minorities, and poor-people's groups all have influence. Pluralists contend that even the poor and racial minorities have the ability to organize get-out-the-vote drives and protest and can be "effectively heard,"[4] as evident in their ability to get municipal officials to support community health clinics and to partner with community development corporations in the construction of affordable housing. Power is not held only by business officials and wealthy families.

As already observed, a city's business community is seldom a monolithic entity capable of unified action. Globalization has further pluralized and promoted contention among business interests. In Charlotte as in a great many other cities, managers sent on assignment by multinational firms do not share the perspectives of locally rooted business leaders.[5] National corporate executives temporarily residing in a community often lack a strong inclination to get involved in a broad range of municipal affairs, as a national survey of such officials underscores:

> [L]ocal executives are now less engaged in civic life, are rotating cities more frequently and consequently less knowledgeable about their communities, and possess less autonomy to make local civic and financial commitments.[6]

The lack of involvement by corporate leaders in local affairs gives municipal leaders a fair degree of freedom when acting on a broad range of issues. In one important way, however, the relative disinterest of global executives also imposes an important constraint on municipal officials, as a city's elected leaders may have a difficult time enlisting corporate support for key local projects.

Pluralist theory points to the oversimplifications inherent in the power elite model. But the pluralist perspective, itself, suffers from oversimplifications and fails to provide an adequate understanding of power in the metropolis. The local political system is not nearly as "open" as the pluralists claim. While poor people may be "effectively heard" on isolated issues, in a great many cities they still lack the ability to force government to address fundamental concerns regarding gentrification and displacement, persistent inequality, underperforming schools, the persistence of racial segregation and ghettoization, and community-police relations.

The pluralist perspective also understates the influence of business in the urban arena. While business leaders do not simply dictate to city officials, cities nonetheless continue to pursue actions that are heavily tilted toward business needs.

The pluralist perspective fails to recognize the degree of influence exerted by the urban **growth machine**—the coalition of businesses, real estate and financial firms, and even labor unions in the construction trades that benefit from continued public approval of, and subsidies for, growth projects.[7] The growth machine claims that its projects provide jobs and other benefits that serve the entire community. In large and medium-sized cities, the members of the growth machine make sizable campaign donations, an increasingly prominent factor in local elections. (See Chapter 6 for further discussion of the role played by money in local elections). Growth machines can also be found in numerous suburbs; growth interests provided the political impetus for the continuing development of "edge cities" such as Tyson's Corner, Virginia, outside Washington, D.C.[8] Clearly, "business" occupies a privileged position in the urban arena and has a degree of influence that is greater than pluralist theory admits.

"CITY LIMITS": HOW ECONOMIC COMPETITION SHAPES LOCAL POLITICS

THE MOBILITY OF CAPITAL: THE ROOTS OF CITY LIMITS

Why do cities pay so much attention to the concerns of business leaders even when there is no small cabal of business executives that effectively controls city decision making from off stage? Paul Peterson, in his important book *City Limits*, offers one possible explanation.[9] According to Peterson, business influence in the local arena derives from the **mobility of capital**. The owners of a business can locate their facilities in another town or state. Municipal officials, fearing the loss of local jobs and tax contributions, take whatever actions are necessary to attract new businesses and retain existing businesses, actions that are necessary for the city's economic and fiscal health. Business executives can raise the prospect that they will site their facilities elsewhere, a threat that will likely leverage substantial tax abatements and other important concessions from municipal officials.

Business leaders do not exert control over the entire range of municipal affairs but, instead, focus on those areas that most directly affect their enterprises. In policy areas where business executives have little at stake, public officials have great freedom to act.

Corporate executives are most concerned with **developmental policy**, redevelopment plans, infrastructure provision, and other public decisions that directly affect business investment and growth. Cities, according to Peterson, have little choice but to cater to business needs in the development arena; cities provide the land-use plans, regulatory approvals, tax abatements, subsidies, and roads, sewers and other physical infrastructure improvements desired by business. Each city and suburb strives to maintain a reputation for being a place that is "good for business."

Business leaders are also concerned with **redistributive policy**, which encompasses social welfare, health, housing, and other programs of assistance to the poor. Corporate executives do not wish to have their facilities taxed in order to support welfare-type programs. Peterson argues that American cities have little choice but to meet the concerns of business even at the price of ignoring the needs of more vulnerable residents:

> [T]he pursuit of a city's economic interests, which requires an efficient provision of local services, makes no allowance for the care of the needy and unfortunate members of the society. Indeed, the competition among local communities all but precludes a concern for redistribution.[10]

For Peterson, New York City's mid-1970s flirtation with bankruptcy underscores the disastrous consequences that can result when a municipality ignores "**city limits**" and instead of focusing on local economic competitiveness decides to pursue a broad range of social welfare and housing programs aimed at helping the poor.

Corporate officials, however, have no great stake in issues of **allocational policy**, decisions that municipalities make regarding just how various services—such as fire stations, library books, and computer facilities—are distributed among neighborhoods. Such service decisions seldom have a great impact on business well-being; as a result, corporate elites pay little attention to such matters, giving local officials great freedom to act on matters that lie in this broad policy area.

PURSUING GROWTH: WHY CITIES IGNORE THE ACADEMIC STUDIES AND CONTINUE TO BUILD COSTLY NEW STADIUMS

Intercity competition helps to explain why local authorities continue to spend vast sums of taxpayer money to aid the multimillionaire owners of sports franchises who seek new arenas with luxury skyboxes, restaurants, and computerized state-of-the-art scoreboards. Cities provide team owners with generous tax abatements and other subsidies for stadium construction. The signed contracts commit the city to costly land giveaways and cede to team owners the revenues from stadium-naming rights, parking, and other concessions. The stadium deals often saddle taxpayers with the costs of various hidden subsidies that become apparent during the post-construction operation of a facility.[11]

Numerous economic studies show that public investment in sports arenas is a very expensive and inefficient way to create new jobs.[12] Sports-related development suffers from a **substitution effect**; the increased economic activity around a new ballpark is offset by the displacement of existing businesses in the area and a decline in entertainment and dining activity elsewhere in the city. Sports arenas also do not operate 365 days a year; a football stadium may be in operation for very few days each year. On days where there are not sports events, the stadium areas are lifeless "black holes" that drain the economic vitality of the immediate surrounding area.

So, why do most cities pursue such seemingly unwise investment? It is not just that local officials fear the wrath of fans if a team leaves town. A city also gains prestige from hosting a major sports franchise, a presence that tells the global business community that the city is "major league" and worthy of major private investment. A new stadium also provides "intangible benefits," adding to community pride and elevating the image of a city, making a community more attractive to residents as well as to business.[13] In contrast, the loss of a sports franchise signals the economic decline of a city. The loss of a team sends a message to potential investors that the city is not a particularly "good place for business," that municipal officials are not particularly helpful and willing to meet business needs.

Peterson's emphasis on business mobility and intercity competition provides insight as to why municipalities give such lucrative subsidies to sports franchises: team owners secure new benefits by pointing to the "better deal" they can obtain from other cities. The threat to relocate can be quite real. The NBA Seattle Supersonics became the Oklahoma City Thunder. The basketball Nets moved from New Jersey to the showcase Barclays Center in downtown Brooklyn in New York City. The NFL Raiders moved to Los Angeles in 1982 only to pick up and move back to Oakland in 1995. The Cleveland Browns became the Baltimore Ravens (1996), and the Houston Oilers became the Tennessee Titans (1997).

But the threat of franchise relocation is also often highly exaggerated. A great many teams have no real interest in picking up and moving to another metropolitan area, as relocation will require that they build a new fan base to fill stadium seats. In such cases, the threat to leave is simply a "card" that franchise owners play in their effort to gain the maximum public concessions. As Pittsburgh Penguins owner and former NHL superstar Mario Lemieux candidly revealed after the city agreed to fund a new hockey arena:

> Our goal was to remain here in Pittsburgh all the way. Those trips to Kansas City and Vegas was [sic] just to go, and have a nice dinner and come back . . . That was just a way for us to put more pressure, and we knew it would work at the end of the day.[14]

Public officials do not know if a team's threat to leave is real or not. Nor do they know just what concessions franchise owners truly require to keep the team in a city. As a result, elected officials tend to err on the side of safety, agreeing to more generous concessions than what is absolutely necessary to retain a franchise.

The members of a city's growth machine add to the lobbying pressures for stadium approval. Labor union leaders point to the jobs that new construction will generate. Consultants' studies emphasize the new revenue stream that a city will tap as a result of stadium development. These forecasts, often prepared by consulting firms hired by members of the growth coalition, tend to underestimate the costs of a new stadium while overestimating the future revenues that the project will yield. All of this leads local officials to sign legally binding, **one-sided stadium contracts** where local taxpayers, not the team owners, are left "on the hook" when costs rise and revenues are less than what had been predicted.

Cincinnati provides a clear illustration of a one-sided stadium deal. Faced with talk of losing its major-league football team, citizens in Hamilton County (greater Cincinnati) voted to increase the local sales tax to help fund two new riverfront stadiums—for the football Bengals and the baseball Reds. To gain public approval of the ballot measure, the growth machine promised that the new sales tax would not be used only for the stadiums; the new revenues would also fund tax relief for the homeowners and provide additional support for the area's public schools. Downtown business interests created a pseudo-grassroots organization to support the measure, buying a million dollars in television ads to overcome what polls revealed to be great public resistance to the new tax. The ballot measure passed, and the two stadiums were built. When the economy slumped and the sales tax failed to yield the revenues that the consultants had projected, it was only the public schools, county services, and the promise of homeowner relief—and not the subsidies provided the sports franchises—that suffered cutbacks. The one-sided contract committed the government to paying for such upgrades to the Bengals' stadium as a multimillion dollar state-of-the art holographic replay machine. The one-sided contract even barred the county from placing new taxes on tickets, parking, and concessions in an effort to generate additional monies to help to defray the costs of the public's obligations.[15]

A municipality cannot be sure that its substantial investment will bind a team to the city. The football Raiders hopped from Oakland to Los Angeles and then back again to Oakland, only to then demand the construction of a new football-only stadium as the price for continuing to remain in Oakland or surrounding Alameda County. The basketball Miami Heat demanded a new arena with greater seating capacity and additional luxury suites to replace the "obsolete" Miami Arena that local authorities had built only eight years previously.[16]

The Atlanta Braves in 2013 announced that they were moving to suburban Cobb County, leaving central Atlanta and Turner Field, the ballpark that had been built for them as part of the city's construction program for the 1996 Summer Olympics. Cobb County offered a reported $450 million (some reports put the figure as high as $672) in subsidies and infrastructure improvements; still, additional public costs were likely to be incurred as a result of the need to provide upgraded highway and transit access to a site that lacked MARTA rail service. Critics surmised that the Braves were looking forward to moving to a new state-of-the art facility and to leaving the inner-city African-American neighborhood that surrounded Turner Field.[17]

Not every stadium deal is bad for a city.[18] Indianapolis shows that cities can be "major league winners," especially if a city ties its investment in sports facilities to a strategic plan to revitalize a section of the city and to raise the profile of the city, increasing the city's attractiveness to business. In San Diego, public authorities and sports team owners formed a public-private partnership to share the costs of a new downtown baseball park for the Padres.[19] Public authorities paid the bulk of the $450 million costs for land acquisition, infrastructure improvements, and construction. But **memos of understanding** signed by the developers ensured their financial commitment to new projects in "Ballpark Village," the underdeveloped twenty-six-block area lying just beyond the fences of Petco Park.

Although the San Diego partnership is often portrayed as a model of success, the stadium deal is also the subject of intense criticism. Taxpayers paid the up-front costs of the stadium, but the contract gave the private developers—not the public—the ability to control land uses in, and reap the profits from, the Ballpark Village area. As construction proceeded, the developers scaled back their earlier promise to build affordable housing. The developers built a smaller green park than the one that was envisioned when they initially presented the project to the voters. The costs that the city had to pick up also increased when the development did not generate the tax revenues that the project's enthusiasts had projected. Arrangements for Tax Increment Financing (a financing mechanism that will be discussed in greater detail in Chapter 12) served to ensure that any gains in property tax revenues from the project could only be used for improvements in the immediate project area, not for the city's schools or for improved public services in residential areas elsewhere in the city.[20]

The growth coalition does not always emerge victorious. In a number of communities, taxpayer associations, neighborhood groups, and environmental activists have mobilized to oppose new stadium construction. In Seattle, voters, concerned with project costs, environmental impacts, and neighborhood preservation said "No!" to a new basketball arena, accepting the likelihood that its NBA team would relocate to Oklahoma City. In 2008, the Supersonics became the Oklahoma City Thunder.

Typically, when sports interests face local authorities reluctant to approve a new stadium, the growth coalition strategically turns its lobbying efforts to the state government, convincing state officials to intercede by creating a new public entity with the authority to approve construction of the new sports facility. Chicago, Cleveland, Milwaukee, Minneapolis, Phoenix, Pittsburgh, San Jose, and Seattle (where a state-created authority helped build CenturyLink Field—previously known as Qwest Field—for the football Seattle Seahawks and the soccer Seattle Sounders) provide only some of the more prominent cases where state governments kept stadium projects alive by circumventing local opposition.[21]

In Minneapolis, local voters over the years expressed their repeated unwillingness to fund various sports arenas. The Minnesota state legislature eventually intervened, arranging for the construction of Target Field for the baseball Twins. That decision wound up escalating the demands by the NFL Minnesota Vikings for public subsidies for a new football stadium to replace the aging Superdome. (See Box 4.2: "Are There Better Ways to Finance a New Stadium? San Francisco and Minneapolis.")

As this brief review of stadium politics reveals, no behind-the-scenes elite dictates the construction of a new stadium. Public subsidies for new stadiums are increasingly controversial; team owners seldom get the exact facility they want, and, in some cases, a proposed stadium project has suffered defeat. Rather than illustrating the willingness of public officials to implement business-led arrangements that have been hammered out in private, negotiations between franchise owners and public officials often are lengthy and protracted.

Still, despite the difficulties that often characterize negotiations, team owners, more often than not, are generally able to get what they want—or, to be more accurate, more of what they want. The power of franchise owners is rooted in the perceived threat inherent in the team's geographical mobility and the ability of business leaders to convince local and state officials of the harm that a team's transfer will inflict on the local and state economy. The growth coalition does a good job of persuading public officials of the dire nature of the economic threat, even when the forecast of dire consequences is not supported by solid data analysis.

Box 4.2
Are There Better Ways to Finance a New Stadium?
San Francisco and Minneapolis

Stadium deals are not all equally one-sided and bad for a city and its taxpayers. Some cities negotiate a better deal than do others.

In San Francisco, the hesitancy of citizens to approve corporate-oriented growth projects strengthened the hand of local officials in their negotiations with sports team owners. As a result, public authorities in San Francisco paid only 14 percent of the capital costs of a new baseball stadium, as compared to 44 percent in Detroit and 95 percent in Baltimore!

In a number of ways, the city of Santa Clara, south of San Francisco in the heart of Silicon Valley, did an even better job in negotiating an agreement with the NFL football 49ers. The 49ers had announced their intention to leave San Francisco for a site in the middle of Silicon Valley, just thirty-five miles to the south. A voter initiative barred Santa Clara from levying new taxes to support the project. As a result, team owners could only get their desired stadium by agreeing to pick up a greater share of project costs than was typical in other cities. Moving to an area of well-paid technology workers, the team owners had no problem in raising $40 million for construction, largely from the sale of **seat licenses**, with willing fans paying thousands of dollars just for the right to buy tickets for future games and events. The sale of **naming rights** to Levi Strauss & Sons generated an additional $220 million over the five-year period during which the facility would be called Levi's Stadium. The public authority in charge of the project also issued bonds at favorable interest rates to help reduce the costs of construction. All of these features minimized the burden the new stadium placed directly on homeowners and local taxpayers.

In Minnesota, the reluctance of local voters to approve subsidies for a new stadium, similarly strengthened the hands of city officials in bargaining with team owners. The owners of the baseball Twins had hinted that they would relocate the team to Charlotte or another city if they could not get a new ballpark to replace the aging Metrodome. Still, local citizens refused to endorse the commitment of taxpayer money to what is essentially a private profit-making venture. Faced with such resistance, franchise owners and their growth coalition allies switched their lobbying efforts to state officials. State government action led to the construction of Target Field, but without the expensive retractable dome that team owners had sought.

The construction of the new Twins ballpark led the Minnesota Vikings to hike (pardon the pun) their own demands for a new downtown football facility to replace the three-decades-old Mall of America Field (popularly known as the Metrodome). Team owners intimated that, if a new field were not built, they would sell the franchise and relocate the team out of state. Once again, the state government intervened, arranging the financing for the new stadium. As was the case in Santa Clara, the owners of the Vikings turned to the sale of seat licenses to help cover their half of the estimated billion dollar cost of the facility.

Compared to stadium agreements in cities like Cincinnati, the deals struck in Minnesota, San Francisco, and Santa Clara put less of a financial burden on homeowners and ordinary citizens. In these cities, team owners agreed to bear a sizable portion of the stadium's costs or pass the costs along to stadium users via the team's imposition of seat license fees.

But even in these cases, the public incurred substantial costs, picking up roughly half the costs of the construction of each project. In Minneapolis, the city was also responsible for building 1,400 parking spaces for the Vikings. The Minnesota state legislature authorized a citywide sales tax surcharge to help cover the public's costs of a new Vikings stadium. A sales tax is a regressive revenue-raising instrument that places a disproportionate burden on a city's poorer residents. A new state tax on "pull tab" gambling was also enacted in an attempt to find new revenues without directly burdening homeowners. Taxpayers, however, still wound up having to pay additional sums when pull-tab gaming failed to produce the proceeds that the growth coalition consultants had so confidently projected.

The San Francisco, Santa Clara, and Minnesota cases illustrate some of the guiding principles for a public-serving stadium deal. First, follow the **benefit principle**: persons and interests who benefit from a project should directly contribute to the project. The benefit principle justifies the imposition of seat license fees, a tax surcharge on tickets, and the levy of special hotel, restaurant, and bar taxes on enterprises that enjoy greater patronage as a result of stadium events. Santa Clara, for instance, placed a room surcharge on hotels located within two miles of the stadium. Targeted fees and surcharges represent a more equitable means of financing stadiums as compared to increasing sales and property levies that are borne by a much broader range of local residents.

A second principle is just as simple: **spread the responsibility for financing** a new stadium over a larger geographical area rather than placing the financial burden on a single city. If a new stadium truly contributes to the "major league" image and economic marketability of a state or metropolitan area, then the state or larger region should share in the costs of construction. State action is often required to set up financing arrangements that extend beyond the borders of a single city.

When it comes to stadium construction, there is no simple system of elite rule. Instead, politics counts. In San Francisco, Santa Clara, and Minneapolis, the recalcitrance of citizens strengthened the ability of public leaders to fashion more equitable stadium deals—especially when contrasted to the more one-sided financing arrangements found in other cities.

Sources: The San Francisco, Detroit, and Baltimore figures are cited by Judith Grant Long, *Public-Private Partnerships for Major League Sports Facilities* (New York: Routledge, 2013), 14; also see chap. 7. For discussions of the Santa Clara and Minnesota stadium deals, see: Robert Selna, "Stadium a Great Deal—Or Is It?" *San Francisco Chronicle,* July 14, 2009; Neil deMause, "Levi's to Pay $11 Million a Year to Put Name on 49ers Stadium," *Field of Schemes,* December 11, 2013, www.fieldofschemes.com/category/nfl/san-francisco-49ers/; and Richard Meryhew, "Doubts, Controversy Exist over $975 Million Vikings Stadium Deal," *Minneapolis Star Tribune,* September 27, 2013; and Michael Powell, "Sniffing for Dollars at Home of the Vikings," *New York Times*, October 3, 2014.

WHO PUSHES THE OVERINVESTMENT IN CONVENTION CENTERS?

Cities once focused on the provision of basic services like streets, sewers, and police and fire protection. Today, as we have already seen, cities have moved beyond basic service provision to the construction of sports stadiums. Cities also build and modernize convention centers in an effort to lure economic growth.

Downtown businesses and their growth machine allies often play a key role in pushing cities to construct and enlarge local convention centers. These boosters argue that an updated convention center is essential for a city to meet its economic competition and prevent the loss of conventions and tourism-related jobs to other communities. Prestigious consulting firms (including KPMG Peat Marwick, PriceWaterhouse, and Conventions, Sports and Leisure International) present allegedly objective analyses with extensive statistics and tables that purport to document the benefits that a city will derive from investing in a new convention center.

But are new convention centers really good for cities? Do they deliver the benefits their backers promise? In most cases, convention centers fail to produce the jobs and extensive economic benefits that growth advocates had predicted. Convention centers often fail to produce a full calendar of events and wind up offering discounts and other subsidies in an effort to fill "dark" days where no activity is already scheduled. Heywood T. Sanders, an urbanist who has spent a large part of his professional life comparing the promises with the reality of convention centers, observes:

> But while communities have proven remarkably capable of building new and larger centers, they have proven remarkably unsuccessful in filling them. From Atlanta to Seattle, Boston to Las Vegas, the promises of local officials and the forecasts of consultants have come up short. State and local governments have built modern new centers, only to see half or less of the convention attendees promised by the consultants. Other cities have expanded their existing centers, yet failed to see any consistent increase in business. Indeed, there is substantial evidence that the supply of convention center space substantially exceeds demand (a "buyer's market"), with cities desperately competing by offering their center space rent free.[22]

The growing competition for the convention business means that even in a major city like Chicago, a convention center will have difficulty in filling its schedule with top-rate conventions. Even McCormick Place, Chicago's premier tradeshow space, faced declining business and attendance despite expensive modernization and expansion. Las Vegas, Orlando, and other competitors upgraded their own facilities, seizing conventions that once went to Chicago. McCormick Place once hosted a majority of the nation's major tradeshows; by 2008, that number fell to only two. The State of Illinois stepped in, offering $10 million in incentives and rebates in an effort to lure tradeshows to the facility.[23]

How do cities—big and small cities and many suburbs, too—wind up in such unenviable positions, investing lavishly in new convention centers when there is too little convention and tradeshow business to fill all of the centers that are built? Local tourism officials, hotel owners, downtown businesses, and their growth machine allies hire expensive consulting firms that produce market analyses with very precise figures that convincingly substantiate the economic return that a city will receive on its investment. However, such figures often are actually little more than guesses based on highly optimistic assumptions that almost invariably overstate the growth of the convention business, local tradeshow attendance, a city's ability to attract major conventions, the number of hotel beds that visitors fill, and tourist spending.[24] When a convention center fails to perform as predicted, the growth machine calls for more—for new subsidies, the further modernization of convention space, and the construction of additional hotel rooms to allow the city to meet its competition.

Even in cities facing difficult times, the claims of growth advocates and the exaggerated statistical forecasts made by hired-gun consultants largely go unchallenged. Detroit, facing the prospects of bankruptcy and having to make drastic cutbacks in basic services, continued with plans to renovate Cobo Center, the city's major meeting and convention facility. Business advocates turn their attention to independent bodies, such as the Detroit Regional Convention Facility Authority, and to the state government for authorization and financial assistance in instances where local officials are unwilling—or, in Detroit's case, unable—to aid convention center expansion.

ARE LOW TAXES THE ONLY WAY TO WOO BUSINESSES?

Peterson's theory of "city limits" rightfully points to the constraints that economic competition imposes on local officials. But Peterson overstates his case, especially in his contention that cities must maintain their competitiveness by keeping taxes low and by minimizing local spending for redistributive programs, including social welfare, health care for the poor, and affordable housing.

A politics of low taxes and reduced provision of social services does not provide the only path—or in all cases the most viable path—to local economic prosperity. In the postindustrial city, the promise of tax cuts does not always constitute a winning local economic strategy. Technology-oriented firms do not always desire locations in low-tax, low-service communities. "Knowledge" enterprises look favorably on communities that have quality schools and effective job-training programs. The provision of quality recreational facilities and lifestyle amenities helps to attract creative workers and technology oriented industries. In such cases, "smart" public investment provides the setting for local economic growth.

Peterson also overstates the mobility of businesses. Not every business is free to pick up and relocate to a community that offers a better package of subsidies and tax abatements. Local tax rates are *not* the Number One factor in a business-siting decision. Businesses give greater consideration to the quality of the local labor force and a site's transportation infrastructure, including the accessibility of a site to suppliers and markets.[25] A business may also be hesitant to uproot—and possibly lose—top executives and talented personnel. Cities like San Francisco and Seattle also enjoy the competitive advantage provided by their scenic setting, a factor that reduces the willingness of many top-end businesses to relocate elsewhere.

In cases where a business is not "rootless" and free to move, municipal leaders have greater policy discretion and bargaining leverage than Peterson avers. In such instances, cities and suburbs can pursue more balanced priorities—more fair development deals and continued spending for social services, subsidized housing, and environmental protection—without worrying that each progressive policy choice will result in an exodus of business.

REGIME THEORY: POWER AS SOCIAL PRODUCTION

Still, as urban theorist Clarence Stone asks, "Why, when all of their actions are taken into account, do officials over the long haul seem to favor upper-strata interests, disfavor lower-strata interests, and sometimes act in apparent disregard of the contours of electoral power?"[26] The answer lies in the dependence of municipal leaders on private business to "get things done," what Stone has called **social production**. Even in the absence of an all-powerful private elite, a city's top officials eventually come to recognize that they need the cooperation of business leaders to get important things done. Business leaders cannot impose their will on a city. Still, city officials recognize that businesses are important municipal assets, that business leaders can be important partners for a city that seeks to strengthen its downtown, revive troubled neighborhoods, and create mentoring opportunities for at-risk youth. In these and a great many other policy areas, the accomplishment of municipal objectives is largely dependent on the willingness of private actors to cooperate.

Business executives, in turn, find that they require government approvals (i.e., zoning and land-use approvals) and public subsidies to achieve many of their growth objectives. As a result, public-private cooperation can even emerge in a city where public and private leaders have different political philosophies and different partisan allegiances. Public officials and private business leaders recognize that they need one another, that it is in their mutual interest to enter into a functional working relationship.

In some cities, business cooperation is so crucial to the realization of public projects that business leaders can be seen as having **preemptive power**; the refusal of civic leaders to cooperate can effectively doom a civic project. Such power, however, does not guarantee businesses the ability to get things they want done across a broad range of policy areas. Preemptive power is veto power, not the ability to force action or to get things done.[27]

LOOKING BEYOND ELECTORAL COALITIONS TO GOVERNING REGIMES

Elections by themselves do not determine how things get done in a city. To get important things done, a mayor, once in office, will often find it necessary to gain the cooperation of actors who were not among his or her most ardent supporters in the previous election campaign. An **urban regime** (also called a **governing regime**) exists when an informal working coalition of governmental and nongovernmental actors persists over a significant number of years with the capacity to decide the overall policy direction and projects that a city will pursue.

A public-private partnership of convenience that is temporarily formed during a single mayoral term in office does *not* constitute an urban regime. The concept of an urban regime denotes a working alliance of greater duration and significance: the emergence of a relatively *stable* alliance among public officials and private actors that governs a city from one municipal administration to the next.

Regime theory shifts the focus of the study of urban politics. Regime analysis focuses less on elections and more on the post-election arrangements for city governance. The election of an African-American or Latino mayor and city council, for instance, does not guarantee that a city's government will succeed in pursuing policies that will increase the opportunities available to African-American and Hispanic residents. Instead, black and Latino mayors often find that they must reach an accommodation with business leaders who control investment resources critical to the future health of the city and its various ethnic communities.[28]

The members of a city's governing regime can be quite different from the electoral coalition that put the mayor and city council into office. In Atlanta, the city's black popular majority dominates municipal elections, leading ill-informed observers to mistakenly claim that Atlanta is a "black power" city where officials give little respect to the concerns of whites. A closer examination of decision making in Atlanta, however, reveals that local business leaders have been able to maintain their privileged position in the biracial regime—not a black-power system—that governs Atlanta. (See Box 4.3, "Atlanta's Biracial Governing Regime.")

A similar story can be told about Charlotte, North Carolina. A biracial coalition composed of white business leaders and African-American elected officials has worked to defuse racial tensions and thereby set the stage for the Charlotte area's dynamic economic growth. The governing regime had to respond to the concerns of both sets of parties. As a result, Charlotte pursued busing for school integration while also issuing bonds to finance new development projects, a policy demanded by growth interests. Over the years, however, the informal governing alliance in Charlotte has begun to fray, especially as local leaders retreated from their earlier commitment to school integration. In both Charlotte and Atlanta, community activists have questioned the degree to which the city's biracial governing regime truly served the interests of more disadvantaged members of the community.[29]

DIFFERENT REGIME TYPES

Regime theory recognizes that business leaders often occupy key positions in a local governing partnership. Still, regime theory does not view business interests as all-powerful. A city's elected officials have their own policy concerns and their own electoral needs and, as a result, do not always choose to cede to business demands. Business interests do not always get their way in the contemporary city.

There is also no guarantee that corporate leaders will be dominant members in the informal alliance that governs a city. A great many cities, of course, give corporate officials great respect. Still, there exist alternative possible governing arrangements, alliances that do not afford business leaders such a privileged position.

In some cities, municipal officials spurn the growth plans of major national and global corporations; in these cities, elected officials may choose to govern in partnership with a city's locally rooted businesses, businesses that may not wish to be taxed to pay for the growth plans desired by global corporations. In other cities, local officials may be responsive to the concerns of homeowners and taxpayers. In still other cities, an alliance of homeowners, taxpayers, racial minorities, and environmentalists may succeed in electing public officials committed to environmental protection and responding to the needs of poorer- and middle-class neighborhoods.

Broadly speaking, there are three alternative types of local governing regimes.[30] A **corporate regime** (also called a **development regime**) reflects the growth-oriented policies preferred by major corporations and businesses, slighting equity ("fairness") concerns and the needs of a city's more distressed neighborhoods. A development regime is often marked by the actions of a city's growth machine, with labor unions interested in construction jobs joining with businesses, real estate firms, the editors of the local newspaper, and other city "boosters" to push for city-funded growth projects. In booming suburbs, real estate firms and development interests can similarly dominate a local agenda committed to growth.

In recent years, Louisville has been governed by a corporate regime, led by a mayor and top municipal staff working with the support of local business organizations (the Chamber of Commerce and Greater Louisville, Inc.), construction unions, the local

Box 4.3
Atlanta's Biracial Governing Regime

Compared to other cities in the Deep South during the civil rights era, Atlanta remained relatively calm. Atlanta was the self-proclaimed "City Too Busy to Hate." A biracial governing regime ruled Atlanta. Whites occupied elected municipal offices and worked with local business leaders who sought the cooperation of church leaders and other representatives of the city's large middle-class African-American community. The two racial groups did not see eye to eye on a great many issues. Nonetheless, they recognized a mutual interest that led them to work together, forging a path of moderate progress on civil rights that averted the civil unrest that scared off downtown customers in other cities.[1]

Atlanta has changed considerably over the years. African Americans have gained effective control of city hall, with a majority-black electorate consistently choosing a black mayor and a black-majority city council. Still, despite these changes, the city's biracial governing regime has largely remained intact. As a result, members of the business community have been able to maintain a considerable influence in the New Atlanta.

Maynard Jackson, the city's first African American to be elected mayor (1973), was a political outsider who initially challenged Atlanta's reliance on elite-led accommodation. Much to the horror of white business leaders, Jackson insisted on strong affirmative-action hiring policies, including a requirement that 20 percent of the contracts on development projects be awarded to minority firms. He also reformed the police department. White business leaders greatly disliked Jackson but also recognized the necessity of maintaining a working relationship with city hall. Jackson, in turn, discovered that he needed their assistance on important civic projects. The city approved the construction of a new international airport, the business community's number-one priority. In return, businesses acceded, despite serious misgivings, to new affirmative-action requirements in hiring and contracting. Mayor Jackson gave new attention to concerns for economic development, backing away from his earlier avowal of neighborhood-oriented planning. He opposed wage increases demanded by black-dominated municipal labor unions.

Jackson's successors were even more supportive of business partnerships for economic growth and working with business. Andrew Young backed efforts to bring the Summer Olympics to Atlanta. The city demolished homes and small businesses in a low-income section of town, clearing the area for a gathering place for visitors to the games. The city built a new ballpark (which, after the Olympics, served as the home of the Atlanta Braves), displacing inner-city homeowners and ousting the area's homeless. Mayors Bill Campbell, Shirley Franklin, and Kasmin Reed similarly recognized the importance of maintaining good relations with business leaders.[2]

But how effectively does the biracial regime govern Atlanta today? Globalization and demographic shifts have weakened the biracial partnership. Corporate managers newly assigned to Atlanta lack the trust and sense of familiarity necessary to maintaining smooth working relations with the local black leaders. The African-American community has splintered along class lines, with leaders in the city's poorest neighborhoods arguing that the biracial partnership has largely forsaken poor neighborhoods in order to promote growth projects favored by business leaders and the city's large population of black professionals.[3] Low black voter turnout, the outmigration of black middle-class voters to the suburbs, the onset of white gentrification, and the new arrival of Hispanics have all weakened the bargaining position of the city's African-American officials.

In 2009, Kasim Reed, an African American, won Atlanta's mayoralty by a mere 714 votes against a white challenger. The narrowness of Reed's victory pinpointed the weakened position of African Americans in Atlanta.[4]

Reed's administration underscores the biracial nature of governance in Atlanta. Reed embraced local growth projects, including a new billion-dollar Atlanta Falcons football stadium to replace the Georgia Dome (which was not yet twenty years old). Reed even demonstrated an ability to work cooperatively with the state's Republican governor, Nathan Deal, on economic development projects. Working with major corporate contributors such as Coca Cola, Reed created a Super PAC to aid the election of his allies, ousting his critics from the city council and school board. In 2013, Reed coasted to reelection victory, announcing that "growing business" was the Number One priority for his second term as mayor.[5]

1. Clarence N. Stone, *Regime Politics—Governing Atlanta: 1946–88* (Lawrence: University of Kansas Press, 1989), esp. 77–159.

2. Cynthia Horan, "Racializing Urban Regimes," *Journal of Urban Affairs* 24, no. 1 (2002): 25–27; Matthew J. Burbank, Gregory D. Andranovich, and Charles H. Heying, *Olympic Dreams: The Impact of Mega-Events on Local Politics* (Boulder, CO: Lynne Rienner, 2001); Larry Keating, *Atlanta: Race, Class and Urban Expansion* (Philadelphia, PA: Temple University Press, 2001); Heywood T. Sanders, *Convention Center Follies* (Philadelphia: University of Pennsylvania Press, 2014), 447–448.

3. Lawrence J. Vale, *Purging the Poorest: Public Housing and the Design Politics of Twice-Cleared Communities* (Chicago: University of Chicago Press, 2013) describes how some of the city's poorest communities in Atlanta have fared under the city's biracial governing regime.

4. Todd C. Shaw, Kasim Ortiz, James McCoy, and Athena King, "'The Last Black Mayor of Atlanta?' Kasim Reed and the Increasing Complexities of Black Politics," in *21st Century Urban Race Politics: Representing Minorities as Universal Interests*, ed. Ravi K. Perry (Bingley, UK: Emerald Publishing Group, 2013), 201–230; Michael Leo Owens and Jacob Robert Brown, "Weakening Strong Black Political Empowerment: Implication from Atlanta's 2009 Mayoral Election," *Journal of Urban Affairs* 36, no. 4 (October 2014): 663–681.

5. Jonathan Shapiro, "Super PAC Backed by Atlanta Mayor and Business Leaders Draws Criticisms," WABE 90.1FM (NPR), October 28, 2013, http://wabe.org/post/super-pac-backed-atlanta-mayor-and-business-leaders-draws-criticism; Katie Leslie and Ernie Suggs, "Reed Returns to His 'Dream' Job," *Atlanta Constitution*, November 5, 2013.

newspaper, and even the NAACP (concerned with the need to bring new jobs to low-income and minority communities). Louisville's corporate regime gave new emphasis to stadium construction, waterfront projects, and downtown renewal. An alliance of public officials and private officials backed growth projects and the shared goal of "Putting Louisville on the map."[31]

Corporate regimes, while quite commonplace, do not emerge and dominate every city and suburb. In many smaller and medium-size cities and better-off dormitory suburbs, a **caretaker regime** (also called a **maintenance regime**) reflects the concerns of small-business owners and homeowners who oppose growth projects that require greater taxes and that threaten to increase congestion and disrupt established patterns of local life. Caretaker cities focus on the provision of routine municipal services, not the initiation of major renewal and development projects.

The least commonly found municipal governing arrangement is the **progressive regime**, where growth interests are forced to take a back seat as environmentalists, homeowner associations, community development corporations (CDCs), and other nonprofit organizations and community groups gain access to city hall.[32] In San Francisco, Seattle, Boston, and Santa Monica, a large, well-educated, and politically active population of creative professionals has led to the emergence of city governments that give greater weight to "green" environmental policies, regulations that limit the scale of new development, the affirmation of gay and lesbian rights, and, at times, even social welfare programs that aid the city's poor.[33]

There are actually two variants of the progressive regime. A **middle-class progressive regime** represents the concerns of environmentalists and homeowners critical of the financial costs of, and the ecological damage inflicted by, growth projects. A **regime devoted to lower-class opportunity expansion**, by contrast, does not give similar emphasis to slow-growth policies and environmental protection. Instead, the opportunity-oriented variant of a progressive regime pursues growth projects that can provide jobs and opportunities for a city's poorer residents.

Progressive regimes are typically unstable. As middle-class homeowners, environmentalists, poor-people's groups, and minority and gay rights activists do not share the exact same interests and policy preferences, their alliance often frays over time. Progressive regimes also lose support when voters, during economic hard times, demand new growth projects and job creation.

Boston provides an illustration of a progressive regime that had a relatively short life. In 1983, community activists helped elect the self-styled progressive Raymond Flynn as mayor. Flynn was committed to balanced development and neighborhood protection; he promised growth restrictions, affordable housing, and job training for the poor. But faced with both an economic recession and federal aid cutbacks, Flynn soon gave renewed priority to growth projects. Thomas Menino, Flynn's successor who served as mayor for twenty years (1993–2013), returned Boston to a more traditional posture toward economic development.[34] Menino reorganized the local redevelopment authority in order to expedite the approval of growth projects. Critics argued that the new process was developer-friendly and lacked sufficient public transparency. African-American activists accused both mayors, especially Menino, of co-opting black influence and failing to challenge the racial hierarchy of Boston politics.[35]

Chicago's progressive regime was similarly short-lived. Harold Washington, the first African American to be elected mayor of the city, embraced programs of neighborhood equity and empowerment.[36] Mayor Washington held his lower-class-opportunity coalition together through the force of his own charisma and leadership skills. When Washington died in office (the result of a heart attack), Chicago's progressive regime seemingly died with him, as no other leader had the same ability to unite African Americans, Latinos, and white liberals. The election and long tenure of Mayor Richard M. Daley (1989–2009) marked the return of growth coalition interests to city hall.[37] Mayor Daley's singular achievement was refashioning postindustrial Chicago into a global corporate city. Rahm Emanuel, Daley's successor, was able to win African-American electoral support (a result of his closeness to Barack Obama) while facilitating downtown growth projects, a pattern inconsistent with a progressive regime.

Some cities have no governing regime; there is no stable governing alliance that persists from one mayoral administration to the next. With no effective semi-permanent working coalition, such cities often lack the capacity to get important things done. In mid-twentieth-century Milwaukee, continuing frictions between the municipal officials and downtown business leaders thwarted efforts to revitalize the city's declining downtown.[38] In pre–Hurricane Katrina New Orleans, city leaders, suburban officials, and private and nonprofit providers lacked the long-term relationship and sense of trust necessary to develop effective disaster preparedness plans. When Hurricane Katrina struck, there was no prearranged emergency ride-sharing program to evacuate the city's carless poor. There were no coordinated, practiced arrangements to provide food, water, and medicine to people trapped inside the city.[39] There simply was no governing regime and no set of effective working relationships to get things done.

THE TRANSFORMATION OF SAN FRANCISCO: POLITICAL POWER AND ECONOMIC DEVELOPMENT IN THE POSTINDUSTRIAL CITY

Modern San Francisco would seem to be the perfect example of a pluralist city open to emergent political voices: environmentalists, neighborhood activists, Chinese Americans, African Americans, Hispanics and other new immigrants, and gays and lesbians. Ed Lee, an Asian American, was elected mayor in 2011, having been chosen earlier to fill out the mayoral term of Gavin Newsom who had used his public defense of same-sex marriages as a stepping-stone to become Lieutenant Governor of California. Over the years, San Francisco has gained international attention for having enacted numerous growth-control measures over the objections of development interests. Clearly, no business elite controls politics in modern San Francisco.

Yet a pluralist perspective seriously understates the influence of corporations and other pro-growth forces. As the following brief review of contemporary San Francisco reveals, activist neighborhood organizations and a variety of counterculture groups have won numerous victories in San Francisco. Still, corporate influence is quite evident, especially in the construction of major development projects that have transformed the face of the city.

The Yerba Buena Center, a large downtown development project centered on a proposed Moscone Convention Center, was advanced "by the city's ruling forces to expand the city's downtown boundaries" across Market Street into SOMA, the low-income South of Market Area. The Yerba Buena project contained important cultural facilities; it entailed much more than a mere convention center. Yet the overwhelming purpose of the project was to lure businesses and visitors to San Francisco and to generate new hotel, office, and residential development in the fading warehouse area lying just south of the city's central business district.[40]

The Manhattanization of San Francisco: The Transamerica Pyramid and the New Downtown.
Copyright © Jesse Garcia. http://commons.wikimedia.org/wiki/File:San_Francisco_skyline_-a.jpg.

Grassroots neighborhood, counterculture, and environmental groups sought to halt the impending "Manhattanization" of their city. Antigrowth forces were able to limit building heights, control rents, restrict condominium conversion, scale back development projects, and protect much of the city's stock of low-income residential hotels. Yet as the construction of the Yerba Buena Center and, later, the nearby ballpark and Mission Bay project reveal, the corporate-led transformation of San Francisco continued.

Community groups seemingly gained control of city hall in 1987 with newly elected mayor Art Agnos promising to protect the city's neighborhoods from unfettered development. Agnos was a progressive who "turned over the keys of City Hall to people who in the past often had the door slammed in their face."[41] Yet Agnos wound up disappointing many of his grassroots supporters by endorsing a number of major growth projects favored by business elites, including new waterfront development and the construction of a downtown ballpark for the baseball Giants.[42]

Agnos was succeeded by the more conservative Frank Jordan, who promised to reverse the city's "anything goes" philosophy. Jordan even initiated an effort to take back the city's streets from panhandlers. Liberals regained control of city hall in 1995 with the election of legendary California house speaker Willie Brown, an African American and a Democrat, as mayor. But Brown was no progressive neighborhood activist; an old-style power broker, Brown maintained political ties to development interests and construction unions that favored growth projects. The growth machine succeeded in its push for new commercial intrusions into the Presidio (a large green area and former army base on San Francisco Bay), the construction of a new Giants ballpark, and the huge Mission Bay project that created an entirely new office and upscale residential section of the city beyond the ballpark.[43]

Yerba Buena Gardens and Center, San Francisco: This major urban redevelopment project extended the city's downtown into the South of Market neighborhood, opening an area of old warehouses and low-income housing to new corporate and convention-related development.

Courtesy of Sebastian Wallroth through Wikimedia Commons. http://commons.wikimedia.org/wiki/File:San_Francisco_Yerba_Buena_Gardens_006.jpg.

Over the years, progressives have not fared well in their attempts to regain control of city hall. Brown quashed a 1999 electoral challenge from neighborhood populist Tom Ammiano, who had promised to "declare war" on gentrification and the city's continued transformation. Contributions from business interests and labor unions allowed Brown to outspend Ammiano by more than 10 to 1. Faced with the strident antibusiness rhetoric of Ammiano, even the Republican Party threw its support to Brown in the city's nonpartisan mayoral contest.[44]

In 2003, "socially connected entrepreneur" Gavin Newsom won a runoff election for mayor, defeating the "[s]haggy-haired Matt Gonzalez, darling of the young, the hip and the non-propertied classes,"[45] who stressed tenants' rights and neighborhood preservation. Newsom, by contrast, promised a balanced approach that would allow downtown and waterfront development to continue while increasing requirements for affordable housing. Newsom, who enunciated a progressive stance on gay marriage and other social issues, had the backing of the city's growth coalition, including the construction unions.

Ed Lee, who succeeded Newsom, continued to woo dot.com and other technology firms that helped to fuel San Francisco's economic dynamism, but at the cost of accelerating the pace of gentrification in the city. When Twitter threatened to leave the city in 2011, Lee and the city Board of Supervisors responded by offering the social media giant $16 million in tax breaks. The city reduced payroll taxes on businesses choosing to locate in the precise Mid-Market area of the city that, not coincidentally, Twitter sought

Whose City? Protest Against the Google Bus in San Francisco. San Francisco activists complain that market-oriented development is making their city a playground for technology-oriented workers, squeezing out lower-income residents in neighborhoods that traditionally housed the working-class and the poor. On various occasions, local protestors attempted to block private buses that carry technology-savvy workers to Google's headquarters located forty miles south of the city.

From Wikimedia Commons by Chris Martin (Flickr user cjmartin), December 9, 2013, http://en.wikipedia.org/wiki/File:Google_bus_protest.jpg.

as its site.[46] Lee even backed the removal of the homeless from Mid-Market in order to make the area more desirable to cutting-edge media firms and housing developers.[47]

The vibrant activity of gay and lesbian, neighborhood, and antigrowth groups serves to make politics in San Francisco quite different from the vast majority of U.S. cities.[48] Yet, as this brief review of politics in contemporary San Francisco reveals, despite their numbers and intense activism, progressive forces were unable to establish a governing regime with the capacity over time to enact a more balanced growth agenda. Instead, neighborhood activists and progressive voices on the city's Board of Supervisors (San Francisco's name for its city council) found that they were faced with a series of mayors and other elected and career officials who had a fairly high tolerance for new growth projects. Overall, the transformation of San Francisco continued despite the regulatory restrictions, delays, and alterations that neighborhood groups forced on development projects.

In San Francisco, neither the growth machine nor progressive community groups were able to establish a stable governing regime committed to their overall vision of the city. Instead, San Francisco is an **anti-regime city** where a loose alliance of activist groups was able to block a number of the projects it disliked, but progressive groups could not take effective control of local government and steer the city toward neighborhood preservation.[49]

Conclusion: Constrained Local Politics

Local political systems are not as closed as power elite theory asserts, nor are they as open as the pluralists assume. Even in San Francisco, a city that is hospitable to the voices of neighborhood activists, gays and lesbians, racial and ethnic minorities, and environmental activists, the influence of corporate leaders is still clearly felt.

Business elites are not all-powerful. Nor is the business community a monolith that is united in its actions. Business leaders also need the cooperation of governmental leaders to get important projects done. This gives local officials the opportunity to exert leverage. A city's elected officials, planners, and redevelopment staff, for instance, can join residents of a development area in negotiating a **community benefits agreement** (CBA) with developers to ensure that a major development project will include affordable housing, environmental safeguards, job opportunities for local residents, and corporate donations to community-oriented charities and the arts in return for municipal subsidies and the city's granting of regulatory approval of the project.[50]

Still, cities are seldom in a very strong position to challenge major businesses. Capital mobility imposes severe constraints on municipal officials. Municipal leaders do not strongly question business' claims, as the city fears losing a sports franchise, important trade show, or a major firm to another city. Businesses ask for generous tax abatements, major infrastructure improvements, and other concessions. City officials can seldom accurately assess just what tax abatements and concessions a business truly requires to locate or stay in a city. Consequently, cities wind up giving a business more than what was likely needed, diverting resources that could have been used for other public purposes.

Even the provisions written into community benefits agreements often prove rather weak and do not effectively hold developers accountable. In San Francisco, the CBA negotiated with Twitter specified the dollar commitments expected of Twitter in certain specified community-oriented actions but not in other areas. The CBA also contained relatively loose language regarding the firm's support of community-based job training. The vague language of the CBA said that Twitter was to "encourage" its employees to volunteer in the community and to patronize local businesses.[51] San Francisco did not bargain with Twitter from a position of strength. Fearing that Twitter would locate its headquarters elsewhere, the city entered into negotiations over a CBA only *after* having already granted Twitter enormous tax concessions.

Similarly in New York, critics contend that developers "hijacked" the CBA process, having used the negotiation of a CBA and other community engagement processes as political "cover" that helped win approval for controversial projects. The developers pointed to the existence of community agreements in arguing that it was safe for the city to approve controversial projects for the development of the Atlantic Yards in downtown Brooklyn, a new Yankee Stadium, and the expansion of Columbia University.[52]

Regime analysis underscores the "weakness in the foundation for democratic politics" in the American city.[53] Cities tend to give special attention to the demands made by important businesses. Corporate regimes (or development regimes) dominate a great many big cities and suburbs.

Yet this does not mean that a private elite rules U.S. cities. Corporate regimes are not inevitable. Political leaders with the will and skill can bargain effectively with elite interests and, in some cases, even build an alternative political regime committed to neighborhood concerns and minority empowerment.

The next chapter explores how the formal structure of local government affects the possibilities of leadership and just whose interests are represented in city hall.

KEY TERMS

allocational policy (*p. 86*)

anti-regime city (*p. 102*)

benefit principle when financing a new stadium (*p. 91*)

caretaker regime (also called a maintenance regime) (*p. 98*)

city limits theory (*p. 85*)

community benefits agreement (*p. 103*)

corporate regime (also called a development regime) (*p. 95*)

developmental policy (*p. 86*)

growth machine (*p. 85*)

memos of understanding (*p. 88*)

middle-class progressive regime (*p. 98*)

mobility of capital (*p. 85*)

naming rights for a stadium (*p. 90*)

one-sided stadium contracts (*p. 87*)

pluralism or pluralist theory (*p. 84*)

power elite theory (*p. 82*)

preemptive power (*p. 94*)

progressive regime (*p. 98*)

redistributive policy (*p. 86*)

regime devoted to lower-class opportunity expansion (*p. 98*)

regime theory (*p. 95*)

seat licenses (*p. 90*)

social production, power as (*p. 94*)

spread the responsibility for financing a new stadium (*p. 91*)

substitution effect (*p. 86*)

urban regime (also called a governing regime) (*p. 94*)

5 Formal Structure and Leadership Style

Local government is not simply a smaller sized version of the national government or even state governments. Local government is quite different, as municipalities possess formal powers that are vastly more limited. Constitutionally speaking, a state creates its local governments and defines just what powers a municipality possesses and just what a locality may and may not do. Cities do not even possess the full authority to raise the funds needed to combat local problems. Instead, state laws determine what a locality may or may not tax and just how much money a local entity may borrow.

Each state's government even has the power to determine if a fiscally troubled municipality has the option to file for federal Chapter 9 bankruptcy protection. In nearly half of the states, municipalities in crisis are not eligible to file for Chapter 9 protection that would place a "freeze" on creditor demands and thereby buy a locality time to restructure its finances. Two states explicitly prohibit municipal bankruptcy filings; another twenty-one states provide no authorization for such actions.[1]

MUNICIPAL INCORPORATION, CITY CHARTERS, AND LOCAL FRAGMENTATION

Each state establishes the requirements for **municipal incorporation**, the conditions that an area must meet to become a city, village, township, town, or county, a recognized administrative subunit of the state with specified state-granted governing powers. A **city charter**, issued or approved by the state, is the rough equivalent of a city constitution. The charter spells out the structure of a municipality's government (for instance, whether a city will operate under the weak-mayor, strong-mayor, council-manager, or commission arrangement) and the powers that the municipality possesses.

State-issued city charters generally serve to **fragment local power**, as the states tend to create a multitude of local jurisdictions and municipal offices, each possessing limited powers. An elected mayor, for instance, typically does not possess full control over a city's executive branch; instead, the mayor often shares executive-branch authority with independently elected officials (i.e., an elected city treasurer or prosecutor), city-council-appointed executives (most notably, in many cities, a council-appointed city manager), and professional and civil-service-protected managers (i.e., the city's budget director or planning and redevelopment director) whom the mayor does not appoint. The mayor also shares authority with numerous boards and commissions (i.e., the parks commission, the police and fire commission, and often an independent school board) whom the mayor does not directly control. As a consequence, a mayor cannot depend on the formal authority of office alone to get things done. To effectively lead, the mayor must convince others to act and to use the authority they possess to help achieve the goals that the mayor sees as good for the city. This, of course, is no easy task.

DILLON'S RULE

The United States Constitution recognizes only two levels of government, the national government and the states. The Constitution contains no mention of local governments and their powers. In terms of constitutional law, municipalities are the **administrative subunits of a state**. Each state creates local governments and decides just what powers a local government may exercise.

Iowa Judge John F. Dillon in 1868 wrote a judicial opinion that articulated the quite limited position of municipal governments in the American constitutional system. **Dillon's Rule**, as the legal doctrine is popularly called, observes that, under the United States Constitution, municipalities are the mere "creatures of the states" and possess only those powers expressly delegated to them by the states.

Dillon's Rule denotes a hierarchical arrangement where a state possesses total legal authority over the local governments it creates. A state even has the power to eliminate cities, townships, counties, and other municipalities, a power that the states have used to force the closing and consolidation of tiny school districts. As Judge Dillon observed, the state's power is so complete that "the Legislature might, by a single act, if we can suppose it capable of so great a folly and so great a wrong, sweep from existence all municipal corporations in a state."[2] As a state possesses the authority to destroy a local government, the state also has the right to abridge, amend, or revoke any power that it has granted a city.

Dillon's Rule means that local governments in general do not possess expansive powers. Dillon's Rule requires that the powers delegated to local government be strictly construed, that is, narrowly interpreted. If there is a dispute as to whether or not a local government possesses a particular power, that power is denied to the locality. As Judge Dillon articulated, "Any fair, reasonable, substantial doubt concerning the existence of power is resolved by the courts *against* the [municipal] corporation and the power is denied."[3]

Over the years, the United States Supreme Court has essentially affirmed the principles elaborated in Judge Dillon's ruling.[4] Constitutionally speaking, a local government is a subunit of a state and possesses only those powers given by the state, as spelled out in a state's constitution, state statutes, and the city's charter.

Until the mid-1800s, state legislatures wrote **special-act charters** that detailed the exact structure and unique powers given to each newly incorporated municipality. But the states eventually tired of having to write an individual charter for each new municipality that the state created. The states shifted to **general-act charters** (also called **classified charters**) that divide cities into different general classes based on population (and, in some cases, also on the value of the local tax base), with different powers granted to the different classes of local government. Larger cities are assigned a wider range of service responsibilities and given greater taxing and borrowing authority than are smaller cities.

Grouping cities by class also helps to protect a city against arbitrary treatment by a state legislature. By having to pass laws that apply to all cities in the specified class, a state cannot single out a city and enact a law that imposes special service and taxing burdens only on a single community. The classification system helps to protect cities against partisan actions, where a state legislature may seek to single out and punish a locality governed by the opposing political party.

Yet the classification system does not afford complete protection against political discrimination. The history of state-city relations is filled with instances where a state has only one city—a Baltimore, Boston, Chicago, Des Moines, New Orleans, or New York—in its top class; the state legislature can single out its major city simply by imposing new service burdens that apply only on the state's top class of cities.

In more recent years, the states have also used the classification system in a helpful way, to facilitate innovative action by granting new powers to the city (or cities) in its highest class. The State of Maryland, for instance, enacted a quick-take law that enabled its largest city, Baltimore, to experiment with new ways of acquiring tax-delinquent abandoned properties and stem the free-fall decline of blighted neighborhoods.[5]

PREEMPTION

States also possess the power of **preemption**, the authority to bar localities from taking specified actions or from acting in designated policy areas. Localities levy an individual income tax in only fourteen states. Why isn't this important revenue source used more extensively by local governments? Simply, the majority of states preempt or bar localities from taxing individual incomes, as state legislators prefer to preserve this lucrative source of revenue for state programs. Likewise, only thirteen states permit local governments to tax fuel; only ten states allow the local taxation of cigarettes; fewer than half of the states (eighteen) permit local taxes on alcoholic beverages.[6]

Powerful interest groups also push the states to enact legislation to effectively preempt or prohibit specified local actions. The political muscle of the gun lobby has led forty-five of the fifty states to prohibit or limit the reach of local gun-control ordinances.[7] The tobacco lobby over the years also pushed for state legislation that barred localities from enacting strong anti-smoking restrictions, including local measures designed to reduce tobacco use by minors. In more recent years, however, numerous states rescinded or modified their preemption on local actions to restrict smoking, a response to the activism of pro-health organizations.[8]

In Massachusetts, California, Georgia, and Tennessee, landlords pushed for state measures to bar local rent-control laws.[9] Wisconsin and New Jersey legislators considered state laws to restrict municipal actions from interfering with the controversial siting of cell phone towers.[10] In Florida, critics of red-light cameras argued in court that the local installation of the cameras was preempted by the state's Uniform Traffic Control Act.[11]

More than forty states impose limits on the ability of local entities to exercise **eminent domain** powers, that is, to take land for public purposes.[12] State statutes, passed at the urging of property rights groups, protect homeowners against overly aggressive local development officials. Such laws, however, also pose an impediment to local economic revitalization projects.[13]

HOME RULE

Provisions for *home rule* can give a municipality greater freedom to act, easing much (but not all) of the seeming tightness of Dillon's Rule. Virtually every state has enacted some version of **home rule**, which empowers cities (and, in most cases, counties as well) to make numerous decisions without having to go to the state for explicit permission for each new action, just as long as the actions are not contrary to state (and federal) law.

In home rule states, a municipality possesses the ability to act in a broad range of policy areas. Cities across the country, for instance, have used home rule discretion to legislate green building codes to require increased energy efficiency and greater sustainability in new home and office construction.

Such expansive use of home rule powers has enabled cities to act in policy areas that extend way beyond the traditional municipal provision of services. In the 1980s and 1990s, more than 150 cities across the country took it upon themselves to provide domestic partner benefits and recognize gay and lesbian unions, part of a national movement that led to greater recognition of the rights of same-sex couples.[14] New York City Mayor Michael Bloomberg's efforts to combat obesity by limiting the cup size of sodas and other sugared drinks, too, was an attempt at exercising local home rule authority.[15]

The extent of local home rule authority varies greatly from one state to another.[16] A handful of state supreme courts have ruled that the language of home rule provisions written into the state's constitution require that the powers of local government be liberally construed. In this small set of states, the state constitution's provisions for home rule effectively neutralize much of the confining nature of Dillon's Rule.

At the other end of the spectrum, an equivalent number of "Dillon's Rule states" require that the exercise of local powers first gain expressed permission from the state government. Even if such a state generally chooses to grant a broad range of power to localities,[17] the necessity of securing expressed state approval may still constrain innovative local action. In Nevada, the difficulty of securing expressed state permission served to deter cities from adopting vacant property registration ordinances even in the face of a rising tide of abandoned properties.[18]

But even in states with a strong home rule tradition, the state government still has the capacity to intrude into local affairs. A state government can even reverse a municipal action, although its exact ability to do so depends on the specific provisions of the state's constitution. In Ohio and Michigan, public-sector labor unions lobbied to have the state government bar the enforcement of locally enacted **residency laws** that required a municipality's workers to reside within the city. The Ohio legislature barred local enforcement of such local provisions. The Ohio Supreme Court upheld the state's restrictions, which the court did not view as a violation of the home rule provisions of the Ohio constitution.[19]

In New York, the state legislature effectively overrode the efforts of New York City Mayor Bill de Blasio to curtail what he believed was the unfair competition that privately-administered charter schools posed to the city's more traditional classrooms. The mayor sought to curb the past practice where the city provided free space in public school buildings to independent charter schools led by administrators who wished to share a building with an existing public school. When de Blasio denied space for three charter schools run by Eva Moskowitz, a notable local politico and charter school enthusiast, Moskowitz organized lobbying efforts and a mass rally in the state capital that led Governor Andrew Cuomo to declare his support for charter schools. A new provision written into the state budget required the city to provide available space for the charter academies or otherwise help pay for their rental of private space.[20]

Home rule traditions have not prevented the states from intruding in the affairs of local governments facing crisis situations. Michigan's home rule traditions did not prevent state takeovers of troubled school districts, takeovers that obliterated much of the authority of elected local school boards. Nor did home rule in Michigan impose a serious barrier to the state's appointment of an emergency fiscal manager for financially-plagued Detroit. The state gave its appointed manager the authority to void provisions of municipal labor contracts that had been approved by local elected officials.

Home rule is important. But it does not alter the fundamental constitutional reality. Despite home rule, Dillon's Rule remains the dominant doctrine of municipal law in four-fifths of the states.[21] State constitutions and statutes define and continue to limit the problem-solving reach of municipal governments. In more recent years, more activist states have "chipped away" at home rule.[22] The following brief review of state actions in key policy areas will underscore the dependent nature of municipal authority.

STATE REGULATIONS REGARDING LOCAL ANNEXATION AND SECESSION

Each state sets the criteria and procedures that a city must meet in order to expand via **annexation**, that is, to grow by extending its borders, making adjoining territory a part of the city. For many decades, North Carolina and Texas gave their major cities liberal authority to grow via annexation. In more recent years, however, protests from suburban areas have led state legislatures to modify the rules in order to make annexation more difficult (a matter that is discussed in greater detail in Chapter 10).

State constitutions and statutes also detail the requirements for **secession**, the conditions that must be met for the residents of an area to separate or detach from a city. California statutes put severe obstacles in the path of San Fernando Valley residents who sought to break away from Los Angeles and establish what, in terms of population, would have been the sixth largest city in the United States. California state law requires approval by **dual majorities**, that the larger city and the seceding area must both give their consent for a detachment to proceed. While popular among Valley residents, secession of this sizeable part of the city was not likely to win approval in the rest of Los Angeles. California law further requires that secession be "revenue neutral," that the detachment must not hurt the larger city financially. Enthusiasm for secession declined as Valley residents discovered that this provision meant that a new Valley city would likely have to pay millions of dollars in "alimony" to Los Angeles, compensating L.A. for past services and infrastructure improvements and for the revenue losses the larger city would suffer as a result of detachment. On the East Coast, efforts by Staten Island to secede from New York City were similarly stymied by provisions of the state constitution that gave the city the power to veto detachment efforts.[23]

LOCAL GOVERNMENT FINANCE: STATE LIMITATIONS ON LOCAL TAXING AND BORROWING

Unlike the national and state governments, localities in the United States are not free to levy taxes, impose fees, and borrow money as they wish. As already noted, Dillon's Rule applies: each state determines what a local jurisdiction may and may not tax, the maximum tax rates that a locality may levy, and the fees for municipal services that a locality may and may not charge citizens and businesses. A state can also set a ceiling on the amount of money that a local government may borrow for infrastructure improvements and other purposes.

State laws have a great influence on a city's revenue structure. Dallas, Oklahoma City, and Shreveport are able to take advantage of state laws that permit a local sales tax. In contrast, state laws lead New York, Philadelphia, Baltimore, and Louisville to be more reliant on locally-imposed income taxes.[24]

State restrictions on local government serve to make local taxation quite different from national taxation. In sharp contrast to the national government's reliance on the income tax, localities get only a meager 2 percent of their revenues from the individual income tax. Only very few localities are greatly reliant on the individual income tax. In general, the states bar extensive municipal use of the income tax, forcing localities to rely on property taxes, a local add-on to the sales tax (where state law permits), and various small service charges and "nuisance fees"

Limited in their taxing authority, municipalities are greatly reliant on **intergovernmental assistance** (state and federal aid) as an important part of their budgets. Intergovernmental assistance accounts for 38 percent of local budgets, even surpassing the 30 percent that localities continue to raise from property taxes.

LOCAL INCOME AND EARNINGS TAXES

An expanded income tax would provide cities with a reliable and fair source of revenues for public services. But the majority of states prohibit municipalities from relying on the personal income tax. As previously noted, the individual income tax accounts for only a paltry 2 percent of local revenues.

In only fourteen states do localities use the income tax.[25] Even where the tax is utilized, state laws sharply cap municipal income-tax rates. Michigan, for instance, limits the city levy to a maximum 1 percent tax on income of residents and only a half-of-one-percent tax on the income of nonresidents who work in the city. Only in very few states, notably Ohio and Pennsylvania, do cities rely to any significant degree on a local income tax or earnings tax. Local officials are also hesitant to hike local income tax rates, fearing that the tax will drive residents and economic activity to neighboring communities.

An income levy can be a **progressive tax** based on an individual's ability to pay; if structured similarly to the federal income tax, people in higher income brackets pay a greater tax rate than do the middle class and the poor. But, state laws generally bar such sharply graduated tax brackets. As a result, the local income tax is not really a progressive tax but has a strong resemblance to a **flat-rate tax**, where people of all income levels pay essentially the same rate of taxation.[26]

PROPERTY TAX

The property tax continues to be the workhorse of local government finance. Property levies make up nearly half (45 percent) of own-source local tax collections[27] and 30 percent of total local budgets including intergovernmental assistance.

Independent school districts (school districts that are not funded directly by a city's general-purpose government) are especially reliant on the property tax. The property tax accounts for a whopping 96 percent of the locally-collected tax revenues for K–12 education (a figure that excludes state and federal aid).[28]

Over the years, a revolution in school finance has reduced some of the dependence of public education on the local property tax base (a matter that is discussed in much greater detail in Chapter 9). State aid to public education now surpasses school property tax collections. The states provide 47 percent of all revenues for public schools as compared to the 29 percent that comes from local property taxes.[29] The levels of state aid and the reliance of the schools on the local property tax, however, vary considerably from state to state. In Texas, 44 percent of school money comes from the property tax; in New Hampshire the figure is a whopping 61 percent! In California, voter-imposed limitations on tax levies reduced property tax reliance: only 23 percent of school funds in California come from property levies.[30]

As a local revenue source, the property tax suffers from major shortcomings. "Property poor" jurisdictions have a difficult time finding the revenues to support essential services. During troubled economic times, when property values are not rising, the property tax fails to generate sufficient revenues to meet the demand for municipal services. Citizen ballot initiatives to roll back property taxes further make the property tax a less-than-reliable revenue source for public education and other important local services.[31] The advocates for greater equity in education argue that the states need to assume a still greater share of school costs so that a child's education is not dependent on the wealth of the property situated within a community.

LOCAL SALES TAXES

Thirty-eight states have local sales taxes.[32] The sales tax accounts for 10 percent of local own-source revenues, a figure that, while quite substantial, still represents only 6 percent of local budgets. Local sales taxes represent less than a fourth of the revenues collected in local property taxes.[33]

The sales taxes is often attacked for being **regressive**, for placing a disproportionate burden on persons who can least afford to pay the tax. Unlike the income tax, there is no "zero" tax rate for the very poor; they, like other citizens, pay a sales tax on whatever they buy. The regressivity of the sales tax, however, is greatly reduced if a government decides not to tax the sale of food and medicines.

A local sales tax can lead to an exodus of customers to neighboring communities. Chicago's whopping 9.25 percent sales tax (combining city and state levies) serves to drive purchasers to other jurisdictions. Delaware, the self-proclaimed "Home of Tax-Free Shopping," draws shoppers away from Philadelphia.[34] In Minnesota in 2014, the combined state and local sales tax can be as high as 7.9 percent. But the state does not levy the tax on the sale of clothing and shoes, part of its efforts to lure visitors from out of state to the Mall of America. A number of states and cities also schedule **sales tax holidays**, usually in the weeks preceding the opening of a new school year, temporarily suspending the sales tax in order to compete with surrounding low-tax communities.

The growing volume of e-commerce poses a new threat to the municipal sales tax. Internet retailers gain a significant competitive advantage in cases where no sales tax is paid on e-transactions. The move to e-commerce represents a significant threat to municipal sales tax collections. As a consequence, the National League of Cities, the National Association of Counties, and the U.S. Conference of Mayors joined traditional retailers in demanding the enactment of a measure they labeled the **Marketplace Fairness Act**, national legislation to require large online retailers to collect sales taxes. In 2013 alone, New York City lost an estimated $235 million in sales revenues due to the failure to collect sales taxes online. Los Angeles County lost $95 million in foregone revenues, and Cook County, Illinois (surrounding Chicago) lost more than $55 million.[35] Internet enthusiasts, however, counter that the collection of e-taxes is an unwise intrusion that would interfere with the growth of the e-economy.

NUISANCE TAXES, DEVELOPMENT IMPACT FEES, AND USER CHARGES

Denied the ability to effectively tap more lucrative sources of revenue, cities have had to impose a miscellany of small-yield **nuisance taxes** (relatively small taxes levied on items such as entertainment admissions, hotel room occupancy, and automobile parking in a pay garage); licensing fees (to operate a taxicab or limousine, to sell alcohol, etc.); **user charges and fees**[36] (for plumbing and electrical inspections or for the use of the public swimming pool, picnic shelter, or local baseball diamond); and **special assessments** (where property owners pay an additional fee to support nearby street paving, lighting, and other infrastructure upgrades).[37] Faced with voters' unwillingness to pay higher taxes, municipal officials have turned to user fees. Revenues from nuisance taxes and user fees and charges make up a quarter of local own-source collections.[38]

Advocates argue that user fees and charges represent a "fair" way to finance public services; according to the **benefit principle**, persons who benefit from a service should be asked to contribute to the costs of service provision. Benefit-related fees are preferable to levying a tax that residents have to pay whether they use a service or not. Political conservatives further argue that user fees help to reveal the price of a public service, eliminating some of the overgrowth of government that results when citizens view municipal services as "free."

Local governments have also been turning more and more to the imposition of **development impact fees**, where new development pays a special assessment to help finance the sewers, roads, parks, schools, and other facilities required by a project. Development fees represent an attractive political strategy that lifts the cost burden of new development off the shoulders of property owners who live elsewhere in a community. The courts have generally upheld such fees as long as the fee is reasonable ("proportional," to be precise) and there is a clear connection between the fees and the services provided a new development.[39]

STATE LIMITATIONS ON LOCAL BORROWING

State laws also restrict how much a municipality may borrow. The New York State Constitution, for instance, limits the total indebtedness of a county, city, town, or village to no more than 7 percent or 9 percent of its taxable real estate valuation, with the exact ceiling dependent on the size of a city's population. A school district is similarly permitted to borrow a total of no more than 9 or 10 percent of the district's property valuation.[40]

The states also often require voter approval by means of a public referendum before a city or school district can borrow money through the issuance of bonds. In many communities, such referenda are not easily won.

In general, such bonding limitations seek to keep local governments from amassing more debt than they can repay. Such state-imposed restrictions, however, also limit the ability of local governments to undertake important projects, especially capital improvements and the construction of new school facilities.

THE VOTER TAX REVOLT AND RECENT TRENDS IN FINANCING LOCAL GOVERNMENT

The citizens' **tax revolt** that started in California in 1975 soon spread nationwide and led the enactment of new state curbs across the nation on local spending and borrowing. California's **Proposition 13** rolled back property levies to what they had been in earlier years and further limited any annual increase to just 2 percent. Proposition 13 also required a two-thirds vote by the citizens for new local taxes, fees, and user charges, a threshold that is exceedingly difficult to achieve. The measure eased the tax burdens on homeowners. It also impaired the ability of California municipalities to find the revenues to fund service programs.

As a result of the new restrictions, per-pupil school spending in California plummeted. Outraged parents protested, and the California legislature responded by mandating that local governments reallocate billions of dollars in local property taxes to the schools. Such a shift in funding coupled with an infusion of state assistance helped alleviate the emergency; but it did not stem the free-fall as California lost its national preeminence in K–12 education. Once "Number One" in the nation in terms of money spent per child in the public schools, California by 2013 tumbled to 49th place, ahead of only Nevada and Utah in terms of school funding per pupil.[41]

By diverting revenues to the schools, new state laws succeeded in helping schools only by worsening the ability of municipalities to provide nonschool services. In California, home rule lost much of its significance as state-imposed tax limitation measures and spending mandates "crippled local government finance"[42] by denying municipalities the flexibility to make meaningful program choices. Even a major local government like Los Angeles County became, in the eyes of critics, little more than an "embattled 'service delivery arm' of the State."[43]

A 2010 national survey documents that city managers nationwide complain about what they see as the growing state intrusion into local affairs. The local executives are especially scornful of state measure that dictate spending patterns or impose additional service responsibilities on municipalities without providing municipalities with the fiscal resources for quality service provision.[44]

Across the country, local leaders desperate to find the money for local services have searched for loopholes in the state- and voter-imposed restrictions. One strategy has seen municipalities shift responsibility for service provision to **special districts**, independent bodies not subject to the taxing and borrowing restrictions placed on general-purpose cities and counties (see Chapter 10).[45] In Ohio, independent port districts issued revenue bonds and otherwise helped raise the capital necessary for the construction of sports arenas, museum extensions, the Cleveland Rock and Roll Hall of Fame, and various other economic development projects not directly related to port activities.[46] Such subterfuges raise important questions of local accountability and democratic control, especially when borrowing and spending decisions are placed in the hands of unelected and politically invisible special-district officials.

In California, Florida, and numerous other states, cities have turned to imposing special assessments, user charges, and service fees for solid waste disposal, street improvements, fire protection, and similar services.[47] Local impact and developer fees tap developers to help pay for the costs of roads, sewers, schools, and other infrastructure provided new subdivisions.[48] The developers, in turn, shift the burden of the fees to homebuyers, adding thousands of dollars to the cost of a home.

Caught between state-imposed tax limitations and the continuing demand for public services, a number of localities chose to engage in the **high-risk strategy of borrowing money to invest** in what they believed were high-return opportunities. If things go as planned, the investments will yield sufficient funds to repay the loans while earning additional funds to support local service provision without the need to ask voters to support new taxes. But should the value of an investment unexpectedly decline, the municipality may find itself facing extreme fiscal distress, unable to repay its creditors as the loans become due.

Orange County, California, in 1994, gambled and lost nearly $2 billion in its creative, high-risk investment strategy. The result was a fiscal crisis that led to emergency measures. The county filed for bankruptcy, closed library branches, cut school programs, reduced social programs and policing, and even stopped testing for fecal coliform bacteria at its beaches.[49]

Facing their own financial squeeze, a number of local school districts across the nation similarly gambled in high-risk investment efforts. In the greater Denver and Milwaukee areas, school districts borrowed money to fund financial investments that officials hoped would yield earnings to help the districts meet their quite costly pension obligations. The school districts, however, wound up in a crisis situation when, in the midst of an underperforming recession economy, the investments lost value.[50]

"ACADEMIC BANKRUPTCY" LAWS: THE STATE TAKEOVER OF SCHOOLS IN CRISIS

School districts are narrow-focused units of local government subject to Dillon's Rule. A local school board possesses only the authority that a state permits. Normally, states give school districts considerable decision-making powers, a reflection of the strong preferences that Americans have for the grassroots control of K–12 school systems. In recent years, however, states have breached local autonomy in an effort to turn around academically failing schools and fiscally insolvent school districts.

By the beginning of the twenty-first century, twenty-four states had **academic bankruptcy laws** that allowed for direct state intervention in, and even state takeover of, poorly performing school systems.[51] In some instances, the state appointed a manager to take charge of a troubled school or district, reducing the authority of elected school officials. In other cases, states placed troubled schools under the direct control of a mayor who, reformers hoped, would have the political clout to challenge vested interests and to shake up school operations. This, too, reduced the power of elected school officials.

Takeovers were once relatively rare, but the list of instances where a state has stepped in to force a change in local school operations is now fairly long. A partial list includes: California (with school takeovers, in Compton, Emery, Inglewood, Oakland, and West Fresno), Alabama (Birmingham), Connecticut (Bridgeport and Hartford), Indiana (Gary and Indianapolis), Maryland (Baltimore), Louisiana, Massachusetts (Boston, Chelsea, and Lawrence), Michigan, New Jersey (Newark, Jersey City, and Paterson), New York (where the state appointed a management team to run the Roosevelt, Long Island, schools, reducing the elected school board to an advisory role), Ohio (Lorain), Pennsylvania (Philadelphia), South Carolina (Allendale), and Virginia (Hampton Roads). In some cases, the state reconstituted the operations of a single school; in other instances, the state assumed greater control over an entire school district.

The State of Pennsylvania took charge of troubled schools in Philadelphia, replacing the elected school board with an appointed School Reform Commission and a chief executive officer who, in turn, hired private educational management firms to run the schools.[52] Neighborhood activists in Philadelphia opposed the loss of local democracy and the "marketization" of public education.[53] The State of Massachusetts turned to Boston University to run the troubled Chelsea school district.

Michigan in 1999 took over Detroit's public schools, replacing the elected school board, which had faced charges of mismanagement, with a board appointed by the governor and the mayor. But in the face of bitter criticism from local residents, the state reversed course, allowing school board elections to once more take place in 2005. But continuing episodes of mismanagement and corruption led the state to reverse course yet again, this time appointing an emergency fiscal manager to run the city's schools.[54]

A number of states have given extensive authority for school operations to big-city mayors, most notably in New York, Chicago, Boston, Cleveland, Harrisburg, Providence, New Haven, Trenton, Hartford, Oakland, and Jackson (Mississippi).[55] The conditions of inner-city schools had deteriorated so badly that state officials broke with the long-standing American tradition of strictly separating the public schools from the political arena. Advocates of change hoped that the **new breed of "education mayor"** would act as the "prime mover" of reform, forcing changes that would lead to gains in scores on student achievement exams.[56]

In Illinois, a Republican-led Illinois legislature was even willing to hand over control of the city's schools to Mayor Richard M. Daley, a Democrat. Daley gained the power to name the school system's chief executive, top financial officers, and a five-member board of trustees; the mayor was also granted additional authority to oversee the school system's $3 billion annual budget.[57]

Rahm Emanuel, Daley's successor, found that mayoral control of schools could be quite controversial and politically costly. Emanuel made the reform of city schools a priority. The mayor suffered criticism from the teacher's union. He faced a citywide teachers' strike in 2012 as he shut down underperforming schools, created new charter schools, and placed new emphasis on quantitative measures of a teacher's performance.

Changes in the governing structure of underperforming schools, however, provides no cure-all for the many significant problems that plague public education. In Indianapolis in 2013, four schools taken over by the state continued to receive "F" grades.[58]

THE FORMAL STRUCTURE OF CITY GOVERNMENT

There are three widely-used forms of city government in the United States: the mayor-council plan (with its weak-mayor and strong-mayor variants), the council-manager plan (which places executive authority in the hands of a professional city manager, not an elected mayor), and the commission arrangement (a form that is no longer widely used).

During the first half of the nation's existence, cities were generally governed by the mayor-council arrangement. Since the early 1990s, however, reformers have succeeded in getting cities to switch to the council-manager system. Today, half of the communities in the United States operate under a council-manager plan that places city stewardship in the hands of a professional city manager.[59] The council-manager system is particularly popular among mid-sized communities and in the Pacific West.

The nation's biggest cities (including New York, Los Angeles, Chicago, Houston, and Philadelphia), however, have spurned the council-manager arrangement and instead look to an elected mayor for leadership. Very small communities, too, tend to be governed by the mayor-council plan, as residents see little reason to pay for a full-time professional manager.

WEAK-MAYOR SYSTEM

In the early United States, mayors were denied strong governing powers. Citizens in the new republic remembered the nation's colonial experience and the arrogance of England's King George III; this was reason enough to distrust executive power.

But as the country urbanized, growing cities required stronger governments that could effectively provide streets, sewers, sanitation, and other important municipal services. In the early 1800s, state legislatures acted to assure the provision of such services, but without increasing the authority of the mayor. The states created a variety of independent elected offices and appointed boards and commissions, each given responsibility for the provision of a specific municipal service. Today, the continued existence of such independent executive offices, boards, and commissions is the defining characteristic of the weak-mayor system.

In the **weak-mayor system**, a mayor possesses quite limited administrative authority; the mayor lacks the power to appoint and dismiss key administrative personnel and to direct the operations of executive branch offices. Unlike the president of the United States, the mayor of a weak-mayor city cannot even name the heads of major executive departments. Instead, the mayor must govern with a number of other executives whom he or she does not appoint or control: independently elected executives (such as a directly elected local prosecutor or city treasurer); appointees made by the city council (and, in some states, even local appointees of the state's governor); and the members of independent boards and commissions (see Figure 5.1). The existence of elected department heads

Figure 5.1 **Two Variants of the Weak-Mayor Structure**

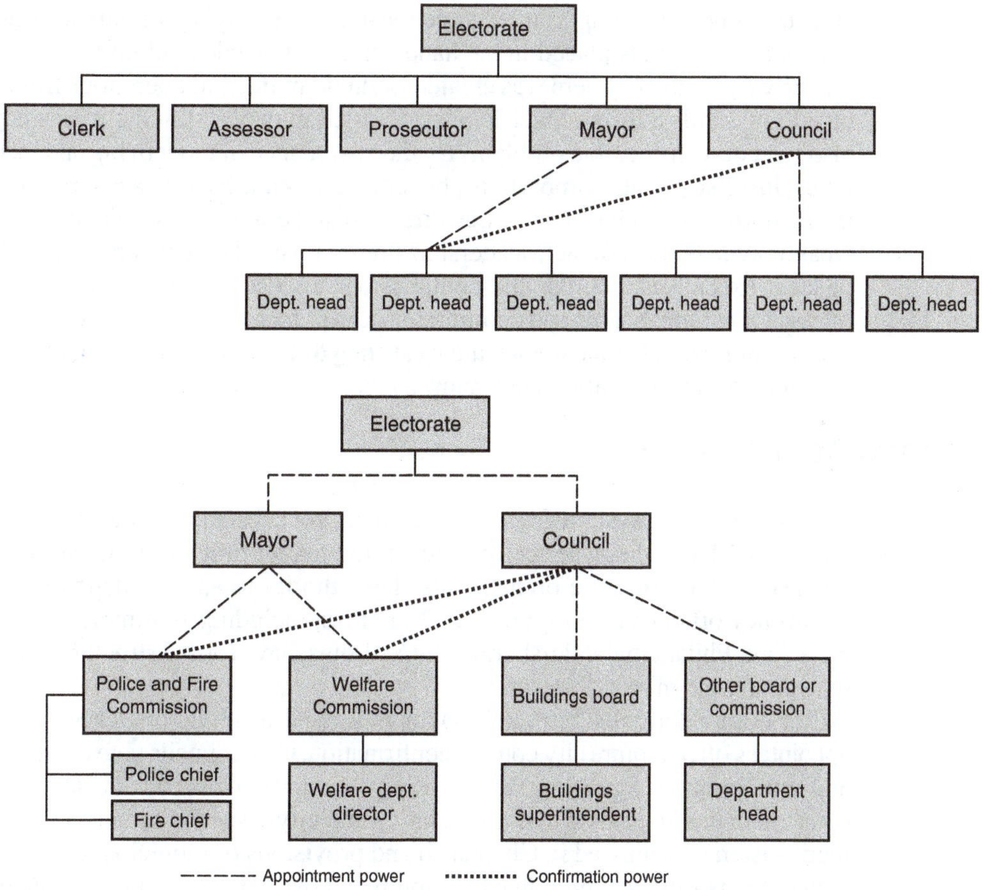

(a) The mayor does not possess total control over the executive branch but shares it with independently elected officials. Other departmental heads are subject to city council confirmation or are appointed directly by the council.

(b) Departmental heads are appointed not by the mayor but by the independent boards and commissions. The members of these boards and commissions serve long, fixed terms, even when appointed by the council and the mayor.

and numerous independent bodies produces a **fragmentation of executive power**; the mayor of a weak-mayor city is denied nominal control over executive branch agencies.

In a weak-mayor city, the members of independent boards and commissions serve long fixed terms of office that insulate the boards from mayoral control. In the absence of resignations, a mayor may be able to appoint only one member a year to a public board or commission; the mayor must govern with board members who do not share his or her point of view. In a great many cities, the city council also has the right to approve or reject mayoral appointments and dismissals. The mayor cannot simply dismiss an uncooperative appointee.

The classic weak mayor also possesses only the most limited legislative and budgetary responsibilities. Smaller communities (with a population below 25,000) typically do not even give the mayor the ability to veto council-passed legislation.[60] In the majority of U.S. communities, the mayor does not control the preparation of the city budget, possibly the single most important vehicle for setting the city's program priorities. Instead, budget preparation is placed in the hands of an independent administrative officer.[61]

The weak-mayor system was created to shield municipal operations from the unwise actions of an ill-trained, power-hungry, or partisan mayor. But the weak-mayor system also presents considerable problems for the governance of modern big and medium-sized cities. Just like private corporations, big cities and suburbs need a central executive with the authority to provide clear policy direction and effective program coordination. The weak mayor is denied such leadership prerogatives. The existence of multiple independent executives, boards, and commissions also adds to policy confusion; without mayoral direction, boards and commissions can pursue their own agendas, often working at cross-purposes. On the whole, the weak-mayor form of government does not provide for capable, strong, unified leadership.

STRONG-MAYOR SYSTEM

The **strong-mayor system** grants the elected mayor substantial authority over city departments. Similar to the American president, the mayor of a strong-mayor city is clearly the head of the executive branch, with the authority to appoint department heads and top agency officials (see Figure 5.2). Big cities, including Baltimore, Boston, Denver, New York, Philadelphia, Pittsburgh, and St. Louis, have formal structures of government that emphasize mayoral power.

But even a formally "strong" mayor is subject to numerous checks. Top mayoral appointees often require city council confirmation. City councils vote on the city's budget and appropriations (spending) bills. The city council can override the mayor's veto. City councils may also review major purchases and city-issued contracts. Civil service and merit systems (discussed in Chapter 6) and provisions of municipal collective bargaining contracts further limit a mayor's command over executive-branch personnel. State laws can narrow—or expand—a mayor's policy reach.

A strong-mayor charter does not guarantee a mayor the ability to lead. Truly effective mayors do not rely solely on the powers of their office. True leadership, as we shall see, also depends on a mayor's ability to build and maintain governing coalitions.

Figure 5.2 **Strong-Mayor Structure**

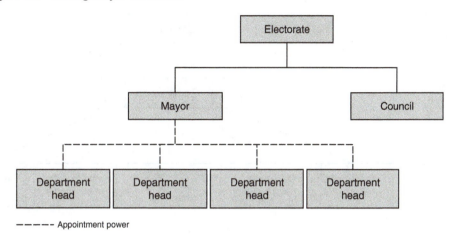

––––– Appointment power

COMMISSION GOVERNMENT

When local officials in Galveston, Texas, proved incapable of responding to the 1900 hurricane and flood that devastated the city, a new commission of experts took charge of the city's clean-up and recovery. This was the beginning of the *commission system* of government. In Galveston, five members each oversaw the operations of a different municipal department, coming together to serve as the city council (usually referred to as the city commission). For a time, Galveston's successful governmental innovation was widely copied. However, Houston and other cities eventually turned away from commission government, having discovered the arrangement's shortcomings.

The **commission form** has no separation of powers; instead, a five- to nine-member city commission governs the city, with each member having both legislative and executive responsibilities. Each commissioner serves both as the head of a city department and as a member of the city's legislature (Figure 5.3). The commission selects one of its members to serve as mayor and preside over commission meetings and ceremonial gatherings. The mayor possesses no more authority than does any other commissioner.

In theory, the commission system provides for quick action as the city's legislators and heads of executive departments are one and the same. Yet the disadvantages of the arrangement are fairly overwhelming. A commissioner may be an advocate of the narrow view of his or her department. Each commissioner may be reluctant to scrutinize the budget requests of other departments, fearing that such actions will produce retaliation by other commissioners. An elected commissioner also does not necessarily possess the administrative skills to manage a large city department, especially as voters rarely cast their ballots on the basis of a candidate's administrative record.

Portland (Oregon) is the only large city in the United States to retain the commission system.[62] Forest Park (Illinois) and Sunrise (Florida) are notable suburbs with the

Figure 5.3 **Commission Structure**

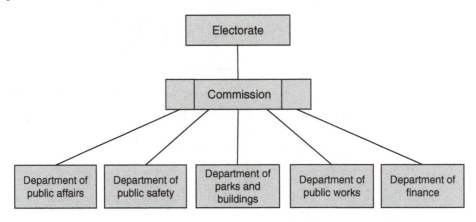

commission plan. The commission arrangement is more commonly found in county government. More than one-third of United States counties are governed under some variant of the commission system.[63]

THE COUNCIL-MANAGER (CITY MANAGER) SYSTEM

In 1908, Staunton, Virginia, experimented with a new form of government that gave extensive administrative authority to an appointed city manager. Staunton's innovation proved so successful that the National Municipal League made the council-manager system a key element in the League's *Model City Charter*. Dayton, Ohio, in 1913 became the first city of significant size to adopt this "good government" reform. The council-manager plan was soon adopted by communities across the nation.

Under the **council-manager system**, the city council appoints a professionally trained manager who is given charge of the daily affairs of the city. The city council enacts laws and sets overall policy; but decisions regarding day-to-day program operations, personnel, and other administrative matters fall under the domain of the appointed manager.

The council selects one of its own members to serve as mayor; alternatively, in some council-manager cities, the mayor is elected citywide. However the mayor is chosen, the powers given the mayor of a council-manager city are quite limited. The mayor presides over council meetings, signs federal aid agreements, and represents the city in public ceremonies. But department heads report to the city manager, not to the mayor. The city manager—not the mayor—appoints key personnel and gives instructions to the various municipal agencies (see Figure 5.4).

The council-manager system emulates the structure of private businesses: the city council functions much like a private corporation's board of directors that sets a corporation's overall goals. The board (or city council) then delegates substantial operational authority to a chief executive officer (CEO). A city manager is a municipality's CEO. The city council, like a private company's board of directors, can dismiss and replace a chief executive whose service proves disappointing.

Figure 5.4 **Council-Manager Structure**

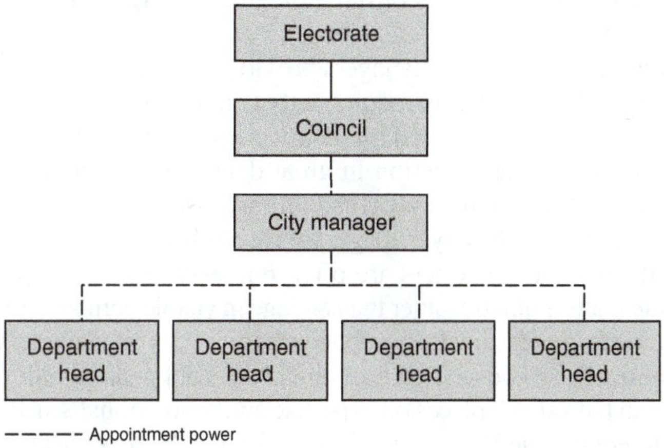

The council-manager system is quite popular, and is a common feature of governments in medium-sized communities, suburbs, and in the South and the West. A number of larger cities, too, operate under the council-manager plan: Phoenix, Dallas, San Antonio, San Jose, Sacramento, Long Beach, Santa Ana, Las Vegas, Tucson, Austin, Fort Worth, Oklahoma City, Jacksonville, Charlotte, Memphis, Virginia Beach, Kansas City and Wichita.

The advantages of the council-manager plan are obvious: it places the highly complex tasks of government in the hands of a well-trained professional. City managers possess considerable **expertise** (detailed technical knowledge) in such areas as accounting, budgeting, public finance, long-term planning, personnel management, and civil engineering. Also, in contrast to a mayor who must face election, the decisions made by a manager are less likely to be influenced by short-term electoral and partisan considerations. City managers generally exhibit a commitment to high ethical standards.

Still, the nation's biggest cities have, for the most part, spurned the council-manager arrangement, fearing that an appointed manager will lack important political skills and resources necessary to getting things done in a diverse community. In a large contentious city, an executive needs the legitimacy that derives from democratic election. Compared to an elected mayor, an appointed manager has much less ability to command media attention and rally public support behind a project.

The council-manager system operates smoothly when all participants recognize their assigned roles. The city council establishes a city's overall **mission** or sense of direction, setting forth the city's general philosophy regarding taxing, spending, and growth. The council and city manager jointly decide specific questions of **policy**, for instance, determining the exact level of services that will be provided and which projects will be built. The city manager, however, has charge over program **management and administration**: matters dealing with personnel, budgeting, purchasing, contracting, data processing, and the daily workings of municipal programs. Council members are not supposed to intrude in matters of program administration. Nonetheless, council members often do intervene, especially in response to constituent complaints.[64]

The city-manager model attempts to separate administration from politics. Yet, to get things done, the city manager must exhibit considerable political skill. The city manager is unavoidably involved in controversial policy areas and project advocacy.[65] The successful manager devotes considerable time to forging a political consensus behind key program changes.[66]

The most successful managers provide information and policy advice that members of the city council dearly require. City council members, who typically serve part-time and are poorly remunerated for their work, often lack the capacity to analyze and review alternative courses of action in great detail. In most cities, council members are not even provided with the assistance of a well-staffed legislative research office. Council members rely on the city manager for research, analysis, and program recommendations.

Effective city managers are often reluctant to take the public stage. They prefer to handle matters quietly rather than engage in visible combat with members of the council.[67] Like other professionals in public service, a city manager commands respect by being "apolitical": "however, being apolitical does not mean avoiding difficult policy issues."[68]

With the value it places on expertise and professionalism, the council-manager system often reduces the level of conflict in city hall.[69] Yet conflict can emerge, as there is no clear line that separates politics and policy formulation from administrative matters. In some cities, the mayor and manager are competitors for influence. The public expects a mayor—especially a mayor elected directly by the voters citywide—to lead. Mayors accuse more aggressive city managers of improperly venturing into policy decisions that lie beyond matters of administration. City managers, in turn, charge that the mayor and council members too frequently and improperly interfere in administrative matters.

Does the ability of the city council to fire a mayor give the council effective control over a city manager? Not always! Not every manager lives in fear of being fired. City councils are often quite hesitant to dismiss the city's top executive, as a city that gains a reputation for being "hostile" to city managers will find it difficult to recruit a truly talented manager. In small- and medium-sized communities, part-time council members have no great willingness to commit extensive time and energy to screen candidates and interview candidates to replace a city manager.

THE HYBRID STRUCTURE OF THE MODERN U.S. CITY

The formal structures of city government are not fixed but are actually rather "malleable."[70] Over time, cities modify their initial charter-specified governing arrangements, borrowing successful elements from other cities. There are few mayor-council and council-manager cities today that precisely fit the ideal forms of government described in this chapter. Rather, most municipal governments are hybrids that have adopted various features from alternative governmental structures. To cite one commonplace example: even a strong-mayor city may have a number of independent boards and commissions and a civil-service personnel system that serves to limit the power of the mayor (a matter that will be discussed in Chapter 6).

A number of council-manager cities have, in recent years, sought to give the mayors new powers to lead, despite the continuing presence of a professional city manager. Cincinnati and Toledo hoped that a strengthened mayor would be a visible and effective spokesperson for the city in seeking new businesses. Cincinnati's mayor was given enhanced budgetary authority and the authority to name and replace the city manager and the chairs of various council committees.[71]

Sacramento Mayor Kevin Johnson similarly pushed his city to modify its council-manager system, which, according to Johnson, undermined the mayor's ability to initiate strong economic programs. Johnson complained that the council-manager system forced the mayor to do "everything by committee." He argued that a mayor who is little more than just one vote on the city council lacks the "clout" to provide effective policy direction.[72]

In California, San Jose, Oakland, Sacramento, and Hayward all moved to the city-wide election of the mayor in order to increase the responsiveness of city hall to racial minorities and homeowner groups. The change sought to offset some of the influence wielded in city hall by business elites and members of the local growth machine.[73]

San Diego under Pete Wilson (who served as mayor from 1971 to 1982 before moving on to become California's governor then U.S. senator) granted its mayor increased authority to set the city council agenda and to name the chairs and members of council committees. Wilson urged still greater changes, arguing that the city's council-manager form of government imposed a "structural straitjacket" on a mayor's ability to lead.[74] In 2004 and again 2010, voters approved changes in San Diego's system of government, abandoning its council-manager system in favor of the strong-mayor form of government.

Oakland similarly abandoned its council-manager system and adopted a strong-mayor plan that gave then-mayor Jerry Brown (the past and also future California governor) the authority to dismiss Oakland's city manager. Fresno, Miami, Hartford, Richmond, St. Petersburg, and Spokane are other cities that have similarly sought to increase mayoral leadership, adopting the mayor-council arrangement in place of the traditional local council-manager arrangement.

Municipal moves, however, are not all in one direction. El Paso, Topeka, and Cedar Rapids switched to the council-manager form. Revelations of local scandal and corruption fuel demands for a reform that embodies the professionalism and higher ethical standards of managerial government.[75]

An increasing number of mayor-council cities make good use of a city-manager-like figure, a **chief administrative officer (CAO)**. The CAO is an experienced city-hall hand who can offer expert advice and help tutor a new mayor in the intricacies of budget preparation and other governmental processes. The CAO is usually a careerist who is a source of continuity and institutional memory in city hall.

In New York, however, the mayor names the CAO. The appointive process assures the position's responsiveness to the mayor at the cost of decreasing the position's professional independence.[76] In New York, the CAO functions less like a city manager and more like a top-level mayoral assistant.

CITY COUNCILS: NO MINIATURE REPRODUCTIONS OF THE U.S. CONGRESS

Unlike the U.S. Congress, the members of the city council typically serve part-time and are rather poorly paid. Many small- and even medium-sized communities do not even schedule weekly council meetings. Only in the nation's biggest cities do council members tend to serve full-time and receive generous compensation.

Los Angeles in 2014 paid the highest city council salaries in the nation, an eye-popping $181,000 per year. Houston paid its full-time council members $62,000. By contrast, Dallas paid its part-time council members only $37,500. In other cities, compensation levels are lower still: Mobile (Alabama), $19,800 plus meeting expenses and a $325 per month expense account; Irvine (California), a paltry $10,560; and Fullerton (California) about $9,000 per year.[77]

Quite unlike the U.S. Congress and the pattern observed in the clear majority of state legislatures, city councils are seldom organized along party lines with the leader of the majority party exerting great control over legislative proceedings. The overwhelming majority of city councils are formally nonpartisan; members run for office with no avowed Democratic or Republican party affiliation (see Chapter 6 for a more detailed analysis of municipal nonpartisan systems). City councils in general do not suffer the deep partisan polarizations that plagued the U.S. Congress during the Obama years.

Legislative committees, key components of the U.S. House and Senate legislative processes, play a much less important role in cities. While more and more city councils are making use of **standing committees** (that is, permanent committees that study proposed legislation in a policy area),[78] legislative committee systems are much less developed in city hall than in Congress. City councils are generally too small to be able to divide work among a number of specialized committees. Part-time and underpaid council members are also generally unwilling to devote substantial time to committee work. Compared to the U.S. Congress, city councils conduct relatively few public committee hearings on proposed legislation.

City councils also suffer from frequent turnover. Quite unlike the U.S. House of Representatives, few city council members serve unduly long legislative careers. In most cities, council members typically serve relatively short tenure and then leave voluntarily in order to return to better-paying private careers or to run for higher office. Only half of a newly elected council class will still be serving on a council five years later.[79]

The short duration of a council member's career diminishes the ability of a city council to develop the depth of knowledge necessary for truly informed and independent legislative action. Amateur, part-time legislators are in a poor position to inspect and challenge the reports and recommendations of the city manager, municipal department heads, and professional consultants.

During the 1990s, a grassroots movement demanded the enactment of **term limitations** to prohibit a council member from serving more than two or three consecutive terms. The term limitations movement initially arose as a brushfire reaction against the U.S. Congress, where members serve long careers and seldom risk defeat at the ballot box.

In more recent years, the term limitations movement has waned. As a consequence, only 10 percent of American communities limit the number of terms that a council member may serve.[80]

Why did the movement for municipal term limitations lose steam? There is one simple and fairly obvious explanation: most communities have no real need for term limitations. As we have already observed, members of city councils, with few exceptions, do not serve extended careers; city councils gain substantial "new blood" as the result of voluntary retirements. "Term limits" appears to be medicine for a disease that does not exist in a great many cities. Indeed, local legislatures need members who have gained knowledge and experience on the job; term limits may force a city council's few experienced members to leave office.

What can be done to improve the performance of a city council? First, city councils need greater staff support so that council members can participate as informed and independent voices in city decision making. Second, local legislators need to be paid adequate compensation if they are expected to devote the considerable time necessary to do the public's business. Third, cities that have two-year terms for council members might consider shifting to four-year terms. The burden of frequent election campaigns (and the accompanying burden of fundraising necessitated by electoral campaigns run in bigger cities) can lead talented and capable council representatives to voluntarily leave office. Finally, as a number of city councils have already begun to do, a city's legislature needs to make council committees a regular part of its operations.

WOMEN IN LOCAL GOVERNMENT

As of January 2014, only 13 of the 100 largest U.S. cities had women mayors, the same number as in 2005. Annise D. Parker was the head of Houston, the nation's 5th largest city. Other prominent women mayors included Betsy Price of Fort Worth (18th largest city), Stephanie Rawlings-Blake of Baltimore (26th), Carolyn Goodman of Las Vegas (28th), Ashley Swearengin of Fresno (42nd), Jean Stohert of Omaha (44th), Nancy McFarlane of Raleigh (45th), Jean Quan of Oakland, California (49th), and Betsy Hodges of Minneapolis (50th). Overall, women were mayors in 17 percent of the nation's cities with a population greater than 100,000.[81]

Houston Mayor Annise Parker Was Inaugurated Mayor of Houston in 2010. An openly lesbian candidate, Parker's victory points to the changing demography and the electoral importance of new groups in a city renowned for its conservative politics. Parker's success shows the importance of skillful coalition building. In her campaign, Parker stressed economic development issues, neighborhood responsiveness, and fiscal prudence.

Courtesy of Zblume through Wikimedia Commons. http://commons. wikimedia.org/wiki/File:Annise_Parker.JPG

Women are also underrepresented in municipal legislatures. In 2014, women held 28 percent of city council seats, a number slightly below what it had been two decades previous. Although the figure is low, it nonetheless compares favorably to the 18.5 percent of congressional seats occupied by women in 2014.[82]

What accounts for the underrepresentation of women in local office? A number of the disadvantages that women candidates face in local electoral contests are actually eroding. In large cities, women office seekers generally are able to raise as much money as do men. Women who run for municipal office enjoy a victory rate that is equivalent to that of men. The underrepresentation of women continues for the most part because relatively few women choose to run for public office.[83]

Why are women less electorally ambitious than men? Why are women more willing to run for local positions than for state or national office?[84] Entrenched gendered roles still affect women's choices. Compared to national office, service at the local level poses less conflict with the family and child care responsibilities borne by women.[85] Women also exhibit a greater interest in local office as local governments focus on issue areas—affordable housing, social welfare, health care, and education—of special concern to women in their role as family caretaker: "[T]he local level is where many of the problems that are of most concern to women are addressed, and consequently where many women are introduced to political gladiatorial combat."[86]

The ideological climate of a city also has an impact on women's electoral prospects. A study of 239 cities reveals that women tend to be elected to the city council more frequently in liberal communities than in more politically conservative communities.[87]

Once in office, women tend to exhibit a political style that differs somewhat from that of men. One study of city managers reveals that, compared to men, female managers are more likely to utilize leadership approaches that emphasize communication and conciliation. Women, more than men, try to bring city officials together in an effort to resolve a dispute. Men, by contrast, were more willing to rely on the formal authority of office and, for instance, simply dismiss an agency head who had lost the council's confidence.[88] Other studies similarly point to the more collegial leadership styles of women.[89] The increased participation of women in local government has the potential to alter the prevailing style of politics in a city.

THE DIFFICULT TASK OF MAYORAL LEADERSHIP

Descriptions of a city's charter and formal governing structure only provide the starting point for examining the possibilities of local leadership. Effective leadership requires that an official look beyond the formal prerogatives of office. Chicago, for instance, largely fits the weak-mayor model.[90] Yet, Mayor Richard J. Daley, the legendary "boss" of Chicago in the 1950s and 1960s, and his son Richard M. Daley, the longest-serving mayor in Chicago history, were certainly not weak mayors. Both mayors wielded considerable power, building relationships with developers and using their dominance in the local Democratic Party organization to gain effective control over the city council.

In many cities, mayors are denied key prerequisites for leadership. Only in large cities (with populations greater than 250,000) is the mayor's position even full-time; in smaller communities and council-manager cities, being mayor is only a part-time job.[91] Part-time, poorly paid, and given little staff assistance, the mayors of many cities find it difficult to lead. They lack the resources that would enable them to challenge the recommendations of top managers and planners. They are unable to commit the time necessary to develop strong working relationships with key business leaders and to lobby for state and federal program assistance.

Box 5.1
Rahm Emanuel: Chicago's New-Style Mayor?

Rahm Emanuel, former member of Congress and Barack Obama's first White House chief of staff, was sworn in as Chicago's 46th mayor in 2011. Emanuel won election handily, despite his abrasive political style, his lack of experience in municipal government, and even his lack of familiarity with large sections of Chicago. Emanuel's lawyers successfully squelched a legal challenge to his eligibility to run; his opponents had tried but failed to remove Emanuel's name from the ballot arguing that the candidate resided in Washington, D.C., not Chicago.

Emanuel was no conventional product of Chicago's Irish-dominated political machine that had its roots in ward politics and service provision. Instead, he was a "policy wonk" with a record of national service. Emanuel was also the first Jew to be elected mayor of Chicago.

Emanuel did not rely on the traditional means that Chicago's political machine (an organization that Chapter 6 describes in further detail) used to win office. Emanuel brought a new age of electoral campaigning to Chicago, putting together a personal political organization and fundraising operation (which included Hollywood fundraisers as well as the more than a million dollars left over from a past congressional race) that enabled his campaign to dominate the airwaves and the Internet. Emanuel used his close ties to Obama to cruise to victory in every African-American ward in the city, despite running against African-American and Hispanic opponents. Emanuel succeeded in building a sense that his electoral victory was inevitable: "Rahm Emanuel's intelligence, energy, organization, and fund-raising simply overwhelmed his major opponents."

Emanuel proclaimed that he would not be a "patient" mayor. As mayor, he governed with a highly individualistic, energetic, and combative approach. He pushed school reform, lengthened the school day, closed dozens of underperforming elementary schools, set up new charter schools, visited classrooms, and rebuffed the salary demands of the teachers' union, even suffering through a teachers' strike. Emanuel built strong relations with downtown corporate leaders and with businesses in Mexico and Poland as he proclaimed Chicago to be a global city. Emanuel visited black, Hispanic, and white neighborhoods, greeted road crews as they cleared snow from city streets, and talked with passengers as they rode the elevated trains. He closed traffic lanes to automobiles in order to create new bike paths. He publicized his many actions via Twitter.

Emanuel initially found support among white voters, Hispanics, and the city's business community. His confrontation with the city's teachers, however, seemed to cost him some support in the black community. His stated policy goal of renegotiating and reducing the city's municipal pension contributions in the face of a looming "pension gap" crisis further served to alienate the city's labor unions. Emanuel's standing in public opinion polls fell. Overall, Emanuel had the reputation of a mayor who could "bulldoze" both "buildings and opponents."

Sources: Paul M. Green, "Rahm Emanuel: Beginning a New Mayoral era in Chicago," in *The Mayors: Chicago's Political Tradition,* 4th ed., ed. Paul M. Green and Melvin G. Holli (Carbondale, IL: Southern Illinois University Press, 2013), 238–261; the "intelligence, energy, organization" quotation appears on p. 256. Edward Luce, "Rahm Emanuel: Mayor America," *Financial Times,* February 14, 2013; the "patient" mayor quotation is from this article. The "bulldoze" quotation is from Ben Joravsky, "Mayor Emanuel: A Tough Leader for a Tough City, or Just an A-Hole?" *The Reader (Chicago),* August 27, 2013.

For much of the nation's history, mayors came to city hall from backgrounds in business.[92] Oftentimes, mayors governed as an entrenched ally of the local growth machine. But over the past few decades, the changing demography of cities has toppled these traditional patterns. Contemporary mayors come to office from more diverse backgrounds and have more dynamic change-oriented agendas.

There is no guarantee, however, that a mayor will be able to effectively lead a city. Effective leadership depends on a mayor's skill, orientation, and personality, not just the formal prerogatives of office. (See Box 5.1, "Rahm Emanuel: Chicago's New-Style Mayor?")

MINORITY MAYORS AND THE DEBATE OVER DERACIALIZATION

African-American and Latino mayors often face difficult choices in governing. Should they pursue economic development projects and programs that promise assistance to the entire city? Or should they give greater attention to changing conditions in the city's poorest neighborhoods? Should they pursue programs that win them the support of a multiracial and multiethnic coalition? Or should they pursue policies that help their core constituency, even at the risk of alienating outside groups?

The first-generation of big-city African-American mayors were steeped in the activism of the civil rights era and were ready to battle for change in cities that were polarized along racial lines. Cleveland's Carl Stokes in 1967 became the first African American to be elected mayor of a big city. He came to office backed by a biracial coalition of black voters and white liberals. In office, however, Stokes' agenda for change stalled; Stokes found he could not push for far-reaching changes to aid Cleveland's poor inner-city neighborhoods while also tending to the concerns of white leaders. Stokes eventually chose to pursue a redistributive agenda, a path of action that invited substantial criticism.[93] Detroit Mayor Coleman Young (1973–1993), who came to government after years as a labor organizer and civil rights activist who battled police brutality, chose to govern with an even more combative, polarizing "what goes around comes around" political style that irked whites and suburbanites.[94]

In contrast, San Antonio's Henry Cisneros (1981–1989), the first Mexican-American mayor of a major U.S. city, toned down overt racial appeals and sought to build support across racial and ethnic lines. Cisneros pursued new growth projects to bring much-needed jobs and opportunity to both Latinos and Anglos. Activist Latino organizations like COPS (Communities Organized for Public Services), however, complained that Cisneros was overly concerned with the city's central business district and new stadium construction. Cisneros, they charged, failed to give sufficient attention to the urgent needs of low-income neighborhoods.[95]

In Los Angeles, Tom Bradley made similar choices during his five terms as mayor (1973–1993) and faced similar criticism. An African American, Bradley won the mayoralty with a *deracialized* appeal that stressed his reputation for being a "tough cop" in the Los Angeles Police Department. Bradley, who was no street radical, downplayed racial appeals and instead built an effective working partnership with the city's business community and with white liberal groups, including organized labor and the city's Jewish community.

Both Cisneros and Bradley were generally regarded as successful mayors. Yet critics charged that their agendas were too incremental, that they were too deferential to white business interests, and that the mayors could have done more to help racial minorities and the poor.[96]

Cisneros, Bradley, Atlanta's Andrew Young, New York's David Dinkins, Philadelphia's Wilson Goode, Detroit's Dennis Archer, Denver's Federico Peña, Seattle's Norman Rice, and Charlotte's Harvey Gantt were all fabled African-American and Latino mayors who, during the latter part of the twentieth century, utilized a **deracialized approach to leadership** that toned down racial appeals and deemphasized redistribution. Instead, these mayors emphasized good-government managerialism, partnerships with business leaders for economic development, and other measures that promised benefits across racial lines.[97] These mayors often walked a difficult line.

In 2005, Antonio Villaraigosa won Los Angeles' mayoralty, having narrowly lost the race for mayor four years previous. Villaraigosa could not rely on Latino votes alone. He broadened his appeal, reaching out to liberal whites, organized labor, and Los Angeles' Jewish community.[98] Assembling and sustaining a coalition that included black, Latino, and Asian voters is no easy task.[99] Oftentimes, these minorities prefer to ally with whites than with one another.

In contemporary San Antonio, a city with a population that is majority Latino, Mayor Julián Castro similarly embraced a largely deracialized approach to leadership. Castro initiated a new pre-kindergarten schooling program for the city's most impoverished children, children who are largely from Hispanic families. Mayor Castro argued, however, that the program was not only for the poor, that the investment in education was also good for business and would help attract new jobs to the city. (See Box 5.2: "PreK4SA: San Antonio's Julián Castro Builds a Coalition behind Pre-Kindergarten Education.") In 2014, President Obama named Julián Castro as the Secretary of the Department of Housing and Urban Development, a position that also promised to increase the national profile of the rising Hispanic political star.

Many political analysts argue that deracialization strategies represent a maturation of black and Latino politics. Deracialized appeals enable racial minorities to win office in cities where they do not constitute a clear majority of the active electorate. Barack

Box 5.2
"PreK4SA": San Antonio's Julián Castro Builds a Coalition behind Pre-Kindergarten Education

San Antonio Mayor Julián Castro gained national prominence as a featured televised speaker at the 2012 National Democratic Convention that nominated Barack Obama for his second term as President. Castro was viewed nationally as a young and up-and-coming Latino leader, an articulate, well-educated (with a Stanford undergraduate degree and a Harvard law degree), and highly-skilled Latino official who could appeal across racial and ethnic lines and who also had a national network of supporters.

Although San Antonio's population is nearly 60 percent Mexican-American, Castro adopted a deracialized leadership approach and did not govern as a "Latino mayor." Castro sought to build partnerships with the city's business leaders and Anglo power structure in order to further local economic development.

Castro achieved a noteworthy political and policy victory when, in November 2012, he secured passage, with 53 percent voter approval, of the PreK4SA ballot initiative that created full-day pre-kindergarten programs for at-risk 4-year-olds. The addition of 1/8th of a cent levy to the city sales tax would pay for the creation of new pre-K centers to serve some 20,000 children in low-income areas of the city. In racially polarized San Antonio, the vote, not surprisingly, divided largely along lines of race and class; the ballot initiative garnered great support in Latino and pro-Obama areas of the city while suffering its greatest opposition in better-off Anglo neighborhoods.

Julián Castro had sought to nurture a broad base of support for the pre-K measure by first assembling a "Brainpower Task Force." Castro did not simply stress the fairness aspects of the program and that it would bring new educational opportunities to a largely poor and Latino population of children. Castro and the program's backers poll-tested various ways to "frame" or sell the program. The poll results led Castro to stress that the program was critical to the city's economic future, and that San Antonio needed a more educated, higher-quality workforce to attract new industries and a growing number of jobs in a competitive economic world.

The passage of the PreK4SA reveals a number of strategic calculations that Castro made in his leadership effort. Castro paid special attention to gaining the support of the city manager. The mayor also acted to gain backing for the measure by the city's business elite (including the owners of the NBA basketball Spurs). The city's business elite helped to fund the media campaign that undoubtedly provided the margin of victory for the measure. Castro also chose the initiative route to circumvent the fractious debate that would likely have greeted the proposal had he put it before San Antonio's divided city council. The ballot initiative was also put before voters in a presidential year, when the expected surge in turnout among lower-income and minority voters could help carry the measure to victory—as it did.

Six months after passage of the measure, Castro won overwhelming election to a third term in office. The Brookings Institution and the Rockefeller Foundation named PreK4SA as one of the "Top Ten State and Metropolitan Innovations to Watch" in 2013.

Castro announced his support for center-city initiatives, promising to remake San Antonio's core in the forthcoming "Decade of Downtown." Grassroots activists criticized the mayor for being too cozy with business and for pushing upscale housing plans that would change the nature of the center city. They asked: "Decade of Downtown for whom?"

Sources: Zev Chafets, "The Post-Hispanic Hispanic Politician," *New York Times Magazine,* May 6, 2010; Michael Barajas, "State of the City," *San Antonio Current,* March 11, 2013 (Marisa Cortez's "Decade of Downtown for whom?" comment appears in the Barajas article); and Arturo Vega, "San Antonio's Urban and Mayoral Politics: The Case of PreK4SA," paper presented to the annual meeting of the Urban Affairs Association, San Antonio, Texas, March 20, 2014.

Obama's stunningly successful 2008 presidential campaign illustrates the electoral possibilities inherent in a candidates' deracialized political appeal.

Critics, however, counter that winning isn't everything, that a deracialized approach in a political campaign can lead to compromised goals after the election is won. The proper goal of minority politics, these theorists argue, is not simply to elect a minority mayor but to increase social justice and "improve the quality [of life] of minorities" who live within a city.[100] Moderate black mayors have pursued "policies of fiscal conservatism and downtown development,"[101] while ignoring more far-reaching transformational change targeted to bring relief to poorer neighborhoods: "Black politics is not maturing and may be degenerating."[102] Constant pressure from community organizations, churches, labor unions, and civil rights groups is necessary to keep a black or Latino mayor from caving in to the demands of business leaders and other elite interests.[103]

For a new generation of black mayors, however, the debate over deracialization just does not appear to be all that interesting. The first wave of big-city black mayors to win office faced the obstruction of white politicians and had to govern in a highly polarized political setting. In the 1960s and 1970s, the first wave of black mayors saw their terms in office as a continuation of the civil rights movement struggle for racial justice.

Today's new breed of African-American mayors, however, governs in much different circumstances. While racial equality has yet to be fully achieved, many African Americans have gained entrance into sectors of American society that were previously closed to them. Public opinion polls of African Americans also reveal class divisions; black voters are not as uniformly liberal as they were just decades ago. Polling data, for instance, point to increases in the number of African Americans who endorse work-oriented welfare reforms, strong anti-crime measures, and the introduction of charter schools—initiatives that are usually portrayed as the province of the political right.[104]

Many of the new generation of black mayors also grew up in racially integrated neighborhoods, attended white-dominated schools, and went to the best universities. These black leaders are not street activists but **postracial black mayors** who are comfortable working across racial and ethnic lines.[105] While committed to progressive change, they also recognize the necessity of balancing a city's finances, of bringing jobs to a city, and of maintaining helpful partnerships with the leaders of corporations and nonprofit organizations. (See Box 5.3, "A New Generation of Black Mayors: Newark's Cory Booker and Sacramento's Kevin Johnson.")

Box 5.3
A New Generation of Black Mayors: Newark's Cory Booker and Sacramento's Kevin Johnson

Cory Booker, the Newark mayor who later rose to become U.S. Senator from New Jersey, exemplifies the new generation of African-American urban leaders. A Rhodes Scholar, a graduate of Yale Law School, and a self-fashioned problem solver who paid attention to policy details, Booker was able to draw considerable support from whites and Hispanics.

But Booker initially faced great difficulty in juggling the support of a multiracial coalition. He lost his initial mayoral bid in 2002, when the sixteen-year incumbent Sharpe James, a local "machine" politician (see Chapter 6) and a veteran political street fighter, portrayed Booker as an outsider, an opportunist who only recently came to the Newark scene and who lacked familiarity with the people of Newark. In contrast to Booker, James presented himself as "The Real Deal," an authentic black man in touch with the city's majority-black electorate.

A series of Booker campaign errors reinforced the concerns of older and poorer African Americans that Booker was the political hero of whites and the news media. Booker had raised an extensive campaign war chest from donors outside of Newark, further fueling doubts as to his racial "authenticity."

Booker learned from the mistakes of his first campaign. His second mayoral campaign would be quite different. Booker spent the four years between elections building bridges with Newark's black majority. Booker continued to reside in the low-income Brick Towers housing project. He opened a law office in the city and focused on nonprofit work He sponsored high-profile activities including a holiday turkey giveaway. Booker in his 2006 mayoral campaign also gave strong emphasis to crime reduction, as voter research revealed the issue was a dominant concern of inner-city residents. This time around, the Booker campaign also took special care to name African Americans and Newarkers, not outsiders, to visible campaign positions such as press secretary. The campaign also gave famous black celebrities the spotlight at campaign events. African Americans, not Booker's enthusiastic white supporters, were featured in photo opportunities. Booker won over 70 percent of the vote in 2006, and his allies swept to control of the city council.

Booker's leadership approach can be characterized as "deracialized" or "postracial." His rhetoric was not dominated by pleas for racial justice and solidarity; instead, he continued to stress his professional credentials and his naturalness in working across racial lines with business CEOs and with state government and nonprofit officials. His 2002 defeat had taught Booker to walk a fine line, balancing the concerns of his multiracial political base.

Booker's commitment to managerialism led him as mayor to dismiss hundreds of workers from the municipal payroll, a cost-cutting step necessitated by Newark's deteriorating fiscal position. Booker also endorsed educational vouchers as part of a strategy to shake up the city's failing school system. This move, too, alienated organized labor and members of the black establishment who saw Booker as attacking their hard-earned jobs. As a consequence, Booker in 2010 easily won reelection but saw his support slip a bit in the city's low-income wards.

In 2013, Booker won election to the U.S. Senate. In his maiden speech before the Senate, Booker once again appealed across racial lines. He even quoted a lyric from rock-and-roll legend Bruce Springsteen, a New Jersey native son.

In cities where African Americans are not an overwhelming majority of the electorate, an African-American mayor must give even greater attention to developing an appeal that can cross racial lines. In Sacramento, African Americans are only 20 percent of the population; whites and the rapidly growing Latino and Asian populations are key electoral constituencies. In 2008, Kevin Johnson, the former NBA basketball star and political novice, became the first African American to be elected mayor of Sacramento. Johnson defeated two-term incumbent Heather Fargo, a liberal Democrat who enjoyed strong support from upper-income and better educated white voters.

Johnson won by emphasizing his local roots and his political moderation. He had grown up in one of the city's more marginal neighborhoods, and, during his years in the NBA, devoted substantial time to nonprofit and youth work in the city. Johnson sought support across racial lines by stressing that, unlike Mayor Heather Fargo, he was a moderate Democrat, not a "tax and spend liberal." Johnson also promised to confront entrenched municipal labor unions.

As mayor, Johnson continued to pursue business growth and job creation, spearheading the effort to construct a new arena to keep the NBA Sacramento Kings from relocating elsewhere. Johnson's encouragement of charter schools alienated labor unions but, in the city's nonpartisan mayoral contests, won him votes from more centrist whites and Republicans. In 2012, Johnson easily won reelection.

Cory Booker and Kevin Johnson both exemplify how a new generation of postracial mayors have spurned rhetoric based on racial identify and grievance and instead have fashioned a political appeal based on a politics of managerialism and moderation. They have made "business" an important part of their governing coalition.

Of course, these mayors were also committed to bringing new opportunities to the residents of the city's poorest communities. But they did not present change in racially divisive terms. Instead, Mayor Booker and Mayor Johnson pursued "universalistic" policies that promised benefits for the entire city while providing an extra infusion of assistance to the city's most distressed communities.

Sources: For discussions of Cory Booker's leadership style, see: Andra Gillespie, *The New Black Politician: Cory Booker, Newark, and Post-Racial America* (New York: New York University Press, 2010); Andrew Jacobs, "Newark Mayor Battles Old Guard and Rumors," *New York Times,* July 3, 2007; and Gillespie, "Losing and Winning: Cory Booker's Ascent to Newark's Mayoralty," in *Whose Black Politics? Cases in Post-Racial Black Leadership,* ed. Andra Gillespie (New York: Routledge, 2010), 67–84.

Mayor Kevin Johnson's leadership approach is reviewed by Corey Cook, "Constructing a Moderate Multiracial Coalition in 'America's Most Diverse City': Kevin Johnson and Coalition Politics in Sacramento," in *21st Century Urban Race Politics* (Research in Race and Ethnic Relations, vol. 18), ed. Ravi K. Perry (Bingley: Emerald Publishing, 2013), 13–32; the "tax and spend liberal" quotation appears on p. 21.

Newark Mayor and Soon-to-Be United States Senator Cory Booker at a 2009 Campaign Fundraiser with Former United States Secretary of State Cyrus Vance: Booker was a postracial mayor, an African American who enjoyed strong popularity among non-black audiences. Lower-income Newark residents often found it troubling that Booker gave such great attention to non-black outsiders.

From Wikimedia Commons, by Cy Vance for DA, August 4, 2009, http://commons.wikimedia.org/wiki/File:CyVance_CoryBooker.jpg.

"Deracialization" does not mean that a black or Hispanic mayor will adopt the exact same governing approach as does a white mayor. Nor does deracialization mean that the new generation of black and Hispanic mayors see "race" as irrelevant or that they otherwise forget their identity. Postracial minority mayors pursue "universalistic" agendas that promise benefits to the entire city. But such agendas are not entirely race neutral; instead, they contain programs that provide disproportionate assistance to minority and low-income communities.

Postracial minority mayors walk a fine line. They serve all people in the city; they use rhetoric that appeals across lines of race and ethnicity. Still, they value programs that make a difference in the lives of the disadvantaged. Contemporary minority mayors are postracial as they seek ways to advance the interests of a city's minorities but without resorting to "explicit racial appeals."[106]

CONCLUSION: THE LIMITED POSITION OF CITIES AND THE PROSPECTS FOR EFFECTIVE CITY LEADERSHIP

Each state creates its local governments, determining each municipality's powers and structure of government. A charter grants a city only limited legislative, taxing, spending, and borrowing authority. Even home rule provisions do not fully offset Dillon's Rule, the legal doctrine that recognizes the hierarchical control that a state may exert over its cities, school districts, and other local governing bodies.

The formal structure of city government often reflects a decentralization or fragmentation of power. The existence of numerous independent boards, commissions, and independently elected and appointive offices serves to diffuse power, providing an impediment to the exercise of strong, centralized urban leadership. Municipal mayors seldom have the full range of appointive, budgetary, and veto powers comparable to those possessed by the president of the United States.

The strong-mayor system, which seeks to centralize authority in the mayor's hands, suffers noteworthy shortcomings. An elected mayor may lack the managerial, planning, and budgeting skills needed to capably direct the affairs of a big city. Once in office, an elected mayor may also be unduly influenced by political and partisan considerations.

The council-manager system offers the values of nonpartisan, trained, professional administration. Governance under the council-manager system emphasizes cooperation more than conflict. However, city council members, mayors, and managers often overstep their roles, which are not clearly demarcated, resulting in conflict. The council-manager system also does not always provide the strong leadership that big cities desire; in a tough and diverse political environment, a city may require a strong executive elected citywide, a leader who can command the attention of the media and legitimately claim to speak for the people.

Over the years, cities have modified and adapted their formal governing structures, borrowing structural elements that have worked well in other communities. As a result, there are few pure mayor-council and council-manager cities in the United States. Instead, cities have hybrid governing arrangements. Mayors govern with the assistance of a professional CAO (chief administrative officer). A fair number of council-manager communities elect their mayor citywide. A significant number of council-manager cities have in recent years increased the formal powers of the mayor's office in order to negotiate with major corporate heads and to get things done. Cities find it desirable to have a person who can speak with one voice when dealing with businesses and negotiating deals to bring new jobs to a city.

No mayor can rely solely on the formal powers of office to get things done. Instead, effective leadership derives from an individual's skill and personal style. Effective leadership requires that a mayor (or other city leader) proactively engage in coalition-building efforts. The successful mayor forms working partnerships with the leaders of businesses and nonprofit institutions, with community organizations, and with other public officials in state, national, and local office. But effective mayoral leadership often proves quite elusive, given the intractable nature of many urban problems and the paucity of power granted municipalities and the mayor's office.

African-American and Latino mayors face a particularly difficult dilemma. When they forge cross-racial political coalitions to promote new investment and job creation in the city, they will often be confronted by activist critics who charge that the mayors have overlooked the interests of poorer neighborhoods and citizens. A new generation of postracial mayors, however, appears to have the comfort level, political skills, and willingness to cross racial lines and work with business and nonprofit leaders and suburban and state officials. Still, such mayors face a difficult balancing act: how to represent the entire local community while steering resources and new opportunities to minority communities and a city's poorer neighborhoods.

The manager-council plan was a key element of the agenda of Progressive Era reformers who sought to "clean up" municipal government and bring "good government" to the city. As the next chapter describes, the political reformers also introduced various other changes in their efforts to improve governmental performance and to diminish the hold that political party "machines" and party "bosses" exerted over municipal affairs. But, as the next chapter further describes, the reforms also had a great impact on local power. The reformed rules of city government served to increase the access to city hall enjoyed by some groups while diminishing the access and influence of others.

KEY TERMS

academic bankruptcy laws (*p. 115*)

administrative subunits of a state, local governments as (*p. 106*)

annexation (*p. 109*)

benefit principle as a justification for user fees (*p. 112*)

chief administrative officer (CAO) (*p. 123*)

city charter (*p. 105*)

classified charters (*p. 107*)

commission form of government (*p. 119*)

council-manager system of government (*p. 120*)

deracialized approach to leadership (*p. 129*)

development impact fees (*p. 112*)

Dillon's Rule (*p. 106*)

dual-majorities requirement for an annexation (*p. 109*)

eminent domain (*p. 108*)

expertise (*p. 121*)

flat-rate tax (*p. 111*)

fragmented local power, city charters and (*p. 105*)

fragmentation of executive power (*p. 118*)

general-act charters (*p. 107*)

high-risk strategy of borrowing money to invest (*p. 114*)

home rule (*p. 108*)

intergovernmental assistance (*p. 110*)

management and administration as areas of responsibility assigned to a city manager (*p. 121*)

Marketplace Fairness Act (*p. 112*)

mission, city council role in determining a city's (*p. 121*)

municipal incorporation (*p. 105*)

new breed of "education mayor" (*p. 115*)

nuisance taxes (*p. 112*)

policy, city council and city manager's joint role in setting (*p. 121*)

postracial black mayors (*p. 131*)

preemption (*p. 107*)

6 | The Machine, Reform, and Postreform City

The formal rules and structures of city government affect who has access to city hall. The formal rules and structures help to determine just which groups receive, and which groups do not receive, the benefits they seek in the local arena. As this chapter describes, the rules that govern the operation of a modern United States city have their roots in the battles of an earlier era between the big-city *political machines* and their antagonists, the urban *reformers*. The reformers largely won the war and rewrote the laws governing local elections, representation, and municipal administration. The reform victory, however, was not total; older machine-style patterns and practices did not entirely disappear.

For much of the nineteenth and the twentieth centuries, strong political party organizations or **political machines** dominated big cities, especially in the Northeast and the Midwest. New York, Boston, Philadelphia, Pittsburgh, Jersey City, New Haven, Albany, Chicago, Cincinnati, and Kansas City all had political machines at major points of their histories. While strong political party organizations were less prevalent in the South and West, "boss rule" also emerged in Memphis, New Orleans, San Antonio, Tampa, and San Francisco.

At its peak power, the urban machine was a top-down organization characterized by **centralized control**. The leaders of the local party organizations—the **political bosses**—gave marching orders to city council members and to ward, precinct, and block captains. The Hague political organization, which ruled Jersey City well into the late 1940s, typified the machine's command structure: "Complete obedience is necessary from the bottom to the top; officials are not supposed to have ideas on public policies, but to take orders."[1] In boss-ruled Chicago, local legislators followed the instructions of party bosses: the city council functioned less as an independent legislature and more as a "rubber stamp" that approved the decisions made by the city's Democratic Party leaders.[2] The political boss was not necessarily the mayor; the fabled bosses of **Tammany Hall**, New York's Democratic Party machine—William Marcy Tweed, Richard Croker, John Kelly, and Charles F. Murphy—issued their orders from offstage.

Political reformers criticized the machine's parochialism, disinterest in the public good, and tendency toward corruption. (See Box 6.1 "Is There Such a Thing as 'Honest Graft'? Corruption and Machine Politics.") The reform movement sought rule changes to introduce "good government" that would undercut the power of narrow-focused and corrupt political organizations. The reformers wanted to free city officials to pursue the "public interest" rather than the orders of political bosses. The reformers sought to place decision-making authority in the hands of competently trained, expert administrators.

The reformers introduced a number of political measures that have stood the test of time and continue to shape city politics today. Most notably, the reformers introduced *civil service systems*, where municipal officials are hired according to test scores and merit, not because of the work they did for a political party in the past election campaign. The reformers also emphasized the *nonpartisan ballot, at-large elections*, and the *voter initiative and referendum processes*, which, as this chapter will describe, are now commonplace features of local government across the United States.

The reforms, however, were not perfect; nor did they always produce "good government." As this chapter will detail, the reformers were concerned with their self-interest, not just with the "public interest." They pursued changes in electoral rules and government structures that had a class and ethnic bias.

The reformers succeeded in "cleaning up" city politics, reducing political corruption and partisan parochialism, and increasing the professionalism of local administration. But these achievements came at a cost. The reforms increased the decision-making power of civil service–protected bureaucracies and professional agencies, with no assurance that these officials would be responsive to citizens. Public dissatisfaction with irresponsive government led to the demand for a new generation of reforms and eventually to the rise of the **postreform city**, where a new generation of reformers has introduced an even newer set of rules in an effort to enhance citizen influence in local government.

HOW URBAN MACHINES OPERATED AND HOW THEY LASTED FOR SO LONG

A POLITICAL TRADING ORGANIZATION

Machine politics was an **exchange process**. The political machine traded favors for votes. The machine rewarded its friends and punished its enemies; it dispensed **specific benefits** (such as jobs and building permits) that were denied to people and businesses who failed to support the machine.

In 2014, critics of New Jersey's Chris Christie accused the governor of reviving machine-style politics when the governor's associates attempted to punish unsupportive local officials by unnecessarily closing access lanes to the George Washington Bridge, causing insurmountable traffic tie-ups in communities where officials did not give sufficient support to the governor.

Box 6.1
Is There Such a Thing as "Honest Graft"? Corruption and Machine Politics

Machine politicians at their worst were notoriously corrupt, taking **graft**, this is payoffs, in exchange for political favors. Extensive money grabbing by New York's Tweed Ring, which in the late 1800s drained millions of dollars from the municipal treasury, took the city to the brink of bankruptcy.

Tammany district leader George Washington Plunkitt, who made a fortune in politics, defended the seemingly indefensible practice of taking graft. Plunkitt disingenuously claimed that there was a difference between "honest graft" and dishonest graft, and that no Tammany official ever made a penny through "dishonest graft," by blackmailing saloon keepers or stealing from the public treasury:

> There's an honest graft, and I'm an example of how it works. . . . My party's in power in the city, and it's goin' to undertake a lot of public improvements. Well, I'm tipped off, say, that they're going to layout a new park at a certain place.
> I see my opportunity and I take it. I go to that place and I buy up all the land I can in the neighborhood. Then the board of this or that makes its plan public, and there is a rush to get my land, which nobody cared particular for before.
> Ain't it perfectly honest to charge a good price and make a profit on my investment and foresight? Of course, it is. Well, that's honest graft.[1]

Plunkitt was a boastful and outrageous character who requested that the epitaph on his headstone be written: "He Seen His Opportunities and He Took 'Em." Of course, despite his protestations, "honest graft" is not at all honest. Today, public officials are prosecuted for using insider knowledge to gain personal enrichment.

Unfortunately, party officials in certain cities and states continue to reflect machine-like tendencies toward influence peddling and corruption. In Atlantic City, New Jersey, the mayor and other elected officials were convicted for having accepted bribes from criminal elements associated with the casino industry. In Bridgeport, Connecticut, in 2003, Mayor and Democratic organization leader Joseph Ganim was convicted of bribery, extortion, and racketeering.[2] In 2013, once-promising Detroit Mayor Kwame Kilpatrick was convicted on federal charges of racketeering and extortion, having steered tens of millions of dollars in municipal contracts to political friends in exchange for kickbacks.

In Chicago, Richard M. Daley's reign for two decade as mayor was marred by a stream of revelations that members of his administration (but not Daley himself) had steered municipal business to political friends and had shaken down contractors for bribes and political contributions. In New York in 2013, revelations of misbehavior by both Democratic and Republican officials stirred memories of Tammany corruption. State legislators accepted cash payoffs for helping businesses to secure licenses, contracts, and other development assistance. In New York City, local Republican leaders demanded that a mayoral hopeful make large campaign contributions to the party in exchange for their support of his effort to win the party's mayoral nomination.[3]

1. William L. Riordan, *Plunkitt of Tammany Hall,* ed. Terrence J. McDonald (Boston: Bedford Books of St. Martin's Press, 1994), 49.

2. Peter F. Burns, *Electoral Politics Is Not Enough: Racial and Ethnic Minorities and Urban Politics* (Albany: State University of New York Press, 2006), 15–16.

3. Michael N. Grynbaum, "A G.O.P Candidate Heard His Party's Message: To Run, You Pay," *New York Times,* April 2, 2013; Michael Wilson and William K. Rashbaum, "Lawmakers in New York Tied to Bribery Plot in Mayor Race," *New York Times,* April 2, 2013. Also see the graphic, "Untangling Two New York Corruption Cases," *New York Times,* April 4, 2013. Defenders of the exchange practice in New York argue that as long as party leaders use the donations for legitimate campaign purposes, the process does not constitute bribery. In 2013, however, criminal charges were filed against State Senator Malcolm Smith, a Democrat, and against local Republican leaders, when Smith gave large sums of cash in an effort to have the officials hand him the Republican party nomination for mayor.

The political machine relied greatly on the **patronage** or **spoils system**. The winning party distributed government jobs and lucrative contracts to its supporters, following the old adage: "To the victors belong the spoils of war." Once again, critics have charged that New Jersey Governor Chris Christie revived patronage-style practices, using the Port Authority of New York and New Jersey, the vast bistate agency that runs the region's bridges and tunnels, as a source of jobs to reward his friends and political loyalists.[3]

IMMIGRANTS AND THE BIG-CITY POLITICAL MACHINE

During the 1800s and early 1900s, large numbers of immigrants came to U.S. cities from Europe at a time when there was no national welfare system to aid people in need. Machine captains offered the new arrivals shelter, emergency assistance, help in securing employment, and other favors—and only demanded one thing in return: that the recipients and their families vote for the machine's designated list of candidates. (See Box 6.2, "Film Images of the City: The Tammany Machine and *The Gangs of New York*.")

The operations of Tammany Hall illustrate the political machine's provision of emergency and welfare-style assistance. During the severe winter of 1870–1871, New York boss William M. Tweed "spent $50,000 of his personal funds in his own ward and gave each of the city's aldermen $1,000 out of his own pocket to buy coal for the poor."[4] Between 1869 and 1871 the Tammany-controlled city treasury gave well over a million dollars to the Roman Catholic Church and other religious charities, assistance that helped solidify the machine's hold among the members of this important New York ethnic group.[5] Machine captains attended weddings, funerals, Irish wakes, and Jewish bar mitzvahs, all in the effort to win votes from the city's diverse ethnic groups.

Yet political machines should not be viewed uncritically as the kindly friend of the immigrants, the poor, and the industrial-age working class. Machine leaders also helped slumlords and the owners of factory sweatshops. The political machine rewarded its business allies with building permits, inspections approvals, city licenses, and lucrative franchises and construction contracts, overlooking the harsh working and living conditions of the urban poor. In return, business owners gave machine leaders either a cash

Box 6.2
Film Images of the City: The Tammany Machine and
The Gangs of New York

Martin Scorsese's *The Gangs of New York* (starring Leonardo DiCaprio, Cameron Diaz, and Daniel Day-Lewis) presents pre–Civil War New York at a time when "Boss" William Marcy Tweed was just beginning his rise to power as the first truly powerful Tammany leader. In an era when there was no municipal fire department, both Tweed and his political rivals organized voluntary fire companies that rushed to the scene of a fire in an effort to earn the gratitude of voters. Tammany assistants also "worked the docks," greeting the Irish immigrants upon their arrival in America on the so-called coffin ships, a reference to the large number of passengers who died during the perilous trans-Atlantic voyage.

The film documents the extreme poverty of the new arrivals and their need for assistance. Scorsese does not portray the machine leaders as benevolent or caring; indeed, the machine's henchmen could be brutal and corrupt. Their sole concern was to win votes and claim power. Gangs and saloons served as the machine's recruiting grounds.

As *The Gangs of New York* recalls, Tammany Hall initially started out as a sort of social club, an organization of nativist Protestants who detested the Irish-Catholic new arrivals. But Tammany's ambitious leaders soon recognized the importance of appealing to the city's burgeoning number of Irish voters who could provide the key to electoral victory.

The political machines in New York and elsewhere operated during a time of fierce interethnic prejudices and rivalries. Upper-class Protestant "high society" resented the growing numbers of Irish Catholics and the waves of immigration that would soon follow. By comparison, the big-city political machine, despite its many shortcomings, was more responsive in meeting at least some of the needs of the immigrants.

kickback or control over a number of jobs for the machine to dispense to its supporters in return for their votes. Machine leaders did *not* fight to improve housing conditions in overcrowded slum tenement districts. Instead, in New York and other industrial-age cities, party officials received payoffs and overlooked the dangerous working conditions that the immigrants faced in urban sweatshops.

Some analysts refer to the urban machine as a **rainbow coalition**, as machine bosses dispensed jobs and other favors widely in their efforts to win votes from various ethnic groups in the immigrant city. Such an assessment contains a grain of truth, yet it overly glorifies the machine. The leaders of the urban machine did not seek to generously share benefits with each newly arriving group. For much of the twentieth century, big cities in the East and West were dominated by Irish-led machines with leaders like Boston's

The Political Machine, Sweatshop Labor, and Tenement Conditions: Political party machine leaders often took financial kickbacks from industrialists and landlords. As a result, the machine did little to combat the unhealthy conditions of the slum tenements and sweatshops of the immigrant city. By contrast, social reformers such as Jacob Riis sought improved housing, sanitation, public education, and an end to child labor.

Cigar Makers and Children at Work in a Tenement Home Workshop, New York City, 1890.
Taken by Jacob Riis. http://commons.wikimedia.org/wiki/File:Bohemian_Cigarmakers.jpg.

Young Girls at Work in a Chicago Sweatshop, 1903.
Courtesy of Chicago Historical Society. http://commons.wikimedia.org/wiki/File:1903sweatshopchicago.jpg.

legendary Michael J. Curley, who distributed patronage jobs mostly to the city's working-class Irish, giving relatively few jobs to the members of other ethnic groups. In Chicago, the Irish-led Democratic machine similarly reserved the lion's share of municipal jobs and other benefits for its own ethnic members, dispensing lesser benefits to the machine's Polish, Italian, and African-American supporters.[6]

THE MACHINE AND AFRICAN-AMERICAN VOTERS

In a number of cities, the political machine provided rewards to black supporters in an era where African Americans were otherwise largely excluded from politics. But even in cities where black votes were crucial to the machine's electoral success, machine leaders seldom, if ever, dispensed a commensurate share of benefits to African Americans.

In Memphis in the early and mid-twentieth century, "Boss" E.H. Crump astutely recognized that African Americans could provide his margin of victory. He appointed African Americans to positions in the municipal bureaucracy and even named monuments after prominent local black citizens—actions that were rarities in the segregationist Old South. Crump's political lieutenants encouraged African-American voter registration; the Crump organization even paid the poll tax so that a selected number of blacks would be able to vote. Yet once Crump cemented his power in office, he had less need to cater to black voters. His organization reduced the numbers of African Americans permitted to register to vote; the Crump organization also drew back on the benefits it dispensed to the black community.[7]

The Chicago Democratic organization, led in the 1950s and 1960s by the legendary Richard J. Daley, the city's first Mayor Daley, dispensed jobs and welfare-style benefits to its African-American supporters. The Daley organization also had a number of black lieutenants. But the machine would not push for housing and school desegregation.[8] Chicago built a **second ghetto**, a virtual "wall" of high-rise public housing to keep the city's black population from spilling into white ethnic neighborhoods.[9] The Dan Ryan Expressway "was shifted several blocks during the planning stage to make one of the ghetto walls."[10] According to critics, in Chicago, "The Daley political machine functioned not as a ladder of political empowerment but as a lid blocking African-American political empowerment."[11]

WHY POLITICAL MACHINES DECLINED

Why did political machines decline? A growing **national prosperity** and **gains in education** undermined the machine. As voters became more affluent, they no longer needed the benefits the machine offered. Better-educated voters were less willing to trade their votes for the machine's favors.

The **rise of the welfare state** also undercut the machine's power. The government's expanded provision of social welfare and housing services, beginning with Franklin D. Roosevelt's New Deal, meant that citizens no longer had to work for the machine on Election Day and vote for the machine's slate of candidates in order to obtain public services.

For a long time, **federal laws restricting immigration**, especially those enacted in the 1920s, denied the political machine an important pool of potential supporters. With

the spigot tightened on immigration from Europe, political machines had to look elsewhere for support—to impoverished African Americans and Hispanics already residing
in the United States who needed the jobs and limited benefits the machine could provide.

Racial polarizations, however, eventually also took their toll. Over time, black voters withdrew their support from white-dominated political organizations that refused to
challenge the segregated neighborhoods and schools that white ethnics preferred. In 1983,
Congressman Harold Washington became Chicago's first elected African-American
mayor, having challenged the "plantation politics" of a political machine that provided
jobs and other specific benefits to its African-American supporters who had no choice
but to accept their second-class, segregated status in Chicago.

Changes in the mass media further impaired the ability of machine captains to reach
voters effectively. In an age of television and the automobile, city residents no longer
looked to political clubhouse dances and machine-sponsored picnics for entertainment.
Television and computers further changed the conduct of elections. Even in Chicago, a new
"era of cash-based, candidate-centered electoral politics" eventually emerged.[12] Mayor
Richard M. Daley adapted to the times by creating a new-style political machine where

> old-style patronage and corruption now coexist with multimillion dollar campaign contribu-
> tions from global corporations, high-tech public opinion polling, and media manipulation. . . .
> [R]ich individuals and global businesses, law firms, and financial institutions contribute the
> millions of dollars necessary to hire national political consultants like David Axelrod to do
> public opinion polling, direct mail, and slick TV ads.[13]

Axelrod would later achieve fame in the national arena as the top political strategist in
the 2008 campaign that took Barack Obama from Chicago to the White House.

The political **reform movement** also instituted various changes in the electoral
rules to undercut the power of the big-city political machine. The **direct primary**
virtually eliminated the ability of a political boss to control the selection of a party's
candidates for public office. In a direct primary, the voters themselves—not party
leaders—determine the party's nominees who run for office in the ensuing general
election. **At-large voting rules** sought to limit the ability of district-based machine
captains to win office by delivering projects and specific favors to small geographic
constituencies. **Nonpartisan systems** kept party labels off the ballot, forcing voters
to give their attention to individual candidates rather than blindly voting for the party
slate as urged by machine captains.

The Progressive Era (1890–1920) reformers instituted **voter registration requirements**
not just to eliminate fraudulent voting but also to diminish the votes cast by lower-class
citizens and ethnic immigrants, groups that often voted for the machine's slate of candidates.
The reformers argued that voter registration was "good government," but the reform also had
a clear class and ethnic bias. Today, the debate continues as a new generation of reformers
seek to increase participation and expand democracy by relaxing voter registration restrictions. These new reformers promote such innovations as **early voting**, giving people the
option to cast their ballots in the weeks preceding Election Day Tuesday. Other political
actors, however, seek to impose tighter restrictions on voting. (See Box 6.3, "Who Should
Be Allowed to Vote? Manipulating the Voting Rules in the Progressive Era and Today.")

Box 6.3
Who Should Be Allowed to Vote? Manipulating the Voting Rules in the Progressive Era and Today

Should regulations on voting be modified to make it easier for more citizens to vote? Not all political actors are interested in maximizing voter turnout. In fact, some of the Progressive Era reforms actually discourage voting! As discussed in this chapter, nonpartisan and at-large elections, despite their other virtues, are reforms that reduce voter participation, especially by lower-class citizens.

Voter registration requirements similarly reduce voter turnout. When first introduced, voter registration was intended to "clean up" elections, making it impossible for the political machine to rely on **repeaters**—voters who were paid to go from poll to poll to cast multiple votes (to "vote early and often," as the saying goes). Requiring advance registration was a simple way to eliminate this corrupt practice.

But voter registration was also a weapon that entrenched interests used to diminish the ballot-box power of newly arrived ethnic groups. As political scientist Walter Dean Burnham observes, the introduction of voter registration reflected "that old-stock nativist and corporate-minded hostility to the political machine, the polyglot city, and the immigrant which was so important a component of the progressive mentality." Pennsylvania and other state governments in the early 1900s required advanced voter registration only in their largest cities, not in Protestant small towns and rural areas. Rural politicians and other anti-immigrant forces looked to voter registration laws to reduce the ballot-box power of the urban masses.[1]

The class-bias of requiring voter registration is clear. Lesser-educated, low-income voters often fail to make the attempt to register in advance and hence cannot vote on election day. What can be done? As one classic study of voter turnout concluded, "Liberalizing registration provisions would have by far the greatest impact on the least educated."[2]

Present-day reformers are aware of the barriers that serve to minimize ballot-box participation; the new generation of reformers urges the adoption of measures to make it easier for people to vote. **Motor voter** legislation offers citizens the convenience of registering to vote when they receive or renew their driver licenses; citizens do not need to make a separate trip to city hall. **Mobile registrars** can register people to vote where they live, shop, or work. As of 2013 eight states and the District of Columbia went even further, adopting **election day registration** that allows citizens to add their names to the voter rolls as they show up at the polls to cast a ballot.

Early voting, which allows voters to cast a ballot days or even weeks before election day, has become increasingly popular. Thirty-two states and the District of Columbia allow early voting. **Vote by mail (VBM)** systems eliminate the inconvenience of having to vote in person. The states of Washington and Oregon utilize a system where all votes are cast by mail, which effectively spreads voting over a period of weeks. Mail balloting also eliminates the need of citizens to have to find and travel to their assigned polling sites.[3]

But critics object that such relaxations of the rules can lead to election fraud. Not all these critics, however, are motivated solely by a desire to protect the integrity of the electoral process. Republican and conservative activists also worry about the partisan leanings of the new voters, especially as newly registered black and Latino voters will have a tendency to vote Democratic.

"Talk radio" hosts and activist groups aligned with the Republican party argue that allies of the Democratic Party recruit "phantom voters," illegally registering them to vote and corrupting the election process.[4] But a review of the statistical evidence shows that voter fraud in the United States is quite rare; existing penalties, including the threat of jail, effectively deter registration fraud.[5] Still, Republican controlled state legislatures tightened the restrictions on voting, adding requirements that were likely to deter voter registration among younger voters, college students, minorities, and the poor, all groups whose members tended to support Barack Obama.[6]

The debate over voter registration requirements continues. In 2014, plaintiffs challenged a Texas law requiring a voter to produce a government-issued photo ID. Their lawyers argued that such a voting requirement was discriminatory, that it put an unjustified burden on poor people and minorities who in past elections relied on alternative proof of residence, such as bills from a public utility. Plaintiffs claimed that the white Republican legislature was attempting to reduce the voting power of the state's growing Hispanic and black populations. In Wisconsin, the courts allowed a similar voter ID law to take effect.

The courts have given insufficient guidance on the matter, sometimes approving and sometimes disallowing the new restrictions on participation. In September 2014, the U.S. Supreme Court issued a last-minute three-sentence-long decision that allowed Ohio's Republican-controlled government to order counties to close election offices on Sundays. The Republican-inspired law also eliminated "Golden Week," the week-long period when voters could both register to vote and immediately cast a ballot. Ohio still allowed four weeks of early voting. But the closing of election offices on Sunday meant that African-American church leaders could no longer bus members of their congregation to county hall at the conclusion of Sunday services in order to register and vote, as they had done in mobilizing votes for Obama. The Supreme Court order, however, did not offer states and cities clear guidance on just what would and would not be permitted when changing voting rules; the ruling was only a temporary order that allowed the Ohio law to continue to take effect while the Court waited for the state to file a more formal appeal.

Later that same week, the result in a North Carolina case was much different, as a federal appeals court overturned the provisions of a North Carolina law that had eliminated same-day registration during early voting. A majority of the justices accepted the argument that the elimination of same-day registration had a disproportionate impact on African-American voters.[7]

In October 2014, the Supreme Court, in an unsigned order, allowed Texas to use its new photo ID requirements for the ensuing month's elections. But once again the Court did not enunciate a clear set of guiding principles that would tell states just what was and was not constitutionally permissible when enacting new voter regulations.[8]

1. Walter Dean Burnham, *Critical Elections and the Mainsprings of American Politics* (New York: W.W. Norton, 1970), 79–65.

2. Raymond E. Wolfinger and Steve Rosenstone, *Who Votes?* (New Haven, CT: Yale University Press, 1980), p. 79.

3. National Conference of State Legislatures, "Absentee and Early Voting," September 4, 2012, www.ncsl.org/legislatures-elections/elections/absentee-and-early-voting.aspx.

4. Radio talk show host Rush Limbaugh viewed measures to reduce the long lines at the polls and other measures to ease voting as little more than a partisan power grab by Democrats intent on increasing their voting strength, even by having noncitizens cast ballots. See the transcript of the segment "Democrats Move to Make Voter Fraud Easier," *The Rush Limbaugh Show*, February 5, 2013, www.rushlimbaugh.com/daily/2013/02/05/democrats_move_to_make_voter_fraud_easier.

5. Lorraine C. Minnite, *The Myth of Voter Fraud* (Ithaca, NY: Cornell University Press, 2010); Jane Mayer, "The Voter Fraud Myth," *New Yorker*, October 29, 2012; "Myth of Voter Fraud," *New York Times*, October 9, 2011.

6. Wendy R. Weiser and Lawrence Norden, *Voting Law Changes in 2012* (New York: Brennan Center for Social Justice, New York University School of Law, 2011), www.brennancenter.org/publication/voting-law-changes-2012; Stephanie Saul, "Looking, Very Closely, for Voter Fraud: Conservative Groups Focus on Voters in Swing States," *New York Times*, September 16, 2012.

7. Manny Fernandez, "Plaintiffs Claim Bias During Closing Arguments Against Texas Voter ID Law," *New York Times*, September 23, 2014; Jackie Borchardt, "Supreme Court Blocks Early Voting in Ohio, *Cleveland Plain-Dealer*, September 30, 2014; Richard Fausset, "2 New Limits on Voting Are Rejected by U.S. Court," *New York Times*, October 2, 2014.

8. Robert Barnes, "Supreme Court Allows Texas to Use Controversial Voter-ID Law," *Washington Post*, October 18, 2014; David G. Savage, "High Court Action on Texas ID Law Shows Mixed Record on Voting Rights," *Los Angeles Times*, October 18, 2014.

Most significantly, the Progressive Era reformers instituted **merit employment systems** (also called **civil service systems**) that cut off the political machine's supply of job patronage; the new merit rules required municipal hiring decisions to be based on an applicant's test scores and job qualifications. Civil service rules deprived machine leaders of the most important asset—jobs—that they could offer to recruit its army of canvassers and to convince voters to cast their ballot for the machine's slate of candidates. Today, almost every city in the country uses a system of merit hiring. The U.S. Supreme Court, too, restricted partisan-based hiring, firing, and promotion as an unconstitutional denial of an individual's First Amendment rights of freedom of speech, belief, and association.[14] In Chicago, local officials adapted as best they could, modifying machine practices to an age that had become increasingly intolerant of the mass distribution of job patronage. (See Box 6.4 "Machine Patterns in Post-Machine Chicago.")

WHO WERE THE REFORMERS? THE IDEOLOGY AND BIAS OF THE REFORM MOVEMENT

The Progressive Era reformers argued that a modern big city could not afford patronage, payoffs, and political favoritism. The reformers sought to run a city "like a business," vesting decision making in the hands of highly skilled managers trained in technical areas such as planning, civil engineering, budgeting, accounting, and personnel management.

Box 6.4
Machine Patterns in Post-Machine Chicago

Like all big-city machines, the power of the Chicago Democratic organization has declined over the years. But despite the city transformation, numerous machine-style practices persist in Chicago.

Richard M. Daley, like his father the legendary "Boss" Richard J. Daley, sought to centralize power in city hall throughout his twenty-two years as mayor (1989–2011). Richard M. Daley governed in an age where reform measures and judicial rulings sharply restricted the use of job patronage. He could not amass the patronage armies of his father, even though his administration often skirted civil service and competitive bidding rules in order to steer jobs and favors to supporters.

Richard M. Daley adapted classic machine practices to a new age. His governing approach was "part machine/part reform." He did not project the image of an old-style political boss. Instead, he cast himself in the role of a good-government reformer, a capable city executive who can effectively manage and provide direction to the city. He promoted Chicago's downtown as a major center of global businesses. He built Navy Pier and Millennium Park, monumental and "fun" event spaces, to signify the city's postindustrial rebirth. He appealed to tax-conscious middle-class voters, leasing parking garages and Midway Airport and privatizing parking meter collections in order to take advantage of new service efficiencies.

The mayor did not reject as much as refashion the city's machine-politics heritage. The privatization of services provided Daley with a source of pin-stripe or contract patronage; the mayor rewarded political supporters with no-bid consulting contracts, legal work, and other city favors. He received millions of dollars in campaign donations from members of the financial services industry, insurance companies, construction firms, and labor unions.

Like his father during his early years as mayor, the younger Daley sought to win the votes of Chicago's black citizens. Upon taking office, Richard M. appointed a black woman, Avis LaVelle, as his press secretary. His organization awarded funding to African-American churches and neighborhood organizations that supported his agenda. His campaign organization assisted African-American and Hispanic candidates who worked within the confines of the machine's patronage traditions. Daley reached out to the city's new ethnic groups, winning the backing of Alderman Luis Gutierrez, whom Daley would later endorse for Congress. Daley understood the importance of building bridges to the city's growing Latino community. In one of his reelection efforts, Daley won over 80 percent of the Latino vote, leading one political analyst to conclude: "A White-Latino coalition now governs Chicago."

Rahm Emanuel, President Obama's chief of staff, returned to Chicago and became mayor when Daley at long last retired. Emanuel differed from Daley in important ways. Emanuel was a self-styled policy "wonk" who gave strong emphasis to policy analysis and professional service provision, including the development of a long-term infrastructure trust. Nonetheless, the Chicago City Council still largely functioned as a "rubber stamp" that gave virtually uncritical support to the mayor's measures, much as it did under the two Mayor Daleys. During Emanuel's first two years as mayor, twenty-one of the fifty members on the Chicago City Council did not cast a single "No" vote on any Emanuel-backed measure! Emanuel organized political action committees (PACs) to steer campaign funds to his council friends.

Sources: William J. Grimshaw, *Bitter Fruit: Black Politics and the Chicago Machine* (Chicago: University of Chicago Press, 1992), 206–224; John J. Betancur and Douglas Gills, "Community Development in Chicago: From Harold Washington to Richard M. Daley," *Annals of the American Academy of Political and Social Science* 594, no. 1 (2004): 92–108; Frederick C. Harris, "Black Churches and Machine Politics in Chicago," in *Black Churches and Local Politics: Clergy Influence, Organizational Partnerships, and Civic Empowerment,* ed. R. Drew Smith and Fredrick C. Harris (Lanham, MD: Rowman and Littlefield, 2005); Dick Simpson and Tom M. Kelly, "The New Chicago School of Urbanism and the New Daley Machine," *Urban Affairs Review* 44, no. 2 (November 2008): 228–234; Dick Simpson and Constance A. Mixon, eds., *Twenty-First Century Chicago* (San Diego: Cognella, 2013); Steve Rhodes, "The Yes Men," *Chicago Magazine,* April 2013, 76ff; Melissa Mouritsen Zmuda and Dick Simpson, *Continuing the Rubber Stamp City Council, Chicago City Council Report #6, June 8, 2011–February 13, 2013* (Chicago: University of Illinois at Chicago, April 2013), www.uic.edu/depts/pols/ChicagoPolitics/City_Council_Report_April2013. The figures on "rubber stamp" council voting during Emanuel's first years in office are from Rhodes, "The Yes Men."

The reformers emphasized **neutral expertise**, that expert administrators should be able to do their jobs free from political pressures. The reformers argued that political parties were irrelevant to local government, that there was no Democratic or Republican way to pick up the trash, pave streets, or control the flow of traffic.

Yet the reformers were not motivated only by a belief in the virtues of "good government" that eliminated inefficiency and waste. While many reformers sought good government, others were more interested in reshaping the rules of city politics in order to preserve their own power. These reformers sought to keep the growing numbers of immigrants from gaining control of city hall. The classic battles between the political machine and the reformers took place in the late 1800s and early 1900s, an era of deepseated ethnic and class antagonisms. More established social groups sought rules to "bias the electoral arena in their favor."[15]

Upper-class citizens and business owners often dominated municipal reform organizations.[16] They did not wish to pay taxes to provide services to immigrants and the poor. In Sunbelt communities, business-led reform groups kept taxes low by limiting municipal services in African-American, Latino, and working-class neighborhoods.[17] The rule changes they proposed were political weapons designed to undercut the growing power of more recently arrived groups.

Even a more contemporary analysis reveals how reformed voting rules serve to reduce the power of insurgent minorities. San Francisco, for many decades, utilized a system of at-large elections. Minorities won no seats on the city's Board of Supervisors (San Francisco's city council): with their population concentrated in only a

THE AMERICAN RIVER GANGES,

"The American River Ganges: The Priests and the Children" by Thomas Nast. This savage anti-Irish editorial cartoon, from *Harper's Weekly* in 1871, illustrates the degree to which ethnic tensions and hatreds helped to shape the battle between the urban political machine and the political reformers. This Reform cartoon presents Irish priests as crocodiles ready to devour American schoolchildren. New York's Boss Tweed sits above and idly watches the alleged Irish threat to America's schools and its children.

From Library of Congress, Prints and Photographs Division, Washington, DC 20540 USA. http://www.loc.gov/pictures/resource/cph.3a00747/.

portion of the city, minorities were outvoted in council races run citywide. In 1977, the city changed the rules and switched to the "unreformed" system of district elections: the composition of the Board of Supervisors immediately changed. For the first time a black woman, a Chinese American, and a gay activist—Harvey Milk—all won seats in the city's legislature. Each was elected from a district that a minority group dominated. Harvey Milk won easily in a district that included the Castro district, the center of San Francisco's growing gay population. He had lost earlier races that were conducted at-large.

Metropolitan Miami-Dade County's reformed system of nonpartisan and at-large elections similarly serves to dissuade "candidates from running as strong advocates of minority political interests."[18] Inner-city community activists and racial minorities have difficulty winning the support of voters living in the suburban portions of the county. When judicial action in 1993 forced the county to switch back to the unreformed system of district elections, the results were dramatic. The court-ordered introduction of district elections led to an immediate increase in the number of Hispanics and African Americans to the Miami-Dade Metro Commission.

THE REFORMS AND THEIR IMPACT

Chapter 5 reviewed two reforms in the structure of local government: the council-manager and commission systems of government. We now examine other structural reforms that have had a lasting influence on city politics.

AT-LARGE ELECTIONS VERSUS DISTRICT ELECTIONS

The reformers disliked district elections, which, they argued, led to parochialism, as each council member fought for projects that brought benefits to their small geographic districts rather than the city as a whole. The reformers sought to replace district elections with a system of **at-large elections**, where candidates for legislative office run citywide and must seek out issues that serve the entire city. The reformers further argued that an at-large system would enable more high-quality candidates to be members of the city council, as the best-qualified candidates are not scattered, one per district, throughout the city.

Nearly two-thirds of all local governments in the United States use some variation of at-large ballot rules. About one-fourth of the nation's cities elect their entire city council in at-large contests. Another 21 percent of municipalities use a **combination or mixed electoral system**, where some council members run citywide while others are elected from narrower voting districts. Only 14 percent of U.S. communities elect all council members from more narrow geographical districts.[19]

Over the years, however, at-large elections have received substantial criticism for the impediments they pose to the representation of minority and low-income communities. As the San Francisco and Miami Metro cases described above serve to indicate, at-large voting rules can have a discriminatory impact: at-large systems make it difficult for a geographically concentrated or ghettoized minority group to elect representatives to office.[20] When races are run city- or countywide, a minority can be easily outvoted by the city- or countywide majority. In contrast, where elections are conducted by district, a minority group that dominates a relatively small geographical area can elect "one of their own" to the city council.

Neighborhood activists also find it difficult to run citywide. A neighborhood activist may be well known in his or her immediate community but will have difficulty in raising the vast sums of money required for a citywide campaign with its reliance on paid advertising.

For decades, at-large voting rules worked against African-American representation on the Boston city council. Until the 1980s, only a single black Bostonian, Thomas Atkins, was able to win council election. Boston eventually abandoned its at-large system in favor of a mixed system, with nine of the council's thirteen members elected from districts; the change enabled a greater number of African Americans to win council seats.

At-large and district systems of elections favor different types of candidates. At-large systems favor office seekers who are visible citywide or who are acceptable to big donors and a broad base of voters across the city. A system of district elections, by contrast, puts a lesser premium on money and political moderation. Instead, district elections provide a route to office for grassroots activists who have strong neighborhood backing, even if they are not well known outside the district.

AT-LARGE ELECTIONS, THE VOTING RIGHTS ACT, AND THE DEBATE OVER PRECLEARANCE

In the South (and in some northern cities as well), whites resorted to at-large voting systems as a weapon of discrimination, a means of undermining minority voting rights. In the 1960s, at a time when African Americans in the South were gaining the right to vote, twenty county governments and boards of education in Georgia suddenly switched from district to at-large voting rules, in an effort to limit the electoral chances of black candidates. The white-controlled State of Mississippi even passed legislation requiring that all county boards of supervisors and county school boards be elected at large.[21] In the North and the South, the annexation of white suburbs further undercut black voting power; with elections conducted at large, the whites in the newer, more suburban areas of the city could help whites in the old city to outvote a city's growing African-American population.

The national government responded to such abuses by passing the **Voting Rights Act (VRA) of 1965**. One section of the act prohibits cities with a history of discrimination from manipulating voting rules in order to diminish the possibilities of electing minority candidates. Civil rights groups went to court to challenge local at-large voting systems. Dallas in 1991 responded to judicial pressures by replacing its at-large electoral system with a new "14–1 plan": fourteen council members were elected by district, with only one, the mayor, elected citywide. As a result of the switch to district elections, four African Americans and two Latinos immediately gained seats on the Dallas city council. By 2008, racial minorities (four blacks and three Hispanics) made up nearly half of the city council.[22]

In 2012, the Irving (Texas) Independent School District, in the face of threatened legal action, switched from an at-large to a mixed system of elections. Minority parents had questioned just how the old all-white Irving school board, elected at large, could respond to the needs of the district's growing number of Hispanic children. Irving changed its system to have five of seven school board members elected by district, a move designed to increase minority representation. The next year, just outside of Dallas, Latino parents sued the suburban Grand Prairie Independent School District, contending that the district's use of an at-large ballot enabled the school board to maintain its all-white membership.[23]

For four decades, the Voting Rights Act required **preclearance** by the U.S. Justice Department before a community with a past record of discrimination would be permitted to introduce at-large elections or make other changes in their voting systems. Preclearance sought to prevent local actions that would dilute minority voting power.

But a divided U.S. Supreme Court in **_Shelby County v. Holder_** (2013) freed nine states from preclearance requirements that had been in place since the civil rights era.

The Court ruled that the Justice Department would need more "current" evidence of local discrimination for it to mandate that a locality submit a proposed change in voting rules for the Department's approval.[24] The Court was unwilling to continue to deny a city—in seeming perpetuity—the powers that other cities normally possess, simply because of discriminatory actions that the city had taken in the distant past.

Voting rights activists were troubled by the Court's action. They worried that the decision would lead a number of municipalities, especially in the South and the Southwest and especially where Republicans controlled the legislature, to institute at-large voting rules or even simply redraw district lines in an effort to diminish the ballot-box power of African Americans and Latinos.[25] Beaumont and Pasadena (Texas) were considering a switch to an all at-large council, eliminating election districts that were originally created to help assure that Latinos would have representation on the city council.[26]

DISTRICT ELECTIONS, THE ELECTION OF MINORITIES, AND POSITIVE GERRYMANDERING

In cities where the Latino population is geographically concentrated, district systems help promote the election of Latino officials.[27] Yet, compared to African Americans, the Hispanic population is less concentrated or ghettoized. As a result, a switch to district elections does not always produce the same extensive political gains for Latinos as it does for African Americans.[28]

Throughout the history of the United States, political parties in power have resorted to **gerrymandering**—the creation of strangely drawn voting districts—in an effort to increase their own chances in the next election, diminishing the number of seats that the opposing party is likely to win.[29] In more recent years, however, gerrymandering has served new purposes. In a process that can be labeled **positive racial gerrymandering** or **race-conscious redistricting**, legislatures draw boundary lines to create **minority-majority districts** and thus *increase* the likely election of racial and ethnic minorities.

In Chicago, the Latino minority is spread geographically over large portions of the city, making it difficult for a Latino to win office. The city elected its first Latino to the U.S. House of Representatives only after a uniquely C-shaped congressional district was created to increase the chances of such an outcome: two separate Latino sections of the city were connected by a very narrow strip of land that ran along an interstate highway in order to create a Latino-majority district (see Figure 6.1).

The Supreme Court has issued a complex set of rulings regarding the extent to which a state or city may take race into account when drawing district lines to aid the election of minorities. The Court has struck down districts with overly "bizarre" shapes,[30] especially when race was "the overriding or predominant factor" in drawing district lines.[31] Yet, the Court permits state and local officials to consider minority representation as *one* of a number of factors when drawing legislative districts, even districts with oddly shaped boundaries. Consequently, a number of states and localities continue to shape districts in an effort to aid the election of underrepresented African Americans and Latinos.

Figure 6.1   **Chicago's Hispanic Congressional District, the Fourth Congressional District, Mid-1990s**

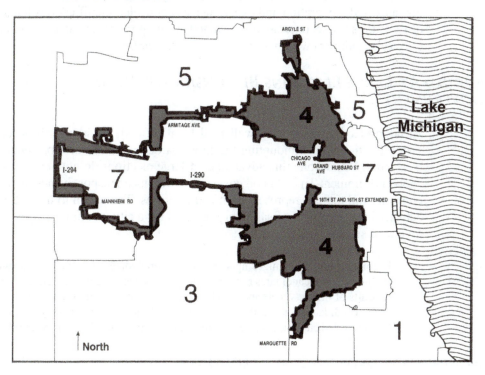

DO AT-LARGE ELECTIONS ADVERSELY AFFECT THE ELECTORAL POWER OF WOMEN, GAYS, AND LESBIANS?

At-large voting rules do *not* discriminate against all underrepresented groups. At-large systems do *not* negatively affect the election of women: studies have discovered that in a number of cities women actually fare slightly better when races are conducted citywide.[32]

Why do at-large elections discriminate against racial minorities but not against women? The reason is simple: at-large election systems hurt geographically concentrated minorities, and women are neither a spatially segregated group nor a minority.

Do at-large elections discriminate against the election of gays and lesbians to local legislative office? Where lesbians and gays reside in a city's identifiable "gay ghetto," a system of district election acts much as it does for African Americans and can aid chances of electoral success.[33] But in cities where the gay and lesbian population is more geographically dispersed, the situation is more analogous to that of women, with district elections providing no clear and consistent advantage.[34] As discussed earlier, San Francisco's switch to district elections led to the 1977 election of gay activist Harvey Milk. Today, however, San Francisco's gay and lesbian population is so large, politically active, and geographically spread throughout the city that gays and lesbians can win local office even when races are conducted citywide.

The 2009 election of Annise Parker as mayor of Houston further indicates the new electability of a gay or lesbian candidate in citywide contests. Parker won by emphasizing her fiscal moderation and experience as controller, qualifications that, in the midst of Houston's hard economic times, gained her support from moderate conservatives and the city's leading newspaper, the *Houston Chronicle*.[35]

SHOULD AT-LARGE ELECTIONS BE CONSIDERED "GOOD GOVERNMENT"?

At-large elections may very well lead local officials to adopt a broader, long-term vision for the city, surmounting the more parochial vision of representatives elected by district. Yet, despite this advantage, at-large elections do not necessarily constitute "good government," if by "good government" we mean responsiveness to neighborhood concerns and the fair representation of minorities. The return to district elections can actually have a number of salutatory benefits for a city, as Amy Bridges reports in her review of southwestern cities:

> Dramatic political changes appeared in the immediate aftermath of changes to district elections. More candidates ran for open seats; issues were more prominent in campaigns; portraits of districts, neighborhoods, and the concerns of their residents appeared in the news; candidates boasted their familiarity with neighborhoods they hoped to represent. Newly elected city councils were more racially diverse than the councils of big-city reform.[36]

NONPARTISAN AND OFF-TIME ELECTIONS

Nonpartisan election is another of the lasting legacies of the reform movement. In a system of **nonpartisan elections** candidates run for office without a party label listed by their names on the ballot. Nonpartisan ballots force voters to focus on the qualifications of the individual candidates and on local issues, not on a candidate's party affiliation or stance on national issues.

Over three-fourths of the local governments in the United States use the nonpartisan ballot.[37] In the West, virtually all local contests for office are nonpartisan. States like Arizona mandate that cities and towns use nonpartisan ballot systems.

Even in Chicago, the city of the legendary Democratic political machine, city council elections are formally nonpartisan. In the mid-1980s, Chicago changed its law to make the contest for mayor nonpartisan as well.

The fact that elections in machine-ridden Chicago are technically nonpartisan underscores the fact that the operations of a nonpartisan system vary greatly from city to city. In communities with a strong nonpartisan tradition, political party organizations play little or no role in the election process. In cities like Chicago, however, partisan activity lurks just below the nonpartisan surface, and party leaders and organizations continue to play important roles in slating candidates, raising funds, and turning out the vote.

Houston is another city where political party activity continues despite the city's nonpartisan electoral system. In 2001, Orlando Sanchez, a registered Republican, ran campaign commercials that featured former president George Herbert Walker

Bush (a Republican and a Houston resident) and post-9/11 hero Rudy Giuliani, the Republican mayor of New York. Incumbent Lee P. Brown, a registered Democrat, was aided by local Democratic organizations.[38]

Nonpartisan election systems have their virtues but also suffer certain shortcomings. The absence of party labels confuses voters: in races for lower offices, a political party label may help voters to choose among candidates about whom they know little. In low-visibility city council and county board races, a party label may provide a helpful clue as to the basic policy orientations of a candidate.

By adding to voter confusion, nonpartisan electoral systems aggravate the **class bias in voting turnout**. Better-educated middle- and upper-class citizens are political self-starters who sort through candidate promises and then go out to vote. In contrast, less-educated and lower-class voters, without the hints provided by party labels, are more likely to be confused and stay home. In cities where elections are truly nonpartisan, there is also no organization of local party workers to telephone, knock on doors, and drive lower-class citizens to the polls on Election Day.

By reducing the turnout of lower-class voters, nonpartisan elections are generally seen to have a partisan bias. Hence it should come as little surprise that Arizona's Republican-controlled state legislature in 2010 passed a measure to force Democrat-dominated Tucson to remove party labels from the local ballot.

Nonpartisan elections for school board are often marred by extremely low voter turnout. Turnout is further reduced when school contests are scheduled for a date when there are no races for other offices on the ballot. Reformers argued that the **off-year** or **off-time** (or **off-cycle**) **scheduling of elections** for school board and other local offices allows voters to focus on the issues unique to the race at hand. The reformers argued that candidates for offices such as a school board should not have to answer questions that arise from more prominent contests.

Yet when nonpartisan local elections are held on dates when no other electoral contests are scheduled, turnout can run as low as 10 to 15 percent—oftentimes even lower! Such poor voter turnout undermines the democratic nature of elections. When voter turnout is extremely low, organized interest groups with a material stake in an issue enjoy increased power. Teachers and other employees of the school system and their immediate families, for instance, make up much of the turnout in local school elections and bond referenda.[39]

Scheduling local and school elections for the same date as national or even state elections would help increase voter participation in local contests.[40] Changes to allow early voting and online voting, too, can be expected to result in small improvements in voting turnout. But Democrats and Republicans continue to be divided when it comes to adopting measures to promote greater voter turnout.

In riot-torn Ferguson, Missouri, habitually low rates of African-American participation were compounded by an electoral system guaranteed to maximize voter disinterest: nonpartisan elections were held in April in odd-numbered years when there were no elections of importance to attract voters to the polls. The off-time scheduling of municipal elections served to diminish African-American representation in Ferguson, the St. Louis suburb that in 2014 suffered an outbreak of civil disorder after the police shot an unarmed young black male. Ferguson has a population that is majority African American, yet whites control the city council (five of six seats) and the city's mayoralty.

INITIATIVE, REFERENDUM, AND RECALL: REFORMS FOR DIRECT DEMOCRACY

Reformers of the Progressive Era of 1890 to 1920 argued that the railroads and other elite interests had effectively seized control of legislatures; elected officials were serving the will of powerful interests, not the people. The Progressives instituted three **direct democracy reforms**—the *initiative, referendum,* and *recall*—to restore the power of the people, that is, to give citizens more direct say in policy making, thereby weakening the grip that powerful private interests held on the political process.

Today, the tools of direct democracy, especially the referendum and recall, can be found in states and communities across the United States. But there are important regional variations. The three institutions of direct democracy are commonplace, almost universal, features of local government in the Southwest and the West. Yet, while 90 percent of cities in the West allow for the initiative and recall, only a third of mid-Atlantic states permit such ballot alternatives.[41]

To a great degree, the direct democracy reforms have delivered on their promise. Citizen groups use the initiative, referendum, and recall to force government officials to be more responsive to citizens' needs. Yet each of the direct democracy tools is imperfect and has also received vast criticism. Quite significantly, in recent years, powerful interest groups, too, have shown the ability to use the tools of direct democracy to advance their interests rather than the people's interest.

THE INITIATIVE AND REFERENDUM

Under the **citizens' initiative**, or more simply the **initiative process**, the voters themselves write and then cast ballots on a proposed piece of legislation, bypassing a legislature that has lost touch with the people. Where the initiative is permitted, the laws (or constitution) of each state and locality specify the number of signatures that citizens must gather to put a proposed piece of legislation or a city charter amendment before the voters.

Critics argue that the initiative process is fundamentally flawed. Initiatives are often poorly drafted and subject to legal challenge. More important, the initiative bypasses the processes of **representative government** that allow elected officials to balance the competing perspectives of different groups of voters. Legislation by initiative does not allow for fine-tuning and compromise; voters simply cast their ballots "Yes" or "No" on the measure as it is written on the ballot. A proposal's backers are likely to exaggerate the measure's benefits. Opponents, in their media advertising, likewise exaggerate the ills likely to result from voter passage of a ballot measure. Amid a flurry of specious claims, popular passion and half-truths may overtake reason.

California's **Proposition 13**, the very important 1978 measure that limited property taxes in the state, illustrates both the virtues and the shortcomings of the initiative process.[42] Voters took the steps to enact Proposition 13 when the state legislature proved irresponsive to the demands of Californians for much-needed relief from soaring property taxes. The tax reduction measures embodied in Proposition 13 and similar measures that followed over the succeeding years garnered strong public approval.

Yet California's voters did not foresee numerous adverse impacts that resulted from the passage of Proposition 13. The initiative did give homeowners significant tax relief, but it also wound up giving the lion's share of the tax reductions to big corporations and other large property holders. The resulting revenue losses forced sharp cutbacks in municipal services and the public schools.[43] In an effort to find new ways to fund basic services, local governments raised user charges and fees, a move that further hurt lower- and middle-income residents and schoolchildren.[44] Proposition 13 even wound up diminishing local control of education: caught in a fiscal bind, school districts accepted additional fiscal assistance and accompanying regulations from the state of California. Education in California became increasingly dependent on decisions made in the state capital.[45]

In San Diego, Proposition 13 virtually paralyzed the city, as municipal officials found that they could not raise the necessary revenues to support popular services. Local officials responded with "creative financing schemes," including the use of city pension funds to fund day-to-day service provision, a "dubious practice" that put pensions at risk and led to a new financial crisis.[46]

Modern-day initiative campaigns can be quite expensive; as a result, this form of direct democracy may represent some people and interests more than others. Business interests, for instance, can hire **paid petition circulators** who secure the required number of signatures to place a measure on the ballot; signature gathering no longer serves as a proxy indicator for the people's genuine interest in a proposed measure.[47] The costs of pollsters, advertising specialists, and other members of a highly-paid, professional **"initiative industry"**[48] further diminishes the grassroots direct-democracy ideal.

The gambling industry effectively financed the ballot campaign that brought a state lottery to California and casinos to Atlantic City (New Jersey) and major cities in Ohio. In the state of Washington, Microsoft cofounder and billionaire Paul Allen, owner of the Seattle Seahawks, spent over $10 million on an initiative drive to have state taxpayers fund a new football stadium. The measure passed with 51 percent voter approval.[49]

The **referendum** is similar to the initiative, except that the process typically starts not with voter signatures but by a decision of the legislature to put an item before the citizens for their approval or disapproval. In some cities and states, citizens can petition for a referendum or public vote on a bill that has previously been passed by the city council or state legislature. In Ohio and Wisconsin in 2011, aggrieved public workers gathered signatures to put on the ballot a referendum to repeal the controversial state laws that restricted the collective bargaining rights and health benefits of schoolteachers and other public servants. In Ohio, voters repealed a recently passed state law that had sought to reduce the benefits offered police officers and firefighters as well as school teachers.

In numerous cities, especially in the Sunbelt, neighborhood, taxpayer, and environmental groups have at times used the initiative and referendum processes to counter the power of local growth coalitions. In a process that has been called **ballot-box planning** or **electoral land-use planning**, voters angered by classroom overcrowding, increased pollution, traffic congestion, and the prospects of additional taxation resorted to the initiative and referendum processes to stop unwanted development projects. In Seattle, grassroots activists pushed for the enactment of Initiative 31, the Citizens' Alternative Plan to slow the pace of downtown skyscraper and office development. Seattle activists also turned to the initiative and referendum routes to commit the city to the construction of a monorail, a system that would be financed largely by a new tax levied on automobiles.[50]

In San Francisco in 2014, Proposition K, the so-called "Housing Affordability Initiative," sought to gain voter endorsement for the construction of 30,000 units of new housing, with at least one-third set aside for low- and middle-income tenants. Housing in this price range was quickly disappearing in San Francisco amid the soaring home prices that accompanied the city's tech boom. But a number of local housing activists and experts decried that the measure, which was advisory only, would actually do little to slow the pace of neighborhood transformation. Proposition K was a watered-down version of an earlier affordable housing measure that developers and city leaders had feared would result in extensive delays that would obstruct the construction of market-rate housing.[51]

Antigrowth measures adopted at the ballot box tend to be more extreme than the measures adopted by city councils.[52] In San Francisco, voters approved Proposition M, which placed a cap on annual new construction and required developers to pay various **linkage fees** to support affordable housing and other public services. Proposition M is one of the toughest antigrowth measures in the United States. Developers and advocates of new construction have, over the years, proposed new laws to replace Proposition M. Yet despite the outcries of developers, in San Francisco, as in San Diego and other California cities, measures such as Proposition M have not brought new development to a halt. Developers simply have provided new public amenities and made whatever other compromises are required by the law.[53]

THE RECALL

When resorting to the **recall process**, citizens sign petitions to hold a special vote to decide whether an official should be removed from office before the normal end of the official's term. The threat of a recall election can lead an elected official to pay greater heed to the wishes of constituents.

In a number of cities and suburbs, recall efforts are commonplace. In 2008, the citizens of tiny Arlington, Oregon (population 600), decided by a narrow vote to remove Mayor Carmen Kontur-Gronquist from office after pictures on MySpace showed the scantily clad single mother posing on a fire truck. In Omaha, Nebraska, mayoral recall elections are so frequent that they are considered a routine feature of the local political landscape.[54]

Where states permit local recalls, a number of big-city mayors have had to deal with the threat of removal. Cleveland's Dennis Kucinich and San Francisco's Dianne Feinstein were two mayors who fended off recall efforts and were able to complete their terms in office. In 2008 anti-immigrant forces attempted to oust Phoenix Mayor Phil Gordon for failing to take aggressive steps against illegal immigrants. But the Phoenix effort fizzled when recall organizers failed to submit the necessary number of signed petitions.[55] Billionaire Norman Braman helped fuel the 2011 effort that recalled Miami-Dade Mayor Carlos Alvarez, a campaign that was prompted by the county's decision to raise property taxes in an effort to reduce its budgetary shortfall—at the same time that the county also awarded large pay hikes to county employees and members of the mayor's staff.[56] An amazing 88 percent of voters chose to oust Alvarez!

Critics argue that recall efforts intrude on responsible, representative government. Under the threat of a recall, an elected official may be more responsive to the demands of recall organizers than to the needs of the general public. Recall efforts can also be overused. In some communities, anti-tax activists begin a recall campaign any time a local official considers raising taxes, even when a revenue increase is needed to keep schools open or to get a community out of a tight fiscal squeeze. In San Jose, a special 2009 local recall election was scheduled after Councilwoman Madison Nguyen voted to refer to the local commercial strip as "the Saigon business district" instead of "Little Saigon,"[57] the name preferred by many of the city's Vietnamese refugees who had fled communism.

Recall elections can also be used to reinforce local exclusion. In wealthy suburban Westport, Connecticut, a recall attempt was launched when school board members voted to admit twenty-five inner-city students to Westport schools. In affluent Birmingham, Michigan, city commissioners who voted to provide subsidized housing to the poor and the elderly were recalled from office.[58]

The nation's most dramatic instance of a successful recall election occurred in 2003, when Californians removed Gray Davis from the governorship, only a year after he had won reelection, replacing him with Arnold Schwarzenegger. Recall advocates argued that Davis had covered up the extent of the state's fiscal difficulties and had failed to initiate steps to alleviate the state's fiscal crisis.[59]

CIVIL SERVICE AND MERIT PERSONNEL SYSTEMS

As mentioned earlier, **civil service personnel systems** provide for the recruitment and advancement of government workers on the basis of merit. Merit-system rules reduced patronage hiring and, instead, enable municipal governments to recruit better-qualified workers. Civil service protections also make it difficult for elected officials to fire municipal workers for partisan reasons; civil service affords career public servants the protection they need to do their jobs free from improper political intrusion.

The introduction of civil service systems changed local government for the better. Still, despite their achievements, civil service protections also come with a cost: they compound problems of governmental performance and accountability. Detailed hiring procedures, fixed pay schedules, and regulations that make it difficult to fire or even transfer a worker to a new position all wind up diminishing the flexibility that a municipal manager requires when attempting to form performance-oriented work teams. The manager of a municipal agency cannot easily dismiss an underperforming worker. Critics charge that civil servants enjoy the equivalent of lifelong tenure protection and, as a result, do not have to work especially hard or even readily follow the directives of superiors.

Management experts often recommend that the civil service protections be relaxed in order to improve the performance and efficiency of government operations. Cities with a strong good-government ethos and an active investigatory media may find that they can modify civil service regulations with little risk. However, in Rhode Island, Delaware, Illinois, Maryland, West Virginia, and New Jersey—states with a relatively current history of political corruption and cronyism—any relaxation of civil service rules could open the door to machine-style abuses.[60]

Nor do municipal hiring systems in all cities truly reward merit. Municipalities that award "bonus points" to veterans effectively discriminate against the hiring of women.[61] In Los Angeles, Mayor Eric Garcetti suspended recruitment by the city's fire department amid revelations that special coaching sessions for LAFD family members and special application procedures were used to give the relatives of existing firefighters a considerable advantage over other applicants who had passed the written exam. Garcetti argued that procedures that allowed for **nepotism** or the hiring of relatives to continue a tradition of family service in a municipal department effectively undermined racial and gender diversity, discriminating against the members of racial minority groups and women applicants who enjoyed no such insider connection.[62]

REFORM'S LEGACY: THE GROWTH OF BUREAUCRATIC POWER

Merit personnel systems and other reforms have had the unfortunate consequence of bureaucratizing city government. As already indicated, mayors and city managers discovered that they could not even easily dismiss officials who refuse to follow their policy leads. (See Box 6.5, "Los Angeles: Can Anyone Fire Chief Gates?") The political reform movement increased the expertise and skill set of city government, but the reforms often also increased the insularity and diminished the accountability of public workers. Civil service and other reforms produced a city that is "well-run but ungoverned." In too many cases, municipal bureaucracies have become "'islands of functional power' before which the modern mayor stands denuded of authority."[63]

Municipal agencies are such important centers of power in the reformed city that political scientist Theodore Lowi refers to them as the **New Machines**.[64] Dissatisfied with the arrogance and "distance" of bureaucratic structures, citizens soon began to seek a new generation of reforms to debureaucratize local government and make it more flexible and responsive to the needs of individual citizens and neighborhoods.

A NEW GENERATION OF REFORM

Racial minorities, middle-class taxpayers, school parents, grassroots activists, and environmentalists all complain about the lack of responsiveness of city officials. Their complaints, beginning in the 1960s and 1970s, resulted in a new generation of reform legislation. In contrast to the reforms of the Progressive Era, the new reformers do not focus so narrowly on cost-cutting efficiency; instead, they seek to enhance the democracy, responsiveness, and fairness of local government.

The new reformers argued for increased citizen participation in government (a matter that will be discussed in greater detail in Chapter 7). Cities reinstalled district elections (or introduced a system that mixed district and at-large representation) in an effort to increase the responsiveness of council members to neighborhood concerns. New ethics laws and campaign finance regulations sought to reduce the influence that "big money" enjoys in the local political arena. In some cities, the new reformers also strengthened the powers of the mayor's office so that the city could act quickly and speak with one voice in the pursuit of jobs and economic development.

Over the past decades, San Jose, Long Beach, Sacramento, Stockton, Oakland, Watsonville, Escondido, Tacoma, San Antonio, Dallas, Fort Worth, El Paso, Albuquerque,

Box 6.5
Los Angeles: Can Anyone Fire Chief Gates?

In 1992, a tense Los Angeles awaited the verdict in the trial of four police officers accused of beating a black motorist, Rodney King. The beating had been caught on videotape and was so dramatic that the footage was aired again and again on television. It showed a circle of officers repeatedly kick and club the fallen King as he attempts to rise from the ground. The trial took place in white suburban Simi Valley, to avoid the turmoil and emotions swirling around Los Angeles.

A tense Los Angeles awaited the verdict. A potential riot situation was in the making, as there was always a chance that, despite the videotape, a jury would fail to convict the officers.

Los Angeles police chief Daryl Gates did not take direct charge of the situation, deciding, instead, to attend a political fundraiser. When the jury announced its "Not guilty!" verdict, inner-city areas of Los Angeles became the sites of spasms of violence. The police quickly withdrew from the South Central riot area, for fear that their continued presence would only serve to precipitate new incidents of violence.

The withdrawal, however, was counterproductive, as it allowed the violence to escalate. One particularly dramatic piece of televised news footage showed a gang of violent thugs pulling a driver, Reginald Denny, from his truck, kicking him, and dropping a cement block on his head. There were no police officers in sight.

Mayor Tom Bradley and other critics sought to remove Chief Gates from office. The chief had refused to discuss riot preparations with the mayor. Mayor Bradley and Chief Gates did not get along. As Gates later revealed in his memoir, he and the mayor "were scarcely on speaking terms"; they had learned over time "to tolerate each other, barely speaking only when we had to, mainly by telephone."[1] But the mayor lacked the formal authority to fire the city's "top cop."

Los Angeles is known as America's most reformed big city. The political reform movement in Los Angeles wrote a charter that gave professional department heads virtual independence from elected leaders. Chief Gates' successor, Willie Williams, observed that the city's top cop was under no legal obligation to meet with the mayor: "I don't have one operating superior. . . . The first six months I thought I was mayor!"[2]

Gates' mishandling of the South Central disturbances coupled with the revelation of other scandals in the Los Angeles Police Department soon led voters to change the city charter, making the police chief subject to reappointment every five years.

1. Daryl F. Gates, *Chief: My Life in the LAPD* (New York: Bantam Books, 1992); see also: Raphael J. Sonenshein, *Politics in Black and White: Race and Power in Los Angeles* (Princeton, NJ: Princeton University Press, 1993), 210–226; and Lou Cannon, *Official Negligence: How Rodney King and the Riots Changed the LAPD* (New York: Books/Random House, 1997), 121–122; Raphael J. Sonenshein, "Memo to the Police Commission: Govern Now and Spin Later," *Los Angeles Times*, December 10, 2001.

2. Los Angeles police chief Willie Williams, comments to the annual meeting of the National Civic League, Los Angeles, November 13, 1992.

Richmond, Montgomery, Charlotte, and Raleigh all reinstituted district elections or created new hybrid or mixed electoral systems. Many of the changes were made in response to lawsuits brought by ethnic and racial minorities. San Mateo County, south of San Francisco, settled a lawsuit brought by Latino and Asian plaintiffs, ending its holdout status as the last California county still using countywide electoral contests. In 2013, Anaheim, the largest city in California still using citywide election, found itself in court facing a similar legal challenge.

The Pasadena Unified School District and numerous other school districts in California, switched to district elections, a result of the 2001 California Voting Rights Act, which prohibits school districts and other local governments from using a system of at-large elections that "impairs" the ability of a minority group "to elect candidates of its choice" or "to influence the outcome of an election."[65] In Seattle a grassroots group sought the passage of a charter amendment to allow for the election of half of the city council by district, a move that would increase the council's responsiveness to neighborhood concerns.[66]

San Diego, Oakland, San Jose, Sacramento, Stockton, Richmond, and Cincinnati all increased the power of the city mayor, diminishing the authority of the city manager.[67] Kansas City Mayor Emanuel Cleaver argued that Kansas City could no longer afford to have a mayor who was little more than a prominent member of the city council:

> Kansas City is now a big-league city, and when the mayor of the city sits around with the president and CEO of a major corporation trying to get them to relocate here, the mayor is at a disadvantage, because other mayors can cut the deal at the table. We are at a disadvantage in many instances when we are out competing.[68]

Sacramento Mayor Kevin Johnson similarly argued for charter changes to give the mayor's office additional powers over budgeting and personnel.[69]

ETHICS LAWS AND CAMPAIGN FINANCE REFORM

Conflict-of-interest laws and **requirements for financial disclosure** seek to increase public awareness of the ties that public officials have with business interests and big campaign donors, ties that may raise questions of impropriety. **Open-meeting laws**, often called **sunshine laws**, prohibit government officials from conducting public business in unofficial gatherings that are closed to the public. Yet, in numerous cities, officials evade legal mandates for transparency. California state law bars public officials from doing business in closed forums. For a number of years, however, the Los Angeles County Board of Supervisors met in informal sessions where it reached a consensus on 90 percent of the board's business that was later formalized in a public vote.[70]

Local **campaign finance reform** measures seek to limit the influence of private money in politics. Albuquerque, New Mexico, has a **limit on campaign spending**, setting a ceiling on the total amount that a candidate can spend in an electoral race. New York, San Francisco, and Austin (Texas) are among the cities that impose a limit or **ceiling on political contributions**. New York City for 2013 set a limit of $2,750 for an individual's contributions to a city council candidate and $4,950 to a candidate for mayor or other citywide office. Contractors and people "doing business" with the city faced even more stringent restrictions: a limit of $250 in donations to a city council candidate and $400 to a mayoral hopeful. Pasadena, Claremont, and Santa Monica (California) and Madison (Wisconsin) are among the cities that bar or impose very strict **limits on the acceptance of gifts by city officials**.[71]

Ceilings on the contributions that an individual can make to a political campaign forces a candidate to search for a broad funding base, decreasing the obligations that an office seeker may owe to a few wealthy donors. Beyond that, however, the reform measures have not had a great impact on local politics. Finance reform rules have not really helped to stimulate new electoral competition by lowering the financial threshold to candidates.[72]

Restrictions on campaign spending, especially limits that are set unduly low, may even lessen the ability of a campaign to reach and educate voters. Austin, Texas, sets a limit of only $350 on the amount that an individual or political action committee can contribute to a candidate for municipal office. Austin also limits the **bundling** of campaign contributions, the total amount in individual donations that a lobbyist assembles and then presents to a candidate. After discovering that a handful of lobbyists had each assembled more than $60,000 in contributions that they then delivered to individual candidates, Austin enacted tough restrictions: a lobbyist cannot bundle more than $1750 in donations to a candidate for local office.[73]

Albuquerque has taken an even stronger approach in its effort to minimize the influence of private money. Albuquerque provides **full public funding** of citywide campaigns: the city's taxpayers pay for the candidates' campaign bills. Portland, Oregon, similarly funded the campaigns of local candidates, but voters in 2010 repealed the system, concerned about its costs.

About a dozen communities (including Austin, Boulder, Long Beach, Los Angeles, Miami-Dade County, New York, Oakland, Petaluma, San Francisco, and Tucson) provide for the **partial public funding** of elections, where taxpayer funds can reduce candidates' reliance on special interest money. Candidates who choose to accept public money voluntarily agree to limit their overall campaign spending and to abide by various accompanying campaign rules. New York City requires recipients of public funding to engage in a series of public campaign debates. The city offers a generous 6:1 match of public money for individual contributions up to $175, an incentive to get candidates to accept public funding and abide by its limits and rules. As participation in New York's incentive system is voluntary, the approach does not violate a candidate's free speech rights.[74]

Still, U.S. Supreme Court rulings have severely undermined local as well as state and national efforts to reduce the influence of money in political campaigns. The Court's very important 1976 ***Buckley v. Valeo*** decision created an **independent expenditures** loophole in campaign finance laws. Candidates and citizens have a First Amendment right of free speech that they cannot be compelled to surrender. Candidates and independent groups (and even political parties, as the Court later added) have a constitutional right to spend unlimited amounts of money in political races, unless they voluntarily choose to participate in a public funding system and surrender that right. In 2010, the Supreme Court overturned federal laws that barred corporations and labor unions from making campaign contributions.[75] The next year, the Court's ruling in *Arizona Free Enterprise* *v. Bennett* (2011) cast doubts as to the constitutionality of state and local public funding systems that give additional funds to a candidate who faces a wealthy or well-financed opponent who refuses to abide by government-established voluntary limits on spending.

In 2013, a federal court, citing First Amendment concerns, voided the limits that New York State had placed on the contributions that an individual can make to an independent-expenditures committee in state and local races. The decision opened the way for wealthy donors to create "super PACs" (political action committees) to influence elections.[76]

The judicial rulings led to a virtual explosion of spending in local elections. In Los Angeles, independent expenditures grew to "unprecedented levels" as spending by businesses, political parties, and labor unions reentered the local arena.[77] Court's rulings have given candidates like billionaire New York Mayor Michael Bloomberg a free-speech right to spend vast sums of their own money on their campaigns, making a mockery of municipal attempts to rein in and equalize campaign spending. In 2001, Bloomberg spent $75 million of his own money in his mayoral race, over $50 million more than the amount spent by his opponent. As his opponent's campaign manager observed, Bloomberg "bought it [the mayoralty] fair and square." Bloomberg spent $90 for each vote he received.[78] Running for reelection in 2005, Bloomberg spent $85 million, four times the total spent by his opponent.[79] In 2009, the billionaire mayor spent over $100 million of his own money—$174 for every vote he won.[80]

"Interested money" finds its way into elections. Billionaire real estate tycoon Donald J. Trump testified how he had circumvented a New York State law that limits a corporation's contributions to $5,000; he simply made the campaign contributions through eighteen subsidiary corporations.[81]

TERM LIMITS

In the 1990s, an anti-incumbency mood led voters across the nation to restrict the number of terms that elected officials could serve. Anti-incumbency sentiment was initially fueled by resentment of members of Congress who enjoyed long careers in office. But quite soon, activists turned their attention to the state and local arenas, imposing ceilings on the length of service by subnational legislators and elected executives.

Local term limits spread like wildfire. In 1992, fewer than 300 municipalities had term limits. By 1998, a mere half dozen years later, the number swelled to nearly 3,000.[82] Cincinnati, Houston, Jacksonville, Kansas City, Los Angeles, New Orleans, New York, San Antonio, San Francisco, San Jose, and Washington, D.C., are among the nation's big cities to enact term limitations. Typically, **term limitation measures** allow city and county legislators to serve only two or three consecutive terms in office.

The nation's largest cities tend to limit the mayor to two terms in office, much like the national model that restricts the president. But when small and mid-sized cities are included, the picture is much different: overall, less than 10 percent of municipalities limit the tenure of mayors.[83]

Advocates of term limitations point to the virtues of having citizen-legislators in government. They argue that unduly long legislative careers tend to insulate officeholders, putting some distance between elected representatives and the people.

The attack on electoral careerism certainly makes some sense when applied to Congress where members often have long tenure. However, the movement makes less sense in cities where substantial legislative turnover is the norm. In small- and medium-size cities, city council positions are poorly paid and understaffed. Each election season sees a number of council members leave office—either from frustration or for the opportunity to run for higher office—which, in turn, brings an infusion of "new blood" to the city legislature.[84] Some smaller communities even have great difficulty in finding people willing to serve for such little compensation. A shortage of candidates led more than sixty Colorado communities to repeal or modify their term limitations statutes.[85]

Critics point to the loss of **institutional memory** when term limitations force the few experienced legislators with deep knowledge of local affairs to leave office. Term limitations can produce a legislature made up of novices who have little ability to challenge the information and advice provided by the city manager, the municipal bureaucracy, legislative staff, and special-interest groups. There is no solid evidence, however, to show that a system of term limits actually results in a shift of power to the city manager and other local administrators.[86]

Term limitations do not really pose an insurmountable obstacle to ambitious "career" politicians. Term limitations result in a game of "musical chairs" when officials facing the end of their allowed period in one public office simply announce their candidacy for another office.[87]

In the past two decades, the local term limitations movement has slowed. Los Angeles voters in 2006 eased restrictions, permitting council members to serve a third four-year term. In 2008, the New York City council relaxed restrictions so that its own members and mayor Michael Bloomberg could run for a third term in office.[88] San Antonio once had one of the strictest term laws in the nation, restricting council members to two two-year terms and then banning them for life from other city offices. But San Antonio eventually modified these measures to permit eight years of service on the city council and another eight years as mayor.[89] Facing tough economic times, cities gave new value to political experience and began to look at ways to strengthen—not to limit—municipal leadership.

CONCLUSION: THE POSTREFORM CITY

The contributions of the reform movement are quite substantial. The reform movement reshaped local politics, reducing corruption, patronage, and partisan favoritism and increasing the technical competence and professionalism of municipal administration. The reforms have been so successful that even cities generally regarded as "unreformed" have adopted numerous reform-style measures to improve managerial capacity and to increase public accountability. Civil service personnel systems, sunshine laws, ethics requirements for auditing, budgeting, purchasing and competitive bidding, and the creation of a city-manager-like chief administrative officer (CAO) position are all commonplace features of contemporary local government.[90]

Despite their achievements, the reforms, especially at-large and nonpartisan elections, have also received criticism for diluting the power of lower-class and minority citizens. Other reforms have vested power in the hands of highly insulated municipal agencies and officials. City residents dislike depersonalized program administration.

This has led to a new generation of reforms to increase the responsiveness of municipal agencies and school systems.

The contemporary generation of reformers no longer sees managerial efficiency as the penultimate expression of "good government." Certainly, cities continue to adopt measures to reduce the costs of public service provision and to do more with less. But the new generation of reformers is cognizant of the class and ethnic biases that plagued the earlier generation of structural reform. The new reformers value citizen participation[91] and the ability of government to respond to the different needs of the diverse population groups that make up the modern city. The new reform movement also seeks to strengthen urban leadership and even the capacity for regional cooperation.[92]

In a global age, localist machine-style practices have ceded way to a "new political culture" where municipal leaders emphasize the effective provision of public services, improvements in the quality of city life, and a high-amenity approach to attracting economic development.[93] Even in Chicago, the last big-city outpost of machine politics in the United States, local leaders can no longer depend on the distribution of job patronage; instead, they run for reelection emphasizing their success in having brought new investment and jobs to the city.[94]

KEY TERMS

at-large elections (also known as at-large voting rules) (*p. 152*)

Buckley v. Valeo (*p. 165*)

bundling (*p. 165*)

campaign finance reform (*p. 164*)

ceiling on political contributions (*p. 164*)

centralized control, political machine as (*p. 138*)

changes in the mass media as a cause of the decline of big-city political machines (*p. 145*)

civil service personnel systems (also known as merit employment systems) (*p. 148*)

class bias in voting turnout, the impact of nonpartisan election systems on (*p. 157*)

combination or mixed electoral system (*p. 152*)

conflict-of-interest laws (*p. 164*)

direct democracy reforms (*p. 158*)

direct primary (*p. 145*)

early voting (*p. 145*)

election day registration (*p. 146*)

electoral land-use planning (*p. 159*)

exchange process, machine politics as an (*p. 139*)

federal laws restricting immigration as a cause of the decline of big-city political machines (*p. 144*)

full public funding of election campaigns (*p. 165*)

gains in education as a cause of the decline of big-city political machines (*p. 144*)

gerrymandering (*p. 154*)

graft (*p. 140*)

independent expenditures (*p. 165*)

initiative industry (*p. 159*)

initiative process (also known as citizens' initiative) (*p. 158*)

institutional memory (*p. 167*)

limits on campaign spending (*p. 164*)

limits on the acceptance of gifts by city officials (*p. 165*)

linkage fees (*p. 160*)

minority-majority districts (*p. 154*)

mobile registrars (*p. 146*)

motor voter law (*p. 146*)

7 Citizen Participation

Professional planners and "expert" public servants do not always know best. Despite their advanced training, experts are not always fully familiar with neighborhood conditions and the policy desires of the people they serve. Ordinary community residents have a "practical wisdom"[1] gained from their life experiences and daily living. **Citizen participation** refers to the variety of arrangements that allow local residents to have a greater say in the making of municipal decisions that have an important impact on their daily lives.

Today, citizen participation is a regular feature of municipal life. Federal urban aid programs routinely require recipient jurisdictions to involve citizens when deciding how to spend program monies. Municipal agencies, too, initiate participatory strategies as they attempt to copy the practices of successful private businesses: to serve your customers better, you must first find out what they truly want. But as the advocates of urban democracy point out, the residents of cities and suburbs are no mere *customers* whose preferences a decision maker may find useful to survey. The residents of local communities are *citizens* who have a democratic right to have a say in decisions that affect their lives.[2]

THE EVOLUTION OF CITIZEN PARTICIPATION

The roots of the modern urban participation movement go as far back as the 1950s and 1960s, when top-down urban renewal and highway construction decisions devastated large sections of cities, tearing down housing and displacing core-city residents. Massive land clearance programs unwittingly accelerated the decline of socially fragile urban communities; redevelopment, housing, and highway officials were outsiders who did not live in or understand the communities that they were reshaping. These officials did not see the social fabric that existed in the low-income neighborhoods that were being torn down: they did not see how, especially in low-rise portions of the city, friends and family members helped to care for children and watch over life on the streets. These interpersonal networks were not reestablished in the new high-rise public housing environments that the planners created.

Jane Jacobs, a Fighter for Neighborhoods. In the 1950s and the 1960s Jane Jacobs led the fight against various urban renewal projects, including a proposed new highway that would cut through her Lower Manhattan East Village neighborhood. Jacobs argued for the importance of bringing citizen voices into the decision-making process. She argued that redevelopment projects conceived by outsiders often destroyed the sense of community that existed in poor and working-class neighborhoods.

Photo by Phil Stanziola. From the Library of Congress, Prints and Photographs Division, Washington, DC 20540 USA, http://www.loc.gov/pictures/resource/cph.3c37838/.

State highway officials similarly gave little deference to the objections raised by residents whose homes and communities lay in the path of progress. In New York, San Francisco, Boston, Baltimore, Miami, and Portland (Oregon), to name just a few, the residents of low-income and working- and middle-class neighborhoods rebelled against the destruction being wrought by highway as well as by urban renewal projects.[3]

The revolt against mid-century urban renewal and highway programs led governmental officials to alter program rules to give affected residents a more substantial voice in decisions that would directly impact their neighborhoods. Federal rules required the "maximum feasible participation of the poor" in antipoverty programs.[4] Soon, participatory requirements were made part of the Community Development Block Program, the nation's largest urban aid program, and virtually every other major urban and environmental program.

State ordinances, too, have helped promote citizen participation; but state requirements are generally less extensive than are federal requirements. Only half the states,

Box 7.1
**Who Participates in Citizen Participation? New York,
Minneapolis-St. Paul, and Los Angeles**

Do requirements for citizen participation empower racial minorities and the urban poor? Or do upper-middle-class citizens and higher-educated professionals take maximum advantage of the opportunities created by participatory processes? A review of the evidence reveals that upper-status groups have enjoyed considerable success in utilizing processes designed for citizen engagement.

New York City created fifty-nine community boards to enhance citizen influence in decisions concerning neighborhood land use, budgeting, and service delivery. The boards are only advisory, and final decision-making authority rests with municipal agencies. Still, activist community boards have been able to force developers to scale back the size of a development or add off-street parking and other community amenities in return for a favorable board recommendation. In the Red Hook section of Brooklyn, the giant Swedish retailer IKEA gained community board support for a big-box superstore only after agreeing to offer job training for local residents and to set up a shuttle bus to link the store to a nearby subway station in an effort to minimize traffic congestion.[1] In gentrifying neighborhoods, upper-status residents have also turned to community boards to oppose the issuance of liquor licenses to bars that residents fear will be public nuisances. On a more far-reaching matter, New York Community Board 4 played a pivotal role in proposing alternatives that helped bring a halt to Mayor Michael Bloomberg's efforts to build a Jets football stadium and new high-rise office towers in the Hudson Yards area of the City's Upper West Side.[2]

Developers complain that New York's community board system gives too much power to self-anointed citizen activists. But the record shows that the boards mostly seek minor adjustments in a developer's plans and seldom pose a serious impediment to a major growth project.[3]

Evidence from other cities further points to the class bias of participatory systems. In Minnesota, middle-class homeowners, especially in predominantly white communities, used participatory processes to secure their budget priorities.[4] Lower-class residents were less effective. St. Paul's citizen engagement program actually gave funds to a white middle-class homeowner association that resisted participation by low-income tenants.[5] In Los Angeles, homeowners dominated the system of eighty-six neighborhood boards that the city created in an effort to decentralize government. The boards did not adequately reflect the region's considerable ethnic diversity and the concerns of the poor. One study concluded: "Latinos are underrepresented, and boards are disproportionately wealthy, white, and highly educated."[6]

Certainly, in numerous instances, participatory mechanisms do provide an important channel for the voices of disadvantaged residents. In New York City, middle-class professionals joined with their working-class neighbors in community board meetings to fight the pace of gentrification in the gritty industrial Gowanus Canal section of Brooklyn.[7]

Overall, what can we conclude? While participatory mechanisms can help empower marginal groups, participatory devices tend to empower the urban middle and professional classes even more.

1. Bruce F. Berg, *New York City Politics: Governing Gotham* (New Brunswick, NJ: Rutgers University Press, 2007), 24–31.

2. Sumathi Reddy, "A Backlash Against Bars," *Wall Street Journal,* April 19, 2011; Julian Brash, *Bloomberg's New York: Class and Governance in the Luxury City* (Athens, GA: University of Georgia Press, 2011), 161–195.

3. Mark Berkey-Gerard, "Community Board Reform," *Gotham Gazette,* March 6, 2006, www.gothamgazette.com/article/issueoftheweek/20060306/200/1779; Tom Angotti, *New York for Sale: Community Planning Confronts Global Real Estate* (Cambridge, MA: MIT Press, 2008).

4. Susan S. Fainstein and Clifford Hirst, "Neighborhood Organizations and Community Planning: The Minneapolis Neighborhood Revitalization Program," in *Revitalizing Urban Neighborhoods,* ed. W. Dennis Keating, Norman Krumholz, and Philip Star (Lawrence: University Press of Kansas, 1996), 86–111.

5. Mark Schuller, "Jamming the Meatgrinder World: Lessons Learned from Tenants Organizing in St. Paul." In *Homing Devices: The Poor as Targets of Public Housing Policy and Practice,* ed. Marilyn M. Thomas-Houston and Mark Schuller (Lanham, MD: Lexington, 2006), 165–166.

6. Juliet Musso, Christopher Weare, Mark Elliot, Alicia Kitsuse, and Ellen Shiau, *Toward Community Engagement in City Governance: Evaluating Neighborhood Council Reform in Los Angeles* (Los Angeles: USC Civic Engagement Initiative, 2007), 1, www.usc-cei.org/userfiles/file/Toward%20Community.pdf.

7. Hamil Pearsall, "Superfund Me: A Study of Resistance to Gentrification in New York City," *Urban Studies* 50, no. 11 (August 2013): 2293–2310.

for instance, require local governments to publish proposed local budgets or otherwise make such documents available for public inspection.[5]

Given the roots of the citizen participation movement, it is little wonder that citizen participatory requirements are often misperceived as tools intended only to empower the poor. In reality, middle- and upper-class groups are often the primary beneficiaries of participatory initiatives. Middle-class citizens and professionals have the education, skills, and motivation to take advantage of the new channels that governments create to enhance citizen engagement. (See Box 7.1, "Who Participates in Citizen Participation? New York, Minneapolis-St. Paul, and Los Angeles.") Suburban and middle-class citizens have used participatory mechanisms to force changes in the local school curriculum, to stop the construction of projects that they deem harmful to the natural environment, and to fight tax hikes and expensive new stadiums and other growth projects that will bring increased traffic and congestion to their communities.

In more recent decades, efforts at citizen participation have transcended the conflict-based paradigm of the 1960s that saw neighborhood residents and municipal officials as antagonistic opponents. Rather than continuing to view power as a zero-sum game, where one party gains power only if the other party loses, more contemporary perspectives seek "win-win" gains when citizens and public officials work in partnership in sustained **collaboration** that gets things done, and that helps identify effective remedies to quite difficult urban problems.[6]

LEVELS OF CITIZEN PARTICIPATION

As already noted, the past half century has seen a virtual revolution in citizen participation as participatory requirements have become a commonplace feature of public programs. Yet too often, citizen engagement has proven more illusory than real. Entrenched bureaucracies and privileged interests do not always want new players at the table; in such instances, residents are allowed to participate in the decision-making process without being given any real power to affect outcomes.

Sherry Arnstein's eight-rung **ladder of citizen participation** (see Figure 7.1), developed a half century ago, still provides a useful tool to sort through the vast maze of participatory arrangements.[7] As Arnstein describes, all participatory mechanisms are not equal; many are created with no real intent to empower ordinary citizens.

On the bottom of the ladder are participatory devices that she labels *manipulation* and *therapy*, participatory vehicles so rudimentary that they can even be viewed as

Figure 7.1 **Eight Rungs on a Ladder of Citizen Participation**

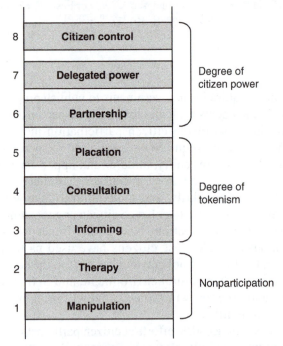

Source: Sherry R. Arnstein, "A Ladder of Citizen Participation," *Journal of the American Institute of Planners* 35 (July 1969): 217. Reprinted with permission from the *Journal of the American Planning Association.* Copyright © July 1969 by the American Planning Association.

nonparticipation. **Manipulation** occurs when agency officials are not concerned with learning what citizens think. Instead, the agency establishes a participatory process as a strategy to make citizens more willing to accept a course of action that an agency has already adopted. The process can be labeled **co-optation**: citizens are brought into the decision-making process and given the illusion of power but are denied any real ability to influence important outcomes.

When participation is viewed as **therapy**, officials again have no great interest in listening to citizens; instead, officials see citizen engagement as a means of helping individuals to overcome their own problems, to help poor people, for instance, to develop a sense of competency and thereby overcome the "pathologies" of their daily lives.

Informing is a one-way flow of information where, for instance, a public official makes a time-consuming presentation at a public meeting (maybe even employing Power-Point technology) that reviews a community problem and outlines the agency's response. The official presentation shapes the meeting agenda and ensuing discussion, allowing members of the audience little time to present and discuss concerns of their own. Such one-way informational sessions offer participants only the most limited opportunity to affect a course of action that in all likelihood has been previously set. As we shall see, citizens require a more structured series of meetings if they are truly to have influence.

On the middle rungs of the ladder are the participatory devices that fall under the categories of *consultation* and *placation*. **Consultation** does embody the willingness of public officials to solicit and listen to community voices. Municipal officials survey the residents of a neighborhood, distribute a questionnaire to the users of a municipal service, and hold public forums and neighborhood meetings in an attempt to uncover residents' concerns. **Community policing** is a noteworthy program that emphasizes public consultation. "Beat meetings" with residents bring neighborhood concerns to the attention of local patrol officers. "Citizen councils" provide a forum for greater discussion between residents and law enforcement officials and help draw the attention of the police to specific problems that a neighborhood faces.[8]

Consultation, however, is no guarantee of power. Effective consultation requires more than a one-time-only mass meeting or even the administration of a questionnaire or survey.[9] A series of meetings or, better yet, the formation of a residents' steering committee or task force that meets regularly with city officials, allows for mutual education, understanding, and compromise. A series of joint work sessions enables residents and public officials to learn about each other's concerns and to jointly fashion collaborative solutions.

Placation occurs where citizen boards and other participatory processes are created with the purpose of muting citizen discontent. Such processes, created in response to bottom-up pressure, can at times provide real channels of influence for local residents. However, such arrangements fall to a lower rung on Arnstein's ladder if a board or committee is constituted so that other members can outvote a neighborhood's representatives.

Placation and even consultation, when inadequately executed, entail the danger of tokenism. **Tokenism** occurs when citizens are given only a few seats on a decision-making board or are allowed to influence only minor aspects of an agency's plans. A good example is provided by the effort of Cincinnati to redesign Washington Park, lying just across from Music Hall, the city's opera house. Washington Park had become a haven for drug users and the homeless. Private and public planners saw the potential of a cleaned up, redesigned, and expanded green space to host public concerts and neighborhood festivals. They envisioned a reclaimed park as key to the rebirth of the low-income Over-the-Rhine neighborhood that abuts the city's central business district. The parks department structured meetings where neighborhood residents were given the opportunity to comment on the designs of park benches, playground equipment, and the park's water-spray play feature. But the meetings did not offer residents an opportunity to challenge the planners' goal of repurposing the park, to have it serve as a centerpiece for the area's gentrification. The expanded park, opened in 2012, provided a new band shell, an outdoor film screen, and underground parking for visitors, but no basketball courts that would attract young African Americans.

Highest on Arnstein's ladder are those forms of participation—*partnership, delegated power,* and *citizen control*—that denote genuine power sharing, a real opportunity for local residents to join city officials in making important decisions. **Partnership** denotes mutual power, where citizens and municipal officials share in decision making. Partnership, in the extreme, may even take the form of a mutual veto, where action requires the consent of both the city and the neighborhood. Such a mutual veto exists when a city superintendent of schools is required to select a new local school principal only from a list of qualified candidates screened by a local community board.

In St. Louis and its Ferguson suburb, in the wake of protests and civil disturbances over the 2014 police shootings of unarmed African-American youth, officials and community activists in both cities discussed the creation of a **police-civilian review board** to help set policing priorities and to review possible instances of police misconduct. While city officials and community leaders recognized the desirability of creating a new process for citizen participation, it was not clear if the board would constitute a true city-community partnership or if it would be only an advisory body. City and community leaders debated the extent to which the new board would have any meaningful say in officer training and departmental policy, as well as the authority, staff, and budget necessary to conduct hearings, gather information, and respond to citizen complaints.[10]

Today, partnership also denotes more positive collaborative opportunities for neighborhood groups and municipal agencies to work hand in hand.[11] As we will discuss in further detail later in this chapter, many **community development corporations (CDCs)** embody the ideal of a working partnership. These neighborhood-based organizations work collaboratively with municipal, nonprofit, and private-sector actors in order to find the funds to build new housing, health clinics, and even supermarkets and other vital commercial facilities in underserved neighborhoods.

Under **delegated power**, municipal officials devolve to a community organization the authority to make a number of significant decisions. Chicago in the 1980s and 1990s experimented with school decentralization, giving citizen-community boards specified budgetary and personnel powers. Dayton, Ohio, similarly gave neighborhood Priority Boards a limited ability to fund local projects. The delegation of governmental authority can be controversial and, at times, even undesirable. In Chicago, numerous school reformers had only limited faith in the wisdom of local parents and the ability of grassroots organizations to turn around failing schools. When the community boards failed to produce results, these reformers changed the law and the direction of school reform in the city, abridging decentralization efforts in order to give the mayor greater control over the city's schools.[12]

Community control exists when residents possess final authority over a program. A neighborhood board—not city officials—operates a facility or otherwise retains final authority in deciding how a program is run and how funds are spent. Not surprisingly, community control is a rather rare occurrence. Public officials are unwilling to abdicate responsibility and cede decision-making and spending powers to citizen groups that lack professional training, that may act on parochial concerns, and that may not even truly represent the larger population they claim to serve. In Los Angeles, the ability of the city's eighty-plus neighborhood councils to develop effective service-delivery partnerships has been undercut by the "disinterest" and "resistance" of administrative officials who see the councils "as annoying distractions from their main work."[13]

TREATING THE PUBLIC NOT ONLY AS CONSUMERS BUT AS CITIZENS AND PARTNERS

As Arnstein observed, many bureaucratic officials are often content with participatory mechanisms that lie on the lower rungs of the participatory ladder. Even public servants who value public participation often view citizen involvement through the limiting lens of consumerism. These public officials use surveys, focus groups, and face-to-face meetings to find out what services users want and just how services can be improved. Such an approach is valuable, but it does not respect residents as citizens.

In a democracy, citizens are not merely **consumers** or persons who receive services provided by the local bureaucracy. In a democracy, local officials should not simply "provide for" people; instead, local agencies must also "work with" citizens. **Citizens** have rights that must be respected, including the right to be effectively heard in agency decisions that have an impact on their lives. Neighborhood and client organizations can also be viewed as **partners** who work with city officials to co-provide improved public services (for instance, by organizing a neighborhood watch to abet community safety). The mobilization of citizens in a public-private collaboration can be critical to the success of a local service program.[14]

Recognition of citizens and citizen rights leads agencies to move beyond the administration of questionnaires and focus groups. An agency that sees itself as working with citizens will exhibit a greater willingness to incorporate citizen-partners into decision-making processes and to have ordinary members of the community serve on committees that meet on a regular basis.

KEYS TO MAKING CITIZEN ENGAGEMENT WORK

What can be done to enhance citizen engagement?[15] First, neighborhood residents are more willing to participate when a city turns over real authority to the citizen bodies rather than simply establishes committees that yield advisory recommendations that municipal officials can ignore. Engagement processes are more attractive to residents when they offer an opportunity to enter into sustained collaboration on the making of important decisions. Los Angeles' system of elected neighborhood councils, by contrast, is structurally weak as the boards possess only advisory power and lack clear channels for routinized interaction with the mayor, city council, and municipal departments.[16]

Second, participatory processes are better received when cities have a demonstrated record of working with community groups and building a culture of participation. In such cities, elected officials and top managers clearly communicate the importance of citizen engagement and dispense rewards that persuade departments to engage in collaborative processes. A municipality's commitment to citizen engagement can also be demonstrated by a line-item in city budgets that provides financial support for participatory efforts.[17]

Third, participatory processes are best instituted throughout the city as opposed to being introduced in only a few troubled neighborhoods. Participatory arrangements created only in a select handful of neighborhoods fail to signify city hall's full commitment to participation.

Fourth, outside assistance is often critical to the success of participatory efforts.[18] (See Box 7.2, "Learning from the Pacific Northwest: Supporting Neighborhood Engagement."). Governmental grants, corporate philanthropy, and nonprofit sponsorship help provide community groups with the financial resources for newsletters, local surveys, the maintenance of community headquarters, and the rental of space for larger community meetings and events. Without outside financial support, neighborhood organizations often find that they are unable to communicate effectively with residents.

The City of Indianapolis created a Neighborhood Resource Center to foster grassroots activism. Nonprofit institutions—including the Lilly Endowment, the Ford Foundation, and the Annie Casey Foundation—played a critical role in funding a Neighborhood Power Initiative that provided staff and training assistance to community groups.[19]

Finally, cities need to develop a variety of tools to promote citizen engagement and dialogue and not be satisfied with crude public hearings that meet statutory program requirements to involve citizens. Government's use of the Internet, as this chapter will soon describe, offers the potential for more extensive information sharing and, if creatively used, for deeper interactions between agency officials and citizens.

What do other innovative participatory strategies look like? In 2006 Oakland, California, Mayor Ronald Dellums sought bottom-up policy development. He appointed 800 residents who met in forty-one separate **citizen task forces**, each focused on making policy recommendations in a fairly narrow issue area. Each task force involved ordinary citizens who met, without pay, for six sessions. The discussions were facilitated by the work of a convener, an ordinary citizen who had interest in the issue and who had received additional training.[20]

Rochester, New York, similarly established a Neighbors Building Neighborhoods (NBN) program, a **bottom-up visioning process** in which the city invited thirty-seven neighborhood organizations to investigate ten "planning sectors," generating reinvestment and service ideas that found their way into the city budget. A city liaison was assigned to each group. Municipal agencies were ordered to respond to each committee's draft plans. The mayor's strong public backing was necessary to ensure the commitment of other city officials to the process.[21]

Box 7.2
Learning from the Pacific Northwest: Supporting Neighborhood Engagement

In Portland, Seattle, and other Pacific Northwest cities, grassroots activism is a prominent feature of local politics. Citizen groups in the Northwest are particularly engaged in efforts to preserve the region's natural environment and fabled quality of life, opposing the threats posed by unbridled growth.

Citizen engagement in the Pacific Northwest is ingrained in the local culture and is an expected part of local decision making. King County (greater Seattle) routinely conducts a series of small-group forums across the county, using volunteers to solicit public feedback on various policy issues. The participants share their opinions, after having first viewed a video and read a summary of the key facts and competing perspectives on an issue. Municipal officials are careful not to manipulate the forums. A citizens' steering committee, not a municipal agency, selects the topics for group discussion.[1]

The City of Seattle offers extensive assistance to help neighborhood groups develop their own plans while respecting the needs of the larger city. A Neighborhood Planning Office and a Neighborhood Matching Fund provide community groups with the staff and financial assistance and technological support in geographic information system (GIS) mapping "to help neighborhood groups do good planning work." The city encourages the building of a long-term collaborative relationship between neighborhood groups and city hall. Seattle also has thirteen district councils. The decentralization of departments further encourages municipal administrators to work with neighborhood groups. The city supports a variety of collaborative efforts, hoping to offer a constructive alternative to grassroots militancy and oppositional politics.[2]

The Seattle and Portland models embody the ideal of grassroots democracy. Still, critics worry that that extensive deference to neighborhood groups can give excessive voice to NIMBY ("not in my backyard") activists opposed to growth, including efforts to bring a halt to new office growth to Seattle's old downtown.

1. "King County, WA Initiates Community Forums Program," *PA Times* (April 2008): 8.
2. Carmen Sirianni, "Neighborhood Planning as Collaborative Democratic Design: The Case of Seattle," *Journal of the American Planning Association* 73, no. 4 (Autumn 2007): 373–387; the quotation appears on p. 374. See also Seattle Planning Commission, *Citizen Participation Evaluation: Executive Summary* (March 2000), www.seattle.gov/planningcommission/docs/part_EXECSM.pdf.

Planning charrettes offer citizens a structured series of sessions in which they work with planning officials on a project's design. **Joint steering committees** and citizen review panels are other devices that enable a small group of residents and public officials to negotiate a project's direction and details.

A few cities have begun to experiment with **citizen juries**, an innovative process where a group of ordinary citizens is given detailed information regarding policy choices. The group then discusses its preferences and possible trade-offs in an attempt to come up with the best, and maybe even the most creative, solution to a difficult problem.

Another participatory technique, **deliberative polling**, takes a similar approach. A deliberative poll does not seek to uncover the present state of public opinion. Instead, the pollster seeks *informed* opinion. The deliberative pollster asks for the respondent's opinion only after the respondent is given detailed and balanced information on the policy issue.[22]

Numerous cities, including Madison, Wisconsin, have turned to technology, using a computer-assisted **geographic information system (GIS)** to generate charts and maps that reveal service patterns and allow for the visualization of development proposals. The materials, which can easily be shared on the Internet, give citizens greater technical information and break the bureaucracy's monopoly hold on information.[23]

THE NEW STYLE OF COMMUNITY ORGANIZATIONS: MOVING FROM PROTEST TO PARTNERSHIP

Formal participatory processes do *not* always allow for effective citizen participation. Sometimes, neighborhood organizations must act outside of official channels. **Community organizing** refers to grassroots efforts by which neighborhood organizations mobilize residents and discover their power resources and other assets. Community organizing refers to "what people can do for themselves," how neighborhood groups press others for action, build their own capacity to run community programs, and, in doing so, "change power relations" to get important things done.[24]

The election of President Barack Obama brought renewed attention to the role played by community organizing in the American city. After finishing college, Obama moved to the South Side of Chicago, where he worked as an organizer for the Calumet Community Religious Conference and its Developing Communities Project. Obama "helped build and guide a small network of grassroots groups that agitated for better playgrounds, improvements in trash pickup and the removal of asbestos from public housing."[25] After finishing law school, Obama returned to Chicago and taught classes on the community organizing techniques publicized by social activist Saul Alinsky.[26]

Alinsky was a renowned and often feared community organizer who worked for the Industrial Areas Foundation (IAF). Alinsky sought to empower the "have-nots" and "have-little-want-mores"[27] by allowing these ignored groups to uncover their own resources and the ability to pressure city officials for action.

Under the **Alinsky/IAF method of community organizing**, the organizer works in tandem with church and religious leaders, union organizers, and other members of a neighborhood who command local respect.[28] Together, they seek to uncover residents' most salient grievances. Identifying injustices, the organizer **rubs wounds raw**, drawing attention to a grievous inequity in order to spur the community to action. The organizer **freezes the target** of the protest action, refusing to accept the target's excuses or otherwise allow the target to shift blame or responsibility to other parties. The organizer selects tactics that disorient and intimidate the target of the protest action.

Box 7.3
What Went Wrong with ACORN?

Strong neighborhood organizations are a vital element of democracy. Yet conservative political groups and Republicans often oppose government efforts to extend funding to activist community organizations that push for increased social spending and whose leaders take actions to support the election of Democratic candidates. The critics further charge that neighborhood organizations are too often dominated by corrupt poverty "hustlers" who are more interested in profiting from publicly funded programs than in building programs that effectively serve people in need. Conservative activists focused their guns on ACORN (the Association of Community Organizations for Reform Now), a prominent nationwide organization of 174 poor-people's groups.

ACORN had a record of combating the redlining of communities by banks and other financial institutions. In more recent years, ACORN documented the predatory lending practices of more unscrupulous home finance companies that led to a wave of home foreclosures in low-income neighborhoods. In New Orleans, ACORN pushed for the reconstruction of homes in the poorest sections of New Orleans after Hurricane Katrina. Local ACORN organizations also fought for a "living wage" for workers. In numerous cities, ACORN also registered poorer Americans to vote.[1]

Like other community groups, ACORN over the years moderated its actions, becoming increasingly involved with running job training and service programs in poor neighborhoods. Yet, in important ways, ACORN was still a throwback to the more confrontational organizing model of the 1960s. ACORN chose to emphasize high-profile protests and political actions as opposed to building stable working partnerships with more established groups.

Conservatives scorned ACORN for corruption, the embezzlement of funds,[2] and blatant politicization. Republicans accused ACORN of voter registration fraud: of misusing public monies to help noncitizens and other unqualified voters to register and vote for Barack Obama and other Democratic candidates.

A 2009 undercover "sting" operation, arranged and video-recorded by a couple of conservative activists, seemed to confirm some of the worst suspicions about ACORN. Conservative activists, in one case even pretending to be a prostitute and a pimp, went to an ACORN office and asked for advice in applying for federal assistance. The local ACORN official counseled the pair and, according to conservatives, even offered advice as to how to obtain federal assistance for their prostitution business. The mass media quickly latched onto the ACORN pimp-and-prostitute story.

In the wake of the scandal, Congress withdrew the support that it had previously extended ACORN. New laws restricted ACORN's participation in government-funded programs. The Census Bureau dropped ACORN as a partner in aiding the decennial count in poorer neighborhoods. Cut off from funding, ACORN shut the doors of regional and local offices and faced bankruptcy. ACORN's misbehavior put the organization at political risk. The conservative political activists had unfairly and severely edited the videotape to show ACORN officials in the worst possible light, omitting such important details as an ACORN official's call to the police reporting the applicants' intentions.[3] Still, as a result of the organization's insensitivity to the enmity it had earned by its past excesses, ACORN had left itself vulnerable to attack, even to an exaggerated attack.

How did ACORN go wrong? ACORN's continued involvement in electoral politics and aggressive protest politics raised its national profile and earned the scorn of the political right. ACORN did not follow the principles of good management that a nonprofit organization must follow: it did not root out misbehavior and "trim its sails" in an era when its dependence on outside funding should have dictated caution.

Nonprofit and community groups that do the public's work and rely on outside funders must show a concern for ethical behavior in order to maintain the public's trust. ACORN failed to institute the appropriate controls to assure the probity of its actions. ACORN was insensitive to the special care that a nonprofit organization must take to safeguard its public image and its reputation for integrity.

Community activist and theorist Harry Boyte offers an additional insight that helps to explain how ACORN ran off course. According to Boyte, ACORN spurned the IAF organizational approach of working with a neighborhood's more established organizations such as churches and labor unions.[4] ACORN chose to go it alone and not be tied to the more staid ways of older groups. As a result, ACORN was not anchored in the values of faith-based service or in the democratic dialogue of labor unions. Nor did ACORN have friends that could strongly caution the organization of the dangers posed by its excesses.

1. Robert Fisher, ed., *The People Shall Rule: ACORN, Community Organizing, and the Struggle for Economic Justice* (Nashville, TN: Vanderbilt University Press, 2009); John Atlas, *Seeds of Change: The Story of ACORN, America's Most Controversial Antipoverty Community Organizing Group* (Nashville, TN: Vanderbilt University Press, 2010); Maude Hurd and Steven Kest, "Fighting Predatory Lending from the Ground Up: An Issue of Economic Justice," in *Organizing Access to Capital: Advocacy and the Democratization of Financial Institutions*, ed. Gregory D. Squires (Philadelphia: Temple University Press, 2003), 119–134; Pablo Eisenberg, "Dropping Acorn: What About the Other Side of the Story?" *Journal of Philanthropy*, September 18, 2009; John Atlas and Peter Dreier, "The Acorn Scandal Offers Key Lessons to All Charities," *Journal of Philanthropy*, December 10, 2009.

2. Stephanie Strom, "Funds Misappropriated at 2 Nonprofit Groups," *New York Times*, July 9, 2008.

3. Ryan Witt, "VIDEO: Release of Unedited ACORN Tapes Reveals Glaring Distortions by Big Government and Fox News," *San Francisco Examiner*, April 7, 2010. In 2013 the producer of the highly deceptive videotape agreed to settle a lawsuit by paying the ACORN employee $100,000 in damages.

4. Harry C. Boyte, *Everyday Politics: Reconnecting Citizens and Public Life* (Philadelphia: University of Pennsylvania Press, 2004), 49.

The organizer does not always choose to fight the biggest problems that face a community. Big battles are not easily won, and failed efforts for change can reinforce a community's sense of hopelessness and defeatism. At least initially, the organizer will choose small, winnable targets that allow for a **quick victory** that will build the community's spirit, a sense of victory that will help mobilize followers for future battles.

In Los Angeles and in cities throughout Texas and the Southwest, community organizers in the Latino neighborhoods pursued mobilizing strategies that built on the community's strong attachments to the Catholic Church.[29] In El Paso, a city with a population that is two-thirds Hispanic, EPISO (the El Paso Interreligious Sponsoring Organization) conducted grassroots actions with the assistance of local churches. In San Antonio, Communities Organized for Public Services (COPS), a federation of more than twenty neighborhood groups, fought to correct the underprovision of infrastructure and other services in the Mexican sections of the city. COPS received the largest part of its budget from local parishes, with San Antonio's Archbishop giving his blessing to COPS participation.[30] COPS, like other IAF organizations, also used **mass accountability meetings** crowded with large numbers of neighborhood residents to press public officials to make policy commitments.[31]

COPS' evolution over the years helps illustrate the changing balance in the activities undertaken by many community groups. While COPS still engages in protest actions when the situation requires, COPS nonetheless has deemphasized public combat in favor of building more enduring and cooperative relationships with governmental bodies, banks and financial institutions, nonprofit funders, and other organizations that have resources critical to neighborhood housing, job training, economic development, health care, and school programs.[32] For COPS and a great many community organizations, protest has ceded way to a new emphasis on "values-based organizing" and "collaborative leadership."[33] (See Box 7.3, "What Went Wrong with ACORN?") COPS also emphasized voter registration; by building a formidable electoral base, COPS gained invitations to decision-making councils.

In San Antonio, COPS is no longer an outsider but a community organization that has gained the power advantages that derive from building long-term, collaborative relationships with public officials and private-sector leaders.[34] Municipal leaders that had once dismissed COPS as a rabble-rousing group came to bestow numerous honors on COPS for its history of public service.

Women have assumed leadership roles in community-based groups, especially those that are active in providing housing, education, and health-care services, service areas that fall within the realm of family caregiving that has traditionally be assigned to women. Women continue to provide much of the back-office, clerical, and detail work that sustains community organizations. With women leading community groups, community organizing has lost much of the "conflict orientation"[35] and "macho" posturing that characterized the work of Saul Alinsky and an earlier generation of community organizers. (See Box 7.4, "Women and Community Organizing.")

"From Protest to Programs" is the slogan that encapsulates the changed orientation of The Woodlawn Organization (TWO), a grassroots organization in the poor African-American South Side of Chicago. In the 1960s and 1970s, TWO, reflecting its IAF roots,

Box 7.4
Women and Community Organizing

As Larry Bennett observed in his study of Chicago, "women are important participants in virtually every neighborhood organization. . . . [P]olitical work directed at neighborhood-, housing-, and school-related issues represents a field where women, for generations, have had a conspicuous impact."[1] In Chicago, in Baltimore, and in cities across the nation, poor black women have been the leaders of public housing tenant organizations, and have used those organizations to address a variety of issues faced by poor women and their children.[2]

Why do women play a prominent role in tenant organizing? The answer is simple. Subsidized housing is, to a great extent, a women's issue. Poverty in the United States is linked to female-headed families, a condition popularly referred to as the **feminization of poverty**. Female-headed households make up an overwhelmingly large portion of the population that lives in subsidized housing.

Cynthia Reed, the president of the Sheridan-Gunnison Tenants' Association in Chicago's Uptown neighborhood, explained her involvement as a matter of self-interest: Low-income, single mothers raising children have few real alternatives in their search for quality housing. They must battle to preserve the conditions of their subsidized housing, even if it means that they have less time for work and their children.[3]

Community-based organizations are often led by the "invisible tier of community leaders, most frequently women who worked behind the scenes." Women build their political skills through activity in PTA groups, church groups, and other neighborhood associations. As one member of San Antonio's Communities Organized for Public Services (COPS) related, women are "community sustainers" who focus not on theatrical political combat but on doing whatever it takes to provide improved schools and family services.[4]

Yet the engagement of women in community groups varies greatly according to nationality and ethnic customs. In Chicago, African-American women played dominant leadership roles in the fight to maintain quality housing. Among the city's Nigerian, Ethiopian, and South Asian populations, however, men were more likely to get involved. Women from the Middle East were most restrained when it came to the neighborhood efforts to preserve affordable housing.

1. Larry Bennett, *Neighborhood Politics: Chicago and Sheffield* (New York: Garland, 1997), 246.
2. Rhonda Y. Williams, *The Politics of Public Housing: Black Women's Struggles Against Urban Inequality* (New York: Oxford University Press, 2004), 174–187, 212–213.
3. The Reed interview is related by Philip Nyden and Joan Adams, *Saving Our Homes: The Lessons of Community Struggles to Preserve Affordable Housing in Chicago's Uptown* (Chicago: Loyola University of Chicago and Organization of the NorthEast, April 1996).
4. The quotations in this paragraph are from Harry C. Boyte, *Everyday Politics: Reconnecting Citizens and Public Life* (Philadelphia: University of Pennsylvania Press, 2004), 52.

undertook mobilizing actions in the Alinsky tradition, organizing boycotts of merchants who cheated community members (i.e., merchants who "short-weighed" the meat and other products they sold) or who refused to expand programs to hire local residents. Over the years, TWO refocused much of its energies, giving less attention to protest actions and more focus and greater devotion to administering a variety of programs that deliver vital services to community residents. The organization helps run low-income housing programs, operate day-care centers, and even bring dental services to area families. TWO established working relationships with public, private, and nonprofit organizations to provide the finances for such community-based services.[36]

In Baltimore, Baltimoreans United in Leadership Development (BUILD) has similarly balanced IAF-style protest actions with the organization's newer responsibilities, as it has taken charge of the operation of community service programs. BUILD worked with nearly fifty churches in Baltimore's African-American community to combat redlining and unfair auto insurance rates. BUILD also led the battle for the payment of a "living wage" to workers. But a focus solely on the group's advocacy efforts overlooks the extensive responsibilities that BUILD assumed in the daily management of extended-day after-school programs, homework assistance, and other education and human resource programs. BUILD has worked in partnership with private businesses that offer job training—and the promise of jobs—to students who stay in school and who graduate with good grades.[37] In El Paso, EPISO gave a similar focus to finding partner organizations for improved public education.[38]

COMMUNITY DEVELOPMENT CORPORATIONS

A **community development corporation (CDC)** is a neighborhood-based organization that works in partnership with public- and private-sector actors for new investments to improve conditions in low-income communities.[39] Many CDCs focus on providing affordable housing. Others pursue local economic development efforts. Still others operate health clinics and food pantries, offer youth activities and after-school programs, and run day-care centers and job training programs. In 2005, an estimated 4,600 CDCs operated in the fifty states.[40] The work of community development corporations is clearly one of the pieces of "good news" for cities.

CDCs have had their greatest success in the area of housing, rehabilitating dwelling units and building new units of affordable housing. Over 90 percent of all CDCs engage in housing activities. CDCs work with government agencies, mortgage lenders, and corporate officials to piece together the financing for low- and moderate-priced units.

CDCs follow a **bridge-building approach**[41] that forms partnerships with institutions that usually lie outside the neighborhood. CDCs ask banks, private investors, corporate managers, nonprofit organizations, and government agencies each to pick up a piece of the financing necessary for a neighborhood project. Banks, private credit institutions, and other organizations are often quite willing to commit to a neighborhood project when they see that a CDC has rounded up the participation of others. CDCs in post–Hurricane Katrina New Orleans formed links with partnering organizations to provide new units of affordable housing and limit the extent of gentrification in the rebuilding city.[42]

CDCs, though, have paid a price for their success. In their efforts to establish partnerships, CDCs have adopted a "consensus organizing"[43] and "conflict-free"[44] vision of community advancement. CDCs, according to their critics, exhibit a "disdain"[45] for political advocacy and "have lost their grassroots mentality."[46] Whatever their imperfections, CDCs have nonetheless enjoyed great success in building affordable housing and bringing improved community services to inner-city areas.[47]

What role will CDCs play in the future? Much depends on the federal government's renewal of the **Low-Income Housing Tax Credit (LIHTC)**, a program that offers tax advantages to private institutions that invest in CDC housing projects. Should the LIHTC be substantially reduced or even abandoned, CDCs would likely have great difficulty in finding investment partners.

The collapse of local housing markets has also hurt CDCs. In Detroit, Cleveland, Youngstown, and other "shrinking cities," CDCs confront the argument that there is simply no need to rehabilitate or build new affordable units when a city already has an extensive supply of vacant housing. In such cities, CDCs have had to turn to smaller initiatives, such as providing assistance for weatherization and home repairs and aiding the development of community gardens. A number of CDCs have also begun to "think strategically," targeting their efforts to communities where new projects are likely to enjoy the greatest chances of success, as opposed to trying to improve housing in neighborhoods suffering the most extreme disinvestment.[48]

E-GOVERNMENT AND E-DEMOCRACY: FROM WEB 1.0 TO WEB 2.0 (AND 3.0)

E-government (or "electronic government") provides a number of tools to bring government closer to the people. Municipal agencies use e-mail, Web sites, Webcasts of public meetings, and even blogs and social media sites (such as Facebook, YouTube, and Twitter) to inform citizens of local events and municipal regulations. Citizens use the new technology to register service requests and complaints without having to visit city hall. Citizens can renew licenses on the Web; they no longer have to travel downtown, take a seat, and wait endlessly for a bureaucrat to call their number.

Cities, however, are only just beginning to tap the interactive and two-way communications capacity of the Web.[49] A survey of New Jersey municipalities reveals that governments use the Web for a variety of purposes, but **"e-democracy"** is the "least practiced" element of e-government.[50] National surveys essentially come to the same conclusion: few cities use the Internet to offer citizens important new opportunities for interactive democratic participation.[51]

Technology enthusiasts, however, observe that local governments are beginning to move beyond Web 1.0, where municipal agencies did little more than post public announcements on city Web pages in a very crude effort at one-way information sharing. **Web 2.0** (also called **Government 2.0**), by contrast, offers the opportunity for interactive exchanges. Web 2.0 gives citizens new opportunities to speak their mind and for citizens and public officials to collaborate in identifying solutions to local problems. Web 2.0

enables citizens to interact with one another, discussing problems and solutions, without a government agency in total control of the discussion that appears on the Web. Public agencies can serve to promote such idea sharing, creating **digital neighborhoods**, online forums where citizens interact with one another and with agency officials.[52]

What do the more innovative local initiatives for e-democracy look like? West Hartford, Connecticut, utilized an interactive, real-time citizen survey that gave respondents policy-related information and then asked them to choose their desired levels of municipal service provision and taxation. As a respondent chose to increase or decrease the level of a specified service, a computerized program revealed just how the choice affects the respondent's tax bill.[53] Only a relatively small handful of cities have made similar efforts to sustain online dialogue and interactive planning.[54]

Seattle is a leader in the e-democracy field, a city where municipal officials work in a supportive environment to promote the interactive capacities of the Web. Seattle established a municipal department, the Office of Electronic Communications, to deepen e-democracy. The city also set up a Web site for e-participation (www.seattlechannel.org) that is separate and distinct from the city's main Web site with its numerous departmental announcements. The "Democracy Portal" (as the city government refers to the e-participation Web site) organizes city-oriented information and news by issue area in order to provide citizens with the means for effective participation. The site also has links to connect viewers to various municipal meetings televised on the city's cable channel. In Seattle, citizens are invited to submit their opinions to public hearings via e-mail.[55]

But Web-based interactions raise important concerns regarding representativeness and democracy, especially as narrow interests can "hijack" online discussions.[56] Municipal administrators fear that online discussion boards and other forms of e-participation may serve to amplify the most strident antigovernment voices in a community, raising controversy that intrudes on an agency's ability to perform its job.

A government agency can use various Web-based "metrics" to assess its success in reaching its audience, for instance, by tabulating Facebook "hits" and "Likes" and other social media comments. Yet such tabulations also underscore the limited nature of e-participation mechanisms, as such tallies and summaries lack the intensity, depth of discussion, and mutual learning that accompanies face-to-face participation. Even **crowdsourcing**,[57] where a government agency throws a problem before the "collective intelligence" of an Internet audience in order to generate a wide array of public comments and citizen-initiated solutions, has its limits; it is still government officials who have the power to decide just which comments are seriously considered and which are ignored.

E-government is not the equivalent of e-democracy.[58] Many municipal agencies use the Web for one-way public announcements and as a tool that conveniently allows citizens to apply for license renewals and to report service problems.[59] Web 2.0 goes further, creating new avenues for citizen-government consultation, interaction, and, at times, even collaboration. But even where municipal agencies use e-tools to facilitate citizen input and agency-citizen interaction, e-participation is a pale substitute for community organizing. E-forums and Web-based commenting cannot be expected to establish a culture where citizens can mobilize an effective political challenge to administrative decisions that ignore a neighborhood's concerns.

Commentators on the new digital society have observed that a **digital divide** separates the technologically competent from the less competent, the young from the old, and the well-off from the poor. Yet the divide may be diminishing, as digital communication has become so commonplace that even the elderly and the poor have picked up habits of e-communication. Municipal governments can also help bridge the digital divide. Chicago has partnered with community-based organizations in its "Smart Communities" outreach and training programs to cultivate a "culture of technology use" in low-income neighborhoods.[60]

Many low-income families, however, lack a computer in the home. When it comes to "digital citizenship," including searches on the Internet for information, a "smart phone" is a poor substitute for the high-speed and reliable broadband access of a home computer.[61] E-democracy is diminished when a group lacks the modern tools that others use to make service demands and press their e-advocacy campaigns. Overall, more sophisticated audiences have the interest and the resources to take advantage of the new engagement opportunities presented by government's expanded use of the Web and social media.

The e-world changes very quickly. Even before cities have become fully comfortable with Web 2.0, they are finding it necessary to adapt to the expectations of a **Web 3.0** world of mobile smart phones, text messages, and tablet technology where citizens expect immediate updates and announcements as soon as a news event breaks. Citizens also demand the opportunity to express their concerns in real time, whether they are home or away from home.

Conclusion: Bottom-Up Participation, Deep Democracy, and the Facilitating Role That Government Can Play

Over the past half century, municipal politics has been reshaped by a virtual revolution in citizen participation. Top-down decision making has yielded to participatory processes as citizens expect to be heard when a municipal decision directly affects their lives. Federal and state program regulations, too, have created an expectation for participation. As a result, procedures for citizen engagement are now a routine part of urban governance. A new generation of urban professionals has also been schooled in the importance of being responsive to citizen-customers. These public servants see themselves as citizen-educators and advisers who work in partnership with neighborhood groups.[62]

The style of community organizations, too, has altered considerably over the years. While protest will always be an important tactic for relatively powerless groups, contemporary neighborhood organizations are less interested in fighting city hall than in building partnerships with public and private officials to provide vitally needed services. Protest actions can increase the level of conflict in a city, impeding the ability of neighborhood groups to reach out to partners across geographical boundaries and across racial and ethnic lines.[63]

Still, while participatory vehicles can make decision makers more aware of neighborhood concerns, citizen participation "is rarely transformative." Participatory arrangements are often cooptative. Participatory processes are also prone to being captured by middle-class and professional groups. Participatory arrangements cannot by themselves make a city just or "equitable."[64] Many municipal bureaucrats are content with one-way information sharing and public hearings that offer little real citizen engagement. Public officials also tend to dismiss citizen input when they regard citizens as having an incomplete understanding of the issues and budgetary constraints.[65]

Bottom-up processes by themselves are not an answer to the urban crisis. CDCs have an impressive record in bringing affordable housing to disinvested areas of the city; still, these organizations lack the resources necessary to rebuild core-city neighborhoods. In times of fiscal stress, when a CDC's partners phase down their fiscal commitments, the limited problem-solving reach of CDCs becomes even more apparent.

CDCs and other community-based organizations require financial support from public, corporate, and philanthropic agencies. This dependence on outside assistance has also led to a "new moderation of community organizing" where community groups adopt business-like practices and refrain from actions that could disrupt partnerships.[66]

Community organizing and citizen participation efforts deepen democracy. Yet when formalized processes are dominated by established neighborhood leaders, ordinary residents can feel excluded.[67]

As Chapter 8 will explore in greater detail, municipal officials have also turned to citizen involvement as one of a number of routes to do "more with less." In a time of fiscal constraint, citizen involvement and partnerships with community groups are seen as means to deliver public services both more effectively and efficiently.

KEY TERMS

Alinsky/IAF method of community organizing (*p. 180*)
bottom-up visioning process (*p. 178*)
bridge-building approach of CDCs (*p. 185*)
citizen juries (*p. 179*)
citizen participation (*p. 170*)
citizen task forces (*p. 178*)
citizens as distinct from consumers (*p. 177*)
collaboration (*p. 174*)
community control (*p. 177*)
community development corporation (CDC) (*p. 176*)
community organizing (*p. 180*)
community policing
consultation (*p. 175*)
co-optation (*p. 175*)
crowdsourcing (*p. 187*)
delegated power (*p. 176*)
deliberative polling (*p. 180*)
digital divide (*p. 188*)

digital neighborhoods (*p. 187*)
e-democracy (*p. 186*)
e-government (*p. 186*)
feminization of poverty (*p. 184*)
freeze the target (an Alinksy/IAF organizing principle) (*p. 180*)
geographic information system (GIS) (*p. 180*)
informing (*p. 175*)
joint steering committees (*p. 179*)
ladder of citizen participation, Sherry Arnstein's (*p. 174*)
Low-Income Housing Tax Credit (LIHTC) (*p. 186*)
manipulation (*p. 175*)
mass accountability meetings (an Alinksy/IAF organizing principle) (*p. 181*)
partnership (viewing citizens as partners) (*p. 176*)
placation (*p. 175*)

planning charrettes (*p. 179*)
police-civilian review board (*p. 176*)
quick victory (an Alinksy/IAF
  organizing principle) (*p. 181*)
rubs wounds raw (an Alinksy/IAF
  organizing principle) (*p. 180*)

therapy, citizen participation as
  (*p. 175*)
tokenism (*p. 175*)
Web 2.0 (also called Government 2.0)
  (*p. 186*)
Web 3.0 (*p. 188*)

8 | Improving Urban Services

THE POWER OF MUNICIPAL SERVICE AGENCIES: THE BUREAUCRATIC CITY-STATE

The reform movement cleaned up much of the favoritism, abuse, and partisanship that plagued big cities during the era of the political machine. The reformers reduced the authority of elected officials by shifting decision-making authority to careerist experts residing in civil-service-protected municipal agencies. In doing so, the reformers inadvertently created a new generation of city problems. Protected by tenure and civil service regulations, teachers, tax assessors, and other municipal officials do not have to respond to citizen requests in order to keep their jobs.

"The legacy of reform," as political scientist Theodore Lowi observed, "is the bureaucratic city-state." The urban service bureaucracies are the city's "new machines," a phrase that underscores their newfound power.[1]

The power of local bureaucrats is the product of the **administrative discretion** they possess. Administrative officials have a fair degree of leeway in deciding how a law's vague provisions and broad accompanying program rules are applied to specific situations. A police officer decides when to issue a traffic citation and when to overlook a moving violation. A housing inspector decides when a building violation notice will be issued and what, if any, follow-up action will be pursued. A public school teacher decides exactly how to conduct the lessons in the classroom each school day and how his or her limited time will be allocated among a diverse group of children with different educational abilities and needs. No law or supervisory official can fully dictate action and remove the discretionary authority that such lower-ranking officials possess.

Bureaucrats also derive power from their **expertise**, their possession of a detailed technical body of knowledge gained from performing specialized tasks. Expertise is desirable but can also result in parochialism, especially when administrators view problems only from the vantage point of their narrow training. Police officers, for instance, traditionally approached matters of domestic violence from a law enforcement perspective. It took the passage of the 1994 Violence Against Women Act (reauthorized in 2013) coupled with continued pressure from women's groups to get police officers to work more closely with health-care providers, child-welfare workers, and substance-abuse counselors in order to provide a fuller range of services to meet the emotional and health needs of battered women.[2]

The more strident critics of local government do not see much hope of breaking the hold that the bureaucratic power centers hold on municipal affairs. Such critics do not see much prospect of improving the performance of urban public servants; they see the bureaucratic condition as hopeless, a malady that cannot be cured. But more far-reaching public policy innovations, they argue, can allow citizens to bypass underperforming public bureaucracies. As this chapter will explore, these critics propose a number of measures to *privatize* city services—to "contract out" and otherwise have private firms and nonprofit organizations do the jobs once performed by municipal agencies. The critics also seek to offer citizens increased *choice*, ending their reliance on the public schools and other irresponsive and poorly performing municipal institutions.

THE IMPORTANCE OF STREET-LEVEL BUREAUCRATS

Street-level bureaucrats are the "foot soldiers" of city government—the police officers, teachers, building inspectors, nurses, social-welfare caseworkers, and lower-court judges who, in "face to face encounters" make important determinations that affect people's lives.[3] Too often, casual observers of local politics overlook the collective power of street-level bureaucrats; these observers mistakenly believe that the foot soldiers on the bottom rungs of the bureaucracy have no choice but to follow in robot-like fashion an agency's policies and the orders issued from above.

Such a misperception is blind to the fact that the street-level foot soldiers often possess considerable discretion in determining how they perform their jobs and how they will respond to citizen needs. Police officers, classroom teachers, housing inspectors, public-health nurses, social-service outreach workers, and other public servants who work "in the field" possess a high degree of administrative discretion or autonomy, especially as their actions are not easily reviewed by superiors.[4] Clients, too, want service providers to have the flexibility to provide personalized attention responsive to their unique needs; they do not want bureaucrats to give unquestioned obedience to a rulebook.

Clear and precise laws and program rules can reduce **unauthorized discretion** and the goal displacement that result when bureaucrats use the freedom they possess to make decisions that are not truly public serving. A street-level bureaucrat typically develops **shortcuts and stereotypes** that allow the bureaucrat to allocate his or her time effectively. A police officer, for instance, may look closely at the "wrong" type of person walking down a residential street late at night. Street-level bureaucrats see such shorthands and shortcuts as the necessary judgments made by an expert in the field. However, to an African-American or Hispanic youth who is questioned for being in the wrong neighborhood at the wrong time of day, such categorizations and stereotyping are resented as blatant discrimination, as **racial profiling**.

Street-level bureaucrats often work under quite difficult conditions: teachers face large class sizes; social workers handle large caseloads; police confront potential threats and face conflicting expectations as to how they should perform their job. Many of these lower-level public servants are quite devoted to serving their clients but simply lack the time, resources, and support to respond to each individual client's needs.[5] Caring and creative bureaucrats chafe at agency rules that constrain innovative actions and individualized service.

Agency rules and effective oversight are necessary to guide bureaucratic performance and prevent misbehavior and wasteful practices. Yet public-spirited bureaucrats need a measure of flexibility to do their job well. A balanced approach to public management will seek to control unauthorized discretion while providing bureaucrats with sufficient room to make legitimate judgment calls in the performance of their jobs. Managers can help by providing updated training that enhances the skills and problem-solving capacities of public-oriented professionals.[6] Dedicated public servants require supportive resources, including the public's respect, in order to do their jobs well.[7]

PROFESSIONALISM: AN IMPERFECT CURE FOR THE URBAN BUREAUCRACY PROBLEM

Classic organizational theory does not recognize a bureaucrat's discretion; strictly speaking, the job of a bureaucrat is to "go by the book," to strictly follow an agency's rules so that all persons are treated the same and there is no deviation from official agency policy. But, as discussed above, such rule-book-driven behavior fails to provide for the flexibility that a citizen desires when seeking a response from a municipal agency. We each want a personal response from a public servant; we want municipal officials with the freedom to respond to the unique situation of each individual case.

As a result, a new model for public service has displaced the older, classic model of rule-driven conformity. A **professional**, in contrast to a bureaucrat, is no mere rule follower but an inner-guided, highly trained, capable public servant who is committed both to client well-being and to a higher ethic of service. A professional does not simply "go by the book" but is given greater freedom to act; a professional has the higher education and ethical obligations to use discretion wisely.

Professionalization offers a partial cure for the street-level bureaucracy problem.[8] As discretion in urban administration is often unavoidable, professionalism seeks to create a cadre of public servants who can be trusted to make judgment calls that are in the best interest of the client and the public. Better pay is necessary to recruit a higher caliber of workers to public service. Higher education can also help lead officials to make better quality decisions. But professionalism denotes more than attractive salaries and advanced education and training. A professional also adheres to a code of conduct articulated by his or her profession. The true professional follows the expectations of ethical conduct and client-oriented service even in cases where peer pressure and the difficulty of the job would seem to demand shortcuts.

Public health, public education, civil engineering, and social work are all among the urban service fields characterized by a high degree of professionalization. By comparison, police officers and firefighters are **semiprofessionals** who are clearly experts in their jobs but who do not always have a professional's advanced education, broader understanding of society, and respect for the constitutionally-protected civil rights and liberties of each person served.

Police officers, like a great many public workers, claim to be professionals. They desire the pay levels, the respect, and the on-the-job deference generally accorded to professionals. Yet while protective officers are expert in their work (work that can be very demanding and even dangerous), police officers confuse narrow job expertise with the larger perspectives and obligations that society expects of professionals. Police officers, for instance, too often abide by an unwritten code that prohibits an officer from "ratting out" a partner by reporting his or her misdoings. The culture of a police department teaches officers to support one another, as officers must make quick decisions in very difficult situations. Such an informal code of conduct, however understandable, runs contrary to a profession's obligation to pursue actions that serve the public and clients rather than the interests of its own members. Deference to claims of professionalism by law enforcement officials can insulate police departments from effective external review, undermining the accountability of law enforcement agencies to the public.[9]

PERFORMANCE MEASUREMENT: EFFICIENCY, EFFECTIVENESS, AND EQUITY IN MUNICIPAL GOVERNMENT

How do citizens and program managers know when a public agency is doing a good job or if changes need to be made? Cities across the country are turning to **performance measurement**, the use of statistical indicators, to provide insight as to an agency's progress over time.[10] **Comparative performance measurement** ranks aspects of local service delivery against that of peer cities. Do local housing inspectors perform fewer or more inspections per week as compared to similar cities in a state? How long does it take for a city to issue a building permit, and how does that compare to the performance of other cities?

What gets measured gets done. Hence, public officials must be careful in choosing what they measure. Indeed, angry parents criticized No Child Left Behind, a program first initiated by President George W. Bush, for relying on a system of performance measurements and sanctions that virtually forced school systems to "teach to the test," draining class time away from social studies and other valuable aspects of a child's education. (See Box 8.1 "No Child Left Behind: What Did We Learn?")

In assessing performance, agencies must utilize **multiple indicators** to reveal just how well an agency is meeting various aspects of its assigned mission. Agencies should not rely on numbers that are easy to amass, such as measures of the **inputs** or the resources devoted to a job (i.e., an agency's number of workers or the amount of money it spent in a particular year). Input measures provide no indication if an agency is actually accomplishing its mission, or if it is using resources well or wasting them.

Rather than merely detail inputs, evaluations should stress service **outcomes or program effectiveness**, just what difference an agency is making in the lives of citizens. Effectiveness measures are concerned with whether a department is doing a good job in reaching clients and in solving problems. What percentage of eligible children in a community do Head Start preschool programs serve? Does Head Start increase children's readiness to learn, as seen in test scores and in measures of appropriate social behavior? Does a new reading program actually improve schoolchildren's reading abilities? These are all questions of program effectiveness.

Box 8.1
No Child Left Behind: What Did We Learn?

President George W. Bush sought to be the nation's "education president." No Child Left Behind (NCLB) was the centerpiece of Bush's schools strategy. NCLB virtually mandated that states and school districts implement a series of annual performance measures, based largely on student achievement tests in math and reading. Bush hoped that the performance data would empower parents to press for changes in poorly performing schools. Parents and guardians could even pull their children from schools that proved incapable of change. NCLB also held out the promise of increased tutoring and other supplemental services for children in failing schools.

But NCLB was met by immediate pushback by parents and teachers who argued that the program was sucking the creativity and spirit out of the classroom. School districts were devoting too many hours in the school day to rote exercises, drills, and "teaching to the test" in order to improve student scores on standardized exams. Schools gave increased attention to reading and math, the two areas covered by NLCB testing, taking time away from the sciences, history, the arts, theater, current affairs, and "even recess."[1] A number of school administrators resorted to fraudulent practices, leaking achievement exam questions in advance and falsifying student test results. These misdeeds testified to the severe pressures that NCLB's high-stakes testing imposed on schools. States and localities also failed to provide the resources for the full range of supplemental services and new "choice" programs that were promised to the children in failing schools.

In the face of unrelenting criticism from parents and educators and test results that revealed vast numbers of schools that failed to meet NLCB standards, a number of states revised their achievement tests, easing the level of difficulty. President Barack Obama, too, issued waivers and otherwise scaled back NLCB requirements.

NLCB did have some positive results. It forced schools to give renewed attention to performance and to give extra focus to students who are not learning. The program also raised student math scores, at least in states that took steps to meet NLCB goals. The program seemed to improve graduation rates, even if the improvement was not dramatic.[2] Still, overall the program failed to achieve its goals; it did not significantly increase student academic performance or narrow the achievement gaps faced by more disadvantaged students.[3] As the program's critics argued, the program's relatively small gains were not worth the huge disruption of the classroom. NCLB was not moving classroom instruction in the right direction.

NCLB failed as it largely measured performance measures in a select few areas—notably math and reading—which led schools to distort classroom practices by taking time away from activities and subject areas not directly measured by NCLB. The history of NCLB further points to the difficulty of making effective policy change in a federal system that allows ample opportunities for goal displacement and foot-dragging by state and local actors who do not fully agree with national policy goals.

1. Diane Ravitch, *The Death and Life of the Great American School System: How Testing and Choice Are Undermining Education* (New York: Basic Books, 2010); see especially Chapter 6, "NCLB: Measure and Punish."

2. Thomas S. Dee and Brian A. Jacob, "The Impact of No Child Left Behind on Students, Teachers, and Schools," Brookings Papers on Economic Activity (Fall 2010): 149–194; John E. Chubb, *Learning from No Child Left Behind* (Stanford, CA: The Hoover Institution, Stanford University, 2010).

3. Lisa Guisbond with Monty Neill and Bob Schaeffer, *NCLB's Lost Decade for Educational Progress: What Can We Learn from This Policy Failure?* (Jamaica Plain, MA: National Center for Fair and Open Testing, January 2012), http://fairtest.org/sites/default/files/NCLB_Report_Final_Layout.pdf.

For instance, instead of merely reporting the number of officers on patrol (a mere measure of inputs), evaluations of law enforcement should give greater attention to outcome indicators, whether crime in a neighborhood is increasing or decreasing. Other outcome measures would seek to assess whether citizens are reporting an increased sense of safety and a willingness to walk the streets without fear. Outcome indicators for a fire department would focus on the actual number of fires that occur, the containment of fires, and the extent of property loss due to fire. Outcome measures for a nursing outreach program might focus on the birth weights of babies born at risk.

Efficiency measures are concerned with saving money, with achieving government performance at a lower cost. Efficiency measures reveal how much it costs the sanitation department to collect a ton of garbage, or how much a city spends to keep a police officer on the beat. As larger cities spend more than smaller cities, an examination of the *total* spending by an agency does not allow for easy comparison. Hence, efficiency is almost always measured on a "cost *per unit*" basis. A city can see if it is paying more or less than comparable cities in terms of how much it spends to inspect a dwelling unit or to resurface a mile of a city street.

Taxpayers and other budget-minded constituencies demand that cities give great attention to efficiency and to finding ways to save money. As a result, municipalities widely use indicators that assess program efficiency.

But there is a danger when city officials rely too heavily on efficiency measures and ignore other important aspects of public service. Efficiency measures provide no indication of program quality or how effective a program may be in reaching important objectives. Nor do efficiency measures reveal whether a city is treating all citizens fairly, an important standard for judging government performance in a democracy.[11] Potentially troubling is the fact that actions taken to improve service efficiency can undermine service effectiveness and program fairness or equity.

Equity measures are quite important, as they seek to ascertain whether programs fairly serve all demographic groups and neighborhoods. Equity, however, is a difficulty concept to define and measure, as different people have quite different definitions of fairness.[12] Some citizens argue that fairness requires that all clients and neighborhoods receive the same level of service. By this definition, inequity arises when some children have new textbooks and a range of classes and extracurricular activities denied to children attending schools in other areas of the city. The standard of **strict equity** entails giving all citizens the same level of service. Trash, for instance, may be collected in all neighborhoods once a week, regardless of the values of homes in an area and the amount that property owners pay in taxes.

Yet equity does not always require the strictly equal provision of services. In many instances, the unequal provision of services can be justified as fair and desirable. Some children have greater needs and require more extensive tutoring and support services than do other children. This is not very troubling. Similarly, academically gifted children desire specialized science, math, and music and arts classes that are of little interest to other students. Some parents may criticize the diversion of school resources to support such specialized programs; yet other parents will defend the classes as a fair and reasonable response to the needs of gifted students.

The concept of **social equity** justifies spending disproportionate resources in order to aid people on the bottom rungs of American society. A more demanding variant of the social equity standard calls for **equal results**: targeting assistance and attention to help equalize health care, student test scores, and job opportunity throughout the city.

Municipal agencies will do well to utilize a **balanced scorecard** that includes indicators of an agency's progress in three quite different areas: *efficiency, effectiveness,* and *equity*.[13] Balanced scorecards seek to avoid the trap of responding to efficiency concerns while neglecting program effectiveness and fairness. The balanced scorecard used by the Oregon Benchmarks Report reveals program efficiency and effectiveness scores but gives special attention to social equity concerns, documenting just how minority communities are progressing in areas such as education and health care.[14]

Good assessment of local service almost always requires public servants to obtain measures of citizen satisfaction.[15] Municipal departments utilize community surveys, user questionnaires, and program evaluation cards filled out by clients—all in an attempt to gauge if local programs are meeting the public's expectations.

Municipal agencies also employ **focus groups**, where a moderator helps to guide a select handful of citizens as they freely talk about their perceptions of an agency's work.[16] Focus groups are generally a much cheaper alternative to a full-fledged community survey. While a focus group does not permit a researcher to claim that the results are scientifically representative of the community as a whole, a well-designed focus group allows for in-depth discussion and gives citizens greater freedom to express what is on their minds, important elements that are often sacrificed in a community survey built upon numerous closed-ended (that is, fixed-choice) questions.

Municipal departments also use **trained observers** to rate the levels of trash on streets, the physical condition of roads, and the serviceability of playground equipment in local parks.[17] Observers often take photographs to document the physical conditions they report. In New York, the Center on Municipal Government Performance uses state-of-the-art laser technology to provide precise, objective measures ("smoothness scores" and "jolt scores") of the condition of city streets.[18]

Box 8.2
CompStat and CitiStat: Advanced Systems of Performance Measurement and Management

New York City Police Chief William Bratton gained national attention for instituting **CompStat**, a weekly reporting system that tracked crime rates on a precinct-by-precinct, and sometimes even on a block-by-block, basis. District commanders had to explain their unit's performance in departmental meetings conducted before the chief and the mayor or top mayoral assistants. Pushed by "the numbers" and aggressive questioning, district commanders altered work shifts and reassigned personnel to target high-crime areas; these commanders did not wish to repeatedly defend their unit's repeated poor performance when called upon in regularly scheduled, high-level accountability meetings.

After leaving New York, Bratton was hired by Los Angeles to see if his techniques could bring similar reductions in crime in that city.[1] In 2014 Mayor Bill de Blasio brought the renowned police chief back to New York.

The move, however, was not without controversy. Both Chief Bratton and Mayor de Blasio received continuing criticism as a result of their emphasis on **broken windows policing**, a performance-oriented approach to crime reduction that stresses the importance of making arrests even for misdemeanor transgressions such as consuming alcohol in public and "turnstile jumping" (the failure to pay the required fare in the city subway). Advocates argue that the broken windows approach helps build greater respect for the law and enables the police to remove from the streets numerous miscreants who then are discovered to have outstanding warrants for more serious offenses. Critics, however, point out that aggressive order maintenance criminalizes behavior in minority neighborhoods, adds to police-citizen tensions, and saddles minority youths with criminal records that are an impediment to future employment.[2] In extreme cases, an altercation over a minor transgression can even result in the accidental death of the person stopped for the violation: in New York in 2014 Eric Garner died in a chokehold as police confronted him over his street sale of untaxed cigarettes.

Baltimore Mayor (and later Maryland Governor) Martin O'Malley used a similar data-driven system, **CitiStat**, with detailed maps that revealed patterns of need and service provision throughout the city. As with CompStat, the data became part of a system of "relentless management,"[3] where regularly scheduled meetings with the mayor and other top officials kept constant pressure on municipal departments to initiate program changes.

San Francisco, St. Louis, Buffalo, Syracuse, Providence, Somerville and Springfield (Massachusetts), Warren (Michigan), and King County (Washington) are only a few of the many municipalities across the United States to adopt CompStat- and CitiStat-style systems of data-driven performance.[4] The Atlanta Dashboard system similarly tracks departmental indicators in an effort to force local administrators to initiate corrective action.

But many cities lack the expert staff, resources, and commitment by leadership to implement advanced performance management systems with their heavy data demands. Data collection is time-consuming and expensive. CitiStat requires extensive training to teach managers how to collect, interpret, and utilize data. In bigger cities, a CompStat or CitiStat operation requires the creation of a central data-support office. Over time, the commitment to such an arduous process sometimes fades.

Line personnel also do not fully "buy into" the new reporting systems. Patrol officers and their immediate supervisors, for instance, often misunderstand the purposes behind CompStat and view the collection of data solely as an effort to increase arrest rates.[5] Also, as helpful as CompStat and CitiStat can be in having departments use their resources to maximum advantage, data-driven management systems do not compensate for deficiencies in resources that are at the root of service problems in distressed communities.[6]

1. William J. Bratton and Sean W. Malinowski, "Police Performance Management in Practice: Taking COMPSTAT to the Next Level," *Policing* 2, no. 3 (January 2008): 259–265. Bratton left New York and brought his enthusiasm for CompStat to Los Angeles. See the CompStat section of the official Web site of the Los Angeles Police Department, www.lapdonline.org/crime_mapping_and_compstat/content_basic_view/6363.

2. Bernard E. Harcourt, *Illusion of Order: The False Promise of Broken Windows Policing* (Chicago: University of Chicago Press, 2001). Patricia J. William, "It's Time to End 'Broken Windows' Policing," *The Nation* magazine, January 27, 2014.

3. Paul D. Epstein, Paul M. Coates, and Lyle D. Wray, with David Swain, *Results That Matter: Improving Communities by Engaging Citizens, Measuring Performance, and Getting Things Done* (San Francisco: Jossey-Bass, 2006), 53. Also see Robert D. Behn, *What All Mayors Would Like to Know About Baltimore's CitiStat Performance Strategy* (Washington, DC: IBM Center for the Business of Government, 2008), www.businessofgovernment.org/report/Behn-CitiStat.

4. Teresita Perez and Reese Rushing, *The CitiStat Model* (Washington, DC: Center for American Progress, 2007), www.americanprogress.org/issues/2007/04/pdf/citistat_report.pdf; Robert D. Behn, "The Varieties of CitiStat," *Public Administration Review* 66, no. 3 (2006): 332–340.

5. Dean Dabney, "Observations Regarding Key Operational Realities in a Compstat Model of Policing," *Justice Quarterly* 27, no. 1 (2010): 28–51.

6. Beth Weitzman, Diana Silver, and Caitlynn Braill, "Efforts to Improve Public Policy and Programs through Data Practice: Experiences in 15 Distressed American Cities," *Public Administration Review* 66, no. 3 (2006): 386–399.

The widespread utilization of trained observer rating systems shows that even relatively simple data collection can help improve municipal performance. Yet systems of data-driven performance management can also be quite sophisticated and complex. New York's CompStat program and Baltimore's CitiStat system provide "real-time" data analysis to spur agencies to initiate immediate changes in response to reported problems. (See Box 8.2: "CompStat and CitiStat: Advanced Systems of Performance Measurement and Management.") These advanced managerial systems have been so successful that they have spawned imitators across the country. But many cities, especially smaller cities, find these systems difficult to implement. Such cities lack the technology and staffing assistance necessary to integrate sophisticated data analysis into their departments' daily decision making.

COPRODUCTION AND BUSINESS IMPROVEMENT DISTRICTS (BIDs)

Citizens and businesses alike have come to realize that overburdened municipal agencies cannot always provide high-quality services. As a result, neighborhoods and businesses have come to see the virtues of working in partnership with governmental agencies in the **coproduction** of improved public services.[19] Neighborhood Watch programs have residents partner with the police to reduce crime. In Detroit, parents and community activists, armed only with flashlights, walk the streets the night before Halloween, bringing a virtual end to the reign of "Devil's Night" arson that once plagued the city. Neighborhood cleanup days entail trash pickup by volunteer groups, which city haulers then cart away. Community groups also raise the funds and provide the labor to install new playground facilities that the local parks department may not otherwise be able to afford. Parents assist schools teachers in tutoring and in student enrichment programs.

Coproduction is also a valuable part of local strategies to "repurpose" vacant lots. In Flint, Michigan, when a neighbor complains about the junk piling up in a vacant lot, the government responds: "Would you like to take care of it? We'll help you." In Pennsylvania, Pittsburgh Mayor Luke Ravenstahl introduced a "Green Up Pittsburgh" program that provides soil, grass seed, and the advice of a landscape architect to community groups that seek to transform vacant properties into gardens, play spaces, and attractive side lots. The city also provides volunteers with liability assistance and helps community groups gain title to the land.[20]

San Francisco relies on volunteers and nonprofit organizations in the gay community to provide risk-reduction counseling and home-based care to persons with AIDS.[21] Similarly, in numerous cities neighborhood-based organizations reach out to Latina women in an effort to increase their willingness to use emergency shelter and protective services. Neighborhood-based organizations assist women who have little command of English and whose distrust of authorities may keep them from seeking assistance.[22]

Businesses, too, have discovered the virtues of coproduction, in supplementing the services that municipalities provide. Across the country, cities have granted businesses in a commercial area the ability to form a **business improvement district (BID)**, a self-taxing, self-help arrangement where the city collects an additional fee from area property owners so that a business council can arrange for supplemental services that businesses desire.[23] The city collects the additional charge and hands it over to the BID's **district management association**, which decides how the money should be spent. Cities are happy to have businesses help pay for improved service provision. Business leaders are willing to contribute, as one downtown Los Angeles business spokeswoman observed: "These aren't like taxes that get lost in the general fund. . . . The money stays inside the business district . . . where businesses can see results."[24]

BIDs undertake a variety of actions to promote an area's business climate. BIDs help pay for additional street security personnel, improved trash collection, more frequent street cleaning, the installation of new street lamps, and the placement of signs to help direct visitors to businesses. BIDs also help sponsor local festivals and concerts that will entice visitors to an area.

It is not quite accurate to view a BID as a purely voluntary organization. Commercial property owners in a district who oppose the creation of a BID must nonetheless pay the additional assessment or surtax imposed by the city on behalf of a BID. In tourist-oriented Hyannis, Massachusetts, dissident property owners organized "RidtheBid.org" in an effort to dissolve the city's Main Street BID.[25]

BIDs are a relatively new but increasingly important form of local governance.[26] The first BID was created in the 1970s. By the early 1990s, more than 1,200 BIDs were created in cities across the United States. Today the figure is closer to 2,000. In 2013, New York City had 678 BIDs that invested over $100 million annually in neighborhood improvement and economic development projects.[27] Los Angeles had 38 BIDs, most of which sought heightened public safety as part of the effort to attract new consumers to graying areas of the city.[28] San Francisco's Union Square Business Improvement District is the largest of the city's 11 BIDs. Atlanta, Baltimore, Boston, Cleveland, Denver, Mesa, Milwaukee, Pasadena, Philadelphia, San Diego, San Francisco, Seattle, and Washington, D.C., are only a few of the cities in which BIDs have been established. In Chicago, BIDs are called Special Service Areas.

Each state determines the exact rules for local BID formation and governance. Typically, a BID is *not* run according to one-person-one-vote ballot rules. Instead, as a business association, votes in a BID are weighted according to the value of an owner's property. The more property an owner possesses, the greater the vote that he or she can cast at BID meetings. Even the vote to create a BID is weighted according to the *value* of the commercial property owned. Residents of a neighborhood do not have a vote on BID formation and activities, even though a BID will make decisions that affect the quality of life of the neighborhood.

BIDs of different sizes serve different purposes.[29] The largest are **corporate BIDs** dominated by major national and international businesses and with budgets that exceed $1 million. In New York City, the Grand Central Partnership undertook a "Clean and Safe" effort to help to revitalize the area surrounding the famed midtown Manhattan train station. In 2011 alone, the Partnership spent over $13 million on activities covering a seventy-block area of midtown Manhattan.[30] In Pennsylvania, the Center City District similarly supports enhanced public safety, streetscape improvements, and improved sanitation services in a 120 city-block section of downtown Philadelphia.[31]

A **Main Street BID**, by comparison, is a smaller organization that seeks to revitalize declining shopping areas in a city that have lost retail customers. Main Street BIDs typically have budgets in the $200,000 to $1 million range and cover five to twenty square blocks.

The **community BID** is the smallest type of BID and is usually found in declining neighborhoods. Working with budgets of only $200,000 or so, the activities of a Community BID may cover only a few city blocks. Community BIDs lack the ability to finance extensive capital improvements and major promotional campaigns.[32]

The rise of BIDs raises questions of power, democracy, and fairness. As previously noted, only the owners of commercial property, not the ordinary residents living in an area, have voting rights when it comes to BID decisions. The courts view BIDs not as general-purpose governments but as private associations created for business promotion. Consequently, a BID, quite unlike a public body like a city council, does not have to meet the one-person-one-vote standard of democratic representation.[33]

Fiscally strapped cities look to BIDs as a means of providing a level of public services that the city itself cannot afford. California cities, squeezed by Proposition 13 and other

Box 8.3
The Debate over BIDs in New York: Should Wall Street Get More Cops?

Business Improvement Districts (BIDs) across the United States have an enviable record in supplementing service provision to aid the revitalization of commercial districts. In New York, the Times Square BID transformed the image of the city's once-gritty entertainment and theater district by funding increased trash pickup, graffiti removal, and new street guides and safety patrols. Yet a city's increased reliance on BIDs also raises important questions regarding service equity. Critics ask just whom BIDs serve and whom BIDs ignore.

In New York, the Grand Central Partnership attempted to remove the homeless from the train station and the surrounding area.[1] Across the continent, in San Francisco, critics similarly charged that the red-and-blue uniformed street "ambassadors" of the Union Square BID harassed the homeless in an attempt to oust them from the city's upscale downtown shopping district.

The Alliance for Downtown New York is a corporate BID funded by the multinational corporate giants that inhabit New York's Lower Manhattan financial district. The BID helped secure the placement of a new police substation in Lower Manhattan, despite the fact that the area has one of the lowest rates of street crime in the city. The Alliance got its wish by offering the city $5 million to help set up and maintain a new substation with 200 officers, with 40 or more assigned to the immediate area. Neighborhoods elsewhere in the city complained that the establishment of the new substation meant the redeployment of officers away from residential areas that suffered greater rates of crime. Queens Councilmember Sheldon Leffler decried that affluent Wall Street was able to buy a level of police protection denied to poorer neighborhoods: "It raises very disturbing questions about whether city resources are going to be allocated where they're needed or auctioned off to the highest bidder."[2]

1. Heather Barr, "More Like Disneyland: State Action, 42 U.S.C. 1 1983, and Business Improvement Districts in New York," *Columbia Human Rights Law Review* 28 (Winter 1997); Evelyn Nieves, "Cities Try to Sweep Homeless Out of Sight," *New York Times,* December 7, 1999.

2. David Kocieniewski, "Wall St. to Pay to Add a Base for the Police," *New York Times,* February 17, 1998. Also see Dan Barry, "Mayor Orders Review of Plan for Substation," *New York Times,* February 19, 1998.

tax limitation measures, turned to BIDs—nongovernmental associations—to enhance trash pickup and downtown security patrols.

The proliferation of BIDs raises serious concerns regarding service inequity and urban dualism.[34] BIDs enable commercial districts to receive a higher level of services that is denied to poorer areas of the city. (See Box 8.3, "The Debate over BIDs in New York: Should Wall Street Get More Cops?")

SERVICE CONTRACTING AND PRIVATIZATION

Cities have looked to the private sector for ways to improve efficiency and performance. Loosely used, the term *privatization* refers to any application of private-sector techniques to public management. Strictly defined, however, **privatization** refers to an even more serious attempt at urban transformation: the effort to replace public bureaucracy with private-sector provision, where services once provided by governmental agencies are turned over to private firms and nonprofit organizations. The privatization movement is driven by the belief that private firms can provide services better and less expensively than can government agencies. The advocates of privatization also believe in the superiority of **market mechanisms**; privatization enables increased competition and citizen choice, freeing citizens from their reliance on an irresponsive and inefficient public bureaucracies.

Under **service contracting**, a municipal government signs a legally binding agreement for a private firm or nonprofit agency to provide a service. Local governments "contract out" a diverse range of services: private haulers pick up trash; community-based organizations assist in drug-abuse counseling and operate shelters for the homeless; private janitorial firms clean governmental offices; and private information technology companies update a city's data processing systems. New York City turned over the daily management of Central Park to the Central Park Conservancy, a not-for-profit private group that turned to extensive corporate fundraising to help finance park improvements.[35] Even certain law enforcement and correctional activities can be privatized. (See Box 8.4, "The Privatization of Policing?")

Privatization is based on the distinction between the decision to *provide* a service to the public, and the decision as to who can best deliver or *produce* the desired service:

> [T]o provide a service is to decide that a service shall be made available and to arrange for its delivery. This is an integral part of a local government's policy-making process. To deliver a service is to actually produce the service. Although a local government may decide to provide a service, it does not necessarily have to be directly involved in its delivery.[36]

Municipal government does not have to produce every service that citizens require; instead, it can arrange for capable private firms and nonprofit agencies to provide the service.

THE ADVANTAGES OF PRIVATIZATION

For many physical and administrative services—including trash collection, fire protection, automotive fleet maintenance, the upkeep of local parks, the performance of inspections, and the modernization of record keeping—private firms often offer similar or better service at lower cost than do municipal agencies.[37] Contracting encourages **competition** that can reduce the costs of service delivery. A private firm must adopt newer and more modern service delivery practices, or else find that it has little chance to submit the winning bid on a contract to perform services for the city. A municipal agency, by contrast, is a **public monopoly** that faces no real competition; its workers

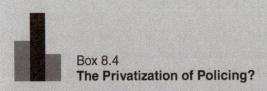

Box 8.4
The Privatization of Policing?

Even a service as seemingly "public" as law enforcement can be privatized or at least partially privatized. There is no reason why protective services must be delivered solely by officers who work directly for the government. Private security firms can assist in maintaining the safety of downtown entertainment districts and large public housing projects. Communities can hire a for-profit firm to run the local jail.

Privatized policing arrangements are largely driven by the search for efficiency. In an age where public dollars are stretched thin, cities have begun to look for ways to carry out important tasks without making expensive long-term commitments. Cities have looked for more flexible options than the hiring of new officers who may earn tenure rights under civil service. A municipality's contract to a private law enforcement firm, by contrast, entails no similar long-term commitments; the city can choose not to renew the contract when a short-term need fades. Facing budget constraints, police departments in Fresno (California), Mesa (Arizona), and Charlotte (North Carolina) have even recruited volunteers to respond to low-level service calls and to collect evidence and interview witnesses, tasks that were previously performed by salaried police officers.

Critics, however, worry about the loss of public control when private companies and volunteers are utilized to help provide for public safety and to run prisons. Private firms may not give their officers the same extensive training that public law enforcement officers receive. Private officers and volunteers may also lack the commitment to respecting civil rights and civil liberties that is expected of law enforcement officials in a democracy.

Sources: Jesse McKinley, "Police Departments Turn to Volunteers," *New York Times,* March 1, 2011; Brian Forst and Peter K. Manning, *The Privatization of Policing: Two Views* (Washington, DC: Georgetown University Press, 1999); James F. Pastor, *The Privatization of Police in America: An Analysis and Case Study* (Jefferson, NC: McFarland, 2003).

do not have to update their skills and perform well and efficiently in order to keep their civil-service-protected jobs.

Former Indianapolis mayor Stephen Goldsmith argues that competition is the key to privatization's ability to produce cost savings. Only when a number of qualified firms bid on a municipal contract will each hopeful feel compelled to submit bids with no excess or "fat." A city will not likely reap cost savings when only one private firm has the capacity to perform requested services. Privatization without competition seldom saves money; in such cases, privatization replaces an inefficient public monopoly with an inefficient private monopoly.[38]

A city can receive the benefits of competition without actually turning over service to a private firm. Under a process known as **managed competition**, public agencies are allowed to bid on a contract: the city can then choose to award the contract to either the municipal agency or a private contractor. In order to win the contract and keep their jobs, workers in a municipal agency will have to "shape up," redesigning work processes and adopting new efficiency-oriented practices. In Phoenix, a reenergized public sanitation department won back many of the contracts that had previously been awarded to private haulers. In Indianapolis, the municipal public works department implemented new cost-savings practices to beat out private competitors in neighborhoods where trash collection was put out for bid.[39]

Contracting also enables new flexibilities that are not normally found in public agencies constrained by civil-service personnel rules. Compared to civil-service-protected agencies, private firms have a greater ability to transfer workers from one division to another and to penalize or dismiss workers who fail to perform effectively. Private firms can also dispense large rewards to top managers for outstanding performance; in public agencies, civil service rules severely constrain such awards in order to limit the dangers of partisan manipulation. Private firms also can save money by hiring part-time employees and paying workers less than does the government.

Financial exigency is driving a number of municipalities to look more deeply at privatization. Cash-strapped cities like Harrisburg, Pennsylvania, look to privatization as a means of gaining much needed revenues. Facing over $300 million in debt and teetering on the edge of bankruptcy, Harrisburg in 2011 sought to sell the city incinerator and have private companies bid for the privilege of operating the city's parking meters and garages. The private companies saw the potential for profit over the longer term. The city, in turn, received an immediate cash windfall to help repay creditors and cover shortfalls in the municipal budget.

Private companies pay substantial sums for city assets that have a profit-making potential. Chicago in 2005 received $1.8 billion for a lease that gave an Australian-Spanish entity a 99-year right to operate and collect the tolls on the Chicago Skyway, a major toll road connecting the city to neighboring Indiana. The private company was obligated to make improvements in the important but physically deteriorating roadway. Two years later, the city received another $1.15 billion from a different private contractor in return for a 75-year lease to run the city's parking meters.

Contractual arrangements enable municipalities to gain the benefit of the extensive experience of renowned global firms and the commitment of nonprofit organizations that work with the elderly, troubled youth, drug users, and the homeless.

THE DISADVANTAGES AND RISKS OF PRIVATIZATION

The advocates of privatization often present an overly idealized portrait of a private sector virtue contrasted with the waste and inefficiency of public bureaucracy. But as the revelations of corporate scandals pointedly underscore, the performance of private corporations, too, can suffer from extensive waste, including **payoffs, skimming, and corruption**. In Chicago, service contracting is not simply a means to improve service efficiency: the local Democratic organization also dispensed contracts to its friends as

Box 8.5
Service Contracting: "Pin-Stripe Patronage" and Corruption in Chicago

Civil service regulations prevented Chicago Mayor Richard M. Daley from amassing the large patronage armies of his father, Richard J. Daley, the legendary political "boss" of the city. Instead of relying on patronage, Richard M. won the public's favor by demonstrating his ability to effectively manage and lead the city. Privatization was one of the tools that Richard M. used. During his two-decade tenure as mayor, Daley reduced the size of the city's workforce and increased service efficiency by contracting out various services: parking meter collections, automobile fleet maintenance, tree stump removal, window cleaning, the towing of abandoned cars, the management of the municipal golf course, and even the treatment of drug addicts.

Yet critics offer a less charitable view of Richard M. Daley's fondness for contracting. They charge that the mayor's loyalists used contracting as a form of **pin-stripe patronage**, steering contracts for legal work and business services to the mayor's financial contributors and political friends. Potential contractors who desired to do work for the city had to "pay to play," receiving very profitable contracts after having made large political contributions.

At its worst, the award of contracts in Chicago was plagued by blatant corruption. The Hired Truck Scandal revealed that the city paid bills for work that was never performed. Operation Incubator, a federal investigation, uncovered a system in which municipal officials took bribes when deciding just which firms would win the competition to collect water bills and unpaid parking tickets.

Sources: Rowan A. Miranda, "Privatization in Chicago's City Government," in *Research in Urban Policy,* vol. 4, ed. Kenneth K. Wong (Greenwich, CT: JAI Press, 1992); Thomas J. Gradel, Dick Simpson, and Andris Zimelis, "Curing Corruption in Illinois: Anti-Corruption Report Number 1," University of Illinois at Chicago, Department of Political Science, February 3, 2009, www.ilcampaign. org/docs/Anti-corruptionReport.pdf; Dick Simpson and Constance A. Mixon, eds., *Twenty-First Century Chicago* (San Diego: Cognella, 2013).

a form of patronage. (See Box 8.5, "Service Contracting: 'Pin-Stripe Patronage' and Corruption in Chicago.")

Nor does privatization always save money. Contracting often entails **hidden costs**, including the costs that a municipality incurs in preparing a contract for bid and the costs of having to monitor the work performed by the contractor.[40] Not all costs go away when the city privatizes a service: the municipality has to maintain buildings that are no longer in use; it also may have continuing salary and pension obligations to municipal workers who are no longer needed by the city. The city also faces the potential problem of a service interruption if a contractor is unable to perform as promised or if the city has to dismiss a contractor.

Unscrupulous contractors may seek to maximize profits by "cutting corners" and lowering service quality. In order to win the city's business, a private firm may submit a **lowball contract bid**, that is, an unrealistically low bid that does not represent the full cost of services provided over the life of the contract. Dependent on a contractor to provide important services, a city may find that it has no real alternative but to pay the cost overruns that a contractor later bills the city.

Bid-rigging, too, can diminish the competitive nature of a process that relies on the submission of "blind bids." In New York City and in cities on neighboring Long Island, trash haulers acted to "fix" bids, to "collusively decide the low bid and low bidder." In Connecticut, James Galante, the head of a trash-hauling empire, was imprisoned for racketeering conspiracy and bid-rigging that drove up trash-hauling rates.[41]

The problems that can result from a **municipality's reliance on a private contractor** are evident in Scottsdale, Arizona, where, for nearly half a century, the city contracted with a private company, Rural/Metro, to provide fire-fighting and emergency medical services. When Rural/Metro decided to leave the fire-fighting business to concentrate on the ambulance services it provided in communities across the nation, Scottsdale had no real alternative but to reestablish a municipal fire department. The city was not fully prepared to assume such a responsibility and had to rush to set up training programs and even buy protective clothing for workers. Suddenly, with Rural/Metro gone, the city found that it had no experienced manager on staff who possessed expertise on such important technical matters as determining equipment needs and developing an appropriate schedule to replace fire equipment.[42]

Service contracting is also criticized for being **anti-union**. Faced with competition from low-cost nonunion bidders, unionized municipal and private workforces find it necessary to restrain salary and workplace demands.

New York Mayors Rudy Giuliani and Michael Bloomberg turned to private cleaning companies in their efforts to break the fabled power of the school custodians' union. School custodians often earned extra money by charging school and community groups high fees for using school facilities after normal school hours. Giuliani and Bloomberg sought to privatize about a third of the school janitorial jobs, using the threat of further privatization to pressure the custodians to accept a reduction in their benefits and job privileges. But the custodians' union fought back, securing judicial intervention that blocked some of the mayors' efforts.[43]

Contracts that allow private companies to run city parking operations have been especially controversial. In their efforts to find resources to alleviate a city's budget crisis and avoid the layoff of police officers and other critical municipal personnel, municipal leaders have shown a new willingness to turn city parking lots and meters over to private operators. The private firms also agree to make substantial investments to modernize services, for instance, replacing aging and often broken coin-operated meters with a new generation of "smart" meters that accept credit cards and that charge rates that can easily be adjusted by the hour of the day. Privatization theorists argue that such fee adjustments allow a city to capture greater revenues from assets such as parking.[44]

But Chicago residents were not buying such justifications, and their outrage mounted when a report issued by the city's Inspector General seemed to document that the city had received nearly a billion dollars less than its parking assets were worth, despite the competitive bidding process. Residents felt they were being "ripped off" when the private firm continued to hike parking prices and extended the hours and days of paid parking—even requiring payment on the July 4th national holiday. The city, too, much to its surprise, found that the contract contained hidden costs; the city was obligated to pay millions of dollars each year to the company for parking spaces lost to parades, festivals, and the necessity of making street repairs. The city sought arbitration to lessen the amount the private company billed the city for parking spaces used by city police, by other municipal workers, and by disabled citizens.[45]

In New York, Los Angeles, Cincinnati, Pittsburgh, and Harrisburg, elected officials and city managers looked to parking privatization as a source of new revenues to help balance municipal budgets. But public officials beat a retreat (in some cities only temporarily) in the face of voter outrage.[46] Cincinnati backed down in the face of disgruntled citizens who demanded the right to vote on the issue. The city's new mayor campaigned on the promise of reexamining parking privatization. Residents intuitively understand that the long-term leasing of parking and private operation of such assets like the Chicago Skyway and toll roads in Texas is an **intergenerational transfer of funds**: the city receives a one-time bounty of revenues while the private operator raises prices and imposes a financial burden on citizens in the future.[47] Critics also questioned the loss of public control and a competitive environment when contracts ran as long as 75 and 99 years.

THE PRIVATE MANAGEMENT OF PUBLIC SCHOOLS

A number of states and cities have turned to private management firms to run troubled local schools. Compared to public schools ensnared by a myriad of state regulations, privately managed schools have greater freedom to act when it comes to curriculum and personnel. Private management firms also utilize cost-savings techniques adopted by other businesses. Most importantly, the advocates of private management hope that new leadership will shake up school operations and instill a new "culture of achievement"[48] in failing schools.

Yet the record shows that privately managed public schools do not consistently produce the results that privatization enthusiasts promise. Miami contracted with a private firm, Educational Alternatives, Inc. (EAI), to take over the operations of a failing public school. EAI developed an individualized learning plan for each student. EAI subcontracted maintenance and building repair tasks to partner firms, allowing principals and teachers to devote greater attention to their core mission. EAI promised to create a "dream school" with the latest in computers and innovative instructional programs in math and reading. Baltimore and Hartford also turned to EAI to run a number of their city's troubled schools.

But teachers complained of EAI's all-out assault on tenure, as the company hired low-cost instructional personnel instead of qualified teachers to fill a number of classroom support positions. Teachers further complained that EAI forced educators to work a longer school day with no extra pay.[49] The continuing conflict between EAI and the teachers' unions impeded reform. In Baltimore, African-American activists decried decisions that placed control over instruction in the hands of outside white managers. The activists objected that EAI's corporate form of instruction was intended to prepare children to be little more than cogs in the workplace.[50]

All three cities eventually decided not to renew their contracts with EAI. In each city, the introduction of private management was a quite tumultuous affair that did not produce dramatic improvements in student test scores.

In the nation's most extensive experiment with the private management of public schools, the State of Pennsylvania in 2002 turned over forty-five Philadelphia elementary and middle schools to three for-profit educational companies—including Edison Schools, the nation's largest private educational management organization. The private teams introduced a new curriculum. The schools were also given an infusion of additional resources. But evaluation results were disappointing; even with the advantage of increased per-pupil expenditures, private management of Philadelphia's schools did not lead to statistically significant improvement in student math and reading scores.[51] In some cases, the gains in student achievement in the Edison-run schools lagged behind those in publicly run schools in the city.[52] In 2008, Philadelphia terminated its experiment with private school management.

Still, despite this mixed record, advocacy groups like the Bill and Melinda Gates Foundation have urged cities to experiment with increased parental engagement coupled with private school management. In California and other states, Parent Revolution and other Gates-inspired groups have urged the adoption of **parent trigger laws** that allow the signatures of 51 percent of the parents in a failing school to close the school and turn over its operation to a private management organization.[53]

The private management of schools, despite the claims of its advocates, is no magic bullet that will cure the ills of public education. At best, the track record of privately managed public schools is uneven. Private management has demonstrated only the most limited ability to turn around schools facing "academic bankruptcy." In Miami, Baltimore, Hartford, and Philadelphia, the private management of public education did not produce clear gains in student learning. Still, as their defenders point out, private school operators in these cities were not given the full flexibility to run schools as they wished.

VOUCHERS, TAX CREDITS, AND CHARTER SCHOOLS: A VARIETY OF SCHOOL CHOICE PROGRAMS

A variety of **school choice programs** seek to give parents greater ability to decide just which school their child will attend, empowering them to find a school with a curriculum and an approach that matches their child's interests. School choice programs seek to liberate parents and students from dependence on local public schools.

The most far-reaching choice plan entails a system of **school vouchers**, under which students (or, to be more accurate, their parents or guardians) receive a certificate that can be used to help pay tuition at a participating school of their choice. Despite the rhetoric of choice, however, the system does not allow every voucher recipient the free ability to choose schools. The **monetary size of the voucher** is crucial to determining just how much choice parents and students actually possess. A large voucher enables a greater choice of schools. Yet, as choice advocates often seek to contain—not increase—school spending, such generous vouchers are rarely provided. Instead, vouchers tend to cover only part of the costs of a private education and provide working-class and low-income families with only quite limited choices.

A voucher program's **accompanying regulations** also help to determine how much choice a student will actually receive. Regulations can reduce some of the unfairness and discriminations of an unregulated or free-market approach to vouchers. In the absence of strong regulations governing admissions, for instance, some private schools discriminate against voucher applicants with disabilities.[54] A school that has total freedom to set its own admissions criteria may also be tempted to engage in a process known as **creaming**, admitting only the most capable voucher students (the so-called "cream of the crop"), leaving other students with no real alternative but to attend the more troubled public schools.

Eligibility provisions, too, help to determine just who does and does not benefit from a voucher program. In Cleveland and Milwaukee, **targeted voucher programs** restrict benefits to poorer children seeking to escape failing schools; targeted programs provide benefits to inner-city minorities. In contrast, more **universal voucher plans** that seek to dispense assistance more broadly to middle-class families (and not just to the poor) would likely have vastly different impacts, enabling better-off students to flee racially mixed schools.[55] As we shall discuss, the advocates of expansive school choice in Wisconsin are pushing to provide vouchers to large numbers of working- and middle-class beneficiaries, a change likely to greatly alter the workings of the state program of educational assistance that has strictly been targeted for the poor.

Florida and Texas provide **publicly and privately funded scholarships** to increase the options available to students from low-income families. These so-called "opportunity scholarships" are, in essence, a voucher-style program that enables a limited number of students to pay private school tuition. Despite the great publicity it received, the Florida Opportunity Scholarship program did not create substantial choice. The Florida legislature failed to provide the level of funding to allow large numbers of students to leave failing schools. The program was only assisting 730 students with private school tuition at the time the state supreme court struck it down for violating language in the Florida constitution requiring the state maintain an efficient system of "public" schools.[56] Since then, the Florida choice program was modified to give students from failing public schools a new ability to enroll in other public schools, not private schools.

In Georgia, the award of scholarships has done relatively little to increase choice among students who have the greatest need. Instead, Georgia's scholarship program channels financial assistance to parents whose children are already attending private academies and to families who seek schools that provide a strong values and religious education.[57]

Tax deductions and tax credits are other tools that seek to promote school choice. Yet such programs often have a pernicious **class bias**, as they wind up subsidizing the education decisions of the middle class while providing only the most minimal assistance to the poor. Such a bias is clearly evident in the national system of **Education Savings Accounts (ESA)** which allows parents to set aside up to $2,000 a year in interest-free accounts for a child's K–12 tuition. Middle- and upper-income families enjoy the tax benefits of investing such money in educational accounts. The tax incentive does little to help poorer families that lack the resources to set aside money in tuition accounts. A promise of a tax credit also provides no meaningful benefit to parents who are so poor that they have very little or no tax liability.

Georgia uses a controversial system of tax credits to fund its scholarship program. In 2012, at a time when public schools were facing "deep cutbacks," Georgia spent $50 million in dollar-for-dollar tax credits, fully reimbursing a couple for up to $2,500 in donations to private school scholarships. Relatively little of the program's money wound up assisting children in need. Instead, the bulk of the funds was channeled into school-designated scholarships that were awarded to the children of the families that raised the money. Most of the scholarships also helped subsidize attendance at religious schools, including schools with policies to expel gay and lesbian students.[58]

In recent years, one choice program has proven particularly popular and is reshaping K–12 school systems across the United States. A **charter school** is an innovative school that is established or "chartered" by the state and that operates under the supervision of a state-authorized body (i.e., a state university, community college, or even the local public school district). Governmental regulations regarding curriculum and various facets of school operation are relaxed in order to give each charter academy greater freedom to develop curriculum, disciplinary policies, and other practices that best fit the school's unique mission. As charter schools are still public schools, though, they do not possess the full freedoms enjoyed by voucher-funded private schools. Numerous state rules and regulations still apply to charter schools, including, in many states, regulations that limit the ability of charter schools to abridge teacher tenure. Charter schools seem to offer a middle ground between voucher schools and traditional public education.

Defenders of the public schools argue that there is no need to resort to educational vouchers and tax credits as a public school district can offer increased student choice by establishing its own **specialized schools and minischools**, each with a distinctive curriculum. Choice advocates retort that such publicly sponsored minischools are too protective of public-school teachers and too constrained by public rules to permit the degree of competition and curricular innovation offered by more expansive market-based reforms.

DOES SCHOOL CHOICE WORK? THE EVIDENCE ON STUDENT ACHIEVEMENT AND RACIAL SEGREGATION

Numerous studies show that vouchers and other school choice programs have had only the most marginal impact on improving student performance. The prestigious Carnegie Foundation concluded that the movement for school choice was guided more by ideology than by evidence, that "many of the claims for school choice have been based more on speculation than experience."[59] Yet, choice advocates continue to point to other studies that support their programs, including data from Milwaukee that indicates that voucher students enjoy higher graduation rates than do comparable nonvoucher students.[60]

The Carnegie Foundation further warned that choice programs may exacerbate **urban dualism**, widening the gap between the haves and have-nots of American society. Choice programs enable more-capable students and the children of more-vigilant parents to escape troubled schools. Other children wind up being left behind in **dumping-ground schools** with even less funding and even lower prospects of success than before. Voucher programs that permit **add-ons**, that is, they allow families to spend their own funds to supplement the amount provided by the voucher, have the potential to deepen the class and racial stratification of the nation's schools.

There is no evidence that choice plans widely allow for increased voluntary racial integration, as voucher theorists contend. In some cities, choice programs have had the exact opposite effect, facilitating "white flight" from schools undergoing racial change. In Cleveland, vouchers did little to increase racial integration in suburban schools, as suburban districts for the most part refused to participate in the program and admit voucher students. Suburban homeowners are resistant to vouchers and school choice programs.[61]

The good news, however, is that while choice programs as a whole do not greatly increase racial integration they do not seem to promote massive school resegregation, as critics contend. Especially when a voucher or choice program is tightly targeted, as in Milwaukee and Cleveland where voucher participation is restricted to the inner-city poor, vouchers do not add greatly to white flight from a city's schools. Instead, such choice programs succeed in enabling some minority students to attend classes in less stratified, church-related parochial schools.[62]

DO SCHOOL VOUCHERS VIOLATE THE SEPARATION OF CHURCH AND STATE?

In Cleveland and Milwaukee, large numbers of students use government-funded vouchers to enroll in **parochial schools**, the Catholic-run schools in the inner city that teach religion during parts of the school day. Critics argue that such aid is a violation of the constitutional requirement for the separation of church and state.

A sharply divided U.S. Supreme Court in 2002 decided the question, ruling in ***Zelman v. Simmons-Harris***[63] that the Cleveland program's inclusion of parochial schools is constitutionally permissible. According to the Court, the voucher program does *not* violate the U.S. Constitution's First Amendment prohibition against the state establishment of religion. Even though many families use the assistance to enroll their children in parochial schools, the Court did not view the program as providing state support of religious instruction. Instead, the Court viewed the Cleveland voucher program as "neutral" in terms of its respect toward religion. The government did not provide aid directly to church schools; rather, parents freely chose which schools their children would attend. The voucher program also had a clear **secular purpose**—to assist children trapped in failing public schools; the program did not intend to advance religious instruction.

Dissenters responded that the Court ignored the on-the-ground reality, that vouchers provide the money that keeps big-city parochial schools open and hence supports religious instruction. At the time of the Court's decision, 96 percent of state-provided voucher funds were spent in Cleveland's parochial schools! In Milwaukee, a quarter of the schools participating in the Choice Program—a group dominated by parochial schools—reported that every one of their students received voucher support![64]

A CASE STUDY: MILWAUKEE'S LOW-INCOME SCHOOL VOUCHER PLAN—THE EVIDENCE AND RECENT CHANGES

In the early 1990s, the State of Wisconsin enacted the first—and the largest—school voucher program in the nation. For the 2012–2013 school year, the program gave $6,442 each in assistance to more than 24,000 Milwaukee students to attend private and parochial schools instead of the city's public schools.

For the first two decades of the program's existence, the distribution of vouchers in Milwaukee was highly **targeted**: vouchers were given only to students whose families were poor or near the poverty line. State regulations sought to avoid selection bias or creaming, where receiving schools would seek to admit only the more talented voucher students. Schools that accepted vouchers were prohibited from selecting students on the basis of a student's prior educational or behavioral record.

Evaluations of the Milwaukee program show mixed results. On the plus side, the vouchers were utilized by students who had been performing poorly in the public schools. The program enhanced the options available to low-income students and their parents. African-American parents expressed their satisfaction with a program that enabled their children to escape problem schools.[65] As the parent of a seventh-grade voucher student who chose a new school explained, "As soon as I came here it was a big change. Here teachers care about you. . . . [In public schools] the teachers were too busy to help."[66] The targeted voucher program did not lead to higher levels of racial segregation, as opponents had feared; nor, however, did it advance racial integration.[67]

Yet voucher students showed few gains on standardized tests.[68] The small edge that the voucher students exhibited was a product of self-selection and not clearly the result of vouchers: the children of more-concerned parents enrolled in the voucher schools and, as could be expected, scored better than the children of less-involved parents. Quite surprisingly, a large number of students chose not to reenroll in the program, indicating some dissatisfaction with the program.[69] Overall, as the Carnegie Foundation summarized, the Milwaukee experience "failed to demonstrate that vouchers can, in and of themselves, spark school improvement."[70]

Looking at the evidence, some prominent political conservatives have begun to question the decision to continue to fight for voucher systems that have not delivered as promised. These conservatives argue that instead of fighting for the expanded use of vouchers, change efforts should be directed at improving the instruction received in the public schools, the schools that the vast majority of poor children attend.[71]

Voucher advocates respond that it often takes years for the new schools to shake off students' bad public-school habits. By their fourth year of participation, voucher students begin to show moderate gains in achievement scores.[72]

Educational restructuring also does not always deliver the healthy competition that voucher enthusiasts had promised. In Florida, the creation of Opportunity Scholarships awarded to students from failing schools did help generate some competitive pressures that led the schools to revamp their curriculum and give heightened attention to low-performing students.[73] But the effects that were observed were relatively modest. Similarly in Milwaukee, the loss of students to voucher schools did not push existing public schools to introduce major reforms. The Milwaukee teachers' union blocked attempts to modify seniority rules, close poorly performing schools, and strengthen processes for evaluating teachers.[74]

In sum, the Milwaukee system of targeted vouchers produced limited results. Despite the testimony of parents affirming the importance of school vouchers to the lives of their children, statistical evidence reveals that voucher students showed few gains on achievement tests. Gains in student achievement scores were inconsistent and rather small.

Governor Scott Walker and a Republican-dominated Wisconsin state legislature largely ignored concerns raised by the evidence and decided in 2011 to expand the state's voucher program. Vouchers were offered to children not only in Milwaukee but also in nearby Racine. The new law relaxed eligibility provisions, allowing families that earned up to three times the poverty line to participate in the program. A family of four with an income of nearly $71,000 was eligible for voucher assistance. A family of six could earn up to $95,395 and still have its children receive school vouchers.[75] The state also gave private schools permission to charge voucher students certain fees for activities not covered by the amount of the voucher. The program changes led to a surge in taxpayer-supported enrollments at parochial and private schools in greater Milwaukee.

Governor Walker and choice enthusiasts proposed that school vouchers be dispensed in a greater number of communities, not just in the low-income neighborhoods in Milwaukee. Opponents feared that even a small statewide program would be a "foot in the door" to the expanded use of vouchers across the state, as the state legislature each year could simply increase the program's enrollment cap.

The Wisconsin changes constitute a bold experiment that merits watching. Governor Walker sought to expand school choice to working- and middle-class families. The new program modifications diminish the tight targeting that had characterized the Milwaukee voucher effort since the program's inception. While the expansion was initially accompanied by increases in state school aid, doubters worried that future expansion of school vouchers would require the redirection of funding away from traditional public schools. The impact that expanded voucher usage will have on the class and racial composition of school populations remains to be seen.

CHARTER SCHOOLS: A MIDDLE WAY?

School vouchers, steeped in controversy, have not gained widespread adoption across the United States. In contrast, a great many states and school districts have turned to charter schools, a less revolutionary but more pragmatic "choice" program.

A **charter school** is authorized and funded by the state but run by an independent group; compared to regular public schools, the operator of a charter school is given greater flexibility in the choice of curriculum and other matters of school operation.[76] A charter school may also have a unique specialization—instruction in science, the arts, military-like discipline, or specialized ethnic history

As a public school, a charter school is nonsectarian (that is, nonreligious) and does not charge student tuition. Each charter school receives state aid based on the number of pupils enrolled. In many states the per-pupil aid is roughly equivalent to the student-based aid that the state provides regular public schools. States also offer grants to assist the start-up of charter schools.

President Barack Obama and First Lady Michelle Obama Pose with Students at a Charter School in Washington, D.C.

From Wikimedia Commons, by Joyce N. Boghosian, February 3, 2009, http://commons.wikimedia.org/wiki/File:Barack_%26_Michelle_Obama_at_Washington_DC_public_charter_school_2-3-09_1.jpg.

Charter schools are popular because of their smaller-size classes and their emphasis on academics and innovative teaching. Many charter schools emphasize the use of computers and technology-assisted instruction. Charter schools also typically make a concerted effort to involve families in the educational process.

Charter schools represent an important way to increase the variety of offerings available to students while maintaining state authority:

> In some ways, charter schools are the middle-way response in the twenty-plus year arguments over school choice. While they are not the free-range schools of choice that some voucher proponents have advocated (. . . charter schools are still moderately to heavily regulated), neither are they the traditional, shop-worn school down the street.[77]

The charter approach is a less far-reaching reform than vouchers. While deregulation allows charter school managers newfound freedom in important areas, nonetheless charter schools must still follow numerous other rules that do not apply to private schools. The process of chartering clearly denotes continuing state authority; a student can only choose to attend an innovative school that the state has decided to charter. States also typically "cap" or limit the number of new schools that can be created each year.

The educational establishment has come to accept charter schools as a moderate form of choice that it finds preferable to vouchers. But teacher unions still see charters as a threat. Consequently teach unions often seek to limit charter school funding and to impose a cap on the number of charter schools that can be created in a state. Public school teachers have also fought against allowing for-profit educational management firms to play an expanded role in charter school operations.[78] In Los Angeles, public school teachers threatened litigation to block charter-school takeovers by outside groups.[79]

In New York, Bill de Blasio won the mayoralty in 2014, promising to rein in charter schools that had a "destructive impact" on regular schools. De Blasio proposed charging rents to the charter academies for the space they occupied in regular city schools. But de Blasio's efforts were initially blunted by New York Governor Andrew Cuomo who declared his intention to "save" charter schools.[80]

The growth of charter schools has been explosive. In 1995, only 250 charter schools existed in the United States. By 2013, approximately 6,000 charter schools enrolled over 2.3 million children. The largest number of charter schools are found in California (1,065), Florida (583), Arizona (535), Texas (623), Ohio (369), Michigan (280), Wisconsin (243), Colorado (184), and Pennsylvania (175).[81]

CHARTER SCHOOLS AND THE QUESTION OF RACE

Do charter schools serve poor and minority children? Or do charter academies exacerbate the racial inequalities of present-day schooling? Does the creation of charter schools offer an important route to voluntary school integration? Or do charter schools create new opportunities for "white flight" that will lead to the resegregation of public school systems? The answers to these questions are not always clear.

Enrollment data reveal that charter schools do, in fact, serve inner-city, low-income, and racial minority students. Nationwide, about half of the students in charter schools come from minority backgrounds.[82] Numerous charter academies are located in inner cities and offer low-income and minority students both college-prep courses and specialized programs in the industrial and the creative arts.

Yet in a number of metropolitan areas, charter academies enable white families to flee schools that have a large concentration of racial minorities.[83] In Pontiac, Michigan, and the inner-ring Detroit suburb of Ferndale, charter schools offered white parents a route of escape that undercut court-ordered school desegregation in neighboring districts.[84]

In Arizona, the creation of charter schools diminished racial integration, as students attended charter academies that were less racially integrated than the district schools the students had exited.[85] In Durham, North Carolina, school choice programs enabled more advantaged students to move to schools with a less racially diverse student body. In New York City, the existence of single-race charter schools reveals that charter academies do not provide a reliable tool for racial desegregation.[86]

Yet there is good news: despite the cases cited above, national statistical data documents that, on the whole, charter schools have not promoted substantial white flight. Why is this so? As already discussed, a great many charter schools are focused on inner-city communities with large minority populations. The racial imbalance found in charter schools does not differ greatly from the racial imbalance that characterizes many big-city school systems.[87]

AN ASSESSMENT OF CHARTER SCHOOLS AND THEIR IMPACT

A wide variety of school approaches exist under the umbrella of charter schools. Some, like the KIPP (Knowledge Is Power Program) academies have a demonstrated record of success. Others do not. In places like Washington, D.C., charter academies have not produced the major gains in student performance that the most enthusiastic backers of charter schools had promised.[88]

The first national assessment of reading and math scores in charter schools revealed data that is particularly troubling. Students in charter schools actually lagged behind the gains that were being achieved by students attending conventional public schools! The Department of Education released the data with little fanfare and tried to bury the more disappointing evidence amid a mountain of data.[89] A RAND Corporation analysis of charter schools in eight states similarly found that chartering had little positive impact on student performance, with one noteworthy exception: charter school students have improved graduation rates.[90]

Despite the disappointing results reported in such studies, other studies point to the successes achieved by charter schools. In Milwaukee, a city that has charter academies as well as the city's renowned voucher program, charter academies gave specialized attention to at-risk students and outperformed the city's regular public schools.[91] Parents expressed their satisfaction with charter schools, but levels of satisfaction diminished over time, as the new schools proved unable to remedy the many educational difficulties that children continued to face.[92]

Critics even question the degree of instructional innovation that can be expected from charter schools. Initially, choice advocates had painted the picture of charter schools as ideal places where innovative young teachers, concerned parents, and community activists could join together in experimenting with new and exciting classroom approaches. Much of that vision of bottom-up creativity has been lost as cities have given national **education management organizations (EMOs)** the right to manage local charter academies. An EMO, which can be a nonprofit organization or even a for-profit private company, seeks cost-savings by insisting that a standardized educational package be implemented in each of its schools. The result is a system where corporate rules promote uniformity but stifle teacher creativity. About one-third of the nation's charter schools are run by EMOs.[93]

Advocates argue that competition from charter schools will spur more conventional public schools to reform their curriculum and practices. However, data from Texas and other states reveal that the impact of charter schools on a city's regular public schools is far less than imagined.[94] Public school teachers and officials often resist copying charter-style practices.

The growth of charter academies also raises questions concerning the separation of church and state. A growing number of charter schools are "quasi-religious," despite explicit requirements that, as public schools, they provide a nonsectarian education. The National Heritage Associates, founded by J.C. Huizenga, a wealthy and devout Christian, creates charter schools with a stress on morals, values, and character development consistent with a Christian education, even though the schools disavow an explicitly religious curriculum.[95] In New York City and Washington, D.C., low-enrollment Catholic schools converted to charter schools but maintained much of their previous staff and classroom stress on the importance of faith and Catholic values—but without the formal recitation of prayers.[96]

In sum, charter schools have a moderate impact on education. While some perform quite well, others do not. Evidence from Wisconsin and other states indicates generally positive, but far from overwhelming and uniformly positive, results. Significantly, charter schools appear to increase graduation rates. The parents of charter school children also generally express their satisfaction with charter schools. Charter schools have also not posed the great dangers that their critics have posited. Especially when the growth in the number of charter schools is capped by state law, charter schools do not pose an extensive threat to conventional public schools.

CONCLUSION: IMPROVING PUBLIC SERVICES

Coproduction, neighborhood-based delivery systems, business improvement districts, contracting out, vouchers, tax credits, and school choice are all strategies that seek to improve municipal service provision or, failing that, to allow citizens to make an "end run" around irresponsive and ineffective local bureaucracies. The new service reformers seek to break the "public monopoly" by introducing market-like systems that create an environment of choice and competition. Competition, they hope, will not only improve service delivery; it will also restrain the wage demands of service providers and provide a motivation for cost efficiency However, the emphasis on cost reduction often overshadows concerns for the equitable provision of municipal services.

In the field of education, the advocates of markets and choice have clearly oversold what privatization can accomplish. Programs of vouchers, private scholarships, tax credits, and charter schools seldom deliver the extensive gains—especially increased student achievement scores—that choice enthusiasts promise. Even where school reforms have produced gains, conservative ideological groups often overstate and oversell the results. The more extensive school reform efforts are driven by ideological groups hostile to public-sector unions and the public-sector monopoly in education.

In the field of housing policy, vouchers do not offer the extensive benefits promised by choice advocates. **Housing choice vouchers (HCV)** are the backbone of the present-day federal strategy to provide housing assistance, having superseded the older national strategy of government construction of public housing. Housing vouchers are meant to promote mobility, to enable low-income families to flee dilapidated housing and find better housing in better neighborhoods. Choice vouchers do not restrict assisted families to public housing. Instead, the award of an HCV assists a low-income family in the private rental market, increasing the financial ability of the family to find satisfactory housing that meets their needs. But studies show that in many cities, especially cities with "tight" housing markets with few vacant units, vouchers give tenants little ability to find housing in nondistressed neighborhoods.[97]

In Broward County, Florida (greater Fort Lauderdale), housing choice vouchers did not greatly promote residential mobility and the dispersal of low-income tenants to low-poverty and racially integrated neighborhoods, as choice enthusiasts had theorized. Instead, Broward's overwhelmingly black population of HCV recipients wind up clustered in the impoverished "low opportunity" neighborhoods in the central core of the county.[98]

"Choice" may be preferable to residents' continued reliance on housing managed by public agencies. Choice by itself, however, fails to produce the opportunities that market advocates promise.

Choice programs do not replace the need for government. Oftentimes, choice strategies work only with the backing of strong government. Choice programs do not substitute for the need to have government invest in education. Housing choice vouchers work capably only when they have the support of municipal officials who convince landlords in better neighborhoods to rent units to voucher families. Effective choice also requires that vouchers be of substantial size, so that they give low-income families sufficient buying power to escape distressed neighborhoods and segregated failing schools.

Effective and efficient service provision also has a metropolitan dimension. As the next two chapters will discuss, effective service provision often requires that communities cross political boundaries and work with their neighbors. Municipal leaders in a region have come to recognize the importance of collaborating for both cost savings and more effective service provision.

KEY TERMS

accompanying regulations, a school voucher program's (*p. 210*)

add-ons to school vouchers (*p. 212*)

administrative discretion (*p. 191*)

anti-union, the accusation that municipal contracting of services is (*p. 207*)

balanced scorecard (*p. 197*)

bid-rigging (*p. 207*)

broken windows policing (*p. 198*)

business improvement district (BID) (*p. 200*)

charter school (*p. 211*)

CitiStat (*p. 198*)

class bias of tax deductions and tax credits for school choice (*p. 210*)

community BID (*p. 201*)

comparative performance measurement (*p. 194*)

competition as a critical element in the success of municipal service contracting (*p. 203*)

CompStat (*p. 198*)

coproduction (*p. 200*)

corporate BIDs (*p. 201*)

creaming (*p. 210*)

district management association, a BID's (*p. 200*)

dumping-ground schools, the charge that school choice programs will result in (*p. 212*)

education management organizations (EMOs) (*p. 217*)

Education Savings Accounts (ESA) (*p. 210*)

efficiency measures (*p. 196*)

equal results standard of service provision (*p. 197*)

equity measures (*p. 196*)

expertise (*p. 191*)

focus groups (*p. 197*)

hidden costs of a service contract (*p. 206*)

housing choice vouchers (HCV) (*p. 218*)

input measures (*p. 196*)

intergenerational transfer of funds, toll road privatization as an (*p. 208*)

lowball contract bid (*p. 207*)

Main Street BID (*p. 201*)

managed competition (*p. 205*)

market mechanisms, privatization's reliance on (*p. 203*)

minischools and other specialized public schools (*p. 211*)

monetary size of the voucher, the critical importance of the (*p. 209*)

9 A Suburban Nation

The United States is a suburban nation.[1] Since the 1960s, the number of people living in the nation's suburbs has exceeded the number in central cities. Even gentrification, the much celebrated "return" to the cities discussed in Chapter 3, poses only a relatively small countertrend that does not offset the long-term drift of population, economic resources, and political power to the suburbs.

Between 2000 and 2009, the population of outer suburban areas in the United States grew at three times the rate of central cities and inner suburbs. The nation's fastest-growing communities are found on the edges of the metropolis: North Las Vegas and Henderson (Nevada), Victorville (sixty miles northeast of Los Angeles), McKinney and Denton (outside of Dallas), and Gilbert and Chandler (outside of Phoenix). McKinney doubled its population in just seven years! Riverside and San Bernardino (outside of Los Angeles), Clark (Nevada), and Maricopa (Arizona) are suburban counties that have experienced explosive growth rates.[2]

Boomburbs—rapidly growing suburbs—can be as big as more established cities. Mesa (Arizona) has a larger population than does Minneapolis, Miami, or St. Louis; Arlington (Texas) surpasses Pittsburgh. Anaheim, Riverside, Santa Ana, San Bernardino, Chula Vista, and Fremont (all in California); Glendale, Scottsdale, and Tempe (Arizona); and Aurora (Colorado) are other notable boomburbs in the American Southwest, where the limited availability of water serves to concentrate patterns of suburban development.[3] Naperville (Illinois), west of Chicago, is a boomburb that has enjoyed rapid growth in the Midwest.

Recent data from the U.S. Census data reveals a somewhat surprising anomaly: from 2009 to 2011, for the first time in decades, a number of big cities experienced greater rates of population growth than did their suburbs.[4] The sluggishness of the national economy coupled with the crisis in housing finance markets acted to depress suburban home buying; potential buyers were hesitant to commit to the purchase of a home, and home finance institutions raised their requirements for mortgages.

Some urban observers argue that the 2009–2001 data point to a fundamental change in urban development patterns: a new generation of younger Americans is showing a

Box 9.1
TV and Hollywood's Schizophrenic View of Suburbia

For much of the second half of the twentieth century, television and Hollywood presented suburbia as a string of well-to-do bedroom communities. *The Donna Reed Show, Father Knows Best, Leave It to Beaver,* and *The Dick Van Dyke Show* all presented conventional two-parent families living the "good life" in large single-family homes. Well-coiffed mothers happily tended to the children and drank coffee with neighbor ladies who lived next door, idling their time, awaiting their commuting husbands to return from work. Hollywood movies such as *Miracle on 34th Street* (1947; remade in 1994) similarly portrayed suburbia as the embodiment of the American Dream: At the end of the movie, a little girl gets her Christmas wish; with Santa's help, she leaves crowded New York City for a manorial suburban home with a fireplace and a large backyard.

Hollywood, however, did not fully embrace suburbia. More critical movies sought to reveal the underside of suburban life that existed beneath the public veneer of normalcy. *Rebel Without a Cause* (1955), *The Man in the Gray Flannel Suit* (1956), *Peyton Place* (1957), *The Graduate* (1967), and *American Beauty* (1999) all attacked the materialism, conformity, sterility, and hypocrisy of suburban lives. *The Stepford Wives* (1975; remade 2004) attacked the isolation and vacuity of suburban life, presenting the "ideal" suburban housewife as a robot, wedded to her husband with no mind of her own. Other films showed husbands and wives desperately seeking to escape the boredom of suburbia through alcohol and meaningless sexual affairs, a theme that also appears in television's more contemporary and tongue-in-cheek *Desperate Housewives*.

In *Edward Scissorhands* (1990), Tim Burton's charming take on the Frankenstein tale, the boy/monster (played by Johnny Depp) represents every person who has ever felt out of place amid the enforced conformity of suburbia. In *Pleasantville* (1998), life in midcentury suburbia is represented as being so mind-numbingly dull and colorless that portions of the film are actually shot in black and white. In *The Truman Show* (1998), the normalcy of suburban life is depicted as highly ordered and antiseptic, so much so that Truman Burbank (Jim Carrey) actually believes that he lives in an ideal suburban community when, in fact, he has spent his entire life on a huge, fabricated, television stage set.

Do Americans share elite Hollywood's distaste for suburbia? Not really. Polls show that most residents are satisfied with life in the suburbs, a view that is reflected in a countercurrent of films that present a more affectionate portrait of suburbia. Steven Spielberg's *E.T.: The Extra-Terrestrial* (1982) reveals a suburbia of family love and contentment, a place where children grow up in relative safety and with a brimming self-confidence.

Ferris Bueller's Day Off (1986) is the rare movie that mixes both positive and negative assessments of suburbia. A hip, fast-talking high-school student (played by Matthew Broderick) skips classes in order to taste the vitality of life that can only be found in the big city, Chicago. The father of his best friend is so blinded by the trappings of suburban materialism that he cares more for his luxury sports car than for his son. Yet the film is no caustic anti-suburban diatribe. Bueller clearly enjoys the privileges of being a teenager who lives in, and goes to school in, a top-end, North Shore community. Life in the suburbs is quite good, even though the city beckons with the enticements of ethnic diversity and adventure.

Only in more recent years have TV and cinema begun to explore the diversity of suburban communities and the people who reside there. *E.T.* and *Close Encounters of the Third Kind* (1977) featured the actions of single mothers, revealing a suburbia where the two-parent family is no longer the norm. *American Beauty* and the television series *Modern Family* went even further showing a suburbia that has become home to same-sex couples. The long-running cartoon *The Simpsons* features a suburb with a diversity (including an African-American doctor and a South-Asian store manager) that was unimaginable at midcentury.

Sources: Robert Beuka, *SuburbiaNation: Reading Suburban Landscape in Twentieth-Century American Fiction and Film* (New York: Palgrave Macmillan, 2004); Douglas Muzzio and Thomas Halper, "Pleasantville? The Suburb and Its Representation in American Movies," *Urban Affairs Review* 37, no. 4 (March 2002): 542–574; and Stanley J. Solomon, "Images of Suburban Life in American Films," in *Westchester: The American Suburb*, ed. Roger Panetta (New York: Fordham University Press; and Yonkers, NY: Hudson River Museum, 2006), 411–441; Timotheus Vermeulen, *Scenes from the Suburbs: The Suburb in Contemporary U.S. Film and Television* (Edinburgh, Scotland: Edinburgh University Press, 2014).

renewed appreciation for urban lifestyles and is less interested than preceding generations in living the "American Dream" in the suburbs.

That observation is in part true. Still, the numbers do not likely portend a significant curtailing of suburban growth. In fact, as the nation's economy at long last began to improve, mid-sized suburban communities and far-off exurban communities reported strong population growth.[5] Further revival of the nation's economy and housing markets will likely see a return of suburban growth rates to their normal levels. Simply put, the majority of Americans continue to prefer the low-density lifestyle of suburbia.

This chapter describes the evolving suburban landscape, with special attention to how public policies—at the national, state, and local levels—shape suburban growth. As schools often are at the heart of life in suburban America, this chapter also explores trends in school finance and racial integration. The chapter concludes by assessing two contemporary movements—Smart Growth and New Urbanism—which promise to build a "better" and more sustainable suburban America.

SUBURBAN DIVERSITY: THE CHANGING FACE OF SUBURBIA

The reality of contemporary suburbia is quite different from popular images of suburbia. Television shows and Hollywood movies, with few exceptions, present suburbia as a homogeneous string of privileged, largely white, middle- and upper-class **bedroom or dormitory communities** (see Box 9.1, "TV and Hollywood's Schizophrenic View of Suburbia.") The award-winning television series *Mad Men*, for instance, presents glimpses of 1950s–1960s suburbia as an upper-class ideal that imperfectly embodies a "familial" ideal: the suburbia of the mid-twentieth century had no room for independent working women, single mothers, gays, and lesbians.[6]

But contemporary suburbia, and even suburbia of the 1950s, had greater diversity than presented in the Hollywood stereotype. Even at midcentury, an era when suburbia was just beginning to flourish, there existed a number **blue-collar and industrial suburbs** centered on manufacturing plants.[7]

Today, the 1950s stereotype of suburban homogeneity is clearly dated. Contemporary suburbia encompasses a wide variety of communities: affluent bedroom or dormitory residential suburbs; **privatopias** or **common-interest developments** with security-controlled gated entrances and rules established by homeowner associations;[8] industrial suburbs centered around factories; **bedroom-developing suburbs**,[9] that is, lower-middle-class communities that lack the tax base to provide quality schools and the infrastructure to keep up with their rapid growth; and boomburbs and far-flung **exurbs** located at some distance from the metropolitan center. **Minority-dominated suburbs** can be found in Prince George's County, Maryland (outside of Washington, D.C.), and East Chicago Heights. Declining inner-ring suburbs suffer vacant storefronts and have a stock of antiquated housing—with small kitchens, tiny backyards, and no attached garage—that has no great appeal to the present generation of homebuyers. So-called **disaster suburbs**—including East St. Louis (Illinois), East Cleveland, Compton (California), and Camden (New Jersey, just across the river from

Edge City: The USA Today/Gannett Communications Headquarters at Tyson's Corner, in Northern Virginia, outside of Washington, D.C. Major corporations no longer have to locate in the city center. Advances in transportation and telecommunications haves freed businesses to move to the suburbs.

From Wikimedia Commons, User Patrickneil, June 30, 2008, http://commons.wikimedia.org/wiki/File:USA_Today_building.jpg.

Edge City: Tyson's Corner, in Northern Virginia, outside of Washington, D.C. The suburbs are no longer "sub" in terms of their economic dynamism. The photo also illustrates how edge cities are built for the automobile, with roads and vast expanses of parking that are almost impossible to cross by foot.

From Wikimedia Commons, User BenjPHolm, August 23, 2009, http://en.wikipedia.org/wiki/File:2009-08-23_Tysons_Corner_skyline.jpg.

Philadelphia)—suffer economic and social problems that are usually associated with the central cities they border.

Edge cities—suburban concentrations of office towers, research parks, college campuses, shopping galleries, and entertainment complexes—are lively centers of commercial activity, as evident in Valley Forge and King of Prussia (outside of Philadelphia), Monroeville (Pittsburgh), Towson (Baltimore), Bloomington (Minneapolis-St. Paul), La Jolla (San Diego), Bellevue (Seattle), Tempe/Scottsdale (Phoenix), North Atlanta, North Dallas, and the Houston Galleria, to name only a few. The New York region has multiple centers of edge-city development, including: Morristown (New Jersey); the Route 1 corridor by Princeton (New Jersey); Huntington, Long Island, and White Plains (New York); and Stamford (Connecticut).[10]

But even recognition of the rise of edge cities does not fully capture the economic dynamism of suburbia. Substantial commercial growth can also be found outside of edge cities in the **edgeless development** of unglamorous strip malls and clusters of offices spread along access roads and side streets near highway interchanges. As seen in the chaotic sprawl of central New Jersey, edgeless development can spill over hundreds of square miles, eating up green space, wetlands, and agricultural acreage.[11]

A new immigration from Asia and Latin America has joined with the continuing out-migration from central cities to increase the population diversity of suburbia. Suburbia is no longer a string of "white" communities: racial and ethnic minorities comprise over a third of the population of the nation's suburbs.[12] Census data reveals an important and much-awaited demographic change: younger African-American families have begun to exhibit the same residential preferences long exhibited by whites, choosing to leave the central city for a home in the suburbs.[13] Immigrants from abroad account for nearly a third (30 percent) of the population increase of suburbs between 2000 and 2009.[14]

While many minority families enjoy all the benefits that suburban living represents, minority families as a whole reside in a different suburbia than do whites. African

Americans and Hispanics tend to be concentrated in declining industrial suburbs and troubled **spillover communities** adjacent to the central city; in contrast, a region's better-off communities and exurbs have populations that are disproportionately white. The degree of minority concentration found in suburbia, however, varies considerably from one metropolitan area to the next. The suburbs of Washington, D.C., and Atlanta are significantly stratified by race. By contrast, suburbs in greater Los Angeles, San Diego, Phoenix, and in the West exhibit greater racial balance, with the population of the suburbs tending to mirror the racial composition of the larger region.[15]

A brief look at California suburbs underscores the new suburban diversity. Orange County, California, the home of Disneyland, was once the iconic image of white suburbia. Although the stereotype of an upscale and largely white suburbia continues to be propagated by shows like the Bravo reality-TV series *The Real Housewives of Orange County*, in fact, contemporary Orange County is "minority majority" with a population that is only 43 percent white but 34 percent Hispanic and 19 percent Asian (although still only 2 percent African American). "Little Saigon," centered in Westminster and Garden Grove in suburban Orange County, advertises itself as the "Capital of Vietnamese America." Cupertino in northern California, the home of Apple computers in the heart of Silicon Valley, has a population that is over 63 percent Asian.[16]

In the Midwest, the new immigration has brought increased racial and ethnic diversity to the suburbs surrounding Minneapolis and St. Paul. But new immigrants are more commonly found in inner-ring suburbs than in the region's better-off communities and far-off exurbs. When it comes to the racial integration of suburbs of the Twin Cities, the glass is only "half full."[17] The enactment of strong public policies will be required to maintain the **stable integration** of suburban communities that will, in the absence of such policies, quickly resegregate as whites pick up and move elsewhere: "Integrated communities have a hard time staying integrated for more than 10 or 20 years."[18]

The new suburban diversity is also evident in the increase in suburban poverty. One-third of the nation's poor reside in the suburbs. A greater number of low-income people live in the suburbs than in central cities. During the national economic recession of the early 2000s, the suburbs—not central cities or rural areas—experienced the largest growth in poverty rates.[19]

Many suburbs are not well equipped to respond to the needs of a growing population of low-income families. In many communities, suburban buses run infrequently or connect only with the downtown; the working class and the poor cannot rely on such bare-bones public transit to go to work, especially when lower-skill jobs are often found at dispersed suburban locations.[20] Many suburbs also offer only minimal local job-training programs. Other suburbs lack a sufficient stock of affordable, quality rental units. Still others lack programs and trained personnel to give poorer schoolchildren the assistance they need, especially children of families where English is not spoken in the home.

The numbers of gays and lesbians living in suburbia, too, has increased, especially as same-sex couples have the money to buy suburban homes. In general, suburbia has shown a new tolerance for nontraditional households. Census data indicates that while younger gays and lesbians prefer to live in active central cities, more mature GLBs and same-sex couples with children prefer the suburbs.[21] Some suburbs have even actively courted same-sex couples. Berwyn, just west of Chicago, has looked to the arrival of same-sex couples as a means of bringing new vitality to a declining community that was once a blue-collar stronghold.[22]

After a prolonged delay, television has at long last begun to reflect the changing suburb. The award-winning series *Modern Family* presents the diversity of family structures found in contemporary suburbia.

RACIAL STRATIFICATION: IS IT RACE OR INCOME THAT DETERMINES WHERE PEOPLE LIVE?

Despite changes in demography, metropolitan America continues to be marred by racial imbalances. Of course, much of the imbalance simply reflects money: people with greater wealth "buy into" better communities while people with less buying power must reside elsewhere. Still, suburban housing patterns do not simply reflect differences in buying power. People of different races with the same buying power do not tend to reside in the same communities.

In greater St. Louis, Kansas City, and Chicago, blacks and whites of equivalent income, education, and professional status reside in different geographical areas.[23] The 2000 Census and the 2006–2010 American Community Survey both reported that increases in income and education among Asians and Hispanics led to higher levels of residential integration, but similar increases in the income of African Americans did not produce equivalent gains in integration. African Americans are the nation's most racially segregated group; even more affluent black families face limits on their residential choice beyond those faced by other affluent home seekers.[24] In greater Detroit, middle- and upper-income African Americans continue to face housing discrimination.[25] Differences in income do not fully explain why different racial groups are concentrated in different portions of the American metropolis.

Nor does voluntary choice fully explain why black and white Americans live in different communities. The vast majority of African Americans do not choose self-segregation. Survey after survey reveals that the clear majority of African Americans prefer to live in mixed-race, as opposed to all-black, neighborhoods. African Americans, as do whites, value communities with high-quality, single-family, detached homes. Whites, however, tend to prefer communities with much lower levels of racial integration.[26]

For many decades, suburbia was shaped by a process known as **racial steering**, where real estate agents and home loan officers helped to direct white and minority home seekers to different communities. A real estate agent would show a prospective white buyer a home in certain communities while showing a minority buyer houses in other communities.

Does racial steering continue today? Fortunately, federal **fair housing laws** and changed community norms have led to the virtual elimination of the most blatant discriminatory real estate and rental practices. Today, it is rare that a real estate agent will show homes in a preferred neighborhood only to whites and not to blacks and other minorities.

Yet more subtle variants of racial steering continue, as they are not easily detected or fought.[27] African Americans do not have the same housing search experiences as whites. Evidence even points to **linguistic profiling**, where a real estate agent's response to a phone query about the availability of a home or apartment varied with the agent's reaction to the home seeker's dialect and accent.[28] A real estate agent may also show fewer homes in predominantly white neighborhoods to an African-American buyer than to prospective white buyers. Real estate agents, mortgage lenders, and insurers also present minority buyers with less assistance in finding financing for a home in what members of the real estate industry view to be a racially incompatible area.[29]

Victimized parties seldom file a complaint about such subtle discriminatory actions. How can a person know just what homes are being shown and what financing information is being provided to other people looking to buy a home? Individuals, especially low-income minorities, also seldom have the money to pursue fair housing enforcement through the courts.

Housing discrimination is primarily detected through a housing audit process known as **paired testing**, where closely matched white and minority individuals pose as home seekers in order to compare the treatment they receive from landlords, real estate agents, and home financial lenders. Evidence from more than 2,000 paired tests conducted in twenty major metropolitan areas (during the years 2000 and 2001) underscores the extent to which differential treatment by race and ethnicity continues to affect the search for housing:

> [I]n roughly one of five visits to a real estate or rental agent, black and Hispanic customers were denied some of the information and assistance that comparable white customers received as a matter of course. Whites were more likely to find out about available houses and apartments, more likely to be given the opportunity to inspect these units, more likely to be offered favorable financial terms, more likely to be steered toward homes for sale in predominantly white neighborhoods, and more likely to receive assistance and encouragement in their housing search.[30]

As a 2013 Urban Institute study concluded, "Prejudice by no means has disappeared ... (M)inorities still face significant barriers to housing search, even when they are well-qualified as renters or homebuyers."[31] Other analysts have similarly concluded: "discriminatory real estate practices clearly contribute to continued patterns of racial and ethnic segregation in the United States."[32]

SCHOOLS AND SUBURBIA

A community's schools often lie at the focal point of a suburb's identity and politics. Suburbanites defend their choice of residence by pointing to quality of the schools. This section explores the suburban response to two possible "threats" to suburban schools: school finance reform and measures to increase school integration.

WHY SCHOOL FINANCE REFORM IS SO DIFFICULT TO BRING ABOUT

In the vast majority of the states, the funding of a community's schools is heavily reliant on local property tax levies. Such local-based financing produces severe inequalities in school funding, with wealthier districts able to provide educational activities that are denied to children in property-poor communities.

Over the last four decades, however, the states have reshaped school funding systems to decrease the extent to which schools are dependent on locally generated revenues. State action was a response to the nationwide campaign for school finance equalization that essentially began in the 1970s, when the outraged of parents in Baldwin Park, a low-income suburb of Los Angeles, challenged that California's system of local-based financing discriminated against their children. Baldwin Hills had levied a school tax that was twice the rate of exclusive Beverly Hills, yet property-poor Baldwin Hills wound up with less than half of what Beverly Hills spent per school child. The California Supreme Court in *Serrano v. Priest* (1971) ruled that such unequal school spending violated the **equal protection clauses** of both the federal and state constitutions.[33]

The threat of Serrano-style challenges and judicial intervention forced states across the nation to act.[34] State governments increased assistance and tweaked the aid formulas that determined just how much assistance a school district received from the state. As a result of these actions, state assistance came to equal—and even narrowly surpass—local revenues for the schools. In 2011, the states provided 44 percent of the funds for K–12 education; local governments provided 43 percent; the federal government 12 percent.[35] The national government plays only a secondary role in school finance, as education is traditionally considered to be a state and local responsibility.

The changes in state aid reduced but did not eliminate disparities in school spending. A school district's local property wealth still remains an important factor that determines the overall sum of money that a community has to spend on its children.

The U.S. Supreme Court dealt the movement for school finance equalization a major setback in *Rodriguez v. San Antonio* (1973). The Court ruled 5–4 that reliance on local property taxes for school funding does *not* violate a person's "equal protection" rights guaranteed by the Fourteenth Amendment of the U.S. Constitution.[36] As "education" is nowhere mentioned in the U.S. Constitution, the Court did not consider spending for education to be a "fundamental right" deserving of special federal protection. The Court was also reluctant to order the equalization of school dollars, as a number of experts contended that money was of no great importance, that school spending was less critical to student learning than were other influences such as parental expectations and student peer pressure.

After the *Rodriguez* ruling, advocates of more equal school funding continued their fight in state courts, pressing claims based on the education provisions written as a part of state constitutions. In California, Texas, New Jersey, Ohio, Kentucky, and other states, courts found that the specific language of a state's constitution, such as wording that requires a state to provide a "thorough and efficient" system of education, meant that a state legislature had to enact measures to reduce (but not necessarily eliminate) school finance disparities.

The school finance equalization movement further stalled in the face of a second political obstacle: a populist taxpayers' rebellion that opposed new tax levies. Legislators from better-off suburbs and other property-rich communities opposed changes in school finance that would increase the taxes paid by their constituents or that would undermine the advantages enjoyed by their schoolchildren.

In California, voters used the initiative process to enact new laws that curtailed the ability of local governments—including school districts—to raise taxes. When the new laws led to steep reductions in school spending, pressure from outraged parents led the State of California to step in to assume primary responsibility for funding schools. The state actions brought new levels of equality to school spending across California, but such extensive state intrusion also resulted in diminished local control over school operations.[37] Critics, especially from wealthier communities, charged that the new parity was achieved by **equalizing down** school spending as wealthier districts faced new limits on the amounts of money that they could raise on behalf of their schoolchildren.[38] In 2014, California once more altered its school financing system, this time approving changes proposed by Governor Jerry Brown to target additional assistance to local programs serving low-income children.[39]

State activism in school finance has reduced the great disparities that had marred school funding in past decades. But the reforms did not produce equalization; school spending continues to vary considerably from district to district. In a suburban nation, the states were reluctant to create new funding rules to channel aid to school districts with the greatest need. In fact, a large portion of the new state assistance is dispensed to suburban and better-off districts. Various elements in a state's school aid formula—such as the provision of a "flat grant" given to districts irrespective of need and state guarantees that provide a minimum of "basic aid" to a district no matter the district's size or wealth—perpetuate interdistrict disparities. In North Carolina, more affluent county districts receive just about as much state aid per pupil as do high-poverty districts.[40]

SCHOOLING IN THE METROPOLIS: RACIAL INTEGRATION OR RESEGREGATION?

Suburbs generally do not have to participate in efforts to increase the racial integration of a region's public schools. In its all-important 1974 *Milliken v. Bradley* decision,[41] the U.S. Supreme Court ruled that the busing of students across district lines is not required, even if cross-district busing is the only means capable of desegregating overwhelmingly minority central-city schools.

A suburb can be forced to participate in a desegregation plan only if plaintiffs first prove that the suburb intentionally undertook segregative actions. Racial "intent," however, is nearly impossible to prove. The advocates of greater school integration can easily document where a suburb's schools have a racial make-up that is vastly different from neighboring communities. But it is next to impossible for the plaintiffs to demonstrate that such imbalances are the result of actions taken by suburban officials who acted with an explicit intent to keep minority enrollments to a minimum. Suburbanites respond that their actions reflect no racial motivation at all. Instead, they argue that local schools serve the members of a local community with no regard at all to race. If a suburban school has an overwhelmingly white student body, it is simply because the suburb itself has an overwhelmingly white population. Racial imbalances in the schools, they argue, are merely the reflection of housing imbalances in the metropolis.

The *Millikin* decision put an end to strong efforts at school desegregation. In most cases, residence in a suburb generally offers a family an escape from school integration efforts.

Over the past quarter century, Supreme Court decisions have also given local districts new leeway to bring an end to school desegregation efforts. The Court's 1991 **Oklahoma City decision**, which dealt with a school district that had been found guilty of past discrimination, permitted local districts to halt desegregation efforts that had been attempted for a "reasonable" period of time. That same year, in **Freeman v. Pitts**, a DeKalb County, Georgia, case, the Court placed severe limits on metropolitan desegregation plans, even in instances where "white flight" to the suburbs undermined court-ordered efforts to integrate central-city schools. The Court's rulings led communities across the nation to terminate or diminish metropolitan desegregation efforts. Charlotte, Seattle, Denver, Kansas City, Minneapolis, Indianapolis, Cleveland, Pittsburgh, Buffalo, Dallas, Austin, Savannah, Nashville, Norfolk, and Wilmington (Delaware) all ended programs aimed at school integration.[42]

National data reveals a substantial increase in segregated classrooms, although not a return to the segregation levels of the pre–civil rights era. The data is troubling. Nationwide, 43 percent of Latinos and 38 percent of African Americans attend **intensely segregated schools** with a student population that is less than 10 percent white. Approximately 15 percent of Latino and African-American students attend **apartheid schools** where whites make up less than one percent of the student population.[43]

Suburban schools are experiencing a **resegregation** of public school classrooms, as African-American, Latino, and Caucasian students in many suburbs have only the most limited interaction with one another. The schools of inner-ring suburbs and outer-ring communities have student bodies with vastly different demographics. Latino and African-American students attend classes in suburban environments that are very different from those where white suburban students attend school. White students in suburbia, not just minority students, suffer from a lack of substantial exposure to students of different ethnic and racial origins.[44]

Local plans for school choice (discussed in Chapter 8) have also undercut the prospects for school integration. In suburban San Antonio, school choice plans offered families the ability to escape schools that were experiencing substantial racial and ethnic integration.[45] The same impact was also apparent in the Minneapolis-St. Paul Twin Cities region where two-thirds of the charter schools located in the suburbs had enrollments that were 80 percent or more white. These charter schools offered students an outlet to escape schools with more diverse student bodies; the charter schools were "facilitating white flight from increasingly diverse traditional schools in the suburbs."[46]

School desegregation no longer occupies a prominent place on the metropolitan agenda. In Charlotte-Mecklenburg and in other cities, leaders in the African-American community have come to accept school resegregation as a political fact of life and have shifted their attention to finding the resources to strengthen "neighborhood schools."[47]

SUBURBAN LAND USE AND EXCLUSION

ZONING POWERS AND SUBURBAN EXCLUSION

A suburb can use its zoning and land-use powers to determine just what types of housing and commercial establishments will be permitted within its jurisdictional borders. Land-use and zoning ordinances are not simply tools for the orderly development of a community. By determining the types of housing that can be built within a community, land-use and zoning ordinances also help determine who can—and who cannot—afford to live in a community. **Exclusionary zoning** refers to local zoning and land-use measures that effectively serve to "keep out" people who have a lower income, and who may be of a different race or ethnicity, than the existing residents of a community. A suburb that prohibits the construction of apartment buildings and other multifamily dwellings will exclude the poor and the working-class residents and the racial and ethnic minorities who are found disproportionately in low-income brackets.

Of course, suburbia is quite diverse, and not every suburb seeks to exclude racial minorities, the working class, and the poor.[48] Nor are land-use and zoning measures enacted solely for reasons of exclusion. Local communities also use land-use and zoning measures to achieve legitimate goals. Planning and zoning, properly used, enhance a community's livability by separating manufacturing activity from residential areas. Land-use regulations and construction codes also promote public safety. The lack of appropriate land-use regulations helps to explain the lethality of wildfires in communities in the Oakland Hills in the San Francisco Bay area and in communities in Colorado, Arizona, Texas, and Washington. In the absence of strong local zoning and land-use regulations, homeowners unwisely build residences in highly flammable woodland areas, even in the brushy areas of the "wildland-urban interface."[49]

Land-use plans can also safeguard a community from overdevelopment. Suburban communities use their land-use and zoning measures to ward off unwanted growth, traffic congestion, crime, and the general "citification" of a community. A suburb's residents also look to zoning to protect the substantial financial investment that they have made in their homes:

> Suburban home owners believe that such [low-density] zoning will maximize the value of their homes. Open-space, low-density zoning adds to existing home values in many ways. Open space may be a substitute for parks and viewscapes. Low density may keep congestion down, at least within one's own community. Larger lots may price out supposedly undesirable residents and promote own-lot privacy. Less development means fewer substitutes for existing housing and thus the possibility of larger capital gains when the home is sold.[50]

But suburban exclusion can also reflect racist, nativist, and classist sentiments. In Los Angeles' San Gabriel Valley, residents of Monterey Park, San Gabriel, Arcadia, and Alhambra organized "slow-growth" campaigns in an effort to limit apartment construction and thereby slow the rapid influx of Latino, Chinese, and Vietnamese newcomers.[51]

THE CONSTITUTIONALITY OF LOCAL ZONING AND EXCLUSIONARY PRACTICES

Many Americans mistakenly believe that a property owner has the total freedom to build whatever he or she wishes on a piece of property. The Supreme Court, however, has ruled to the contrary, upholding the constitutionality of local zoning codes that restrict the use of property. Beginning with the 1926 **Euclid case** (*Village of Euclid, Ohio,* *v. Ambler Realty Co.*),[52] the Supreme Court has viewed zoning as a legitimate exercise of the state's **police powers** to protect the public well-being against unwanted noise, congestion, and changes in a community's character.

Yet, as has already been discussed, more affluent suburbs do not use their zoning powers simply to maintain public health and safety and to eliminate nuisance uses of property. Instead, suburban communities also use zoning as a tool to keep out less-advantaged people.

Is such a discriminatory use of local zoning powers constitutional? The short answer is "Yes!" The U.S. Constitution does not bar discrimination on the basis of income or buying power. There is no constitutional violation per se when a poor or middle-class family is unable to "buy into" a wealthier community. The courts will strike down a local zoning ordinance only if a litigant can prove that the community's *intent* to discriminate was racial, not economic, in nature.

The Supreme Court's 1977 **Arlington Heights decision** affirmed the ability of suburbs to enact land-use plans that had exclusionary impacts.[53] A church group had sought to build subsidized housing units in Arlington Heights, an affluent, overwhelmingly white suburb northwest of Chicago. But Arlington Heights' zoning regulations prohibited multifamily housing in almost all sections of the suburb. The Supreme Court upheld the constitutionality of the zoning restrictions, observing that a community may use its zoning powers to preserve a peaceable environment, promote orderly land development, and protect local property values. The plaintiffs were able to show that the zoning regulations impeded the movement of less-well-off minority citizens into Arlington Heights. But, according to the Court, proof of a discriminatory effect was not enough: the housing advocates would also have to produce evidence that Arlington Height's zoning and land-use regulations were enacted not for legitimate purposes but with a clear intent to discriminate on the basis of race. This the open suburbs advocates could not prove.

The significance of the *Arlington Heights* ruling cannot be overstated. Suburbs are generally under no obligation to modify exclusionary zoning and land-use ordinances in order to promote class and racial integration. A suburb's legal counsel can always argue that exclusionary ordinances reflect no racial intent but are simply tools to protect local housing values and preserve a community's tranquil, congestion-free environment. As historian Charles Lamb observes, the Supreme Court

> transformed the vision of low-income suburban housing into a pipe dream in *Arlington Heights*. Its policy prevents federal judges from inferring intent from disproportionate impact . . . and therefore makes a finding of racial discrimination very difficult to prove . . . . The fundamental problem with this approach, however, is all too obvious: local legislators and administrators are too politically conscious to exhibit their racial prejudices openly.[54]

THE TECHNIQUES OF SUBURBAN EXCLUSION

Many suburbs keep poorer persons out simply by refusing to take the necessary steps to allow for the construction of publicly assisted housing units. Exclusive suburbs also have zoning and land-use ordinances that **prohibit the construction of multifamily housing**.

Such provisions price a community beyond the means of people who can only afford to rent an apartment or buy a small condominium as opposed to a single-family home.

Exclusive suburbs further drive up the price of entry to their community through **large-lot zoning**, which requires that a home be built on no less than a half acre, one acre, or even two acres of land. Such ordinances restrict entry into a community to only those people who can afford the steep price of large-lot homes.[55]

Suburban governments also drive up the price of entry by legislating **minimum room/space requirements** that go beyond concerns for health and safety. **Regulations requiring the use of expensive construction technologies and materials** similarly add to construction costs and increase the price of entry into a community. Many suburbs require that homes be built piece by piece on-site, a practice that inflates home prices as it does not allow for the time and cost savings that come from utilizing preassembled modular home components. Construction regulations further drive up home costs, for instance, by requiring the use of expensive copper pipes instead of serviceable plastic pipes.

A **moratorium on the extension of sewer and water lines** effectively limits the supply of land available for new home construction. The designation of **agricultural preserves** and **open-space and green-space areas** likewise limit the acreage available for new homes. Of course, local communities argue that their efforts are motivated by concern for the natural environment, not exclusion. But in New Jersey, suburban communities did not buy natural areas of exceptional beauty or acreage critical for open-space preservation; instead, local officials acquired land parcels that developers had targeted for construction, sometimes land that was already equipped with sewers and other municipal infrastructure![56]

Suburban jurisdictions can also defeat new development projects through a **strategy of delays** and constantly **shifting development standards**. When a developer meets one set of conditions, a city council or planning commission can stall a project by imposing newer and even more expensive ones. A developer can go to court to challenge the new requirements. But judicial action takes quite a bit of time and can be expensive. Good business sense will often lead developers to cede to exclusionary pressures rather than have their developments entangled in extensive government-imposed delays and judicial battles.

Some suburbs have gone so far as to enact **limited-growth and no-growth ordinances**. Petaluma (California), Boulder (Colorado), and Livermore (California) have each set an annual quota or otherwise limited the annual construction of new residential dwellings.[57] Ramapo, a town in Rockland County about thirty-five miles outside New York City, gained fame for its policy of slow-growth zoning. The municipality issued permits for new residential development only in instances where the required municipal services were readily available and a construction proposal was especially meritorious. Decades later, in the face of evidence that the stringency of its strict no-growth regulations were serving to drive new commercial development and job growth to neighboring communities, municipal officials in Ramapo at long last decided to relax the community's growth restrictions.[58]

Suburban municipalities can impose thousands of dollars in developer fees and access charges that a developer will pass on to homebuyers. These fees burden new homeowners with the costs of new streets, sewers, and schools, services that are provided to other community residents who do not have to pay additional fees.

While suburbs are generally willing to impost developer fees, they are unwilling to raise property taxes as a means of increasing the cost of entry into a community. Why the difference? Developer fees and access charges are shouldered only by newcomers. A suburb's existing residents quite naturally oppose raising property tax rates that they, too, will have to pay!

CAN JUDICIAL POWER "OPEN" THE SUBURBS? NEW JERSEY'S MOUNT LAUREL DECISIONS

Activists seeking to "open" the suburbs have turned to litigation in state courts, arguing that exclusionary practices violate a state's constitution and statutes. But such lawsuits seldom bring the extensive gains that advocates desire.

In New Jersey, open-suburbs advocates appeared to have won a major victory when the state supreme court, in a series of rulings known as the *Mount Laurel* **decisions**, struck down the exclusionary practices of a broad range of communities. The New Jersey court ruled that, under the state's constitution, Mount Laurel Township (a New Jersey suburb of Camden and Philadelphia) and all growing communities in the state were obligated to change their land-use and zoning ordinances to allow the construction of a "fair share" of a region's low- and moderate-income housing units.[59]

The initial 1975 court ruling had little immediate impact. Suburban communities simply dragged their feet and rezoned as few parcels of land as possible, producing no real increase in the availability of affordable housing.

After eight years, the court again intervened.[60] The court sought to incentivize developers to bring legal challenge against exclusionary practices. In instances where a developer could demonstrate that local ordinances improperly obstructed new home-building efforts, the court allowed developers to construct higher densities and thereby earn additional profit. The New Jersey Supreme Court also set up a special system of housing courts to expedite the legal challenges brought by developers.

Outraged suburbanites countermobilized against the reform measures, which they saw as a broad attack on their communities. New Jersey's governor and legislature responded by passing state laws to narrow the impact of the *Mount Laurel* rulings. The state abolished the special housing courts and created, in their place, an appointed Council on Affordable Housing. Despite its name, the Council did not aggressively promote the construction of affordable housing. Instead, the Council devoted much of its time to hearing appeals from suburbs that sought to reduce the number of affordable housing units that they were required to build. The new state laws also allowed suburbs to reserve a number of affordable units for established residents and the elderly, a provision that reduced the number of dwelling units for newcomers and the poor.[61]

Quite significantly, state legislation reduced the number of affordable units that a suburb actually had to build within its borders. A suburb could, if it wished, shift half of its fair-share obligation to other communities, helping to pay for subsidized housing in economically troubled cities like Newark, Paterson, and Jersey City. In 1993, suburban

Wayne Township gave $8 million to low-income Paterson in order to avoid having to build an additional 500 units of affordable housing inside the township.[62]

The *Mount Laurel* decisions did produce some positive results. The process led numerous suburbs, including Mount Laurel, to permit the construction of some new housing for working- and lower-middle-class families. The intermunicipal agreements also provided fiscally strapped core cities with substantial assistance for their own housing efforts. Between 1987 and 1996, intermunicipal agreements transferred more than $92 million and enabled the construction of 4,700 units of affordable housing.[63]

Yet despite these achievements, the *Mount Laurel* decisions did little to truly open the suburbs.[64] Eighty percent of the units built as a result of *Mount Laurel* were owner-occupied, not rental. The new condominiums, town houses, and garden apartments built in suburban communities seldom went to central-city residents and the poor. Instead, suburbs gave the affordable units to the grown children of suburban residents, essential public service workers (the police, fire, and hospital personnel that suburban communities need), divorced mothers, and rising middle-class young couples—anyone but the poor.[65]

INCLUSIONARY APPROACHES TO BUILD MORE BALANCED SUBURBS

Massachusetts' Chapter 40B **Anti-Snob Zoning law** allows the state to invalidate local land-use controls that unreasonably interfere with the construction of low- and moderate-income housing. The Massachusetts law seeks to ensure that at least 10 percent of the housing stock in each local community is within the financial reach of working-class and poorer families. The state can deny development-related assistance to offending municipalities. A developer can go to the state board and argue that a local community had failed to develop a housing plan that includes a sufficient number of affordable units. Connecticut, Rhode Island, and New Hampshire are among the states that have similar state ordinances.

Anti-snob zoning laws work. They have led to the production of affordable housing units in communities that would otherwise have zoned out such construction.[66] Yet suburban power severely limits the reach of the Massachusetts law, which is not aggressively enforced. Suburbanites object that the law impedes their ability to protect the character of their communities, especially as developers have a route that allows them to bypass locally enacted zoning restrictions. In Massachusetts, the protests from suburbanites led to modifications of 40B, exempting smaller projects from the full application of the law and giving new weight to the concerns of residents as well as developers. As a result of these changes, Massachusetts 40B has favored the construction of new housing units for moderate-income families and not units for the poor.[67]

Montgomery County (Maryland), Fairfax (Virginia), Orange and San Diego Counties (California), and Seattle are among the communities that have gone beyond state legislation to initiate their own **inclusionary programs**: relaxing zoning ordinances, modifying building codes, and providing expedited permitting and public financial assistance to developers who agree to build affordable multifamily housing.[68] Inclusionary efforts often promise **density bonuses** that enable a developer to build a greater number of housing units than is normally allowed, in return for a signed agreement that sets aside a specified number of units for low- and moderate-income families.

Minneapolis and St. Paul have an even stronger approach, imposing **mandatory inclusionary** requirements on developers who receive municipal assistance. The Twin Cities regulatory approach is quite rare. More commonplace is the approach taken by hundreds of communities across the country, where participation is purely voluntary; the developer ultimately decides if it is worth taking the proffered bonus in exchange for designating additional units of affordable housing.

In communities like Montgomery County, Maryland, inclusionary programs have resulted in the construction of thousands of affordable units. Still, skeptics question whether the promise of a density bonus would, in most communities, be sufficient to incentivize developers to include additional affordable units in their construction plans. The presence of low-income units can adversely affect a developer's ability to sell a complex's market-rate homes. In Durham, North Carolina, the offer of density bonuses did not work as anticipated as developers refused to participate. Developers complained of the administrative costs of working with government and of the risks that the inclusion of low-income units posed to their ability to market a new development.[69]

Inclusionary programs that require "affordable" units with rents that are unrealistically low can wind up imposing a fiscal burden that kills a new housing development. California Governor Jerry Brown in 2013 vetoed a measure to strengthen the state's requirements for inclusionary development. Brown noted that his experience as mayor of Oakland led him to worry that such requirements can impede a city's efforts to attract new development.[70]

What can be done to make inclusionary programs work? Some municipalities have purchased a number of the new low-income units in a development, a means of providing a developer with a guaranteed revenue stream when new construction includes affordable dwelling units.[71]

One bias in inclusionary program seems almost endemic. Almost universally, local inclusionary programs favor homeowners over renters. Even programs aimed at affordable housing seldom do much to override the exclusion of poorer families from suburban communities with better schools and job opportunities.[72]

The debate over the relative merits of incentives versus mandates for affordable housing is not limited to the suburbs. New York mayor Bill de Blasio, citing the loss of affordable units in gentrifying areas in his global city, argued that the city should require developers to include affordable units as part of any new housing development.[73]

SUBURBAN AUTONOMY AND METROPOLITAN FRAGMENTATION

Exclusionary zoning statutes are a product of suburban autonomy: local officials respond to the concerns of their own citizens; a suburb's officials have no similar obligation to respond to the needs of persons who live elsewhere in the metropolis. Local autonomy assumes the independence of communities, that the decisions made by one jurisdiction do not affect the well-being of other communities.

But the concept of a **metropolitan area** denotes the economic and social **interdependence** of communities in a region, not their independence. No city or suburb is an island unto itself; instead, each community is dependent on the existence, actions, and resources of its neighbors. Even the most affluent suburb requires the support functions provided by other jurisdictions in the metropolis. Central cities and inner-ring suburbs provide the warehousing, distribution, and manufacturing activities that sustain economic activity throughout the region. Core cities and declining suburbs also house many of a region's low-wage manual and service workers.

The economic dependence of far-off exurbs on their regional neighbors is readily observed in traffic patterns. The streets of Moreno Valley, located seventy miles outside of downtown Los Angeles, are relatively empty during weekday working hours, as one-third of the workers who reside in the exurb have ventured off to jobs elsewhere in Los Angeles, Riverside, and Orange counties.[74]

Metropolitan fragmentation denotes the lack of a broad, overarching governmental body capable of governing the socially and economically interconnected metropolis. The word *fragmentation* underscores that governmental authority in a region is divided among many smaller pieces, autonomous municipal governments and special-purpose governing bodies. Even the creation of new governing arrangements intended to facilitate interlocal cooperation often winds up compounding problems of metropolitan fragmentation by adding to the number of autonomous decision-making councils in a region (a matter that Chapter 10 will discuss in further detail). Governmental powers in the metropolis are exercised by hundreds of independent cities, towns, villages, townships, counties, special authorities, and narrow-purpose service districts. The fragmentation of major metropolitan areas can be even more extensive. The Greater New York metropolitan area sprawls into three states and is governed by a confusing mosaic of more than 2,000 separate units of government, including cities, villages, towns, townships, boroughs, 31 counties, more than 740 special districts (each responsible for providing a service like water or parks), and numerous independent authorities and regional multistate agencies.[75]

The existence of so many governing bodies makes effective, coordinated regional action immensely difficult to achieve. Each locality and special service district looks first to its own interests and does not always give great consideration to the impacts that their actions have on neighboring jurisdictions or even on the natural environment of the region.

Metropolitan fragmentation imposes obstacles to the effective provision of public services across political and administrative boundaries. No metropolitan area can develop an effective system of regional mass transit when bus and rail service stops at the boundary lines of a county or community whose residents are unwilling to help pay for the service. The provision of emergency medical services is similarly impeded when a community's ambulances are not permitted to freely cross a political boundary line in response to a call for assistance.

Metropolitan fragmentation results in the costly **overlap and duplication of services**, as public facilities in a region are not centrally planned or coordinated.[76] Some services in the metropolis are overprovided, as each community has its own fire station and hospital, and, of course, each local hospital must have its own CAT scanner and other expensive state-of-the-art equipment; the region's taxpayers shoulder the costs. Metropolitan fragmentation impedes the realization of **economies of scale**, where cost savings and volume discounts can be gained through the larger-scale provision of a service.

Metropolitan fragmentation is also a root cause of the racial segregation of public schools. As previously discussed, no school district is normally required to participate in actions to promote the racial integration of schools in a metropolis. The Detroit metropolitan area has "115 separate school districts empowered to erect walls around themselves."[77]

CAN "SMART GROWTH" CURB SUBURBAN SPRAWL?

SUBURBAN SPRAWL: WHAT ARE ITS IMPACTS?

In the fragmented metropolis, suburbs pursue land-use actions that exacerbate **sprawled development**, the spread of new development over a wide geographical area.[78] A community lying on the outer edges of a metropolis, for instance, will likely find it in its interest to offer subsidies and other supportive actions to attract a regional shopping mall, as the development will likely be a source of substantial future municipal tax revenues. A fringe community may also approve new residential developments that promise to yield new property tax revenues. Looking primarily at its fiscal self-interest, the edge community will likely show little regard for the adverse environmental impacts of sprawled development: lost wetlands, increased storm-water runoff, and heightened levels of air pollution resulting from lengthened automobile trips.

More affluent inner-ring suburbs, too, pursue land-use and development policies that exacerbate sprawl. The actions of an exclusive inner-ring suburb to limit new commercial and housing development within its borders wind up promoting sprawl as such restrictions push developers to "head for the more rural areas in search of more buildable land."[79]

Sprawled development is expensive, as new development requires the construction of infrastructure and facilities that may duplicate what exists in already-built-up sections of

Urban Sprawl. Automobile-oriented spread development eats up land in the San José, California, region.
From Wikimedia Commons, by U.S. Army Corps of Engineers Digital Visual Library, n.d., http://commons.wikimedia.org/wiki/File:San_Jose_California_aerial_view_south.jpg.

the metropolis. Growth on the edge of the metropolis requires new roadways, sewers, and other infrastructure. Compared to compact development, suburban sprawl increases the costs of municipal service delivery.[80] The Salt Lake City region would save an estimated $4.5 billion in transportation, water, sewer, and utility investments if it could override local decisions and thereby contain sprawled growth.[81]

Suburban sprawl undermines ecological sustainability and also has adverse impacts on human health.[82] Automobile commuting uses nonrenewable energy sources, adds to greenhouse gas emissions that contribute to global warming, and spews tailpipe emissions that degrade air quality.[83] Runoff from the roadways, parking lots, and paved surfaces of suburbia allows oil, road salts, and other contaminants to flow into lakes and streams. Impermeable roads and parking lots interfere with the groundwater seepage that replenishes aquifers. Sprawl eats up greenfields and wetlands, destroying animal habitats and diminishing biodiversity. Sprawl also results in the loss of agricultural acreage. In Wisconsin, new residential subdivisions on the edge of the Milwaukee area served to drive up land prices, prompting farmers to sell off farmland to developers who intended nonagricultural uses.[84]

Urban sprawl even raises questions of racial equity. Sprawled development diminishes metropolitan school integration, as white students disproportionately attend more racially homogeneous schools found in exurban portions of the metropolis. Sprawled development hurts the job prospects of inner-city minorities and the poor, as employment concentrations are increasingly found in edge cities and edgeless developments that are not adequately served by public transit.

Sprawl also raises concerns for **environmental justice**[85] and the health problems faced by urban minorities and the poor. Children and the elderly who live in the poor central-city neighborhoods through which commuter and trucking traffic is funneled suffer high rates of emphysema and other respiratory problems as a result of diesel emissions.[86]

POLICIES FOR SMART GROWTH

Can urban sprawl be contained? More than twenty states pursue some variant of **sustainable development, growth management, and Smart Growth** policies that emphasize compact and transit-oriented development as an alternative to spread development.[87]

Greater Boston provides a case study of the steps that one region has taken in order to reduce the traffic congestion and environmental problems that accompany continued edgeless development beyond the region's I-495 beltway. The regional transit agency played a key role in pushing plans for **compact development**, targeting growth to new town centers that were developed around the rail stations in older suburbs such as Canton, Medford, Newton, Norwood, Salem, and Waltham.[88]

Florida's program of statewide growth management seeks to ward off the extensive ecological damage that spread development can bring to the Everglades and to fragile coastal areas. Florida also seeks to manage growth in order to reduce the costs of new roads and infrastructure construction borne by the state's taxpayers. Florida requires localities to develop comprehensive development plans so that new development will occur only in places where the necessary supporting infrastructure is already in place. But the state's growth management tool has not been fully effective in containing sprawl. Localities seeking growth projects have found ways to circumvent the Florida Growth Management Act. Substantial new growth continues to occur in suburban rim areas where sufficient highway capacity already exists.[89]

Maryland adopted Smart Growth legislation relatively early, as the state faced the pressures on farmland and green space resulting from the more than a million new residents expected by the year 2020. The pressures on open space were further exacerbated by an additional half million residents who were expected to leave central cities and move to the metropolitan rim during the same period of time. If left undirected, new rim growth also threatened to drain the vitality of central cities and inner-ring communities.

Maryland's Smart Growth Areas Act, adopted in 1997, seeks to direct new growth to already-built up areas, including aging communities in need of redevelopment. The state targets its assistance for highways, sewage treatment, new housing, and other programs to already-developed areas. Proposed large-lot subdivisions and projects sited for greenfield areas do not qualify for priority state funding.[90] New Jersey in 1998 adopted a similar approach, prioritizing the award of state aid to developments in communities where the necessary infrastructure is already in place.[91]

Despite the widespread publicity they have received, Smart Growth strategies have been only moderately successful in curbing sprawled development: "Despite the rhetoric, smart growth still means that growth will happen in the suburbs and on the periphery."[92] Maryland and New Jersey have spurned strong-government regulations that would prohibit new development in green areas; instead, these states offer various subsidies to steer growth projects to already-built-up areas. Growth-oriented suburbs simply ignore the incentives and continue to approve new developments outside the state's targeted growth areas. In Maryland, local officials approved the construction of thousands of new residential units in areas that the state had not designated for growth. Also, despite the state's Smart Growth law, more exclusive communities continue to zone out multifamily housing, driving new development to the urban periphery.[93]

Oregon has taken a more direct strong-government approach to regulating land development. Oregon state laws and regional planning measures have succeeded in limiting the extent of new intrusions into forest areas and farmland. However, over the past two decades, **property rights advocates** have used the voter initiative process to weaken the state's much-celebrated land planning controls. The modified rules now require the state to pay compensation to owners who claim that growth control measures diminish the value of their properties.[94]

While environmentalists generally argue that strong state and regional planning is necessary to contain sprawl, not all regional planning processes actually serve to curb sprawl and protect the environment. In Georgia, development interests have allied with sympathetic state officials and have used the Atlanta Regional Commission (ARC) to promote continued highway construction and plans for single-home upper-status communities (with buffers to protect nearby streams and green spaces) far removed from the region's center. In greater Atlanta, unlike Portland, there was no active and strong grassroots environmentalist movement to prevent growth interests from taking control of the region's planning institutions.[95]

PORTLAND'S URBAN GROWTH BOUNDARY

The State of Oregon, as noted above, is a leader in growth management. In contrast to Maryland's strategy of incentives, Oregon relies on a regulatory approach to growth management. During the 1970s, Oregon enacted a series of strong planning laws, including the requirement that Portland and other cities formulate growth boundaries. The Portland **Urban Growth Boundary (UGB)** was created to prevent new residential development from encroaching on green areas and farmland in the Willamette Valley. The UGB draws a line on a map; developers are permitted to build new housing only inside, not outside, the designated growth boundary. The UGB averts sprawl while also promoting infill development to strengthen central Portland, the city's neighborhoods, and the region's older suburbs.[96]

The UGB has clearly succeeded in terms of its major goals. By the 1980s and early 1990s, over 90 percent of single-family homes and 99 percent of multifamily development took place within the confines of the boundary.[97] In terms of sprawl, the Portland metropolitan area ranks as the eighth lowest of eighty-three metropolitan areas.[98] The

The Urban Growth Boundary Promotes Compact Development. Orenco Station, Portland.

Courtesy of user Aboutmovies from Wikimedia Commons. http://commons.wikimedia.org/wiki/File:HillsboroOrencoStation.jpg.

UGB reinforces compact development. As a result, Portlanders drive less and enjoy cleaner air than do the residents of similar communities in other states.

Yet the Portland regulatory approach has its downside: homebuyers get "less house" for their money. Townhouses and relatively small homes or "skinny houses" are "shoe-horned" into small plots of land inside the growth boundary. Homes have tiny backyards and, in most cases, virtually no side yards.

Critics charge that by constricting the supply of developable land, the UGB drives up the costs of housing, diminishing the affordability of housing. Yet the evidence does not clearly support the contention that Portland's UGB has led to home price inflation. As Denver and Salt Lake City, two cities that do not have a growth boundary, experienced a rapid escalation in home prices during the same period that home prices soared in Portland, the extent to which the UGB deserves the blame for rising home prices is unclear. During the 1990s, home prices in Portland climbed as a result of rapid job and wage growth in the region; good wages, not the UGB, bear most of the responsibility for the region's high home prices.[99]

Important features of the law further explain why the blame for rising home prices cannot be attributed to the Portland UGB. Most significantly, the measure does not severely restrict the supply of land available to developers. Oregon state law requires urban communities to adjust the boundary every five years in order to maintain a twenty-year supply of land for expected growth. Rather than limiting the supply of land, as developers contend, the Portland UGB has shifted the location where growth in the region takes place. The lines drawn by the UGB constrain new development on the west side of Portland, forcing builders to look to the east side of the region where developable land inside the boundary is readily available.[100]

As Oregon law requires, the UGB expands to accommodate growth pressures. In 2002, Portland's Metro Council widened the boundary, adding 18,000 acres. In 2009 Metro again expanded the boundary, adding a 7 percent increase in developable space.[101] In 2011, at the behest of developers and despite the outcries of environmentalist organizations, the Metro Council voted to widen the boundary by an additional 2,000 acres to facilitate home building.[102]

Oregon policy makers have also taken other steps to maintain the supply of affording housing. In particular, the state promotes the construction of a mix of housing types in order to assure that a supply of new housing will remain within the price reach of working- and middle-class families. The state also requires all jurisdictions in greater Portland to rezone land so that apartments and multifamily homes will constitute half or more of all new housing.[103] Oregon statutes further prohibit communities in the region from capping new home construction.

"NEW URBANISM": CAN WE BUILD BETTER SUBURBS?

The New Urbanism shares a lot in common with Smart Growth. The **New Urbanism (NU)** is a movement of designers, developers, and urban planners who have reacted against the environmental costs of sprawled suburban development and the diminished sense of "community" evident in contemporary suburbs. The New Urbanism seeks to build a better alternative to conventional suburbs. New Urbanists design communities that are ecologically sustainable and that promote a sense of community as an alternative to the anomie of life in automobile-dominated suburbs. New Urbanists seek to get Americans out of their cars and back on the street and in touch with their neighbors. The New Urbanism "is arguably the most influential movement in city design in the last half-century."[104]

THE GUIDING PRINCIPLES OF THE NEW URBANISM[105]

Conventional suburbs, designed for the convenience of the automobile, pose nearly insurmountable barriers to walking. Homes are located far from commercial destinations. Side yards and driveways add to the distances that a person must walk to get from one destination to another. Fast highway approaches and access ramps make it nearly impossible for pedestrians to cross major streets. High schools and office centers are situated on virtual islands surrounded by acres of parking that are not easily traversed by foot. The workers in a suburban office tower who go out for lunch often find that they have no real alternative but to drive from one parking lot to another. The mass-produced home and highway- and parking-dominated landscape of many suburbs also makes suburbia "an incredibly boring place to walk."[106]

New Urbanism seeks compact development, minimizing the acreage lost to roadways, access ramps, and the sea of parking lots that surround shopping centers, malls, and office gallerias. NU design emphasizes walkability, with homes built close to sidewalks and located within a five-minute walk to schools, convenience stores, and other neighborhood focal points. Attractive, retro-style town centers with cafés and interesting shops and window displays serve to promote pedestrian traffic. Townhomes and garden apartments are essential features of NU communities, providing the population densities to support neighborhood schools and lively town centers.

Front porches on homes restore the "eyes" that watch over streets and make them safe and free of crime. **Traffic-calming measures**, such as low speed limits, traffic bumps, and the preservation of on-street parallel parking, all serve to protect pedestrians, enhancing walkability. Tree-lined walkways and bike paths provide pleasant alternatives to the automobile. Stores, and often houses as well, are located one abutting the other in order to reduce walking distances. Where central facilities require automobile access, parking is pushed to rear garages so that a pedestrian-friendly shopping environment is maintained.

New Urbanists emphasize diversity as opposed to the homogeneity that conventional suburbs enforce through zoning. NU mixes visually attractive apartments and townhomes with single-family homes. Where government monies for subsidized housing are available, New Urbanists seek to "blend in" the subsidized units so that, from the outside, they are not readily distinguishable from market-rate housing.

New Urbanism is not solely a suburban movement. Its principles have also been applied to center-city shopping districts in an effort to bring twenty-four-hour-a-day life back to a city's downtown. The federal government's **HOPE VI** program also adopted a number of New Urbanism design elements in an effort to create more habitable public housing environments. In Chicago, Atlanta, Baltimore, Charlotte, New Orleans, Louisville, and numerous other cities, HOPE VI sought the physical transformation

New Urbanism: The Attractive Downtown of Celebration, Florida. The master-planned community of Celebration in Osceola County, Florida, illustrates a number of features that distinguish New Urbanism design from more typical suburban development: Stores are built close to the street and close to one another to promote walking. Awnings add texture, adding to the "retro" or nostalgic appeal of small-town America. Fountains and places to sit allow people to congregate and meet one another. Streets are narrow and are not built to accommodate high-speed traffic.

From Wikimedia Commons, by Bobak Ha'Eri, February 23, 2006,http://commons.wikimedia.org/wiki/File:022306-CelebrationFL11.jpg.

of public housing, helping to demolish some of the nation's most distressed public housing structures, replacing them with more attractive low-rise housing communities built according to NU principles.[107]

THE LIMITED NATURE OF THE NEW URBANISM REVOLUTION

The New Urbanism's singular achievement has been the construction of aesthetic communities that pose an alternative to automobile-centered suburbia.[108] Developers have also incorporated numerous aspects of New Urbanism into the lively "lifestyle" faux-urban shopping and entertainment villages that are more attractive than the older generation of indoor shopping malls they replaced.[109] Yet despite theses laudable successes, the New Urbanism is unable to contain sprawl or substantially alter the face of suburbia.[110] NU cannot undo patterns of spread land use that have taken root over the years. Also, most

Americans continue to seek homes with multicar garages and spacious side yards and backyards, not the more compact developments of the New Urbanism.

New Urbanists value mixed-income communities and social diversity. But in the absence of public subsidies, NU developers have been unable to include housing for the poor. As a result, NU communities tend to lack the population diversity that was part of the initial NU ideal.[111] To some degree, the New Urbanism has not altered things very much, other than to build "a slightly reconfigured suburb," an "automobile-oriented subdivision dressed up to look like a small pre-car-centered town."[112]

NU design places a high value on ecological sustainability. New Urbanists can build a number of well-designed, aesthetically pleasing, exemplary communities. But overall those communities will have little impact on the continuing sprawled nature of most of suburban development.

CONCLUSION: MOVING FROM SUBURBAN AUTONOMY TO A WORKING REGIONALISM

Suburban communities jealously guard their autonomy, especially their control over schools, zoning, and land-use powers that define a community's identity. Suburban autonomy has also led to sprawled development, raising questions of ecological sustainability and equity.

Each of the regional reform movements described in this chapter—school finance reform, "open suburbs," Smart Growth, growth management, and New Urbanism— has produced important outcomes, and each has served to build a more fair and more ecologically sustainable suburban nation. Still, none of the movements is likely to fundamentally alter the shape of suburbia. American home seekers continue to opt for the "good life" of the suburbs. Developers and home builders will continue to press for the construction of large single-family homes. Together, suburbanites and development interests constitute a quite powerful coalition. Only the most rash or politically naive policy maker will seek to impose strong reform measures that threaten America's suburban majority.

Already-built patterns of settlement cannot practically be changed. Effective growth management programs can help curb new sprawled development; they cannot, however, do much to reverse already established patterns of sprawl. The suburban "facts on the ground" shape public policy choices.

Good public policies must start by first recognizing the physical and political reality of suburbia. In most metropolitan regions, for instance, suburban population densities are just too low to support conventional rail transit and even fixed-guideway bus rapid transit (BRT) systems. What can be done in regions where populations densities do not make rail transit a viable choice? Simply, pursue more limited, less flashy, and more pragmatic transit alternatives: reinvigorate bus service; provide paratransit, where smaller vehicles run flexible routes; limit automobile parking; and increase the charges for parking so that more people will take mass transit. Governments can impose road tolls to reduce commuting during peak times. Municipalities can also establish partnerships with private employers to promote flexible work hours, car pools, and employee use of bicycling and public transit.[113] New mixed residential-commercial town centers with higher population densities can also be planned around public transit hubs.[114]

But will cities and suburbs be willing to cooperate in order to promote job growth, environmental protection, and the cost-efficient delivery of public services? The answer to this question is the subject of our next chapter.

KEY TERMS

agricultural preserves as an
  exclusionary tool (*p. 234*)
Anti-Snob Zoning laws (*p. 236*)
apartheid schools (*p. 231*)
Arlington Heights decision (*p. 233*)
bedroom-developing suburbs (*p. 224*)
bedroom or dormitory suburb
  (*p. 223*)
blue-collar and industrial suburbs
  (*p. 224*)
boomburbs (*p. 221*)
common-interest developments
  (*p. 224*)
compact development (*p. 240*)
density bonuses (*p. 236*)
disaster suburbs (*p. 224*)
economies of scale (*p. 238*)
edge cities (*p. 225*)
edgeless development (*p. 225*)
environmental justice (*p. 240*)
equal protection clause (*p. 229*)
equalizing down, the criticism that
  school finance reform amounts
  to (*p. 230*)
Euclid case (*Village of Euclid, Ohio,
  v. Ambler Realty Co.*), (*p. 232*)
exclusionary zoning (*p. 232*)
exurbs (*p. 224*)
fair housing laws (*p. 227*)
Freeman v. Pitts (*p. 231*)
HOPE VI (*p. 244*)
inclusionary programs (*p. 236*)
intensely segregated schools (*p. 231*)
interdependence of communities in
  a metropolis (*p. 237*)
large-lot zoning (*p. 234*)

limited-growth and no-growth
  ordinances (*p. 234*)
linguistic profiling (*p. 227*)
mandatory inclusionary housing
  requirements, the Minneapolis-
  St. Paul system of (*p. 237*)
metropolitan area (*p. 237*)
metropolitan fragmentation (*p. 238*)
Milliken v. Bradley (*p. 230*)
minimum room/space requirements
  as an exclusionary tool (*p. 234*)
minority-dominated suburbs
  (*p. 224*)
moratorium on the extension of
  sewer and water lines (*p. 234*)
Mount Laurel decisions (*p. 235*)
New Urbanism (NU) (*p. 243*)
Oklahoma City decision (*p. 231*)
open-space and green-space areas
  as exclusionary tools (*p. 234*)
overlap and duplication of services,
  metropolitan fragmentation and
  the (*p. 238*)
paired testing (*p. 228*)
police powers, zoning as an expression
  of local government's (*p. 233*)
privatopias (*p. 224*)
prohibitions on the construction
  of multifamily housing as an
  exclusionary tool (*p. 233*)
property rights advocates (*p. 241*)
racial steering (*p. 227*)
regulations requiring the use of
  expensive construction
  technologies and materials as
  an exclusionary tool (*p. 234*)

10 Regional Governance in a Global Age

As already mentioned in Chapter 9, governing authority in a metropolitan area can be highly fragmented, dispersed among hundreds—in some cases thousands—of autonomous and often overlapping governmental bodies: municipalities, villages, townships, counties, narrow special-purpose governments (including school districts, community college districts, library districts, park districts, fire districts, and water and sewer districts), broad multipurpose districts, and regional planning authorities.

The existence of numerous local governments and autonomous bodies impedes effective regional action. Each jurisdiction and independent agency has the ability to pursue its own interests, with little regard for the well-being of neighboring communities or the region as a whole. The fragmentation of governments can even impede the development of a unified mass transit system that can capably serve all parts of the metropolis.

The erratic, unsystematic development of mass transit in the San Francisco Bay Area reveals the impact that fragmented governing structures have on the lives of citizens. For decades, affluent San Mateo and Marin counties objected to the contributions they were expected to make and, as a result, refused to participate in the building of the Bay Area Rapid Transit (BART) system. As a result, BART rail initially did not serve major portions of the region. For a quarter of a century, BART rail did not even serve the region's airport, located south of San Francisco in San Mateo County. Similarly, in the East Bay, decades of contentious interlocal haggling over routes and funding mechanisms impeded the extension of BART rail service to communities in the I-580 corridor. Political fragmentation produced a chaotic and fragmented mass transit system.

Even today, political fragmentation continues to impede the development of a truly integrated and effective system of mass transit for the Bay Area. A trip from the southern suburbs into San Francisco may necessitate that a rider switch from a local bus to Caltrain (a separate commuter rail system) to BART and finally to San Francisco's Muni system, entailing transfers that lengthen commuting times and require the payment of multiple fares, hassles that are a disincentive to travel by mass transit. The various transit agencies in the region have had difficulty in working together even to offer commuters the convenience of purchasing a single transit pass that would be good for rides on all transit systems in the region.

The tale of fragmentation and public transit is not unique to BART. In Georgia, voters in suburban Cobb County blocked the extension of the Metropolitan Atlanta Regional Transit Agency (MARTA) rail service. In the Dallas-Fort Worth metroplex, the objection of suburbanites to new taxes similarly impeded the extension of Dallas Area Rapid Transit (DART) light-rail service to populous Arlington—the home of the University of Texas-Arlington—and other up-county communities.

As this chapter will describe, metropolitan reformers for many years sought to cure the problem of metropolitan fragmentation by creating a new level of government—a strong, centralized metropolitan government with the authority to undertake coordinated action throughout an entire urban region. But the movement toward metropolitan government has stalled in the face of the fierce opposition of suburbanites intent on defending local autonomy. Even where reformers succeeded in creating new metropolitan bodies, the new governments seldom possessed the extensive powers that metropolitan reformers had envisioned. Jacksonville, Nashville, Baton Rouge, Lexington, Louisville, Indianapolis, Miami, Portland (Oregon), Seattle, and the Minneapolis-St. Paul Twin Cities have all adopted various forms of metropolitan government. But a quick review of the new governing institutions points to their incompleteness; regional governing arrangements in practice fall far short of the metropolitan government ideal.

But is it really necessary to create new metropolitan governments? A more politically pragmatic alternative strategy focuses on getting existing governments in a region to work together. The good news is that regional cooperation is quite possible and, in fact, quite commonplace. Interregional and global economic competitive pressures are also leading to a new interest in local joint action and regional collaboration. Communities that work collaboratively with one another improve their chances of piecing together the sort of proposal that can "win" the location of a major corporation.

OLD-STYLE RESTRUCTURING: ANNEXATION, CONSOLIDATION, AND METROPOLITAN GOVERNMENT

Old-style metropolitan reform emphasized the redrawing of local political borders and the creation of new governmental entities with the authority to act effectively over a large geographical area. Annexation (discussed below) continues to be the most commonplace means of realigning local borders. In the 1950s and 1960s, metropolitanists also focused on efforts to consolidate or merge city and county government. In rare instances, metropolitan reformers created multipurpose bodies that could govern beyond the borders of a single county. In recent decades, however, all of these metropolitan restructuring efforts have foundered, confronted by citizens and local officials opposed to the sacrifice of local autonomy.

ANNEXATION

When an **annexation** occurs, a municipality extends its boundaries outward, absorbing neighboring territory. Through the nineteenth century and much of the twentieth century, cities grew extensively, annexing areas of growth located outside their existing borders. Chicago expanded to the south, capturing Hyde Park and industrial Pullman, and to

the north, absorbing Rogers Park and other bungalow neighborhoods. Los Angeles, in a brief ten-year period (1915 to 1925), mushroomed to nearly four times its previous size, expanding from 108 to 415 square miles. Los Angeles pursued an aggressive policy of **water imperialism**, refusing to supply water to outlying communities in arid southern California unless they agreed to incorporation into the city. (See Box 10.1, "Urban Films: *Chinatown* and the Story of Los Angeles Water Imperialism.") Cities in the Northeast and the Midwest, by contrast, were unable to force already established suburbs to unite with the city. Jersey City and Newark, for instance, lacked control over the New Jersey water supply and hence could not force growing suburban communities to accept annexation.[1]

Each state determines the legal requirements for local annexations and just when an annexation may take place. State laws are generally permissive in allowing cities to annex **unincorporated areas** that have not yet established their own municipal governments under state law. State laws also generally enable a municipality to annex small parcels of land for the siting of industrial and commercial facilities critical to a city's economic growth. Numerous states have a state-established boundary commission to approve (or disapprove) relatively minor annexations. The owner of a factory in an unincorporated area may request annexation, discovering that business expansion plans require a level of water, sewage service, and fire protection that only a neighboring city has the capacity to provide.

The age of annexation is over. Compared to the past, cities today lack the ability to annex large geographical areas and tracts with a substantial residential population. When a city attempts to annex a parcel of land from an already-incorporated suburb, state law typically requires **dual approval**: for the annexation to proceed, both the larger municipality and the smaller area being annexed must consent to the boundary change. For many of the nation's most important cities, this requirement makes growth via annexation all but impossible. Los Angeles, San Francisco, Chicago, Detroit, St. Louis, Milwaukee, Pittsburgh, Cleveland, New York, Baltimore, and Boston are all **landlocked cities** completely surrounded by incorporated suburban municipalities. These central cities no longer have any real prospect of expanding through annexation.

For most of the twentieth century, Sunbelt states were quite permissive, even allowing sizable annexations. Texas allowed cities to unilaterally annex an abutting area with a population of 5,000 or less, if the larger city was already providing water and sewer service to the developing community. In the 1970s, Houston gained over 200,000 new residents through annexation. San Antonio, Charlotte, Phoenix, and Portland (Oregon) were other national annexation leaders.[2]

Local economic elites often push for annexations to assist their profit-making ventures. Houston and Denver annexed the acreage to construct new international airports to facilitate global commerce. Albuquerque in the 1950s and early 1960s seized sparsely populated acreage at the request of developers who needed city water and other municipal services for their new residential subdivisions.[3] Municipalities enjoy the tax revenues that come from annexing sites that are then developed for residential and commercial use.[4]

Annexation contributes to the sound fiscal health of central cities. David Rusk, the former mayor of Albuquerque, uses the term **elastic cities** to refer to cities such as

Box 10.1
**Urban Films: *Chinatown* and the Story of Los Angeles
Water Imperialism**

In the arid West, water is scarce and a vital resource. Los Angeles in the early twentieth century used its municipal water as a weapon of territorial expansion. The city forced other communities to consent to annexation in exchange for water.

The power play of municipal water politics provides the backdrop for Roman Polanski's 1974 *cinema noir* classic, *Chinatown*, a film that received eleven Academy Award nominations. The film, despite its name, is not really about the city's Chinese immigrant enclave. Instead, the movie presents a fictionalized version of the efforts undertaken by Los Angeles water chief William Mulholland to construct the Owens Valley aqueduct, a project that, in 1913, brought water from over 200 miles away to Los Angeles. Situated in a desert region, Los Angeles needed an assured supply of water for the city to grow. Control over water enabled L.A. to annex communities in the water-starved San Fernando Valley. The region's orchard growers and ranchers, however, were unhappy with the changes being forced upon them; they charged that Los Angeles had stolen the water from the Owens River and was using it for political extortion. In the 1920s, angry protestors dynamited sections of the new aqueduct.

In *Chinatown*, private detective Jake Gittes (played by Jack Nicholson) explores the mystery of why Los Angeles is secretly dumping water at a time when fruit growers and urban dwellers are suffering from drought conditions. Gittes is shot at by resentful Valley farmers. He uncovers a cesspool of corruption: the city's growth machine, including its leading newspaper, has whipped up a frenzy over water in order to win approval for the city's efforts to gain control over the Owens River water supply, thereby making possible the dynamic growth of Los Angeles.

The film, of course, is a fictional presentation that is loosely based on the story of L.A.'s water wars. The film distorts the timeline of events, moving them to the New Deal era. It also exaggerates the corruption and sinister motives underlying the city's acquisition of water, fabrications that "amp up" the drama of a classic screen detective story.

Sources: For comparisons of the film *Chinatown* with the actual history of L.A.'s water imperialism and events surrounding the Owens Valley water controversy, see: John Walton, "Film Mystery as Urban History: The Case of *Chinatown*," in *Cinema and the City: Film and Urban Society in a Global Context*, ed. Mark Shiel and Tony Fitzmaurice (Oxford, UK: Blackwell, 2001), 46–58; and Gary D. Libecap, *Owens Valley Revisited: A Reassessment of the West's First Great Water Transfer* (Stanford, CA: Stanford University Press, 2007). Also see the work of best-selling novelist/historian Les Standiford, *Water to the Angels: William Mullholland, His Monumental Aqueduct, and the Rise of Los Angeles* (New York: HarperCollins, 2015).

Albuquerque, Charlotte, Houston, and San Antonio that have used annexation to capture much of the tax base of new suburban development. In contrast, Hartford, Cleveland, and Detroit and other landlocked or **inelastic** cities in the Frostbelt suffer continued

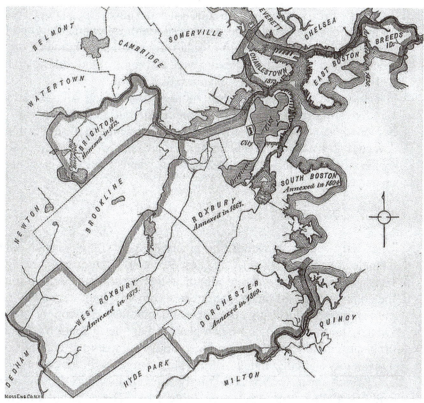

Boston Annexations, 1880. By the beginning of the twentieth century, Boston had taken its present-day shape, having grown through the annexation of Roxbury, Dorchester, East Boston, and other surrounding areas. Brookline, however, spurned annexation and remains outside of Boston. Today, Boston is landlocked by already incorporated areas and no longer can expand via annexation.

http://commons.wikimedia.org/wiki/File:Boston_annexations_1880.jpg.

fiscal distress, as they cannot tap revenues from the extensive economic growth taking place just beyond the city's edge.[5] Columbus, Ohio, is the rare example of a Frostbelt city that was able to use its control over water and sewer hookups to force growing rim areas to agree to annexation. Columbus grew from 39 square miles in 1950 to 210 square miles in 2000. The revenues captured as a result of annexation allowed Columbus to maintain an enviable fiscal position, especially when compared to other major Ohio cities, inelastic Cleveland and Cincinnati.[6]

In recent years, the wave of annexations in the Sunbelt has waned. Charlotte and Oklahoma City have already swallowed up the easy-to-annex acreage. Throughout the Sunbelt, resistance to annexation has stiffened and spurred states to impose new limitations on annexation. The State of Texas enacted changes that made large-scale annexations more time-consuming and difficult. These changes were prompted by the howls of anger from the residents of Kingwood, an upscale community with a population of 50,000, who failed in their attempts to keep Houston from absorbing their community. Virginia, since the late 1980s, has imposed a moratorium on local annexations.

Tennessee in 2013 called a "time out" on annexations, legislating a one-year partial ban on border changes. That same year, the Republican-controlled Ohio legislature placed new obstacles even in the path of relatively small annexations. Fort Worth, Amarillo, Denver, Wilmington, and Asheville were just some of the communities where Tea Party activists mobilized resistance to annexation efforts.[7]

Faced with the prospect of even more restrictive state rules, cities lowered their profile, retreating from major annexation efforts but, nonetheless, still pursuing smaller border adjustments for new economic development and the collection of additional tax revenues. Townships and unincorporated areas, however, continue to contest attempts by the city to take their land, even in cases where a local business needs greater public resources for expansion.[8]

CITY-COUNTY CONSOLIDATION

Under **city-county consolidation**, a city merges with its surrounding county to form a single government; the city and county are no longer separate entities with separate legislative bodies and separate administrative departments. A total consolidation entails the elimination of all municipalities in the county, with the county becoming the sole general-purpose local government. Contemporary city-county consolidations in the United States, however, are incomplete and are never total. Numerous suburban governments and other local governing entities continue to remain in existence even after a major city and other municipalities have merged with the county.

The movement toward city-county consolidation has clearly slowed after a brief mid-twentieth-century spurt (see Table 10.1). The consolidation of Louisville with Jefferson County is the only significant merger to take place in more than three decades. Suburban residents oppose consolidation as a loss of small-scale, accessible government. Advocates promise that consolidation will bring about greater efficiency. But such promises fall on the deaf ears of suburbanites who are more worried about maintaining their community's identity and local control. In Athens–Clarke County (Georgia), Carson City–Ormsby County (Nevada), and Kansas City–Wyandotte County (Kansas), the merger of city and county governments did not produce substantial cost savings.[9]

In the middle of the twentieth century, the residents of newly developing suburban communities sometimes welcomed consolidation as a means of gaining improved municipal services provided by the central city. Homeowners in the rim areas surrounding Nashville and Jacksonville, for instance, saw merger with the city as a means of gaining paved streets, curbs, gutters, and other municipal improvements. Today, however, the situation is quite different; the residents of established suburbs view merger not as a help but as a threat.

Business and political leaders often propose city-county consolidation as a means of altering power arrangements in a community. In midcentury Nashville and Jacksonville, business leaders saw consolidation as a means to wrest power away from parochial municipal officials who were unwilling to finance downtown renewal projects.[10] In Indiana, Republican Party officials and business leaders looked to the creation of **Unigov**, the unification of the City of Indianapolis with Marion County, as a tool that would

Table 10.1
City-County Consolidations, 1805–2012

Year	City-County	State
1805	New Orleans–Orleans Parish	Louisiana
1821	Boston–Suffolk County	Massachusetts
1821	Nantucket–Nantucket County	Massachusetts
1854	Philadelphia–Philadelphia County	Pennsylvania
1856	San Francisco–San Francisco County	California
1874	New York (Manhattan)–New York County	New York
1984	New York–Bronx and Staten Island	New York
1898	New York–Brooklyn, Queens, and Richmond County	New York
1904	Denver–Arapahoe County	Colorado
1907	Honolulu–Honolulu County	Hawaii
1947	Baton Rouge–East Baton Rouge Parish	Louisiana
1952	Hamilton and Phoebus–Elizabeth City County	Virginia
1957	Newport News–Warwick City County	Virginia
1962	Nashville–Davidson County	Tennessee
1962	Chesapeake–South Norfolk–Norfolk County	Virginia
1962	Virginia Beach–Princess Anne County	Virginia
1967	Jacksonville–Duval County	Florida
1969	Indianapolis–Marion County	Indiana
1969	Carson City–Ormsby County	Nevada
1969	Juneau and Douglas–Greater Juneau Borough	Alaska
1970	Columbus–Muscogee County	Georgia
1971	Holland and Whaleyville–Nansemond County	Virginia
1971	Sitka–Greater Sitka Borough	Alaska
1972	Lexington–Fayette County	Kentucky
1972	Suffolk–Nansemond County	Virginia
1975	Anchorage, Glen Alps, and Girdwood–Greater Anchorage	Alaska
1976	Anaconda–Deer Lodge County	Montana
1976	Butte–Silver Bow County	Montana
1984	Houma–Terrebonne County	Louisiana
1988	Lynchburg–Moore County	Tennessee
1992	Athens–Clarke County	Georgia
1992	Lafayette–Lafayette Parish	Louisiana
1995	Augusta–Richmond County	Georgia
1997	Kansas City (KS)–Wyandotte County	Kansas
2001	Hartsville–Trousdale County	Tennessee
2001	Louisville–Jefferson County	Kentucky
2002	Haines City–Haines Borough	Alaska
2003	Cusseta City–Chattahoochee County	Georgia
2006	Georgetown–Quitman County	Georgia
2007	Tribune–Greeley County	Kansas
2008	Statenville–Echols County	Georgia

Sources: National Association of Counties, Research Division, "Research Brief," no date, NACO, Washington, DC, 1999; National Association of Counties, "City-County Consolidation Proposals, 1921–present," 2011, www.naco.org/Counties/learn/Documents/City%20County%20Consolidations.01.01.2011.pdf; Kathryn Murphy, *Reshaping County Government: A Look at City-County Consolidation* (Washington, DC: National Association of Counties, February 2012).

Box 10.2
Indianapolis: Unigov or Unigrab?

The creation of Unigov was motivated by partisan concerns; it was not simply a good-government reform intended to strengthen regional action and catalyze economic investment in Indiana's capital region. Democrats charge that the state's Republican-controlled legislature and governor manipulated a self-serving power grab so brazen that the reform should be referred to not as Unigov but as **Unigrab**.

Demographic trends at the time clearly indicated that if the city boundaries of Indianapolis were left unchanged, the Democrats would likely gain electoral control of city hall as a result of the city's growing numbers of low-income voters and racial minorities. But the Unigov consolidation changed the boundaries for city elections, effectively adding thousands of suburban residents—a largely Republican voting bloc—to the electorate that would choose the Unigov mayor and council.

The results of the elections that immediately followed the merger attest to the success of the Republican strategy. In 1975, Republican votes from the suburbs provided their party's mayoral candidate, William Hudnut, with his margin of victory, despite the Democrats having won the "old city" by 17,500 votes. In 1991, Republican Stephen Goldsmith similarly won Unigov's mayoralty, despite the Democratic candidate having won the old city by 15,000 votes. It was not until 1999, thirty years after the creation of Unigov, that a Democrat, Bart Peterson, was at long last elected mayor. Even the creation of Unigov could not forever hold back the demographic tide that was changing Indianapolis politics.

Source: The vote tallies are from William Blomquist, "Metropolitan Organization and Local Politics: The Indianapolis-Marion County Experience," paper presented at the annual meeting of the Midwest Political Science Association, Chicago, April 9–11, 1992.

help preserve Republican Party control over Indianapolis and its downtown business district in the face of demographic changes that seemed to be leading to an emerging Democratic majority in the city. (See Box 10.2, "Indianapolis: Unigov or Unigrab?").

Just what impact does city-county consolidation have on a region's racial minorities? The answer to the question is subject to much debate. Merger clearly dilutes African-American voting power; by making the city's borders coterminous with those of a county, consolidation effectively adds white suburban voters to the city's electorate, diminishing the prospects that African Americans will gain control of city hall. Yet the adoption of district voting systems (see Chapter 6) helps to ensure that racial minorities have representatives in the new city/county council. Data from Nashville and Jacksonville also indicate that city-county consolidation can help promote new economic growth and new economic opportunities for racial minorities. Consolidation in both Nashville and Jacksonville even helped give business leaders a regional perspective on problem, a perspective that included a more inclusive and welcoming attitude toward citizen participation.[11]

Indianapolis's Unigov: Built for Economic Development

As Indiana lacks a strong home-rule tradition, the state legislature in 1969 was able to order the unification of Indianapolis and Marion County without having to gain the approval of the affected local jurisdictions. Business leaders saw the creation of Unigov as a means of energizing the city, enabling Indianapolis to surmount economic stagnation and escape its "Indiana-no-place" image. Overnight, the merger seemingly made Indianapolis "major league"; civic leaders claimed that the new Unigov Indianapolis instantly became the twelfth largest city in the nation (1990 figures). Extending the city's boundaries also increased the total assessed value of property located within the city's borders, thereby increasing the amount of money that, under state law, the city could borrow to finance downtown redevelopment and other growth projects.[12]

The merger created a county government with a capacity to act cohesively in promoting downtown revitalization and major regional economic development projects. Unigov's mayor presides over one of the strongest regional planning and economic development departments in the country.[13] The city's economic team steered new investment to Indianapolis' center, something that the leaders of the old city could not do as their efforts were often undercut by suburban officials who sought to lure attractive corporations to their own communities. Unigov planners persuaded the developers of Market Square Arena to locate their new sports facility in the center of the city rather than along an interstate highway. Unigov officials similarly convinced American United Life to abandon plans for a suburban headquarters and instead build a thirty-eight-story downtown office tower, the tallest building in the state, bringing an estimated 1,500 employees into the heart of the city. Unigov's ability to speak with one voice also helped the region win the ninety-three-city national competition for an $800 million United Airlines maintenance facility.[14] Indianapolis built a new indoor football stadium and basketball arena and new facilities for amateur tennis, swimming, bicycle racing, and track and field, becoming the self-proclaimed amateur sports capital of the United States and home to the National Collegiate Athletic Association.[15]

Yet despite these noteworthy achievements, Unigov suffers serious limitations. Its planning controls are confined within the borders of a single county. Unigov could not curb the rapid growth of Carmel and Fishers, affluent communities lying just outside the Marion County boundary line.

Unigov has also had much less success in social policy than in economic development. While Unigov's planning efforts have been quite successful in sparking the revival of Indianapolis' once-failing downtown, the consolidated government has not been able to stem the decline of the city's poorer neighborhoods.

The creation of a "unified" countywide governing system did not result in a single government with the capacity to equalize tax rates and services throughout the county. In fact, the name "Unigov" is a misnomer; governmental arrangements in the county are not fully consolidated into a single, unified government. Postconsolidation Marion County has

6 municipalities, 9 townships, and more than 100 separate taxing units and school districts. In 2009, Unigov Mayor, Greg Ballard, called for further governmental consolidation and streamlining efforts,[16] a proposal that the city's surrounding townships vigorously opposed.

The creation of Unigov also did not lead to greater racial integration in the region's public schools, for an obvious reason: the school districts were intentionally left out of the consolidation plan. Any proposed consolidation plan that threatened the local control of schools and raised the prospects of racial integration would have been doomed to political failure.

Louisville: Was the Merger Necessary?

The 2003 merger of Louisville with surrounding Jefferson County gained the city instant national prestige. Including the residents of an outlying portion of the county, the merger made Louisville the sixteenth largest city in the nation, a significant leap from the old city, which ranked only at number sixty-four. Indeed, civic pride helped drive the consolidation effort. Louisville residents feared that, without the merger, Lexington-Fayette would soon surpass Louisville as Kentucky's most populous city. Advocates further argued that the merger would provide the regional vision and leadership necessary to reverse the area's declining economic fortunes.

As was the case in Indianapolis' Unigov, the consolidation of governments in Louisville-Jefferson County was incomplete. The old City of Louisville lost its independent existence, but eighty-four smaller suburban municipalities continue to exist postconsolidation.[17]

Critics argue that the Louisville consolidation was not really necessary. Studies of city-county mergers across the nation reveal that consolidations seldom produce the extensive gains in service efficiency, economic development, and racial desegregation that consolidation enthusiasts promise.[18] Consolidation also is not necessary for cost savings; interlocal arrangements allow communities to cooperate in ways that save money even in the absence of merger. Preconsolidation Louisville even enjoyed limited tax-base sharing. In 1986, Louisville and Jefferson County agreed to a formal "compact" that reduced the interlocal competition for new economic development and that redistributed $5 million a year in fiscal assistance to the city.[19] Why would Louisville's suburbs extend such help to the city? Suburban officials hoped that the compact would be sufficient to deter threats by the city to annex surrounding areas.[20]

The new Metro government has succeeded in promoting new investment in both the downtown and in suburban areas in the county. The revival of downtown Louisville is, in some ways, rather amazing. However, as was the case in Unigov, Metro brought little new investment to inner-city residential neighborhoods.[21] The residents of Louisville's troubled neighborhoods are "just as poor after consolidation as before."[22] The merger also adversely affected the prospects of black electoral power. African Americans were a third of the population of Louisville prior to the merger; in the election held immediately after consolidation, African Americans won less than a fourth (six of twenty-six) of the seats on the new Metro Louisville council.

Overall, the creation of Louisville's Metro had limited economic effects; the merger was not the "breakthrough" event that jump-started the local economy. The years immediately following consolidation saw no sharp growth in employment, payrolls, or other measures of regional economic health.[23] Yet the merger did have a positive impact on downtown and tourist-related development. Consolidation also improved the fiscal position of the city, a factor that led private financial houses to upgrade the city's bond rating.[24]

Miami's Two-Tiered System

Miami's **two-tiered system** of metropolitan government, created in 1957, has been in existence for more than half a century. Initially hailed as a model for metropolitan areas across the nation, more sober evaluations since that time have identified the limitations as well as the advantages of a two-level arrangement that assigns a number of important planning responsibilities to a strengthened Dade County government while leaving daily service responsibilities in the hands of local government. In contrast to city-county consolidation, the two-tier system does not remove any municipality from the map.

The creation of Metro-Dade led to improvements in such service areas as mass transit, highway construction, countywide land-use planning, social service provision, voter registration, and countywide tax assessment and administration. Metro-Dade brought a new professionalization to municipal government, an upgrade that posed quite a contrast to the episodes of corruption, maladministration, and patronage abuses that continued to plague the City of Miami, Hialeah, and other municipalities in the region.

Over the half century since Metro-Dade's creation, no U.S. region has copied the two-tiered model, a reflection of the strong political opposition to such metropolitan restructuring. It is doubtful that the two-tiered system could be created today in the Miami area. Dade County's more wealthy communities—Miami Beach, Surfside, Golden Beach, Bal Harbour, and North Bay Village—have repeatedly attempted, without success, to secede from the arrangement. Hundreds of lawsuits have also been filed in an attempt to diminish the authority of the regional government.[25]

Like Indianapolis' Unigov, Metro-Dade is also limited in terms of its geographic reach. As the governing arrangement for a single county, Metro-Dade lacks the ability to plan or control development in a dynamically growing region that spills into neighboring Broward (Fort Lauderdale), Palm Beach, and Monroe counties.

CREATING NEW METROPOLITAN GOVERNMENTS: PORTLAND AND THE TWIN CITIES

The Greater Portland (Oregon) Metropolitan Service District and the Twin Cities (Minneapolis–St. Paul) Metropolitan Council are the most prominent examples of the three-tiered approach to metropolitan government, which adds a new regional government atop the existing municipal and county levels of government.

Portland

The Portland Metropolitan Service District (commonly called "Metro") is unique, as it is the only directly elected multicounty regional government in the United States. Metro's authority cuts across twenty-four cities and three counties.

Oregon state law gives Metro real authority in areas such as land use, environmental protection, and transportation planning. Oregon law mandates that local land-use and zoning regulations comply with the overall framework set by Metro. As described in Chapter 9, Metro sets the region's urban growth boundary. Metro planners seek to "build up" rather than "build out" the Portland area, with downtown revitalization and infill projects as an alternative to sprawl. Portland planners have also channeled new development to growth nodes along light-rail lines.

Oregon state law also gives Metro the responsibility to formulate an affordable housing plan that details how each of the district's twenty-four cities will accept their share of low- and moderate-income housing units. Metro's actions in this area have led to the greater availability of apartments and small-lot housing in Portland's suburbs than in suburbs elsewhere in the United States.

While Portland arguably has the most powerful metropolitan government in the nation, in important ways its authority is still quite limited: Metro "is at once pathbreaking as a mode of regional governance yet benign in its functions."[26] Metro's "budget is piddling by comparison to many other governmental units."[27] Existing municipalities, not Metro, retain responsibility for most service provision. Conservative political forces have also gone to the ballot box to impose new limitations on Metro's land-use powers, requiring, for instance, that the government pay owners for planning decisions that diminish the economic value of a piece of property. Suburban jurisdictions have also gone to court to challenge Metro's plans for fair-share affordable housing.[28]

The Twin Cities Met Council

In 1969 the Minnesota state legislature created the Twin Cities Metropolitan Council (the Met Council, for short) to help cope with the rapid growth taking place in the seven-county capital region. Over the years, the Met Council has gained additional powers in areas such as sewers, wastewater management, open space protection, transportation, airport construction, and the development of stadiums and sports facilities. The Met Council can also levy property taxes and issue bonds, important financial powers that distinguish the Twin Cities regional entity from COGs (council of governments, a weaker arrangement for regional cooperation that will be discussed later in this chapter) and the more commonplace regional planning bodies found in other U.S. metropolitan areas.

The Met Council formulates a **metropolitan development guide**, a "blueprint" or "binding plan" that designates certain areas of the county for concentrated development while safeguarding farmland and other areas from development incursions and sprawl. A visitor to the Twin Cities region can look out an airplane window and see the difference that the Met Council has made: despite the region's immense population growth, large green and natural areas are preserved and sprawl is minimized.

The Met Council also serves as the region's housing authority. The regional government has had limited success in dispersing subsidized housing units into the region's suburbs.

Unlike Portland's Metro and Indianapolis' Unigov, however, the members of the Twin Cities Met Council are not elected; instead, the council's members are appointed by the Minnesota governor. The absence of election places an important limitation on the Met Council's power: the Met Council lacks the legitimacy, visibility, and leadership potential that derives from popular election. Members of the Met Council felt that they had little alternative but to approve the construction of the suburban Mall of America, despite the adverse effects that the megamall was predicted to have on older shopping centers in the region. The Met Council simply lacked the political stature to challenge a major development project favored by the governor.[29]

The Met Council has also been quite restrained in its efforts to convince the region's better-off suburbs to allow construction of affordable housing. Despite the goals set by the Met Council in its fair-share housing plans, more affluent suburbs still employ exclusionary zoning to keep out low-income housing. In the face of intense opposition— including the opposition of state legislators—to its fair-share housing efforts, the Met Council turned to a policy of noninterference, in effect, seeking the construction of public housing only in communities willing to accept new units. In 1986, the council even defined houses costing $120,000 as "affordable," a move that enabled virtually all communities in the region to meet their assigned affordable-housing goals without really opening their communities to families in need.[30]

The Twin Cities area is also renowned for its system of **regional tax-base sharing**, another initiative enacted by the Minnesota state legislature. Under the state's tax-base sharing or **fiscal disparities law**, a local government does not receive all of the increase

Indoor Amusement Park at The Mall of America, The Twin Cities. The Met Council had no ability to challenge the building of the suburban Mall of America, a mega–economic development project that had the backing of the state's governor and other pro-growth officials.

Copyright © Jeremy Noble. http://commons.wikimedia.org/wiki/File:Mall_of_America-2005-05-29.jpg.

in property tax revenues generated by new commercial development located inside its borders; instead, 40 percent of the new revenues are placed in a pool for distribution to localities throughout the region, with each jurisdiction's share determined by its population and need.

Tax-base sharing has smoothed out some of the inequalities of local government finance, providing additional assistance to poorer communities and especially to blue-collar suburbs. The region's two major cities, however, are not always the beneficiaries of tax-base sharing. While St. Paul continues to receive assistance from the program, since 2011 Minneapolis, the site of substantial new downtown development, has been a net "loser" under the law, having to contribute to the pool of money that is redistributed to other communities.[31] The region's better-off suburbs continue to bitterly attack the plan, although, in some cases, small but wealthy bedroom communities actually receive financial assistance under the program's unique distribution formula.[32]

The Twin Cities Met Council and Portland's Metro represent the most expansive efforts to create a multicounty regional government in the United States. The creation of such strong regional bodies, however, evokes strident opposition. They are not likely to be copied by other metropolitan areas across the nation. Were they not already in existence, it is highly questionable whether the Minnesota state government would be willing today to vote for the creation of the Met Council and regional tax-base sharing.[33]

IS METROPOLITAN GOVERNMENT REALLY DESIRABLE? TWO CONTRASTING SCHOOLS OF THOUGHT

Is the creation of strong metropolitan governments a goal worth pursuing? There are two sharply contrasting schools of thought. **Metropolitanists** argue that a centralized government can provide more efficient, uniform, and equitable service provision across the metropolis. Environmentalists, too, argue for a strong regional authority to constrain the self-seeking actions by local governments that encourage sprawled development.

Metropolitanists point to the costs savings that result from **economies of scale** when a large government gains discounts by making large purchases, or when overhead costs are shared among communities when services are provided over a relatively large geographic area. A regional police or fire force, for instance, would allow for the closing of a number of unnecessary police and fire stations that each separate municipality maintains.

Polycentrists, by contrast, see great virtue in having a multitude of local governments in a region. They oppose the creation of powerful regional governing bodies; instead, they argue that smaller-scale governments work best. Polycentrists cite the responsiveness of smaller governments as compared to bureaucratized large-scale government.

DEFENDING THE POLYCENTRIC METROPOLIS: PUBLIC CHOICE THEORY

Polycentrism is rooted in **public choice theory**, which observes that citizens vary considerably in their willingness to pay taxes for public services. A single centralized government that provides the same level of taxes and services throughout a metropolitan area cannot possibly respond to the great variety of citizen preferences. Smaller-scale local governments, in contrast, offer citizens choice. Citizens who desire quality parks and recreational services can choose to live in a community that offers high-level amenities at a high rate of taxation. Citizens who do not wish to pay high taxes can choose to reside in a community that provides only more basic public services.

Polycentrists reject the metropolitanists' contention that bigger is better: that a metropolitan government saves taxpayer money by taking advantage of economies of scale. Public choice theorists observe that economies of scale seldom exist. Instead, urban service delivery is often characterized by **diseconomies of scale**, as large-scale production is plagued by new inefficiencies. Public choice theorists argue that large-scale governments are bloated, wasteful, bureaucratized, and unresponsive.

Evidence from the history of city-county mergers provides some support for the arguments of public choice theorists: major political consolidations seldom produce the extensive cost savings that metropolitanists predicted. Where savings result, they tend to be concentrated in a few administrative areas. Many of the initial cost savings gained from city-county consolidation also fade over time as service providers "level up" municipal wages and benefits across the region to the highest levels found in the metropolis.[34] In a consolidated system, it is difficult for municipal officials to justify giving lower remuneration to a firefighter or bus driver in one part of the region while offering better pay and benefits to workers performing the same jobs in other parts of the region.

Public choice theory essentially applies market theory to defend the fragmented or polycentric metropolis.[35] Public choice theorists contend that **interlocal competition** for businesses and better-off residents spurs communities to place greater emphasis on effective and efficient service delivery. To attract good businesses and residents, municipal leaders have to search for new ways to provide high-quality services while keeping taxes low.

Polycentrists further argue that there is no need to create a centralized metropolitan government to capture the economies of scale that do exist. Instead, local communities can voluntarily enter into joint purchasing agreements and other cooperative arrangements to save money.

THE BLIND SPOTS IN PUBLIC CHOICE THEORY

Public choice theorists present a highly articulate defense of the polycentric metropolis. They emphasize the virtues of grassroots democracy and the shortcomings of big government. Yet public choice theory suffers shortcomings of its own.

While bigger is often bureaucratic, there are also times when consolidation does actually produce efficiencies and cost savings. The consolidation movement achieved its greatest success in public education, where mergers dramatically slashed the number of school districts in the United States from 117,000 (in 1940) to 14,200 (in 2005).[36] Consolidation eliminated thousands of tiny school districts that were too small to take advantage of economies of scale. The mergers allowed for the elimination of redundant administrative positions. Students also gained the ability to choose from a variety of programs that the tiny districts could not offer.[37]

The critics of public choice theory also ask: Who gets to choose? The choices exercised by more privileged residents may reduce the choices available to the working class and the poor. More affluent suburbs enact exclusionary zoning and land-use regulations that limit the free-market production of more affordable dwelling units, denying working- and even middle-class families the opportunity to choose housing in better communities.

Interlocal competition also does not always motivate lagging communities to upgrade their performance, as public choice theorists contend. A region's more distressed communities often find that they lack the resources necessary to make much-needed improvements in protective services and recreational programs; rather than improve, poorer communities fall further behind the competition.

Public choice theorists correctly point out that extensive intergovernmental cooperation already exists in metropolitan areas. Yet jurisdictions cooperate only when they find it to their mutual advantage to do so. There is little voluntary resource sharing or joint action to combat such serious social problems as the isolation of the poor or the racial imbalance of public school systems. Nor, as we have already seen, do localities always find it in their self-interest to cooperate in efforts to constrain local development in order to minimize urban sprawl and the loss of green space. In such areas, stronger regional institutions are necessary to reach regional goals.

REGIONAL COOPERATION, OLD STYLE

As public choice theorists observe, regional action does not necessarily require the creation of a new metropolitan government. Instead, a fairly large variety of interlocal cooperative arrangements offer flexible responses to regional problems.

INFORMAL COOPERATION AND JOINT POWERS AGREEMENTS

Informal cooperation occurs when two or more localities share equipment or work together with no agreement spelled out in writing. Casual arrangements, however, often evolve into a formalized **joint powers agreement**, a legally binding arrangement that spells out each community's contribution, say, to support a shared training center for firefighters. In many metropolitan areas, fairly simple joint powers agreements enable residents to patronize the libraries of neighboring communities. In other cases, a joint powers agreement can be quite complex and detailed. The agreement between Dallas and Fort Worth that set the terms for the financing and operations of the region's international airport runs well over 100 pages.[38]

Mutual aid agreements, where localities commit to helping one another in times of emergency, are typified by the compact signed by Thornton and Westminster, Colorado, to back up each other's computer system in the event of a disaster.[39] The inadequacy of the immediate response to the 9/11 terrorist attacks on the New York World Trade Center underscores the importance of mutual aid agreements. Prior to 9/11, neighboring jurisdictions were leery about entering into agreements with an agency as huge as the Fire Department of New York (FDNY). As a result, on 9/11 the FDNY had no clear procedures or practiced routines to direct the utilization of first responders from other communities in the region; the initial response to the emergency was poorly coordinated.[40]

Box 10.3
San Diego and Tijuana: Collaboration in a Cross-Border Metropolis

Over the years, cooperation between San Diego, California, and Tijuana, Mexico, has become increasingly commonplace. Officials from the two cities meet to coordinate disaster response plans, to regulate traffic, to share intelligence on street gangs, to arrange ride-along exchanges for police officers, and to promote tourism and the economic development of the region. They have even arranged a joint effort to promote recycling.

Local law-enforcement agencies work, often informally, with their counterparts across the border. Under Mexico's centralized political system, municipalities generally lack the authority to enter into formal joint efforts to combat drug trafficking and to maintain homeland security.[1] The United States Constitution bars state and local governments from negotiating their own agreements with foreign nations. As a result, in law enforcement and other service areas, many of the cooperative efforts by Tijuana and San Diego are limited to informal understandings.

The interdependence of two cities, however, does at times require joint action that extends beyond informal understandings. The commitments of huge sums of money to construct a light-rail system to connect the two downtowns necessitated a binding cooperative arrangement. The Agreement on Binational Cooperation formalized a number of joint cross-border actions. San Diego residents pressed for the construction of new sewage facilities to lessen untreated effluent from Tijuana that washes up on California beaches. Local officials have also discussed the construction of an international airport that would straddle the border.

In 2013 San Diego mayor Bob Filner called on the two cities to join together in submitting a bid to host the 2024 Summer Olympic Games. Filner even set up a municipal office located in Tijuana, testifying to the geographic reality: the two cities were interdependent parts of a single region. San Diego's bid for a bi-national Olympic bid, which may never have had much of a chance from the beginning, suffered a major setback when Filner resigned from office in the face of allegations of sexual harassment.

To relieve congestion at San Diego's one-runway airport, a public-private partnership proposed a novel solution: new parking lots would be built on the United States side of the border, with passengers crossing the border via a new 325-foot enclosed walkway to Tijuana International. Travelers from the United States would gain increased access to the Tijuana airport. The pedestrian bridges would operate like any of the six other border crossings in the region.[2]

---

1. José María Ramos, "Managing Transborder Cooperation on Public Security: The Tijuana-San Diego Region," paper presented at Research Seminar on Mexico and U.S.-Mexican Relations, The Center for U.S.-Mexican Studies, University of California, San Diego, La Jolla, California, October 15, 2003, http://repositories.cdlib.org/usmex/ramos/.

2. Billy Witz, "Tijuana Airport Parking, Just Over the Border," *New York Times,* January 20, 2014.

Informal cooperation is especially important for communities that lie on an international border, as the intricacies of constitutional and international law often preclude a city from signing formal agreements with its neighbors in other countries.[41] Globalization denotes the interdependence of areas on both sides of an international border, an interdependence that requires a coordinated response to mutual problems, as evident in the collaborative undertaking of San Diego and Tijuana. (See Box 10.3, "San Diego and Tijuana: Collaboration in a Cross-Border Metropolis.") In El Paso and its cross-border neighbor Ciudad Juárez, nongovernmental organizations have called for joint actions by law enforcement agencies to combat both the serious problem of femicides—the murder of hundreds of women—and drug-gang violence.[42]

INTERGOVERNMENTAL SERVICE CONTRACTING

A municipality does not always have to use its own workers to provide a public service. Where state law allows, a locality can sign an **intergovernmental service contract**, agreeing to buy a service that will be provided by another city or a county. Smaller communities contract for services that they cannot afford to provide on their own, for instance, purchasing water for the central city. Contracting enables governments to save money on equipment and overhead costs. By joining together, governments can also obtain discounted prices from vendors.

In 2013, financially strapped Camden, New Jersey, a city suffering both extreme fiscal distress and a high number of murders, disbanded its local police department, transferring responsibility to the county. A signed shared-services agreement gave responsibility for police protection in the city to a new metropolitan division of the county's police force. The financially troubled city had no viable alternative, as fiscal urgency had previously forced the municipality to dismiss a number of local police officers despite the city's high crime rates. The city had even stopped responding to citizen calls reporting property crime.

Camden's shift of police activities to the county was assisted by a state grant to help pay for new equipment and the hiring of additional officers. Figures just a year after the new arrangement was put into place appeared to show a dramatic drop in murders and in police response times (from more than 60 minutes to only 4.4 minutes). New Jersey Governor Chris Christie argued that the consolidation of local police departments would save taxpayer money in the long term by eliminating duplicate services and reducing unnecessary bonuses and other incentives that some localities offered officers. The city's police union opposed the transfer of functions to the nonunionized county protective force, a move that it labeled "union busting." A number of suburban officials, too, opposed the move, as they saw no need to assume responsibility for service provision in the troubled central city.[43]

The **Lakewood Plan** is the most expansive variant of intergovernmental service contracting in the United States. The Lakewood Plan offers communities in Los Angeles County an extremely large "menu" of services that they can purchase from the county. As a result of the Lakewood Plan, a municipality does not even have to maintain its own police force; the municipality can arrange for the county to provide police services, with a legally binding contract specifying the frequency of patrols, the number of officers

Box 10.4
The Lakewood Plan: Cure or Contributor to Metropolitan Fragmentation?

Under the **Lakewood Plan**, Los Angeles County offers local governments a large menu of services. A municipality can choose to have the county provide police patrols, fire protection, and any of a large number of other municipal services. The arrangement allows local communities—especially smaller communities—to save money. A community can secure high-quality and professionalized services without having to incur the expense of setting up its own municipal departments and hiring and training its own workers.

The Lakewood Plan emphasizes the increase in efficiency gained from the county-wide provision of services. But the plan also exacerbated metropolitan fragmentation by facilitating the formation of new autonomous local governments. The years following the creation of the Lakewood Plan saw a rash of new municipal incorporations: previously unincorporated areas organized as new units of local government, enjoying home rule protections, while relying on the county for the provision of important local services. The City of Lakewood itself was formed as residents sought municipal incorporation as a means to avoid annexation by the neighboring Long Beach.

The Lakewood Plan led to the creation of a number of **minimal cities**—small, independent suburban jurisdictions that purchase many municipal services from the county. The newly incorporated suburbs became centers of "white flight," places of escape from the region's troubled core cities. The more affluent suburbs used their newfound zoning and land-use powers to price out low-income and renter populations. Rancho Palos Verdes restricted new development, preserving the community's exclusive, estate-like character.

Business interests engineered a number of the early municipal incorporations, creating small municipalities that relied on the county for service provision. Business executives sought to avoid the higher taxes—especially school taxes—that they would have to pay if a populous neighbor were to annex the community. The strange names of some of the newly created Lakewood communities reflect their industrial and commercial roots. The City of Industry was created as a tax shelter for local railroad yards, factories, and warehouses. In order to meet the minimum population of 500 required by state law for incorporation, the community even had to include the 169 patients and 31 employees of a local psychiatric sanitarium in its population count. By the year 2000, the City of Industry, with a population of only 777, was still not much of a city. The city levied no taxes on industrial and residential property.

The Lakewood Plan likewise prompted the incorporation of the City of Commerce, a tax haven for railroad and industrial property. The City of Dairy Valley was similarly created as a **tax island** to protect large agricultural land holdings. As Dairy Valley grew over the years, and agricultural interests profited by selling their acreage to developers, the city adopted a new name, Cerritos.

As these case studies demonstrate, the Lakewood Plan did not simply allow for cost savings through service contracting. The plan helped to exacerbate inequality in the Los Angeles region, shielding large landowners from taxation while denying revenues to minority-dominated neighboring cities.

Sources: Gary J. Miller, *Cities by Contract: The Politics of Municipal Incorporation* (Cambridge, MA: MIT Press, 1981); Christopher G. Boone and Ali Modarres, "Creating a Toxic Neighborhood in Los Angeles County: A Historical Examination of Environmental Inequity," *Urban Affairs Review* 35, no. 2 (November 1999): 163–187; William A. Fischel, *The Homevoter Hypothesis: How Home Values Influence Local Government Taxation, School Finance, and Land-Use Policies* (Cambridge, MA: Harvard University Press, 2001), 221–228; Michan Andrew Connor, "'Public Benefits from Public Choice': Producing Decentralization in Metropolitan Los Angeles, 1954–1973," *Journal of Urban History* 39, no. 1 (January 2013): 79–100.

in each patrol car, and the price that the city will pay. The plan takes its name from the City of Lakewood, which incorporated in 1954 and became the first community in the region to contract with L.A. county for law enforcement and other services.

The Lakewood Plan enables municipalities to upgrade services while saving money. Yet the plan is also subject to various criticisms. Municipalities sometimes complain about a loss of control as the county decides many of the details of service delivery. Initially, the Lakewood Plan also served to exacerbate metropolitan fragmentation by facilitating the incorporation of new suburban municipalities. In a number of instances, the newly created suburbs shielded large landholdings—factories and rail yards—from the prospects of annexation and the higher taxes that large corporations would have likely paid to support schools and local services in the region. (See Box 10.4, "The Lakewood Plan: Cure or Contributor to Metropolitan Fragmentation?") The Lakewood Plan is incomplete regionalism, as it reinforces a sense of "localism";[44] middle- and upper-class suburbs resort to contracting to reduce service costs with no concern for the quality of schools and service provision in neighboring Latino and African-American communities.

COUNCILS OF GOVERNMENTS AND REGIONAL PLANNING COUNCILS

A **council of governments (COG)** is a voluntary association of the top-elected official of each municipality in a region. A COG functions much like the United Nations, bringing together top city and suburban officials to discuss matters of mutual interest. The COG's staff helps to identify potential solutions to problems that regional leaders discuss. Similar to the United Nations, a COG possesses little authority or ability to enforce action on unwilling members.

Some of the more noteworthy COGs include the Metropolitan Washington Council of Governments, the Baltimore Metropolitan Council (BMC), the Association of Bay Area Governments (ABAG) in greater San Francisco, the San Diego Association of Governments (SANDAG), the Houston-Galveston Area Council, the Southeast Michigan Council of Governments (SEMCOG) in greater Detroit, and the Southern California Association of Governments (SCAG). SCAG serves 6 counties, 91 cities, and 18 million residents.

COGs are not directly elected and, consequently, lack the strength and legitimacy that derive from popular election. As an unelected organization, a COG does not abide by the one-person-one-vote principle; instead, each member jurisdiction, regardless of the size of its population, has a single vote. Such voting apportionment underrepresents a region's more populous cities and suburbs.[45]

A **regional planning council (RPC)** is a staff-dominated organization that operates in a manner quite similar to a COG. An RPC lacks the assembly of a region's mayors and city managers at its top. Instead, an appointed executive director determines the areas of RPC research and planning activities.

COGs and RPCs are weak regional organizations. First and foremost, these bodies are advisory only: they possess no legislative authority, no ability to raise money through taxes, and no power to force local governments to follow a regional plan. In the greater Chicago area, the Northeastern Illinois Planning Commission has been unable to impose any serious anti-sprawl measures to limit the growth of suburban communities. In California, suburban jurisdictions are often out of compliance with the fair-share housing plans developed by SCAG and ABAG; jurisdictions fail to meet the local construction targets outlined in the region's affordable housing plan. Residents of nearby areas also harshly criticized ABAG's plans to build 188,000 new homes largely in high-density "stack and pack" developments located in "transit villages" surrounding suburban rail stations.[46]

At times, local officials have been so upset by a COG's actions that they have threatened to pull out of the COG. In 1989, Orange County actually stopped paying its dues and withdrew from SCAG.

Faced with such serious limitations, COGs tend to shy away from far-reaching and controversial housing and social policy initiatives that may estrange dues-paying members. COGs do not push their member jurisdictions to act. Instead, COGs serve member jurisdictions by providing technical assistance that will help communities secure federal and state grants. The Baltimore Metropolitan Council (BMC) avoided hard choices on transportation projects that would alienate member communities; instead, the BMC helped members pursue federal funding for their "wish lists" of transportation projects.[47]

In one policy area, regional planning bodies have gained increased prominence. Under the **Intermodal Surface Transportation and Efficiency Act (ISTEA**, commonly pronounced "Ice Tea"), which was later reformulated as **TEA-21** (the Transportation Equity Act for the 21st Century) and **SAFETEA-LU** (Safe, Accountable, Flexible, Efficient Transportation Act: A Legacy for Users), a COG or RPC may serve as the region's **Metropolitan Planning Organization (MPO)**, "a voice for metropolitan areas"[48] in promoting more balanced transportation systems for a better environment. MPOs have even been able to take some of the monies initially intended for highways and shift the funds to commuter rail development and improved bus service. In Salt Lake City, Denver, Dallas, Charlotte, Las Vegas, San Jose, and San Diego, MPOs used the ISTEA/TEA-21 process to target new funds to light-rail systems.[49] Yet in other metropolitan areas, weak and understaffed COGs have not been willing to battle state highway departments, construction unions, and other interests tied to continued highway construction.[50]

Despite its quite limited powers, the COG/RPC/MPO approach still is of value. In the greater Pittsburgh area, dialogue among the members of the Southwestern Pennsylvania Commission (SPC) shifted over time from the "parochial protection of individual governments' self-interests to a more enlightened discussion of the needs of the (ten-county) region."[51]

SCAG has walked a fine line in its efforts to avoid controversy in formulating southern California's 2012–2035 Regional Transit Plan and Sustainable Communities Strategy. Rather than try to force unwilling suburbs to accept new transit-related development, SCAG sought to meet southern California's affordable housing needs and reduce greenhouse gas emissions by giving priority funding to those communities willing to develop housing and job sites in close proximity to bus stops and rail stations.[52]

SPECIAL DISTRICTS

There are nearly 90,000 units of local government in the United States (see Table 10.2), but most are not cities, counties, villages, or townships, the **general-purpose governments** that provide a wide variety of municipal services. Instead, the great bulk of local governments have more narrow responsibilities. More than 37,000 are **special districts** that exist to provide a single specific service (such as drainage and flood control, solid waste management, fire protection, water supply, community college classes, or assisted housing) or a set of related services. Another 13,000 **independent school districts** provide K–12 education and are not directly controlled by the local mayor or city council.[53] Special districts are important units of local government that lack the public visibility of cities and other general-purpose governments.

The number of school districts in the United States has shrunk considerably over the years due to consolidation. In contrast, as Table 10.2 reveals, nonschool special districts are the fastest-growing type of government in the United States.

The size of a special district depends on the service it provides. Special districts for libraries, fire protection, and local recreation often serve relatively small geographic areas. By contrast, the Metropolitan Sanitary District of Greater Chicago and the Forest Preserve District of Cook County each serves an area that is much larger than the city of Chicago.

Table 10.2
Number of Local Governmental Units in the United States

Type of government	1952	1962	1972	1982	1992	2002	2012
County	3,052	3,043	3,044	3,041	3,043	3,034	3,031
Municipal	16,807	18,000	18,517	19,076	19,279	19,429	19,522
Town/Township	17,202	17,142	16,991	16,734	16,656	16,504	16,364
School district	67,355	34,678	15,781	14,851	14,422	13,506	12,883
Special district	12,340	18,323	23,885	28,078	31,555	35,052	37,203

Source: U.S. Census Bureau, 2002 and 2012 Census of Governments.

Each state determines the exact boundaries and powers of special districts. Special districts can be established across conventional local political boundary lines, allowing for cost-savings that come from economies of scale. On occasion, special districts even help address regional questions concerning service equity. Suburban taxpayers, for instance, help to fund the Milwaukee Technical College, a special-district institution that disproportionately serves central-city residents.[54]

The majority of special districts and independent school districts have the authority to levy taxes. Other districts rely on user fees and charges. In recent years, voters in numerous states have imposed restrictions on the taxing and borrowing authority of cities and other general-purpose governments. In such states, local leaders turn to special districts to raise revenues and to "get things done."

Yet the existence of so many special districts also causes problems. Numerous independent bodies can compound political fragmentation, making it difficult to coordinate action in the metropolis. Special districts are also relatively **invisible and unaccountable governments**. Most citizens are unaware of the existence of, and cannot name the officials in charge of, community college districts, sewer and water districts, and other specialized units of local government. Newspapers and television devote little coverage to the actions of narrow-purpose district boards. Such insularity creates conditions where highly motivated special interests can seize control of special districts. In Texas and other states, private developers and real estate interests have been able to dominate the boards of urban fringe districts, having the boards issue bonds and otherwise securing the funding for new sewers, water mains, and other infrastructure improvements essential for new construction on the rim of the metropolis.[55] Developers like the Disney Corporation have looked to the creation of special districts to support growth projects without having to answer directly to local voters. (See Box 10.5, "Was Walt Disney World Given Its Own Government?")

The invisibility of special districts raises important questions regarding democracy and accountability.[56] In Ohio, anti-tax groups have criticized local port districts for deceiving voters in committing funds to affordable housing projects, new sports arenas, arts museums, and other economic development projects—projects that are not directly related to the operation of a river or Great Lakes port facility.[57]

REGIONAL DISTRICTS AND AUTHORITIES

States also establish **regional districts and authorities** that are broader and more powerful variants of the special district. The Bay Area Rapid Transit District, the Southern California Metropolitan Water District, the Massachusetts Bay Transit Authority, the Chicago Metropolitan Sanitary District, and the Seattle Port District are all important regional districts.

The Port Authority of New York and New Jersey possesses broad powers in a number of service areas, with policy responsibilities that go well beyond maintaining the freight terminals and shipping facilities in the New York–New Jersey region. The Port Authority is involved in highway and bridge construction, commuter rail and airport operations, the maintenance of a giant bus terminal in midtown Manhattan, and regional planning.

Box 10.5
Was Walt Disney World Given Its Own Government?

When the Disney Corporation sought to build Walt Disney World, one of its first actions was to get the Florida legislature to create a forty-square-mile special district, the Reedy Creek Improvement District. The 1967 establishment of the tourism-related special district meant that Disney did not have to ask the elected officials of Orlando, Kissimmee, or any other municipality for approval of its development plans. Within the forty-square-mile zone of the Reedy Creek Improvement District, Disney effectively assumed the powers of local government, with the ability to make decisions concerning land use, building codes, police and fire service, drainage, sewer line extensions, and other infrastructure investment. As a unit of local government, Disney has even used Reedy Creek to issue public bonds, borrowing money at low cost to finance theme park development. Having gained control of its own special local government, the Disney Corporation does not have to worry that other local political actors, who are not loyal to the Disney vision, will impose unwanted taxes, impact fees, environmental safeguards, and requirements for subsidized housing.

Disney officials adopted a strategy to limit the voting power of residents in the district. As a special district and not a general-purpose local government (even though the district was granted a fairly broad range of municipal powers, including the ability to operate an airport and a heliport), Reedy Creek was not obliged to follow one-person-one vote principles of representation. Instead, votes in the district were allocated according to property acreage; the Disney Corporation, as the most sizable property owner, possessed effective control of the district. Renters and small landowners had no voting rights in district elections.

The Disney Corporation also sought to limit contending voices by limiting the construction of housing. Housing was essentially restricted to Disney executives and employees, assuring that the Disney Corporation's interests would continue to enjoy primacy in local affairs. When the Disney Corporation built the new residential town of Celebration, Florida, it took care to de-annex or detach the development from the Reedy Creek District, assuring that the growing number of homeowners in Celebration would have no say over Disney's actions and plans for expansion.

Sources: Richard Foglesong, "When Disney Comes to Town," in *The Politics of Urban America: A Reader,* ed. Dennis R. Judd and Paul P. Kantor (Boston: Allyn and Bacon, 1998), 238–241; Richard E. Foglesong, *Married to the Mouse: Walt Disney World and Orlando* (New Haven, CT: Yale University Press, 2003); Chad D. Emerson, "Merging Public and Private Governance: How Disney's Reedy Creek Improvement District 'Re-imagined' the Traditional Division of Local Regulatory Powers," *Florida State University Law Review* 36 (2009): 177–213.

The Port Authority built the original World Trade Center in Lower Manhattan and was a major player in the post-9/11 reconstruction efforts at Ground Zero.

Regional authorities such as the Port Authority of New York and New Jersey help to get important things done, but their actions also raise important questions of accountability. To whom do these districts answer? Regional authorities "are frequently as accountable to bond buyers as to the localities and the citizen consumers."[58] During the 1970s, the directors of the Port Authority of New York and New Jersey neglected the region's ailing commuter rail system, which was deemed a never-ending "bad" investment, and instead continued to promote road construction.[59] In 2013 the Port Authority was charged with excessive partisanship after its appointees closed approach lanes to the George Washington Bridge, causing massive traffic jams in communities where local officials had failed to give their enthusiastic support to New Jersey Governor Chris Christie.

Despite the Port Authority's impressive powers in a number of program areas and its responsibilities for regional planning in the bi-state region, the Authority overall provides only a weak vehicle for regional cooperation.[60] The Port Authority could not get state and local governments in the New York–New Jersey region to abide by the "nonaggression pact" to which state and local officials had earlier agreed. State and local leaders had promised that they would not offer tax incentives and other subsidies in an effort to lure businesses away from neighboring communities. The agreement, however, lacked teeth and was repeatedly broken. New York officials were outraged when state and local officials in New Jersey offered to help pay for the cross-river relocation of over 1,000 First Chicago Trust jobs from the corporation's offices in Lower Manhattan.[61]

STRENGTHENED COUNTY GOVERNMENT

In the middle of the twentieth century, counties were viewed as America's "forgotten governments"[62]—backward, rural-oriented, understaffed, and generally incapable of providing the quality services demanded by an increasingly urban society. In more recent years, however, the position of counties has changed considerably. Urban and suburban counties modernized their structures and increased their problem-solving capacities. They tapped new sources of revenue, restructured their operations to provide stronger executive leadership, and assumed new responsibilities in law enforcement, social services, housing assistance, workforce training, and economic development.[63]

But even a strengthened and modernized urban county faces a very important limitation when it comes to regional action. No county can govern beyond its borders. In the more than 150 metropolitan areas that spill over two or more counties, even a reinvigorated county government can provide, at best, only a subregional basis for action.

A NEW REGIONALISM FOR THE TWENTY-FIRST CENTURY: IMPROVING REGIONAL GOVERNANCE, NOT CREATING REGIONAL GOVERNMENT

Clearly, the array of informal and formal cooperative arrangements described above allows municipalities to cooperate for more effective and cost-efficient service delivery. Still, in important ways, these vehicles of cooperation are limited and do not provide the more extensive collaboration that a region requires in the highly competitive global marketplace of the twenty-first century.

The more normal interlocal cooperative arrangements do not provide for the "deeper" collaborations that enable a region to reposition itself to develop the comprehensive proposals that can win the interregional and global competition for businesses. The United States is comprised of a number of **local economic regions** where the "economic fates and fortunes of cities and suburbs are inextricably interwoven."[64] As Theodore Hershberg has observed, "The most important lesson that the global economy teaches is that regions—not cities or counties—will be the units of economic competition."[65]

Local borders are almost irrelevant when a major corporation seeks to assess the extent to which a specific location meets its needs. The corporation does not look at what an individual municipality can provide; instead, it seeks to determine whether the entire region can offer the quality labor, transportation, infrastructure, and even housing and cultural activities that would aid the firm's continued growth. A high-tech firm, for instance, will locate its headquarters in a well-to-do technoburb only if it is reasonably certain that transportation arrangements, education and job training efforts, and affordable housing programs will allow the firm to draw qualified workers from surrounding communities. A region stands its greatest chances of winning a major new investment if it can present a clear plan for "holistic economic development,"[66] a multifaceted strategy that details how various communities will work together to provide the transportation, trained labor, infrastructure improvements, and workforce housing that meet a firm's needs.

Acting alone, no city or suburb has the capacity to provide the airport facilities, university research, roadways, and qualified labor demanded by a major corporation.[67] Communities that join together to meet the needs of potential businesses will attract new development and growth. Regions in which communities are unable to collaborate face the prospect of economic stasis and decline.

New Regionalism denotes the move toward regional collaborations that extend beyond the more formalized structures of cooperation described in previous sections of this chapter. The Allegheny Conference on Community Development, Cleveland Tomorrow, and the Greater Houston Partnership are all early examples of new-style **public-private partnerships**, forums of corporate leaders and public officials that have convened, oftentimes outside the halls of government, to develop strategies for a region's economic rebirth.[68]

What do New Regional partnerships look like? The Allegheny Conference brought together private, nonprofit, and public institutions in an effort to "re-vision" a Pittsburgh region not as a declining center of an aging steel manufacturing industry but as an important high-tech and office-headquarters city in a postindustrial global economy. Private-sector groups helped to underwrite a planning process that overcame the severe political fragmentation of a region that has over 300 units of government in Allegheny County alone.[69]

A similar collaborative process took place on the other side of the continent, as BIO-COM (an industry association) and the San Diego Regional Economic Development Corporation joined with local governments, the San Diego Association of Governments, and local universities in a public-private effort to direct the transformation of the region's post–Cold War economy. With the end of the Cold War, the greater San Diego area was suffering extensive jobs losses in its defense-related industries. The New Regional partnership sought a strategy to replace disappearing defense-related industries with new biotechnology and biomedical jobs.[70]

The declining significance of local political borders was also demonstrated when the Boeing Corporation announced that it was moving its headquarters out of Seattle. Boeing's officers announced that the corporation wanted to relocate in a culturally diverse community with a probusiness environment. Rather than receive development proposals from thousands of communities across the United States, Boeing requested that communities in three regions—the Denver, Dallas-Fort Worth, and Chicago metropolitan areas—come up with joint proposals that would describe just how each region would meet Boeing's needs. Compared to Denver and Dallas, the greater Chicago area suffers from the lack of a strong tradition of interlocal collaboration. Individual localities in the Chicago area initially—and unsuccessfully—attempted to approach Boeing on their own. Faced with the prospects of failure, Illinois Governor George Ryan and Chicago Mayor Richard M. Daley quickly acted to impose regional discipline, organizing a Blue Ribbon Commission that put together the joint incentive package that brought Boeing's headquarters to downtown Chicago.[71]

The Boeing case study illustrates the approach of the New Regionalism, how ad hoc public-private partnerships are able to cross existing political boundaries in an effort to mount a regional collaboration in response to a specific economic problem. The search for economic growth and new jobs provides much of the driving force behind the New Regionalism—quite a contrast to the Old Regionalism that was focused largely on gaining cost savings and improved effectiveness in service delivery. The New Regionalism is less obsessed with efficiency and more concerned with economic development.

The New Regionalism stresses *governance*, finding ways for governments and nongovernmental bodies to work together. As the Pittsburgh, San Diego, and Boeing cases all demonstrate, New Regionalism efforts do not normally entail the creation of new bodies or agencies of metropolitan government. New Regionalism seeks pragmatic solutions: ad hoc and less rule-bound means of cooperation that lie outside the formal structures of government. New Regionalism seeks to get things done—gover*nance*—without creating new units of govern*ment*.

But even many of the advocates of New Regionalism recognize the risks incurred by creating business-dominated forums of action outside the halls of government. Such business-led partnerships can act as **shadow governments**, making important decisions regarding the future of a region, with no clear accountability to voters and the general public.[72] Such business-led collaborations often lack the full insistence on transparency and extensive public participation that distinguishes the public sector from the private sector.

BUILDING REGIONAL COALITIONS

Who are the potential partners who can be expected to join a New Regional coalition? Can successful New Regional action be organized in policy areas beyond the economic development arena?

Former Minnesota state legislator Myron Orfield argues that creative regional alliances can be assembled even in controversial policy areas such as taxing and environmental and social policy. Orfield's insight is clear: metropolitan politics does not have to feature antagonisms between a central city and its suburbs. Instead, numerous suburbs are beginning to find that they have much in common with the region's central city and share an interest in pursuing policies that work to their mutual advantage. Declining inner-ring suburbs and working- and middle-class suburbs that are growing too rapidly (and cannot afford the quality schools and services that residents expect) have a common interest in joining with central cities to redirect state aid and development programs away from a region's "favored quarter" communities, those fortunate localities that corporations and higher-status citizens find attractive.[73]

Smart Growth policies for infill development, green space protection, and farmland preservation have the potential to unite a broad coalition of central cities, inner-ring suburbs, environmentalists, and agriculture interests. In Ohio, the First Suburbs Consortium joined with farmers and environmentalists in support of the state's Agricultural Preservation Act, a measure that preserved farmland by steering investment to central cities and older suburbs. In Portland, Oregon, environmentalists and farmers joined downtown business interests and neighborhood activists to legislate growth management measures that preserved agricultural acreage and green space by steering new development to already built-up areas.

Central cities, working-class suburbs, and declining first suburbs may all benefit from a program of regional tax sharing. The political "trick," as the Minnesota experience with the Twin Cities' fiscal disparities law reveals, is to produce maps and other documentation that convinces legislators from a wide swath of constituencies that their districts will benefit from a measure that shares part of the tax proceeds from new private investment in a region. GIS (geographic information system) data and computer-generated maps can be quite powerful in documenting just which communities have unmet needs and which will emerge as winners if regional tax sharing is enacted.[74]

Interlocal sharing also provides the basis for Ohio's **Joint Economic Development Districts (JEDDs)**, which enable municipalities and unincorporated suburban townships to work together to provide the sewers, upgraded roads, and other infrastructure improvements needed to attract a new business. As the Ohio state code prohibits townships from levying a local earnings (income) tax on workers, townships often find that they lack the ability to pay for expensive site improvements, as their expected gain in property taxes will not cover the costs of expensive infrastructure upgrades.

The establishment of a JEDD allows for intercommunity collaboration to pay for, and to share the revenues from, a new development. The township in which the new business is located reaps the increased property tax revenues resulting from the new commercial investment; the participating city, in turn, collects specified fees and an earnings (income) tax imposed on workers in the district.

The formation of a JEDD is not easy. Cities and suburbs continue to distrust one another. Of course, each suburb and city would prefer to "go it alone" rather than share revenues. Still, however difficult the negotiations over a JEDD contract, a JEDD represents a more collaborative approach to economic development, one that is certainly less bitter and less antagonistic than the **annexation wars** of past years where cities and townships battled over potential growth sites.

In Arizona, "landlocked" Tempe, suburban Chandler (Tempe's rapidly growing neighbor), and the Town of Guadalupe (which borders the mall site) agreed to share the sales tax revenues gained from a new mall with 200-plus stores, easing the competitive pressures that at one time had led each locality to launch its own campaign to win the location of the regional retail plaza. The innovative agreement was business-led; in order to begin construction, the competing development groups came together to arrange a compromise that would be agreeable to officials of the feuding local communities. In 2009, Phoenix and suburban Glendale similarly agreed to share the construction costs and sales tax revenues of a new 15,000-seat baseball spring training stadium built on land that Glendale owned, even though the land was situated inside the city limits of Phoenix.[75]

Yet despite their potential, interlocal agreements that allow for tax sharing remain relatively rare. Too often, local communities continue to view one another as competitors rather than as partners.[76] Vocal constituents also charge that local officials who sign a tax-sharing agreement have "sold out" the community. Such collaborations are more likely to occur where local officials trust one another and have faith that an agreement will fairly meet each community's needs.[77]

Is New Regional coalition building possible in areas outside of the economic development arena? Myron Orfield argues that the activism of church groups and nonprofit associations can add a "justice" dimension to New Regional action. In the mid-1990s, for instance, church congregations and religious organizations pushed the Minnesota state legislature for regional fair-share-housing and social justice legislation.[78] Similarly, in northwest Indiana, an interfaith federation cut across racial and jurisdictional lines in their efforts to block plans to relocate the county's juvenile courts outside the troubled central city of Gary.[79] On Chicago's poor African-American West Side, Bethel New Life, a faith-based CDC, built an alliance with nearby suburbs to fight for the preservation of a light rail line that served both areas.[80]

CONCLUSION: GOVERNING REGIONS IN A GLOBAL AGE

In most regions of the country, city-county consolidation and the creation of strong metropolitan government no longer pose politically viable solutions to the problems posed by metropolitan fragmentation. Even annexation represents a viable strategy for only relatively small land parcels; states that were once permissive now impose new limits on annexation.

Is metropolitan restructuring a strategy worth pursuing? In some cases the answer is "Yes," especially when reform produces great cost savings or new capacity for regional economic development. Still, suburbanites resent having to surrender local autonomy. Local officials oppose restructuring measures that threaten their jobs or that even diminish their authority. Racial minorities remain suspicious of metropolitan reform plans that undermine their chances of winning control of city hall.

Studies reveal that many of the benefits promised from metropolitan restructuring prove illusory. City-county consolidation seldom yields clear and consistent cost savings.

In many cases, communities have already picked the low-hanging fruit of cost savings by arranging cooperative actions especially in cases where the financial advantages were obvious.

At best, consolidation has only a mild impact on promoting local economic fortunes.[81] The creation of Unigov did help spur the rebirth of downtown Indianapolis, just as the new Metro government facilitated the economic takeoff of downtown Louisville. The merger of Kansas City (Kansas) with Wyandotte County was largely spurred by the region's failure in the mid-1990s to land a NASCAR racetrack, a project that was seen as vital to the region's economy. The newly consolidated Kansas City government eventually gained the NASCAR tourist facility and the tourism-related development it so greatly desired.[82]

Yet these cases, especially Unigov, are fairly exceptional. In Louisville and in other metropolitan areas across the United States, city-county consolidation has had, at most, only a modest impact on economic growth.

Despite the rather disappointing evidence regarding the impact of consolidation on economic development, business leaders continue to argue that merged government will energize a region's economy and attract new jobs. These leaders are oftentimes the prime beneficiaries of the policies pursued by the consolidated county governments.

In most metropolitan areas, the key to a more prosperous economic future lies not in the creation of a new regional government but in more creative partnerships for regional governance. A fairly large range of cooperative arrangements enable local governments to work across borders to take advantage of economies of scale and to provide more professionalized service. The New Regionalism, often business-led, is helping to arrange for deeper collaborations for a region's economic growth.

Denver provides a prime example of a region where collaboration has produced economic success. Adams County allowed the City of Denver to annex land for a new Denver International Airport, enabling direct air service to Tokyo and Mexico City, routes that made the entire Denver region more accessible to global investors and markets. Residents of areas outside the city also voted for ballot measures to support mass transit, various cultural facilities, and new sports stadiums, many of which were located in downtown Denver. These votes "indicated that the people who lived and worked in Denver, Aurora, Littleton, and the other communities that made up the region were starting to understand that they were united for better or worse."[83] The Denver Metro Chamber of Commerce formed a new civic leadership group, which evolved into the Metro Denver Economic Development Corporation, to get the airport built and to press for collaborative undertakings and the creation of global ties that would bring new jobs to the Denver region.

The New Regionalism points to the importance of creating informal, flexible partnerships (public-private partnerships) outside the formal channels of government. New Regionalism creates ad hoc forums for cooperation in response to specific problems. The emphasis is on partnerships, not processes dominated by government officials.

The private-led nature of much of the New Regionalism, however, raises important questions of democracy and accountability, questions that are also raised by the operations of special districts and other "invisible" metropolitan authorities. Just who does, and does not, exert power in these "shadow" decision-making bodies? Developers and major corporations enjoy privileged access to special districts, regional planning commissions, and business-led associations focused on planning for a region's future. By contrast, neighborhood groups often face great difficulty in mobilizing efforts to pressure seemingly distant regional bodies and nearly invisible quasi-governmental associations. In numerous cases, public-private partnerships and quasi-governmental regional organizations have given elites living in suburbia new channels to influence the operation of central-city museums, educational enrichment programs, and inner-city health and social service programs.[84] Latino and African-American activists have at times been hesitant to embrace regional environmental measures and other New Regional initiatives that seem to offer very little to improve the lives of the inner-city poor.[85]

In Detroit, in the face of looming bankruptcy, numerous good-government civic leaders argued that regional organizations and private-led associations could pick up some of the costs of operating the Detroit Institute of Arts, the Cobo Convention Center, the municipal water system, and the Detroit Zoo. But members of Detroit's city council objected that the black-dominant city was being shown no respect, that outsiders were virtually forcing the city to sell off its jewels, that is, to cede control of its assets to non-Detroiters.[86]

Requirements for transparency, public election, and citizen participation are necessary to ensure the democratic nature of regional decision making. Continued pressure from community-based organizations, for instance, led a number of MPOs (Metropolitan Planning Organizations) to include, as part of their regional transportation plan, specific job training and hiring measures targeted to the region's more disadvantaged citizens.[87] As Myron Orfield and others have argued, the active engagement of community-based organizations and church groups is essential to adding a degree of balance—that is, equity and justice concerns—to a private-led metropolitan agenda.

KEY TERMS

annexation (*p. 250*)
annexation wars (*p. 277*)
city-county consolidation (*p. 254*)
council of governments (COG) (*p. 268*)
diseconomies of scale (*p. 263*)
dual approval requirement for an
   annexation to proceed (*p. 251*)
economies of scale (*p. 262*)
elastic cities (*p. 251*)
fiscal disparities law (*p. 261*)
general-purpose governments (*p. 270*)
govern*ance* (as opposed to
   government) (*p. 275*)
independent school districts (*p. 270*)
inelastic cities (also called
   "landlocked cities") (*p. 251*)
informal cooperation (*p. 264*)
intergovernmental service contract
   (*p. 266*)

interlocal competition (*p. 263*)
Intermodal Surface Transportation
   and Efficiency Act (ISTEA)
   (*p. 269*)
invisible and unaccountable
   governments, special districts as
   (*p. 271*)
Joint Economic Development
   Districts (JEDDs) (*p. 276*)
joint powers agreement
   (*p. 264*)
Lakewood Plan (*p. 266*)
local economic regions (*p. 274*)
metropolitan development guide,
   the Met Council (Minnesota)
   (*p. 260*)
Metropolitan Planning Organization
   (MPO) (*p. 269*)
metropolitanists (*p. 262*)

11 | The Intergovernmental City

State and National Policy

Cities and suburbs exist in an **intergovernmental system** where they are greatly affected by the actions of the national and state governments. The federal and state governments provide considerable fiscal assistance to local communities. Federal and state regulations also impose costly service obligations on cities and suburbs. The states, as discussed in Chapter 5, play a particularly prominent role in urban affairs: each state essentially determines the territorial borders and governing powers and responsibilities of its municipalities.

This chapter provides a more in-depth look at the role played by the national and state governments in urban affairs. As Tea Party activists and other outspoken critics often question the basis for federal aid to cities, the chapter begins by describing the constitutional underpinnings for an active federal role in domestic and urban affairs. In the contemporary United States, the national, state, and local governments share responsibility for fighting domestic problems. The central government does indeed possess the constitutional authority to aid local communities.

As this chapter also describes, the contemporary debate in Washington over domestic program responsibility has to a great extent been shaped by Republican criticisms of the role played by the federal government in domestic affairs. The critics correctly point out that intergovernmental action is often marred by overly rigid program rules and excessive paperwork and reporting requirements that stifle local creativity, increase costs, and undermine program effectiveness. Over the past four decades, the Republicans have succeeded in their call for a **New Federalism**. New Federalism sees great virtue in program **decentralization**, that is, in enhancing the program authority of states and localities while decreasing the program reach of Washington and its bureaucracies. Since the 1990s, however, budget-cutting Republicans have taken the New Federalism ideal one step further. They see program decentralization as a means to cut federal domestic spending and taxes and to reduce the overall size of the public sector. Democratic leaders and advocates of cities work in a Washington that has become increasingly hostile to developing strong, big-spending programs of aid to local communities in need.

THE CONSTITUTIONAL BASIS FOR FEDERAL URBAN PROGRAMS: COOPERATIVE FEDERALISM

The U.S. Constitution established a **federal system** of government, which simply means that more than one level of government has the right to exist: a central government with meaningful powers exists alongside the states.

The very existence of state governments, of course, serves as a limit on the power of the national government. Yet despite the contention of Tea Party and "states' rights" activists, a federal system does not necessarily establish the states as the dominant partners. The framers of the Constitution actually assembled in Philadelphia to strengthen the national government, to create a governmental system with a greater ability to govern, correcting the glaring weaknesses of the Articles of Confederation. The framers of the Constitution threw out the then-existing system of **confederation**, where the states were the dominant actors and the central government lacked meaningful decision-making authority. In its place, the framers created a federal system, with the central government given new powers.

Does the U.S. Constitution permit the national government to play an active role in fighting urban problems? Critics of the central government say "No." These critics argue that the Constitution sets up a system of **dual federalism** that gives the national government only a few specified powers with all other policy areas falling within the realm of the states. Dual federalists argue that the national government possesses only the few **expressed powers** (also called **delegated powers** or **enumerated powers**) explicitly listed for it in Article I, Section 8 of the Constitution, including the powers to coin money, regulate interstate commerce, raise an army, declare war, enter into treaties with other nations, and establish post offices. All other powers, dual federalists argue, are **reserved powers** given to the states by the **Tenth Amendment**, which reads:

> The powers not delegated to the United States by the Constitution, nor prohibited by it to the States, are reserved to the States respectively, or to the people.

Dual federalists contend that most urban and social program responsibilities are not explicitly listed under the federal government's enumerated powers; hence action in these areas properly belong to the states, not to the national government.

But the dual federalist perspective is clearly out of date. Nor is it based upon a reading of all of the provisions in the Constitution, some which give the national government a more expanded domain of program responsibilities than the dual federalists admit. The dual federalist perspective certainly does not describe the system of **cooperative federalism** that has evolved and taken root in the United States over the past two centuries. Cooperative federalism does not limit the national government to a few, narrowly construed powers. Instead, cooperative federalism allows for more expansive areas of national government power and shared program responsibilities: the national, state, and local governments work together (although not always smoothly or easily) to combat important domestic problems. Dual federalists, with their emphasis on the Tenth Amendment, slight other provisions of the Constitution as well as Supreme Court interpretations of the Constitution that, especially in the more than eighty years since the Great Depression, allow the national government to play an active role in domestic and urban policy.

The **supremacy clause** (Article VI of the Constitution) declares that national laws and treaties are the supreme law of the land. National laws are superior to state and local laws: no state or locality may contradict a national law. The Constitution's **interstate commerce clause** effectively gives the national government the authority to act in a broad range of policy areas that affect commerce, including public education, job training, local economic development, environmental protection, and even programs to help maintain the health of citizens and workers.[1]

The Constitution's **necessary and proper clause** expands the range of actions that the central government may undertake. At the very end of the list of enumerated powers given the national government, Article I, Section 8 declares that the national government has the right "to make *all* laws which shall be *necessary and proper* for carrying into execution the foregoing powers" (emphasis added). The necessary and proper clause indicates that the federal government possesses a whole host of unstated but **implied powers** that are related to the few broad functions listed for the central government. The necessary and proper clause can be viewed as an **elastic clause**: it vastly stretches the list of policy areas in which the central government can take action. In doing so, it greatly narrows the policy areas reserved for the states by the Tenth Amendment.

As already indicated, the miseries of the Great Depression led Americans to welcome the relief provided by the expanded domestic aid programs of President Franklin Delano Roosevelt's New Deal. A second surge in national government domestic programs commenced beginning in the 1960s with President Lyndon Johnson's War on Poverty and Great Society programs. Beginning at about the same time, in what can be called the **Fourteenth Amendment Revolution**, the federal government began to take strong civil-rights-oriented actions to ensure that all citizens receive the "equal protection of the laws" guaranteed by the Fourteenth Amendment of the Constitution. Beginning in the 1970s, the national government also assumed greater responsibility for environmental protection.

While the U.S. Supreme Court has generally affirmed the central government's extended reach in domestic policy, the Court has not approved every instance of federal program expansion. Republican victories in presidential elections during the second half of the twentieth century led to the appointment of Supreme Court justices who argue that the very nature of the federal system imposes some limits on the program reach of the central government.

In *United States v. Lopez* (1995),[2] the Court invalidated the Gun Free School Zones Act, because Congress had made no attempt whatsoever to show how the prohibition of firearms in school zones was related to interstate commerce. Two years later, in *Printz v. United States*,[3] the Supreme Court again referred to the doctrine of federalism in striking down a provision of the Brady Handgun Prevention Act. A local sheriff had objected to the act's requirement that law-enforcement officials conduct background checks on handgun buyers. The Court ruled that the states are independent and autonomous units of government with the freedom to act as they see fit within their own spheres of authority. State and local officials cannot be "dragooned" by the national government into administering federal law. In these and a small set of related decisions,[4] the Supreme Court breathed new life into the concept that a federal system imposes some outer limit on the federal government's claim of powers.[5]

Still, despite these rulings, the Court has not reduced in any significant way the federal government's reach in domestic policy. The Court even affirmed the constitutionality of the Affordable Care Act (popularly known as "Obamacare") and the national requirement that Americans purchase health insurance. The Court, however, did strike down the portion of the act that threatened to withhold a portion of federal Medicaid assistance from states that refused to participate in efforts to increase health care coverage for the medically needy.[6] The Court would not permit the central government to wield its grant monies in a coercive manner that denies the basic autonomy of state and local governments in their respective policy areas.[7]

In sum, the more recent decisions handed down by a Supreme Court dominated by Republican appointees has not demolished the system of cooperative federalism. Nor has the Court revived the old doctrine of dual federalism.[8] The Court has not in any significant way rolled back the reach of the central government in domestic—and urban—affairs.

GRANTS-IN-AID: THE FUEL OF COOPERATIVE FEDERALISM AND INTERGOVERNMENTAL RELATIONS

The contemporary intergovernmental system is built around money, or, more precisely, the transfer of money. A **grant-in-aid** (or **grant**, for short) is a transfer of money from one level of government to another to accomplish specified purposes. As Table 11.1 underscores, the federal government provides substantial grant assistance to state and local governments. In 2010 alone, federal grants to states and localities surpassed $608 billion and accounted for 37 percent of state and local expenditures.[9] Much of the growth in aid in more recent years has been for Medicaid, the giant program that helps provide health care assistance for low-income persons. Table 11.1 also reveals that, despite New Federalism antigovernment sentiment, national assistance to states and localities remains substantial. However, the federal government's role is not increasing in importance even to the extent that a quick scan of the annual spending figures would seem to indicate. When measured as a percentage of the national budget (a calculation that is not presented in Table 11.1), the level of assistance that the central government provides states and localities is roughly the same today as it was three decades earlier.[10]

The lobbying efforts of the U.S. Conference of Mayors, the National League of Cities (NLC), and the National Association of Counties (NACO)[11] all served to promote the provision of federal assistance to cities and counties. These and similar associations of state governments are often referred to as **public interest groups** (or **PIGs**, for short). The PIGs lobby for increases in federal program assistance and for a relaxation of program rules that hinder subnational flexibility. A number of big cities and states also maintain their own individual offices in Washington, offices that provide valuable assistance when a city seeks federal program dollars.

Table 11.1
Federal Grants-in-Aid to State and Local Governments, 1990 to 2011

	Total grants, in current year dollars ($mill.)	Percent change from prior year	Grants as percent of state and local own-source expenditures	Total grants,in constant(2005) dollars ($bill.)	Percent change from prior year
1960	7,019	8.6	34.6	45.3	7.6
1970	24,065	19.3	29.1	123.7	12.3
1980	91,385	9.6	39.9	227.1	−1.9
1990	135,325	11.0	25.2	198.1	6.2
1991	154,519	14.2	26.6	216.6	9.3
1992	178,065	15.2	28.7	242.2	11.8
1993	193,612	8.7	29.6	256.4	5.9
1994	210,596	8.8	30.9	272.9	6.4
1995	224,991	6.8	31.5	283.6	3.9
1996	227,811	1.3	30.8	280.5	−1.1
1997	234,160	2.8	30.2	283.1	0.9
1998	246,128	5.1	30.3	293.9	3.8
1999	267,886	8.8	31.2	314.8	7.1
2000	285,874	6.7	27.4	326.8	3.8
2001	318,542	11.4	28.4	354.9	8.6
2002	352,895	10.8	29.5	387.4	9.2
2003	388,542	10.1	30.5	416.2	7.4
2004	407,512	4.9	30.9	424.3	1.9
2005	428,018	5.0	30.8	428.0	0.9
2006	434,099	1.4	29.7	417.3	−2.5
2007	443,797	2.2	28.4	412.4	−1.2
2008	461,317	3.9	27.4	411.0	−0.3
2009	537,991	16.6	33.1	476.6	16.0
2010	608,390	13.1	37.5	527.1	10.6
2011 (est.)	625,211	2.8	(NA)	532.7	1.1

Source: Extracted from U.S. Census Bureau, *The 2012 Statistical Abstract: The National Data Book,* Table 431, Excel version, www.census.gov/compendia/statab/2012/tables/12s0431.pdf.

TYPES OF GRANTS

The vast majority of the federal aid dollars dispensed to states and cities comes in the form of **categorical grants**, narrowly focused grants that seek specific program objectives and that have numerous accompanying program rules or "strings" to constrain how the states and localities can spend program funds. Categorical grants allow only limited subnational discretion. A municipality that receives a categorical grant to upgrade its police communications equipment, for instance, must use program funds only for that purpose; it cannot use the grant money for any other police or nonpolice purpose.

A federal grant system dominated by categorical grants suffers from excessive rigidity and waste. As a consequence, a new form of federal aid, **block grants**, was introduced beginning in the mid-1960s to allow greater program flexibility in order to give state and local governments greater freedom to decide just how to spend federal aid dollars within a broad functional or program area. A contemporary block grant, SAFE-TEA (commonly referred to as the Transportation Equity Act), serves as a case in point. SAFE-TEA was created to remove the **program silos** that result when separate categorical grants serve to support a variety of relatively small and uncoordinated transportation programs, each administered by a different federal agency. SAFE-TEA merged the narrow categorical programs into a larger block grant in order to give states and cities a greater choice of program activities.[12] President Obama's Energy Efficiency and Conservation Block Grant is another contemporary block grant: the program allows each recipient community the freedom to formulate its own initiatives to promote mass transit usage and to reduce fossil fuel emissions.

Republican presidents emphasized block grants as part of their New Federalism agenda. President Richard Nixon introduced the first significant block grants in the 1960s and the 1970s. President Ronald Reagan went further. Reagan did not simply seek to decentralize program administration, he wanted to reduce the overall level of public domestic spending. For Reagan and his Republican successors, block grants were a "transitional device," a "halfway house" on the road to withdrawing federal support from unessential program areas.[13]

Contemporary Republican "budget hawks" similarly do not simply seek to enhance state and local power in the running of jointly funded domestic programs; instead, the budget hawks seek to shrink the overall size of the public sector. To do so, the budget hawks in Congress changed key facets of the block grant approach. They drew up **new-style block grants** that gave states and localities greater program authority but with substantial reductions in the accompanying levels of federal assistance! The budget hawks argued that the states and localities could get by with less, as the new block grants gave subnational governments the freedom to introduce cost-saving innovations in program administration.[14] State and local officials countered that enhanced discretion does not always produce extensive savings. When the savings are less than expected, the new-style block grants saddle cities and suburbs with costly program responsibilities but not the levels of assistance that would allow for effective problem solving.

Changes in the **Community Development Block Grant (CDBG)** program clearly reveal both the transformation of the block grant ideal and the shrinking of federal urban aid programs. President Nixon created the CDBG program by consolidating (that is, by merging together) urban renewal monies and a number of smaller categorical urban-aid programs. Nixon wanted to give cities greater freedom to devise their own community-building initiatives. Democrats in Congress, however, added "strings" (accompanying regulations) to assure that cities spent the bulk of CDBG monies to aid low- and moderate-income neighborhoods.[15] Democrats opposed unbridled program decentralization out of fear that public officials in many states and cities would be tempted to use their newfound discretion to cut social programs and to shift program activities away from poorer inner-city communities.

In 1978, at the peak of CDBG funding, the program provided $12.7 billion in assistance to cities (expressed in 2012 constant dollars). By 2012, budget cutters had slashed CDBG funding to a mere $3 billion (in constant dollars), "less than a fourth of what it was in 1978."[16] The cutback in federal assistance led municipalities to reduce housing inspections, the provision of affordable housing assistance, day care programs, substance abuse treatment, and urban infrastructure replacement.[17]

Contemporary Republican leaders continue to emphasize the block grant concept. Former Republican vice-presidential candidate and chair of the House Budget Committee Paul Ryan proposed a radical transformation of federal antipoverty efforts, seeking to combine eleven federal programs, including CDBG assistance, food stamps, housing vouchers, and child care support, into a single **Opportunity Grant**, a mega-block grant that would give states new freedom to spend federal aid in a very broad program area. The states would not be told what to do, but they would be expected to produce measureable results. Ryan argued that the complex structure of the federal aid system, with so many distinctly separate programs, too often prevents state officials from undertaking coordinated approaches and innovative strategies that could lift families out of poverty.[18]

Critics immediately noted the dangers that they saw in Ryan's approach. Despite Ryan's claim that the program would not cut social spending, critics observed that Opportunity Grants would clearly be a budget-cutting (or at least a budget-stabilizing) device. In contrast to such programs as food stamps, the amount of assistance provided by Ryan's Opportunity Grants remains fixed and does not increase with heightened levels of need or during an economic recession. Critics also worried that state and local officials would spend Opportunity Grant money on economic development projects, diverting funds away from food stamps and social services for the poor. As Republican sponsors proposed to give the Opportunity Grants directly to the states, the program did not assure that city officials would have a meaningful voice in project selection.[19]

Despite suspicions that block grants are a tool that is being used to slash antipoverty and urban program spending, Democrats have nonetheless come to recognize the importance of program decentralization and flexibility. As a consequence, in his economic stimulus program, President Barack Obama utilized both categorical grants and block grants. Categorical grant "strings" required state and local governments to spend stimulus grant money as quickly as possible on highway construction, mass transit improvements, and other "shovel ready" infrastructure projects that would get the economy moving and provide immediate job creation. Other program strings in the American Recovery and Reinvestment Act (ARRA) sought to target funding to activities that served children at risk, to K–12 and higher education, and to communities with the greatest need. Other parts of ARRA, however, gave states and localities considerable discretion to design their own job-creation projects. ARRA's Energy Efficiency and Conservation Block Grants empowered states and cities to develop their own initiatives to reduce energy consumption and fossil-fuel emissions.[20]

The federal grant system is indeed quite complex. Even the distinction between "categorical grants" and "block grants" does not provide a full understanding of the different types of federal grants. Federal grants-in-aid programs can also be typed according to the method used to distribute funds. A **formula grant** distributes money in relatively automatic fashion to all eligible states and local governments; statistical criteria determine just how much money each jurisdiction receives. The size of the grant is determined by such formula factors as a jurisdiction's population, per capita income, rate of poverty, tax effort, age of the local housing stock, or daily school attendance. Formula grants are popular with local officials, as a municipality does not have to devote considerable resources to filling out a detailed application or to out-competing other jurisdictions seeking program assistance.

A **project grant**, in sharp contrast, establishes a competitive process as the award of project grant money is not at all automatic. Each jurisdiction submits an application that details exactly how it plans to use program monies. Only the "winning" applications are awarded funding. The Obama administration relied on the competitive offering of Race to the Top (RTT) project grants to incentivize the states to come up with creative K–12 educational strategies. Neighborhood Stabilization Program 2 (NSP2) funds were similarly awarded on a competitive basis in an effort to spur cities to find new ways to deal with their large volume of vacant properties.

THE GRANT SYSTEM: ITS ACCOMPLISHMENTS AND PROBLEMS

The federal grant system has received its fair share of criticism, but it is important to recognize that federal grants have also produced quite significant accomplishments. Federal assistance has reduced the gross state-to-state and city-to-city disparities that once plagued the nation when it came to providing citizens with health care, income assistance, and social services. Federal grants also prompted municipalities to upgrade local service provision and their physical infrastructure. Federal grants and regulations spurred subnational action for clean air and water and for toxic cleanup. Federal programs also led to increased subnational action in numerous other areas, including Head Start, special education, child nutrition, the fair treatment of the disabled, homeland security, and the construction of hospitals, mass transit, and solid waste disposal facilities, to name only a few.

Still, the federal grant-in-aid system is heavily criticized, especially for a rigidity that results from its **overreliance on categorical grants**. Despite the introduction of block grants, the vast majority of federal aid to states and cities continues to take the form of categorical grants. In 2009, there were 928 categorical grant programs as compared to only 25 block grants.[21] Congress favors narrow-purpose grants in order to assure accountability; Congress wants to assure that recipient governments actually spend the money on the activities for which they requested assistance. States and localities, however, complain of the **paperwork and administrative costs** entailed by federal program rules. They resent the loss of program flexibility, especially when the provisions of narrow-purpose grants prevent local officials from shifting program monies to higher-priority needs.

Categorical grants often contain **matching requirements** that a recipient government spend some of its own money on a program as a condition of receiving federal funds. The federal government uses matching stipulations to force state and localities to contribute monetarily to problem-solving efforts, rather than have the national government bear the entire cost of a program. Matching requirements, however, **distort subnational program priorities**, as state legislatures and city councils begin to shift their own spending toward projects that can earn generous federal matching funds, ignoring more pressing needs in program areas where local spending does not generate additional federal assistance.

Project grants also result in a **grantsmanship game**. A city or suburb can increase its chances of winning federal money by hiring professional staff members who are expert in the art of filing grant applications. Not all communities have the resources to hire the staff and consultants who can find out about available grants and inform the municipality of the steps that must be taken to compete effectively in the "game" to win federal money.

Block grants are popular because they increase the authority of state and local officials who would seem to know a locality's needs. Yet the history of Community Development Block Grants reveals that subnational governments do not always use their discretion wisely. (See Box 11.1, "Can the Cities Be Trusted? The Case of Community Development Block Grants.") Local officials oftentimes spend the money where projects are popular and where spending wins votes for reelection, not where assistance is most needed.

In the aftermath of Hurricane Katrina, the federal government waived program rules that normally prohibit the use of CDBG funds for commercial projects. Established program rules sought to force communities to focus on efforts to improve housing and services in low- and moderate-income neighborhoods. After Katrina, however, the City of Gulfport and the State of Mississippi received a waiver so that they could reallocate CDBG funds to rebuild Gulfport's commercial center. Gulfport wound up rebuilding and expanding its gambling boat district, siphoning off funds that had earlier been directed toward affordable housing and other low- and moderate-income projects.[22]

Democrats in Washington often respond to the abuses of local discretion by tightening program rules and oversight. Such tightening of program rules represents a **creeping categorization** of block grants that diminishes the subnational flexibility that was so much a part of the original block grant ideal. But in the case of the Community Development Block Grant program, the long-term trend has clearly been in the opposite direction, toward loosening federal oversight, a reflection of the degree to which New Federalism sentiment has become entrenched in Washington.[23]

"Cooperative federalism" is not always very cooperative. At times, the federal-subnational partnership can be quite quarrelsome and unwieldy, as the different governmental partners each have a different perspective on how a program should be run and what exact goals should be achieved. Local officials also protest against a system

Box 11.1
Can the Cities Be Trusted? The Case of Community Development Block Grants

Do state and local governments act responsibly in their exercise of program discretion? The history of local government action in the **Community Development Block Grant (CDBG)** program raises considerable concern.

The CDBG program was created in 1974 by folding a number of urban-related grants—including urban renewal, urban parks, and Model Cities social services monies—into a single program that would give recipient municipalities new freedom to determine the exact projects to be funded. CDBG, however, did not allow cities and counties complete freedom. The Democratic Congress succeeded in listing certain priorities, including the elimination of slums and blight and providing aid to low- and moderate-income families. These program strings sought to ensure that local decision makers would not ignore the needs of poorer neighborhoods.

Bridgeport, Connecticut, officials made little attempt to target community development spending to low-income communities. Instead, municipal leaders spent a sizable chunk of CDBG funds for parks development and improved recreational facilities in the better-off parts of town. The city council even earmarked funds for new tennis courts on the city's affluent north side. Such parks and recreational spending allowed council members to claim political credit with their voters. Bridgeport largely ignored low- and moderate-income housing projects; instead, the city allocated CDBG funds for an upscale pier and marina project. The federal Department of Housing and Urban Development eventually overrode Bridgeport's actions, ruling the marina project as ineligible.

Many localities choose CDBG projects wisely. Other communities, however, continue to fund projects that provide little assistance to poorer neighborhoods. From 2005 to 2009, affluent Hamilton County, outside of Indianapolis, spent over half of its community development program funds (excluding administrative costs) on sidewalks and infrastructure improvements that were of little benefit to the county's low-income residents.

Despite these abuses, federal oversight of CDBG spending has waned over the years. HUD (the U.S. Department of Housing and Urban Development) no longer reviews local plans for the use of community development funds. Federal on-site monitoring of local community development programs has virtually disappeared. Federal regulations no longer even require that a city target a large portion of community development spending in low-income communities.

In 2011 and 2012, the congressional Republican Study Group called for the elimination of the CDBG program. The conservative members of Congress argued that the program had become a "slush fund for pet projects" of local politicians and politically-connected developers. House Budget Committee Chairman Paul Ryan called for deep cuts in the CDBG program.

Democrats and affordable housing activists responded that the proposal was part of the continuing assault by Republicans on urban aid programs. Rather than cut CDBG spending still further, city advocates called for a return to previous funding levels so that communities would once again be able to undertake meaningful assisted housing and community development initiatives. They also called for a renewal of program requirements for the spending of CDBG funds in low-income neighborhoods, a targeting provision that Republican decentralization under the New Federalism had undermined.

Sources: Donald F. Kettl, *Government By Proxy: (Mis?)Managing Federal Programs* (Washington, DC: CQ Press, 1988), 54–66; Maureen Groppe, "Critics: Block Grants Designed for Needy End Up in Wealthier Communities," *Indianapolis Star,* August 17, 2011; W. Paul Farmer, Chief Executive Officer, American Planning Association (APA), "The Stakes Are High in Washington," *APA Domestic Policy Watch,* September 2011, http://planning.org/domesticpolicy/open/sep11.htm; Rep. Tom McClintock (R-CA), "Draining a Slush Fund: Community Development Block Grants," June 27, 2012, http://mcclintock.house.gov/2012/06/draining-a-slush-fund-community-development-block-grants.shtml; Michael J. Rich, "Community Development Block Grants at 40: Time for a Makeover," *Housing Policy Debate* 24, no. 1 (2014): 46–90.

of **regulatory federalism** or **coercive federalism,** where the national government often *mandates* (i.e., requires) local action without always providing sufficient assistance to reimburse communities for the required actions.[24] (See Box 11.2, "Unfunded Mandates.")

State and local officials are quite right to complain about mandates and the constraining nature of federal aid conditions. Yet subnational officials often exaggerate the national government's ability to dictate program administration. State and local officials do not simply cede to the demands of federal program overseers. Nor can the federal government demote or fire uncooperative state and local officials. Federal officials cannot even easily cut off assistance in cases of state and local noncompliance, as such sanctions will hurt citizens who are dependent on the services supported by intergovernmental funds. Categorical grants often offer an **"illusion of federal control,"**[25] as subnational officials retain considerable leeway in deciding how joint programs are administered.

WHY THE UNITED STATES HAS NO NATIONAL URBAN POLICY

Why is there no national policy in the United States committed to rebuilding communities in need? The answer is simple: a suburban nation has little tolerance for an explicit policy focused on revitalizing central cities and problem neighborhoods. The U.S. Congress, with so many members elected from suburban and Sunbelt districts, lacks the political will to target assistance to big cities, especially to the troubled former industrial centers of the Northeast and Midwest.

The reluctance of Congress to target urban assistance is not new. In the 1960s, President Lyndon Johnson had great difficulty in securing the enactment of a **Model Cities program** that would demonstrate just what could be accomplished by concentrating resources in a coordinated, multifaceted attack on the problems of a select few cities.

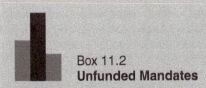

Box 11.2
Unfunded Mandates

An **unfunded federal mandate** is an order or regulation by a higher level of government or the court system that requires a state or locality to undertake an action but does not provide the funding to fully pay for the action. The Clean Air Act, the Clean Water Act, the Endangered Species Act, the Fair Labor Standards Act, the Americans with Disabilities Act, federal historic preservation, national standards for foster care, requirements for brownfields cleanup, and the Homeland Security Act are only a few of the vast number of federal programs that impose costly burdens on the states and localities. The states complain that they have been saddled with more than $29 billion in mandated costs in just a single year (2004). But even Republican presidents, despite their general criticisms of mandates, have added to the mandate burden imposed on states and localities. George W. Bush relied on mandates in a number of policy areas, including school achievement testing, homeland security, and emergency management.

In the mid-1990s, the Congress responded to state and local complaints by passing the **Unfunded Mandates Relief Act (UMRA)**. The law required the Congress to pay fully for any new mandate that had an annual cost in excess of $50 million. The law, however, has had only a limited impact.

Despite UMRA, as Paul Posner observes, "the march of mandates" continues, as UMRA legislation is riddled with numerous loopholes. Most significantly, the Unfunded Mandates Relief Act does not apply to existing programs, even when the costs required of the states and localities dramatically increase each year. Critics charge that the federal government does not even fully compensate localities for the training exercises and protective services required for homeland defense.

The **Individuals with Disabilities Education Act (IWDEA)** imposed expensive new schooling obligations on the states and localities. The **No Child Left Behind Act (NCLB)** entailed new subnational costs for testing and remedial education programs. The State of Connecticut sued the federal government, contending that No Child Left Behind imposed a $40 million burden on the state. The federal Office of Management and Budget (OMB) ruled that IWDEA and NCLB are technically not mandates that are constrained by UMRA; instead, IWDEA and NCLB are grant-in-aid programs to which a state or locality voluntarily applies and then must abide by program rules. State and local officials respond that such a fine distinction is absurd, and that they have no real alternative but to take federal assistance only to find that they are later saddled with costly and unwanted actions as new program rules are developed.

While the states complain about federal mandates, the state governments themselves often impose costly service responsibilities on municipalities. State mandates range from something as small as regulations governing the safety of playground equipment to something as large as requirements for the local provision of special education. The Connecticut Conference of Municipalities claims that state statutes impose more than 1,200 mandates on local governments in the state.

Sources: Paul L. Posner, *The Politics of Unfunded Mandates* (Washington, DC: Georgetown University Press, 1998); Janet M. Kelly, "The Unfunded Mandate Reform Act: Working Well for No Good Reason," *Government Finance Review* 19, no. 1 (February 2003): 28–30; Molly Stauffer and Carl Tubbesing, "The Mandate Monster: Unfunded Federal Mandates Are Back, and They Are Costing States Millions," *State Legislatures* (May 2004): 23; Connecticut Conference of Municipalities, "CT Mandate Watch—2010," www.ccm-ct.org/advocacy/mandates/; Robert J. Dilger and Richard S. Beth, *Unfunded Mandates Reform Act,* CRS Report to Congress R40957 (Washington, DC: Congressional Research Service, 2013), http://assets.opencrs.com/rpts/R40638_20100216.pdf.

Members of Congress were not enthusiastic about a program that promised benefits to other districts and not their own constituencies. To win legislative support, the president broadened the program geographically, proposing the creation of sixty-six model cities in states across the nation. But even that was not enough: Congress in its legislation spread Model Cities money even further, to 140 communities, including communities that just happened to lie in the districts of powerful congressional committee and subcommittee chairs. Model Cities were even created in non-urban Maine, Tennessee, Kentucky, and Montana.[26] Congress spread program funds so thinly that it undermined the entire Model Cities idea: no single city received the critical mass of monies necessary to demonstrate what an effective multipronged attack on urban problems could accomplish.

A similar fate greeted Jimmy Carter's National Urban Policy. Carter was the only president to propose an explicit policy to aid the economic development of troubled communities. But the votes of congressional representatives from the suburbs and the Sunbelt killed the major elements of the Carter program. Congress voted down the president's proposed urban development bank as well as public works and fiscal assistance programs that would give extra help to the nation's most distressed communities. In the wake of the crushing defeat of the urban bank, Carter proposed to have the Department of Commerce's Economic Development Administration (EDA) dispense a much smaller program of local job-creation funds. But Congress would not even accept the mild targeting of EDA assistance that Carter proposed. Instead, Congress moved in the exact opposite direction, spreading benefits by redefining "distress" so broadly that 90 percent of the nation's population lived in areas eligible to apply for EDA assistance!

Future presidents learned the political lesson inherent in the defeat of the Carter urban policy. Jimmy Carter was the first, and last, president to announce an explicit and coordinated set of programs aimed at aiding troubled urban communities. Since then, urban policy efforts have been less far-reaching. Discrete program initiatives in crime control, energy conservation, environmental protection, homeland security, and education have been able to gain popular backing and have had to substitute for national urban policy.[27]

URBAN POLICY FOR AN ANTI-URBAN AGE: BILL CLINTON'S "STEALTH" URBAN APPROACH

Bill Clinton was a self-styled **New Democrat** who sought an alternative approach to the big-government Democratic programs of the 1960s. The politically costly defeat of his national health-care bill in his first year in office reinforced his sense of caution in other domestic policy areas. Midway through his first term in office, Clinton faced a new major obstacle: the election of a Republican-controlled Congress intent on checking his program initiatives.

Clinton pursued a **refrigerator list approach**[28] to urban policy, a "to-do" list of a number of relatively small programs that appealed to middle-class voters yet delivered substantial benefits to urban communities. Clinton called for the federal government to fund 100,000 local police officers. He increased the funding of after-school and summer programs aimed at reducing youth crime. He proposed brownfields reclamation programs that won the support of environmentalists.

Clinton practiced a **stealth urban policy**, pursuing urban goals through "nonurban" means.[29] The Stealth Bomber was a cutting-edge weapon at the time that had a profile that could not be detected by enemy radar. Clinton sought urban aid programs that would similarly fly beneath Congress' radar. The president did not stress that his program initiatives would help cities; instead, he rallied people around the banners of heightened law enforcement, reforms in public schooling, brownfields reclamation, and "ending welfare as we know it." Clinton sought targets of opportunity; he took advantage of Congress' willingness to expand highly popular programs such as Head Start, child nutrition, and efforts to reduce violence against women. He secured new levels of assistance for urban job training, housing vouchers, and day care, all framed in terms of the popular goal of moving people from welfare to work.

Clinton's expansion of the **Earned Income Tax Credit (EITC)** provides an illustration of the stealth urban approach. The EITC provides millions of dollars in income assistance to the working poor, giving low-income workers a refundable tax credit, that is, extra money in their paychecks. Clinton increased EITC eligibility and benefits. A working mother with two children could receive as much as $3,370 annually in income assistance; families earning as much as $27,000 received smaller income supplements. The expansion of EITC helped cities, as that is where concentrations of the working poor are found. In 1998, the EITC pumped an estimated $737 million into the economy of the greater Chicago area, with 60 percent going to families residing in the central city.[30]

As a provision embedded in the tax code, the EITC also enjoyed distinct political advantages as compared to more direct spending programs. Tax provisions are not always easily understood by the public and hence are not as politically salient as "welfare" programs that provide cash assistance to the poor. Also, as the tax benefit provided assistance only to people who worked, opponents could not easily attack EITC as a welfare program that rewarded indolence.

Clinton was a pragmatist. He pursued a number of relatively small and "do-able" **urban policy pieces** rather than a bold, holistic, Carter-like national urban policy.

Clinton's welfare reform, day care, and EITC programs all provided aid directly to *people* in need, no matter where they resided; these programs did not specifically target urban *places*. Only the Clinton empowerment zone program stands out as a major exception; the empowerment zone program was a spatially based strategy aimed at the revitalization of the nation's most distressed communities.[31]

BARACK OBAMA'S HYBRID URBAN APPROACH

LOW VISIBILITY AND PRAGMATIC

President Barack Obama did not announce a major policy effort focused on cities; nor did he propose an overhaul of the federal grant system.[32] While the White House office devoted Web pages to urban policy, Obama did not use the presidential office to seek the enactment of a broad-reaching national urban policy. Instead, he largely continued the "stealth" approach of Clinton, with initiatives "embedded in programs with goals that are not oriented to places per se" but that nonetheless are "indirectly helping cities."[33]

Obama, however, did embrace **spatial targeting**; where possible, he sought to focus assistance on more troubled communities.[34] The **Choice Neighborhoods Program** sought to strengthen areas in close proximity to public housing projects or neighborhoods with a large concentration of subsidized housing.[35] The **Promise Neighborhoods Program** gave aid to help high-risk communities create programs similar to the **Harlem Children's Zone**, the famed program in New York's City that provides for the health, safety, nurturing, and education of children from birth to college. Key White House offices—the Office of Management and Budget, the White House Domestic Policy Council, and the National Economic Council—instructed federal departments and agencies to develop "effective place-based policies" when submitting their annual budget requests.[36]

Yet despite the embrace of targeting apparent in these programs, overall the aid that Obama offered communities was *not* highly targeted. In the midst of an economic recession, a broad range of America's communities had need. The logic of politics, too, dictated the widespread award of federal assistance. Obama's foreclosure assistance programs gave relief to overextended homeowners in the suburbs of Las Vegas and Phoenix and to the buyers of upscale condominiums in Florida, not just to homeowners in hard-hit core areas in cities like Cleveland. Likewise, Obama did not choose between place-based and people-based programs; he pursued both.[37]

Obama's hybrid or combination approach is clearly apparent in the single most important domestic program of his first term in office, the **American Recovery and Revitalization Act of 2009 (ARRA)**. ARRA was a whopping $780 billion package of federal spending programs and tax incentives designed to assist job-creation projects across the nation. In order to create jobs as quickly as possible, ARRA demanded "shovel ready" highway and infrastructure projects, whether located in cities, in rural areas, or even in relatively well-to-do suburbs. Despite the wide spread of program monies, ARRA nonetheless provided billions of dollars in assistance that big cities used to modernize infrastructure, attract industry, improve education, and combat housing foreclosures and various other urban ills. ARRA also contained program elements that were spatially targeted; ARRA offered **Recovery Zone bonds** to provide low-interest-rate financing for new economic development projects in communities with high rates of poverty, joblessness, and home foreclosures.

Obama responded to the meltdown in the home finance industry by announcing a vast $247 billion plan in which the government would buy the "toxic" assets of banks, freeing up capital that the banks could use to make new loans.[38] Once again, the president sought to target disproportionate assistance to areas with the greatest need within a program that otherwise spread benefits quite widely.

The **Neighborhood Stabilization Program (NSP1)**, created just before Obama took office, had previously set aside $3.9 billion to combat property foreclosures and to inject new investment capital into troubled neighborhoods. Obama provided an additional $2 billion in a second round or **NSP2** funds. Compared to the original program, NSP2 gave a greater share of assistance to hard-hit sections of cities such as Cleveland and Detroit. But NSP2 funds were not dispensed strictly to shrinking cities. NSP assistance was also awarded to Phoenix, Las Vegas, Miami, and Sacramento and Riverside (California), Sunbelt communities where new condominium and vacation villa projects had stopped mid-construction, in some cases creating virtual ghost towns in half-completed developments that were barely populated.[39]

Obama's urban actions also embraced a new **metropolitan and regional focus** that differed from the central-city focus of his Democratic predecessors. Obama sought to incentivize cities and suburbs to work together to invest in the infrastructure and other improvements necessary to make an entire metropolitan region competitive in a global age:

> The [Obama] administration has *not* proposed to launch a new round of Empowerment Zones or other initiatives designed to promote job development in distressed neighborhoods. Instead, economic development and jobs policies are being pursued at the metropolitan scale. Low-income communities and their residents are expected to benefit through training, job placement, and transportation policies that strengthen access to metropolitan opportunities.[40]

Obama promoted the development of **regional innovation clusters** to strengthen the competitive advantages that exist in a metropolitan region.[41]

DEBATING THE OBAMA URBAN APPROACH

Obama's programs aided many thousands of financially overstretched homeowners. His program provided an infusion of resources to communities trying to stave off decline. Yet more liberal critics scorned Obama for being excessively cautious and for failing to have a bold vision that would lead to a stronger attack on the root causes of racial segregation, home foreclosures, property abandonment, and inner-city decline.[42] These critics argue that Obama was too politically timid, that he was

THE INTERGOVERNMENTAL CITY

HOPE VI: The Demolition of Chicago's Cabrini-Green and the Rise of Replacement Housing.
Beginning in the 1990s, the federal government's HOPE VI program helped cities tear down their worst-off public housing towers and build more attractive lower-rise structures in their place. The new housing was certainly an improvement compared to the units that were razed. Still, the HOPE VI program proved quite controversial. Many of the residents displaced by demolition were not given units in the replacement housing, which in Cabrini was intended as a mixed-income development. As discussed in Chapter 3, by demolishing the high-rise projects, the city opened nearby areas, located in close proximity to Chicago's downtown, to a new wave of upscale development and gentrification.

Photo by Payton Chung, February 2006, http://commons.wikimedia.org/wiki/File:Cabrini%E2%80%93Green_Tear_Down.jpg.

too deferential to major financial institutions, and that he ceded too much ground to a Republican-led House of Representatives intent on cutting domestic programs. Other political liberals attacked Obama for his misguided approach, which led him to "bail out" troubled banks without first assuring that they would undertake measures to help distressed homeowners remain in their homes. Obama pushed banks to restructure loans to ease the burden on owners who had fallen behind in their payments, but many of the lenders refused to do so; bank participation in his home refinancing program was largely voluntary.[43]

Conservative critics, of course, offer a much different set of criticisms. They argue that Obama's initiatives were a waste of taxpayer money, especially as the history of spatial-based programs reveals a paucity of achievements despite the substantial federal monies spent.[44] Suburban representatives argued that the efforts of HUD (the Department of Housing and Urban Development) to target NSP funds to the hardest-hit urban core neighborhoods slighted the needs of the suburbs that were also hurt by the nation's economic and home finance crises.[45]

THE CONTINUING IMPORTANCE OF THE STATES

The states, with their constitutional authority and resources, play a critical role in urban affairs. State laws determine what revenue sources a municipality is permitted and how much a city may tax or borrow. State statutes can be permissive or restrictive when it comes to annexations, local service contracting, and the creation of interlocal cooperative agreements. As Chapter 9 reviewed, state-enacted Smart Growth and growth management measures can act to contain sprawl and to promote infill development in core urban areas.

As Chapter 9 also observed, the states play a more important role than the national government in K–12 education. Each state establishes a formula to assist local school funding. A state can alter school district lines, force the consolidation of smaller school districts, establish a program of school vouchers, and facilitate or cap the creation of charter schools.

Over half the states have **educational bankruptcy laws** that authorize the state takeover or reconstitution of failing local schools. The list of cities where a state removed powers from the hands of local school offices is fairly long. A partial list includes: New York, Los Angeles, Chicago, Philadelphia, Baltimore, Boston, Camden, Cleveland, Compton, Detroit, Harrisburg, Hartford, Jersey City, Lawrence, Newark, New Haven, Oakland, Paterson, Pontiac, Providence, and Trenton. In some cases the states gave the mayor new authority to appoint school board members and initiate other reforms to shake up underperforming schools.[46] In Chicago, Cleveland, and a number of other cities, school reformers hoped that the mayor would be able to take on entrenched interests. In 2002, New York City Mayor Michael Bloomberg exercised his new authority to abolish the local school board and take direct control of the city's schools and their more than one million students. The State of Maryland took power away from the previously independent school district in Prince Georges County and handed it to the county executive. In other cases, the states appointed an emergency financial manager or receiver to take charge of troubled districts.

One of the most dramatic instances of state intervention occurred when Pennsylvania took charge of Philadelphia's 200,000-student school system in 2002. Pennsylvania's governor appointed a School Reform Board that, in turn, placed the operation of elementary and middle schools in the hands of nonprofit management companies. The new school managers revised the core curriculum and introduced other reforms in their efforts to increase student proficiency scores.[47]

State actions have been helpful to cities in other policy areas. The states have sought to assist municipalities in finding creative ways to deal with the glut of vacant properties. State statutes determine the steps that a city must follow in order to establish a **land bank** that can acquire strategic tax-delinquent properties, rather than allowing speculators to buy distressed properties at rock-bottom prices and skim the profits while running the properties into the ground. Land banking is an important tool to stem the spread of blight. Land banking can also be part of a strategy to repurpose vacant properties to new uses that add to a neighborhood's livability. (See Box 11.3, "Land Banks: The States Enable Cities to Respond to Property Abandonment.") Supportive state laws are necessary to remove delinquent-tax obligations and all liens from problem properties, so that a community-oriented buyer can acquire the property clear of entanglements.[48]

Pennsylvania has established an innovative Tax Increment Financing Guarantee Program to encourage lenders to invest in brownfields reclamation projects. Pennsylvania's state fund takes some of the risk out of financing inner-city redevelopment projects. The state will reimburse creditors in cases where a strategic local project fails to produce sufficient revenues to repay bondholders.[49]

The states have come to recognize that their economic futures are to a great extent intertwined with the fate of their major cities. A blighted major city can drag down the image and economic competitiveness of an entire state. The State of New Jersey simply could not afford to ignore the bleak conditions of much-troubled Newark. The state provided over $100 million in funds and loans—twice the amount garnered by corporate and philanthropic giving—to build a world-class performing arts center in Newark.[50] The arts-based strategy was aimed at jump-starting Newark's rebirth and raising the state's international profile.

Yet when it comes to urban affairs, the states are not uniformly progressive. While the states are extremely interested in promoting new economic development, state legislatures are less receptive to the pleas of local officials for expanding local taxing and bonding authority, a reflection of the states' continuing distrust of municipal officials and their problem-solving abilities.[51] A national survey reports that city managers do not see the states as very helpful; instead the local managers complain that the states have reduced the problem-solving capabilities of local governments by cutting back state aid programs, raiding local revenue sources that are then used to fund state programs, and resorting to mandates and other actions that shift the costs of public program provision to local government.[52]

The states have not always had an exemplary record in responding to the needs of big cities and racial minorities.[53] In the years preceding Hurricane Katrina, state policy makers in Louisiana made little concerted effort to address the needs of the Crescent City's poorer neighborhoods. Even after the devastation wrought by Katrina, state officials intervened in New Orleans' affairs primarily to support economic growth projects, not community development.[54]

Much like the United States Congress, state legislatures often reflect the policy concerns of electorates dominated by middle-class suburban constituencies (and, in some states, rural constituencies as well). Many states, for instance, provide disproportionate funding to lesser-trafficked suburban and rural roadways while failing to provide equivalent levels of assistance for more heavily utilized urban transportation needs.[55]

State enterprise zone programs, often justified as a way to bring new jobs to economically troubled areas, lack targeting. Enterprise zones offer extensive tax breaks and other inducements in an attempt to lure businesses to distressed communities. Yet many states create enterprise zones in communities that exhibit no clear distress.[56] A

Box 11.3
**Land Banks: The States Enable Cities to Respond
to Property Abandonment**

Can cities "repurpose," that is, find new uses for, abandoned and tax-foreclosed properties? A growing number of states have given cities and counties the ability to create a **land bank** in order to "gain control" over the disposition of vacant lots and structures, distressed properties that, if left untended, can lead to the quick decline of a neighborhood. Land banking statutes enable a municipality to acquire, hold, and develop properties in cases where property owners owe substantial back taxes or fail to meet their legal obligations for the care and maintenance of abandoned properties.

In the absence of a local land bank, a city or county typically seizes a tax-delinquent property and attempts to auction it off in order to recoup a minimal amount of money for the public treasury. In too many instances, auction sales are shortsighted, as they set in motion a process that accelerates a neighborhood's decline. Quick-buck speculators buy the properties at low auction prices. These absentee buyers do not make repairs. Instead, they hope to reap rents in the short term and then "flip" a property to make a quick profit. When a property no longer proves profitable and cannot be sold, speculators board up the structure (if they even meet that minimal requirement for maintaining a property) and let it decline.

To avoid having distressed properties fall into the hands of speculators, land banking authority enables a city or county to acquire abandoned property and to put the property in a "bank" for future development. The city assures that the property is properly maintained and that the grass is mowed, so that blight does not spread to neighboring properties. The city then seeks to repurpose the land for more positive uses.

Land banking can facilitate **greening strategies** to make a neighborhood more attractive to residents. A government can offer **side lots** at virtually no cost to the owners of abutting properties, where the new owners agree to maintain the addition as a green lot or garden; the city can further help in aiding landscaping and reseeding. Neighborhood groups can use vacant lots for playgrounds as well as community gardens. In some cases, cities have assembled properties to expand park land. Cleveland does not focus its land banking efforts on areas suffering the greatest distress; instead, the city uses land banking to stabilize and upgrade neighborhoods that still have market potential, where new green spaces and attractive side lots can help attract new owners.

A proactive city can even use land banking for neighborhood transformation. Developers are more willing to invest in troubled neighborhoods if they can be assured that surrounding properties will be similarly upgraded and maintained. Land banking allows a city to assemble a group of properties that can then be offered for coordinated development.

Land banking has its roots in Genesee County, Michigan, where, under Michigan Public Act 123, county treasurer Dale Kildee took control over every new piece of land entering Flint's foreclosure system, preventing, as Kildee phrased it, the "late-night infomercial speculators" from taking title and spreading further ruin in the city's neighborhoods. From 2003 through the beginning of 2009, Genesee County took charge of some 7,400 properties—12 percent of all land in Flint—and demolished over 1,000 abandoned homes.

State law determines whether and under what conditions a locality can acquire and hold on to a nuisance property. State law also determines whether or not a city can use eminent domain powers to acquire a land parcel that is essential to an economic or neighborhood renewal project.

Changes in state statutes are also necessary to streamline excessively lengthy tax foreclosure processes. In Michigan, tax foreclosure on a property used to take from four to seven years! Public Act 123 fast-tracked the process and shortened typical foreclosure proceedings to just a year or two. Ohio House Bill 294 similarly reduced the foreclosure process from two years to only four months.

By 2013, more than a dozen states authorized land banking activities. The list includes Georgia, Illinois, Indiana, Kentucky, Maryland, Michigan, Missouri, Nebraska, New York, Ohio, Pennsylvania and Texas.

Sources: "Genesee County Land Bank," presentation by Genesee County Treasurer Dan Kildee to the Revitalizing Older Cities Capitol Hill Urban Summit, organized by the Northeast-Midwest Institute, Washington, DC, February 12, 2009; Frank S. Alexander, *Land Bank Authorities: A Guide for the Creation and Operation of Local Land Banks* (New York: Local Initiatives Support Corporation, April 2005); "State Policy Toolkit: State Land Bank Enabling Legislation," Restoring Prosperity Initiative, 2008, www.restoringprosperity.org/wp-content/uploads/2008/09/land-bank-policy-package-pdf.pdf; and U.S. Department of Housing and Urban Development, *Revitalizing Foreclosed Properties with Land Banks* (Reston, VA: Sage Computing, August 2009).

number of states make only the barest of efforts to target zone creation to communities in need. Illinois, Ohio, and Texas designated hundreds of enterprise zones; Louisiana created over 1,700 spread throughout the state! Arkansas declared the entire state an enterprise zone.[57] Such broad-scale creation of enterprise zones may help attract business to a state, but such programs do not offer much hope for distressed communities. When so many enterprise zones exist in a state, or when an entire state is designated as an enterprise zone, a business firm has little reason to choose a location in a troubled city or suburb; a business can locate in a fairly well-off community and still gain the program's various tax incentives and subsidies.[58]

CONCLUSION: FINDING WAYS TO CREATE PARTNERSHIPS IN AN ANTI-URBAN POLICY AGE

The New Federalism is rooted in the public's distrust of "big government" and programs that are viewed as wasteful, inefficient, inflexible, and overly complex.[59] The New Federalism is a contemporary reflection of the anti-government political culture of the United States, a culture that helps to explain why the United States has no formal national urban policy capable of revitalizing distressed communities.

In an age where population and power have shifted to the suburbs and to the Sunbelt, the United States Congress is even less inclined than ever to target substantial assistance to communities in need. Even Democratic presidents must be careful of the political need to court a middle-class suburban voting base.

Political logic further leads to a **spread effect** where both the United States Congress and state legislatures spend program monies widely, allowing as many legislators as possible to claim electoral credit for local projects. Even in its response to the threat of terrorism, Congress did not target assistance to the nation's most vulnerable areas; instead, Congress made sure to give every state and virtually every congressional district a share of homeland security assistance. According to one estimate, three-fourths of the initial funds dispensed for homeland security were allocated without regard to a jurisdiction's risk of attack![60]

Politically pragmatic Democrats like Bill Clinton and Barack Obama recognize the political reality of a suburban nation. Clinton and Obama did not pursue the dream of a national urban policy. Nor, despite their preference for targeted urban aid programs, did they insist on strict targeting. Instead, Clinton and Obama chose to pursue more limited but "do-able" urban policy pieces.

The age of National Urban Policy is over; in fact, it never really began. The death of National Urban Policy, however, does not mean the end of effective national and state urban actions. Smaller, well-crafted, and important urban programs are politically possible, especially if the programs contain a promise to aid middle-class communities and families and not just the poor. Such programs will also recognize the importance of mobilizing partnerships that take advantage of the problem-solving capacities of the states, localities, and community-based and nonprofit organizations. In an anti-urban age, national urban programs must also respond to the needs of suburban and Sunbelt communities that have become increasingly diverse.

KEY TERMS

American Recovery and
    Revitalization Act of 2009
    (ARRA) (*p. 295*)
block grants (*p. 286*)
categorical grants (*p. 285*)
Choice Neighborhoods Program,
    Obama's (*p. 295*)
coercive federalism (*p. 291*)
Community Development Block
    Grant (CDBG) (*p. 286*)
confederation (*p. 282*)
cooperative federalism (*p. 282*)
creeping categorization (*p. 289*)
decentralization (*p. 281*)

distort subnational program
    priorities, how categorical grants
    (*p. 289*)
dual federalism (*p. 282*)
Earned Income Tax Credit (EITC)
    (*p. 294*)
educational bankruptcy laws (*p. 298*)
elastic clause, the U.S.
    Constitution's (*p. 283*)
expressed powers (also called
    delegated powers or enumerated
    powers) (*p. 282*)
federal system (*p. 282*)
formula grant (*p. 288*)

12 The Future of Urban America

In an age of global competition, cities and suburbs devote considerable effort to the pursuit of jobs and economic development. Yet urban politics is not solely about local economic development. In the United States, questions of class, racial, and ethnic equity continue to define the urban political arena. While the more blatant forms of racial steering and housing discrimination have disappeared, more subtle discriminations in home finance persist and urban ghettoes continue to exist. Resegregation is occurring in the suburbs and in suburban schools. African Americans have largely gained entrance to inner-ring communities that differ markedly from the exurban communities with their largely white populations.

In an age of limited public resources, municipal leaders are preoccupied with strategies to improve local service effectiveness and efficiency. Cutbacks in governmental assistance further impel the local search for cost-saving innovations. Municipal officials have no choice but to do more with less.

Environmentalists and the American public in general have also come to recognize the importance of *sustainability*, the need to promote patterns of growth and development that minimize resource depletion and environmental harm. Cities and suburbs across the United States have adopted "green" policies to reduce energy consumption, require the use of recycled building materials, preserve wetlands, minimize water runoff and soil contamination, and ensure that the decisions made today do not adversely affect the quality of life for future generations.

"Shrinking" cities that have lost substantial population, too, have adopted their own *greening* strategies, turning vacant lots into green areas that promote natural drainage and flood control while adding to community livability. Atlanta has committed more than $2.8 billion to the Atlanta BeltLine, an effort to transform underutilized and abandoned rail property surrounding the core of the city into a twenty-two-mile extension of parks, greenways, and mass transit that will connect forty-five city neighborhoods to one another. The project will make Atlanta a more livable city. Civic leaders also hope that it will attract new economic investment to the city.[1]

This book concludes with a discussion of the future of cities and suburbs as leaders at the local, state, and national levels attempt to pursue new economic development while also respecting concerns for equity, service effectiveness, and a sustainable urban future.

THE CONTINUING EMPHASIS ON ECONOMIC DEVELOPMENT

Throughout their history, cities in the United States have been concerned with their economic development. Business leaders in early New York City, Buffalo, Chicago, and Dayton pushed states and municipalities to construct canals to promote trade. In the age of the big-city political machine, party bosses supported growth projects that enabled them to dispense valuable contracts, franchises, and job patronage to their loyal supporters. In Houston, Los Angeles, Long Beach, and other Sunbelt cities, local leaders expanded port facilities and shipping channels, built new airports, and otherwise provided the infrastructure necessary for business growth and local prosperity.[2]

The attention that contemporary communities give economic development surpasses the attention such matters received during earlier stages of American urban history. Today, questions of economic development dominate the local agenda to a degree unmatched in previous eras. Economic matters were not always at the top of urban politics. For nearly a hundred years, the battle between the political machine and reformers defined local politics. In the decades that followed World War II, cities devoted considerable attention to the provision of suitable housing, including public housing.[3] Beginning in the 1960s, antipoverty policy, community action, community control, school busing, and law-and-order programs dominated national, state, and local agendas. Governments experimented with a vast array of programs in an attempt to find a solution to the "urban crisis," especially the wave of big- and medium-city riots that had spread across the nation. None of these programs had economic development at their heart. Beginning in the mid-1970s, after New York City's and Cleveland's flirtation with bankruptcy, "cutback management" and other fiscal concerns dominated the urban agenda. Rising voter anti-tax sentiment soon reinforced the pressure for municipal belt-tightening. Once again, questions of urban local economic development did not dominate urban affairs.

By the 1990s, however, postindustrial restructuring had undermined local economies, leading local leaders to give new urgency to the pursuit of jobs. With globalized competition adding to cities' fiscal insecurity, economic development gained a near-hegemonic position in the municipal arena. Only the most affluent communities could afford to be selective, spurning growth projects in order to protect the local quality of life. Today, local economic initiatives are a normal part of municipal government, activities as commonplace as street cleaning and the provision of police and fire service.

Cities across the nation promise infrastructure improvements, tax concessions, and other subsidies in the attempt to attract and retain businesses. Cities establish **tax increment financing (TIF) districts** to help pay for the improvements demanded by business. When a TIF district is created in a designated area in a city, the gains in property tax revenues from business expansion are plowed back into the district, helping to pay for physical improvements that were made. Politicians see TIFs as an attractive "self-financing" means of development. The revenues yielded from a project are used to pay off the obligations that were incurred when the city borrowed money to begin work on the project. Dallas created a 9.5-mile-long TIF district in the Skillman corridor, northeast of the downtown, to promote commercial renewal around the newly opened stations of the DART light-rail system.[4] Businesses in the district, in turn, see a TIF arrangement as quite attractive, as the additional taxes they pay are dedicated to the improvements they desire.

But TIFs also have problems. "Tiffed" business expansion does not yield new tax revenues that can be used to support a city's schools and other general service improvements. The public schools gain little when the revenues received from new development are dedicated to repaying debt and financing even further infrastructure upgrades demanded by businesses in a TIF district.[5]

Many economists argue that TIFs and other tax abatements are wasteful, that such incentives have only a minor influence on business-siting decisions. Tax rates are less critical to business location than are matters of transportation, accessibility to suppliers and markets, and the quality of the local labor force.[6] One study has also found that the growth in value in TIF districts is "unremarkable" and may even come at the cost of diverting development from areas in a city located outside the district.[7]

Trend data from Chicago casts doubts that the city's extensive TIF program should be given credit for the major new developments and job creation taking place in the city; Chicago's expensive TIF approach may not have added much new development and job creation beyond that which would have occurred even in the absence of TIF districts and TIF incentives.[8] Critics also question the desirability of allowing suburbs and exurbs to create TIF districts that give sizable subsidies to already profitable big-box retailers like Cabela's, the outdoors hunting and fishing megastore.[9]

Yet despite the negative assessment of numerous academic studies, local officials continue to offer prospective businesses TIF financing and a seemingly endless array of tax concessions and subsidies. Local officials feel that they are in a competitive race to attract business and that they have no choice but to match what other communities are offering. Few elected officeholders want to risk being blamed for the relocation of a prominent business firm or the loss of the city's professional baseball or football team.

TIFs and other tax concessions awarded to businesses serve to reduce the net revenues that a city gains from a project. When the revenues do not cover the full costs to a city of a new sports arena, convention center, or other development project, the city's taxpayers—residents, small businesses, and business firms located in other areas of the city—wind up paying the difference. School systems find that the revenues for education are diminished by the tax abatements that municipal officials award to industrial and commercial property.

Chicago faces just such a quandary over its use of TIFs. Chicago is the city that loves to TIF, with 154 TIF districts inside the borders of the city and another 281 in the suburban portion of Cook County (2012 figures). Since 1964, Chicago area TIF districts have collected more than $5.5 billion in revenue. But David Orr, the Cook County Clerk, raises questions as to who controls such a large pot of money and for just what purposes the revenues are spent. He proposes that some of the funds be diverted from the business districts in order to support schools and other public service provision. In Detroit various tax incentives offered to businesses and property owners have led to the **erosion of the city's property tax base**, lessening the funds available to support essential municipal services. In Detroit, property owners in ten designated "Renaissance Zones," receive a "property tax reduction of 66% to 74% without even being required to make new investments or even to improve their properties."[10]

Cities have also begun to discover that a development strategy based on TIFs, tax cuts, and other business subsidies is no longer guaranteed to win the "job wars." A city's offer of tax concessions is easily matched by other cities. A city that invests heavily to expand "Wi-Fi" coverage may gain very few new businesses when hundreds of other communities are offering firms the same support.

Improved roads, telecommunications, and transportation infrastructure are the **hard factors** that affect private investment. Studies, however, also point to the critical importance of **soft factors** that a city can manipulate in its efforts to attract employers. Businesses are drawn to communities with good schools, a capable workforce, plentiful parks and recreational facilities, interesting arts and cultural programs, and a pleasant living environment. As the success of Seattle and Portland attests, an excellent local **quality of life** helps to make a region attractive to upscale employers and their **creative class** workforces.[11]

The **shadow governments** of special districts, regional authorities, and business-led public-private partnerships (described in Chapter 10) are often the new forums in which the decisions are made to subsidize development projects. Some states even give these bodies eminent domain authority. The shadow governments "get things done," working with minimal citizen participation and minimal scrutiny from the press.[12] In some cities, however, their pro-development posture has led to a countermobilization of homeowner associations, anti-tax forces, environmental organizations, and minority groups. Particularly in the Sunbelt, neighborhood and taxpayer groups have turned to the voter initiative and referendum processes in an effort to check the growth-oriented actions of shadow governments.

Do cities have any real choice but to give in to the demands of growth forces? Certain public policies, if enacted, can reduce the economic stranglehold that business seems to have on the local arena. Federal revenue sharing, metropolitan tax-base sharing, and state assumption of a greater share of local school expenditures would help to mitigate some of the fiscal pressures that lead localities to uncritically woo new development. Strict land-use regulation, statutes that limit condominium conversion and tenant displacement, and factory-closing laws can similarly serve to constrain the dislocations that accompany unfettered free-market growth.[13] In the privatist United States, however, few cities and states will adopt such strong-government solutions.

The local love affair with economic development will likely continue. Laws for greater transparency, public participation, the provision of affordable housing, environmental protection, and "green" construction, and even campaign finance reform, can all add a measure of balance to a decision-making process that is too often dominated by developers, corporate interests, local chambers of commerce, and other members of the local growth coalition.

THE FUTURE OF MINORITY EMPOWERMENT

THE NEW STYLE OF LATINO AND AFRICAN-AMERICAN POLITICS

Half of the fifteen largest U.S. cities are "majority minority" with Hispanics, African Americans, and Asians comprising more than 50 percent of the local population.[14] The growth of the Hispanic population has been particularly dynamic. At the tail end of the twentieth century, the Hispanic urban population grew by 46 percent in a period of just ten years, the result of both continuing immigration and high birthrates. By 2010 Latinos comprised 22 percent of the population of the 100 largest metropolitan areas in the United States, far surpassing the African-American population.[15] In the Southwest, the Latino "sleeping giant" was awakening to its potential voting and political power.[16]

Poor voter turnout, however, diminishes Latino power.[17] But Latino turnout "is not predestined to such low levels"; the rising numbers of Latino candidates on the ballot for public office, especially for visible public offices like a city's mayoralty, can be expected to draw increased numbers of Latinos to the polls.[18] Continuing immigration, too, is likely to swell Hispanics' share of the vote.[19]

As African Americans and Latinos gain effective representation in city hall, the more militant rhetoric of prior generations has ceded way to the more pragmatic concerns of governance. Black and Latino mayors have had to be concerned with providing improved municipal services, finding new operational efficiencies, and building effective public-private partnerships. The new generation of black and Latino leaders has worked with business and nonprofit leaders in order to bring new jobs and opportunities to the city.

As discussed in Chapter 5, Newark's Cory Booker and San Antonio's Julián Castro worked comfortably across class and racial line and were at ease in using Twitter and other forms of social media to reach out to a broad spectrum of citizens. Castro has been called the "Post-Hispanic Politician"[20] as a result of his coalition-building abilities. In economically distressed Youngstown, Ohio, Jay Williams, the city's first African-American mayor, similarly utilized a soft-spoken approach in forging partnerships with businesses, nonprofit foundations, and the local university.[21] Williams eventually left the mayoralty to serve as the Obama Administration's so-called "auto czar," the administration's point person in promoting new investment in communities hard-hit by the decline of automobile-related manufacturing. Castro was named by Obama to head the Department of Housing and Urban Development.

More activist voices in the African-American and Latino communities criticize the compromises that black and Latino mayors make in their efforts to head diverse governing coalitions. Progressives argue that black and Latino mayors are overly deferential to the business community and to white voters. Critics charge that the pragmatic course of action steered by Latino mayors as "more an achievement of the conservative middle class than of the masses."[22]

Progressives over the years have continued to call for African Americans and Latinos to unite in a biracial coalition in their mutual quest for power. Yet the formation of a black-Latino alliance often proves quite difficult, especially as African Americans and Latinos do not share a common identity.[23] In Miami and Los Angeles, black and Hispanic voters are often polarized; the two groups see one another as competitors for the same slice of the urban political and economic pie.[24] Public opinion data from California further reveals the greater affinity that Latinos have with whites, and not with African Americans, on major public policy questions.[25]

Yet with special care and the proper leadership skills, a biracial coalition can be built. Antonio Villaraigosa won the Los Angeles mayoralty in 2005, garnering nearly half of the votes cast by the city's black citizens, who were upset that his opponent, Mayor James Hahn, had ousted Bernard Parks, the city's African-American chief of police.[26]

LIMITS IN USING RACIAL PREFERENCES FOR MINORITY ECONOMIC EMPOWERMENT

During the age of the political machine, city bosses steered jobs and benefits to various ethnic constituencies. Today, African Americans and Latinos similarly attempt to use their control of city hall to promote minority-owned business and employment in their primary constituencies. But the courts have not looked kindly on the use of racial preferences in municipal contracts.

In a very important decision, the U.S. Supreme Court placed sharp restrictions on municipal **contract compliance** programs, the affirmative-action-style preferences used to steer city contracts to minority-owned firms and to businesses that agree to racial hiring targets. In *Richmond v. Croson* (1989), the Court struck down the City of Richmond's contract compliance program as a noxious racial classification.

African Americans are more than half of the population of Richmond, Virginia, the former capital of the Confederacy. When whites controlled the city government, less than 1 percent of the city-issued contracts was awarded to black-owned firms. When African Americans finally gained control of city hall, they sought to correct this vast imbalance. Richmond established a **minority set-aside program**, specifying that at least 30 percent of the total dollar amount of municipal contracts be awarded to minority firms.

The city's business community was split in its reaction to the program. The more pragmatic white business leaders recognized how the program could help build a political coalition behind their growth projects; black elected officials could show their supporters how new projects were bringing jobs to the black community. Contract compliance set-asides were the "glue" that allowed African Americans and whites to work together on economic development initiatives.[27] But the white owners of other businesses, especially in the construction trades, objected that the program amounted to reverse discrimination; they argued that the city should simply award a contract to whichever qualified firm submitted the lowest bid, with no added preferences for firms that delivered jobs to racial minorities.

According to the Court's *Croson* ruling, a city cannot simply refer to broad societal discrimination in the past to justify its use of a system of racial preferences. A city can only use a system of racial preferences if it first presents clear evidence that the municipality itself had engaged in unconstitutional discriminatory practices in the particular service area in question. **Disparity studies**—statistical analyses that document the failure of minority businesses to receive a fair percentage of city contracts—are an important first step in documenting that a pattern of discrimination *may* have occurred. The Supreme Court further ruled that an acceptable minority set-aside program must be **narrowly tailored**: the program cannot offer preferences to all minority groups but only to individuals and groups proven to have suffered actual discrimination by the city.[28]

Croson poses a difficult set of requirements for a city to meet if it wishes to use contracting for minority economic empowerment. Many cities simply reduced or ended their contract compliance programs. Relatively few cities were willing to assume the costs of preparing the detailed racial disparity studies necessary to justify minority preferences.[29] Cities were also hesitant to continue a program that could lead to costly court proceedings in the face of legal challenges likely to be brought by white-owned firms.[30]

Recent Supreme Court rulings in a related policy area, affirmative action in education, do not bode well for the future of contract compliance programs. In 2014 the Supreme Court upheld a voter initiative in Michigan that banned public universities from considering a candidate's race in their admissions decisions.[31]

RESEGREGATION AND THE PUBLIC SCHOOLS

In the 1950s, the Supreme Court was a force for desegregation, striking down as unconstitutional the *de jure* **segregation** of public schools, the racial segregation of schools mandated by state law. The Court, however, has not taken aggressive action against *de facto* **segregation**, the racial imbalances in school enrollments that are not ordered by state law but are the consequence of residential patterns: blacks and whites tend to live in different areas of the metropolis, leading to great variation in the racial composition of local schools.

In fact, the Court's 1975 *Milliken v. Bradley* decision effectively brought metropolitan school desegregation efforts to a halt. In striking down a busing program that encompassed Detroit and its nearby suburbs, the Court ruled that no suburb has to participate in a plan to correct the de facto segregation of metropolitan schools. The *Milliken* decision "sent the unmistakable message—urban apartheid would not be overcome through judicial decree."[32]

Over the ensuing decades, the Supreme Court has even modified a number of its earlier court-ordered school integration orders. The Court allowed DeKalb County (Georgia), Kansas City (Missouri), Charlotte-Mecklenburg (North Carolina), and a whole host of other cities across the nation, in both the North and the South, to terminate desegregation plans. The Court permitted school systems to curtail integration plans that had been tried for a substantial period of time, even when the city had not yet succeeded in producing racially integrated classrooms. City after city ended major desegregation efforts, and the percentage of students attending racially integrated schools fell.[33]

School officials turned to other techniques—most notably **magnet schools** with their enriched curriculums and the promise of a safe school environment—in an effort to persuade parents to voluntarily send their children to schools with quality educational programs and racially integrated classrooms. But here, too, the Supreme Court eventually intervened, ruling in 2007 that districts could establish magnet schools but could not use race as a factor in order to promote racial balance in the school's enrollment.[34] Once again, the Supreme Court acted to limit local desegregation efforts.

Polling data reveal that African Americans have come to accept the permanence of de facto segregation and have become frustrated with the costs their children bear in school busing programs and the loss of neighborhood schools that could serve as the anchors of black communities.[35] Many minority parents see little worth in continuing a battle for desegregation that just cannot be won. African-American parents, especially middle- and upper-class parents whose children attend integrated schools, have turned their efforts to improving the quality of the schools their children attend rather than continuing the fight for the seemingly impossible dream of city and metropolitan school integration.[36]

In one area, there is clearly good news: the all-white suburb has virtually disappeared. Census data documents the extent to which African Americans have moved to the suburbs. Yet many suburbs remain "almost exclusively" white despite the arrival of a few African Americans.[37]

URBAN POLICY IN A SUBURBAN AGE: THE END OF URBAN POLICY?

Numerous urban scholars have called for an explicit, comprehensive national policy to alleviate urban ills: "Only a total rethinking of the nation's priorities and a reinvestment in social and human capital can transform urban life."[38] However, in a suburban nation, as discussed in the preceding chapter, the formulation and enactment of such a sweeping, national urban policy is not politically possible. The call for a national urban policy has little resonance outside of academic circles.

The 2008 election of Barack Obama brought a new optimism, a sense that the federal government would adopt strong policies of benefit to cities. Obama created a White House Office of Urban Affairs to give new priority to and to coordinate urban policies. His appointees to serve as Secretary of the Department of Housing and Urban Development (HUD)—Shaun Donovan (the former housing commissioner for New York City) and Julián Castro (the mayor of San Antonio)—possessed great familiarity with urban constituencies and cities' needs. Obama's Recovery Act programs offered cities much-needed assistance for street reconstruction, transportation, and other infrastructure projects. The president initiated various efforts to restructure mortgages so that homeowners facing difficulty would not be forced out of their homes. The president's Neighborhood Initiatives also gave core-city neighborhoods an extra measure of assistance in repurposing vacant properties. The Obama Administration also dispensed grant money to support public transportation, transit-oriented development, and Smart Growth practices.[39]

Yet Obama's urban actions were sharply constrained. Obama recognized that most Americans do not live in cities and are not willing to support high-visibility programs that would pour additional resources into cities. Beginning in 2010, Obama also was limited by Republican control of the House of Representatives. Congressional opposition to new domestic spending initiatives and Republican insistence that major cuts be made in domestic spending programs further slammed the door shut; the dream of targeted, coherent, national urban policy was just that, a dream.

URBAN POLICY FOR AN ANTI-URBAN AGE: EIGHT WAYS TO BUILD A REALISTIC URBAN POLICY

In an age where there is no broad public support for national urban programs, the advocates of cities will find the greatest possibilities of success if they pursue "non-urban programs"[40] that, as a side product, deliver substantial aid to cities and distressed communities. Indeed, the call for a "national urban policy" focused on the nation's most distressed communities lacks the capacity to rally public support. But, as the past decades have demonstrated, a more pragmatic attack on urban ills can be launched by identifying discrete and "isolated" programs that have the ability to command broad political support.[41]

The eight suggestions listed below provide tactical advice for enacting a pragmatic urban policy, for finding do-able and meaningful urban programs in an age that is not conducive to strong urban policy.

1. Emphasize a Program's Benefits for America's Middle Class

In a middle-class nation, advocates need to stress the benefits that programs will bring to the middle class, not to central cities and the poor. Educational reforms, for instance, not only help the inner-city poor, they can also empower middle-class parents who are dissatisfied with underperforming public schools. Programs aimed at repurposing vacant properties do not simply concentrate assistance to inner-city communities in Frostbelt cities such as Cleveland, Detroit, and Baltimore. Vacant properties programs also provide extensive aid to California, Florida, Nevada, and Arizona, Sunbelt states that suffered some of the highest rates of foreclosures in the country when the buyers of condominiums and suburban homes could not meet their monthly mortgage obligations.

2. Tie Program Benefits to Participation in the Workplace

Americans are hostile to "welfare." However, despite their opposition to welfare, the public will support assistance programs that emphasize workforce participation, job training, and the transition from welfare to work.[42] The provision of day care, too, can be justified as part of a program than enables poor women to leave welfare and return to work.

3. Pursue "Race-Neutral" and Universal Programs

Americans as a whole disapprove of programs that give benefits to the members of a specific racial group while denying benefits to members of other racial and ethnic groups. Americans give greater support to **race-neutral programs** that promise assistance to all people in need, irrespective of race or ethnicity. Affirmative action and contract compliance programs that emphasize race are highly controversial. Programs that provide opportunity to the economically disadvantaged, irrespective of skin color, are less so. The American public endorses education and job-training programs that promise aid to all citizens in need, not just to racial minorities.[43]

4. Spread Benefits! Target When Possible! Target Within Universalism!

As just discussed, programs that **spread benefits** to a larger population have the potential to garner broad public support. Yet, such programs suffer a major drawback: high cost! The wide spread of program benefits also dilutes the assistance provided to people and communities most in need. As a consequence, many urban advocates argue for the opposite approach, for programs that **target benefits**, that is, programs that concentrate their limited resources on residents and communities with the greatest need. But as seen repeatedly throughout this book, targeted urban policy, however rational and justified in theory, is extremely difficult to achieve politically.

A mixed approach of **targeting within universalism** actually provides the most satisfactory strategy. An aid program can define program eligibility quite broadly, allowing the participation of a great many communities, while allocating a higher level of benefits and additional services to poorer people and communities in need.[44]

The Community Development Block Grant (CDBG) program provides a good example of targeting within universalism. The CDBG program delivers assistance annually to nearly 1,200 communities. Yet the CDBG aid formula ensures that aid is disproportionately given to the nation's big cities and to smaller jurisdictions with the greatest need.

Head Start enjoys overwhelming popularity because it serves all children in need irrespective of where they live. Head Start aids poor children, not poor places. Nonetheless, the program provides disproportionate benefits to central cities and inner-city communities, the sites where large concentrations of poor families reside.

A number of the new generation of African-American mayors have adopted a similar leadership strategy: especially when governing cities with a white majority, African-American mayors justify their program choices in rhetoric that serves to "universalize Black interest," carefully explaining how community development initiatives and other targeted programs will bring benefits to the larger city.[45] These leaders push programs of educational reform that, they argue, will do more than simply improve the conditions of inner-city schools; these leaders emphasize that improved schools will upgrade the quality of the local workforce, a critical factor in the city's future competitiveness and its ability to attract new employers and jobs.

5. Look to the Tax Code!

Bill Clinton expanded the **Earned Income Tax Credit (EITC)**, a program of wage supplements to the working poor. In doing so, he faced virtually none of the harsh debate that accompanies proposals to expand "welfare" programs. As EITC benefits are dispensed only to low-income workers—and not to nonworkers—the change could not easily be attacked as an expansion of welfare. Clinton understood that Americans are willing to support the provision of assistance to persons who hold jobs but who still face difficulties in "getting by." Clinton also recognized the virtues of using the tax code to provide such assistance: embedded in a complex and difficult-to-understand tax code, EITC expansion enjoyed a certain degree of political insulation. Administered through the tax code, EITC expansion flew "under the political radar."

Another tax code program, the **Low Income Housing Tax Credit (LIHTC),** has become arguably the nation's most important program for the construction of housing for families in need. When measured in terms of **tax expenditures,** the revenues lost to the public treasury as a result of the program's tax incentives, LIHTC is clearly a formidable venture. In just a ten-year period (2008–2017), LIHTC is expected to cost the federal government $61 billion in foregone revenues.[46] As a program that gives developers tax credits as an incentive to construct affordable housing, the LIHTC escapes much of the controversy that surrounds more direct government spending efforts to build "public housing." As another quite complex tax incentive that is not easily understood and hence flies under the political radar, LIHTC has had better success than other federal subsidized housing programs when it comes to building new units of low-income housing units in the suburbs.[47]

6. Emphasize the Win–Win Benefits of Regional Cooperation, Especially for Job Creation and Economic Development

The prominence of economic development concerns opens the door to potentially fruitful regional collaborations. Cities and suburbs have a record of cooperating with one another when mutual cost savings are obvious. But cities and suburbs are beginning to recognize that they need one another's help in attracting new businesses and jobs. Neighboring communities enjoy their best chances of attracting a major corporation when they cooperate in providing the roads, sewers, water, transportation, housing, and job training programs that a business firm desires.

Businesses seek the advantages of locating in an **industrial cluster** where they have close proximity to similar businesses and can even draw on the same skilled firms for support services. An industrial cluster is regional in nature and spills over local boundaries. No single city or suburb acting on its own possesses the ability to establish or advance an industrial cluster.

The provision of state and national incentives is often necessary to get communities to surmount past antagonisms and begin the habits of more extensive collaboration. The ISTEA/NEXTEA/TEA-21 programs provide a model of how higher levels of government can promote regional cooperation: the federal government required local governments to work together on regional plans for public transit, requiring the establishment of a metropolitan planning organization (an MPO) as a condition for receiving federal assistance.

The Obama administration provided a small but important stimulus to regional action in its 2010 award of $100 million in **Sustainable Communities Regional Planning grants**. The grants served to incentivize interlocal planning for housing, job sites, and the transportation facilities, and to encourage communities in a region to work together to formulate the best plans to accommodate new growth. Minnesota's Twin Cities used the funds to steer new growth to developments built along transit lines. Austin, Texas, and ten surrounding communities similarly used the federal monies to connect new housing with public transit and schools.[48]

The states, too, have begun to show a heightened interest in promoting regionalism. New Jersey, New York, and Ohio are among the states that offer incentives for interlocal collaboration. Yet the state programs often lack follow-through. State legislatures are interested in promoting regional ventures that will result in taxpayer savings. But elected state officeholders are fearful of incurring the wrath of suburban voters by pushing interlocal action too far.[49]

7. Build Cities Bottom Up Through Community Development Corporations, Nonprofits, and Community-Based Organizations

Urban affairs journalist Neal Peirce observes that the hope for the urban future lies largely with Community Development Corporations (CDCs), mutual housing associations, land trusts, reinvestment corporations, and a myriad of disparate civic, neighborhood, and corporate and citizen-volunteer organizations.[50] State and federal policy can help nurture and extend the problem-solving capacities of the tens of thousands of nonprofit and community organizations that "do the public's work" in urban and suburban America. An urban policy approach that works through community-based, faith-based, and other nonprofit organizations can garner greater legitimacy and public support. Nonprofit and community organizations also possess expertise and accumulated knowledge; these organizations know a neighborhood's needs and unique circumstances, having worked in the community for many years.

CDCs have demonstrated impressive success in leveraging the monetary commitment and other resources necessary to construct and rehabilitate low-income housing. CDCs also have an enviable record in providing job training for low-income residents, in building neighborhood-based health-care centers, and, in general, in building a community's "social capital."[51]

But CDCs cannot do their work in isolation. Their work requires the financial support of corporate philanthropy, nonprofit foundations, and even government agencies. Three key federal programs—the Low Income Housing Tax Credit (LIHTC) program, the Community Development Block Grant (CDBG) program, and the HOME Investment Partnership—have helped to catalyze much of the bottom-up revitalization work that has taken place in lower-income neighborhoods across the nation. The LIHTC program, in particular, provides the financial incentive for corporations to invest as partners in CDC low-income housing.

8. Focus on Powerful Emotional Symbols and "Deserving" Constituencies: Education, Children, the Elderly, Women, and Protecting the Natural Environment

The American public continues to support programs focused on children and education. Children are a particularly sympathetic constituency. Head Start and the Supplemental Food Program for Women, Infants, and Children (WIC) continued to grow even during years when other "welfare" programs were scaled back. The public also supports funding for education to give individuals greater opportunity and to provide the level of human resources necessary for the nation's long-term economic growth.

Spending for education is seen as a cost-efficient alternative to "welfare." If schools do their jobs and children mature and become productive citizens, there will be less future need for expensive social welfare and correctional programs.

Programs aimed at helping the elderly, veterans, families on the street, battered women, and people with AIDS also enjoy considerable public support. Communities, for instance, often build subsidized housing for the elderly and veterans with needs even while refraining from other construction for the nonelderly poor. The elderly also vote, providing policy makers with a political incentive to respond to their needs.

Environmentalism is another powerful symbol that can be used to mobilize support for urban-related programs. Where possible, program initiatives should be framed as environmental policy, not urban policy. Regional growth management and Smart Growth initiatives gain public support for their professed goals of saving green space, natural habitats, and farmland. Programs for sustainable growth, the cleanup of toxic brownfields, and the "greening" of abandoned properties can attract the support of environmentalists and younger persons who might otherwise not be very interested in the subject of urban revitalization.

TOWARD SUSTAINABLE CITIES

Critics like to misrepresent *sustainable development* as "no growth" environmental extremism. Yet the truth is that **sustainable development** *does* seek new growth, but it seeks growth patterns and practices that will minimize the adverse effects of development on the natural environment: "Reduced to its most basic tenets, sustainable urbanism is *walkable and transit-served urbanism integrated with high-performance buildings and high-performance infrastructure.*"[52]

Cities and suburbs across the United States and around the world are giving increased prominence to matters of sustainability. Major cities have even had to address sustainability concerns as part of a locality's application to host the Olympic Games. New York, Madrid, and London all boasted of their "green" bids for the 2012 Olympics, as did Chicago in its bid for the 2016 games. New York's application emphasized the creation of new parkland, reliance on mass transit, and the design of a sustainable "urban village." London's winning bid for the 2012 games promised a 25 percent gain in the energy efficiency of the Olympic Village, increased reliance on renewable sources, reduced water consumption, the use of recycled materials from demolished buildings, reliance on low-carbon-emission mass transit, and the dedication of new bicycling and walking paths.[53]

Chapters 9 and 10 reviewed a number of growth-management efforts, including Smart Growth, Urban Growth Boundaries (UGBs), transit-oriented development, and the New Urbanism. All of these efforts aim to preserve green space and agricultural acreage while promoting the necessary population densities for mass transit, bicycling, and even walking.[54] Compact development also lessens a region's acreage devoted to roadways and parking lots, reducing the runoff of contaminants that pollutes streams and rivers.

THE SUSTAINABILITY TRIANGLE

Concern for the natural environment is only one of three legs in the **sustainable development triangle**. Policies that protect the natural environment will not be politically sustainable unless they also meet the economic and social needs of urban populations, the other two legs of the triangle. Voters will not approve of local environmental measures that decrease jobs and opportunity. Disadvantaged groups will mobilize against policies that decrease the job and housing opportunities available to new workers, recently arrived immigrants, younger families, racial minorities, and the poor. To be truly equitable, sustainability must not only seek a reduction in the overall levels of pollution; sustainable development must also have a focus on reducing the health consequences that pollution imposes on at-risk communities.[55]

Portland's Urban Growth Boundary (UGB) illustrates this larger conceptualization of urban sustainability. At its heart, the UGB seeks to contain the destructive impacts of sprawl. The Portland region has also provided extended assistance for affordable housing and has on occasion expanded the boundary in order to mitigate pressures toward home price inflation that would adversely affect newly marrieds, minorities, working-class citizens, and the poor. Portland also requires developers to include affordable units in new residential developments.

GREEN CONSTRUCTION AND ENERGY REDUCTION

More than 138 U.S. communities (with a population size of 50,000 or greater) have "green" building ordinances to promote sustainable practices in construction.[56] Green cities often condition the issuance of a building permit on a developer's willingness to meet or surpass the federal government's **Energy Star standards** and the U.S. Green Building Council's **Leadership in Energy and Environmental Design (LEED) standards** for energy efficiency, reduced water use, and the use of recycled building materials in construction.[57]

Green building codes award a builder with **tax incentives, expedited permit approvals, and density bonuses** (approval to build at greater floor-to-area ratios than is normally allowed) in return for incorporating design features that reduce a structure's energy consumption.[58] A green city may issue these rewards to a developer for a tight building "envelope" that minimizes the "footprint"[59] or square footage of a structure. A green city also incentivizes other design features to reduce a structure's usage of energy: passive solar heating (i.e., the use of skylights and windows that take advantage of sunlight), natural ventilation, low-flow toilets, the use of recycled building materials, and the installation of energy-efficient heating systems and appliances in new construction. In a few instances, cities have even sought to incentivize the construction of European-style **passive houses** that are thoroughly insulated and have ventilation systems that recycle heat, with the result that a homeowner pays extremely low winter heating bills.[60]

In an increasing number of cities, green building practices have become "normal," an expected part of local development, as municipal administrators have helped train developers to meet LEED standards and other sustainable construction expectations.[61]

Solar Panels on Car Parking Lot, Arizona State University, 2009. Green building construction codes can encourage the utilization of renewable energy.

Copyright © Kevin Dooley and courtesy of Wikimedia Commons. http://commons.wikimedia.org/wiki/File:Solar_panels_on_car_parking.jpg.

Developers enjoy the increased marketability that can accompany LEED-certified structures with their promise of reduced energy costs.

Still, numerous environmentalists charge that the standards of LEED certification, which were formulated by the construction industry, are too easily met. Too often, LEED certification is issued for very modest savings in energy. In too many cases, the structures, when completed, did not achieve the energy savings that had been promised.

Environmental activists, for instance, sharply criticize the award of a "gold" level of LEED certification to the suburban Illinois headquarters for HSBC, the giant banking and financial services firm, despite the building's location far away from mass transit. The structure did incorporate the use of recycled materials and a number of other green construction practices. Yet can the construction of such an edifice be considered truly sustainable when workers must rely on the automobile, especially when the building replaced the corporation's former headquarters that was located on metro transit line? The debate over HSBC approval led to a revised set of certification standards, **LEED-Neighborhood Design (LEED-ND)**, which gives new consideration to a building's location and its access to public transit, not just to the energy efficiency of the building.[62]

GREEN PROMOTION AND PRACTICES AT CITY HALL

Through its own actions, a local government can model sustainable practices. The City of Chicago placed a *green roof* atop its 100-year-old city hall, a demonstration project intended to show builders how such an investment can reduce energy costs. Portland

(Oregon) and Dayton (Ohio) are among other cities with a green roof on city hall. Milwaukee has a green roof on its local library. These cities hope the private building owners will follow. A **green roof** (to be more precise, a layer of grass or vegetation that covers the top of a building) provides natural insulation for a structure, saving on energy costs. Green roofs also reduce the **heat island effect**, where, during summer months, a city's downtown becomes warmer than the surrounding area. Green roofs also retain rainwater, reducing storm-water runoff and the flow of pollutants downstream.[63]

Green cities further seek to reduce storm-water runoff by narrowing the widths of new streets and through incentives for the use of **porous surfaces** instead of impervious concrete in parking lots and public plazas. Porous paving materials permit water to seep into the ground below, allowing the soil to filter contaminants while minimizing the pollution that results when storm water is piped through sewers into nearby rivers and streams. **Green dividers**, strips of trees and low-lying grassy areas between aisles of a parking lot, also help minimize water runoff. Green building codes also reward developers for site design plans that include **rain gardens**, low-lying landscaped areas that capture and absorb storm water.[64] Cleveland, New Orleans, and other "shrinking cities" have adopted **greening strategies** to turn large

Green Roof atop Chicago City Hall.

From Wikimedia Commons, user TonyTheTiger, July 25, 2010, http://commons.wikimedia.org/wiki/File:Chicago_City_Hall_green_roof_edit.jpg.

swaths of vacant property into green swales that aid in storm-water retention, reducing downstream pollution.[65]

Miller Park, the Brewers' baseball field in Milwaukee has three 1,500-gallon rain barrels to collect water draining from the field's 8.5-acre roof, reducing the discharge into storm sewers flowing to the Menomonee River. The water is used for irrigation. The barrels are only a small step in reducing surges in water flow after a storm, a model for others to emulate. The baseball club has even proposed to sell corporate sponsorships—naming rights—for each of the barrels.[66]

Numerous cities make fuel efficiency an important factor in vehicle procurement. Municipalities have even converted their municipal fleets from diesel to **"cleaner" fuels**—natural gas, hybrid electric, biodiesel, or possibly even hydrogen fuel cells—to improve overall air quality and to reduce the incidence of asthma attacks suffered by inner-city children who reside in neighborhoods choked by diesel exhaust fumes.[67] Berkeley, California, is only one of a number of cities to switch its truck fleet from diesel to cleaner-burning **biodiesel** (essentially a fuel made from vegetable oil) as part of the municipal effort to reduce the occurrence of asthma.[68] Of course, municipal governments can also promote mass transit usage by distributing reduced-cost transit passes to city workers and putting an end to free employee parking.

Portland and Seattle are among the national leaders in the use of **performance indicators** to measure environmental progress (an important service-improvement technique that was reviewed in Chapter 8). The collected data do not merely sit on the shelf. Instead, the data are integrated into a system of **performance management** where managers and even activist neighborhood groups are given the information that they need to demand that municipal agencies live up to the environmental standards that the city has set.

SUSTAINABLE URBAN DEVELOPMENT: FIVE CITIES

What do sustainable cities look like? A brief look at Chattanooga, Austin, Boulder, Portland (Oregon), and Seattle[69] gives some indication as to how cities promote continued development while the same time decreasing their "ecological footprint."

Chattanooga

Once a center of coke foundries and textile manufacturing—smokestack industries attracted by low-wage labor in the South—Chattanooga, Tennessee, in the 1960s was reputed to be the most polluted city in the United States. Today, it is a much different community. Chattanooga cleaned up the local environment and cast its future with sustainable development. The clean-up of the Tennessee River, bordered by industrial sites, was critical to the downtown's rebirth. The city also turned to a system of electric buses as a visible expression of the city's newfound livability.

Regional efforts in greater Chattanooga cross municipal borders. Businesses and nongovernmental organizations took the lead in New Regionalism partnerships that developed the vision of a clean and revitalized Chattanooga. The Chamber of Commerce provided the energy behind the Vision 2000 effort to identify sustainable development opportunities capable of transforming the city's national image. Nonprofit organizations took the lead in piecing together the Chattanooga Greenways, a seventy-five-mile network of parks and open space.[70] The city employs a sustainability officer to oversee and coordinate the city's various initiatives; an urban forester is devoted to greening the city.

In Chattanooga, "livability" has become a local "economic development issue."[71] The city has clearly improved the quality of its air and the quality of local life, factors that have also enhanced the city's attractiveness to business. Yet critics charge that Chattanooga's "Cinderella story" is in many ways a "mirage," a corporate-led "rebranding" tool manipulated by local elites to win public support for an agenda of downtown business renewal that has delivered only a modest commitment to sustainability.[72]

Austin

Austin, Texas, utilizes a system of "Sustainable Community" performance indicators to measure the city's progress in areas such as air quality, energy and water conservation, and the reduced use of hazardous materials. The Austin city council set a target of purchasing 5 percent or more of the city's energy from renewable resources. A locally established Office of Sustainability oversees these programs as well as the city's comprehensive plan, which emphasized green space protection and transit-oriented development.

The city gives priority to capital improvement projects that contribute to sustainability. City planners channel new development toward "smart growth zones" rather than to areas lying above the local aquifer.[73] Austin waives fees and provides other incentives to contractors who meet sustainability goals. The local utility offers customers a **Green Choice option**: utility customers can direct that the electricity used in their home be generated by wind, solar, and other renewable sources.

The city's **Green Building Program** provides technical assistance to developers for energy-efficient construction. The program also rates new homes and commercial buildings according to the sustainability of their construction practices. New homes are awarded one to five stars based on such factors as water and energy conservation, indoor air quality, and the use of recycled materials. Austin does more than incentivize; local ordinances require energy efficiency in new building construction.

The Green Building Program got results! It lowered the demand for energy during peak months and hours, reducing emissions from Austin Energy power plants and lessening the need to construct new power-generating facilities. The municipality served as an exemplar, building ten LEED-certified buildings including city hall.[74]

Boulder

Similar to Austin, Boulder (Colorado) established a Department of Community Planning and Sustainability. The city also mandates various green practices in new home construction. Most notably, the city awards **Green Points** to builders and contractors for a wide variety of sustainable construction practices, including: permeable surfacing; water efficiency; roof overhangs to provide natural shading; passive solar heating; enhanced insulation; heat recovery in ventilation; the use of engineered lumber in a floor or roof; the use of local-source materials; and even the employment of a green building consultant.[75] The city issues a building permit only *after* a project has earned a specified number of Green Points.

Also similar to Austin, Boulder's municipal government utilizes a system of statistical performance indicators to monitor environmental quality, to reduce its own energy and water consumption, to reduce the number of miles driven by city employees, and to prompt the increased use of recycled materials and renewable energy sources.

Boulder emphasizes public-private partnership. The Partners for a Clean Environment (PACE) program adopted a nonintrusive, nonregulatory approach to educate business owners as to the variety of actions they can take to help achieve environmental goals. A business can be certified as a "PACE partner" for curbing energy consumption, solid waste, and the use of hazardous materials.

A region-wide Boulder Valley Comprehensive Plan seeks to manage land uses beyond the city's borders. In 2006, the city council enacted (and voters approved!) a **local carbon tax** added to homeowner and business electric bills; the tax was part of the local strategy to reduce energy consumption and greenhouse gas emissions. The proceeds from the tax help to fund energy audits and incentives dispensed to landlords to increase the energy efficiency of rental buildings. In 2012, 60 percent of the voters in environmentally conscious Boulder chose to extend the tax another five years.[76]

Portland (Oregon)

Portland, as discussed in Chapter 9, has gained international recognition for its Urban Growth Boundary and its efforts to promote infill and transit-oriented development. Portland has also taken strong initiatives in other sustainability areas, including measures aimed at reducing carbon dioxide emissions and countering global warming. Portland designates fragile areas as **environmental zones** where development is approved "only in rare and unusual circumstances."[77]

Portland's Comprehensive Plan sets the targets not just for environmental goals such as reduced energy use and increased recycling; the plan also sets social goals such as the construction of new units of multifamily housing. A municipal Office of Sustainable Development oversees and coordinates various energy-savings and sustainability strategies.

Like Austin and Boulder, Portland utilizes a system of **sustainability benchmarks** to track just how well the city is doing in reducing pollution, promoting recycling, and providing citizens with new opportunities and a high quality of life. Portland's system of **comparative performance measurement** allows citizens to gauge just how well progress in Portland stacks up when compared to similar cities across the nation.

Seattle

Seattle has adopted a policy of environmentally friendly purchasing. Seattle further requires municipal agencies to prepare specific plans of action for the safe handling of hazardous wastes, the reduced generation of solid waste, and the conservation of energy and water. Seattle's Sustainable Indicators Project monitors progress and keeps public pressure focused on the achievement of declared policy ends. The King County Benchmark Program and the extensive reporting of performance measurements by the Puget Sound Regional Council further add to the pressures on municipal officials to achieve sustainability goals.[78]

Seattle has gained national renown for the degree to which neighborhood dialogue, citizen organizations, and nonprofit groups play an integral role in the process of achieving sustainability goals. Citizen groups keep the pressure on government to perform. A nonprofit organization, Sustainable Seattle, serves as the public's watchdog, criticizing public agencies when the performance indicators show that environmental goals are not being met.

Building codes and development regulation emphasize sustainable practices. The **Street Edge Alternatives (SEA Street) program** seeks to promote natural drainage by narrowing the width of streets, eliminating curbs and gutters, and adding trees and bordering green swales to increase storm-water retention and minimize runoff, erosion, and stream pollution.[79] A comprehensive plan, *Toward a Sustainable Seattle,* channels growth into a variety of mixed-use residential-commercial **urban villages** with the necessary densities to support mass transit, neighborhood stores, and even walking.[80]

Green Street-side Swale, Seattle, 2008. By allowing for the capture of water runoff from abutting sidewalks and roadways, this low-lying green swale allows for natural on-site filtration of water, minimizing the pollution that accompanies the underground piping and drainage of wastewater.

Courtesy of the Environmental Protection Agency. http://commons.wikimedia.org/wiki/File:Streetside_swale_Seattle.jpg.

AN ASSESSMENT: THE POLITICS OF SUSTAINABLE URBAN DEVELOPMENT

The new interest in sustainability is not limited to medium-sized cities and to university communities. Kent Portney reports that forty-five or more of the fifty-five largest cities in the United States have municipal offices to promote sustainable practices.[81] The nation's Big Five cities have ratcheted up their sustainability efforts, both to protect public health and to promote a local quality of life that will attract world-class businesses.[82]

New York Mayor Michael Bloomberg even attempted to establish a congestion zone that would lessen traffic by imposing a fee on vehicles that entered the city's downtown business district during business hours. But Bloomberg's efforts were ultimately denied by the New York State Assembly, which refused to give the city the legal authority to enact the system.[83] Los Angeles Mayor Antonio Villaraigosa instructed all city departments to develop sustainability plans as part of the "Mayor's Green Agenda." His successor, Mayor Eric Garcetti, named the city's first Chief Sustainability Officer. Chicago Mayor Richard M. Daley announced his intent to make his city the greenest in America, with a Sustainable Development division to promote green construction. Daley and his successor, Rahm Emanuel, created new bicycle lanes on major streets leading to the downtown. Philadelphia emphasizes the use of porous paving material; the city has also purchased municipal vehicles run on biofuels. Even pro-business, antigovernment Houston has established a Green Houston initiative to save energy and reduce pollution. (See Box 12.1, "Antigovernment Houston Turns to Sustainability.")

But despite all the excitement surrounding the vast new array of local green initiatives, cities in the United States generally lag behind their counterparts in Europe, Canada, and East Asia when it comes to sustainability practices.[84] Regional efforts in greater New York to protect the natural environment are relatively weak when compared to big cities elsewhere in the world. United States metropolitan areas continue to suffer a deficit in regional thinking and leadership.[85]

The situation is far from static. As Kent Portney has observed in reviewing the flood of local green initiatives that have emerged in recent years, "the gap" between the United States and cities in the rest of the world "had certainly been greatly narrowed."[86]

Globalization is one factor that has helped to narrow the gap. Transnational communication networks allow local officials in the United States to gain greater familiarity with green practices from abroad.[87] Supranational organizations highlight global environmental concerns and green practices. International environmental conferences, global nongovernmental organizations, consultant who work for cities around the world, and various committees of the United Nations all have spread sustainable development practices. As previously observed, even the International Olympics Committee has pushed host-city hopefuls toward green development.

Yet "politics" or, to be more accurate, the distribution of "power," prevents the adoption of still more formidable sustainability measures in the United States. While green construction codes have enjoyed newfound popularity, more extensive measures to promote energy and land conservation remain quite difficult to enact. The real potential for energy savings lies not in green building codes but, as seen in Europe, in the provision of fast and frequent mass transit coupled with effective land-use and planning

Box 12.1
Antigovernment Houston Turns to Sustainability

Houston is known as the free-enterprise city of the American South, a city that does not look fondly on zoning and other governmental regulations that intrude on self-reliance and business freedom. Hence, Houston's turn to sustainability in recent years is big news. In part, the increased concern for the natural environment reflects the policy agenda of Mayor Annise Parker. Yet something more significant is at work. The new interest in sustainability also reflects the importance of budget savings that a city can obtain by reducing its energy consumption. Also, even a "free market" city built on "Big Oil" must pay attention to the local quality of life in order to remain economically competitive, as world-class businesses have a large choice of locations.

In 2012, the U.S. Conference of Mayors honored Mayor Parker for the city's use of federal stimulus money to fund a variety of green building and energy reduction initiatives: the retrofit of city buildings; assistance to homeowners for weatherization efforts; incentives for commercial owners to reduce energy usage; the procurement of hybrid vehicles for the municipal fleet; and even the introduction of wind turbines for energy production. Houston also teamed up with Blue Cross and Blue Shield and a local nonprofit, Houston Bike Share, to place 200 gray-and-red bikes at 24 self-service kiosks located throughout the city, providing residents and workers with a health-oriented transportation alternative.

Still, despite these notable successes, in other important sustainability areas, free-market Houston lags behind other big cities. Commuter patterns in Houston reveal relatively little use of mass transit. Houston also ranks extremely low in terms of trash recycling but continues to be unwilling to impose a garbage collection fee to pay for recycling efforts.

Sources: City of Houston, "Mayor Annise Parker Announces Major Sponsorship for Houston Bike Share Program," March 2013 press release, www.greenhoustontx.gov/pressrelease20130109.html; Chris Moran, "Houston's Green Efforts Win Accolades," *Houston Chronicle*, April 25, 2012; Kent E. Portney, *Taking Sustainable Cities Seriously: Economic Development, the Environment, and Quality of Life in American Cities*, 2nd ed. (Cambridge, MA: MIT Press, 2013), 131–141, 198–203, 256–271, and 283–297.

regulations to promote in-fill and transportation-oriented development and walkability.[88] A suburban, privatist, car-oriented United States has been unwilling to make such an extensive investment in public transit or give the deference to strong central and regional land-use planning that is commonplace in Europe.

But we must be careful to avoid stereotyping. Local politics counts. Communities with traditions of local activism and citizen engagement—active neighborhood associations, petition signing, and attendance at council meetings—tend to adopt stronger green policies.[89]

THE URBAN FUTURE: U.S. CITIES IN A GLOBAL AGE

The prolonged economic recession of the early twenty-first century hurt cities. But even the return to a growing economy will not solve urban problems that have long-standing structural roots. Also, economic growth rates in the near future will not likely approach those of the boom years of previous decades. Even after the national economy has rebounded, cities and suburbs can expect to face a **new normal** of slow economic growth rates, low returns on investment, depressed housing markets, constricted inter-governmental revenues, anti-tax voter sentiment, and continuing budgetary difficulties. In such a setting, demands for economic development will continue to dominate local politics. City and suburban officials will face an exceedingly daunting task as they try to balance the demands for job creation, downtown revitalization, neighborhood develop-ment, immigrant incorporation, improved schools and public services, fiscal moderation, and the protection of the natural environment.

In important ways, the urban crisis of the early twenty-first century looks quite different from the urban crisis of the 1960s when a wave of riots swept cities and the core areas of big cities emptied as residents and businesses continued to flee to the suburbs. Gentrification has marked the rediscovery of many inner-city neighborhoods. Down-towns, too, have come back as a number of cities have found their place in a global economy. Still, despite these elements of urban health, the problems of inner-city poverty, failing schools, sprawled development, ghettoization, and coping with deindustializa-tion remain. If anything, capital mobility and the intensity of the global competition for businesses have made the economic and fiscal position of cities more tenuous than ever.

Urban leaders face the challenge of building viable political coalitions in support of practical policies that can ameliorate urban ills. A broad, overarching, national policy strictly focused on the revitalization of troubled cities is just not politically possible. Instead, urban leaders need to find workable change strategies that "fit" the political and economic realities of the suburbanized and globalized United States of the twenty-first century.

KEY TERMS

biodiesel and "cleaner" fuels
  (*p. 320*)
comparative performance
  measurement (*p. 322*)
contract compliance (*p. 309*)
creative class (*p. 307*)
de facto segregation (*p. 310*)
de jure segregation (*p. 310*)
disparity studies (*p. 309*)
Earned Income Tax Credit (EITC)
  (*p. 313*)
Energy Star standards (*p. 317*)
environmental zones, Portland's
  designation of (*p. 322*)

erosion of a city's property tax base,
  tax incentives and the (*p. 307*)
Green Building Program (*p. 321*)
Green Choice option, utility
  customers' (*p. 321*)
Green Points program, Boulder's
  (*p. 321*)
green roof (*p. 319*)
greening strategies for "shrinking"
  cities (*p. 319*)
hard factors in local economic
  development (*p. 307*)
heat island effect, a city's (*p. 319*)
industrial cluster (*p. 314*)

Notes

1. THE URBAN SITUATION

1. Robert Lang, *Edgeless Cities: Exploring the Elusive Metropolis* (Washington, DC: Brookings Institution, 2003).

2. Elizabeth Kneebone and Emily Garr, *The Suburbanization of Poverty: Trends in Metropolitan America, 2000 to 2008* (Washington, DC: Brookings Institution, January 2010), www.brookings.edu/~/media/Files/rc/papers/2010/0120_poverty_kneebone/0120_poverty_paper.pdf; Scott W. Allard and Benjamin Roth, *Strained Suburbs: The Social Service Challenges of Rising Suburban Poverty* (Washington, DC: Brookings Institution, October 2010), www.brookings.edu/research/reports/2010/10/07-suburban-poverty-allard-roth; and U.S. Department of Housing and Urban Development, "Meeting the Challenges of Suburban Poverty," *Evidence Matters* (Winter 2012): 16–23, www.huduser.org/portal/periodicals/em/EM_Newsletter_winter_2012_FNL.pdf.

3. Of course, even postindustrial cities are not purely reliant on office, finance, and entertainment functions. Cities can continue to be important centers of light and heavy manufacturing, even as nonindustrial sectors gain in relative importance. Bruce Katz and Jennifer Bradley, *The Metropolitan Revolution* (Washington, DC: Brookings Institution, 2013), argue that United States cities can be resurgent centers of manufacturing, if the national, state, and local governments give priority to making the appropriate investments in technology-oriented infrastructure. Also see Robert Puentes, "Transformative Infrastructure to Boost Exports and Manufacturing," testimony presented to the Joint Economic Committee, United States Congress, November 15, 2011, www.brookings.edu/research/testimony/2011/11/16-infrastructure-puentes.

4. Edward Glaeser, *Triumph of the City: How Our Greatest Invention Makes Us Richer, Smarter, Greener, Healthier, and Happier* (New York: Penguin, 2011).

5. Glaeser, *Triumph of the City*; Saskia Sassen, *The Global City: New York, London, Tokyo* (Princeton, NJ: Princeton University Press, 2001); Sassen, *Cities in a World Economy,* 4th ed. (Los Angeles: Pine Forge Press/SAGE Publications, 2011). For the classic works on the importance of clustering to economic development, see the writings of economist Michael Porter.

6. Ramon Grosfugel, "Global Logics in the Caribbean City System: The Case of Miami," in *World Cities in a World-System,* ed. Paul L. Knox and Peter J. Taylor (New York: Cambridge University Press, 1995), 164.

7. Zach Patton, "New Orleans' Latino Population Boom," *Governing,* February 29, 2012, www.governing.com/topics/health-human-services/gov-new-orleans-latino-population-boom.html.

8. Steven Greenhouse and Mireya Navarro, "The Hidden Victims," *New York Times,* September 17, 2001.

9. See the following writings by Richard Florida: *The Rise of the Creative Class* (New York: Routledge, 2004); *Cities and the Creative Class* (New York: Routledge, 2004); *Who's Your City: How the Creative Economy Is Making Where to Live the Most Important Decision of Your Life* (HarperCollins, 2009); and *The Rise of the Creative Class—Revisited* (New York: Basic Books, 2012).

10. Terry Nichols Clark with Richard Lloyd, Kenneth K. Wong, and Pushpam Jain, "Amenities Drive Urban Growth: A New Paradigm and Policy Linkages," in *The City as an Entertainment Machine,* ed. Terry Nichols Clark (Lanham, MD: Rowman and Littlefield, 2011), 209–239; the "Seine" quotation appears on p. 221. Also see Timothy J. Guilfoyle, *Millennium Park: Creating a Chicago Landmark* (Chicago: University of Chicago Press, 2006); and Dennis R. Judd, ed., *The Infrastructure of Play: Building the Tourist City* (Armonk, NY: M.E. Sharpe, 2002).

11. In Dennis R. Judd, "Constructing the Tourist Bubble," in *The Tourist City,* ed. Judd and Susan S. Fainstein (New Haven, CT: Yale University Press, 1999), 35–53.

12. Population estimates for Stockton and San Bernardino are from the California Departments of Finance, "Population Estimates for Cities, Counties, and the State—January 1, 2012 and 2013," (2013), www.dof.ca.gov/research/demographic/reports/estimates/e-1/. Other noteworthy Chapter 9 municipal bankruptcy filings in recent years include: Orange County, California (which filed for bankruptcy in 1994 and exited in a year and a half); the City of Vallejo, California (which filed in 2008 and exited from bankruptcy in 2011; population 120,000); and Jefferson County, Alabama (home of the City of Birmingham, which filed for bankruptcy in 2011).

13. Mary Williams Walsh and Jon Hurdle, "Harrisburg Sees Path to Restructuring Debts Without Bankruptcy Filing," *New York Times,* July 24, 2013.

14. Jim Christie (Reuters), "Stockton Bankruptcy the Result of 15-Year Spending Binge," *The Huffington Post,* July 4, 2012, www.huffingtonpost.com/2012/07/04/stockton-bankruptcy_n_1648634. html; Mary Williams Walsh, "Creditors of Stockton Fight City Over Pension Funding While in Bankruptcy," *New York Times,* August 24, 2012; Robert C. Pozen, "The Retirement Surprise in Detroit's Bankruptcy," *Brookings Institution,* July 25, 2013, www.brookings.edu/research/opinions/2013/07/25-detroit-bankruptcy-retirement-benefits-pozen; Jess Bidgood, "Plan to End Bankruptcy in Rhode Island City Gains Approval," *New York Times,* September 7, 2012.

15. Matt Bevilacqua, "Five Major Cities with Pension Troubles Worse than Detroit," *Next City,* July 19, 2013, http://nextcity.org/daily/entry/five-major-cities-with-pension-troubles-worse-than-in-detroit; Melanie Hicken, "Moody's Downgrades Chicago Amid Pension Crisis," *CNN Money,* March 4, 2014, http://money.cnn.com/2014/03/04/news/chicago-credit-rating/.

16. John F. McDonald, "What Happened to and in Detroit?" *Urban Studies* 51, no. 16 (December 2014): 3309–3329.

17. George C. Galster, *Driving Detroit: The Quest for Respect in the Motor City* (Philadelphia: University of Pennsylvania Press, 2012).

18. City-Data.com, "Detroit, Michigan," www.city-data.com/city/Detroit-Michigan.html. Also see Reynolds Farley, Sheldon Danziger, and Harry J. Holzer, *Detroit Divided* (New York: Russell Sage Foundation, 2002).

19. Nathan Bomey and John Gallagher, "How Detroit Went Broke: The Answers May Surprise You—and Don't Blame Coleman Young," *Detroit Free Press,* September 15, 2013.

20. Brent D. Ryan, *Design After Decline: How America Rebuilds Shrinking Cities* (Philadelphia: University of Pennsylvania Press, 2012), xii.

21. Mary Williams Walsh and Jonathan Glater, "Contracts Now Seen as Being Rewritable," *New York Times,* March 31, 2009.

22. Michael De Angelis and Xiaowei Tian, "United States: Chapter 9 Municipal Bankruptcy—Utilization, Avoidance, and Impact," in *Until Debt Do Us Part: Subnational Debt, Insolvency, and Markets,* ed. Otaviano Cavuto and Lili Liu (Washington, DC: International Bank for Reconstruction and Development/World Bank, 2013), 326–328.

23. For the distinction between power as "social production" as opposed to "social control," see Clarence N. Stone, *Regime Politics: Governing Atlanta, 1946–88* (Lawrence: University Press of Kansas, 1989), 8–9, 222–226, and 289.

24. Elisabeth Rosenthal, "Across Europe, Irking Drivers Is Urban Policy," *New York Times,* June 26, 2011.

25. Pietro S. Nivola, *Laws of the Landscape: How Policies Shape Cities in Europe and America* (Washington, DC: Brookings Institution Press, 1999); H.V. Savitch and Paul Kantor, *Cities in the International Marketplace: The Political Economy of Urban Development in North America and Western Europe* (Princeton, NJ: Princeton University Press, 2002).

26. For the classic statement that identifies privatism as imposing a severe limit on the actions of U.S. local governments, see Sam Bass Warner Jr., *The Private City* (Philadelphia: University of Pennsylvania Press, 1968).

27. John L. Mikesell, *Fiscal Administration: Analysis and Applications for the Public Sector,* 8th ed. (Boston, MA: Cengage, 2011), 648–649.

28. Jess Bidgood, "Plan to End Bankruptcy of Rhode Island City Gains Approval," *New York Times,* September 6, 2012; Michael Corkery and Matthew Dolan, "Detroit's Bankruptcy Sparks Pension Brawl," *Wall Street Journal,* July 20–21, 2013; Mary Williams Walsh, "Judge Rules Calpers Lien Is Invalid," *New York Times*, October 2, 2014; Melody Petersen, "Cities May Use Bankruptcy to Cut Worker Pensions," *Los Angeles Times*, October 2, 2014.

29. Mary Williams Walsh, "Detroit Turns Bankruptcy into Challenge of Banks," *New York Times,* February 4, 2014; Walsh, "Judge Rules Calpers Lien Is Invalid."

30. Congressional Budget Office, *The Impact of Unauthorized Immigrants on the Budgets of State and Local Governments* (Washington, DC: CBO, 2007),

31. U.S. Census Bureau, *2010 American Community Survey.* See Jill H. Wilson and Audrey Singer, "Immigrants in 2010 Metropolitan America: A Decade of Change," a report of the Metropolitan Policy Program of The Brookings Institution, Washington, D.C., October 2011. Also see Audrey Singer, Susan Wiley Hardwick, and Caroline Brettell, eds., *Twenty-First Century Gateways: Immigrant Incorporation in Suburban America* (Washington, DC: Brookings Institution, 2008).

32. De Angelis and Tian, "United States: Chapter 9 Municipal Bankruptcy—Utilization, Avoidance, and Impact," 317.

33. The figure is for 2008. See "State and Local Tax Policy: What Are the Sources of Revenue for Local Government?" in Tax Policy Center, *The Tax Policy Briefing Book: A Citizens' Guide for the 2012 Election and Beyond* (Urban Institute/Brookings Institution, 2009), www.taxpolicycenter.org/briefing-book/state-local/revenues/local_revenue.cfm.

34. Citizens Budget Commission, *A Poor Way to Pay for Medicaid: Why New York Should Eliminate Local Funding for Medicaid* (New York: December 2011), 12.

35. Critics often unfairly deride the federal assistance extended to New York as an unwise "bailout" of a fiscally imprudent, ultraliberal city. While the federal assistance program was exceedingly helpful, it was not a bailout or an act of charity. Federal taxpayers did not repay the debts that New York City had incurred. In fact, the national government actually made a small profit, charging the city interest on the federal loans. The city also paid a fee for the insurance backing or guarantees that higher levels of government provided each new bond issue. The assistance was also accompanied by new oversight arrangements that infringed on the city's political autonomy. A state-appointed Fiscal Control Board and the U.S. Department of Treasury both gained the authority to review New York City's major taxing and spending plans. As Detroit and other cities and school districts facing a fiscal emergency would later discover, the establishment of a state fiscal control board or federal oversight authority entails a shift in power, with decision-making authority over important matters removed from the hands of local elected leaders and given to state- and federally-appointed overseers.

36. Eric Jaffe, "The Time the Teacher's Union Saved the City from Bankruptcy," *The Atlantic Cities,* July 24, 2013, www.theatlanticcities.com/jobs-and-economy/2013/07/time-teachers-union-save-new-york-city-bankruptcy/6306/; Sam Roberts, "When New York Teetered on the Brink of Bankruptcy,"

New York Times, July 24, 2013; Seymour P. Lachman and Robert Polner, *The Man Who Saved New York: Hugh Carey and the Great Fiscal Crisis of 1975* (Albany, NY: SUNY Press, 2010).

37. Chad Livengood, "Bills for State Aid for Detroit Pensions to Be Introduced Next Week," *Detroit News,* April 29, 2014. Jackie Calmes, "$300 Million in Detroit Aid, But No Bailout," *New York Times,* September 27, 2013, describes the quite limited steps that the Obama administration could take in aiding Detroit without having to win support in Congress for a bailout program.

38. Peter Eisinger, "Is Detroit Dead?" *Journal of Urban Affairs* 36, no. 1 (2014): 2.

39. U.S. Census Bureau, "Population Distribution and Change, 2000 to 2010," 2010 Census Briefs (March 2011), www.census.gov/prod/cen2010/briefs/c2010br-01.pdf.

40. U.S. Census Bureau, *County and City Data Book: 2000,* Table B-1; U.S. Census Bureau, "Large Suburban Cities in West Are Fastest-Growing, Census Bureau Reports," press release, July 10, 2003, www.census.gov/Press-Release/www/2003/ch03-106.html. New Orleans would soon join the list of the nation's quickly growing cities, with population returning to the city after the huge exodus that occurred in the immediate wake of the destruction wrought by Hurricane Katrina and the city's extensive flooding.

41. William H. Frey, "Did the 2010 Census Tell Us Anything New?" *Upfront (The Brookings Institution),* December 22, 2010, www.brookings.edu/blogs/up-front/posts/2010/12/22-census-findings-frey.

42. Frey, "Did the 2010 Census Tell Us Anything New?"

43. Ann Markusen, Peter Hall, Scott Campbell, and Sabina Deitrick, *The Rise of the Gunbelt: The Military Remapping of Industrial America* (New York: Oxford University Press, 1991).

44. Census figures are from 2009, as reported by the U.S. Census Bureau, Statistical Abstract of the United States, 2012.

45. Census figures are from 2009, as reported by the U.S. Census Bureau, Statistical Abstract of the United States, 2012, Table 708: "Household Income, Family, and Per Capita Income and Individuals, and Families Below Poverty Level by City: 2008." The Benton Harbor, Camden, and East St. Louis figures are 2007 U.S. Census estimates, as reported by City-Data.com.

46. Alex Finkelstein, "Highest Foreclosure Rates Remain in CA, FL, NV and AZ, Says Mid-year Reality Track Report," *Real Estate Channel,* July 30, 1998, www.realestatechannel.com/us-markets/ residential-real-estate-1/realtytrac-mid-year-foreclosures-james-j-saccacio-alex-finkelstein-1158.php.

47. See, for instance, Justin B. Hollander, *Sunburnt Cities: The Great Recession, Depopulation, and Urban Planning in the American Sunbelt* (New York: Routledge, 2011).

48. Margery Austin Turner, Rob Santos, Diane K. Levy, Doug Wissoker, Claudia Aranda, and Rob Pitingolo, *Housing Discrimination Against Racial and Ethnic Minorities 2012* (Washington, DC: U.S. Department of Housing and Urban Development, 2013). The full report runs over a hundred pages. An executive summary is available at www.huduser.org/portal/Publications/pdf/HUD-514_HDS2012_execsumm.pdf.

49. Sean F. Reardon and Demetra Kalogrides, "Brown Fades: The End of Court-Ordered School Desegregation and the Resegregation of American Public Schools," *Journal of Policy Analysis and Management* 31, no. 4 (Fall 2012): 876–904.

50. Erica Frankenberg and Gary Orfield, eds., *The Resegregation of Suburban Schools: A Hidden Crisis in American Education* (Cambridge: Harvard Education Press, 2012).

51. Kneebone and Garr, *The Suburbanization of Poverty,* 11, Fig. 4.

52. Annette Steinacker, "Economic Restructuring of Cities, Suburbs, and Nonmetropolitan Areas, 1977–92," *Urban Affairs Review* 34, no. 2 (November 1998): 229; John Brennan and Edward W. Hill, *Where Are the Jobs? Cities, Suburbs, and the Competition for Employment* (Washington, DC: Brookings Institution, November 1999).

53. Kneebone and Garr, *The Suburbanization of Poverty.*

2. THE EVOLUTION OF CITIES AND SUBURBS

1. Edward C. Banfield, *The Unheavenly City Revisited* (Boston: Little, Brown, 1974), 25–51.

2. Kenneth T. Jackson, *Crabgrass Frontier: The Suburbanization of the United States* (New York: Oxford University Press, 1985), 14–15.

3. Jackson, *Crabgrass Frontier*, 12–45, esp. 13.

4. Sam Bass Warner Jr., *Streetcar Suburbs: The Process of Growth in Boston, 1870–90,* 2nd ed. (Cambridge, MA: Harvard University Press, 1978), 164–165. Also see Ronald Dale Karr, "Brookline Rejects Annexation, 1873," in *Suburbia Re-examined,* ed. Barbara M. Kelly (New York: Greenwood Press, 1989), 103–110.

5. Warner, *Streetcar Suburbs*, 165.

6. Joe William Trotter Jr., ed., *The Great Migration in Historical Perspective: New Dimensions of Race, Class, and Gender* (Bloomington: University of Indiana Press, 1991); James N. Gregory, *The Southern Diaspora: How the Great Migrations of Black and White Southerners Transformed America* (Chapel Hill: University of North Carolina Press, 2007).

7. Joel Garreau, *Edge City: Life on the New Frontier* (New York: Doubleday, 1991); Robert Fishman, *Bourgeois Utopias: The Rise and Fall of Suburbia* (New York: Basic Books, 1987).

8. Robert D. Atkinson, "Technological Change and Cities," *Cityscape: A Journal of Policy Development and Research* 3, no. 1 (1998): 135–136.

9. Joseph Schilling and Jonathan Logan, "Greening the Rustbelt," *Journal of the American Planning Association* 74, no. 4 (Autumn 2008): 451–466; Cleveland City Planning Commission, "Re-Imagining Cleveland: A More Sustainable Cleveland: Citywide Strategies for Reuse of Vacant Land," adopted 2008; and John Gallagher, *Reimagining Detroit: Opportunities for an American City* (Detroit: Wayne State University Press, 2010). Justin B. Hollander, *Sunburnt Cities: The Great Recession, Depopulation and Urban Planning in the American Sunbelt* (New York: Routledge, 2011), observes how numerous neighborhoods in otherwise growing Sunbelt cities like Phoenix and Orlando nonetheless experienced extensive home mortgage defaults and property abandonment. Hollander advises that these Sunbelt communities pay increased attention to the land repurposing and greening strategies that are being adopted by shrinking cities in the United States Rustbelt.

10. Janet Rothenberg Pack, ed., *Sunbelt/Frostbelt: Public Policies and Market Forces in Metropolitan Development* (Washington, DC: Brookings Institution Press, 2005), traces the continuing effects of government spending and regulatory actions on the regional population and job shift.

11. Jackson, *Crabgrass Frontier*, 204.

12. The VA program offered no-money-down loans to veterans. In more recent years, the FHA required down payments of around 3 percent or 3.5 percent.

13. Quoted in Jackson, *Crabgrass Frontier*, 207

14. Douglas Massey, "Origins of Economic Disparities: The Historical Role of Housing Segregation," in *Segregation: The Rising Costs for America,* ed. James H. Carr and Nandinee K. Kutty (New York: Routledge, 2008), 72.

15. Ibid., 208.

16. Citizens Commission on Civil Rights, "A Decent Home . . . A Report on the Continuing Failure of the Federal Government to Provide Equal Housing Opportunity" (Washington, DC: 1983), reprinted in *Critical Perspectives on Housing*, ed. Rachel G. Bratt, Chester Hartman, and Ann Myerson (Philadelphia: Temple University Press, 1986), 299.

17. For a good overview of the evolution of FHA anti-city actions and various other practices that produced the racial segregation of the American city, see Massey, "Origins of Economic Disparities," 39–80.

18. Citizens Commission on Civil Rights, "A Decent Home," 301.

19. Thomas J. Sugrue, *The Origins of the Urban Crisis: Race and Inequality in Postwar Detroit* (Princeton, NJ: Princeton University Press, 1996), 64.

20. Mike Davis, "How Eden Lost Its Garden: A Political History of the Los Angeles Landscape," in *The City: Los Angeles and Urban Theory at the End of the Twentieth Century*, ed. Allen J. Scott and Edward J. Soja (Berkeley and Los Angeles: University of California Press, 1996), 169.

21. Rachael A. Woldoff, *White Flight/Black Flight: The Dynamics of Racial Change in an American Neighborhood* (Ithaca, NY: Cornell University Press, 2011), 142.

22. Roger Biles, *The Fate of Cities: Urban America and the Federal Government, 1945–2000* (Lawrence, KS: University Press of Kansas, 2011), 179–180.

23. Edward J. Pinto, "Too Many Americans Are in Homes They Can't Afford," *The Guardian,* October 8, 2013, www.aei.org/article/economics/financial-services/housing-finance/too-many-americans-are-in-homes-they-cant-afford/.

24. David Streitfeld and Louis Story, "F.H.A. Problems Raising Concerns of Policy Makers," *New York Times,* October 8, 2009.

25. David H. Stevens, President and CEO of the Mortgage Bankers Association and former FHA commissioner, "Sustainable Housing Finance: Perspectives on Reforming FHA," written statement prepared for the Subcommittee on Housing and Insurance Services, Committee on Financial Services, U.S. House of Representatives, April 10, 2013, http://financialservices.house.gov/uploadedfiles/hhrg-113-ba04-wstate-dstevens-20130410.pdf.

26. Jeff Crump et al., "Cities Destroyed (Again) for Cash: Forum on the U.S. Foreclosure Crisis," *Urban Geography* 29, no. 8 (2008): 745–784, quote on 749.

27. Ibid.

28. Gregory D. Squires and Charis E. Kubrin, *Privileged Places: Race, Residence, and the Structure of Opportunity* (Boulder, CO: Lynne Rienner, 2006); Dwight M. Jaffee and John M. Quigley, "Housing Policy, Mortgage Policy, and the Federal Housing Administration," paper presented at the NBER Conference on Measuring and Managing Fiscal Risk, Evanston, Illinois, February 2007, updated May 2009, http://faculty.haas.berkeley.edu/jaffee/Papers/MS_ch5_DwightJaffeeJohnQuigley_p163-213.pdf.

29. Margery Austin Turner, Eric Toder, Rolf Pendall, and Claudia Sharygin, *How Would Reforming the Mortgage Interest Deduction Affect the Housing Market?* (Washington, DC: The Urban Institute, March 2013), www.taxpolicycenter.org/UploadedPDF/412776-How-Would-Reforming-the-Mortgage-Interest-Deduction-Affect-the-Housing-Market.pdf; Joint Committee on Taxation, U.S. Congress, *Estimates of Federal Tax Expenditures for Fiscal Years 2012–2017* (Washington, DC: U.S. Government Printing Office, 2013), Table 1.

30. Bruce Bartlett, "The Sacrosanct Mortgage Interest Deduction, *New York Times,* August 6, 2013, http://economix.blogs.nytimes.com/2013/08/06/the-sacrosanct-mortgage-interest-deduction/?_r=0.

31. Will Fischer and Chye-Ching Huang, *Mortgage Interest Deduction Is Ripe for Reform* (Washington, DC: Center for Budget Priorities, June 25, 2013), www.cbpp.org/files/4-4-13hous.pdf.

32. Joint Committee on Taxation figures, reported by Jeanne Sahadi, "Mortgage Deduction: America's Costliest Tax Break," *CNNMoney.com,* April 18, 2010, http://money.cnn.com/2010/04/14/pf/taxes/mortgage_interest_deduction/index.htm.

33. Peter Dreier, "Will President Bush Reform the Mansion Subsidy?" *Shelterforce* 144 (November/December 2005), table titled "Distribution of Tax Benefits for Mortgage Deduction, FY2004," www.nhi.org/online/issues/144/mansionChart1.html. For more current figures that underscore the inequities of the tax deductions for homeowners, see Fischer and Huang, "Mortgage Interest Deduction Is Ripe for Reform."

34. See, for instance, Joseph F.C. DiMento, "Stent (or Dagger?) in the Heart of Town: Urban Freeways in Syracuse, 1944–1967," *Journal of Planning History* 8, no. 2 (2009): 133–161.

35. Raymond A. Mohl, "Planned Destruction: The Interstates and Central City Housing," in *The Making of Urban America,* 3rd ed., ed. Raymond A. Mohl and Roger Biles (Lanham, MD: Rowman and Littlefield, 2012), 294–295.

36. Carlton Wade Basmajian, *Atlanta Unbound: Enabling Sprawl Through Policy and Planning* (Philadelphia: Temple University Press, 2013).

37. John H. Mollenkopf, *The Contested City* (Princeton, NJ: Princeton University Press, 1983), 103–109; Margaret Pugh O'Mara, "Uncovering the City in the Suburb," in *The New Suburban History,* ed. Kevin Kruse and Thomas J. Sugrue (Chicago: University of Chicago Press, 2006), 60–63.

38. Richard M. Bernard and Bradley R. Rice, "Introduction," in *Sunbelt Cities: Politics and Growth Since World War II,* ed. Richard M. Bernard and Bradley R. Rice (Austin: University of Texas Press, 1983), 12.

39. Virginia Mayer and Margaret Downs, *The Pentagon Tilt: Regional Biases in Defense Spending and Strategy* (Washington, DC: Northeast-Midwest Institute, January 1983), 9.

40. Mia Gray, Elyse Golob, Ann R. Markusen, and Sam Ock Park, "The Four Faces of Silicon Valley," in *Second Tier Cities: Rapid Growth Beyond the Metropolis,* ed. Ann R. Markusen, Yong-Sook Lee, and Sean DiGiovanna (Minneapolis: University of Minnesota Press, 1999), 293–299.

41. Joe R. Feagin, *Free Enterprise City: Houston in Political and Economic Perspective* (New Brunswick, NJ: Rutgers University Press, 1988), 54–55, 63–71, 186–188, 203–204.

42. Joe W. Trotter and Jared N. Day, *Race and Renaissance: African Americans in Pittsburgh Since World War II* (Pittsburgh: University of Pittsburgh Press, 2010), 68–71.

43. Meghan McCarthy, "A History of Urban Renewal in San Antonio," *Planning Forum,* vols. 13–14 (2009): 53–56.

44. Melita Marie Garza and Flynn McRoberts, "Addison Settles with Hispanics," *Chicago Tribune,* August 8, 1997.

45. Arnold R. Hirsch, *Making the Second Ghetto: Race and Housing in Chicago, 1940–60* (Chicago: University of Chicago Press, 1983 and 1998) provides the classic statement on the making of the second ghetto in Chicago.

46. Robert Pear, "New York Admits to Racial Steering in Housing Lawsuit," *New York Times,* July 1, 1992.

47. Jonathan Rothwell and Douglas S. Massey, "The Effect of Density Zoning on Racial Segregation in U.S. Urban Areas," *Urban Affairs Review* 44, no. 6 (June 2009): 779–806.

48. Heywood T. Sanders, "The Political Economy of Sunbelt Urban Development: Building the Public Sector," paper presented at the annual meeting of the American Political Science Association, New York, September 2–5, 1994.

49. Steven P. Erie and Scot A. MacKenzie, "The L.A. School and Politics Noir: Bringing the Local State Back In," *Journal of Urban Affairs* 31, no. 5 (2009): 545–552; Steven P. Erie, *Globalizing L.A.: Trade, Infrastructure, and Regional Development* (Stanford, CA: Stanford University Press, 2004).

50. Jackson, *Crabgrass Frontier*, 191.

51. Massey, "Origins of Economic Disparities," 48.

52. David M. Gordon, "Capitalist Development and the History of American Cities," in *Marxism and the Metropolis,* 2nd ed., ed. William K. Tabb and Larry Sawers (New York: Oxford University Press, 1984), 40.

53. David L. Clark, "Improbable Los Angeles," in *Sunbelt Cities: Politics and Growth Since World War II,* ed. Bernard and Rice, 271–272.

54. William Fulton, *The Reluctant Metropolis: The Politics of Urban Growth in Los Angeles* (Baltimore: Johns Hopkins University Press, 1997, 2001 [paperback]), 15.

55. Massey, "Origins of Economic Disparities," 56.

56. *Shelley v. Kraemer,* 334 U.S. 1 (1948).

57. Trotter and Day, *Race and Renaissance*, 66–68.

58. Eliot M. Tretter with M. Anwar Sounny-Slitine, *Austin Restricted: Progressivism, Zoning, Private Racial Covenants, and the Making of a Segregated City,* final report prepared for the Institute for Urban Policy Research and Analysis, University of Texas, 2012, www.academia.edu/1888949/Austin_Restricted_Progressivism_Zoning_Private_Racial_Covenants_and_the_Making_of_a_Segregated_City.

59. The story of Levittown is presented by Thomas J. Sugrue, "Jim Crow's Last Stand: The Struggle to Integrate Levittown," in *Second Suburb: Levittown, Pennsylvania,* ed. Dianne Harris, 175–199; the quotations appear on pp. 175–179.

60. Margery Austin Turner and Stephen L. Ross, "How Racial Discrimination Affects the Search for Housing," in *The Geography of Choice: Race and Housing Choice in Metropolitan America,* ed. Xavier de Souza Briggs (Washington, DC: Brookings Institution, 2005), 79–100, especially 86 and 92. On the persistence of housing discrimination, see Margery Austin Turner, Todd M. Richardson, and Stephen Ross, "Housing Discrimination in Metropolitan America," in *Fragile Rights Within Cities: Government, Housing, and Fairness,* ed. John Goering (Lanham, MD: Rowman & Littlefield, 2007), 39–60.

61. Even one of the nation's most pro-business periodicals has recognized the existing continuing racial disparities in mortgage lending and home insurance. See "The New Redlining," *U.S. News & World Report,* April 17, 1995, 51–58.

62. Joseph P. Treaster, "Insurer Must Pay $100.5 Million in Redlining Case," *New York Times,* October 27, 1998.

63. Gregory D. Squires, "Prospects and Pitfalls of Fair Housing Efforts," in *Segregation*, ed. Carr and Kutty, 317.

64. Christi Harlan, "Why Gramm Strangled Bank Bill," *Austin American-Statesman,* October 23, 1998.

65. Allan J. Fishbein, general counsel for the Center for Community Change, testimony before the Senate Committee on Banking, Housing, and Urban Affairs, Hearings on the "Financial Services Act of 1998," June 24, 1998

66. Alex Schwartz, "The Limits of Community Reinvestment: The Implementation of Community Reinvestment Agreements in Chicago, Cleveland, New Jersey, and Pittsburgh," paper presented at the annual meeting of the Urban Affairs Association, Fort Worth, Texas, April 22–25, 1998.

67. William C. Apgar and Mark Duda, "The Twenty-Fifth Anniversary of the Community Reinvest-ment Act: Past Accomplishments and Future Regulatory Challenges," *Economic Policy Review* (June 2003): 174. See also Michael S. Barr, "Credit Where It Counts: Maintaining a Strong Community Reinvestment Act," Brookings Institution Research Brief, Washington, DC, May 2005, www.brookings. edu/~/media/Files/rc/reports/2005/05metropolitanpolicy_barr/20050503_cra.pdf.

68. Conservative talk radio host Rush Limbaugh, in his February 11, 2010 nationally syndicated broadcast, blamed the CRA for causing lenders to engage in unwise lending practices that led to the nation's housing finance meltdown:

> The Community Reinvestment Act was hatched by Carter, it was expanded by Clinton, it was used by ACORN and their allies to wreck the housing market by wrecking the mortgage market, by demanding that mortgages be given to people who could no way pay them back. Ergo, the sub-prime mortgage crisis. . . . I don't defend AIG [the giant mortgage insurance institution that was unable to pay its obligations on defaulted loans], but they were treating loans—derivatives, if you will—that was based fundamentally on loans developed by liberal policies.

See Greg Lewis, "Limbaugh Resurrects CRA Falsehoods, Claims Affordable Housing Was Designed to Wreck the Whole System," *MediaMatters for America,* February 11, 2010, http:// mediamatters.org/limbaughwire/2010/02/11.

For a more thoughtful conservative critique that argues that the Clinton administration's use of CRA performance measures constituted virtual "quotas" that scared banks into making unwise loans, see Peter J. Wallison, "Cause and Effect: Government Policies and the Financial Crisis," *American Enterprise Institute,* November 25, 2008, www.aei.org/article/economics/financial-services/cause-and-effect-outlook.

69. Alex F. Schwartz, *Housing Policy in the United States,* 2nd ed. (New York: Routledge, 2010), 283.

70. Kathleen C. Engel and Patricia A. McCoy, "From Credit Denial to Predatory Lending: The Challenge of Sustaining Minority Home Ownership," in *Segregation*, ed. Carr and Kutty, 91–99; William Apgar and Allegra Calder, "The Dual Housing Market: The Persistence of Discrimination in Mortgage Lending," in *The Geography of Choice: Race and Housing Choice in Metropolitan America,* ed. Xavier de Souza Briggs, 102–103 and 112. On the concentration and "racialization" of higher-cost subprime loans in Sacramento, see Jesus Hernandez, "Redlining Revisited: Mortgage Lending Patterns in Sacramento 1930–2004," *International Journal of Urban and Regional Research* 33, no. 2 (June 2009): 291–313.

71. Dan Immergluck, *Foreclosed: High-Risk Lending, Deregulation, and the Undermining of America's Mortgage Market* (Ithaca, NY: Cornell University Press, 2009), esp. 55–58, 162–163, and chap. 3.

72. Elizabeth Kneebone and Jane Williams, *New Census Data Shows Metro Poverty's Persistence in 2012* (Washington, DC: Brookings Institution, 2013), www.brookings.edu/~/media/research/files/reports/2013/09/19%20census%20data%20poverty/poverty2012update.pdf. Also see Emily Garr and Elizabeth Kneebone, *The Suburbanization of Poverty: Trends in Metropolitan America, 2000 to 2008* (Washington, DC: The Brookings Institution, 2010), www.brookings.edu/~/media/research/files/papers/2010/1/20%20poverty%20kneebone/0120_poverty_paper.pdf.

73. Wendell Cox, "Core City Growth Mainly Below Poverty Line," *New Geography,* July 12, 2012, www.newgeography.com/content/002956-core-city-growth-mainly-below-poverty-line.

74. Rachael A. Woldoff and Seth Ovadia, "Not Getting Their Money's Worth: African-American Disadvantages in Converting Income, Wealth, and Education into Residential Quality," *Urban Affairs Review* 45, no. 1 (September 2009): 66–91.

75. Charles M. Lamb, *Housing Segregation in Suburban America since 1960: Presidential and Judicial Politics* (New York: Cambridge University Press, 2005).

76. Anne Power, Jörg Ploger, and Astrid Winkler, *Phoenix Cities: The Fall and Rise of Great Industrial Cities* (Bristol, UK: Policy Press, University of Bristol, 2010).

77. Portland's Urban Growth Boundary is a noteworthy exception. The Portland UGB and other U.S. regional growth management measures are discussed in further detail in Chapters 9 and 10.

3. RECENT TRENDS

1. Heather Smith and William Graves, "Gentrification as Corporate Growth Strategy: The Strange Case of Charlotte, North Carolina and the Bank of America," *Journal of Urban Affairs* 127, no. 4 (2005): 403–428.

2. See Japonica Brown-Saracino, ed., *The Gentrification Debates: A Reader* (London and New York: Routledge, 2010); and Loretta Lees, Tom Slater, and Elvin Wyly, eds., *The Gentrification Reader* (London and New York: Routledge, 2010).

3. Neil Smith and Peter Williams, "Alternatives to Orthodoxy: Invitation to a Debate," in *Gentrification of the City,* ed. Neil Smith and Peter Williams (Boston: Allen and Unwin, 1986), 1.

4. For descriptions of how gentrifying is changing New York City's Harlem and Chicago South Side neighborhoods such as Bronzeville, see: Timothy Williams and Tanzina Vega, "As East Harlem Develops, Its Accent Starts to Change," *New York Times,* January 21, 2007; Sam Roberts, "No Longer Majority Black, Harlem Is in Transition," *New York Times,* January 5, 2010; Derek S. Hyra, *The New Urban Renewal: The Economic Transformation of Harlem and Bronzeville* (Chicago: University of Chicago Press, 2008). The focus of Lance Freeman, *There Goes the 'Hood: Views of Gentrification from the Ground Up* (Philadelphia: Temple University Press, 2006), 40–48, goes beyond Harlem to also describe the vast changes that black gentrification is bringing to Brooklyn's Clinton Hill neighborhood.

5. Alan Ehrenhalt, *The Great Inversion and the Future of the American City* (New York: Alfred A. Knopf, 2012). According to Ehrenhalt (p. 233), the rebound of inner-city areas is so extensive that the term gentrification no longer captures it, "as it is a much larger force than the coming of 'gentry' to previously dilapidated neighborhoods . . . 'Gentrification' is too small a word for it." Of course, Ehrenhalt also recognizes that cities continue to face great problems.

Yet, despite this recognition, Ehrenhalt (pp. 6–7) overstates gentrification's impact on changing the balance between cities and suburbs: "The truth is that we are living at a moment in which the massive outmigration of the affluent that characterized the second half of the twentieth century is coming to an end. And we need to adjust our perceptions of cities, suburbs, and urban mobility as a result." Despite Ehrenhalt's exaggerated claim, the truth is that dual migration continues and that gentrification does not alter to a very great degree the overall balance of cities and suburbs. The American middle class continues to leave cities for the suburbs, and central cities continue to have disproportionately large concentrations of the poor who require public assistance. Poorer and working-class families, in large part, continued to be "kept out" of the suburbs by exclusionary zoning and land-use practices. Despite Ehrenhalt's claims (pp. 8–14), the rising price of gasoline and jammed highways will not be sufficient to lead the middle class to forsake their preferences for suburban living. Gentrification does not counterbalance the continuing exodus of middle-class Americans and taxable wealth to the suburbs.

6. 2012 American Community Survey figures, reported by Michael Lewyn, "Gentrification, Shmentrification," *Planetizen,* October 1, 2013, www.planetizen.com/node/65386.

7. Maureen Kennedy and Paul Leonard, "Dealing with Neighborhood Change: A Primer on Gentrification and Policy Choices," discussion paper prepared for the Brookings Institution Center on Urban and Metropolitan Policy, Washington, DC, 2001, www.brookings.edu/es/urban/gentrification/gentrification.pdf.

8. George C. Galster, Roberto G. Quercia, Alvaro Cortes, and Ron Malega, "The Fortunes of Poor Neighborhoods," *Urban Affairs Review* 39 (November 2003): 205–227.

9. Suleiman Osman, *The Invention of Brownstone Brooklyn: Gentrification and the Search for Authenticity in Postwar New York* (New York: Oxford University Press), especially 13–16, 23–37 and 192–206.

10. Japonica-Brown Saracino, *A Neighborhood That Never Changes: Gentrification, Social Preservation, and the Search for Authenticity* (Chicago: University of Chicago Press, 2009).

11. Jason Hackworth, "Post-Recession Gentrification in New York City," *Urban Affairs Review* 37, no. 6 (2002): 815–843; John J. Betancur, "The Politics of Gentrification: The Case of West Town in Chicago," *Urban Affairs Review* 37, no. 6 (July 2002): 780–814.

12. Sharon Zukin, *Naked City: The Death and Life of Authentic Urban Places* (New York: Oxford University Press, 2010), 237–239.

13. Loretta Lees, "A Reappraisal of Gentrification: Towards a 'Geography of Gentrification,'" *Progress in Human Geography* 24, no. 3 (2000): 389–408. See also Hackworth, "Post-Recession Gentrification in New York City"; Betancur, "The Politics of Gentrification."

14. Saracino, in *A Neighborhood That Never Changes: Gentrification, Social Preservation, and the Search for Authenticity*, distinguishes among the prevailing attitudes of three different types of gentrifiers in the contemporary city: pioneers, homesteaders, and social preservationists. Osman, in *The Invention of Brownstone Brooklyn*, in contrast to Saracino, portrays the initial wave of gentrifiers, the urban pioneers, as not very interested in upgrading and changing their neighborhood. These new arrivals rejected the consumerism of mass society and valued the "authenticity" of the inner-city areas that became their home.

15. Patrick Rérat, Ola Söderström, and Etienne Piguet, "New Forms of Gentrification: Issues and Debate," *Population, Space and Place* 16, no. 5 (2010): 335–343; Mark Davidson and Loretta Lees, "New-Build Gentrification: Its Histories, Trajectories, and Critical Geographies," *Population, Space and Place* 16, no. 5 (2010): 395–411.

16. Rowland Atkinson and Gary Bridge, "Introduction," in Atkinson and Bridge, eds. *Gentrification in a Global Context* (London: Routledge, 2005), 4–5, present a brief overview of the pros and cons of gentrification.

17. Daniel Monroe Sullivan, "Reassessing Gentrification: Measuring Residents' Opinions Using Survey Data," *Urban Affairs Review* 42, no. 2 (March 2007): 583–593, especially 586–588.

18. Saracino, *A Neighborhood That Never Changes*, 213–248.

19. Freeman, *There Goes the 'Hood,* esp. 62–74, 92–94, and 190–202.

20. Andrew V. Papachristos, Chris M. Smith, Mary L. Scherer, and Melissa A. Fugiero, "More Coffee, Less Crime? The Relationship Between Gentrification and Neighborhood Crime Rates in Chicago, 1991–2005," *City & Community* 10, no. 3 (2011): 215–240. Other studies have reported mixed results when seeking to ascertain the degree to which gentrification leads to reduced or increased crime rates in a community. By bringing new wealth into a poor community, gentrification may produce new opportunities for property theft and street robberies. Also see Yan Y. Lee, "Gentrification and Crime: Identification Using the 1994 Northridge Earthquake in Los Angeles," *Journal of Urban Affairs* 32, no. 5 (2010): 549–577.

21. Tom Slater, "The Eviction of Critical Perspectives from Gentrification Research," *International Journal of Urban and Regional Research* 30, no. 4 (December 2006): 737–757; Kathe Newman and Elvin K. Wyly, "The Right to Stay Put, Revisited: Gentrification and Resistance to Displacement in New York City," *Urban Studies* 43, no. 1 (January 2006): 23–57.

22. Betancur, "The Politics of Gentrification."

23. Sullivan, "Reassessing Gentrification," 589–591.

24. Neil Smith, *The New Frontier: Gentrification and the Revanchist City* (London: Routledge, 1996).

25. E.K. Wyly and D.J. Hammel, "Islands of Decay in Seas of Renewal: Housing Policy and the Resurgence of Gentrification," *Housing Policy Debate* 10, no. 4 (1999): 716.

26. Mary Pattillo, *Black on the Block: The Politics of Race and Class in the City* (Chicago: University of Chicago Press, 2007), 284. Rachael A. Woldoff, *White Flight/Black Flight: The Dynamics of Racial Change in an American Neighborhood* (Ithaca, NY: Cornell University Press, 2011), describes the tensions and the different expectations regarding proper behavior that can divide middle-class black residents from lower-class blacks in neighborhoods undergoing transition. Her research, though, does not focus on gentrifying areas of the city.

27. John Betancur, "Gentrification and Community Fabric in Chicago," *Urban Studies* 48, no. 2 (2011): 383–406.

28. Loretta Lees, "Gentrification and Social Mixing: Towards an Inclusive Urban Renaissance?" *Urban Studies* 45, no. 12 (2008): 2440–2470.

29. Dax-Devlon Ross, "Separate and Unequal in D.C.," *Next City,* April 8, 2013; a long excerpt from this article can be found, without subscription, at http://nextcity.org/daily/entry/forefront-excerpt-separate-and-unequal-in-d.c.

30. Pauline Lipman, "Mixed-Income Schools and Housing Policy in Chicago: A Critical Examination of the Gentrification/Education/'Racial' Exclusion Nexus," in *Mixed Communities: Gentrification by Stealth?* ed. Gary Bridge, Tim Butler, and Loretta Lees (Bristol, England: Policy Press, 2012), 106. See Lipman's larger discussion, 105–107.

31. Robert J. Chaskin and Mark L. Joseph, "Building 'Community' in Mixed-Income Developments: Assumptions, Approaches, and Early Experiences," *Urban Affairs Review* 45, no. 3 (2010): 299–335; the quotation appears on 323.

32. Renia Ehrenfeucht and Marla Nelson, "Young Professionals as Ambivalent Change Agents in New Orleans after the 2005 Hurricanes," *Urban Studies* 50, no. 4 (2013): 825–841.

33. Hackworth, "Post-Recession Gentrification in New York City," 835–838; Betancur, "The Politics of Gentrification," 806–808.

34. Jason Hackworth, *The Neoliberal City* (Ithaca, NY: Cornell University Press, 2007); Harley F. Etienne, *Pushing Back the Gates: Neighborhood Perspectives on University-Driven Revitalization in West Philadelphia* (Philadelphia, PA: Temple University Press, 2012), especially 90–92. Etienne shows how the University of Pennsylvania shared an interest with the City of Philadelphia in upgrading the much-troubled and crime-ridden inner-city area that surrounded the university's campus.

35. Zukin, *Naked City,* p. xi.

36. Ibid., p. x.

37. Michael Indergaard, *Silicon Alley: The Rise and Fall of a New Media District* (New York: Routledge, 2004), 26–27, 102–112.

38. Zukin, *Naked City,* 23–27 and 137.

39. Edward G. Goetz, "Where Have All the Towers Gone? The Dismantling of Public Housing in U.S. Cities," *Journal of Urban Affairs* 33, no. 4 (2011): 267–287.

40. Costas Spirou, *Urban Tourism and Urban Change: Cities in a Global Economy* (New York: Routledge, 2011), 211–213.

41. Susan J. Popkin, Bruce Katz, Mary K. Cunningham, Karen D. Brown, Jeremy Gustafson, and Margery A. Turner, *A Decade of Hope VI: Research Findings and Policy Challenges* (Washington, DC: Urban Institute and Brookings Institution, 2004), 44–45; Betancur, "The Politics of Gentrification," 790.

42. Betancur, "The Politics of Gentrification," 787–789, 801–803.

43. Roman A. Cybriwsky, David Ley, and John Western, "The Political and Social Construction of Revitalized Neighborhoods: Society Hill, Philadelphia, and False Creek, Vancouver," in *Gentrification of the City,* ed. Neil Smith and Peter Williams, 119.

44. Etienne, *Pushing Back the Gates*, 79.

45. Joyce Gelb and Michael Lyons, "A Tale of Two Cities: Housing Policy and Gentrification in London and New York," *Journal of Urban Affairs* 15, no. 4 (1993): 345–366.

46. Kennedy and Leonard, "Dealing with Neighborhood Change," 30.

47. Murtaza H. Baxamusa, "Empowering Communities through Deliberation: The Model of Community Benefits Agreements," *Journal of Planning and Education Research* 27, no. 3 (March 2008): 261–276.

48. Tony Robinson, "Gentrification and Grassroots Resistance in San Francisco's Tenderloin," *Urban Affairs Review* 30, no. 4 (1995): 483–513.

49. Michelle Boyd, "Defensive Development: The Role of Racial Conflict in Gentrification," *Urban Affairs Review* 43, no. 6 (July 2008): 751–776.

50. Diane K. Levy, Jennifer Comey, and Sandra Padilla, *In the Face of Gentrification* (Washington, DC: The Urban Institute, 2006), 33–43, www.urban.org/UploadedPDF/411294_gentrification.pdf.

51. City of New York Mayor Bill de Blasio, *Housing New York: A Five-Borough 10-Year Plan* (New York: Office of the Mayor, 2014), www.nyc.gov/html/housing/assets/downloads/pdf/housing_plan. pdf; the "mandatory" quote appears on p. 8. Also see Mireya Navarro and Michael M. Grynbaum, "De Blasio Makes Push for Affordable Units in His $8.2 Billion Housing Plan," *New York Times,* May 6, 2014; and Charles V. Bagli, "Plan to Redevelop Brooklyn Sugar Refinery Hits Roadblock: New Mayor," *New York Times,* February 24, 2014.

52. Rolf Pendall, "From Hurdles to Bridges: Local Land-Use Regulations and the Pursuit of Affordable Rental Housing," paper prepared for the conference Revisiting Rental Housing: A National Policy Summit, November 2006, www.jchs.harvard.edu/publications/rental/revisiting_rental_symposium/ papers/rr07–11_pendall.pdf.

53. Levy, Comey, and Padilla, *In the Face of Gentrification*, 53–65.

54. David Imbroscio, "From Redistribution to Ownership: Toward an Alternative Urban Policy for America's Cities," *Urban Affairs Review* 49, no. 6 (2013): 787–820, esp. 800–801.

55. Timothy Williams, "City Helping Residents Resist the New Gentry," *New York Times,* March 4, 2014.

56. Studies generally rank New York, London, and Tokyo as the top three world cities. The ranking presented here draws on Paul K. Knox, "Globalization and Urban Economic Change," *Annals of the American Academy of Political and Social Science* (May 1997), 22–23. Of course, the exact ranking of a city in the world hierarchy depends on just how a researcher measures and weighs each aspect of a city's being "global." One important study ranks New York and London as the top two cities in terms of the "connectedness" of their businesses to other businesses around the world. Tokyo, while still an important global hub, falls to sixth place behind Hong Kong, Paris, and Singapore; see Ben Derudder et al., "Pathways of Change: Shifting Connectivities in the World City Network, 2000–08," *Urban Studies* 47, no. 9 (2010): 1861–1877. For a more detailed explanation of their "globalizing cities index" and how it ranked Tokyo only as the world's 6th most important city on the "Financial Control Index," see the research team's larger study: Peter J. Taylor et al., *Global Urban Analysis: A Survey of Cities in Globalization* (London, UK: Earthscan, 2011).

57. Just how far below New York do Los Angeles and other important U.S. cities ranks in terms of their global significance? By 2008, Chicago ranked as only Number 19 and Los Angeles and San Francisco had dropped to 40th and 46th places, respectively, in terms of the "connectivity" of their firms to enterprises located in other cities. See Derudder et al., "Pathways to Change," 1868.

58. Peter J. Taylor and Robert E. Lang, *U.S. Cities in the "World Cities Network"* (Washington, DC: Brookings Institution, February 2005), www.brookings.edu/~/media/Files/rc/reports/2005/02cities_ taylor/20050222_worldcities.pdf. Taylor and Land rank U.S. cities solely according to their global connectivity.

59. Charles S. Suchar, "The Physical Transformation of Metropolitan Chicago," in *The New Chicago: A Social and Cultural Analysis,* ed. John P. Koval et al. (Philadelphia: Temple University Press, 2006), 56–76.

60. John Rennie Short, *Globalization, Modernity, and the City* (New York: Routledge, 2012), 7.

61. Robert Atkinson and Howard Wial, *The Implications of Service Offshoring for Metropolitan Economies* (Washington, DC: Brookings Institution, February 2007), www.brookings.edu/~/media/Files/rc/reports/2007/02cities_atkinson/20070131_offshoring.pdf.

62. Zachary P. Neal, *The Connected City: How Networks Are Shaping the Modern Metropolis* (New York: Routledge, 2013), 137–142 and 159–161.

63. Susan M. Wachter and Kimberly A. Zeuli, eds., *Revitalizing American Cities* (Philadelphia: University of Pennsylvania Press, 2014).

64. Indergaard, *Silicon Alley.*

65. Joel Kotkin, *The New Geography: How the Digital Revolution Is Reshaping the American Landscape* (New York: Random House, 2000), 9.

66. Leonard I. Ruchelman, *Cities in the Third Wave: The Technological Transformation of Urban America* (Chicago: Burnham, 2000), 91.

67. Matt Richtel, "In Utah, Public Works Project in Digital," *New York Times,* November 17, 2003. While Utah's growth coalition supports investment in the region's technological infrastructure, critics, naturally, respond that UTOPIA is an expensive "drain" on taxpayers. See Vince Horiuchi, "Lawmakers: Is It Time to Let UTOPIA Die?" *Salt Lake City Tribune,* September 19, 2012.

68. Edward Wyatt, "A City Wired for Growth," *New York Times,* February 4, 2014.

69. William M. Rohe, *The Research Triangle: From Tobacco Road to Global Prominence* (Philadelphia, PA: University of Pennsylvania Press, 2011), 96–105 and 178–190.

70. Saskia Sassen, *The Global City,* 2nd ed. (Princeton, NJ: Princeton University Press, 2001), 294–300; Sassen, *Cities in a World Economy,* 4th ed. (Los Angeles: Pine Forge Press/Sage, 2012).

71. Edward Glaeser, *Triumph of the City* (New York: Penguin, 2011), 252.

72. Jacob L. Vigdor, "Immigration and the Revival of American Cities: From Preserving Manufacturing Jobs to Preserving the Housing Market," a report of the Partnership for a New American Economy and the Americas Society/Council of the Americas, September 2013, www.as-coa.org/sites/default/files/ImmigrationUSRevivalReport.pdf.

73. Robert Courtney Smith, "Mexicans: Civic Engagement, Education, and Social Progress Achieved and Inhibited," in *One Out of Three: Immigrant New York in the Twenty-First Century,* ed. Nancy Foner (New York: Columbia University Press, 2013).

74. Brookings Institution, *Phoenix in Focus: A Profile from Census 2000* (Washington, DC, November 2003), www.brookings.edu/reports/2003/11_livingcities_Phoenix.aspx; Audrey Singer and Jill H. Wilson, *The Impact of the Great Recession on Metropolitan Immigration Trends* (Washington, DC: Brookings Institution, December 2010), www.brookings.edu/~/media/Files/rc/papers/2010/1216_immigration_singer_wilson/1216_immigration_singer_wilson.pdf; U.S. Census Bureau, "State & County QuickFacts: Phoenix (city), Arizona," revised June 28, 2013.

75. U.S. Census Bureau, "State & County QuickFacts: New York (city), New York," revised June 27, 2013.

76. Min Zhou, "Chinese: Diverse Origins and Destinies," in Foner, *One Out of Three,* 120–127.

77. Yvonne M. Lau, "Chicago's Chinese Americans: From Chinatown and Beyond," in *The New Chicago,* ed. Koval et al., 168–181.

78. Richard C. Jones, ed., *Immigrants Outside Megalopolis: Ethnic Transformation in the Heartland* (Lanham, MD: Lexington Books, 2008).

79. See the November 2003 reports of the Living Cities Project: *Denver in Focus: A Profile from Census 2000*; and *Kansas City in Focus: A Profile from Census 2000*; both published in Washington, DC, by the Brookings Institution.

80. Jeremy Hein, *Ethnic Origins: The Adaptation of Cambodian and Hmong Refugees in Four American Cities* (New York: Russell Sage Foundation, 2006); Karl Byrand, "The Quest for Home: Sheboygan's Hmong Population," in *Immigrants Outside Megalopolis,* ed. Jones, 189–211.

81. Janet L. Abu-Lughod, *New York, Chicago, Los Angeles: America's Global Cities* (Minneapolis: University of Minnesota Press, 1999), 374; Karin Aguilar-San Juan, "Staying Vietnamese: Community and Place in Orange County and Boston," *City and Community* 4, no. 1 (March 2005): 37–65; Madhulika S. Khandelwal, *Becoming an American, Being Indian: An Immigrant Community in New York City* (Ithaca, NY: Cornell University Press, 2002), 20–21 and 56.

82. Padma Rangaswamy, "Asian Indians in Chicago," in *The New Chicago*, ed. Koval et al., 130–131.

83. U.S. Census Bureau, *2007 American Community Survey*, Table 41.

84. Sassen, *Cities in a World Economy*, chap. 6.

85. U.S. Congressional Budget Office, *The Impact of Unauthorized Immigrants on the Budgets of State and Local Governments* (Washington, DC, December 2007).

86. Partnership for a New American Economy, "Immigrants Boost U.S. Economic Vitality through the Housing Market," press release, June 20, 2013, www.renewoureconomy.org/research/immigrants-boost-u-s-economic-vitality-through-the-housing-market/. See also the larger report: Vigdor, "Immigration and the Revival of American Cities."

87. David Gladstone and Peter Marina, "Stemming Urban Decline in the Most Urbanized State in the United States: Latino Immigration and Urban Revitalization in New Jersey," paper presented at the annual meeting of the Urban Affairs Association, San Antonio, Texas, March 20, 2014.

88. Carol Morello and Luz Lazo, "Baltimore Puts Out Welcome Mat for Immigrants, Hoping to Stop Population Decline," *Washington Post,* July 24, 2012.

89. Fran Spielman, "Emanuel: Police Won't Detain Undocumented Immigrants Except for Serious Crime," *Chicago Sun-Times,* July 10, 2012.

90. Joe Smydo, "Pittsburgh Promise Aims to Lure Hispanics with Financial Aid," *Pittsburgh Post-Gazette,* September 27, 2012.

91. John P. Koval and Kenneth Fidal, "Chicago: The Immigrant Capital of the Heartland," in *The New Chicago*, ed. Koval et al., 102.

92. Jerome Straughan and Pierrette Hondagneu-Sotelo, "From Immigrants in the City, to Immigrant City," in *From Chicago to L.A.: Making Sense of Urban Theory,* ed. Michael J. Dear (Thousand Oaks, CA: Sage, 2002), 199–203, here 201.

93. Reuel R. Rogers, "Race-Based Coalitions Among Minority Groups: Afro-Caribbean Immigrants and African-Americans in New York City," *Urban Affairs Review* 39, no. 3 (January 2004): 283–317.

94. Hank V. Savitch and Paul Kantor, *Cities in the International Marketplace: The Political Economy of Urban Development in North America and Western Europe* (Princeton, NJ: Princeton University Press, 2002), 14–15.

95. William J. Mitchell and Anthony M. Townsend, "Cyborg Agonistes: Disaster and Reconstruction in the Digital Electronic Era," in *The Resilient City: How Cities Recover from Disaster,* ed. Lawrence J. Vale and Thomas J. Campanella (New York: Oxford University Press, 2005), 313–334.

96. Randy Shilts, *And the Band Played On: Politics, People, and the AIDS Epidemic* (New York: St. Martin's Press, 1987).

97. Thomas L. Friedman, *The Lexus and the Olive Tree: Understanding Globalization* (New York: Anchor Books, 2000), 104–106; see also Friedman's discussion, pp. 13–14 and 112–142.

98. Susan E. Clarke and Gary L. Gaile, *The Work of Cities* (Minneapolis: University of Minnesota Press, 1998), 107–214.

99. Mark Purcell, *Recapturing Democracy: Neoliberalization and the Struggle for Alternative Urban Futures* (New York: Routledge, 2008), 109–152.

100. Donald Rosdil, *The Cultural Contradictions of Progressive Politics: The Role of Cultural Change and the Global Economy in Local Policymaking* (New York: Routledge, 2012). Terry Nichols Clark, in *The City as an Entertainment Machine* (Lanham, MD: Lexington Books, 2011), 209–236, also describes the emergence of a "new political culture" that has led cities to give new emphasis to the provision of lifestyle amenities and policies that maintain ecological sustainability. Where it emerges, the new political culture serves as a political counterweight to the demands of local growth coalitions.

101. Michael E. Porter, *The Competitive Advantage of Nations* (New York: Free Press, 1990); Michael E. Porter, "Location, Competition, and Economic Development: Local Clusters in a Global Economy," *Economic Development Quarterly* 14, no. 1 (2000): 15–34; Yasuyuki Motoyama, "What Was New about Cluster Theory? What Could It Answer and What Could It Not Answer?" *Economic Development Quarterly* 22, no. 4 (2008): 353–363.

102. Robert J. Stimson, Roger R. Stough, and Brian H. Roberts, *Regional Economic Development: Analysis and Planning Strategy,* 2nd ed. (Berlin and New York: Springer, 2006), 252.

103. Mark Muro and Bruce Katz, *The New "Cluster Moment": How Regional Innovation Clusters Can Foster the Next Economy* (Washington, DC: Brookings Institution, September 2010), www.brookings.edu/~/media/Files/rc/papers/2010/0921_clusters_muro_katz/0921_clusters_muro_katz.pdf.

104. Larry Ledebur and Jill Taylor, *Akron, Ohio: A Restoring Prosperity Case Study* (Washington, DC: Brookings Institution, September 2008), www.brookings.edu/~/media/Files/rc/reports/2007/05 metropolitanpolicy_vey/200809_Akron.pdf.

105. Porter, "Location, Competition, and Economic Development," 17.

106. Eugenie L. Birch, "Anchor Institutions in the Northeast Megaregion: An Important But Not Fully Recognized Resource," in *Revitalizing American Cities,* ed. Wachter and Zeuli, 207–223.

107. Rosdil, *The Cultural Contradictions of Progressive Politics,* 10.

108. Savitch and Kantor, *Cities in the International Marketplace,* 313–345, esp. 344–345.

4. WHO HAS THE POWER?

1. For the classic statement of power elite theory, see Floyd Hunter's study of mid-century Atlanta (which he referred to as "Regional City"), *Community Power Structure* (Garden City, NY: Anchor Books, 1963, originally published in 1953). A quarter of a century later, Hunter updated the study and came largely to the same conclusions: *Community Power Succession: Atlanta's Policymakers Revisited* (Chapel Hill: University of North Carolina Press, 1980). Also see William G. Domhoff, "Power at the Local Level—Atlanta: Floyd Hunter Was Right," *Who Rules America?* October 2005, www2.ucsc.edu/whorulesamerica/local/atlanta.html.

2. Arnold Fleischmann and Joe R. Feagin, "The Politics of Growth-Oriented Urban Alliances: Comparing Old Industrial and New Sunbelt Cities," *Urban Affairs Quarterly* 23 (December 1987): 207–232.

3. Anthony Knapp and Igor Vojnovic, "Rethinking the Growth Machine: How to Erase a Chinatown from the Urban Core," *Urban Geography* 42, no. 1 (2013): 53–85; Angela Podagrosi and Igor Vojnovic, "Tearing Down Freedman's Town and African American Displacement: The Good, the Bad, and the Ugly of Urban Revival," *Urban Geography* 29, no. 4 (2008): 371–401.

4. The phrase "effectively heard" is from Robert A. Dahl's classic statement of pluralism, *Who Governs? Democracy and Power in an American City* (New Haven, CT: Yale University Press, 1961). For criticisms of Dahl's work and pluralist theory, see G. William Domhoff, "Power at the Local Level—Who Really Ruled in Dahl's New Haven?" in his blog *Who Rules America?* September 2005, www2.ucsc. edu/whorulesamerica/local/new_haven.html. For criticisms of both power elite theory and the pluralist perspective, see Alan Harding, "The History of Community Power," in *Theories of Urban Power,* 2nd ed., ed. Jonathan Davies and David Imbroscio (Thousand Oaks, CA: SAGE Publications, 2009): 27–39.

5. Stephen Samuel Smith, "Hugh Governs? Regime and Education Policy in Charlotte, North Carolina," *Journal of Urban Affairs* 19, no. 3 (1997): 247–274.

6. Royce Hanson, Harold Wolman, David Connolly, Katherine Pearson, and Robert McManmon, "Corporate Citizenship and Urban Problem Solving: The Changing Civic Role of Business Leaders in American Cities," *Journal of Urban Affairs* 22, no. 1 (2010): 8.

7. Harvey Molotch, *Urban Fortunes: The Political Economy of Place,* 20th Anniversary ed. (Berkeley: University of California Press, 2007).

8. Nicholas A. Phelps, "The Growth Machine Stops? Urban Politics and the Making and Remaking of an Edge City," *Urban Affairs Review* 48, no. 5 (September 2012): 670–700.

9. Paul E. Peterson, *City Limits* (Chicago: University of Chicago Press, 1981).

10. Ibid., 37–38.

11. Judith Grant Long, *Public-Private Partnerships for Major League Sports Facilities* (New York: Routledge, 2013).

12. The literature on this subject is vast. See Mark S. Rosentraub, *Major League Losers: The Real Cost of Sports and Who's Paying for It* (New York: Basic Books, 1997), esp. 129–170; Ian Hudson, "Bright Lights, Big City: Do Professional Sports Teams Increase Employment?" *Journal of Urban Affairs* 21, no. 4 (1999): 397–408; Charles A. Santo, "Beyond the Economic Catalyst Debate: Can Public Consumption Benefits Justify a Municipal Stadium Investment?" *Journal of Urban Affairs* 29, no. 5 (December 2007): 455–479; Geoffrey Propheter, "Are Basketball Arenas Catalysts of Economic Development?" *Journal of Urban Affairs* 34, no. 4 (October 2012): 441–459.

13. Mark S. Rosentraub, "The Local Context of a Sports Strategy for Economic Development," *Economic Development Quarterly* 20, no. 3 (August 2006): 278–291; Costas Spirou and Larry Bennett, *It's Hardly Sportin': Stadiums, Neighborhoods, and the New Chicago* (DeKalb: Northern Illinois University Press, 2003), 21–28.

14. Neil deMause, "Stop the Subsidy-Sucking Stadiums," *The Nation,* August 5, 2011.

15. Reed Albergotti and Cameron McWhirter, "A Stadium's Costly Legacy Throws Taxpayers for a Loss," *Wall Street Journal,* July 12, 2011; Craig Fehrman, "A Major League Mistake," *Cincinnati Magazine,* November 1, 2011; Sharon Coolidge, "Tax Rebate from 96's Stadium Plan May Be Gone," *Cincinnati Enquirer,* September 8, 2013. Even a more "balanced" stadium agreement announced in 2014 revealed little real balance. The Bengals consented to higher heights for surrounding downtown buildings; the team also agreed to pick up part of the costs of a new replay system. But governmental bodies assumed most of the costs for stadium improvements (including new Wi-Fi capacity for the stadium) and also gave the Bengals permission to play two "home" games outside the county without compensating the county for lost ticket and parking revenues. See Sharon Coolidge, "Bengals, County Reach Major Deal on The Banks," *Cincinnati Enquirer,* April 17, 2014.

16. Neil deMause and Joana Cagan, *Field of Schemes: How the Great Stadium Swindle Turns Public Money into Private Profit,* rev. and exp. ed. (Lincoln, NE: University of Nebraska Press, 2008), 106. The *Field of Schemes* website also provides links to newspaper articles and various other updates concerning stadium deals in cities across the country: www.fieldofschemes.com.

17. Bill Torpy, "Stadium Move Angers Its Neighbors," *Atlanta Journal-Constitution,* November 13, 2013. Also see the comments of former Atlanta Braves pitcher John Rocker, "Who Wants to Fight Crime on the Way to the Ballpark?" *WND: Commentary,* November 20, 2013, www.wnd.com/2013/11/who-wants-to-fight-crime-on-way-to-ballpark/.

18. Long, *Public-Private Partnerships for Major League Sports Facilities,* chap. 7; Mark S. Rosentraub and David Swindell, "Of Devils and Details: Bargaining for Successful Public/Private Partnerships between Cities and Sports Teams," *Public Administration Quarterly* 33, no. 1 (2009): 118–148.

19. Mark S. Rosentraub, *Major League Winners: Using Sports and Cultural Centers as Tools for Economic Development* (Boca Raton, FL: CRC Press, 2010).

20. Steven P. Erie, Vladimir Kogan, and Scott A. MacKenzie, "'Redevelopment, San Diego Style': The Limits of Public-Private Partnerships," *Urban Affairs Review* 45, no. 5 (2010): 644–678; Steven P. Erie, Vladimir Kogan, and Scott A. MacKenzie, *Paradise Plundered: Fiscal Crisis and Government Failures in San Diego* (Palo Alto, CA: Stanford University Press, 2011), chap. 6.

21. Peter Eisinger, "The Politics of Bread and Circuses: Building the City for the Visitor Class," *Urban Affairs Review* 35, no. 3 (January 2000): 316–333.

22. Heywood T. Sanders, *Convention Center Follies: Politics, Power, and Public Investment in American Cities* (Philadelphia: University of Pennsylvania Press, 2014), p. x.

23. Ibid., 7–8.

24. Ibid., chap. 4, offers persuasive documentation in numerous cases where the economic impact of a new convention center has fallen far short of the predictions made in the seemingly impressive statistical analyses prepared by outside consultants.

25. Todd Swanstrom, "Semisovereign Cities: The Politics of Urban Development," *Polity* 21, no. 1 (1988): 88–96.

26. Clarence N. Stone, "Systemic Power in Community Decision Making: A Restatement of Stratification Theory," *American Political Science Review* 74 (December 1980): 978.

27. Unless otherwise noted, the basic outline of regime theory is taken from Clarence N. Stone's classic work, *Regime Politics—Governing Atlanta: 1946–88* (Lawrence: University of Kansas Press, 1989), 242. For a brief review of the contributions of regime theory, see Karen Mossberger, "Urban Regime Analysis," in *Theories of Urban Power,* 2nd ed., ed. Davies and Imbroscio, pp. 40–54.

28. Cynthia Horan, "Racializing Urban Regimes," *Journal of Urban Affairs* 24, no. 1 (2002): 19–33.

29. Stephen Samuel Smith, *Boom for Whom? Education, Desegregation and Development in Charlotte* (Albany, NY: State University of New York Press, 2004).

30. The classification of regime types presented here was developed by Clarence N. Stone, "Summing Up: Urban Regimes, Development Policy, and Political Arrangements," in *The Politics of Urban Development,* ed. Clarence N. Stone and Heywood T. Sanders (Lawrence: University of Kansas Press, 1987), 272–273.

31. H.V. Savitch, Takashi Tsukamoto, and Ronald K. Vogel, "Civic Culture and Corporate Regime in Louisville," *Journal of Urban Affairs* 20, no. 4 (2008): 437–460. The quoted material can be found on p. 452.

32. David L. Imbroscio, *Reconstructing City Politics: Alternative Economic Development and Urban Regimes* (Thousand Oaks, CA: Sage, 1997), 97–138. Imbroscio advocates decentralized, community-based economic development initiatives. See his *Urban America Reconsidered: Alternatives for Governance and Policy* (Ithaca, NY: Cornell University Press, 2010).

33. Donald L. Rosdil, *The Cultural Contradictions of Progressive Politics: The Role of Cultural Change and the Global Economy in Local Policymaking* (New York: Routledge, 2013).

34. Pierre Clavel, *Activists in City Hall: The Progressive Response to the Reagan Era in Boston and Chicago* (Ithaca, NY: Cornell University Press, 2010), 1–95. For a partial listing of Menino's development projects, see Tom Acitelli, "Mayor Menino's Greatest Real Estate Hits," *Curbed,* March 28, 2013, http://boston.curbed.com/archives/2013/03/mayor-meninos-greatest-real-estate-hits.php; and Tom Acitelli, "It's Go Time for Developers as Menino Exits Office," *Curbed,* July 22, 2013, http://boston.curbed.com/archives/2013/07/its-go-time-for-developers-as-menino-leaves-office.php. Also see Casey Ross, "Businesses Hurry to Win Approval in Boston: Mayoral Change Could Slow Projects," *The Boston Globe,* July 22, 2013.

35. William E. Nelson Jr., *Black Atlantic Politics: Dilemmas of Political Empowerment in Boston and Liverpool* (Albany: State University of New York Press, 2000), 72–78.

36. Pierre Clavel and Wim Wiewel, eds., *Harold Washington and the Neighborhoods: Progressive City Government in Chicago, 1983–87* (New Brunswick, NJ: Rutgers University Press, 1991); Clavel, *Activists in City Hall,* 96–170.

37. John J. Betancur and Douglas C. Gills, "Community Development in Chicago: From Harold Washington to Richard M. Daley," *Annals of the American Academy of Political and Social Science* 594, no. 1 (2004): 92–108; Dan Immergluck, "Building Power, Losing Power: The Rise and Fall of a Prominent Community Economic Development Coalition," *Economic Development Quarterly* 19, no. 3 (August 2005): 211–224.

38. Joel Rast, "Governing the Regimeless City: The Frank Zeidler Administration in Milwaukee, 1948–1960," *Urban Affairs Review* 42, no. 1 (2006): 81–112.

39. Peter Burns and Matthew O. Thomas, "The Failure of the Nonregime: How Katrina Exposed New Orleans as a Regimeless City," *Urban Affairs Review* 41, no. 4 (2006): 517–527.

40. Chester Hartman with Sarah Carnochan, *City for Sale: The Transformation of San Francisco,* rev. ed. (Berkeley: University of California Press, 2002).

41. Dawn Garcia, "Who Holds the Keys to Power in S.F. under Agnos?" *San Francisco Chronicle,* July 11, 1988.

42. Richard Edward DeLeon, *Left Coast City: Progressive Politics in San Francisco, 1975–91* (Lawrence: University of Kansas Press, 1992), 12.

43. G. William Domhoff, "Why San Francisco Is Different: Progressive Activists and Neighborhoods Have Had Big Impact," *Who Rules America?* blog, September 2005, http://sociology.ucsc.edu/whorulesamerica/local/san_francisco.html.

44. Richard E. DeLeon, "San Francisco: The Politics of Race, Land Use, and Ideology," in *Racial Politics in American Cities,* 3rd ed., ed. Rufus P. Browning, Dale Rogers Marshall, and David H. Tabb (New York: Longman, 2003), 168–169, and 186–193.

45. John Ritter, "Green Win Could Have Impact Beyond City Race," *USA Today,* December 4, 2003.

46. Larry N. Gerston, *Not So Golden After All: The Rise and Fall of California* (Boca Raton: FL: CRC Press, 2012), 133–135.

47. Heather Knight, "Swept Off Mid-Market, S.F.'s Homeless Cluster Nearby," *San Francisco Chronicle,* January 11, 2014.

48. Domhoff, "Why San Francisco Is Different."

49. DeLeon, *Left Coast City,* 7–8, 132–133, and 142–149.

50. Laura Wolf-Powers, "Community Benefits Agreements and Local Government: A Review of the Evidence," *Journal of the American Planning Association* 76, no. 2 (2010): 141–159.

51. Joshua Sabatini, "SF Citizens Advisory Committee Recommends Revisions to Mid-Market Community Benefit Agreements," *San Francisco Examiner,* January 6, 2014.

52. Dan Rosenblum, "Building Low, Selling High," *Next City,* February 18, 2013, http://nextcity.org/daily/entry/forefront-excerpt-selling-low-building-high.

53. Clarence N. Stone, "Looking Back to Look Forward: Reflections on Urban Regime Analysis," *Urban Affairs Review* 40, no. 3 (January 2005): 309–341. The quotation appears on p. 326.

5. Formal Structure and Leadership Style

1. Cory Eucalitto, Kristen De Pena, and Shannan Younger, "Municipal Bankruptcy: An Overview for Local Officials," *State Budget Solutions,* February 26, 2013, www.statebudgetsolutions.org/publications/detail/municipal-bankruptcy-an-overview-for-local-officials. Fourteen states require that a municipality receive permission from a state authority before filing for bankruptcy; see National Association of State Budget Officers, "Municipal Bankruptcy & the Role of the States," August 21, 2012, p. 2, www.nasbo.org/sites/default/files/pdf/Municipal%20Bankruptcy%20%26%20the%20Role%20of%20the%20States.pdf.

2. *City of Clinton v. Cedar Rapids and Missouri Railroad Company,* 24 Iowa 455 (1868).

3. John F. Dillon, *Commentary on the Law of Municipal Corporations,* 5th ed. (Boston: Little, Brown, 1911), vol. 1, sec. 237, emphasis added.

4. *Atkins v. Kansas*, 191 U.S. 207 at 220–221 (1903); and *Trenton v. New Jersey*, 262 U.S. 182. 67LEd93j, 43 SCt 534 (1923).

5. John Kromer, "Vacant-Property Policy and Practice: Baltimore and Philadelphia," discussion paper prepared for the Brookings Institution Center on Urban and Metropolitan Policy, Washington, DC, October 2002, www.brookings.edu/es/urban/publications/kromervacant.pdf. Quite significantly, the Maryland Court of Appeals (the state's supreme court) in 2007 narrowly construed the quick-take authority given to the state's cities, observing that a city is obligated to respect other state statutes that protect an owner's property rights.

6. John L. Mikesell, *Fiscal Administration: Analysis and Applications for the Public Sector,* 9th ed. (Boston: Wadsworth, 2014), 349.

7. Law Center to Prevent Gun Violence, "Local Authority to Regulate Firearms Policy Summary," May 18, 2012, http://smartgunlaws.org/local-authority-to-regulate-firearms-policy-summary/. Connecticut, Hawaii, Massachusetts, New Jersey, and New York are the only states that do not preempt local action on gun control.

8. The number of states that preempt local tobacco ordinances has plummeted in more recent years. By 2010, Delaware, Illinois, Iowa, Louisiana, Mississippi, Nevada, New

Jersey, Oregon, and South Carolina rescinded such laws or saw them overturned by judicial action. See Center for Disease Control and Prevention, "State Preemption of Local Tobacco Control Policies Restricting Smoking, Advertising, and Youth Access—United States, 2000–2010," *Morbidity and Mortality Weekly Report* 60 (August 16, 2011): 1124–1127, www.cdc.gov/mmwr/preview/mmwrhtml/mm6033a2.htm.

9. David R. Berman, "State-Local Relations: Authority, Finance, and Regional Cooperation," *The Municipal Year Book 1998 (MYB 1998)* (Washington, DC: International City/County Management Association, 1998), 66.

10. Jason Stein, "Budget Committee: Preempt Local Cell Phone and Radio Tower Ordinances," *Milwaukee-Wisconsin Journal Sentinel,* May 9, 2013, www.jsonline.com/newswatch/206803481.html.

11. Carolina Bolado, "Fla. Residents Say Red-Light Camera Penalties Go Too Far," *Law 360,* November 7, 2013, www.law360.com/articles/466509.

12. David R. Berman, "State-Local Relations: Authority and Finances," *The Municipal Year Book 2010 (MYB 2010)* (Washington, DC: International City/County Management Association, 2010), 47–49; David R. Berman, "State-Local Relations: Authority and Finances," *The Municipal Year Book 2009* (Washington, DC: International City/County Management Association, 2009), 57–58.

13. Myron A. Levine, ed., *Taking Sides: Clashing Views in Urban Studies* (New York: McGraw-Hill, 2013), 41–61.

14. Charles W. Gossett, "Pushing the Envelope: Dillon's Rule and Local Domestic Partnership Ordinances," in *Queer Mobilizations: GLBT Activists Confront the Law,* ed. Scott Barclay, Mary Bernstein, and Anna-Maria Marshall (New York: New York University Press, 2009), 158–186.

15. Paul A. Diller and Samantha Graff, "Regulating Food Retail for Obesity Prevention: How Far Can Cities Go?" *Journal of Law, Medicine and Ethics* 39, no. 1 (Spring 2011), http://works.bepress.com/cgi/viewcontent.cgi?article=1001&context=paul_diller. New York City's ban ran into serious legal challenges, including questions as to the rationale for limiting sugared drinks of a certain size and not of other sizes.

16. For a detailed discussion of the variation in home rule authority permitted in each of the fifty states, see Dale Krane, Platon N. Rigos, and Melvin B. Hill, eds., *Home Rule: A Fifty-State Handbook* (Washington, DC: Congressional Quarterly Press, 2000); and Berman, "State-Local Relations: Authority and Finances," *MYB 2010,* 47–57. For a general overview of the constitutional position of cities, including a discussion of Dillon's Rule, home rule, and the ongoing evolution of state-local relations, see Joseph F. Zimmerman, *Contemporary American Federalism: The Growth of National Power* (Albany, NY: State University of New York Press, 2008), chap. 8.

17. Jesse J. Richardson Jr., "'Dillon's' Rule Is from Mars, Home Rule Is from Venus: Local Government Autonomy and the Rules of Statutory Interpretation," *Publius: The Journal of Federalism* 41, no. 4 (October 2011): 662–685.

18. Yun Sang. Lee, Patrick Terranova, and Dan Immergluck, "New Data on Local Vacant Property Registration Ordinances," *Cityscape: A Journal of Policy Development and Research* 15, no. 2 (2013): 263–264.

19. Henry J. Gomez, "Ohio Supreme Court Rules Against City Residency Requirements," *The Plain Dealer (Cleveland),* June 10, 2009.

20. Kate Taylor, "Mayor Agrees to Accommodate 4 Larger or New Public Schools," *New York Times,* September 10, 2014. See Chapter 8 for a more detailed discussion of the debate over charter schools.

21. Jesse J. Richardson Jr., Meghan Zimmerman Gough, and Robert Puentes, "Is Home Rule the Answer? The Influence of Dillon's Rule on Growth Management," discussion paper prepared for the Brookings Institution Center on Urban and Metropolitan Policy, Washington, DC, January 2003, www.brookings.edu/~/media/Files/rc/reports/2003/01metropolitanpolicy_jesse%20j%20%20richardson%20%20jr/dillonsrule.pdf.

22. David R. Berman, "State-Local Relations: Authority and Finances," *The Municipal Year Book 2010* (Washington, DC: International City/County Management Association, 2010), 48. Berman was

reviewing the Ohio state legislature's overruling a number of local ordinances when he made his "chipped away at home rule authority" statement. It should be also noted, as Berman points out (p. 52), that Ohio's top court also ruled that the ability to install red-light cameras did fall within local home rule authority.

23. Raphael J. Sonenshein and Tom Hogen-Esch, "Bringing the (State) Government Back In: Home Rule and the Politics of Secession in Los Angeles and New York City," *Urban Affairs Review* 41, no. 4 (March 2006): 467–491. For detailed discussion of the politics of the San Fernando Valley's attempt to secede from Los Angeles, see Raphael J. Sonenshein, *The City at Stake: Secession, Reform, and the Battle for Los Angeles* (Princeton, New Jersey: Princeton University Press, 2004), 72–83.

24. Michael A. Pagano, "City Fiscal Conditions in 2002," a report to the National League of Cities, Washington, DC, 4.

25. Mikesell, *Fiscal Administration,* 9th ed., 349.

26. These and other issues concerning the local income tax are discussed by John L. Mikesell, "General Sales, Income, and Other Nonproperty Taxes," in *Management Policies in Local Government Finance,* ed. J. Richard Aronson and Eli Schwartz (Washington, DC: International City/County Management Association, 2004), 305–309.

27. Berman, "State-Local Relations: Authority and Finances," *MYB 2010,* 54.

28. Daphne A. Kenyon, *The Property Tax-School Funding Dilemma* (Cambridge, MA: Lincoln Institute of Land Policy, 2007).

29. Ibid. The figures are from the 2004–2005 school year.

30. Ibid., 13. The figures are for 2005.

31. Various issues related to the property tax are discussed by Roy W. Bahl Jr., "Local Government Expenditures and Revenues," in *Management Policies in Local Government Finance,* ed. Aronson and Schwartz, 90–93; and Mikesell, *Fiscal Administration,* 9th ed., 493–495 and 515–528.

32. Scott Drenkard, "State and Local Sales Tax Rates Midyear 2013," The Tax Foundation Fiscal Fact Sheet No. 392, August 28, 2013, http://taxfoundation.org/article/state-and-local-sales-tax-rates-midyear-2013.

33. Berman, "State-Local Relations: Authority and Finances," *MYB 2010,* 54.

34. Drenkard, "State and Local Sales Tax Rates Midyear 2013."

35. IHS Global Insight, *Impact of "Marketplace Fairness" on Select Jurisdictions—An Update,* report prepared for the National League of Cities, the National Association of Counties, and the U.S. Conference of Mayors (May 2013), http://usmayors.org/metroeconomies/0613/Marketplace FairnessReport.pdf.

36. David L. Sjoquist and Reyna Stoycheva, "Local Revenue Diversification: User Charges, Sales Taxes, and Income Taxes," in *The Oxford Handbook of State and Local Government Finance,* ed. Robert D. Ebel and John E. Petersen (New York: Oxford University Press, 2012), 435–446.

37. For a list of the many small nuisance taxes and fees levied by the City of Philadelphia, see Stu Bykofsky, "City Has 100 Ways to Leave You Poorer," *Philadelphia Daily News,* April 6, 2012, http://articles.philly.com/2012-04-06/news/31300570_1_nuisance-taxes-school-tax-realty-transfer-tax; and City of Philadelphia, "Taxes & Fees," http://media.philly.com/documents/Taxes_Fees2_2012.pdf.

38. Berman, "State-Local Relations: Authority and Finances," *MYB 2010,* 54.

39. Larry L. Lawhon, "Local Government Use of Development Impact Fees: More Fallout from a Poor Economy?" *The Municipal Year Book 2012* (Washington, DC: International City/County Management Association, 2012), 25–35, esp. 28–29.

40. Douglas E. Goodfriend and Thomas E. Myers, *Bond Basics for Towns, Villages, and Cities in New York State* (New York: Orrick, Herrington, and Sutcliffe LLP, 2009), 4, www.orrick.com/Events-and-Publications/Documents/2161.pdf.

41. John Fensterwald, "California Drops to 49th in School Spending in Annual Ed Week Report," *EdSource,* January 14, 2013, http://edsource.org/today/2013/california-drops-to-49th-in-school-spending-in-annual-ed-week-report/25379#.Uuk_yqQo5gE. The *Education Week* data has California as Number 49 in the rankings of the 50 states plus the District of Columbia.

42. David Brunori, *Local Tax Policy: A Federalist Perspective,* 2nd ed. (Washington, DC: The Urban Institute, 2007), 26. For more extensive descriptions of how Proposition 13 and various state ballot initiatives and mandates have diminished or "hollowed out" local authority in California, see Peter Schrag, *The End of Paradise: California's Experience, America's Future,* rev. ed. (Berkeley, CA: University of California Press, 2004), 163–167.

43. Stephen P. Erie, Christopher W. Hoene, and Gregory D. Saxton, "Fiscal Constraints and the Loss of Home Rule: The Long-Term Impacts of California's Post-Proposition 13 Fiscal Regime," *American Review of Public Administration* 32, no. 4 (December 2002): 423–454.

44. Richard C. Kearney, Jodi E. Swicegood, and Ann O'M. Bowman, "Second-Order Devolution? What City Managers Have to Say," *The Municipal Year Book 2011* (Washington, DC: International City/County Management Association, 2011), 13–23; the quotation appears on p. 20.

45. Vladimir Kogan and Mathew D. McCubbins, "The Problem of Being Special: Special Assessment Districts and the Financing of Infrastructure in California," research paper of the University of Southern California Keston Institute for Public Finance and Infrastructure Policy, May 2008, www.usc.edu/schools/sppd/keston/research/documents/McCubinsProblemofBeingSpecial2008.pdf.

46. Steven Litt, "Cleveland Cuyahoga County Port Authority Approves $75 Million Bond Issue for Cleveland Museum of Art Expansion," *The Plain Dealer (Cleveland),* June 8, 2010; James F. McCarty, "Should the Port Authority Be Saved or Dismantled? Critics Say Other Public Entities Could Do the Job Better," *The Plain Dealer (Cleveland),* January 11, 2010.

47. See, for instance, Colin H. McCubbins and Mathew D. McCubbins, "Proposition 13 and The California Fiscal Shell Game," *California Journal of Politics and Policy* 2, no. 2 (2010), www.bepress.com/cjpp/vol2/iss2/6/.

48. Jack Citrin, "Proposition 13 and the Transformation of California Government," *California Journal of Politics and Policy* 1, no. 1 (2009), www.bepress.com/cjpp/vol1/iss1/16/.

49. Mark Baldassare, *When Government Fails: The Orange County Bankruptcy* (Berkeley: University of California Press, 1998).

50. Gretchen Morgenson, "Exotic Deals Put Denver Schools Deeper into Debt," *New York Times,* August 5, 2010; Amy Hetzner, "As the Value of Investments Plunge, 5 School Districts Pressured Over Loans," *Wall Street Journal,* January 3, 2010; Amy Hetzner, "Credit Ratings Lowered for 2 School Districts with Risky Investments," *Wall Street Journal,* April 19, 2010.

51. Rutgers University Institute on Education, Law, and Policy, *50-State Report on Accountability, State Intervention and Takeover,* a policy report prepared for the New Jersey Department of Education (2002), http://ielp.rutgers.edu/docs/developing_plan_app_b.pdf.

52. Brian Gill, Ron Zimmer, Jolley Christman, and Suzanne Blanc, "State Takeover, School Restructuring, Private Management, and Student Achievement in Philadelphia," research paper published by the Rand Corporation, Santa Monica, CA, 2007, http://pdf.researchforaction.org/rfapdf/publication/pdf_file/262/Gill_B_State_Takeover.pdf.

53. Elaine Simon, Eva Gold, and Maia Cucchiarra, "The Prospects for Public Engagement in a Market-Oriented Public School System: A Case Study of Philadelphia, 2001–2007," in *Public Engagement for Public Education: Joining Forces to Revitalize Democracy and Equalize Schools,* ed. Marion Orr and John Rogers (Stanford, CA: Stanford University Press, 2011), 276–300.

54. The earlier stages in the state's fluctuating relations with Detroit schools are described by Wilbur C. Rich, "Who's Afraid of a Mayoral Takeover of Detroit's Public Schools?" in *When Mayors Take Charge: School Governance in the City,* ed. Joseph P. Viteritti (Washington, DC: Brookings Institution Press, 2009), 148–167.

55. Jeffrey R. Henig, "Mayoral Control: What We Can and Cannot Learn from Other Cities," in *When Mayors Take Charge,* ed. Viteritti, 19–45; Kenneth K. Wong. Francis X. Shen, Dorothea Agnostopoulos, and Stacey Routledge, *The Education Mayor: Improving America's Schools* (Washington, DC: Georgetown University Press, 2007).

56. Kenneth W. Wong and Francis X. Shen, "Mayors Can Be 'Prime Movers' of Urban School Improvement," *Education Week,* October 14, 2009, www.edweek.org/ew/articles/2009/10/14/07wallace-wong.

h29.html. The quotations are from Wong and Shen. Also see Jeffrey Henig, "The End of Educational Exceptionalism," in *Education Governance for the Twenty-First Century,* ed. Patrick McGuinn and Paul Manna (Washington, D.C.: Brookings Institution Press, 2013), 187–192.

57. Dorothy Shipps, "Updating Tradition: The Institutional Underpinnings of Modern Mayoral Control in Chicago's Public Schools," in *When Mayors Take Charge,* ed. Viteritti, 117–147.

58. Stephanie Wang, "Four Indianapolis Takeover Schools Get F Grade," *Indianapolis Star,* December 20, 2013.

59. James H. Svara and Jennifer Claire Auer, "Perspectives on Changes in City Government Structure," *The Municipal Year Book 2013* (Washington, DC: International City/County Management Association, 2013), 19.

60. Ibid., 24.

61. Tari Renner and Victor S. DeSantis, "Municipal Form of Government: Issues and Trends," *The Municipal Year Book 1998* (Washington, DC: International City/County Management Association, 1998), 30–41.

62. Tulsa, was another large city with the commission arrangement, that is until 1989 when Tulsa switched to the mayor-council system.

63. Edgar E. Ramirez de la Cruz, "County Form of Government: Trends in Structure and Composition," *The Municipal Year Book 2009* (Washington, DC: International City/County Management Association, 2009), 23.

64. James H. Svara, *Official Leadership in the City: Patterns of Conflict and Cooperation* (New York: Oxford University Press, 1990).

65. John Nalbandian, Robert O'Neill Jr., J. Michael Wilkes, and Amanda Kaufman, "Contemporary Challenges in Local Government: Evolving Roles and Responsibilities, Structures, and Processes," *Public Administration Review* 73, no. 4 (July/August 2013): 567–574.

66. Jerri Killian and Enamul Choudhury, "Continuity and Change in the Role of City Managers," *The Municipal Year Book 2010* (Washington, DC: The International City/County Management Association, 2010), 10–18, esp. 13; Tansu Demir and Christopher G. Reddick, "Understanding Shared Roles in Policy and Administration: An Empirical Study of Council-Manager Relations," *Public Administration Review* 72, no. 4 (July/August 2012): 526–535.

67. Siegrun Fox Freyss, "Matching City Power Structures and City Managers' Leadership Styles: A New Model of Fit," *The Municipal Year Book 2009* (Washington, DC: International City/County Management Association, 2009), 3–10.

68. Ron Carlee, "The Politics of Apolitical Leadership: Professional Management in a Digital and Divided Society," *The Municipal Year Book 2012* (Washington, DC: International City/County Management Association, 2012), 7.

69. Karl Nollenberger, "Cooperation and Conflict in Governmental Decision Making in Mid-Sized U.S. Cities," *The Municipal Year Book 2008* (Washington, DC: International City/County Management Association, 2008), 9–15; Kimberly L. Nelson and Karl Nollenberger, "Conflict and Cooperation in Municipalities: Do Variations in Form of Government Have an Effect?" *Urban Affairs Review* 45, no. 5 (September 2011): 696–720.

70. The material presented here on the hybrid city borrows largely from H. George Frederickson, Gary A. Johnson, and Curtis H. Wood, *The Adapted City: Institutional Dynamics and Structural Change* (Armonk, NY: M.E. Sharpe, 2004).

71. John T. Spence, "Charting Progress of the Empowered Mayor: The 'Stronger Mayor' in Cincinnati, Ohio," in *The Facilitative Leader in City Hall*, ed. James H. Svara (Boca Raton, FL: CRC Press, 2009), 253–279.

72. Stu Woo, "'Weak' Mayor Seeks Assistance to Reshape Sacramento," *Wall Street Journal,* December 5, 2009.

73. Rufus P. Browning, Dale Rogers Marshall, and David H. Tabb, *Protest Is Not Enough: The Struggle of Blacks and Hispanics for Equality in Urban Politics* (Berkeley: University of California Press, 1984), 201–202.

74. Glen W. Sparrow, "San Diego: Switch from Reform to Representative," in *More Than Mayor or Manager: Campaigns to Change Form of Government in America's Large Cities,* ed. James H. Svara and Douglas J. Watson (Washington, DC: Georgetown University Press, 2010), 103–120.

75. See the various case studies in Svara and Watson, eds., *More Than Mayor or Manager.* A list of cities that switched from one form of government to another can be found on p. 12.

76. Kimberly L. Nelson and James H. Svara, "Adaptation of Models versus Variations in Form: Classifying Structures of City Government," *Urban Affairs Review* 45, no. 4 (2010): 552–554.

77. Salary figures from 2013 and 2014 were obtained from the individual cities via their Web sites.

78. Svara and Auer, "Perspectives on Changes in City Government Structure," 29–30.

79. Timothy Bledsoe, *Careers in City Politics: The Case for Urban Democracy* (Pittsburgh: University of Pittsburgh Press, 1993), 113–119 and 126–128.

80. Svara and Auer, "Perspectives on Changes in City Government Structure," 29.

81. Center for American Women in Politics, "Women in Elective Office 2014," fact sheet, May 2014, www.cawp.rutgers.edu/fast_facts/levels_of_office/documents/elective.pdf.

82. National League of Cities, "City Councils," www.nlc.org/build-skills-and-networks/resources/cities-101/city-officials/city-councils; Center for American Women in Politics, "Women in Elective Office 2014."

83. Brian E. Adams and Ronnee Schreiber, "Gender, Campaign Finance, and Electoral Success in Municipal Elections," *Journal of Urban Affairs* 33, no. 1 (2010): 83–97.

84. Jennifer L. Lawless and Richard L. Fox, "Why Are Women Still Not Running for Local Office?" *Brookings Institution Issues in Governance Studies,* no. 16 (May 2008); www.brookings.edu/~/media/research/files/papers/2008/5/women%20lawless%20fox/05_women_lawless_fox.pdf; Jennifer L. Lawless and Richard L. Fox, *It Still Takes a Candidate: Why Women Don't Run for Office* (New York: Cambridge University Press, 2010), 50.

85. See the fuller discussion in Lawless and Fox, *It Still Takes a Candidate*, and Susan J. Carroll and Kira Sanbonmatsu, *More Women Can Run: Gendered Pathways to the State Legislatures* (New York: Oxford University Press, 2013).

86. M. Margaret Conway, Gertrude A. Steuernagel, and David W. Ahern, *Women and Political Participation* (Washington, DC: CQ Press, 1997), 113.

87. Adrienne R. Smith, Beth Reingold, and Michael Leo Owens, "The Political Determinants of Women's Descriptive Representation in Cities," *Political Research Quarterly* 65, no. 2 (2012): 315–329.

88. Robert A. Schumann and Richard L. Fox, "Women Chief Administrative Officers: Perceptions of Their Role in Government," *The Municipal Year Book 1998* (Washington, DC: International City/County Management Association, 1998), 116–122.

89. Susan Abrams Beck, "Acting as Women: The Effects and Limitations of Gender in Local Government," in *The Impact of Women in Public Office*, ed. Susan J. Carroll (Bloomington: University of Indiana Press, 2001), 49–67. For an overview discussion of women's ambition (or, rather, limited ambition) and leadership styles at the local level, see Laura Van Assendelft, "Entry-Level Politics? Women as Candidates and Elected Officials at the Local Level," in *Women and Elective Office: Past, Present, and Future*, ed. Sue Thomas and Clyde Wilcox (New York: Oxford University Press, 2014), 199–215.

90. Melvin G. Holli, "Mayors," *The Electronic Encyclopedia of Chicago* (Chicago: Chicago Historical Society, 2005), http://encyclopedia.chicagohistory.org/pages/795.html.

91. Svara and Auer, "Perspectives on Changes in City Government Structure," 24.

92. Andrew D. McNitt, "Big City Mayors: Political Specialization and Business Domination in the 19th and 20th Centuries," *Journal of Urban Affairs* 33, no. 4 (October 2011): 431–449.

93. Charles H. Levine, *Racial Conflict and the American Mayor* (Lexington, MA: Lexington Books, 1974).

94. The quotation is from Mayor Young. See also Wilbur C. Rich, *Coleman Young and Detroit Politics: From Social Activist to Power Broker* (Detroit: Wayne State University Press, 1999).

95. Rodolfo Rosales, *The Illusion of Inclusion: The Untold Story of San Antonio* (Austin: University of Texas Press, 2000), esp. chap. 7.

96. Raphael J. Sonenshein, *Politics in Black and White: Race and Power in Los Angeles* (Princeton, NJ: Princeton University Press, 1993); J. Phillip Thompson III, *Double Trouble: Black Mayors, Black Communities, and the Call for a Deep Democracy* (New York: Oxford University Press, 2006), 136–139.

97. See, for instance, Huey L. Perry, ed., *Race, Politics, and Governance in the United States* (Gainesville: University Press of Florida, 1997), and Richard A. Keiser, "Philadelphia's Evolving Biracial Coalition," in *Racial Politics in American Cities*, 3d ed., ed. Rufus P. Browning, Dale Rogers Marshall, and David H. Tabb (New York: Longman, 2003), 77–112.

98. Raphael J. Sonenshein and Susan H. Pinkus, "Latino Incorporation Reaches the Urban Summit: How Antonio Villaraigosa Won the 2005 Los Angeles Mayor's Race," *PS: Political Science and Politics* 38, no. 4 (2005): 713–721. See also Raphael J. Sonenshein, *The City at Stake: Secession, Reform, and the Battle for Los Angeles* (Princeton, NJ: Princeton University Press, 2004),214–226; the "high road" comment appears on p. 219.

99. Frédérick Douzet, *The Color of Power: Racial Coalitions and Political Power in Oakland* (Charlottesville, VA: University of Virginia Press, 2012).

100. Ravi K. Perry, "Deracialization Reconsidered: Theorizing Target Universalistic Urban Policies," in *21st Century Urban Race Politics*, ed. Ravi K. Perry (Bingley, United Kingdom: Emerald Publishing, 2013), xxiv.

101. David C. Smith, "Recent Elections and Black Politics: The Maturation or Death of Black Politics?" *PS: Political Science and Politics* 23 (June 1990): 161.

102. Ibid., 160.

103. Thompson, *Double Trouble*, esp. 15–16, 156, and 265–267.

104. This paragraph is based largely on the study of longitudinal changes in black public opinion presented by Michael C. Dawson, *Not in Our Lifetimes: The Future of Black Politics* (Chicago: University of Chicago Press, 2011).

105. The preceding two paragraphs draw heavily on the works of Andra Gillespie, "Meet the New Class: Theorizing Young Black Leadership in a 'Postracial' Era," in *Whose Black Politics? Cases in Post-Racial Black Leadership*, ed. Andra Gillespie (New York: Routledge, 2010); and Andra Gillespie, *The New Black Politician: Cory Booker, Newark, and Post-Racial America* (New York: New York University Press, 2012).

106. Ravi K. Perry, "Epilogue: Future Prospects for Targeted Universalism," in *21st Century Urban Race Politics*, ed. Perry, 300.

6. THE MACHINE, REFORM, AND POSTREFORM CITY

1. Dayton David McKean, *The Boss: The Hague Machine in Action* (Boston: Houghton Mifflin, 1940), 271.

2. Dick Simpson, *Rogues, Rebels, and Rubber Stamps: The Politics of the Chicago City Council from 1863 to the Present* (Boulder, CO: Westview Press, 2001).

3. Bob Dreyfuss and Barbara Dreyfuss, "Inside the Port Authority: Governor Christie's Vast Patronage Machine," *The Nation*, February 14, 2014.

4. Martin Shefter, "The Emergence of the Political Machine: An Alternative View," in *Theoretical Perspectives on Urban Politics*, ed. Willis D. Hawley and Michael Lipsky (Englewood Cliffs, NJ: Prentice Hall, 1976), 22.

5. John M. Allswang, *Bosses, Machines, and Urban Voters* (Port Washington, NY: Kennikat Press, 1977), 52.

6. Steven P. Erie, *Rainbow's End: Irish Americans and the Dilemmas of Urban Machine Politics, 1840–1985* (Berkeley: University of California Press, 1988); Tomasz Inglot and John P. Pelissero, "Ethnic Political Power in a Machine City: Chicago's Poles at Rainbow's End," *Urban Affairs Quarterly* 28, no. 4 (June 1993): 526–543.

7. Marcus D. Pohlmann and Michael P. Kirby, *Racial Politics at the Crossroads: Memphis Elects Dr. W.W. Herenton* (Knoxville: University of Tennessee Press, 1996), 62–63 and 100–104; G. Wayne

Dowdy, *Mayor Crump Don't Like It: Machine Politics in Memphis* (Jackson: University Press of Mississippi, 2006).

8. William J. Grimshaw, *Bitter Fruit: Black Politics and the Chicago Machine, 1931–1991* (Chicago: University of Chicago Press, 1992); Peter Sherry, "Political Institutions and Minority Mobility in the USA," in *Ethnicity, Social Mobility, and Public Policy: Comparing the US and UK*, ed. Glenn C. Loury, Tariq Mood, and Steven M. Tales (Cambridge: Cambridge University Press, 2005), 479–481.

9. Arnold R. Hirsch, *Making the Second Ghetto: Race and Housing in Chicago Politics, 1940–1960*, rev. ed. (Chicago: University of Chicago Press, 1998), describes the complicity of the Chicago machine in public housing segregation.

10. Mike Royko, *Boss: Richard J. Daley of Chicago* (New York: Signet, 1977), 137.

11. Richard A. Keiser, "Explaining African-American Political Empowerment: Windy City Politics from 1900 to 1983," *Urban Affairs Quarterly* 29 (September 1993): 84–116; quotation on p. 112.

12. Anthony Gierzynski, Paul Kleppner, and James Lewis, "Money or the Machine? Money and Votes in Chicago Aldermanic Elections," *American Politics Quarterly* 26, no. 2 (April 1998): 160–173; quotation on p. 171.

13. Dick Simpson and Tom M. Kelly, "The New Chicago School of Urbanism and the New Daley Machine," *Urban Affairs Review* 44, no. 2 (November 2008): 229–231. J. Cherie Strachan, *High-Tech Grass Roots: The Professionalization of Local Elections* (Lanham, MD: Rowman and Littlefield, 2003), observes the rise of "new-style campaigns" in cities across the United States. Local races are no longer dominated by volunteers and party organization. Instead, candidates for local office need to raise substantial sums of money in order to pay for media and the assistance of professional campaign consultants.

14. For a review as to how Chicago responded to court rulings on patronage, see Dick Simpson and Constance A. Mixon, eds., *Twenty-First Century Chicago* (San Diego, CA: Cognella, 2013), esp. "Patronage: Shakman to Sorich," 85–94.

15. Jessica Trounstine, *Political Monopolies in American Cities: The Rise and Fall of Bosses and Reformers* (Chicago: University of Chicago Press, 2008).

16. Amy Bridges and Richard Kronick, "Writing the Rules to Win the Game: The Middle-Class Regimes of Municipal Reformers," *Urban Affairs Review* 34, no. 5 (May 1999): 691–706; Glenda Elizabeth Gilmore, ed., *Who Were the Progressives?* (Boston: Bedford/St. Martin's, 2002).

17. Amy Bridges, *Morning Glories: Municipal Reform in the Southwest* (Princeton, NJ: Princeton University Press, 1997), esp. 151–174.

18. Christopher L. Warren, John G. Corbett, and John F. Stack Jr., "Hispanic Ascendancy and Tripartite Politics in Miami," in *Racial Politics in American Cities*, 2nd ed., ed. Rufus P. Browning, Dale Rogers Marshall, and David H. Tabb (New York: Longman, 1990), 158.

19. National League of Cities, "Municipal Elections," www.nlc.org/build-skills-and-networks/resources/cities-101/city-officials/municipal-elections.

20. A system of district voting can aid the election of a racial minority only when a group's population is highly concentrated (or ghettoized) and voting patterns in a city or county are highly polarized by race. See Jessica Trounstine and Melody E. Valdini, "The Context Matters: The Effects of Single-Member versus At-Large Districts on City Council Diversity," *American Journal of Political Science* 57 (July 2008): 554–569.

21. Chandler Davidson, "Minority Vote Dilution: An Overview," in *Minority Vote Dilution*, ed. Chandler Davidson (Washington, DC: Howard University Press, 1989), 11.

22. Gromer Jeffers Jr., "20 Years After Lawsuit, Debate over Dallas City Council's 14–1 System Persists," *Dallas Morning News*, May 16, 2008.

23. Jackie Hardy, "The Verdict Is Finally in as Irving ISD Moves to Adopt a 5–2 Single-Member/At-Large Mixed Voting System," *North Dallas Gazette*, January 19, 2012.

24. *Shelby County v. Holder*, 570 U.S. (2013). Shaun Bowler and Gary M. Segura, *The Future Is Ours: Minority Politics, Political Behavior, and the Multiracial Era of American Politics* (Los Angeles: SAGE/CQ Press, 2012), 155–165, reviews the importance of the Voting Rights Act, and how the

VRA sought to fight "cracking," "packing," and other techniques that localities turned to in an effort to dilute minority voting power.

25. Jonathan Martin, "New Face of South Rises as an Extralegal Force," *New York Times,* June 26, 2013.

26 Ana Campoy and Nathan Koppel, "Voting-Rights Fights Crop Up," *Wall Street Journal,* November 2–3, 2013.

27. Timothy B. Krebs and John P. Pelissero, "City Councils," in *Cities, Politics, and Policy,* ed. John P. Pelissero (Washington, DC: CQ Press, 2003), 174; David L. Leal, Valerie Martinez-Ebers, and Kenneth J. Meier, "The Politics of Latino Education: The Biases of At-Large Elections," *Journal of Politics* 66 (November 2004): 1224–1244; Belinda I. Reyes and Max Neiman, "System of Elections, Latino Representation, and School Policy in Central California Schools," in *Latinos and the Economy: Integration and Impact in Schools, Labor Markets, and Beyond,* ed. David L. Leal and Stephen J. Trejo (New York: Springer, 2011), esp. 43–53.

28. Trounstine and Valdini, "The Context Matters," 563–565. Rodney E. Hero, *Latinos and the U.S. Political System: Two-Tiered Pluralism* (Philadelphia: Temple University Press, 1992), 141–142.

29. Bowler and Segura, *The Future Is Ours,* 166–183, review the evolving Supreme Court decisions regarding the creation of minority-majority districts and the political and societal consequences that result from such gerrymandering.

30. *Shaw v. Reno* 509 U.S. 630 (1993).

31. *Miller v. Johnson* 515 U.S. 900 (1995). See also *Shaw v. Hunt* 517 U.S. 899 (1996).

32. Susan A. MacManus, "How to Get More Women in Office: The Perspectives of Local Elected Officials (Mayors and City Councilors)," *Urban Affairs Quarterly* 28 (September 1992), 164–165 and 167n2; Susan A. MacManus and Charles S. Bullock III, "Women and Racial/Ethnic Minorities in Mayoral and Council Positions," *Municipal Year Book 1993* (Washington, DC: International City/County Management Association, 1993), 78; Trounstine and Valdini, "The Context Matters," 563–565.

33. James W. Button, Kenneth D. Wald, and Barbara A. Rienzo, "The Election of Openly Gay Public Officials in American Communities," *Urban Affairs Review* 35, no. 2 (November 1999): 188–209, esp. 199–203.

34. Gary M. Segura, "Institutions Matter: Local Electoral Laws, Gay and Lesbian Representation, and Coalition Building Across Minority Communities," in *Gays and Lesbians in the Democratic Process,* ed. Ellen D.B. Riggle and Barry L. Tadlock (New York: Columbia University Press, 1999), 225.

35. Bradley Olson, "Annise Parker Elected Houston's Next Mayor: Nation Watches as City Becomes the Largest in U.S. to Choose an Openly Gay Leader," *Houston Chronicle,* December 15, 2009.

36. Bridges, *Morning Glories,* 200.

37. The data is from a 2001 survey of communities. See National League of Cities, "Partisan vs. Nonpartisan Elections," www.nlc.org/build-skills-and-networks/resources/cities-101/city-officials/partisan-vs-nonpartisan-elections.

38. Jim Yardley, "In Houston, a 'Nonpartisan' Race Is Anything But," *New York Times,* November 30, 2001.

39. Sarah F. Anzia, "Election Timing and the Electoral Influence of Interest Groups," *Journal of Politics* 73, no. 2 (April 2011), 412–427.

40. Zoltan L. Hajnal and Paul G. Lewis, "Municipal Institutions and Voter Turnout in Local Elections," *Urban Affairs Review* 38, no. 5 (May 2003): 645–668; Neal Caren, "Big City, Big Turnout? Electoral Participation in American Cities," *Journal of Urban Affairs* 29, no. 1 (2007): 31–46. Interestingly, Caren finds that council-manager cities also suffer depressed turnouts, as voters apparently see less at stake in municipal elections when a manager is given substantial authority in a city's affairs.

41. Tari Renner and Victor S. DeSantis, "Contemporary Patterns and Trends in Municipal Government Structures," *The Municipal Year Book 1993* (Washington, DC: International City/County Management Association, 1993), 68–69.

42. Jack Citrin and Isaac William Martin, eds., *After the Tax Revolt: California's Proposition 13 Turns 30* (Berkley, CA: Institute of Government Studies Press, 2009).

43. David O. Sears and Jack Citrin, *Tax Revolt: Something for Nothing in California* (Cambridge, MA: Harvard University Press, 1982); Peter Schrag, *Paradise Lost: California's Experience, America's Future* (New York: Norton, 1998), 188–256; James Sterngold, "Hard Times Fuel Debate on the Initiative Process," *San Francisco Chronicle,* August 18, 2003.

44. Christopher Hoene, "Fiscal Structure and the Post–Proposition 13 Fiscal Regime in California's Cities," *Public Budgeting and Finance* 24, no. 4 (December 2004): 51–72.

45. Ibid., 70–72.

46. Steven P. Erie, Vladimir Kogan, and Scott A. MacKenzie, *Paradise Plundered: Fiscal Crisis and Governance Failures in San Diego* (Stanford, CA: Stanford University Press, 2011). The quotations, respectively, appear on pp. 66 and 70.

47. Richard J. Ellis, *The Democratic Delusion: The Initiative Process in America* (Lawrence: University Press of Kansas, 2002), 49–61; Dennis F. Thompson, *Just Elections: Creating a Fair Electoral Process in the United States* (Chicago: University of Chicago Press, 2002), 139.

48. Mark Baldassare and Cheryl Katz, *The Coming Age of Direct Democracy: California's Recall and Beyond* (Lanham MID: Rowman & Littlefield, 2008), 17.

49. Galen Nelson, "Putting Democracy Back into the Initiative and Referendum," in *Democracy's Moment: Reforming America's Political System for the 21st Century,* ed. Ronald Hayduk and Kevin Mattson (Lanham, MD: Rowman and Littlefield, 2002), 159. A reasonably balanced assessment of the initiative process is presented by Larry J. Sabato, Howard R. Ernst, and Bruce R. Larson, eds., *Dangerous Democracy? The Battle Over Ballot Initiatives in America* (Lanham, MD: Rowman and Littlefield, 2001).

50. Anne F. Peterson, Barbara S. Kinsey, Hugh Bartling, and Brady Baybeck, "Bringing the Spatial In: The Case of the 2002 Seattle Monorail Referendum," *Urban Affairs Review* 43, no. 3 (January 2008): 403–429.

51. John Coté, "Prop. K Will Do Little to Ease S.F.'s Housing Crisis," *San Francisco Chronicle,* September 24, 2014.

52. Elisabeth R. Gerber and Justin H. Phillips, "Evaluating the Effects of Direct Democracy on Public Policy: California's Urban Growth Boundaries," *American Politics Research* 33, no. 2 (2005): 310–330.

53. Elisabeth R. Gerber and Justin H. Phillips, "Direct Democracy and Land Use Policy: Exchanging Public Goods for Development Rights," *Urban Studies* 41, no. 2 (2004): 463–479.

54. A.G. Sulzberger, "For Omaha Mayors, Recall Elections Are Almost Routine," *New York Times,* January 26, 2011.

55. Casey Newton, "Group Organizes Recall Against Gordon," *Arizona Republic,* April 30, 2008,

56. Matthew Haggman and Martha Brannigan, "In Dramatic Revolt, Miami-Dade Voters Fire Mayor Carlos Alvarez over Pay Hikes, Tax Increase," *Miami Herald,* March 15, 2011.

57. John Woolfolk, "Both Sides in San Jose's 'Little Saigon' Furor Plotting Next Moves," *San Jose Mercury News,* October 10, 2008.

58. Joseph F. Zimmerman, *The Recall: Tribunal of the People* (Westport, CT: Praeger, 1997), 97–130 for the details of this and other local recall efforts.

59. Larry N. Gerston and Terry Christensen, *Recall! California's Political Earthquake* (Armonk, NY: M.E. Sharpe, 2004).

60. Robert Maranto and Jeremy Johnson, "Bringing Back Boss Tweed: Could At-Will Employment Work in State and Local Government and, If So, Where?" in *American Public Service: Radical Reform and the Merit System,* ed. James S. Bowman and Jonathan P. West (Boca Raton, FL: CRC Press, 2007), 77–100.

61. For evidence as to the success of veteran preferences in increasing the hiring of military veterans by state and local governments, see Gregory B. Lewis and Rahul Pathak, "The Employment of Veterans in State and Local Government Service," *State and Local Government Review,* 46. 2 (June 2014): 91–105.

62. Robert J. Lopez and Ben Welsh, "LAFD Recruitment Program Is Suspended," *Los Angeles Times,* March 20, 2014; Ben Welsh, "LAFD Gets New Anti-Nepotism Rules in Wake of Hiring Controversy," *Los Angeles Times,* September 16, 2014.

63. The quotations are from Theodore Lowi, "Machine Politics-Old and New," *Public Interest* 9 (Fall 1967): 86–87.

64. Ibid.

65. California Voting Rights Act of 2001, Election Codes Section 14027. Also see: Nora Fleming, "Districts Abandoning At-Large School Board Elections," *Education Week,* May 17, 2013; and Eric Lindgren, "Violating the California Voting Rights Act? Uncovering Racially Polarized Voting in a Majority Latino City's At-Large Council Elections," American Political Science Association, annual meeting paper, New Orleans, August 2012, http://ssrn.com/abstract=2107848.

66. Bob Egelko, "San Mateo County Shifts to District Elections," *San Francisco Chronicle,* February 20, 2013.

67. Rufus P. Browning, Dale Rogers Marshall, and David H. Tabb, *Protest Is Not Enough* (Berkeley: University of California Press, 1986), 201–202, in their study of ten communities in northern California, found that "minority incorporation" was strengthened in cities that modified their old reformed structures of government.

68. Rob Gurwitt, "Nobody in Charge," *Governing* (September 1997), 20–24.

69. Ryan Lillis, "Johnson Starts Push for Strong Mayor," *Sacramento Bee,* December 12, 2008; Loretta Kalb, "Sacramento Judge Intends to Bar Strong-Mayor Proposal from Ballot," *Sacramento Bee,* January 15, 2010.

70. Evelyn Larrubia, "Supervisors' Decisions Made Mostly Behind Closed Doors," *Los Angeles Times,* March 26, 2002.

71. For a more full discussion of limits on gift giving, disclosure requirements, requirements for transparency, and other local government ethics laws, see Institute for Local Government (ILG), *Understanding the Basics of Public Service Ethics Laws: Principles and California Law* (Sacramento, CA: ILG, 2013), www.ca-ilg.org/sites/main/files/file-attachments/understandingbasicsethicslaws_finalproof_0.pdf.

72. Jeffrey Kraus, "Campaign Finance Reform Reconsidered: New York City's Public Finance Program at Twenty," in *Public Financing in American Elections,* ed. Costas Panagopoulos (Philadelphia: Temple University Press, 2011), 147–175.

73. Sarah Coppola, "Austin Approves New Campaign Finance Rules," *Austin American-Statesman,* April 26, 2012.

74. Michael J. Malbin, Peter W. Brusoe, and Brendan Glavin, "Small Donors, Big Democracy: New York City's Matching Funds as a Model for the Nation and States," *Election Law Journal* 11, no. 1 (2012), 3–20, www.cfinst.org/pdf/state/NYC-as-a-Model_ELJ_As-Published_March2012.pdf.

75. *Citizens United v. Federal Election Commission,* 558 U.S. 876 (2010).

76. Thomas Kaplan, "Court Upends New York Cap on Donations," *New York Times,* October 25, 2013.

77. Los Angeles City Ethics Commission, *Campaign Finance Reform in Los Angeles: Lessons from the 2001 City Elections,* Executive Summary, October 2001, 3, http://ethics.lacity.org/news.cfm.

78. Michael Cooper, "At $92.60 a Vote, Bloomberg Shatters an Election Record," *New York Times,* December 4, 2001; Michael Cooper, "Final Tally: Bloomberg Spent $75.5 Million to Become Mayor," *New York Times,* March 30, 2002. For a more detailed analysis, see New York City Campaign Finance Board, *An Election Interrupted . . . The Campaign Finance Program and the 2001 New York City Elections,* Part I (New York, 2002).

79. Michael D. Shear, "N.Y. Mayor Bloomberg Leaves GOP," *Washington Post,* June 20, 2007.

80. Michael Barbaro, "Bloomberg Spends $102 Million to Win 3rd Term," *New York Times,* November 27, 2009.

81. Joyce Purnick, "Koch to Limit Contributions in Race," *New York Times,* June 21, 1988.

82. See the work and advocacy of the U.S. Term Limits Organization, https://termlimits.org.

83. Evelina R. Moulder, "Municipal Form of Government: Trends in Structure, Responsibility, and Composition," in *Municipal Year Book 2008* (Washington, DC: International City/County Management Association, 2008), 31.

84. Victor S. DeSantis and Tari Renner, "Term Limits and Turnover Among Local Officials," in *Municipal Year Book 1994* (Washington, DC: International City/County Management Association, 1994), 36–42. Mayraj Fahim, "Arguments For and Against Term Limits," provides a good review of the arguments pro and con regarding the adoption of term limits at the local level: www.citymayors.com/government/term-limits.html.

85. Peggy Lowe and Ellen Miller, "Term Limits Hurt Small Towns," *Rocky Mountain News,* December 2, 2002, www.msnbc.com/local/rmn/DRMN_1581934.asp?cp1=1.

86. Mark P. Petracca and Karen Moore O'Brien, "Municipal Term Limits in Orange County, California," *National Civic Review* (Spring-Summer 1994): 192–193.

87. Courtney Gross, "Musical Chairs: Shuffling Seats in City Government," *Gotham Gazette,* March 29, 2008, www.gothamgazette.com/article/issueoftheweek/20080329/200/2479.

88. Sewell Chan, "Council Votes, 29 to 22, to Extend Term Limits," *New York Times,* October 23, 2008.

89. Josh Baugh, "Effects of New Term Limits Are Beginning to Take Hold: Council Seats Are Becoming More Attractive with a Chance to Serve Longer," *San Antonio Express-News,* April 17, 2011.

90. H. George Frederickson, Gary A. Johnson, and Curtis Wood, *The Adapted City: Institutional Dynamics and Structural Change* (Armonk, NY: M.E. Sharpe, 2004), 52–67.

91. Pradeep Chandra Kathi and Terry L. Cooper, "Democratizing the Administrative State: Connecting Neighborhood Councils and City Agencies," *Public Administration Review* 65, no. 5 (September 2005): 559–567.

92. Alan L. Saltzstein, Colin Copus, Raphael J. Sonenshein, and Chris Skelcher, "Visions of Urban Reform: Comparing English and U.S. Strategies for Improving City Government," *Urban Affairs Review* 44, no. 2 (November 2008): 155–181. Megan Mullin, Gillian Peele, and Bruce E. Cain, "City Caesars? Institutional Structure and Mayoral Success in Three California Cities," *Urban Affairs Review* 40, no. 1 (September 2004): 19–43, describes the structural measures instituted in San Francisco, Oakland, and San Jose in an effort to strengthen city leadership.

93. Terry Nichols Clark, "Old and New Paradigms for Urban Research: Globalization and the Fiscal Austerity and Urban Innovation Project," *Urban Affairs Review* 36, no. 1 (September 2000): 3–45.

94. Simpson and Kelly, "The New Chicago School of Urbanism and the New Daley Machine," 213–238.

7. CITIZEN PARTICIPATION

1. Harry C. Boyte, *The Citizen Solution: How You Can Make a Difference* (Minneapolis: Minnesota Historical Society, 2008), 152; in particular, see pp. 143–158 on "Citizen Professionals."

2. Janet V. Denhardt and Robert B. Denhardt, *The New Public Service: Serving, Not Steering,* exp. ed. (Armonk, NY: M. E. Sharpe, 2007).

3. Raymond A. Mohl, "Stop the Road: Freeway Revolts in American Cities," *Journal of Urban History* 30, no. 5 (2004): 674–706.

4. Alice O'Connor, "Swimming Against the Tide: A Brief History of Federal Policy in Poor Communities," in *The Community Development Reader,* ed. James DeFilippis and Susan Saegert (New York: Routledge, 2008), 9–27.

5. Maureen Bernier and Sonya Smith, "The State of the States: A Review of State Requirements for Citizen Participation in the Local Government Budget Process," *State and Local Government Review* 36, no. 2 (Spring 2004): 140–150.

6. Terry L. Cooper, "Citizen-Driven Administration," in *The State of Public Administration,* ed. Donald C. Menzel and Harvey L. White (Armonk, NY: M.E. Sharpe, 2011), 238–256.

7. Sherry R. Arnstein, "A Ladder of Citizen Participation," *Journal of the American Institute of Planners* 35 (July 1969): 216–224.

8. Wesley G. Skogan, *Police and Community in Chicago: A Tale of Three Cities* (New York: Oxford University Press, 2006); Peter Grabosky, "Democratic Policing," in *Community Policing and*

Peacekeeping, ed. Peter Grabosky (Boca Raton, FL: CRC Press, 2009), 33–54; Michael J. Palmiotto, *Community Policing: A Police-Citizen Partnership* (New York: Routledge, 2011), 210–243.

9. Brian Adams, "Public Meetings and the Democratic Process," *Public Administration Review* 64, no. 1 (February 2004): 43–54; Barbara Faga, *Designing Public Consensus: The Civic Theater of Community Participation for Architects, Landscape Architects, Planners, and Urban Designers* (Hoboken, NJ: Wiley, 2006), 107–114.

10. Alex Stuckey, "Ferguson, St. Louis Contemplate Police Review Boards," *St. Louis Post-Dispatch,* September 22, 2014; Matt Pearce, "Ferguson Plan for Police Oversight Board Is Derided as 'Insulting.'" *Los Angeles Times,* September 11, 2014.

11. For a contemporary reworking of Arnstein's ladder of participation that recognizes the potential for administrators and citizens to work collaboratively, see Paul D. Epstein, Paul M. Coates, and Lyle D. Wray, with David Swain, *Results That Matter: Improving Communities by Engaging Citizens, Measuring Performance, and Getting Things Done* (San Francisco: Jossey-Bass, 2006), 198–201. The potential for collaborative efforts to promote grassroots empowerment is also described by Tom Wolfe, *The Power of Collaborative Solutions: Six Principles and Effective Tools for Building Healthy Communities* (San Francisco, CA: Jossey-Bass, 2010), and E. Franklin Dukes, Karen E. Firehock, and Juliana E. Birkhoff, eds., *Community-Based Collaboration: Bridging Socio-Ecological Research and Practice* (Charlottesville: University of Virginia Press, 2011).

12. Dorothy Shipps, *School Reform, Corporate Style: Chicago, 1880–2000* (Lawrence: University Press of Kansas, 2006).

13. Cooper, "Citizen-Driven Administration," 246–247.

14. John Clayton Thomas, *Citizen, Customer, Partner: Engaging the Public in Public Management* (Armonk, NY: M. E. Sharpe, 2012).

15. Much of this section relies on the insights offered by Jeffrey Berry, Kent Portney, and Ken Thomson, *The Rebirth of Urban Democracy* (Washington, DC: Brookings Institution Press, 1993), esp. 34–39, 47–51, 61–63, and 295–299.

16. Juliet Musso, Christopher Weare, Mark Elliot, Alicia Kitsuse, and Ellen Shiau, "Toward Community Engagement in City Governance: Evaluating Neighborhood Council Reform in Los Angeles," an Urban Policy Brief of the USC Civic Engagement Initiative and USC Neighborhood Participation Project, 2007, 2–8, www.usc-cei.org/userfiles/file/Toward%20Community.pdf.

17. Robert Mark Silverman, "Sandwiched Between Patronage and Bureaucracy: The Plight of Citizen Participation in Community-Based Housing Organizations in the United States," *Urban Studies* 46, no. 1 (January 2009): 3–25, esp. 20.

18. Carmine Sirianni, *Investing in Democracy: Engaging Citizens in Collaborative Governance* (Washington, DC: Brookings Institution Press, 2009), esp. chap. 3, which describes the extensive support provided for neighborhood engagement in Seattle.

19. Stephen Goldsmith, *The Twenty-First Century City: Restructuring Urban America* (Lanham, MD: Rowman and Littlefield, 1999), 159–163.

20. Kitty Kelly Epstein, with Kimberly Mayfield Lynch and J. Douglas Allen-Taylor, *Organizing to Change a City* (New York: Peter Lang, 2012), 27–31, 125–133.

21. Kiran Cunningham, Phyllis Furdell, and Hannah McKinney, *Tapping the Power of City Hall to Build Equitable Communities: 10 City Profiles* (Washington, DC: National League of Cities, 2007), 195–220.

22. For a description of how "deliberative polling" gives citizens information before seeking their responses, see James S. Fishkin, "Consulting the Public Through Deliberative Polling," *Journal of Policy Analysis and Management* 22, no. 1 (2003): 128–133.

23. Eleonora Redaelli, "Cultural Planning in the United States: Toward Authentic Participation Using GIS," *Urban Affairs Review* 48, no. 5 (September 2012): 642–669.

24. Loretta Pyles, *Progressive Community Organizing: A Progressive Approach for a Globalizing World,* 2nd ed. (New York: Routledge, 2014), 9–10.

25. Peter Slevin, "For Clinton and Obama, a Common Ideological Touchstone," *Washington Post,* March 25, 2007.

26. Ryan Lizza, "The Agitator: Barack Obama's Unlikely Political Education," *New Republic,* March 9, 2007. Partisan Obama critics wrote broadsides that noted Obama's affiliation with Alinsky-style groups in an attempt to discredit Obama as a "radical." See, for instance, Jerome R. Corsi, *Saul Alinsky: The Evil Genius Behind Obama* (New York: Paperless Publishing LLC, 2012).

27. Saul D. Alinsky gave the clearest description of his principles for organizing in his *Rules for Radicals* (New York: Vintage Books, 1971).

28. Even though Alinsky/IAF organizers often work with local churches, advocates of faith-based organizing argue that the Alinsky approach places too much power in the hands of lay organizers and that the approach fails to fully exploit the power inherent in the religious language, prayer, and biblical imagery that characterizes congregation-based organizing. See Richard L. Wood, *Faith in Action: Religion, Race, and Democratic Organizing in America* (Chicago: University of Chicago Press, 2002), and Helene Slessarev-Jamir, *Prophetic Activism: Progressive Religious Justice Movements in Contemporary America* (New York: New York University Press, 2011), 77–80. Loretta Pyles, *Progressive Community Organizing: A Critical Approach for a Globalizing Word* (New York: Routledge, 2009), reviews faith-based and other alternative models to the Alinsky organizing approach.

29. Mark R. Warren, *Dry Bones Rattling: Community Building to Revitalize America* (Princeton, NJ: Princeton University Press, 2001), esp. 20–22, 191–210, and 239–247.

30. Ibid., 48–50.

31. Donald C. Reitzes and Dietrich C. Reitzes, *The Alinsky Legacy: Alive and Kicking* (Greenwich, CT: JAI Press, 1987).

32. Mike Eichler, *Consensus Organizing: Building Communities of Mutual Self-Interest* (Thousand Oaks, CA: Sage, 2007).

33. Harry C. Boyte, *Everyday Politics: Reconnecting Citizens and Public Life* (Philadelphia: University of Pennsylvania Press, 2004), 51 and 122. See also Robert Fisher, "Neighborhood Organizing: The Importance of Historical Context," in *The Community Development Reader,* ed. DeFilippis and Saegert, 191; and Mark Warren, "A Theory of Organizing: From Alinsky to the Modern IAF," in *The Community Development Reader,* ed. DeFilippis and Saegert, 194–203.

34. J. Rick Altemose and Dawn A. McCarty, "Organizing for Democracy Through Faith-Based Institutions: The Industrial Areas Foundation in Action," in *Alliances Across Difference: Coalition Politics for the New Millennium,* ed. Jill M. Bystydzienski and Steven P. Schacht (Lanham, MD: Rowman and Littlefield, 2001), 133–145; Warren, *Dry Bones Rattling,* 56–57.

35. Susan Stall and Randy Stoecker, "Community Organizing or Organizing Community: Gender and the Crafts of Empowerment," in *The Community Development Reader,* ed. DeFilippis and Saegert, 245.

36. Richard C. Hula and Cynthia Jackson-Elmoore, "Nonprofit Organizations, Minority Political Incorporation, and Local Governance," in *Nonprofits in Urban America,* ed. Hula and Jackson-Elmoore (Westport, CT: Quorum Books, 2000), 121–150.

37. Marion Orr, "BUILD: Governing Nonprofits and Relational Power," *Policy Studies Review* 18, no. 4 (Winter 2001): 71–90; Marion Orr, "Baltimoreans United in Leadership Development: Exploring the Role of Governing Nonprofits," in *Nonprofits in Urban America,* ed. Hula and Jackson-Elmoore, 151–167; and J. Phillip Thompson III, *Double Trouble: Black Mayors, Black Communities, and the Call for a Deep Democracy* (New York: Oxford University Press, 2006).

38. Kathleen Staudt and Clarence N. Stone, "Division and Fragmentation: The El Paso Experience in Global-Local Perspective," in *Transforming the City: Community Organizing and the Challenge of Political Change,* ed. Marion Orr (Lawrence, KS: University Press of Kansas, 2007), 94.

39. Ross Gittell and Avis Vidal, *Community Organizing: Building Social Capital as a Development Strategy* (Thousand Oaks, CA: Sage, 1998); Robert J. Chaskin et al., *Building Community Capacity* (New York: Aldine de Gruyter, 2001).

40. Census of Industry figures from 2005, cited by Community-Wealth.org, "Overview: Community Development Corporations (CDCs)," www.community-wealth.org/strategies/panel/cdcs/index.html.

41. Barbara Ferman and Patrick Kaylor, "The Role of Institutions in Community Building: The Case of West Mt. Airy, Philadelphia," in *Nonprofits in Urban America*, ed. Hula and Jackson-Elmoore, 93–120. Also see Warren, *Dry Bones Rattling*, 98–123.

42. Myung-Ji Bang, "Understanding Gentrification: The Role and Abilities of Community-Based Organizations in Changing Neighborhoods," paper presented at the annual meeting of the Urban Affairs Association, New Orleans, March 16–19, 2011.

43. Gittell and Vidal, *Community Organizing,* 51–54. Thad Williamson, David Imbroscio, and Gar Alperovitz, *Making a Place for Community: Local Democracy in a Global* Era (New York: Routledge, 2003), 212–222 and 226–235, provide a sober yet positive overall assessment of the potential inherent in CDCs.

44. James DeFilippis, "Community Control and Development: The Long View," in *The Community Development Reader,* ed. DeFilippis and Saegert, 34.

45. Larry Lamar Yates, "Housing Organizing for the Long Haul: Building on Experience," in *A Right to Housing: Foundation for a New Social Agenda*, ed. Rachel G. Bratt, Michael E. Stone, and Chester Hartman (Philadelphia: Temple University Press, 2006), 222.

46. Randy Stoecker, "The CDC Model of Urban Development: A Critique and an Alternative," in *The Community Development Reader,* ed. DeFilippis and Saegert, 303. See also Robert Mark Silverman, "Caught in the Middle: Community Development Corporations (CDCs) and the Conflict between Grassroots and Instrumental Forms of Citizen Participation," *Community Development* 36, no. 3 (2005): 35–51; and Silverman, "CBOs and Affordable Housing," *National Civic Review* 97, no. 3 (Fall 2008): 26–31.

47. Chaskin et al., *Building Community Capacity;* Rachel G. Bratt, "Community Development Corporations: Challenges in Supporting a Right to Housing," in *A Right to Housing,* ed. Bratt, Stone, and Hartman, 340–359; Norman Krumholz, W. Dennis Keating, Philip D. Star, and Mark C. Chupp, "The Long-Term Impact of CDCs on Urban Neighborhoods: Case Studies of Cleveland's Broadway-Slavic Village and Tremont Neighborhoods," *Community Development* 37, no. 4 (2006): 3–52.

48. Alan Mallach, "Where Do We Fit In? CDCs and the Emerging Shrinking City Movement," *Shelterforce: The Journal of Affordable Housing and Community Building* (Spring 2011), www.shelterforce.org/article/2180/where_do_we_fit_in_cdcs_and_the_emerging_shrinking_city_movement/.

49. Darrell M. West, "E-Government and the Transformation of Service Delivery and Citizen Attitudes," *Public Administration Review* 64, no. 1 (February 2004): 15–27; Sharon S. Dawes, "The Evolution and Continuing Challenges of E-Governance," *Public Administration Review* 68, S1 (December 2008): S86–S102.

50. Tony Carrizales, "Functions of E-Government: A Study of Municipal Practices," *State and Local Government Review* 40, no. 1 (2008): 15.

51. James K. Scott, "'E' the People: Do U.S. Municipal Government Web Sites Support Public Involvement?" *Public Administration Review* 66, no. 3 (May/June 2006): 341–353.

52. Ines Mergel, *Social Media in the Public Sector* (San Francisco: Jossey-Bass, 2013), 34 and 146–152.

53. Mark D. Robbins, Bill Simonsen, and Barry Feldman, "Citizens and Resource Allocation: Improving Decision Making with Interactive Web-Based Citizen Participation," *Public Administration Review* 68, no. 3 (May/June 2008): 564–575.

54. Dawes, "The Evolution and Continuing Challenges of E-Governance," S96–S97.

55. Rona Zevin, "The Interface of PEG and the Internet," *Journal of Municipal Telecommunications Policy* (Summer 2005), www.cityofseattle.net/html/citizen/edemocracy.htm.

56. Epstein et al., *Results That Matter*, 205.

57. Daren C. Brabham, "Crowdsourcing the Public Participation Process for Planning Projects," *Planning Theory* 8, no. 3 (August 2009): 242–262; Mergel, *Social Media in the Public Sector,* 50–51, 172–174.

58. Marc Brenman and Thomas W. Sanchez, *Planning as if People Matter: Governing for Social Equity* (Washington, DC: Island Press, 2012), 117–118.

59. Donald F. Norris and Christopher G. Reddick, "Local E-Government in the United States: Transformation or Incremental Change?" *Public Administration Review* 73, no. 1 (January/February 2013): 165–175.

60. Karen Mossberger, Caroline J. Tolbert, and William W. Franko, *Digital Cities: The Internet and the Geography of Opportunity* (New York: Oxford University Press, 2013), 195–199.

61. Ibid., 63–84.

62. Thomas A. Bryer, "Explaining Responsiveness in Collaboration: Administrator and Citizen Role Perceptions," *Public Administration Review* 69, no. 2 (March/April 2009): 271–283.

63. Clarence N. Stone, Jeffrey Henig, Bryan Jones, and Carol Pierannunzi, *Building Civic Capacity: The Politics of Reforming Urban Schools* (Lawrence: University Press of Kansas, 2001), 154.

64. Susan S. Fainstein, *The Just City* (Ithaca, NY: Cornell University Press, 2010), 67.

65. Maureen M. Berner, Justin M. Amos, and Ricardo S. Morse, "What Constitutes Effective Citizen Participation in Local Government: Views from City Stakeholders," *Public Administration Quarterly* 35, no. 1 (Spring 2011): 128–163.

66. Robert Fisher and Eric Shragge, "Contextualizing Community Organizing: Lessons from the Past, Tensions in the Present, Opportunities for the Future," in *Transforming the City: Community Organizing and the Challenge of Political Change,* ed. Orr, 202–203.

67. Elaine B. Sharp, *Does Local Government Matter? How Urban Policies Shape Civic Engagement* (Minneapolis: University of Minnesota Press, 2012), 53–56.

8. IMPROVING URBAN SERVICES

1. Theodore J. Lowi, "Machine Politics—Old and New," *Public Interest* (Fall 1967): 83–92; quotations are on p. 86.

2. Sandra J. Clark, Martha R. Burt, Margaret M. Schulte, and Karen Maguire, *Coordinated Community Responses to Domestic Violence in Six Communities: Beyond the Justice System* (Washington, DC: Urban Institute, October 1996), www.urban.org/publications/406727.html.

3. Michael Lipsky, *Street-Level Bureaucracy: Dilemmas of the Individual in Public Services,* 30th anniv. ed. (New York: Russell Sage Foundation, 2010). Also see Janet Coble Vinzant and Lane Crothers, *Street-Level Leadership: Discretion and Legitimacy in Front-Line Public Service* (Washington, DC: Georgetown University Press, 1998).

4. Peter Hupe and Michael Hill, "Street-Level Bureaucracy and Public Accountability," *Public Administration Review* 83, no. 2 (2007): 279–299.

5. Evelyn Z. Brodkin, "Reflections on Street-Level Bureaucracy: Past, Present, and Future," *Public Administration Review* 72, no. 6 (November/December 2012): 940–949.

6. Peter J. May and Søren C. Winter, "Politicians, Managers, and Street-Level Bureaucrats: Influences on Policy Implementation," *Journal of Public Administration Research and Theory* 19, no. 3 (2009): 453–476.

7. Evelyn Z. Brodkin, "Policy Work: Street-Level Organizations Under New Managerialism," *Journal of Public Administration Research and Theory* 21 (2011): 253–277.

8. Tony Evans, "Professionals, Managers and Discretion," *British Journal of Social Work* 41, no. 2 (2011): 368–386.

9. Samuel Walker, *The New World of Police Accountability* (Thousand Oaks, CA: Sage, 2005), 22–26.

10. David N. Ammons, *Leading Performance Management in Local Government* (Washington, DC: International City/County Management Association, 2008); Patria de Lancer Julnes and Marc Holzer, eds., *Performance Measurement: Building Theory, Improving Practice* (Armonk, NY: M.E. Sharpe, 2008); Patricia Keehley and Neil N. Abercrombie, *Benchmarking in the Public and Nonprofit Sectors: Best Practices for Achieving Performance Breakthroughs,* 2nd ed. (San Francisco: Jossey-Bass, 2008).

11. Beryl A. Radin, *Challenging the Performance Movement: Accountability, Complexity, and Democratic Values* (Washington, DC: Georgetown University Press, 2006), 91–102.

12. James H. Svara and James R. Brunet, "Filling the Skeletal Pillar: Addressing Social Equity in Introductory Courses in Public Administration," *Journal of Public Affairs Education* 10, no. 2 (2004): 99–109, discuss various definitions of the concept of "social equity."

13. Harry P. Hatry, *Performance Measurement: Getting Results,* 2nd ed. (Washington, DC: Urban Institute, 2007), urges managers and citizens to pay greater attention to outcome measures (indicators of a program's reach and effectiveness) as opposed to input measures that merely indicate the resources (i.e., budgetary dollars or number of personnel). Output measures seek to ascertain just what has and has not been accomplished by the money spent on a program.

14. Radin, *Challenging the Performance Movement,* 100–102.

15. Kathe Callahan, "Performance Measurement and Citizen Participation," in *Public Productivity Handbook,* rev. ed., ed. Marc Holzer and Seok Hwan-Lee (New York: Marcel Dekker, 2004), 31–42; Thomas I. Miller, Michelle M. Kobayashi, and Shannon E. Hayden, *Citizen Surveys for Local Government: A Comprehensive Guide to Making Them Matter* (Washington, DC: International City/County Management Association, 2008).

16. Richard A. Krueger and Mary Anne Casey, "Focus Group Interviewing" in *Handbook of Practical Program Evaluation,* 3rd ed., ed. Joseph S. Wholey, Harry P. Hatry, and Kathryn E. Newcomer (San Francisco: Jossey-Bass, 2010), 378–403; and Richard A. Krueger and Mary Anne Casey, *Focus Groups: A Practical Guide for Applied Research*, 4th ed. (Thousand Oaks, CA: Sage, 2009).

17. Barbara J. Cohn Berman, Julie Brenman, and Verner Vasquez, "Using Trained Observer Ratings," in *Handbook of Practical Program Evaluation,* ed. Wholey, Hatry, and Newcomer, 298–320.

18. The Fund for the City of New York, Center on Municipal Government Performance, *How Smooth Are New York City's Streets?* (2008), http://venus.fcny.org/cmgp/streets/pages/indexb.htm.

19. Tony Bovaird, "Beyond Engagement and Participation: User and Community Coproduction of Public Services," *Public Administration Review* 67, no. 5 (2007): 246–260.

20. Remarks of Daniel Kildee, former treasurer of Genesee County (Flint), Michigan, and Kim Graziani, director of neighborhood initiatives, Pittsburgh, at the Conference on Reclaiming Vacant Properties, Cleveland, Ohio, October 14, 2010.

21. Anne Elder and Ira Cohen, "Major Cities and Disease Crises: A Comparative Perspective," paper presented at the annual meeting of the Midwest Political Science Association, Chicago, April 14–16, 1988; P. Arno, "The Nonprofit Sector's Response to the AIDS Epidemic: Community-Based Services in San Francisco," *American Journal of Public Health* 76 (1986): 1325–1330.

22. Anna M. Santiago and Merry Morash, "Strategies for Serving Latina Battered Women," in *Gender in Urban Research, Urban Affairs Annual Review,* vol. 42, ed. Judith A. Garber and Robyne S. Turner (Thousand Oaks, CA; Sage, 1995), 228–233.

23. Jerry Mitchell, *Business Improvement Districts and the Shape of American Cities* (Albany: State University of New York Press, 2008).

24. Maria Dickerson, "Improvement Districts Spur Revival—and Division," *Los Angeles Times,* January 20, 1999.

25. Tina Carey, "Dissolution of the Hyannis Main Street Improvement District (commonly called the BID)," *RidtheBig.org,* March 7, 2013, http://ridthebid.org/?q=node/1.

26. Göktuğ Morçöl and James F. Wolf, "Understanding Business Improvement Districts: A New Governance Framework," *Public Administration Review* 70, no. 6 (November/December 2012): 906–913.

27. Figures from 2013 are from the Department of Small Business Services, The City of New York, "Help for Neighborhoods: Business Improvement Districts," www.nyc.gov/html/sbs/html/neighborhood/bid.shtml.

28. Cerrell Associates, *The State of Los Angeles' Business Improvement Districts: Why BIDs Matter* (Los Angeles, April 2009), www.slideshare.net/andrewwilliamsjr/los-angeles-bid-consortium-report-2009.

29. Edward T. Rogowsky and Jill Simone Gross, "To BID or Not to BID?" *Metropolitics* 1, no. 4 (Spring 1998): 7–8; Jill Simone Gross, "Business Improvement Districts in New York City's Low-Income and High-Income Neighborhoods," *Economic Development Quarterly* 19, no. 2 (2005): 174–189. Also see Robert J. Stokes, "Business Improvement Districts and Small Business Advocacy: The Case of San Diego's Citywide BID Program," *Economic Development Quarterly* 21, no. 3 (2007): 278–291.

30. Grand Central Partnership, *Annual Report 2011* (New York: GCP, 2012), www.grandcentral-partnership.org/wp-content/uploads/2012/05/GCP_2011AR.pdf.

31. Center City Philadelphia, "Life: Center City District," www.centercityphila.org/about/CCD.php.

32. Jill Simone Gross, "Business Improvement Districts in New York City's Low-Income and High-Income Neighborhoods," *Economic Development Quarterly* 19, no. 2 (May 2005): 174–189.

33. Carol J. Becker, "Democratic Accountability and Business Improvement Districts," *Public Performance and Management Review* 36, no. 2 (December 2012): 187–202, explores the extent to which BIDs meet various standards of democratic accountability.

34. Nathaniel M. Lewis, "Grappling with Governance: The Emergence of Business Improvement Districts in a National Capital," *Urban Affairs Review* 46, no. 2 (November 2010): 180–217.

35. For criticisms of the partial privatization of Central Park, that the Central Park Conservancy's reliance on private fundraising has "commodified" a precious public resource and that the park no longer serves as a peaceful green haven, see Oliver D. Cooke, *Rethinking Municipal Privatization* (New York: Routledge, 2008), chap. 4.

36. Carl F. Valente and Lydia D. Manchester, *Rethinking Local Services: Examining Alternative Delivery Approaches* (Washington, DC: International City Management Association, 1984), xi. Ronald J. Oakerson, *Governing Local Public Economies: Creating the Civic Metropolis* (Oakland, CA: Institute for Contemporary Studies Press, 1999), 7–9, further explains the distinction between the provision and the production of urban services.

37. E.S. Savas, *Privatization in the City: Success, Failures, Lessons* (Washington, DC: CQ Press, 2005), esp. chap. 6.

38. Stephen Goldsmith, *The Twenty-First Century City: Resurrecting Urban America* (Lanham, MD: Rowman and Littlefield, 1999), esp. 18–19.

39. David Osborne and Peter Plastrik, *The Reinventor's Fieldbook: Tools for Transforming Your Government* (San Francisco: Jossey-Bass, 2000), 183–187; Jeffrey D. Greene, *Cities and Privatization: Prospects for the New Century* (Upper Saddle River, NJ: Prentice Hall, 2002), 42–43; Goldsmith, *The Twenty-First Century City*, 96–99.

40. Kelly LeRoux, *Service Contracting: A Local Government Guide* (Washington, DC: ICMA Press, 2007), details some of the costs and work that a government still incurs when contracting out a service. The city must determine the scope of the work to be contracted out, prepare a Request for Proposals, circulate the bid document, establish the criteria by which the bids will be rated, select a panel to evaluate the bids, formulate the legal documents that will govern the city's relationship with the winner, arrange for insurance, monitor contract performance, intervene to deal with poor performance, and, upon the end of the contract, decide whether to renew the contract or to make a change in service delivery.

41. James B. Jacobs with Coleen Friel and Robert Radick, *Gotham Unbound: How New York City Was Liberated from the Grip of Organized Crime* (New York: New York University Press, 1999), the quotation appears on p. 91; "Connecticut Trash Hauler Pleads Guilty in Mob Case," *Associated Press,* June 4, 2008.

42. Richard Upham, *Develop an Apparatus Replacement Plan for the Scottsdale Fire Department* (Scottsdale: Scottsdale Fire Department, August 2007).

43. Elissa Gootman, "School Custodians Object as City Hires Private Firms," *New York Times,* September 26, 2003; Elissa Gootman, "Education Department Plans Nearly 500 Job Cuts," *New York Times,* December 9, 2003.

44. Stephen Goldsmith, "Chicago's Parking Meter Mishap: Successful 'Fiasco,'" *Governing,* January 20, 2010, www.governing.com/columns/mgmt-insights/Chicago-Parking-Meters.html.

45. Dan Mihalopoulos and Chris Fusco, "Chicago Parking Meter Company Wants More Money; Mayor Balks," *Chicago Sun-Times,* May 4, 2012.

46. Caroline Porter and Ted Mann, "New York Scraps Privatizing Parking Meters," *Wall Street Journal,* January 26, 2013.

47. John B. Gilmour, "The Indiana Toll Road Lease as an Intergenerational Transfer," *Public Administration Review* 72, no. 6 (November/December 2012): 856–864; Molly Ball, "The Privatization Backlash," *The Atlantic,* April 23, 2014, www.theatlantic.com/politics/archive/2014/04/city-state-governments-privatization-contracting-backlash/361016/.

48. Brian P. Gill et al., *Inspiration, Perspiration, and Time: Operations and Achievements in Edison Schools* (Santa Monica, CA: RAND Corporation, 2005).

49. James G. Cibulka, "The NEA and School Choice," 165–166, and William Lowe Boyd, David N. Plank, and Gary Sykes, "Teachers Unions in Hard Times," 204–206, both in *Conflicting Mission? Teachers, Unions, and Educational Reform,* ed. Tom Loveless (Washington, DC: Brookings Institution Press, 2000).

50. Marion Orr, "The Challenge of School Reform in Baltimore: Race, Jobs, and Politics," in *Changing Urban Education,* ed. Clarence N. Stone (Lawrence: University of Kansas Press, 1998), 106–113.

51. Brian Gill, Ron Zimmer, Jolley Christman, and Suzanne Blanc, *School Restructuring, Private Management, and Student Achievement in Philadelphia* (Santa Monica, CA: RAND Corporation, 2007), www.rand.org/pubs/monographs/MG533.html. In contrast to the Rand Education study, the advocates of private management take a different view. They argue that the evidence on achievement scores is mixed but on the whole still favorable to the management of public schools by for-profit firms; see Paul E. Peterson and Matthew M. Chingos, "For-Profit and Nonprofit: Management in Philadelphia Schools," *Education Next* (Spring 2009): 64–70, http://educationnext.org/for-profit-and-nonprofit-management-in-philadelphia-schools/educationnext.org/files/ednext_20092_64.pdf.

52. Vaughan Byrnes, "Getting a Feel for the Market: The Use of Privatized School Management in Philadelphia," *American Journal of Education* 115 (May 2009): 437–455. For a detailed assessment of the performance of Edison Schools, the largest nongovernmental Education Management Organization (EMO) in the United States, see Brian Gill, Laura S. Hamilton, and Ron Zimmer, "Perspectives on Education Management Organizations," in *Handbook of Research on School Choice,* ed. Mark Berends et al. (New York: Routledge, 2009), 555–568.

53. Philip E. Kovacs, ed., *The Gates Foundation and the Future of U.S. "Public" Schools* (New York: Routledge, 2011); Diane Ravitch, "Another Battle in the War Against Public Schools," *New York Times,* March 20, 2012, www.nytimes.com/roomfordebate/2012/03/18/hopes-and-feard-for-parent-trigger-laws/another-battle-in-the-war-against-public-schools; Center for Education Organizing, *Parent Trigger: No Silver Bullet* (Providence, RI: Annenberg Institute for School Reform at Brown University, 2012); Andrew Ujifusa, "More States Consider 'Parent Trigger' Laws," *Education Week,* March 27, 2013.

54. American Civil Liberties Union, "Justice Department Says State Voucher Programs May Not Discriminate Against Students with Disabilities," press release, May 2, 2013, www.aclu.org/racial-justice/justice-department-says-state-voucher-programs-may-not-discriminate-against-students.

55. John F. Witte, *The Market Approach to Education: An Analysis of America's First Voucher Program* (Princeton, NJ: Princeton University Press, 2000), 205.

56. Sam Dillon, "Florida Supreme Court Blocks School Vouchers," *New York Times,* January 6, 2006.

57. Stephanie Saul, "Public Money Finds Back Door to Private Schools," *New York Times,* May 21, 2012.

58. Ibid.

59. Ernest L. Boyer, "Foreword," in The Carnegie Foundation for the Advancement of Teaching, *School Choice: A Special Report* (Princeton, NJ: Carnegie Foundation, 1992), xv. For a competing collection of studies that present a more positive assessment of school vouchers, see William G. Howell

and Paul E. Peterson, *The Education Gap: Vouchers and Urban Schools*, rev. ed. (Washington, DC: Brookings Institution Press, 2002).

60. John R. Warren, *Graduation Rates for Choice and Public School Students in Milwaukee* (Milwaukee: School Choice Wisconsin, January 2008), www.heartland.org/custom/semod_policybot/pdf/22908.pdf.

61. Frederick M. Hess, "School Vouchers and Suburbanites," *FrederickHess.org,* April-May 2013, www.frederickhess.org/5042/school-vouchers-and-suburbanites.

62. Brian P. Gill, P. Michael Timpane, Karen E. Ross, and Dominic J. Brewer, *Rhetoric Versus Reality: What We Know and What We Need to Know About Vouchers and Charter Schools* (New York: RAND Education, 2001), reviews the effect of school choice programs on racial integration.

63. *Zelman v. Simmons-Harris,* 536 U.S. 639 (2002).

64. Erin Richards and Kevin Crowe, "Vouchers a Boon for Private Schools in Milwaukee, Racine Counties," *Milwaukee-Wisconsin Journal Sentinel,* May 4, 2013.

65. Howell and Peterson, *The Education Gap,* 168–184; Witte, *The Market Approach to Education,* 117–118.

66. For the words of parents who express their profound thanks for choice programs, see Paul Peterson, "School Choice: A Report Card," *Virginia Journal of Social Policy and the Law* 6, no. 1 (1998): 47–80.

67. Jay P. Greene, Jonathan N. Mills, and Stuart Buck, *The Milwaukee Parental Choice Program's Effect on School Integration,* School Choice Demonstration Project Report #20 (Department of Education Reform, University of Arkansas, April 2010), www.uark.edu/ua/der/SCDP/Milwaukee_Eval/Report_20.pdf.

68. Carnegie Foundation, *School Choice: A Special Report,* 70; Witte, *The Market Approach to Education,* 119–143.

69. Witte, *The Market Approach to Education.* Also see John F. Witte, Joshua M. Cowen, David J. Fleming, and Patrick J. Wolf, "The Second Year of the Longitudinal Educational Growth Study of the Milwaukee Parental Choice (Voucher) Program," paper prepared for the conference on School Choice and School Improvement: Research in State, District, and Community Contexts, Vanderbilt University, Nashville, October 25–27, 2009, www.vanderbilt.edu/schoolchoice/conference/papers/Witte_etal_COMPLETE.pdf.

70. Carnegie Foundation, *School Choice: A Special Report,* 73.

71. Sol Stern, "School Choice Isn't Enough: Instructional Reform Is the Key to Better Schools," *City Journal* 18, no. 1 (Winter 2008); Diane Ravitch, *The Death and Life of the Great American School System* (New York: Basic Books, 2010).

72. Jay P. Greene, Paul E. Peterson, and Jiangtao Du, "School Choice in Milwaukee: A Randomized Experiment," in *Learning from School Choice,* ed. Paul E. Peterson and Bryan C. Hassel (Washington, DC: Brookings Institution Press, 1998), 338 and 345. Also see the arguments made by Jay Greene and other choice advocates in their responses to Sol Stern in a special forum, "Is School Choice Enough?" *City Journal,* January 24, 2008, www.city-journal.org/2008/forum0124.html.

73. Cecilia E. Rouse, Jane Hannaway, Dan D. Goldhaber, and David N. Figlio, *Feeling the Florida Heat? How Low-Performing Schools Respond to Voucher and Accountability Pressure,* NBER Working Paper No. w13681 (Cambridge, MA: National Bureau of Economic Research, December 2007), http://ssrn.com/abstract=1077807.

74. Martin Carnoy et al., *Vouchers and Public School Performance: A Case Study of the Milwaukee Parental Choice Program* (Madison: University of Wisconsin Economic Policy Institute, 2007).

75. Wisconsin Department of Public Instruction, "2013–14 Income Limits for New Students: Milwaukee Parental Choice Program and Parental Private School Choice Program," http://sms.dpi.wi.gov/files/sms/pdf/pcp_income_limits_2013-14.pdf.

76. Paul T. Hill, ed., *Charter Schools Against the Odds: An Assessment of the Koret Task Force on K–12 Education* (Stanford, CA: Hoover Institution Press, 2006), 1. A copy of the book is available online at www.hoover.org/publications/books/8322.

77. John F. Witte, Arnold F. Shober, Paul A. Schlomer, Pär Jason Engle, *The Political Economy of School Choice,* La Follette School of Public Affairs Working Paper no. 2004–002 (University of Wisconsin-Madison, August 2004): 4–5, www.lafollette.wisc.edu/publications/workingpapers/witte2004–002.pdf.

78. Hill, *Charter Schools against the Odds.*

79. Howard Blume, "Teachers Union Files Lawsuit over Charter Takeovers," *Los Angeles Times,* December 22, 2009; Howard Blume, "Teachers Seek Control at Up-for-bid L.A. Unified Schools," *Los Angeles Times,* January 2, 2010.

80. Al Baker and Javier C. Hernandez, "De Blasio and Builder of Charter School Empire Do Battle," *New York Times,* March 5, 2014.

81. National Alliance for Public Charter Schools, *Back to School Tallies: Estimated Number of Public Charter Schools and Students, 2012–2013* (January 2013), http://www.charterschoolcenter.org/resource/back-school-tallies-estimated-number-public-charter-schools-and-students-2012-2013.

82. Peterson, "School Choice: A Report Card," 10–11.

83. Robert Bifulco, Helen F. Ladd, and Stephen L. Ross, "Public School Choice and Integration: Evidence from Durham, North Carolina," *Social Science Research* 38, no. 1 (2009): 71–85. Also see Gary Miron, Jessica L. Urschel, William J. Mathis, and Elana Tornquist, "Schools Without Diversity: Education Management Organizations, Charter Schools, and the Demographic Stratification of the American School System," University of Colorado Education and the Public Center (EPIC) and the Great Lakes Center for Education Research and Practice, policy brief, February 2010, http://nepc.colorado.edu/publication/schools-without-diversity.

84. Tamara Audie, "Desegregation an Issue in Charter School Plan," *Detroit Free Press,* September 3, 1998.

85. David R. Garcia, "The Impact of School Choice on Racial Segregation in Charter Schools," *Educational Policy* 22, no. 6 (2008): 805–829.

86. N. R. Kleinfield, "Why Don't We Have Any White Kids?" *New York Times,* May 11, 2012.

87. Ron Zimmer et al., *Charter Schools in Eight States: Effects on Achievement, Attainment, Integration, and Competition* (Washington, DC: RAND Corporation, 2009), 12–19, www.rand.org/pubs/monographs/2009/RAND_MG869.pdf; Jeffrey R. Henig, *Spin Cycle—How Research Is Used in Public Policy Debates: The Case of Charter Schools* (New York: Russell Sage Foundation, 2008), 6–7. Also see Matthew M. Chingos, "Does Expanding School Choice Increase Segregation?" *The Brown Center Chalkboard Report,* May 15, 2013, www.brookings.edu/blogs/brown-center-chalkboard/posts/2013/05/15-school-choice-segregation-chingos.

88. Jack Buckley and Mark Schneider, *Charter Schools: Hope or Hype?* (Princeton, NJ: Princeton University Press, 2007).

89. The U.S. Department of Education was hesitant to release the results of a study that seemingly undermined President George W. Bush's agenda for charter schools. See Diana Jean Schemo, "Nation's Charter Schools Lagging Behind, U.S. Test Scores Reveal," *New York Times,* August 17, 2004.

90. Zimmer et al., *Charter Schools in Eight States,* esp. 35–39.

91. John F. Witte, David L. Weimer, Paul A. Schlomer, Arnold F. Shober, "The Performance of Charter Schools in Wisconsin," University of Wisconsin-Madison La Follette School of Public Affairs (2004), www.lafollette.wisc.edu/wcss/docs/persum.doc.

92. Buckley and Schneider, *Charter Schools: Hope or Hype?* chap. 10.

93. Gary Miron, "Testimony Prepared for the June 1, 2011, hearing of the House Committee on Education and the Workforce," U.S. House of Representatives, http://edworkforce.house.gov/uploadedfiles/06.01.11_miron.pdf.

94. Amy Brandon and Gregory Weiher, "The Impact of Competition: Charter Schools and Public Schools in Texas," paper presented at the annual meeting of the Midwest Political Science Association, Chicago, April 12, 2007, www.allacademic.com/meta/p198562_index.html.

95. Peggy Walsh-Sarnecki, "National Heritage-Run Charter Schools Making Profits," *Manatee-Bradenton-Sarasota Herald Today,* January 15, 2003.

96. Javier C. Hernandez, "Secular Education, Catholic Values," *New York Times,* March 8, 2009.

97. Martha M. Galvez, *What Do We Know About Housing Choice Voucher Program Location Outcomes? A Review of Recent Literature, a Report of the What Works Collaborative* (Washington, DC: The Urban Institute, August 2010), www.urban.org/uploadedpdf/412218-housing-choice-voucher.pdf.

98. Rebecca J. Walter, Yanmei Li, Serge Atherwood, and Auntaria Brown-Davis, "Moving to Opportunity? An Examination of the Impact of the Housing Choice Voucher Program on Reducing Urban Inequality," paper presented at the annual meeting of the Urban Affairs Association, San Antonio, Texas, March 22, 2014.

9. A Suburban Nation

1. Robert A. Beauregard, *When America Became Suburban* (Minneapolis: University of Minnesota Press, 2006), ix and 14.

2. Alan Berube et al., *State of Metropolitan America: On the Front Lines of Demographic Transformation* (Washington, DC: Brookings Institution Press, 2010), 7, www.brookings.edu/~/media/Files/Programs/Metro/state_of_metro_america/metro_america_report.pdf; U.S. Census Bureau, "New Orleans Population Continues Katrina Recovery; Houston Leads in Numerical Growth," press release CB08–106, July 10, 2008, www.census.gov/newsroom/releases/archives/population/cb08-106.html.

3. Robert E. Lang and Jennifer E. LeFurgy, *Boomburbs: The Rise of America's Accidental Cities* (Washington, DC: Brookings Institution Press, 2007); Robert E. Lang and Jennifer E. LeFurgy, "Boomburb 'Buildout': The Future of Development in Large, Fast-Growing Suburbs," *Urban Affairs Review* 42, no. 4 (May 2007): 533–552.

4. William H. Frey, "A Big City Growth Revival?" *Brookings Institution,* May 28, 2013, www.brookings.edu/research/opinions/2013/05/28-city-growth-frey.

5. Joel Kotkin, "America's Fastest-Growing Cities Since the Recession," *New Geography,* June 18, 2013, www.newgeography.com/content/003779-americas-fastest-growing-cities-since-the-recession; Todd Gardner and Matthew C. Marlay, "Population Growth in the Exurbs Before and Since the Great Recession," *Metro Trends,* 2012, http://metrotrends.org/commentary/Exurban-Population-Growth.cfm; and Nate Berg, "Exurbs, the Fastest Growing Areas in the U.S.," *CityLab* (*The Atlantic* magazine), July 18, 2012, www.theatlanticcities.com/neighborhoods/2012/07/exurbs-fastest-growing-areas-us/2636/. For the competing point of view, that the nation's economic rebound will not bring with it a demand for exurban housing, see Christopher B. Leinberger, "The Death of the Fringe Suburb," *New York Times,* November 25, 2011.

6. Lynn M. Appleton, "The Gender Regimes of American Cities," in *Gender in Urban Research,* vol. 42, ed. Judith A. Garber and Robyne S. Turner (Thousand Oaks, CA: Sage, 1994), 44–59; Stephanie Coontz, "Why 'Mad Men' Is TV's Most Feminist Show," *Washington Post,* October 10, 2010.

7. The 1950s stereotype of suburbia as a stream of bedroom communities was the result of such celebrated books as William H. Whyte Jr., *The Organization Man* (New York: Simon and Schuster, 1956); David Riesman, *The Lonely Crowd* (Garden City, NY: Doubleday, 1957); and J. Seeley, R. Sim, and E. Loosley, *Crestwood Heights* (New York: Basic Books, 1956). Bennett M. Berger's *Working-Class Suburb* (Berkeley: University of California Press, 1960) was a noteworthy exception: a book that detailed life in a blue-collar suburban community. Suburbia today denotes a quite diverse set of communities, including "first suburbs" and politically progressive communities described in Christopher Niedt, ed., *Social Justice in Diverse Suburbs* (Philadelphia: Temple University Press, 2013).

8. Evan McKenzie, *Privatopia: Homeowner Associations and the Rise of Residential Private Government* (New Haven, CT: Yale University Press, 1994).

9. Myron Orfield, *American Metropolitics: The New Suburban Reality* (Washington, DC: Brookings Institution Press, 2002), 2–3.

10. Joel Garreau, *Edge City: Life on the New Frontier* (New York: Doubleday, 1991).

11. Robert E. Lang, *Edgeless Cities: Exploring the Elusive Metropolis* (Washington, DC: Brookings Institution Press, 2003).

12. William H. Frey, *Melting Pot Cities and Suburbs: Racial and Ethnic Change in Metro America in the 2000s* (Washington, DC: The Brookings Institution, May 2011), www.brookings.edu/~/media/research/files/papers/2011/5/04%20census%20ethnicity%20frey/0504_census_ethnicity_frey.pdf.

13. William H. Frey, "The 2010 Census: America on the Cusp," *The Milken Institute Review* (Second Quarter 2012), 56–57, www.milkeninstitute.org/publications/review/2012_4/47–58MR54.pdf.

14. Robert Suro, Jill H. Wilson, and Audrey Singer, *Immigration and Poverty in America's Suburbs* (Washington, DC: The Brookings Institution, 2011), www.brookings.edu/~/media/research/files/papers/2011/8/04%20immigration%20suro%20wilson%20singer/0804_immigration_suro_wilson_singer.pdf.

15. Thomas I. Phelan and Mark Schneider, "Race, Ethnicity, and Class in American Suburbs," *Urban Affairs Review* 31, no. 5 (May 1996): 307–309.

16. U.S. Census Bureau, *State and County QuickFacts,* January 6, 2014; the numbers are U.S. Census population estimates for 2012. Also see Karin Aguilar-San Juan, "Staying Vietnamese: Community and Place in Orange County and Boston," *City and Community* 4, no. 1 (2005): 37–65.

17. Myron Orfield and Thomas Luce, *America's Racially Diverse Suburbs: Opportunities and Challenges* (Institute on Metropolitan Opportunity, University of Minnesota Law School, July 20, 2012), www.law.umn.edu/uploads/e0/65/e065d82a1c1da0bfef7d86172ec5391e/Diverse_Suburbs_FINAL.pdf.

18. MaryJo Webster, "Twin Cities Suburbs Diversifying at Rate among Fastest in Nation," *Twin Cities Pioneer Press,* July 19, 2012.

19. Elizabeth Kneebone and Alan Berube, *Confronting Suburban Poverty in America* (Washington, DC: Brookings Institution, 2013). Much of the discussion in this paragraph and the paragraph that follows is based on Kneebone and Berube.

20. Yonah Freemark, "As Suburban Poverty Grows, U.S. Fails to Respond Adequately," *Next American City,* October 12, 2010, http://americancity.org/columns/entry/2670/; Adie Tomer, Elizabeth Kneebone, Robert Puentes, and Alan Berube, *Missed Opportunity: Transit and Jobs in Urban America* (Washington, DC: The Brookings Institution, May 12, 2011), www.brookings.edu/research/reports/2011/05/12-jobs-and-transit.

21. Robert W. Bailey, *Gay Politics, Urban Politics: Identity and Economics in the Urban Setting* (New York: Columbia University Press, 1999), 122; Gary J. Gates, *Geographic Trends Among Same-Sex Couples in the U.S. Census and the American Community Survey* (The Williams Institute, November 2007), http://williamsinstitute.law.ucla.edu/wp-content/uploads/Gates-Geographic-Trends-ACS-Brief-Nov-2007.pdf ; Associated Press, "Census: More Same-Sex Couples Living in NJ Suburbs," *NBC New York,* August 14, 2011, www.nbcnewyork.com/news/local/Census-More-same-sex-couples-living-in-NJ-suburbs-127687643.html.

22. Rex W. Huppke, "Berwyn Pushes to Attract Gay Community," *Chicago Tribune,* September 2, 2010.

23. John E. Farley, "Race Still Matters: The Minimal Role of Income and Housing Cost as Causes of Housing Segregation in St. Louis, 1990," *Urban Affairs Review* 31, no. 2 (November 1995): 244–254; Casey J. Dawkins, "Recent Evidence on the Continuing Causes of Black-White Residential Segregation," *Journal of Urban Affairs* 26, no. 3 (2004): 379–400.

24. Gregory Sharp and John Iceland, "The Role of SES in Shaping the Residential Patterns of Whites in U.S. Metropolitan Areas," paper presented at the annual meeting of the Population Association of America, San Francisco, May 2–5, 2012, http://paa2012.princeton.edu/papers/121203.

25. Joe T. Darden, "Black Access to Suburban Housing in America's Most Racially Segregated Metropolitan Area: Detroit," paper presented at the conference on Adequate and Affordable Housing for All, Toronto, Canada, June 24–27, 2004, www.urbancentre.utoronto.ca/pdfs/housingconference/Darden_Black_Access_Housing.pdf. Also see Joe T. Darden and Richard W. Thomas, *Detroit: Race Riots, Racial Conflicts, and Efforts to Bridge the Racial Divide* (East Lansing, MI: Michigan State University Press, 2013), chap. 6.

26. Ingrid Gould Ellen, "Continuing Isolation: Segregation in America Today," in *Segregation: The Rising Costs for America,* ed. James H. Carr and Nandinee Kutty (New York: Routledge, 2008), 265–271.

27. Margery Austin Turner et al., *Housing Discrimination against Racial and Ethnic Minorities 2012* (Washington, D.C.: U.S. Department of Housing and Urban Development, 2013), www.huduser.org/portal/Publications/pdf/HUD-514_HDS2012.pdf.

28. John Baugh, "Linguistic Profiling in Housing Markets and Lending Institutions Based on Racial Inferences from Telephone Calls," paper presented at the annual meeting of the Urban Affairs Association, March 20, 2014, San Antonio, Texas; and Gregory D. Squires and Jan Chadwick, "Linguistic Profiling: A Continuing Tradition of Discrimination in the Home Insurance Industry?" *Urban Affairs Review* 41, no. 3 (January 2006): 400–415. In contrast, Meena Bavan, "Does Housing Discrimination Exist Based on the 'Color' of an Individual's Voice?" *Cityscape* 9, no. 1 (2007): 109–130, finds no real evidence of "linguistic profiling," at least as measured by the success of members of different racial groups in using the telephone to arrange appointments with real estate agents.

29. Gregory D. Squires, Samantha Friedman, and Catherine E. Saidat, "Experiencing Residential Segregation: A Contemporary Study of Washington, DC," in *Desegregating the City: Ghettos, Enclaves, and Inequality,* ed. David P. Varady (Albany: State University of New York Press, 2005), 127–144; George Galster and Erin Godfrey, "By Word and by Deed: Racial Steering by Real Estate Agents in the U.S. in 2000," *Journal of the American Planning Association* 71, no. 3 (Summer 2005): 251–268; Margery Austin Turner and Stephen L. Ross, "How Discrimination Affects the Search for Housing," in *The Geography of Opportunity: Race and Housing Choice in Metropolitan America,* ed. Xavier de Souza Briggs (Washington, DC: Brookings Institution Press, 2005), 81–100; Gregory D. Squires and Charis E. Kubrin, *Privileged Places: Race, Residence, and the Structure of Opportunity* (Boulder, CO: Lynne Rienner, 2006), 69–93.

30. Turner and Ross, "How Discrimination Affects the Search for Housing," 86.

31. Margery Turner, "Housing Discrimination Today and the Persistence of Residential Segregation," *MetroTrends,* June 12, 2013, http://blog.metrotrends.org/2013/06/housing-discrimination-today-persistence-residential-segregation/. For further details, see Turner et al, *Housing Discrimination against Racial and Ethnic Minorities 2012.*

32. Shanna L. Smith and Cathy Cloud, "Welcome to the Neighborhood? The Persistence of Discrimination and Segregation," in *The Integration Debate: Competing Futures for American Cities,* ed. Chester Hartman and Gregory D. Squires (New York: Routledge, 2010), 18.

33. *Serrano v. Priest,* 5 Cal. 3d 584,487 (1971).

34. Deborah A. Verstegen and Teresa S. Jordan, "A Fifty-State Survey of School Finance Policies and Programs: An Overview," *Journal of Education Finance* 34, no. 3 (Winter 2009): 213–230.

35. U.S. Census Bureau, *Public Education Finances 2011* (Washington, DC: Government Printing Office, 2010), 5, Table 5.

36. *Rodriguez v. San Antonio Independent School District* 411 U.S. 1 (1973).

37. Michael W. Kirst, "The Evolution of California's State School Finance System and Implications from Other States," Stanford University Institute for Research on Education Policy and Practice, March 2007. Frank Kemerer and Peter Samson, *California School Law,* 3rd ed. (Stanford, CA; Stanford University Press, 2013), 112, report that assistance from the state in California accounts for 60 percent of the funds for public schools.

38. William A. Fischel, *The Homevoter Hypothesis: How Home Values Influence Local Government Taxation, School Finance, and Land-Use Policies* (Cambridge, MA: Harvard University Press, 2001), 131–133 and 140–143.

39. Teresa Watanabe, "Big Changes to California's School-Funding Rules Are Approved," *Los Angeles Times,* January 16, 2014.

40. "How State Aid Formulas Undermine Educational Equity in the States," in Bruce D. Baker and Sean P. Corcoran, *The Stealth Inequities of School Funding: How State and Local School Finance Systems Perpetuate Inequitable Student Spending* (Washington, DC: Center for American Progress, September 2012), esp. 19, www.americanprogress.org/wp-content/uploads/2012/09/StealthInequities.pdf.

41. *Milliken v. Bradley,* 418 U.S. 717 (1974).

42. For further details on how resegregation occurs in districts released from desegregation plans, see: John Charles Boger and Gary Orfield, eds., *School Resegregation: Must the South Turn Back?* (Chapel Hill: University of North Carolina Press, 2005); and Sean F. Reardon, Elena Tej Grewal, Demetra Kalogrides, and Erica Greenberg, "Brown Fades: The End of Court-Ordered Desegregation and the Resegregation of American Public Schools," *Journal of Policy Analysis and Management* 31, no. 4 (Fall 2012): 876–904.

43. Gary Orfield, John Kucsera, and Genevieve Siegel-Hawley, *E Pluribus . . . Separation: Deepening Double Segregation for More Students* (Los Angeles: UCLA Civil Rights Project/Proyecto Derechos Civiles, September 2012), 9, http://civilrightsproject.ucla.edu/research/k-12-education/integration-and-diversity/mlk-national/e-pluribus . . . separation-deepening-double-segregation-for-more-students/orfield_epluribus_revised_omplete_2012.pdf. The word "apartheid" is a reference to the infamous system of strict racial separation that once characterized white-ruled South Africa.

44. Erica Frankenberg and Gary Orfield, eds., *The Resegregation of Suburban Schools: A Hidden Crisis in American Education* (Cambridge, MA: Harvard Education Press, 2012); Orfield and Kucsera, *E Pluribus . . . Separation,* 57–71; Adai Tefera, Erica Frankenberg, Genevieve Siegel-Hawley, and Gina Chirichigno, *Integrating Suburban Schools: How to Benefit from Growing Diversity and Avoid Segregation* (Los Angeles: UCLA Civil Rights Project/Proyecto Derechos Civiles, 2011), http://civilrightsproject.ucla.edu/research/k-12-education/integration-and-diversity/integrating-suburban-schools-how-to-benefit-from-growing-diversity-and-avoid-segregation/tefera-suburban-manual-2011.pdf.

45. Jennifer Jellison Home, Anjale Welton, and Sarah Diem, "Pursuing 'Separate But Equal' in Suburban San Antonio," in *The Resegregation of Suburban Schools*, ed. Frankenberg and Oldfield.

46. Institute on Metropolitan Opportunity, *Charter Schools in the Twin Cities: 2013 Update* (Minneapolis: University of Minnesota Law School, October 2013), 1, http://www.law.umn.edu/uploads/16/65/1665940a907fdbe31337271af733353d/Charter-School-Update-2013-final.pdf.

47. Stephen Samuel Smith, "Hugh Governs? Regime and Education Policy in Charlotte, North Carolina," *Journal of Urban Affairs* 19, no. 3 (1997): 247–274; Damien Jackson, "Here Comes the Neighborhood: Charlotte and the Resegregation of America's Public Schools," *In These Times,* December 20, 2002, reprinted in Myron A. Levine, ed., *Annual Editions: Urban Society,* 16th ed. (New York: McGraw-Hill, 2014), 118–120. For documentation of the resegregation of schools that has taken place in Charlotte-Mecklenburg County, see Laura Simmons and Claire Appaliski, "Mapping de facto Segregation in Charlotte-Mecklenburg Schools," *UNC Charlotte Urban Institute,* September 23, 2010, http://ui.uncc.edu/story/mapping-de-facto-segregation-charlotte-mecklenburg-schools.

48. See Niedt, ed., *Social Justice in Diverse Suburbs.*

49. Jim Malewitz, "West's Record Wildfires Raise Questions about Development," *USA Today,* August 19, 2013.

50. Fischel, *The Homevoter Hypothesis,* 230.

51. Mike Davis, *City of Quartz* (New York: Random House, 1990), 206–209.

52. *Village of Euclid, Ohio, v. Ambler Realty Co.,* 272 U.S. 365 (1926). Robert H. Nelson, *Private Neighborhoods and the Transformation of Local Government* (Washington, DC: Urban Institute, 2005), 139–152, argues that contemporary communities are no longer concerned with safeguarding against nuisance and incompatible uses of land; instead, communities primarily use zoning for exclusionary purposes to maintain income and class segregation, thereby preserving property values.

53. *Arlington Heights v. Metropolitan Housing Development Corporation,* 429 U.S. 252 (1977).

54. Charles M. Lamb, *Housing Segregation in America since 1960* (Cambridge, UK and New York: Cambridge University Press, 2005), 220–224.

55. Nelson, *Private Neighborhoods and the Transformation of Local Government,* 144–146.

56. Stephan Schmidt and Kurt Paulsen, "Is Open-Space Preservation a Form of Exclusionary Zoning? The Evolution of Municipal Open-Space Policies in New Jersey," *Urban Affairs Review* 45, no. 1 (2009): 111–112.

57. For a review of various state and local growth management strategies, see Douglas R. Porter, *Managing Growth in America's Communities,* 2nd ed. (Washington, DC: Island Press, 2008).

58. Alexander Garvin, *The American City: What Works, What Doesn't*, 2nd ed. (New York: McGraw-Hill, 2002), 454.

59. *Southern Burlington County NAACP v. Township of Mount Laurel* 67 N.J. 151,336 A. 2d 713 (1975). Charles M. Haar, *Suburbs Under Siege: Race, Space, and Audacious Judges* (Princeton, NJ: Princeton University Press, 1996), presents an in-depth discussion of the *Mount Laurel* decisions; Haar offers the *Mount Laurel* approach as a model for the judicial assault on exclusionary practices.

60. *Burlington County NAACP v. Township of Mount Laurel*, 92N.J. 158, 336A. 2d 390 (1983).

61. In 2013, the New Jersey Supreme Court rejected an effort by Governor Chris Christie to weaken the *Mount Laurel* process still further. See Salvador Rizzo, "N.J. Supreme Court Blocks Christie's Plan to Abolish Affordable-Housing Agency," *The Star-Ledger (New Jersey)*, July 10, 2013.

62. Patrick Field, Jennifer Gilbert, and Michael Wheeler, "Trading the Poor: Intermunicipal Housing Negotiation in New Jersey," *Harvard Negotiation Law Review* (Spring 1997): 1–33.

63. David L. Kirp, John P. Dwyer, and Larry A. Rosenthal, *Our Town: Race, Housing, and the Soul of Suburbia* (New Brunswick, NJ: Rutgers University Press, 1995), 175, present a detailed discussion of the *Mount Laurel* decisions and their impact.

64. For a review of the *Mount Laurel* decisions and a positive assessment of the program's ability to promote improved living conditions and the social mobility of poorer families who gained access to new suburban environments, see Douglas S. Massey, Len Albright, Rebecca Casciano, Elizabeth Derickson, and David N. Kinsey, *Climbing Mount Laurel: The Struggle for Affordable Housing and Social Mobility in an American Suburb* (Princeton, NJ: Princeton University Press, 2013).

65. Allan Mallach, "The Rise and Fall of Inclusionary Housing in New Jersey: Social Policy, Judicial Mandates, and the Realities of the Real Estate Marketplace," paper presented at the annual meeting of the Urban Affairs Association, March 16, 1996.

66. Spencer M. Cowan, "Anti-Snob Land-Use Laws, Suburban Exclusion, and Housing Opportunity," *Journal of Urban Affairs* 82, no. 3 (2006): 295–313.

67. Ravit Hananel, "Can Centralization, Decentralization, and Welfare Go Together? The Case of Massachusetts Affordable Housing Policy (Ch. 40B)," *Urban Studies* 51, no. 12 (September 2014): 2487–2502.

68. Gerrit-Jan Knaap, Antonio Bento, and Scott Lowe, *Housing Market Impacts of Inclusionary Zoning* (National Center for Smart Growth Research and Education, University of Maryland, 2008); Robert Hickey, "After the Downturn: New Challenges and Opportunities for Inclusionary Housing," Inclusionary Housing Policy Brief, February 2013, www.nhc.org/media/files/InclusionaryReport201302.pdf.

69. Jim Wise, "'Affordable' Housing Bonus an Incentive to Lose Money," *Durham News (North Carolina)*, December 20, 2013.

70. "Inclusionary Zoning Bill Vetoed in California," *Affordable Housing Finance*, October 2013, www.housingfinance.com/affordable-housing/inclusionary-zoning-bill-vetoed-in-california.aspx.

71. The Urban Institute and the U.S. Department of Housing and Urban Development, *Expanding Housing Opportunities through Inclusionary Zoning: Lessons from Two Counties* (Washington, DC: HUD, 2013), www.huduser.org/portal/publications/HUD-496_new.pdf.

72. Heather L. Schwartz, Liisa Ecola, Kristin J. Leuschner, and Aaron Kofner, *Is Inclusionary Zoning Inclusionary? A Guide for Practitioners*, technical report TR-1231 (Santa Monica, CA: The Rand Corporation, 2012), www.rand.org/content/dam/rand/pubs/technical_reports/2012/RAND_TR1231.pdf.

73. Sophia Rosenbaum, "De Blasio Pins Affordable Housing Hopes on Mandatory Inclusionary Zoning," *Gotham Gazette*, November 3, 2013, www.gothamgazette.com/index.php/housing/4700-de-blasio-pins-affordable-housing-hopes-on-mandatory-inclusionary-zoning; Jonathan Lemire, "Bill de Blasio Turning to Big Push on Affordable Housing," *Huffington Post*, March 30, 2014, www.huffingtonpost.com/2014/03/30/bill-de-blasio-affordable-housing_n_5059210.html.

74. William Fulton, *The Reluctant Metropolis* (Baltimore: Johns Hopkins University Press, 2001), 2–4.

75. Benjamin and Nathan, *Regionalism and Realism*, 3–26.

76. Robert W. Burchell et al., *Sprawl Costs* (Washington, DC: American Planning Association, 2005) provides detailed estimates of the extensive costs of sprawl.

77. David Rusk, "Growth Management: The Core Regional Issue," in *Reflections on Regionalism,* ed. Bruce Katz (Washington, DC: Brookings Institution Press, 2000), 88.

78. Of course, not all metropolitan areas are equally sprawled. Metropolitan areas in the Northeast and the Midwest tend to have more compact development than is found in metropolitan areas in other regions. Still, metropolitan areas in all regions show considerable variation in terms of their level of compact development, population density, and the access of citizens to public transit. Reid Ewing and Shima Hamidi, *Measuring Sprawl 2014* (Washington, DC: Smart Growth America, 2014) ranks 221 metropolitan areas and nearly a thousand counties on various indicators of sprawl: www.smartgrowthamerica.org/measuring-sprawl.

79. Fischel, *The Homevoter Hypothesis,* 230. See also Matthew E. Kahn, *Green Cities: Urban Growth and the Environment* (Washington, DC: Brookings Institution Press, 2006), 127–129.

80. Smart Growth America, *Building Better Budgets: A National Examination of the Fiscal Benefits of Smart Growth Development* (Washington, DC, May 2013), www.smartgrowthamerica.org/documents/building-better-budgets.pdf.

81. American Planning Association, *Planning for Smart Growth: 2002 State of the States* (Washington, DC: APA, 2002).

82. Kahn, *Green Cities,* 110–129; Sarah Gardner, "The Impact of Sprawl on the Environment and Human Health," in *Urban Sprawl: A Comprehensive Reference Guide,* ed. David C. Soule (Westport, CT: Greenwood Press, 2006), 240–259.

83. Christopher Jones and Daniel M. Kammen, "Spatial Distribution of U.S. Carbon Footprints Reveals Suburbanization Undermines Greenhouse Gas Benefits of Urban Population Density," *Environmental Science and Technology* 48, vol. 2 (2014): 895–902.

84. Mark Edward Brown, "Subdivision Sprawl in Southeastern Wisconsin: Planning, Politics, and the Lack of Affordable Housing," in *Suburban Sprawl: Culture, Theory, and Politics,* ed. Matthew J. Lindstrom and Hugh Bartling (Lanham, MD: Rowman and Littlefield, 2003), 263.

85. Robert D. Bullard, "Smart Growth Meets Environmental Justice," in *Growing Smarter: Achieving Livable Communities, Environmental Justice, and Regional Equity,* ed. Robert D. Bullard (Cambridge, MA: MIT Press, 2007), 23–50.

86. Swati R. Prakash, "Beyond Dirty Diesels: Clean and Just Transportation in Northern Manhattan," in *Growing Smarter,* ed. Bullard, 273–298.

87. Andres Duany and Jeff Speck, with Mike Lydon, *The Smart Growth Manual* (New York: McGraw-Hill, 2010), describe the various urban planning, traffic calming, green construction, and architectural design strategies that constitute Smart Growth.

88. James C. O'Connell, *The Hub's Metropolis: Greater Boston's Development from Railroad Suburbs to Smart Growth* (Cambridge, MA: MIT Press, 2013), 7–8; also see 225–251.

89. Peter Calthorpe and William Fulton, *The Regional City: Planning for the End of Sprawl* (Washington, DC: Island Press, 2001).

90. James R. Cohen, "Maryland's 'Smart Growth': Using Incentives to Combat Sprawl," in *Urban Sprawl: Causes, Consequences, and Policy Responses,* ed. Gregory D. Squires (Washington, DC: Urban Institute Press, 2002), 293–324.

91. Katz, "Smart Growth: Future of the American Metropolis?" 18.

92. Christopher G. Boone and Ali Modarres, *City and Environment* (Philadelphia: Temple University Press, 2006), 181. See also Jerry Anthony, "Do State Growth Management Regulations Reduce Sprawl?" *Urban Affairs Review* 39, no. 3 (January 2004): 376–397.

93. Anthony Downs, "Smart Growth: Why We Discuss It More Than We Do It," *Journal of the American Planning Association* 71, no. 4 (Autumn 2005): 367–378.

94. Hannah Gosnell, Jeffrey D. Kline, Garrett Chrostek, and James Duncan, "Is Oregon's Land Use Planning Program Conserving Forest and Farm Land? A Review of the Evidence," *Land Use Policy* 28 (2011): 185–192. My thanks go to Innisfree McKinnon for sharing her insights on various aspects of land policy in Oregon.

95. Carlton Wade Basmajian, *Atlanta Unbound: Enabling Sprawl Though Policy and Planning* (Philadelphia: Temple University Press, 2013).

96. It should also be noted that more than one study has found that urban growth boundaries and other "urban containment" strategies have an impact on reducing residential racial segregation in a metropolis. See Arthur C. Nelson, Thomas W. Sanchez, and Casey J. Dawkins, "The Effect of Urban Containment and Mandatory Housing Elements on Racial Segregation in U.S. Metropolitan Areas, 1990–2000," *Journal of Urban Affairs* 26, no. 3 (2004): 339–350.

97. Nancy Chapman and Hollie Lund, "Housing Density and Livability in Portland," in *The Portland Edge: Challenges and Successes in Growing Communities,* ed. Connie P. Ozawa (Washington, DC: Island Press, 2004), 210.

98. Reid Ewing, Rolf Pendall, and Don Chen, *Measuring Sprawl and Its Impact* (Washington, DC: Smart Growth America, 2002), www.smartgrowthamerica.org/sprawlindex/sprawlindex.html.

99. Arthur C. Nelson, Rolf Pendall, Casey J. Dawkins, and Gerrit J. Knapp, "The Link Between Growth Management and Housing Affordability: The Academic Evidence," discussion paper prepared for the Brookings Institution Center on Urban and Metropolitan Policy (Washington, DC, 2002), www.brookings.edu/dybdocroot/es/urban/publications/growthmanagexsum.htm.

100. William K. Jaeger, Cyrus Grout, and Andrew J. Plantings, "Evidence of the Effects of Oregon's Land Use Planning System on Land Prices," Working Paper WP08WJ1 (Cambridge, MA: Lincoln Institute of Land Policy, 2008).

101. Peter A. Walker and Patrick T. Hurley, *Planning Paradise: Politics and Visioning of Land Use in Oregon* (University of Arizona Press, 2011), 160. As Walker and Hurley observe, not all of the land added to an expanded urban growth boundary is ready for development, especially where localities refuse to provide the sewers and other infrastructure essential for new development.

102. Eric Mortenson, "Metro Approves Urban Growth Boundary Expansion for the Portland Area," *The Oregonian,* October 20, 2011.

103. Rolf Pendall et al., "Connecting Smart Growth, Housing Affordability, and Racial Equity," in *The Geography of Opportunity,* ed. de Souza Briggs, 237–239.

104. Alex Marshall, *How Cities Work: Suburbs, Sprawl, and the Roads Not Taken* (Austin: University of Texas Press, 2000), xix.

105. For a review of the guiding principles of the New Urbanism, see: Andres Duany, Elizabeth Plater-Zyberk, and Jeff Speck, *Suburban Nation: The Rise of Sprawl and the Decline of the American Dream,* 10th anniv. ed. (New York: North Point Press, 2010); and Emily Talen (ed.) and the Congress for the New Urbanism, *Charter of the New Urbanism,* 2nd ed. (New York: McGraw-Hill, 2013).

106. Duany, Plater-Zyberk, and Speck, *Suburban Nation,* 30.

107. For a review of the transformation that HOPE VI brought to public housing in Louisville, see James Hanlon, "Success by Design: HOPE VI, New Urbanism, and the Neoliberal Transformation of Public Housing in the United States," *Environment and Planning Annual* 42, no. 1 (2010): 80–98.

108. For an in-depth assessment of the various achievements and limitations of New Urbanism, sustainable design, and green urban planning, see: Tigran Hass, ed., *New Urbanism and Beyond: Designing Cities for the Future* (New York: Rizzoli, 2008); and Tigran Hass, *Sustainable Urbanism and Beyond: Rethinking Cities for the Future* (New York: Rizzoli, 2012).

109. Ellen Dunham-Jones and June Williamson, *Retrofitting Suburbia: Urban Design Solutions for Redesigning Suburbs* (Hoboken, NJ: Wiley, 2009), 112–134.

110. Myron A. Levine, "The New Urbanism: A Limited Revolution," in *Redefining Suburban Studies: Searching for New Paradigms,* ed. Daniel Rubey (Hempstead, NY: National Center for Suburban Studies at Hofstra University, 2009), 25–30.

111. Jill L. Grant, "Two Sides of a Coin? New Urbanism and Gated Communities," *Housing Policy Debate* 18, no. 3 (2007): 481–501.

112. Marshall, *How Cities Work,* xx and 6. Also see Alex Krieger, "Arguing the 'Against' Position: New Urbanism as a Means of Building and Rebuilding Our Cities," in *The Seaside Debates: A Critique of the New Urbanism,* ed. Todd W. Bressi (New York: Rizzoli, 2002), 51–58.

113. Robert Cervero, *Suburban Gridlock* (New Brunswick, NJ: Transaction Books, 2013), 226–230.

114. Judith K. De Jong, *New SubUrbanisms* (New York: Routledge, 2014).

10. REGIONAL GOVERNANCE IN A GLOBAL AGE

1. Richardson Dilworth, *The Urban Origins of Suburban Autonomy* (Cambridge, MA: Harvard University Press, 2005), 108–193.

2. Rodger Johnson, Marc Perry, and Lisa Lollock, "Annexation and Population Growth in American Cities, 1990–2000," *Municipal Year Book 2004* (Washington, DC: International City/County Management Association 2004).

3. Howard N. Rabinowitz, "Albuquerque: City at a Crossroads," in *Sunbelt Cities: Politics and Growth Since World War II,* ed. Richard M. Bernard and Bradley R. Rice (Austin: University of Texas Press, 1983), 258–259.

4. Carol E. Heim, "Border Wars: Tax Revenues, Annexation, and Urban Growth in Phoenix," *International Journal of Urban and Regional Research* 36, no. 4 (July 2012): 831–859.

5. David Rusk, *Inside Game/Outside Game: Winning Strategies for Saving Urban America* (Washington, DC: Brookings Institution Press, 1999), 3–10 and 126–145; David Rusk, *Annexation and the Fiscal Fate of Cities* (Washington, DC: Brookings Institution, August 2006), www.brookings. edu/reports/2006/08metropolitanpolicy_rusk.aspx.

6. The importance of annexation to economic growth and inclusion in Columbus is detailed by Chris Benner and Manuel Pastor, *Just Growth; Inclusion and Prosperity in America's Metropolitan Regions* (New York: Routledge, 2012), 96–109.

7. See, for instance, Monte Whaley, "'Tea Party' to Fight City's Annexation," *Denver Post,* February 7, 2008.

8. John Johnston, "More Border Battles as Cities Search for Cash," *Cincinnati Enquirer,* June 10, 2012; Lisa Wakeland, "New Annexation Bill on Its Way," *Cincinnati Enquirer,* May 23, 2013.

9. Suzanne Leland and Kurt Thurmaier, "When Efficiency Is Unbelievable: Normative Lessons from 30 Years of City-County Consolidations," *Public Administration Review* 65, no. 4 (July–August 2005): 475–489; Suzanne M. Leland and Kurt Thurmaier, eds., *City-County Consolidation: Promises Made, Promises Kept?* (Washington, DC: Georgetown University Press, 2010).

10. For an easy-to-read brief review of city-county consolidation efforts, see John F. Freie, *The Case for Government Consolidation* (Syracuse, NY: Syracuse 20/20, September 2005), www.syracuse2020. org/LearnAboutConsolidation/tabid/77/Default.aspx.

11. Chris Benner and Manuel Pastor, *Just Growth: Inclusion and Prosperity in America's Metropolitan Regions* (New York: Routledge, 2012), 77–96.

12. Mark Rosentraub, "City-County Consolidation and the Rebuilding of Image: The Fiscal Lessons from Indianapolis's UniGov Program," *State and Local Government Review* 32, no. 3 (Fall 2000): 180–191.

13. C. James Owen and York Willbern, *Governing Metropolitan Indianapolis: The Politics of Unigov* (Berkeley: University of California Press, 1985), 1–2.

14. Ibid. Former Indianapolis Mayor Stephen Goldsmith, *The Twenty-First Century City: Resurrecting Urban America* (Lanham, MD: Rowman & Littlefield, 1999), 75–94, describes his success in shepherding regional cooperation for economic development. The figures he reports for the airport can be found on p. 36.

15. Suzanne M. Leland and Mark S. Rosentraub, "Consolidated and Fragmented Governments and Regional Cooperation: Surprising Lessons from Charlotte, Cleveland, Indianapolis, and Wyandotte/Kansas City, Kansas," in *Governing Metropolitan Regions in the 21st Century,* ed. Donald Phares (Armonk, NY: M.E. Sharpe, 2009), 143–163.

16. Mayor Greg Ballard, speech to the Rotary Club of Indianapolis, January 28, 2009, www. insideindianabusiness.com/newsitem.asp?ID=33672. The continued existence of numerous taxing and service zones is a notable feature of a number of consolidations.

17. Hank V. Savitch, Ronald K. Vogel, and Lin Ye, "Beyond the Rhetoric: Lessons from Louisville's Consolidation," *American Review of Public Administration* 40, no. 1 (2010): 3–28.

18. Leland and Thurmaier, eds., *City-County Consolidation.*

19. H.V. Savitch and Ronald K. Vogel, "Metropolitan Consolidation versus Metropolitan Governance in Louisville," *State and Local Government Review* 32, no. 3 (Fall 2000): 201. This paragraph relies on pp. 198–212, and the authors' argument for a "New Regionalism" based on innovative forms of interlocal cooperation instead of the creation of new metropolitan government plans.

20. H.V. Savitch and Ronald K. Vogel, "Suburbs Without a City: Power and City-County Consolidation," *Urban Affairs Review* 39, no. 6 (2004): 758–790; H.V. Savitch, Takashi Tsukamoto, and Ronald K. Vogel, "Civic Culture and Corporate Regime in Louisville," *Journal of Urban Affairs* 30, no. 4 (2008): 437–460, esp. 441.

21. Joseph Gerth, "Merger: One Year Later," *Courier-Journal (Louisville),* December 22, 2003; Savitch and Vogel, "Suburbs Without a City."

22. Savitch and Vogel, "Metropolitan Consolidation versus Metropolitan Governance in Louisville," 210.

23. Savitch, Vogel, and Ye, "Beyond the Rhetoric: Lessons from Louisville's Consolidation." 3–28.

24. Janet M. Kelly and Sarin Adhikari, "Indicators of Financial Condition in Pre- and Post-Merger Louisville," *Journal of Urban Affairs* 35, no. 5 (December 2013): 553–567; Patricia Atkins, Pamela Blumenthal, Adrienne Edisis, Alec Friedhoff, Leah Curran, Lisa Lowry, Travis St. Clair, Howard Wial, and Harold Wolman, *Responding to Manufacturing Loss: What Can Economic Development Policy Do?* (Washington, DC: The Brookings Institution, June 2011), 28–33; and Barry Kornstein, Prakitsha Bhattarai, Sarah Ehresman, and Janet M. Kelly, *Destination Tourism: Economic and Community Impacts of Tourism* (Louisville: University of Louisville Urban Studies Institute, 2012), http://usi.louisville.edu/images/Publications/Destination%20Louisville.pdf.

25. Raymond A. Mohl, "Miami: The Ethnic Cauldron," in *Sunbelt Cities,* ed. Bernard and Rice, 82–83.

26. Arthur C. Nelson, "Portland: The Metropolitan Umbrella," in *Regional Politics: America in a Post-City Age,* ed. H.V. Savitch and Ronald K. Vogel (Beverly Hills, CA: SAGE Publications, 1996), 253.

27. Ibid., 263–220, presents more detailed discussion of Metro's limitations.

28. John Provo, "Risk-Averse Regionalism: The Cautionary Tale of Portland, Oregon, and Affordable Housing," *Journal of Planning Education and Research Urban Affairs* 28, no. 3 (March 2009): 369–381.

29. John J. Harrigan, "Governance in Transition: Regime Under Pressure in the Twin Cities," paper presented at the annual meeting of the American Political Science Association, New York, September 2, 1994.

30. Edward G. Goetz, *Clearing the Way: Deconcentrating the Poor in Urban America* (Washington, DC: Urban Institute Press, 2003), 98–99 and 189–190; Edward G. Goetz, Karen Chapple, and Barbara Lukermann, "Enabling Exclusion," *Journal of Planning Education and Research* 22, no. 3 (2003): 213–225; Myron Orfield, Nick Wallace, Eric Myott, and Geneva Finn, "Governing the Twin Cities," in *Region: Planning the Future of the Twin Cities,* ed. Myron Orfield and Thomas F. Luce Jr. (Minneapolis: University of Minnesota Press, 2010), 57–59.

31. The potential for this to occur was even foreseen by the state legislator most responsible for the creation of the Twin Cities fiscal disparities law. See Myron Orfield, *Metropolitics: A Regional Approach for Community and Stability* (Washington, DC: Brookings Institution Press, 1997), 109–111.

32. David Peterson, Katie Humphrey, and Laurie Blake, "Twin Cities Tax-Share Program Receives Scrutiny," *StarTribune (Minneapolis),* January 31, 2012.

33. Remarks of George Latimer, former mayor of St. Paul, Minnesota, to the annual conference of the National Civic League, Denver, Colorado, October 27, 1989.

34. Dagney Faulk and Michael Hicks, *Local Government Reform in Indiana* (Muncie, IN: Ball State University, Miller College of Business, January 2009), https://cms.bsu.edu/-/media/WWW/

DepartmentalContent/MillerCollegeofBusiness/BBR/Publications/LocalGovReform.pdf; and Leland and Thurmaier, *City-County Consolidation: Promises Made, Promises Kept?*

35. For classic statements of public choice theory applied to metropolitan areas, see: Vincent Ostrom, Charles Tiebout, and Robert Warren, "The Organization of Government in Metropolitan Areas," *American Political Science Review* 55 (December 1961): 831–842; Robert L. Bish, *The Public Economy of Metropolitan Areas* (Chicago: Markham, 1971); Robert L. Bish and Vincent Ostrom, *Understanding Urban Government: Metropolitan Reform Reconsidered* (Washington, DC: American Enterprise Institute, 1973); and Vincent Ostrom and Elinor Ostrom, "Public Choice: A Different Approach to the Study of Public Administration," *Public Administration Review* 31 (March/April 1971): 203–216. For a more readable overview of the public choice debate see Kathryn A. Foster, *The Political Economy of Special-Purpose Governments* (Washington, DC: Georgetown University Press, 1997), 35–41.

36. William Duncombe, "Strategies to Improve Efficiency: School District Consolidation and Alternative Cost-Sharing Strategies," presented at the Conference on School Finance and Governance in Providence Rhode Island, November 13, 2007.

37. All of these successes were gained in school consolidation in Pennsylvania. See Standard & Poor's, *Study of the Cost-Effectiveness of Consolidating Pennsylvania Districts* (New York: Standard & Poor's School Evaluation Services, 2007).

38. Patricia S. Atkins, "Local Intergovernmental Agreements: Strategies for Cooperation," MIS Report (Washington DC: International City/County Management Association, 1997), 2–3.

39. Atkins, "Local Intergovernmental Agreements: Strategies for Cooperation," 5.

40. Donald F. Kettl, *System Under Stress: Homeland Security and American Politics* (Washington. DC: CQ Press, 2003), 30–31 and 63–66.

41. Mauricio Covarrubias, "The Challenges of Interdependence and Coordination in the Bilateral Agenda: Mexico and the United States," in *Networked Governance: The Future of Intergovernmental Management,* ed. Jack W. Meek and Kurt Thurmaier (Los Angeles: SAGE/CQ Press, 2012), 250–257.

42. Kathleen Staudt, *Violence and Activism at the Border: Gender, Fear, and Everyday Life in Ciudad Juárez* (Austin: University of Texas Press, 2008).

43. Darran Simon and Claudia Vargas, "Financial Details Outlined for Camden Regional Police Force," *Philadelphia Inquirer*, August 30, 2012; Charlie Ban, "Regional Police Force in Camden County, N.J. Nears Launch Date," *County News*, a publication of the National Association of Counties, March 11, 2013, available at www.naco.org/newsroom/countynews/Current%20Issue/3-11-2013/Pages/Regional-police-force-in-Camden-County,-N-J--nears-launch-date.aspx; and Kate Zernike, "Camden Turns Around with New Police Force," *New York Times*, September 1, 2014. The figures on the dramatic decrease in response times can be found in the Zernike article.

44. Connor, Michan Andrew, "Public Benefits from Public Choice: Producing Decentralization in Metropolitan Los Angeles, 1954–1973," *Journal of Urban History* 39, no. 1 (January 2013): 79–100.

45. Thomas W. Sanchez and James F. Wolf, "Environmental Justice and Transportation Equity: A Review of MPOs," in *Growing Smarter: Achieving Livable Communities, Environmental Justice, and Regional Equity,* ed. Robert D. Bullard (Cambridge, MA: MIT Press, 2007), 249–271.

46. Tony Barboza, "Irvine Is Told to Accommodate 35,000 Homes in 7 Years," *Los Angeles Times,* July 25, 2007; Paul G. Lewis, *California's Housing Element Law: The Issue of Local Non-compliance* (San Francisco: Public Policy Institute of California, 2003), www.ppic.org/content/pubs/report/R_203PLR.pdf; Eric Young, "New Housing Targets Spur a Bay Area Backlash," *San Francisco Business Times,* May 30, 2013, www.bizjournals.com/sanfrancisco/print-edition/2013/05/31/new-housing-targets-spur-a-bay-area.html?page=all.

47. Donald F. Norris and Carl W. Stenberg, "Governmental Fragmentation and Metropolitan Government: Does Less Mean More? The Case of the Baltimore Region," in *Governing Metropolitan Regions in the 21st Century,* ed. Phares, 132–133.

48. Bruce Katz, Robert Puentes, and Scott Bernstein, *TEA-21 Reauthorization: Getting Transportation Right for Metropolitan America* (Washington, DC: Brookings Institution, March 2003), 4,

www.brookings.edu/research/reports/2003/03/transportation-katz. The MPO process is also part of the 2005 Safe, Accountable, Flexible, Efficient Transportation Act: A Legacy for Users (SAFETEA-LU), which succeeded TEA-21.

49. Katz, Puentes, and Bernstein, *TEA-21 Reauthorization,* 4. See also Thomas A. Horan, Hank Dittmar, and Daniel R. Jordan, "ISTEA and the New Era in Transportation Policy: Sustainable Communities from a Federal Initiative," in *Toward Sustainable Communities: Transition and Transformations in Environmental Policy,* ed. Daniel A. Mazmanian and Michael E. Kraft (Cambridge, MA: MIT Press, 1999), 217–245.

50. Bruce Katz, Robert Puentes, and Scott Bernstein, "Getting Transportation Right for Metropolitan America," in *Taking the High Road: A Metropolitan Agenda for Transportation Reform,* ed. Bruce Katz and Robert Puentes (Washington, DC: Brookings Institution Press, 2005), 21–25; Kate Lowe, "Bypassing Equity? Transit Investment and Regional Transportation Planning," Building Resistant Regions Working Paper No. 210–07, Institute of Governmental Studies, University of California, Berkeley, December 10, 2010, http://brr.berkeley.edu/brr_workingpapers/2010–07-lowe_bypassing_equity.pdf.

51. David Y. Miller and Raymond W. Cox III, "Reframing the Political and Legal Relationships between Local Governments and Regional Institutions," in *Network Governance: The Future of Intergovernmental Management,* ed. Jack W. Meek and Kurt Thurmaier (Los Angeles: Sage/CQ Press, 2012), 112–114. The quotation appears on p. 113.

52. Josh Stephens, "Southern California Adopts $524 Billion Regional Housing Plan," *California Planning & Development Report,* April 4, 2011.

53. U.S. Census Bureau, "2012 Census of Governments," Table 2, "Local Governments by Type and State: 2012," http://www2.census.gov/govs/cog/2012/formatted_prelim_counts_23jul2012_2.pdf.

54. Brett W. Hawkins and Rebecca M. Hendrick, "Do Metropolitan Special Districts Reinforce Sociospatial Inequalities? A Study of Sewerage and Technical Education in Milwaukee County," *Publius: Journal of Federalism* 27, no. 1 (Winter 1997): 135–143.

55. Martin V. Melosi, *Precious Commodity: Providing Water for America's Cities* (Pittsburgh: University of Pittsburgh Press, 2011), 144–145 and 165–166.

56. Of course, some special districts do seek to consult the people they serve. The administrators of modern special districts use surveys, focus groups, and various other methods to engage citizens. See Tanya Heikkila and Kimberley Roussin Isett, "Citizen Involvement and Performance Management in Special-Purpose Governments," *Public Administration Review* 67, no. 2 (March/April 2007): 238–248.

57. Darin Painter, "Hoop Dreams," *IBmag.com,* June 2008, http://ibmag.com/Main/Archive/Hoop_Dreams_9776.aspx; Steven Litt, "Cleveland Cuyahoga Port Authority Approves $75 Million Bond Issue for Cleveland Museum of Art Expansion," *The Plain Dealer (Cleveland),* June 8, 2010; James F. McCarty, "Should the Port Authority be Saved or Dismantled? Critics Say Other Public Entities Could Do the Job Better," *The Plain Dealer (Cleveland),* January 11, 2010; Nancy Bowen-Ellzey, "Community Development Fact Sheet: Port Authorities as an Economic Development Tool for Local Government," Fact Sheet CDFS-1567–10, The Ohio State University Extension, 2010, http://ohioline.osu.edu/cd-fact/pdf/1567.pdf; Jason Williams, "Port Authority Test New Muscle with Development," *Cincinnati Enquirer,* May 30, 2012.

58. David Walker, "Snow White and the 17 Dwarfs: From Metro Cooperation to Governance," *National Civil Review* 76 (January/February 1987). See also Dennis R. Judd and James M. Smith, "The New Ecology of Urban Governance: Special-Purpose Authorities and Urban Development," in *Governing Cities in a Global Era: Urban Innovation, Competition, and Democratic Reform,* ed. Robin Hambleton and Jill Simone Gross (New York: Palgrave Macmillan, 2007), 151–160.

59. Jamieson Doig, *Empire on the Hudson: Entrepreneurial Vision and Political Power at the Port of New York Authority* (New York: Columbia University Press, 2002), 379–386 and 397–402; Gerald Benjamin and Richard P. Nathan, *Regionalism and Realism: A Study of Governments in the New York Metropolitan Area* (Washington, DC: Brookings Institution Press, 2001), 126–134.

60. Susan Fainstein, "The Port Authority of New York and New Jersey and the Rebuilding of the World Trade Center," paper presented at the annual meeting of the Urban Affairs Association,

Washington, DC, April 1, 2004. See also Bruce Berg and Paul Kantor, "New York: The Politics of Conflict and Avoidance," in *Regional Politics: America in a Post-City Age,* ed. Savitch and Vogel, 39.

61. Berg and Kantor, "New York: The Politics of Conflict and Avoidance," in *Regional Politics*, 39–50.

62. Vincent L. Marando and Robert D. Thomas, *The Forgotten Governments: County Commissioners as Policy Makers* (Gainesville: Florida Atlantic University/University Presses of Florida, 1977).

63. Linda Lobao and David S. Kraybill, "The Emerging Roles of County Governments in Metropolitan and Nonmetropolitan Areas: Findings from a National Survey," *Public Administration Review* 19, no. 3 (August 2005): 245–259.

64. William R. Barnes and Larry C. Ledebur, *Local Economies: The U.S. Common Market of Local Economic Regions* (Washington, DC: National League of Cities, 1994), 11.

65. Theodore Hershberg, "Regional Imperatives of Global Competition," in *Planning for a New Century,* ed. Jonathan Barnett (Washington, DC: Island Press, 2001), 13.

66. Beverly A. Cigler, "Economic Development in Metropolitan Areas," in *Urban and Regional Policies for Metropolitan Livability,* ed. David K. Hamilton and Patricia S. Atkins (Armonk, NY: M.E. Sharpe, 2008), 296–323, here 311.

67. Savitch and Vogel, eds., *Regional Politics: America in a Post-City Age.*

68. Norman Krumholz, "Regionalism Redux," *Public Administration Review* 57, no. 1 (1997): 83–89, esp. 88.

69. Louise Jezierski, "Pittsburgh: Partnerships in a Regional City," in *Regional Politics: America in a Post-City Age,* ed. Savitch and Vogel, 159–181; H.V. Savitch and Ronald K. Vogel, "Perspectives for the Present and Lessons for the Future," in *Regional Politics: America in a Post-City Age,* ed. Savitch and Vogel, 292.

70. Joan Fitzgerald, David Perry, and Martin Jaffe, *The New Metropolitan Alliances: Regional Collaboration for Economic Development,* Kitty and Michael Dukakis Center for Urban and Regional Policy, Paper 22 (2002), Northeastern University, Boston, http://hdl.handle.net/2047/d20003672.

71. Joel Rast and Virginia Cohen, "When Boeing Landed in Chicago: Lessons for Regional Economic Development," paper presented at the annual meeting of the Urban Affairs Association, Washington, DC, April 2, 2004.

72. Judd and Smith, "The New Ecology of Urban Governance: Special-Purpose Authorities and Urban Development," 151–161. Jonathan S. Davies, "Against 'Partnership': Toward a Local Challenge to Global Neoliberalism," raises many of the same concerns as he reviews public-private development bodies in England and Scotland; his work can be found in *Governing Cities in a Global Era,* ed. Hambleton and Gross, 199–210.

73. Myron Orfield, *Metropolitics: A Regional Agenda for Community and Stability* (Washington, DC: Brookings Institution, 1997, 1998), 104–172. Also see Hal Wolman, Todd Swanstrom, Margaret Weir, and Nicholas Lyon, "The Calculus of Coalitions: Cities and States and the Metropolitan Agenda," a discussion paper prepared for the Center on Urban and Metropolitan Policy, The Brookings Institution, Washington, DC, April 2004, www.brookings.edu/~/media/research/files/reports/2004/4/politics%20wolman/20040422_coalitions.pdf.

74. Myron Orfield, *American Metropolitics: The New Suburban Reality* (Washington, DC: Brookings Institution, 2001); Myron Orfield and Thomas F. Luce Jr., *Region: Planning the Future of the Twin Cities* (Minneapolis: University of Minnesota Press, 2010).

75. Heim, "Border Wars: Tax Revenues, Annexation, and Urban Growth in Phoenix," 831–859.

76. Victoria Gordon, "Partners or Competitors? Perceptions of Regional Economic Development Cooperation in Illinois," *Economic Development Quarterly* 21, no. 1 (February 2007): 60–78.

77. Raymond W. Cox III, "Building Trust and Developing a Vision: Akron, Ohio," in *The Facilitative Leader in City Hall,* ed. James H. Svara (Boca Raton, FL: CRC Press, 2009), 318–319; Christopher V. Hawkins, "Competition and Cooperation: Local Government Joint Ventures for Economic Development," *Journal of Urban Affairs* 32, no. 2 (2010): 253–275; Rosemary D'Apolito, "Can't We All Get Along? Public Officials' Attitudes toward Regionalism as a Solution to Metropolitan Problems in a Rustbelt Community," *Journal of Applied Social Science* 6, no. 1 (March 2012): 103–120.

78. Orfield, *Metropolitics*, 129–131, 140–141, and 169–170.

79. Rusk, *Inside Game/Outside Game*, 278.

80. Manuel Pastor Jr., Chris Benner, and Martha Matsuoka, *This Could Be the Start of Something Big: How Social Movements for Regional Equity Are Reshaping Metropolitan America* (Ithaca, NY: Cornell University Press, 2009), 9–10.

81. In addition to the works of Leland and Thurmaier, see Patricia S. Atkins, "Metropolitan Forms, Fiscal Efficiency, and Other Bottom Lines," in *Urban and Regional Policies for Metropolitan Livability,* ed. Hamilton and Atkins, 78–79; and Samuel R. Staley, *The Effects of City-County Consolidation: A Review of the Recent Academic Literature* (Ft. Wayne, IN: Indiana Policy Review Foundation November 16, 2005), www.in.gov/legislative/interim/committee/2005/committees/prelim/MCCC02.pdf.

82. Suzanne M. Leland, "Kansas City/Wyandotte County, Kansas," in *Case Studies of City-County Consolidation,* ed. Leland and Thurmaier, 266; Susan M. Leland and Curtis Wood, "Improving the Efficiency and Effectiveness of Service Delivery in Local Government: The Case of Wyandotte County and Kansas City, Kansas," in *City-County Consolidation: Promises Made, Promises Kept?* ed. Leland and Thurmaier, 251 and 255.

83. Bruce Katz and Jennifer Bradley, *The Metropolitan Revolution: How Cities and Metros Are Fixing Our Broken Politics and Fragile Economy* (Washington, DC: Brookings Institution, 2013), chap. 3. The quotation appears on p. 43.

84. Carolyn Adams, "How the Suburbs Are Reshaping the City: A Philadelphia Case Study," paper presented at the annual meeting of the Urban Affairs Association, New Orleans, March 17, 2011.

85. Joel Rast, "Environmental Justice and the New Regionalism," *Journal of Planning Education and Research* 25, no. 3 (2006): 249–263.

86. George Galster, *Driving Detroit: The Quest for Respect in the Motor City* (Philadelphia: University of Pennsylvania Press, 2012), 263–266.

87. Todd Swanstrom and Brian Banks, "Community-Based Regionalism, Transportation, and Local Hiring Agreements," *Journal of Planning Education and Research* 28, no. 3 (March 2009): 355–367; Pastor, Benner, and Matsuoka, *This Could Be the Start of Something Big*.

11. The Intergovernmental City

1. At the height of the New Deal, the U.S. Supreme Court ruled in *United States v. Darby,* 312 U.S. 100 (1941), that the Tenth Amendment's "reserved" powers language states only a "truism" that states the obvious, that "all is retained which has not yet been surrendered." Such a statement, which by its very definition is true, does not necessarily impose severe limits on the national government. As the Court explained, the central government is entitled to the full exercise of its powers found elsewhere in the Constitution. Six decades later, the Court's logic in *Darby* remains the subject of controversy. Texas Governor Rick Perry and other conservatives argue that the Supreme Court misconstrued the Constitution's provisions on federalism, improperly undermining the Tenth Amendment.

2. *United States v. Lopez,* 514 U.S. 549 (1995).

3. *Printz v. United States* 117 S. Ct. 2365 (1997).

4. In *United States v. Morrison,* 120 S. Ct. 1740 (2000), the Supreme Court again recognized the existence of a boundary that separates national and state authority. The Court voided a provision of the federal Violence Against Women Act that allowed victims of rape to sue their attackers in federal court as opposed to state courts.

5. Timothy J. Conlan and Francois Vergniolle De Chantal, "The Rehnquist Court and Contemporary American Federalism," *Political Science Quarterly* 116, no. 2 (Summer 2001): 253–275; John Dinan and Dale Krane, "The State of American Federalism, 2005: Federalism Resurfaces in the Political Debate," *Publius: Journal of Federalism* 36, no. 3 (Summer 2006): 327–374.

6. Paul L. Posner, "The Supreme Court and the Remaking of Federalism," *Governing,* July 18, 2012, www.governing.com/columns/mgmt-insights/col-supreme-court-health-care-ruling-coercion-states-federalism.html.

7. See the January 2012 amicus or "friend of the court" brief in the Obamacare case, *National Federation of Independent Business v. Sebelius,* 132 S. Ct. 2566 (2012), filed by the Cato Institute, a politically conservative "think tank," www.cato.org/sites/cato.org/files/pubs/pdf/FvHHS-Brief.pdf.

8. Christopher C. Banks and John C. Blakeman, *The U.S. Supreme Court and New Federalism: From the Rehnquist to the Roberts Court* (Lanham, MD: Rowman & Littlefield, 2012); Christopher Shortell, "The End of the Federalism Five? Statutory Interpretation and the Roberts Court," *Publius: The Journal of Federalism* 42, no. 3 (Summer 2012): 516–537.

9. U.S. Census Bureau, *The 2012 Statistical Abstract: The National Data Book,* Tables 431 and 432; www.census.gov/compendia/statab/2012/tables/12s0431.pdf and www.census.gov/compendia/statab/2012/tables/12s0432.pdf.

10. U.S. Government Accountability Office, *Grants to State and Local Governments: An Overview of Federal Funding Levels and Selected Challenges,* GAO report 12–1016, September 2012, 8–9, www.gao.gov/assets/650/648792.pdf.

11. In addition to the three organizations mentioned in the paragraph, the ranks of the public interest groups (PIGs) also include the International City/County Management Association (ICMA), the National Governors Association (NGA), the National Conference of State Legislatures (NCSL), and the Council of State Governments (CSG).

12. Robert J. Dilger, *Federalism Issues in Surface Transportation Policy: Past and Present,* Congressional Research Service Report R40431 (Washington, DC: CRS, July 27, 2012), 26, www.fas.org/sgp/crs/misc/R40431.pdf.

13. Timothy Conlan, *New Federalism: Intergovernmental Reform from Nixon to Reagan* (Washington DC: Brookings Institution Press, 1988), 160.

14. Carl W. Stenberg, "Block Grants and Devolution: A Future Tool?" in *Intergovernmental Management for the Twenty-First Century,* ed. Timothy J. Conlan and Paul L. Posner (Washington, DC: Brookings Institution, 2008), 271.

15. Charles J. Orlebeke and John C. Weicher, "How CDBG Came to Pass," *Housing Policy Debate* 24, no. 1 (2014): 14–45.

16. William M. Rohe and George C. Galster, "The Community Development Block Grant Program Turns 40: Proposals for Program Expansion and Reform," *Housing Policy Debate* 24, no. 1 (2014): 3–13, esp. 6.

17. Michael Cooper, "Cities Face Tough Choices as U.S. Slashes Block Grants Program," *New York Times,* December 11, 2011; National Association of Development Organizations, "HUD CDBG: FY2013 Appropriations Update," July 13, 2012, www.nado.org/hud-cdbg-fy13-appropriations-update.

18. Expanding Opportunity in America: A Discussion Draft from the House Budget Committee, Chairman Paul Ryan, July 24, 2014, http://budget.house.gov/uploadedfiles/expanding_opportunity_in_america.pdf.

19. Robert Greenstein, "Commentary: Ryan 'Opportunity Grant' Would Likely Increase Poverty and Shrink Resources for Poverty Programs over Time," Center on Budget and Policy Priorities, Washington, DC, July 24, 2014, www.cbpp.org/cms/index.cfm?fa=view&id=4176.

20. John Dinan and Shama Damkhar, "The State of American Federalism 2008–2009: The Presidential Election, the Economic Downturn, and the Consequences for Federalism," *Publius: Journal of Federalism* 39, no. 3 (2009): 369–407, esp. 376.

21. Robert Jay Dilger, *Federal Grants-in-Aid: A Historical Perspective on Contemporary Issues,* CRS Report to Congress R40638 (Washington, DC: Congressional Research Service, 2010), 32, http://assets.opencrs.com/rpts/R40638_20100216.pdf.

22. Kevin Fox Gotham, "Reinforcing Inequalities: The Impact of the CDBG Program on Post-Katrina Rebuilding," *Housing Policy Debate* 24, no. 1 (2014): 192–212.

23. Michael J. Rich, "Community Development Block Grants at 40: Time for a Makeover," *Housing Policy Debate* 24, no. 1 (2014): 46–90.

24. Timothy J. Conlan, "Between a Rock and a Hard Place: The Evolution of American Federalism," in *Intergovernmental Management for the Twenty-First Century,* ed. Conlan and Posner, 33–34.

For the argument that even such views as "cooperative federalism" and "coercive federalism" fail to capture the nuances of an intergovernmental system that has become extremely complex, see Cynthia J. Bowling and J. Mitchell Pickerill, "Fragmented Federalism: The State of American Federalism 2012–2013," *Publius: Journal of Federalism* 43, no. 3 (Summer 2013): 315–346.

25. Charles J. Orlebeke, "The Evolution of Low-Income Housing Policy, 1949 to 1989," *Housing Policy Debate* 11, no. 2 (2000): 505–506.

26. Bernard Frieden and Marshall Kaplan, *The Politics of Neglect* (Cambridge, MA: MIT Press, 1975); Benjamin Kleinberg, *Urban America in Transformation: Perspectives on Urban Policy and Development* (Thousand Oaks, CA: Sage, 1995), 175–184.

27. This argument is also made by Joshua Sapotichne, "National Urban Policy: Is a New Day Dawning?" paper prepared for the Comparative Urban Studies Project Seminar, the Woodrow Wilson Center for International Scholars, Washington, DC, January 25, 2010, http://www.wilsoncenter.org/sites/default/files/Sapotichne.pdf.

28. Robert J. Waste, *Independent Cities: Rethinking U.S. Urban Policy* (New York: Oxford University Press, 1998), 90.

29. Myron A. Levine, "Urban Policy in America: The Clinton Approach," *Local Economy* 9 (November 1994): 278–281.

30. Alan Berube and Thacher Tiffany, *The "State" of Low-Wage Workers: How the EITC Benefits Urban and Rural Communities in the 50 States* (Washington, DC: Brookings Institution, February 2004), www.brookings.edu/es/urban/publications/eitc/20040203_berube.htm. See also Alan Berube and Benjamin Forman, *Rewarding Work: The Impact of the Earned Income Tax Credit in Greater Chicago* (Washington, DC: Brookings Institution, November 2001), www.brookings.edu/es/urban/eitc/chicago.pdf.

31. The empowerment zone program, passed with much fanfare, did not live up to expectations that it would revive troubled communities. See Deirdre Oakley and Hi-Shien Tsao, "A New Way of Revitalizing Distressed Urban Communities? Assessing the Impact of the Federal Empowerment Zone Program," *Journal of Urban Affairs* 28, no. 5 (2006): 443–471. Michael J. Rich and Robert P. Stoker, *Collaborative Governance for Urban Revitalization: Lessons from Empowerment Zones* (Ithaca, NY: Cornell University Press, 2013), report uneven results across the nation, with the empowerment zones accomplishing some good in cities that were committed to public-private collaboration.

32. Robert Jay Dilger and Eugene Boyd, *Block Grant: Perspectives and Controversies,* CRS Report to Congress R40486 (Washington, DC: Congressional Research Service, 2013), 15.

33. Hilary Silver, "Obama's Urban Policy: A Symposium," *City & Community* 9, no. 1 (March 2010): 3–12; quotations on p. 6.

34. The White House, "The White House Neighborhood Revitalization Initiative," www.whitehouse.gov/sites/default/files/nri_description.pdf.

35. Rolf Pendall and Leach Hendey, *A Brief Look at the Early Implementation of Choice Neighborhoods* (Washington DC: The Urban Institute, 2013), www.urban.org/UploadedPDF/412940-A-Brief-Look-at-the-Early-Implementation-of-Choice-Neighborhoods.pdf.

36. See, for instance, The White House, "Memorandum for the Heads of Executive Departments; Subject: Developing Effective Place-Based Policies for the FY 2012 Budget," June 21, 2010.

37. See, for instance, the prepared remarks of Department of Housing and Urban Development Secretary Shaun Donovan at the Fifth National Conference on Housing Mobility, The Urban Institute, Washington, DC, June 12, 2012; Donovan defended the importance of both place-based housing programs and people-based mobility programs, http://portal.hud.gov/hudportal/HUD?src=/press/speeches_remarks_statements/2012/Speech_06122012.

38. Sheryl Gay Stolberg and Edmund L. Andrews, "$275 Billion Plan Seeks to Address Housing Crisis," *New York Times,* February 18, 2009; U.S. Department of Treasury, "Homeowner Affordability and Stability Plan: Executive Summary," February 18, 2009, www.ustreas.gov/press/releases/tg33.htm.

39. Dan Immergluck, "The Foreclosure Crisis, Foreclosed Properties, and Federal Policy: Some Implications for Housing and Community Development Planning," *Journal of the American Planning Association* 75, no. 4 (2009): 406–423, esp. 408.

40. Margery Austin Turner, "New Life for US Housing and Urban Policy," *City & Community* 9, no. 1 (March 2010): 32–40; quotation on pp. 34–35.

41. Bruce Katz, "Obama's Metro Presidency," *City & Community* 9, no. 1 (March 2010): 23–32.

42. See, for instance, Paul Kantor, "City Futures: Politics, Economic Crisis, and the American Model of Urban Development," *Urban Research and Practice* 3, no. 1 (March 2010): 1–11; Matt Chaban, "Can Obama's Office of Urban Affairs Carrion?" *Architect's Newspaper,* June 2, 2010, http://archpaper.com/e-board_rev.asp?News_ID=4588; and Dan Immergluck, "Too Little, Too Late, and Too Timid: The Federal Response to the Foreclosure Crisis at the Five-Year Mark," *Housing Policy Debate* 23, no. 1 (2013): 199–232.

43. John B. Judis, "Foreclosure? For Shame: Obama Is Making a Historic Mistake," *New Republic,* October 21, 2010; Gregory D. Squires and Derek S. Hyer, "Foreclosures—Yesterday, Today, and Tomorrow," *City & Community* 9, no. 1 (March 2010): 50–60.

44. Economist Edward L. Glaeser, "Can Buffalo Ever Come Back?" *City Journal* 17, no. 4 (Summer 2007): 95–99, also makes the argument for people-based programs—for education programs that would allow workers to move to areas of job growth, instead of spatially oriented programs that attempt to restore places that residents and businesses no longer value.

45. Juan-Pablo Velez, "Suburbs United in Quest of Federal Housing Aid, But Are Shut Out," *New York Times,* May 7, 2010.

46. Kenneth K. Wong, Francis X. Shen, Dorothea Anagnostopoulos, and Stacey Rutledge, *The Education Mayor: Improving America's Schools* (Washington, DC: Georgetown University Press, 2007). For a readable overview of the actions taken by the states to increase the mayor's control over failing school systems, see Frederick M. Hess, "Assessing the Case for Mayoral Control of Urban Schools," *American Enterprise Institute,* 4 (August 2008), www.aei.org/outlook/28511. For an analysis of mayoral takeover efforts, see Joseph P. Viteritti, ed., *When Mayors Take Charge: School Governance in the City* (Washington, DC: Brookings Institution Press, 2009).

47. Brian Gill, Ron Zimmer, Jolley Christman, and Suzanne Blanc, *State Takeover, School Restructuring, Private Management, and Student Achievement in Philadelphia* (Santa Monica, CA: RAND Education, 2007), www.rand.org/pubs/monographs/2007/RAND_MG533.pdf.

48. Jim Rokakis, Cuyahoga County (Ohio) treasurer, remarks at the Reclaiming Vacant Properties Conference, Cleveland, Ohio, October 14, 2010.

49. Evans Paull, "Vacant Properties, TIFs, and What's Working Now," presentation to the Reclaiming Vacant Properties Conference, Cleveland, Ohio, October 14, 2010.

50. Elizabeth Strom, "Let's Put on a Show! Performing Arts and Urban Revitalization in Newark, New Jersey," *Journal of Urban Affairs* 21, no. 4 (1999): 423–435.

51. Gerald E. Frug and David J. Barron, *City Bound: How States Stifle Urban Innovation* (Ithaca, NY: Cornell University Press, 2008).

52. Ann O'M. Bowman and Richard C. Kearney, "Second-Order Devolution: Data and Doubt," *Publius: The Journal of Federalism* 41, no. 4 (October 2011): 563–585, especially 572 and 576.

53. John A. Ferejohn and Barry R. Weingast, eds., *The New Federalism: Can the States Be Trusted?* (Stanford, CA: Hoover Institution Press, 1997).

54. Peter Burns and Matthew O. Thomas, "Governors and the Development Regime in New Orleans," *Urban Affairs Review* 39, no. 6 (2004): 791–812.

55. Edward Hill et al., "Slanted Pavement: How Ohio's Highway Spending Shortchanges Cities and Suburbs," in *Taking the High Road: A Metropolitan Agenda for Transit Reform,* ed. Bruce Katz and Robert Puentes (Washington, DC: Brookings Institution Press, 2005), 101–135.

56. Gary Sands, Laura A. Reese, and Heather L. Kahn, "Implementing Tax Abatements in Michigan: A Study of Best Practices," *Economic Development Quarterly* 20, no. 1 (February 2006): 44–58.

57. Robert T. Greenbaum, "Siting It Right: Do States Target Economic Distress When Designating Enterprise Zones?" *Economic Development Quarterly* 18, no. 1 (February 2004): 67–80, esp. 70.

58. Alan H. Peters and Peter S. Fisher, *Enterprise Zones: Have They Worked?* (Kalamazoo, MI: Upjohn Institute, 2002), 218–219; Jim F. Couch and J. Douglas Barrett, "Alabama's Enterprise Zones: Designed

to Aid the Needy?" *Public Finance Review* 32, no. 1 (January 2004): 65–81; Robert C. Turner and Mark K. Cassell, "When Do States Pursue Targeted Economic Development Policies? The Adoption and Expansion of State Enterprise Zone Programs," *Social Science Quarterly* 88, no. 1 (March 2007): 86–103.

59. John Kincaid and Richard L. Cole, "Public Opinion on Issues of Federalism in 2007: A Bush Plus?" *Publius: Journal of Federalism* 38, no. 3 (Summer 2008): 469–487.

60. Hillary Rodham Clinton, "Give New York Its Fair Share of Homeland Money," *New York Times,* August 22, 2004. See also Sewell Chan, "Bloomberg Criticizes Security Fund Distribution," *New York Times,* January 9, 2007; and Peter Eisinger, "Imperfect Federalism: The Intergovernmental Partnership for Homeland Security," *Public Administration Review* 66, no. 4 (July 2006): 537–545.

12. THE FUTURE OF URBAN AMERICA

1. Atlanta BeltLine, Inc., "Atlanta BeltLine Overview," http://beltline.org/BeltLineBasics/Belt-LineBasicsOverview/tabid/1691/Default.aspx; Robbie Brown, "Now Atlanta Is Turning Old Tracks Green," *New York Times,* February 14, 2013.

2. Steven P. Erie, *Globalizing L.A.: Trade, Infrastructure, and Regional Development* (Stanford, CA: Stanford University Press, 2004), details the history of actions taken by Los Angeles decision makers in support of the city's and the region's growth.

3. Roger Biles, *The Fate of Cities: Urban America and the Federal Government, 1945–2000* (Lawrence, KS: University Press of Kansas, 2011), provides a detailed description of the shifting tides of national urban policies since the end of World War II.

4. Evans Paull, "Vacant Properties, Tax Increment Financing, and What's Working Now," presented at the Reclaiming Vacant Properties conference, Cleveland, October 14, 2010; City of Dallas, Office of Economic Development, "Skillman Corridor TIF District," brochure, 2009, www.dallas-ecodev.org/SiteContent/66/documents/Incentives/TIFs/Skillman/skillman_marketing.pdf.

5. Robert G. Lehnen and Carlyn E. Johnson, "The Impact of Tax Increment Financing on School Districts: An Indiana Case Study," in *Tax Increment Financing and Economic Development: Uses, Structures, and Impact,* ed. Craig L. Johnson and Joyce Y. Man (Albany: State University of New York Press, 2001), 137–154.

6. Local taxes may have a considerable impact on a corporation's choice of sites within a metropolitan area, inasmuch as the corporation's access to suppliers, a qualified labor force, and markets is relatively the same throughout much of the metropolis. See Harold Wolman, "Local Economic Development Policy: What Explains the Divergence Between Policy Analysis and Political Behavior?" *Journal of Urban Affairs* 10, no. 1 (1988): 19–28.

7. Richard Dye and David Merriman, "Tax Increment Financing: A Tool for Local Economic Development," *Land Lines*, a publication of the Lincoln Institute of Land Policy 18, no. 1 (January 2006), http://www.lincolninst.edu/pubs/1078_Tax-Increment-Financing.

8. T. William Lester, "Does Chicago's Tax Increment Financing (TIF) Program Pass the 'But-for' Test? Job Creation and Economic Development Impacts Using Time-Series Data," *Urban Studies* 51, no. 4 (March 2014): 655–674.

9. Daniel McGraw, "Giving Away the Store to Get a Store: Tax Increment Financing Is No Bargain for Taxpayers," *Reason* (January 2006), http://reason.com/archives/2006/01/01/giving-away-the-store-to-get-a.

10. Gary Sands and Mark Skidmore, "Making Ends Meet: Options for Property Tax Reform in Detroit," *Journal of Urban Affairs* 36, no. 4 (2014): 682–700; quotation on p. 689. Cook County Clerk David Orr's 2013 TIF report can be accessed at Cook County Clerk; see "Chicago TIF revenue up 1%, down 3% in suburbs," press release, 2012, www.cookcountyclerk.com/newsroom/newsfromclerk/Pages/2012TIFreport.aspx.

11. Signe M. Rich, "How Important Is 'Quality of Life' in Location Decisions and Local Economic Development," in *Dilemmas of Urban Economic Development: Issues in Theory and Practice*

(Urban Affairs Annual Review, vol. 47), ed. Richard D. Bingham and Robert Mier (Thousand Oaks, CA: Sage, 1997), 56–73; Richard Florida, *The Rise of the Creative Class* (New York: Basic Books, 2002); Richard Florida, *Who's Your City: How the Creative Economy Is Making Where to Live the Most Important Decision of Your Life* (New York: Basic Books, 2008). For an essay that points to the limitations of local strategies designed to attract the "creative class," see Allen J. Scott, "Creative Cities: Conceptual Issues and Policy Questions," *Journal of Urban Affairs* 28, 1 (2006), 1–17.

12. Kathryn A. Foster, *The Political Economy of Special-Purpose Government* (Washington, DC: Georgetown University Press, 1997), 103; David Ranney, *Global Decisions, Local Collisions: Urban Life in the New World Order* (Philadelphia: Temple University Press, 2003), 106–107, 111–118.

13. David L. Imbroscio, "Overcoming the Economic Dependence of Urban America," *Journal of Urban Affairs* 15 (1993): 173–190, discusses a number of these strategies. Also see Thad Williamson, David Imbroscio, and Gar Alperowitz, *Making a Place for Community: Local Democracy in a Global Era* (New York: Routledge: 2003).

14. Stephanie Czeckalinski and Doris Dhan, "7 of 15 Most Populous U.S. Cities Are Majority-Minority," *National Journal,* July 2, 2012, www.nationaljournal.com/thenextamerica/demographics/7-of-15-most-populous-u-s-cities-are-majority-minority-20120702; Nate Berg, "U.S. Metros Are Ground Zero for Majority-Minority Populations," *The Atlantic Cities,* May 18, 2012, www.theatlanticcities.com/neighborhoods/2012/05/us-metros-are-ground-zero-majority-minority-populations/2043/.

15. The numbers, respectively, are reported by: *Racial Change in the Nation's Largest Cities: Evidence from the 2000 Census* (Washington, DC: The Brookings Institution Center on Urban and Metropolitan Policy, April 2001), www.brookings.edu/research/reports/2001/04/demographics; William H. Frey, "The New Metro Minority Map: Regional Shifts in Hispanics, Asians, and Blacks from Census 2010," State of Metropolitan American Report No. 37, Brookings Institution, August 31, 2011, www.brookings.edu/research/papers/2011/08/31-census-race-frey.

16. Alexandra Cole, "The 'Sleeping Giant' Shifts: Latinos and Orange County Politics," paper presented at the annual meeting of the American Political Science Association, Washington, DC, August 31–September 3, 2000.

17. In the 2008 presidential election, Hispanics voted in record numbers. Still, figures presented by the Pew Research Center (www.pewsocialtrends.org/2012/12/26/the-growing-electoral-clout-of-blacks-is-driven-by-turnout-not-demographics/) reveal that the Hispanic turnout rate stood at only 49.9 percent, well below the 66.1 percent for Caucasians and the 65.2 percent for African Americans driven to new heights by the Obama presidential candidacy. In 2012, the 49 percent for eligible Latinos continued to lag behind the 64 percent for non-Hispanic whites and the 66 percent turnout for African Americans again driven by Obama's presence on the ballot. The 2012 figures are based on respondents' self-reports in census surveys and hence are likely to be somewhat exaggerated. See Thom File, "The Diversifying Electorate: Voting Rates by Race and Hispanic Origin in 2012 (and Other Recent Elections)," Current Population Survey Reports, P20–569, May 2013, U.S. Census Bureau, Washington, DC, www.census.gov/prod/2013pubs/p20-568.pdf.

18. Matt A. Barreto, "¡Sí Se Puede! Latino Candidates and the Mobilization of Latino Voters," *American Political Science Review* 101, no. 3 (August 2007), 425–441; the quotation appears on p. 439. The presence of a nonviable Latino candidate for top office, of course, does little to draw Latino voters to the polls.

In the 2013 first-round or primary election for mayor of Los Angeles, overall voting turnout was dismal, with only 16 to 21 percent of the eligible electorate bothering to vote, according to estimates released in the wake of the balloting. The Latino turnout rate appeared to be even lower. The nonpartisan ballot and off-schedule timing of the election, held in March on a date when no other high-level races were before voters, dampened voter enthusiasm. Nor were Angelenos enthusiastic about the choice of contenders vying to succeed term-limited Mayor Antonio Villaraigosa. The single Hispanic candidate among the top-five candidates was a "long shot" who did not come close to making it to the second-round or runoff election. Latino voters did show some affinity for City Councilmember Eric Garcetti, who wound up making it to the final round and eventually to winning the mayoralty. Garcetti, who was seeking to become

L.A.'s first Jewish mayor, stressed his Mexican roots: his mother was Jewish, while his father was of Mexican and Italian heritage.

19. Paul Taylor, Ana Gonzales-Barrera, Jeffrey Passel, and Mark Hugo-Lopez, "An Awakened Giant: The Hispanic Electorate Is Likely to Double by 2030," *Pew Research Hispanic Trends Project,* November 14, 2012, www.pewhispanic.org/2012/11/14/an-awakened-giant-the-hispanic-electorate-is-likely-to-double-by-2030/.

20. Zev Chafets, "The Post-Hispanic Politician," *New York Times Magazine,* May 6, 2010; Andrew Romano, "Can Castro Turn Texas Blue?" *Newsweek,* April 15, 2013.

21. Luke Mullins, "How Youngstown Is Tackling the Housing Crisis," *U.S. News and World Report,* December 15, 2008.

22. Roberto E. Villarreal and Howard D. Neighbor, "Conclusion: An Overview of Mexican-American Political Empowerment," in *Latino Empowerment: Progress, Problems, and Prospects,* ed. Roberto E. Villarreal, Norma G. Hernandez, and Howard D. Neighbor (New York: Greenwood Press, 1988), 128. Michael Leo Owens and Jacob Robert Brown observe that the compromises in office made by black city officials may be contributing to the low turnout rates of a large portion of the black electorate who have become frustrated with the inability of black mayors to produce meaningful progressive results. Owens and Brown see black alienation and demobilization, coupled with the migration of the black middle-class to the suburbs and the return of white gentrifiers to the central city, as weakening prospects for black electoral power even in cities with a population that is majority African-American. See their article "Weakening Strong Black Political Empowerment: Implications from Atlanta's 2009 Mayoral Election," *Journal of Urban Affairs* 36, no. 4 (2014): 663–681.

23. Ali Modarres and Greg Andranovich, "Local Context for Understanding Poverty and Segregation," paper presented at the annual meeting of the Urban Affairs Association, Washington, DC, April 1, 2004.

24. Paula D. McClain and Steven C. Tauber, "Racial Minority Group Relations in a Multiracial Society," in *Governing American Cities: Inter-Ethnic Coalitions, Competition, and Conflict,* ed. Michael Jones-Correa (New York: Russell Sage Foundation, 2001), 111–136. For a description of the polarization between Cubans and African Americans in Miami, see Guillermo J. Grenier and Max Castro, "Blacks and Cubans in Miami: The Negative Consequences of the Cuban Enclave on Ethnic Relations," in *Governing American Cities: Inter-Ethnic Coalitions, Competition, and Conflict,* ed. Jones-Correa, 137–157.

25. Mark Baldassare, *California in the New Millennium: The Changing Social and Political Landscape* (Berkeley: University of California Press, 2000), 99–127. Other studies, however, argue that blacks and Latinos share a number of commonalities, that the two groups do not perceive each other as economic competitors, and that there may be a greater potential for a biracial or multiracial alliance than is commonly thought. See Matt A. Barreto, Benjamin F. Gonzalez, and Gabriel R. Sanchez, "Rainbow Coalition in the Golden State? Exposing Myths, Uncovering New Realities in Latino Attitudes towards Blacks," in *Black and Brown Los Angeles: A Contemporary Reader,* ed. Laura Pulido and Josh Kun (Berkeley: University of California Press, 2010).

26. Raphael J. Sonenshein and Susan H. Pinkus, "Latino Incorporation Reaches the Urban Summit: How Antonio Villaraigosa Won the 2005 Los Angeles Mayor's Race," *PS: Political Science and Politics* 38, no. 4 (2005): 713–721.

27. W. Avon Drake and Robert D. Holsworth, *Affirmative Action and the Stalled Quest for Black Progress* (Urbana and Chicago: University of Illinois Press, 1996), 71–79 and 120–125.

28. Mitchell F. Rice, "State and Local Government Set-Aside Programs, Disparity Studies, and Minority Business in the Post-*Croson* Era," *Journal of Urban Affairs* 15, no. 6 (1993): 529–553, esp. 533. In its 1995 *Adarand v. Pena* decision, the Court struck a further blow against minority set-aside programs, applying the *Croson* logic to federal preference programs. For a detailed discussion of the Court's *Croson* and *Adarand* rulings and what local governing bodies can do within the constraints of those decisions, see "Legal Analysis," in Mason Tillman Associates, Ltd., *Los Angeles County Metropolitan Transportation Authority DBE Disparity Study Update* (Oakland, CA: Mason Tillman

Associates, March 2013), www.metro.net/about_us/disparity_study/images/gcp_final_la_metro_chapter_1.pdf.

29. The 2009–2010 Disparity Study prepared for the City of Milwaukee illustrates how a city can determine whether or not the statistical evidence on the disparities in the issuance of municipal contracts is sufficient to meet the *Croson* standards that would allow the use of race- and gender-conscious preferences in municipal contracting: D. Wilson Consulting Group, *Disparity Study for the City of Milwaukee: Final Report* (Jacksonville, FL: December 20, 2010), http://city.milwaukee.gov/ImageLibrary/Groups/doaEBEP/Events/Disparity_Study_-_Full_Report.pdf.

30. Heather Martin, Maureen Berner, and Frayda Bluestein, "Documenting Disparity in Minority Contracting: Legal Requirements and Recommendations for Policy Makers," *Public Administration Review* 67, no. 3 (May/June 2007): 511–520.

31. *Schuette v. Coalition to Defend Affirmative Action,* 12–682 (1984). The case is also cited as *Schuette v. BAMN.*

32. David L. Kirp, "Retreat into Legalism: The Little Rock School Desegregation Case in Historical Perspective," *PS: Political Science and Politics* 30, no. 3 (September 1997): 443–447; quotation on p. 446.

33. Megan Twohey, "Desegregation Is Dead," *National Journal,* September 18, 1999, 2614–2619; Valerie G. Johnson, *Black Power in the Suburbs* (Albany: State University of New York Press, 2002), discusses the dramatic resegregation of schools in Prince George's County, outside of Washington, D.C. African Americans constituted 24.5 percent of the school population when desegregation efforts began in 1973; by 2001, they were 75 percent of Prince George's school population.

34. *Parents Involved in Community Schools v. Seattle School District No. 1* and *Meredith v. Jefferson County Board of Education,* 551 U.S. 701 (2007).

35. Susan Welch, Michael Combs, Lee Sigelman, and Timothy Bledsoe, "Race or Place? Emerging Public Perspectives on Urban Education," *PS: Political Science and Politics* (September 1997): 454–458; Sarah Garland, *Divided We Fail: The Story of an African American Community that Ended the Era of School Desegregation* (Boston: Beacon Press, 2013).

36. Johnson, *Black Power in the Suburbs,* 119–121.

37. Daniel J. Monti Jr., "The Numerology of Racial Segregation," paper presented at the annual meeting of the Urban Affairs Association, San Antonio, Texas, March 20–22, 2014.

38. Edward J. Blakely and David L. Ames, "Changing Places: American Urban Planning Policy for the 1990s," *Journal of Urban Affairs* 14, no. 3–4 (1992): 423–446; quotation on p. 423. This was only one of a number of articles in the *Journal of Urban Affairs* Special Issue to call for a national urban policy.

39. More conservative voices criticized the extra focus that Obama gave core-city communities. See Joel Kotkin, "The War Against Suburbia," *The American,* January 21, 2010, www.american.com/archive/2010/january/the-war-against-suburbia.

40. Marshall Kaplan and Franklin James, eds., *The Future of National Urban Policy* (Durham, NC: Duke University Press, 1990).

41. Joshua Sapotichne, "The Evolution of National Urban Policy: Congressional Agendas, Presidential Power, and Public Opinion," paper prepared for the Woodrow Wilson International Center for Scholars project "National Urban Policy: Is a New Day Dawning?" Washington, DC, January 25, 2010, www.wilsoncenter.org/sites/default/files/Sapotichne.pdf.

42. Robert Greenstein, "Universal and Targeted Programs to Relieving Poverty," in *The Urban Underclass,* ed. Christopher Jencks and Paul E. Peterson (Washington, DC: Brookings Institution Press, 1991), 437–459.

43. William Julius Wilson, *The Truly Disadvantaged* (Chicago: University of Chicago Press, 1981); William Julius Wilson, "Public-Policy Research and the Truly Disadvantaged," in *The Urban Underclass,* 460–481. See also Greenstein, "Universal and Targeted Programs to Relieving Poverty," 437–459.

44. Theda Skocpol, "Targeting Within Universalism: Politically Viable Policies to Combat Poverty in the United States," in *The Urban Underclass,* ed. Jencks and Peterson, 411–436, esp. 414.

45. Ravi K. Perry and Andrea Owens-Jones, "Balancing Act: Racial Empowerment and the Dual Expectations of Jack Ford in Toledo, Ohio," in *21st Century Urban Race Politics: Representing Minorities as Universal Interest,* ed. Ravi K. Perry (Bingley, UK: Emerald Group Publishing, 2013), 185.

46. President's Economic Recovery Advisory Board, "Report on Tax Reform Options, August 2010. For a description of how the LIHTC works and its impact on housing investment and construction, see Alex F. Schwartz, *Housing Politics in the United States,* 2nd ed. (New York: Routledge, 2006), 103–124.

47. Kirk McClure, "The Low-Income Housing Tax Credit Program Goes Mainstream and Moves to the Suburbs," *Housing Policy Debate* 17, no. 3 (2006): 419–446. For the limits that even LIHTC faces as a tool for the geographic dispersion of subsidized housing, see Lance Freeman, *Siting Affordable Housing: Location and Neighborhood Trends of Low Income Housing Tax Credit Developments in the 1990s* (Washington, DC: Brookings Institution Center on Urban and Metropolitan Policy, April 2004), www.brookings.edu/urban/publications/20040405_freeman.htm; Lance Freeman, "Comment on McClure's 'The Low-Income Housing Tax Credit Program Goes Mainstream and Moves to the Suburbs,'" *Housing Policy Debate* 17, no. 3 (2006): 447–459; and David P. Varady, "Comment on McClure's 'The Low-Income Housing Tax Credit Program Goes Mainstream and Moves to the Suburbs,'" in *Housing Policy Debate* 17, no. 3 (2006): 461–490.

48. Yonah Freemark, "HUD Unveils Winners of Sustainable Communities Awards," *Next American City,* October 15, 2010, http://americancity.org/columns/entry/2680/.

49. See, for example, The Ohio Commission on Local Government Reform and Collaboration, *Building a Better Ohio: Creating Collaboration in Governance* (August 27, 2010), www.morpc.org/pdf/Commission_Final_Report_Press_Quality.pdf.

50. Neal Peirce, "An Urban Agenda for the President," *Journal of Urban Affairs* 15 (1993): 457–467.

51. Ross Gittell and Avis Vidal, *Community Organizing: Building Social Capital as a Development Strategy* (Thousand Oaks, CA: Sage, 1998), esp. 33–56. Thad Williamson, David Imbroscio, and Gar Alperovitz, *Making a Place for Community: Local Democracy in a Global Era* (New York: Routledge, 2003), 213–235, reviews the potential and limitations of the CDC approach.

52. Douglas Farr, *Sustainable Urbanism: Urban Design with Nature* (Hoboken, NJ: Wiley, 2007); emphasis in original.

53. "London Olympics 2012—Going for Green?" *EurActive.com,* January 30, 2007, www.euractiv.com/en/sports/london-olympics-2012-going-green/article-161197; Global Forum for Sports and Environment, "New York City's 2012 Olympic Bid," www.g-forse.com/archive/news326_e.html; Nick Swift, "The Cities Bidding for the 2012 Olympics Have Learnt from the Salt Lake City Scandal," *City Mayors,* November 28, 2004, www.citymayors.com/sport/2012olympics_nov04.html; ICLEI-Local Governments for Sustainability, "ICLEI Joins The Climate Group and Chicago 2016 to Announce Olympic 'Green' Program," press release, June 25, 2008, www.icleiusa.org/news-events/press-room/press-releases/iclei-joins-the-climate-group-and-chicago-2016-to-announce-olympic-201cgreen201d-program.

54. Governments can adopt a variety of policies to promote greater densities in development and the use of public transit, walking, and biking as alternatives to automobiles. For easy-to-understand overviews of the variety of approaches tried around the globe, see Timothy Beatley, *Green Urbanism: Learning from European Cities* (Washington, DC: Island Press, 2000), 29–106; and Robert Cervero, *The Transit Metropolis: A Global Inquiring* (Washington, DC: Island Press, 1998).

55. Robert D. Bullard, *Dumping in Dixie: Race, Class, and Environmental Quality* (Boulder, CO: Westview Press, 2000).

56. Figures from 2009 provided by American Institute of Architects, *Local Leaders in Sustainability—Green Building Policy in a Changing Economic Environment* (Washington, DC: AIA, 2009), 13, www.aia.org/aiaucmp/groups/aia/documents/document/aiab081617.pdf.

57. Allyson Wendt, "Cities Mandate LEED But Not Certification," *GreenSource,* July 30, 2008, http://greensource.construction.com/news/080730CitiesMandateLEED.asp; Margot Roosevelt, "L.A. and San Francisco Vie for Title of 'Greenest City,'" *Los Angeles Times,* April 22, 2008.

58. The American Institute of Architects and the National Association of Counties, *Local Leaders in Sustainability: Green Building Incentive Trends* (Washington, DC: AIA, 2012), 47, www.aia.org/aiaucmp/groups/aia/documents/pdf/aiab093472.pdf, reviews the large variety of green building incentives and requirements adopted by cities across the United States.

59. For a brief review of the concept of a city's "ecological footprint," see Peter Newman and Isabella Jennings, *Cities as Sustainable Ecosystems: Principles and Practices* (Washington, DC: Island Press, 2008), 80–91.

60. Elisabeth Rosenthal, "No Furnaces But Heat Aplenty in 'Passive Houses,'" *New York Times*, December 28, 2008.

61. American Institute of Architects and the National Association of Counties, *Local Leaders in Sustainability: Green Building Incentive Trends*, 47.

62. Austin Troy, *The Very Hungry City: Urban Energy Efficiency and the Economic Fate of Cities* (New Haven, CT: Yale University Press, 2012), 169–171, 225–230. Also see Aaron Welch, Kaid Benfield, and Matt Raimi, *A Citizen's Guide to LEED for Neighborhood Development: How to Tell If Development Is Smart and Green* (New York: Natural Resources Defense Council, 2011), https://www.nrdc.org/cities/smartgrowth/files/citizens_guide_LEED-ND.pdf.

63. For a discussion of rainwater catchment systems, green roofs, rain gardens, the use of natural and artificially constructed wetlands, and pervious alternatives to pavement, see: Raquel Pinderhughes, *Alternative Urban Futures: Planning for Sustainable Development in Cities throughout the World* (Lanham, MD: Rowman and Littlefield, 2004), 38–46; and Christopher G. Boone and Ali Modarres, *City and Environment* (Philadelphia: Temple University Press, 2006), 101–106 and 124–126.

64. Ibid.

65. Neighborhood Progress, Inc., and Cleveland City Planning Commission, *Reimagining a More Sustainable Cleveland: Citywide Strategies for Reuse of Vacant Land* (Cleveland, OH: 2008), www.scribd.com/doc/64257913/Re-Imagining-A-More-Sustainable-Cleveland-Report.

66. Don Behm, "Brewers Plan Rain Barrel Rollout," *Milwaukee Journal Sentinel*, December 24, 2013.

67. Swati R. Prakash, "Beyond Dirty Diesels: Clean and Just Transportation in Northern Manhattan," in *Growing Smarter: Achieving Livable Communities, Environmental Justice, and Regional Equity*, ed. Robert D. Bullard (Cambridge, MA: MIT Press, 2007), 273–298; Pinderhughes, *Alternative Urban Futures*, 176–179; New York University Medical Center and School of Medicine, "Asthma Linked to Soot from Diesel Trucks in Bronx," *ScienceDaily*, October 30, 2006, www.sciencedaily.com/releases/2006/10/061017084420.htm.

68. Pinderhughes, *Alternative Urban Futures*, 178–179. Boone and Modarres, *City and Environment*, 106–114, review the potential advantages that biodiesel and other alternative fuels offer urban communities.

69. Except where otherwise noted, the description of the sustainability efforts of the five cities draws heavily on Kent E. Portney, *Taking Sustainable Cities Seriously: Economic Development, the Environment, and Quality of Life in American Cities*, 2nd ed. (Cambridge, MA: MIT Press, 2013), 131–141, 198–203, 256–271, and 283–297.

70. For a discussion of the importance of greenways to urban populations and to ecological systems, see: Boone and Modarres, *City and Environment*, 170–175; and Rob Jongman and Gloria Pungetti, eds., *Ecological Networks and Greenways: Concept, Design, Implementation* (Cambridge: Cambridge University Press, 2004).

71. Portney, *Taking Sustainable Cities Seriously*, 289.

72. Ernest Y. Yaranella and Richard S. Levine, *The City As Fulcrum of Global Sustainability* (New York: Anthem Press, 2011), esp. 123–126.

73. Beatley, *Green Urbanism*, 70–72.

74. For the steps taken by Austin and other leading "green building" communities, see: Eric Mackres, Kate Johnson, Annie Downs, Rachel Cluett, Shruti Vaidyanathan, and Kaye Schultz, *The 2013 Energy Efficiency Scorecard* (Washington, DC: American Council for an Energy Efficient

Economy, 2013), http://aceee.org/files/pdf/summary/e13g-summary.pdf, with the full report available at http://www.lawandenvironment.com/wp-content/uploads/sites/5/2013/09/energy-scorecard.pdf; and Dan York and Martin Kushler, *America's Best: Profiles of America's Leading Energy Efficiency Programs* (Washington, DC: American Council for an Energy Efficient Economy, 2003), www.aceee. org/press/2003/04/aceee-recognizes-nations-top-energy-efficiency-programs.

75. Beatley, *Green Urbanism,* 320–321; Portney, *Taking Sustainable Cities Seriously,* 284–285.

76. "Boulder Extends Carbon Tax; Washington County Bans GMOs," *SustainableBusiness.com News,* November 12, 2012, www.sustainablebusiness.com/index.cfm/go/news.display/id/24266.

77. Portland zoning ordinances, as cited by Portney, *Taking Sustainable Cities Seriously,* 133.

78. Donald Miller, "Developing and Employing Sustainability Indicators as a Principal Strategy in Planning: Experiences in the Puget Sound Urban Region of Washington State," in *Towards Sustainable Cities: East Asian, North American and European Perspectives on Managing Urban Regions,* ed. André Sorensen, Peter J. Marcotullio, and Jill Grant (Hampshire: Ashgate, 2003), 112–131.

79. Eran Ben-Joseph, *The Code of the City: Standards and the Hidden Language of Place Making* (Cambridge, MA: MIT Press, 2005), 122–123.

80. Portney, *Taking Sustainable Cities Seriously,* 135; City of Seattle, *Toward a Sustainable Seattle* (Seattle's Comprehensive Plan), "Urban Village Element," 2005, updated 2013, www.seattle.gov/dpd/cs/groups/pan/@pan/documents/web_informational/dpdd016663.pdf. An interesting overview of the Seattle program is also provided by a graduate student project: Max Blume, "Seattle's Vision for Sustainability: Implementing an Urban Village Strategy," prepared for the Urban and Regional Planning Program, UP734, the University of Michigan, Ann Arbor, April 2012, www-personal.umich. edu/~bieri/docs/UP734_BlumeFinalDoc_W12.pdf.

81. Portney, *Taking Sustainable Cities Seriously,* 23.

82. Ibid. 234–244.

83. For a summary of the arguments for and against the establishment of a congestion zone and a review of the political forces that led to its defeat in New York, see Myron A. Levine, ed., *Taking Sides: Clashing Views in Urban Studies* (New York: McGraw-Hill, 2013), 151–271, especially the Environment Defense Fund, "Road Pricing Makes Sense: Taming Traffic in London, Singapore, and Norway," and The Keep NYC Congestion Tax Free Coalition, "Congestion Pricing in the Manhattan Central Business District: Let's Look Hard Before We Leap."

84. Beatley, *Green Urbanism;* Sorensen, Marcotullio, and Grant, eds., *Towards Sustainable Cities.*

85. For a detailed comparison of regional actions in the New York, London, Paris, and Tokyo metropolitan areas, see Paul Kantor, Christian Lefèvre, Asato Saito, H.V. Savitch, and Andy Thornley, *Struggling Giants: City-Region Governance in London, New York, Paris, and Tokyo* (Minneapolis: University of Minnesota Press, 2012), esp. 248–250 and 255–251.

86. Portney, *Taking Sustainable Cities Seriously,* 23.

87. Sofie Bouteligier, *Cities, Networks, and Global Environmental Governance: Spaces of Innovation, Places of Leadership* (New York: Routledge, 2013).

88. John Norquist, president of the Council on New Urbanism, as cited in Troy, *The Very Hungry City,* 8.

89. Kent E. Portney and Jeffrey M. Berry, "Participation and the Pursuit of Sustainability in U.S. Cities," *Urban Affairs Review* 46, no. 1 (September 2010), 119–139; Elaine B. Sharp, Dorothy M. Daley, and Michael S. Lynch, "Understanding Local Adoption and Implementation of Climate Change Mitigation Policy," *Urban Affairs Review* 47, no. 3 (May 2011), 433–457. Edgar E. Ramirez de la Cruz, "Local Political Institutions and Smart Growth: An Empirical Study of the Politics of Compact Development," *Urban Affairs Review* 45, no. 2 (November 2009), 218–246, similarly traces the impact that local activism has had on the adoption of Smart Growth practices by Florida counties.

Index

Page numbers in **bold** refer to figures, page numbers in *italic* refer to tables